译者简介

潘 琪

1957年出生，北京市人。1982年春毕业于北京大学国际政治系，获法学学士学位。在对外经济贸易大学取得法学硕士学位，师从沈达明、冯大同教授。后赴美国学习法律，获耶鲁大学法学硕士学位(LL.M)及华盛顿大学(Washington University)法律博士学位(JD)。1988年取得中国律师资格，1994年取得美国律师资格(宾夕法尼亚州)。曾任教于对外经济贸易大学法律系，后长期在国际律师事务所（O' Melveny & Myers; White & Case）及通用汽车公司（General Motors）、强生公司（Johnson & Johnson）的法律部从事律师工作。1990年出版《美国统一商法典》中译本（中国对外经济贸易出版社）；著有《美国破产法》(法律出版社1999年)。

美国
统一商法典
UNIFORM COMMERCIAL CODE

（中英双语）

潘琪 译

法律出版社
LAW PRESS · CHINA

1990 年 5 月版《美国统一商法典》中译本

THE AMERICAN LAW INSTITUTE
OFFICE OF THE DIRECTOR
YALE LAW SCHOOL
401A YALE STATION
NEW HAVEN, CT 06520

GEOFFREY C. HAZARD, JR.
DIRECTOR

(203) 432-4971

November 15, 1989

Professor Pan Qi
5-162
33 Foreign Ministry St.
Beijing 10005
People's Republic of China

Dear Pan Qi:

I received the text of the Chinese translation of the Uniform Commercial Code about a month ago. I submitted the text to a professional colleague and former student, who is conversant in Mandarin. He in turn consulted with another colleague who is more fully fluent and also an expert in Chinese law and culture. Their report is highly favorable. Hence, on behalf of the American Law Institute I am greatly pleased to grant permission for the publication of this translation.

You are authorized to publish the translation as you sent it to me. However, I enclose an excerpt from the report by my colleagues that you may find helpful. You may wish to include their observations in the publication of the translation. You may do so if you wish, but you should not feel required to do so.

It is a welcome opportunity to celebrate this occasion of international legal and cultural exchange.

Best wishes.

Sincerely,

Geoffrey C. Hazard, Jr.

GCH:mg
cc Paul Wolkin
Mike Klausner

三十年的历程

《美国统一商法典》在美国法律体系和商业活动中占据着显著地位，在国际上有较大影响，对中国相关法律的制定和发展亦有重要参考意义。我初次翻译这部法典是在 1985 年，当时在对外经济贸易大学法律系读硕士研究生，至 1988 年毕业时，译稿基本完成。经导师冯大同教授作保，导师沈达明教授作序，译稿得以顺利出版。

当年，译稿的出版还得到美国法学会的大力支持。美国法学会时任会长哈泽德教授（Geoffrey Hazard，Jr.）专门委托两位法律专家对译稿进行审阅，一位是后来在斯坦福大学法学院任教的克劳斯纳教授（Michael Klausner），另一位是后来任谢尔曼斯特灵律师事务所合伙人的李小琼律师（Hsiao Chiung Li）。1990 年我去耶鲁大学法学院读硕士研究生时，拜见了在那里任教的哈泽德教授，对他的支持和授权表示感谢，并送了他一本已出版的法典中文版。

从初次翻译统一商法典到现在已时隔三十余年，能够有机会在法律出版社的支持下重新翻译这部法典，我感到非常高兴。重译的想法很多年前即已产生，因为法典已历经多次重大修改，重译可使读者更方便地了解法典的现状。同时，也希望这部具有经典意义的法典有一个更好的中译本。

统一商法典的雏形可以追溯至美国统一州法全国委员会（也称统一法委员会）于 1896 年公布的统一流通票据法，以及随后公布的一系列单独领域的统一法示范本。统一法委员会的愿望是通过美国各州把这些示范本采纳为本州法律，使各州的商法达到事实上的统一。统一法委员会之后与美国法学会合作，将单独领域的统一法示范本进行整合，于 1952 年形成综合性的统一商法典。在经历一番波折后，法典在 20 世纪 60 年代得到美国几乎所有各州立法机构的采纳，达到了预期目的。

统一商法典代表了美国顶尖法律人士一百多年来为规范和完善美国商法体系所作的不懈努力。法典及其前身单行示范本的起草工作均由相关领域的知名学者和律师承担，并经过各界法律人士的反复讨论和修改。统一法委员会和美国法学会还专门设立了统一商法典常设编辑委员会，根据商业实践对法典不断进行修改。在美国法律界，统一商法典亦成为单独的研究领域，著述浩繁。

统一商法典问世之后，依照修订时间存在不同版本。1985年我初次翻译时使用的是1972年版本，即当时美国各州普遍采纳的版本。之后的法典修订分篇进行，不再有统一的修订年份。法典每篇最后一次实质性修改的年份：第1篇《总则》为2001年；第2篇《买卖》为1995年；第2A篇《租赁》为1990年；第3篇《流通票据》为2002年；第4篇《银行存款和收款》为2002年；第4A篇《资金转账》为1989年；第5篇《信用证》为1995年；第7篇《所有权凭证》为2003年；第8篇《投资证券》为1994年；第9篇《担保交易》为2010年。法典近年已较少修改，说明其结构和内容已基本稳定，能够较好地适应美国的商业实际。上述不同年份的各篇组成了法典的“最新”版本。法典第6篇《整体转让》没有列入，是因为美国法学会因其内容已失去现实意义而建议将其废除，且很多州实际上已将其废除；第2篇《买卖》曾有过2003年版，但后被美国法学会撤销，因此第2篇目前的最新版本仍为1995年版。

此次重译依据的英文原文是美国得克萨斯州通过立法程序所实际采纳的统一商法典，只在个别地方作了技术性调整。之所以选择该州，是因为该州采纳的统一商法典非常接近美国法学会最新的标准文本。一般而言，各州在将法典采纳为本州法律时，都会根据本州情况作出某些修改，并且不一定对法典的每一篇都使用该篇的最新版本。

法典的这个中译本采用中英对照的形式，使读者在阅读中文时，可以根据自己的需要方便地看到英文原文。相信这对读者更加准确地理解法典会有极大的帮助。无论译者尽多大努力，由于翻译水平的限制、中美法律制度的差异以及语言某些内在的不可翻译性，译文必定存在相当的局限，因此，参考原文有时是非常必要的。此外，中英对照的形式可以使有兴趣的读者将本书作为法律英语的参考资料。

虽然我在三十多年前曾翻译过法典，并在最近二十多年的律师工作中一直使用法律英语，现在仍然感到法典翻译并非易事。专业词汇是首先遇到的困难。由于中美两国的法律制度存在巨大差异，因此，作为反映两种不同制度的专业词汇，常常无法一一对应，有时甚至完全无法对应。例如，法典大量使用的“enforce”这个词，在很多翻译中（包括在我自己以前的翻译中）都被译为“强制执行”，但两者的含义其实有很大差别。在中国法律中，“强制执行”的概念相对狭窄，主要指当事方不主动履行法院判决时，法院通过强制措施使判决得到履行；而在美国法律中，“enforce”泛指当事方通过法律上承认的任何措施（包括非司法措施和自助措施，也包括被动的应诉措施）来实现自己的权利或免除自己的义务。中文里实际上没有真正对应“enforce”的词汇。这次将其译为“强制履行”，只是希望比“强制执行”稍好。同样，译文中将“lien”这个词译为“留置权”也是无奈之举。在中国法律中，“留置”意味着担保物的占有；但在美国法律中，“lien”的含义很广，包括占有和不占有。虽然“lien”这个词也有一些其他译法，但都有各自的问题。此外，还有一些词汇则属于完全不能对应。例如，法典第9篇中有关担保交易的“attach”和“perfect”这两个词，在中国法律中没有相应概念，在中文里也没有惯用的表达。

在这种情况下，如何翻译这些专业词汇呢？我认为首先应该坦率承认，绝对准确或完美对应有时是不现实的，是虚幻的概念，因此不应强求，而应退而求其次。我采用的方法是尽量顺其自然，并力争相对合理。对于不能完全对应的词汇，尽量使用相对而言最接近和最合理的中文词汇，如上述提到的“强制履行”和“留置权”。所谓相对合理，就是在无法做到绝对合理的情况下，综合考虑各种因素后找到相对较好的译法。最接近理想的不理想，暂且可以视为理想。对于完全不能对应的词汇，则在尊重原文基本含义的原则下，尽量顺其自然。法典使用的绝大多数专业词汇，实际上在英文中也是日常用词，有大体对应的中文词汇。例如，上面提到的“attach”和“perfect”这两个词，不仅在英文中是日常用词，而且法典从专业的角度也是借用了它们的自然含义，因此，虽然中国法律或中文惯用表达中没有相应词汇，但顺其自然地将它们直译为“附着”和“完善”，应该说既符合原文，亦不失原意。偏离自然含义太远的译法，有时会超出翻译的范畴，而且效果未必更好。

对于译文中与法典原文不完全对应的中文词汇，以及中国法律或中文惯用表达中没有的中文词汇，应该如何加以理解呢？我认为应该在承认翻译具有局限性的基础上，避免过度解读中文词汇的字面含义，并避免过度套用中国或其他国家的法律概念。应该把法典中所有的专业词汇，都放到法典自身环境和美国法律制度中去理解，并仔细注意法典对这些词汇的定义。专业词汇在一定意义上是一个符号，关键不在于如何画这个符号，而在于赋予这个符号什么意义。很多词汇，即使从英文原文的角度看，如果缺少定义，缺少使用环境，其含义也是不确定的。正因如此，对专业词汇进行定义，是美国法律界的标准做法。例如，法典第9篇中“chattel paper”的含义比较复杂，所以法典需要仔细加以定义。相应地，译文中无论将其译为“动产契据”还是任何其他词，要准确理解其含义，都离不开定义。所以，对专业词汇的理解，除去翻译因素，更重要的是方法和角度。只要认真注意法典对专业词汇的定义，认真注意它们在法典中的使用，就能比较容易和比较准确地理解这些词汇在法典和美国法律中的真实含义。

在阅读译文时，读者还应注意词汇之间的细微差别，以减少混淆和误解。例如，票据的“holder”和“bearer”被分别译为“执票人”和“持票人”，而“maker”、“drawer”和“issuer”被分别译为“制票人”“出票人”和“立票人”。从中文角度，“执”和“持”的含义几乎没有区别，而“制”“出”和“立”也没有明显区别，但在法典中，这些词的定义是完全不同的。又如，“agreement”和“contract”被分别译为“协议”和“合同”。这两个词在中文里常被用作同义词，但它们在法典中的定义却是不同的。“购买”（purchase）这个词在法典中不仅指买卖，也包括赠予等其他取得方式。因此，“购买”不等于“买进”（buy），而“购买人”（purchaser）也相应地不同于“买方”（buyer）。“权利”和“权力”看上去比较接近，但对应的英文 right 和 power 具有不同含义。“票据”（instrument）和“票证”（item）的含义也不完全相同，而“所有权凭证”（document of title）和“产权证书”（certificate of title）的含义则完全不同。“价值”虽然基本上等于“对价”，但英文使用的是“value”和“consideration”两个不同的词，含义也有一定差别。为了减少可能给读者造成的混淆或误解，译文中尽量做到专业词汇的表述一致，即同一个英文词汇尽量在全书中始终对应同一个中文词汇。但是，有些地方由于上下文和其他限制，未能完全做到这一点。例如，“claim”被分别译为“索赔”或“主张”，而“obligation”则被分别译为“债务”或“义务”。但在第 9 篇中，“债务人”（debtor）和“义务人”（obligor）是两个不同的概念，需要注意区分。此外，还应注意法典对标点的使用。在涉及排列的内容时，如果法典的表述是“甲、乙或丙”，即指甲乙丙任何一者。如果是“甲、乙及丙”，则指甲乙丙全部。

除去上面谈到的专业词汇，法典翻译的真正难题，在于如何准确理解法典每一句话所要表达的真实含义和细微含义，并在尽可能接近原文含义、措辞、风格、排列和韵律的原则下，把那些与中文表达方式有巨大差异的英文句子，组装成符合中文阅读和思维习惯的简洁、清晰、通顺和易读的中文句子。法典英文整体较为艰涩曲折，很多细节不易把握，因此准确理解已有相当难度；但相较而言，中文的完美表达则更为重要和更为困难。中文作为我们的母语，本来最应把握好，但恰恰最难把握好。英文理解的错误通常是个别的，而中文表达的不足则可能是整体的。英文理解决定译文的对错，而中文表达则决定译文的优劣。尽管每个方面都有程度之分，而且相互制约，但总体而言先有对错后有优劣，错的不可能是优的，而对的也有可能是劣的。这是以匠人精神追求完美的过程，一分耕耘，一分收获，没有止境。

影响译文对错优劣的另一个重要因素是法律和专业知识。法典涉及多个法律和专业领域，从比较常见的货物买卖和货物租赁，到不常接触的流通票据和银行业务，比较专门的所有权凭证和投资证券，以及高度复杂的担保交易，每个领域都包含各自的专业概念和法律问题。翻译法典的过程，实际上也是我学习的过程。有时为了一个词汇或一个概念，花费很大精力，但也未必获得满意结果。不足之处，只好留给未来改进。

无论如何，法典重译工作暂告一个段落。首先要感谢我的导师沈达明教授和冯大同教授，他们是带我进入这个领域的启蒙老师，并在起步阶段给予我巨大的帮助，他们对我的教诲和提携使我受益终生。还要感谢我在对外经济贸易大学的研究生同学吴兴光教授。吴教授长期从事美国统一商法典的研究，是国内这个领域的专家，著述颇丰。他当年即对我初次翻译法典的尝试给予了很多鼓励和支持。在担任广东外语外贸大学法学院院长和资深教授后，还是一直不断鼓励我重译法典，并多方给予帮助。重译完成后，他花费大量时间对译稿进行了审阅，提出了很多重要的改进建议。可以说，吴兴光教授是我重译法典最坚定的支持者和推动者。特别要感谢美国的汉宁 (William H.Henning) 教授。汉宁教授是统一商法典的权威专家，曾任美国统一州法全国委员会执行主任以及法典第2篇和第2A篇修订委员会主任。我十年前产生重译统一商法典的想法后，一直得到汉宁教授的热情帮助和支持。对于一些非常具体的问题，汉宁教授也给予耐心的解答，令我十分感动。同时感谢法律出版社的黄琳佳编辑。她对法典重译所给予的巨大支持，是这个译本得以顺利出版的基础。从开始讨论重译事项到完成法律出版社的出版安排，只用了一个多星期的时间。这样的热情和专业效率，十分令人钦佩。在编辑和排版过程中，她花费了大量心血，只是为了向读者呈现一部更好的图书。此外，感谢对外经济贸易大学法学院的李喆同学，她从繁忙的学业中抽出时间进行了大量校对工作，并帮助准备了专业词汇索引。

我希望并相信此次重译的《美国统一商法典》比前次有所进步，但是，由于前面提到的诸多原因，译文必定存在种种不足和缺陷。我愿与对美国统一商法典有兴趣的读者进行交流和讨论，互相学习。我的电子邮箱是: panqichina@163.com。

潘　琪

2018 年 10月于北京

目　　录

第1篇　总　则

ARTICLE 1. GENERAL PROVISIONS

第1章　总　则

PART 1. GENERAL PROVISIONS

第 1.101 条　简称

（a）本法被引用时可称为《统一商法典》。

（b）本篇被引用时可称为《统一商法典——总则》。

第 1.102 条　本篇适用范围

如果一项交易受本法另一篇的约束，本篇即在相应范围内适用于该交易。

第 1.103 条　本法的解释应促进本法之基本宗旨的实现；补充性法律原则的适用

（a）必须灵活地解释和适用本法，以促进本法之基本宗旨的实现。本法的基本宗旨是：

（1）使管辖商业交易的法律更加简洁、明确和现代；

（2）使商业做法能够通过惯例、实践和当事方协议不断发展；以及

（3）使各州法律归于统一。

§ 1.101.Short Titles.

（a）This Act may be cited as the Uniform Commercial Code.

（b）This Article may be cited as Uniform Commercial Code—General Provisions.

§ 1.102.Scope of Article.

This Article applies to a transaction to the extent that it is governed by another Article of this Act.

§ 1.103.Construction of Act to Promote Its Purposes and Policies; Applicability of Supplemental Principles of Law.

（a）This Act must be liberally construed and applied to promote its underlying purposes and policies, which are:

（1）to simplify, clarify and modernize the law governing commercial transactions;

（2）to permit the continued expansion of commercial practices through custom, usage and agreement of the parties; and

（3）to make uniform the law among the

various jurisdictions.

（b）除被本法特定条款排除外，各种法律原则和衡平原则，包括商人法，以及涉及合同能力、被代理人和代理人、禁止自相矛盾、欺诈、不实陈述、胁迫、强制、误解或破产的法律，或其他涉及生效或失效原因的法律，应作为本法条款的补充。

（b）Unless displaced by the particular provisions of this Act, the principles of law and equity, including the law merchant and the law relative to capacity to contract, principal and agent, estoppel, fraud, misrepresentation, duress, coercion, mistake, bankruptcy, or other validating or invalidating cause shall supplement its provisions.

第 1.104 条　不作默示废除解释

§ 1.104.Construction Against Implied Repeal.

本法是旨在对其适用领域提供统一规则的一般法，因此不应将本法的任何部分视为被本法之后的立法所默示废除，只要可以合理避免此种废除解释。

This Act being a general act intended as a unified coverage of its subject matter, no part of it shall be deemed to be impliedly repealed by subsequent legislation if such construction can reasonably be avoided.

第 1.105 条　可分割性

§ 1.105.Severability.

如果本法的任何条款或其对任何人或任何情况的适用被判决无效，只要在排除该无效条款或无效适用后，其他条款或其适用仍有可能被赋予效力，该无效即不影响本法的其他条款或其适用。在此意义上，本法各条款是可分割的。

If any provision or clause of this Act or its application to any person or circumstance is held invalid, the invalidity does not affect other provisions or applications of this Act which can be given effect without the invalid provision or application, and to this end the provisions of this Act are severable.

第 1.106 条　单数和复数的使用；词性

§ 1.106.Use of Singular and Plural; Gender.

在本法中，除条款的上下文另有所指外：

In this Act, unless the statutory context otherwise requires:

（1）单数词包含复数含义，复数词包含单数含义；并且

（1）words in the singular number include the plural, and those in the plural include the singular;and

（2）任何词性的词，都包含任何其他词性。

（2）words of any gender also refer to any other gender.

第 1.107 条 各条的标题

各条的标题系本法的组成部分。

§ 1.107.Section Captions.

Section captions are parts of this Act.

第 1.108 条 与《国际及国内商业电子签名法》的关系

本法修改、限制并取代联邦《国际及国内商业电子签名法》，但不修改、限制或取代该法第 7001 条（c）款，也不授权以电子交付方式作出该法第 7003 条（b）款所述的通知。

§ 1.108.Relation to Electronic Signatures in Global and National Commerce Act.

This Act modifies, limits, and supersedes the federal Electronic Signatures in Global and National Commerce Act, but does not modify, limit, or supersede Section 7001（c）of that Act, or authorize electronic delivery of any of the notices described in Section 7003（b）of that Act.

第2章 通用定义和解释原则

PART 2. GENERAL DEFINITIONS AND PRINCIPLES OF INTERPRETATION

第 1.201 条 通用定义

（a）除上下文另有所指外，本条对任何词语作出的定义，或本法其他篇对该词语作出的适用于特定篇或其任何部分的补充定义，使该词语具有所说明的含义。

（b）除本法其他篇为适用于特定篇或其任何部分而作出补充定义外：

（1）“诉讼”包括扣减、反诉、抵销、衡平诉讼，以及确认权利的任何其他法律程序。

（2）“受损方”指有权寻求

§ 1.201. General Definitions.

（a）Unless the context otherwise requires, words or phrases defined in this section, or in the additional definitions contained in other Articles of this Act that apply to particular Articles or parts thereof, have the meanings stated.

（b）Subject to definitions contained in other Articles of this Act that apply to particular Articles or parts thereof:

（1）“Action,” in the sense of a judicial proceeding, includes recoupment, counterclaim, set-off, suit in equity, and any other proceeding in which rights are determined.

（2）“Aggrieved party” means a party

救济的当事方。

entitled to pursue a remedy.

（3）相对于“合同”而言，“协议”指当事方的实际约定。此种约定应通过当事方使用的语言确定，或通过其他客观情况（包括第1.303条所述的履约过程、交易过程或行业惯例）推定。

(3) "Agreement," as distinguished from "contract," means the bargain of the parties in fact, as found in their language or inferred from other circumstances, including course of performance, course of dealing, or usage of trade as provided in Section 1.303.

（4）“银行”指从事银行业务的人，包括储蓄银行、储贷协会、信贷合作社和信托公司。

(4) "Bank" means a person engaged in the business of banking and includes a savings bank, savings and loan association, credit union, and trust company.

（5）“持票人”指控制流通电子所有权凭证的人，或占有流通票据或流通实体所有权凭证的人，或占有持票式或被空白背书之票式证券的人。

(5) "Bearer" means a person in control of a negotiable electronic document of title or a person in possession of a negotiable instrument, a negotiable tangible document of title, or a certificated security that is payable to bearer or indorsed in blank.

（6）“提单”指直接或间接从事货物运输或递送业务的人所出具的，证明收到待运货物的所有权凭证。该词不包括仓单。

(6) "Bill of lading" means a document of title evidencing the receipt of goods for shipment issued by a person engaged in the business of directly or indirectly transporting or forwarding goods.The term does not include a warehouse receipt.

（7）“分行”包括银行在国外独立注册的分行。

(7) "Branch" includes a separately incorporated foreign branch of a bank.

（8）对一项事实承担“举证责任”，指有义务使事实审的审理人相信，该事实存在的可能性大于其不存在的可能性。

(8) "Burden of establishing" a fact means the burden of persuading the trier of fact that the existence of the fact is more probable than its nonexistence.

（9）“正常业务中的买方”指以善意买进货物的人，且其不知道该销售侵犯了另一人对

(9) "Buyer in ordinary course of business" means a person that buys goods in good faith, without knowledge that the sale violates the

货物的权利，并以正常方式向从事该类货物销售的卖方（典当商除外）买进。如果卖方向任何人作出的销售符合卖方行业的通常或惯用做法，或符合卖方自己的通常或惯用做法，后者即属于以正常方式买进货物。在井源或矿源销售石油、天然气或其他矿产品的人，属于从事该类货物销售的人。正常业务中的买方在买进时，可以支付现金，也可以使用其他财产交换，或利用有担保或无担保的信贷，也可以根据前存买卖合同取得货物或所有权凭证。买方只有根据第 2 篇取得货物的占有，或有权追索货物，才可能成为正常业务中的买方。“正常业务中的买方”不包括通过整体转让取得货物的人。涉及为担保金钱债务或为全部或部分清偿金钱债务所作的转让时，“正常业务中的买方”不包括通过该转让取得货物的人。

rights of another person in the goods, and in the ordinary course from a person, other than a pawnbroker, in the business of selling goods of that kind.A person buys goods in the ordinary course if the sale to the person comports with the usual or customary practices in the kind of business in which the seller is engaged or with the seller’s own usual or customary practices. A person that sells oil, gas, or other minerals at the wellhead or minehead is a person in the business of selling goods of that kind.A buyer in ordinary course of business may buy for cash, by exchange of other property, or on secured or unsecured credit, and may acquire goods or documents of title under a preexisting contract for sale.Only a buyer that takes possession of the goods or has a right to recover the goods from the seller under Article 2 may be a buyer in ordinary course of business. “Buyer in ordinary course of business” does not include a person that acquires goods in a transfer in bulk or as security for or in total or partial satisfaction of a money debt.

（10）如果一项条款的书写、展示或表达方式，对于作为其受众且通情达理的人而言，本应引起该类人注意，该条款即为“醒目”。条款是否“醒目”，由法院判定。醒目的条款包括下列情况：

（10）“Conspicuous,” with reference to a term, means so written, displayed, or presented that a reasonable person against which it is to operate ought to have noticed it.Whether a term is “conspicuous” or not is a decision for the court.Conspicuous terms include the following:

（A）字母尺寸等于或大于周围文字并使用大写字母的标题，或字母尺寸等于或大于周

（A）a heading in capitals equal to or greater in size than the surrounding text, or in contrasting type, font, or color to the

围文字并使用对比之式样、字体或颜色的标题；以及

surrounding text of the same or lesser size;and

（B）记录或展示之正文中的用语，只要其字母尺寸大于周围文字，或字母尺寸等于周围文字但风格、字体或颜色与周围文字存在对比，或字母尺寸等于周围文字，但通过符号或其他标注与周围文字有所区别，以致能够引起对该用语的注意。

（B）language in the body of a record or display in larger type than the surrounding text, or in contrasting type, font, or color to the surrounding text of the same size, or set off from surrounding text of the same size by symbols or other marks that call attention to the language.

（11）“消费者”指主要因个人、家庭或家用目的达成交易的个人。

（11）“Consumer” means an individual who enters into a transaction primarily for personal, family, or household purposes.

（12）相对于“协议”而言，“合同”指基于当事方协议而产生的，并根据本法确定且由任何其他适用法补充的全部法律义务。

（12）“Contract,” as distinguished from “agreement,” means the total legal obligation that results from the parties’agreement as determined by this Act as supplemented by any other applicable laws.

（13）“债权人”包括无担保债权人、担保债权人、留置权债权人，以及债权人的任何代表人，包括代表债权人利益的受让人、破产受托人、衡平法中的清算人，以及破产债务人或转让人之财产的执行人或管理人。

（13）“Creditor” includes a general creditor, a secured creditor, a lien creditor and any representative of creditors, including an assignee for the benefit of creditors, a trustee in bankruptcy, a receiver in equity and an executor or administrator of an insolvent debtor’s or assignor’s estate.

（14）“被告”包括在反诉、相向索赔和第三方索赔中处于被告地位的人。

（14）“Defendant” includes a person in the position of defendant in a counterclaim, cross-claim, or third-party claim.

（15）涉及电子所有权凭证时，“交付”指自愿转移控制；涉及票据、实体所有权凭证或动产契据时，“交付”指自愿转

（15）“Delivery,” with respect to an electronic document of title, means voluntary transfer of control, and with respect to an instrument, a tangible document of title, or

移占有。

chattel paper, means voluntary transfer of possession.

（16）"所有权凭证"指具有全部下列特征的记录：在正常业务或融资中，被认为足以证明其占有人或控制人有权接收、控制、持有或处置该记录及其所覆盖的货物；显示系由货物保管人出具，或系出具给货物保管人；覆盖由货物保管人占有的货物；该货物已特定化，或系已特定化的批量货物中一定份额的种类物。"所有权凭证"包括提单、运输文件、码头收货单、码头收据、仓单和交货命令。电子所有权凭证系由储存在电子介质中之信息组成的记录予以证明。实体所有权凭证系由记录在实体介质中之信息组成的记录予以证明。

（16）"Document of title" means a record that in the regular course of business or financing is treated as adequately evidencing that the person in possession or control of the record is entitled to receive, control, hold, and dispose of the record and the goods the record covers, and purports to be issued by or addressed to a bailee and to cover goods in the bailee's possession which are either identified or are fungible portions of an identified mass. The term includes a bill of lading, transport document, dock warrant, dock receipt, warehouse receipt, and order for delivery of goods. An electronic document of title is evidenced by a record consisting of information stored in an electronic medium. A tangible document of title is evidenced by a record consisting of information that is inscribed on a tangible medium.

（17）"过错"指违约、不当行为或疏漏。

（17）"Fault" means a default, breach, or wrongful act or omission.

（18）"种类物"指：

（18）"Fungible goods" means:

（A）根据货物性质或行业惯例，其任何一个单位都等于任何一个其他同等单位的货物；或

（A）goods of which any unit, by nature or usage of trade, is the equivalent of any other like unit; or

（B）根据协议被视为相同的货物。

（B）goods that by agreement are treated as equivalent.

（19）"真实"指不存在伪造或仿造。

（19）"Genuine" means free of forgery or counterfeiting.

（20）除第5篇另有规定外，

（20）"Good faith," except as otherwise

"善意"指事实上的诚实，以及对公平交易之合理商业准则的遵守。

（21）"执票人"指：

（A）占有向持票人付款之流通票据的人；或占有向特定人付款之流通票据的人，且占有人即为该特定人；

（B）占有流通实体所有权凭证的人，只要货物应交付给持票人，或应交付给凭证占有人的指定人；或

（C）控制流通电子所有权凭证的人。

（22）"破产程序"包括为债权人利益所作的转让，或其他旨在清算或重组相关人之财产的程序。

（23）"破产"指：

（A）在正常业务中总体停止清偿债务，但因正当争议引起的停止清偿除外；

（B）在债务到期时无力偿付；或

（C）根据联邦破产法的定义，失去偿付能力。

（24）"金钱"指当前由本国或外国政府授权或采纳的交换媒介。"金钱"也包括由政府间组织设立的或通过两国或多国间协议设立的记账货币单位。

（25）"组织"指除个人外

provided in Article 5, means honesty in fact and the observance of reasonable commercial standards of fair dealing.

（21）"Holder" means:

（A） the person in possession of a negotiable instrument that is payable either to bearer or to an identified person that is the person in possession;

（B）the person in possession of a negotiable tangible document of title if the goods are deliverable either to bearer or to the order of the person in possession; or

（C）a person in control of a negotiable electronic document of title.

（22）"Insolvency proceeding " includes an assignment for the benefit of creditors or other proceeding intended to liquidate or rehabilitate the estate of the person involved.

（23）"Insolvent" means:

（A）having generally ceased to pay debts in the ordinary course of business other than as a result of a bona fide dispute;

（B）being unable to pay debts as they become due; or

（C）being insolvent within the meaning of the federal bankruptcy law.

（24）"Money" means a medium of exchange currently authorized or adopted by a domestic or foreign government.The term includes a monetary unit of account established by an intergovernmental organization or by agreement between two or more countries.

（25）"Organization" means a person other

的其他人。

(26)相对于"第三方"而言,"当事方"指从事了受本法约束之交易的人,或订立了受本法约束之协议的人。

(27)"人"指个人、公司、商业信托、遗产、信托、合伙、有限责任公司、协会、合资企业、政府、政府部门、政府代理机构、政府控制机构、上市公司或其他任何法律或商业实体。

(28)"现值"指将一笔或多笔应在未来支付的款项,按照一定利率折现到某个特定日期时的金额。该利率可以由当事方商定,只要在达成交易的当时,所商定的利率不是明显不合理;或如果不存在商定利率,则应根据达成交易当时的事实和客观情况,确定一个商业上系属合理的利率。

(29)"购买"指通过下列方式取得:买卖、租赁、贴现、流通、不动产抵押、质押、留置、设立担保权益、发行或再发行、赠予,或任何其他在财产上设立权益的自愿交易。

(30)"购买人"指作出购买行为的人。

(31)"记录"指记录在实体介质上的信息,或存储在电子介质或其他介质上并可读取

than an individual.

(26)"Party," as distinguished from "third party," means a person that has engaged in a transaction or made an agreement subject to this Act.

(27)"Person" means an individual, corporation, business trust, estate, trust, partnership, limited liability company, association, joint venture, government, governmental subdivision, agency, or instrumentality, public corporation, or any other legal or commercial entity.

(28)"Present value" means the amount as of a date certain of one or more sums payable in the future, discounted to the date certain by use of either an interest rate specified by the parties if that rate is not manifestly unreasonable at the time the transaction is entered into or, if an interest rate is not so specified, a commercially reasonable rate that takes into account the facts and circumstances at the time the transaction is entered into.

(29)"Purchase" means taking by sale, lease, discount, negotiation, mortgage, pledge, lien, security interest, issue or reissue, gift, or any other voluntary transaction creating an interest in property.

(30)"Purchaser" means a person that takes by purchase.

(31)"Record" means information that is inscribed on a tangible medium or that is stored in an electronic or other medium and is

的信息。

（32）“救济”指受损方享有的通过或不通过裁决机构而行使的救助性质的权利。

（33）“代表人”指被授权代表他人作为的人，包括代理人、公司或协会的行政官，以及遗产的受托人、执行人或管理人。

（34）“权利”包括救济。

（35）“担保权益”指对动产或不动产附着物享有的，作为付款或履约义务之担保的权益。涉及受第9篇约束的交易时，“担保权益”包括寄售委托人的权益，还包括应收款、动产契据、无形支付或本票之买方的权益。“担保权益”不包括第2.401条所述的特殊财产权，即在货物特定于买卖合同项下后买方对货物享有的特殊财产权；但是，买方也可以通过满足第9篇的要求而取得“担保权益”。除第2.505条另有规定外，在第2篇或第2A篇中，货物的卖方或出租方保留或取得的对货物的占有权，不属于“担保权益”；但是，卖方或出租方也可以通过满足第9篇的要求而取得“担保权益”。在第2.401条中，在货物已发运或已交付给买方后，卖方所保留的货物所有权，效力上只相当于

retrievable in perceivable form.

(32) “Remedy” means any remedial right to which an aggrieved party is entitled with or without resort to a tribunal.

(33) “Representative” means a person empowered to act for another, including an agent, an officer of a corporation or association, and a trustee, executor, or administrator of an estate.

(34) “Right” includes remedy.

(35) “Security interest” means an interest in personal property or fixtures which secures payment or performance of an obligation. “Security interest” includes any interest of a consignor and a buyer of accounts, chattel paper, a payment intangible, or a promissory note in a transaction that is subject to Article 9. “Security interest” does not include the special property interest of a buyer of goods on identification of those goods to a contract for sale under Section 2.401, but a buyer may also acquire a “security interest” by complying with Article 9.Except as otherwise provided in Section 2.505, the right of a seller or lessor of goods under Article 2 or 2A to retain or acquire possession of the goods is not a “security interest,” but a seller or lessor may also acquire a “security interest” by complying with Article 9.The retention or reservation of title by a seller of goods notwithstanding shipment or delivery to the buyer under Section 2.401 is limited in effect to a reservation of a “security interest.” Whether a transaction in the form of

保留“担保权益”。采用租赁形式的交易是否属于设立“担保权益”，应根据第1.203条确定。

a lease creates a security interest is determined pursuant to Section 1.203.

（36）涉及书面文件、记录或通知时，“发送”指：

（36）“Send” in connection with a writing, record, or notice means:

（A）在落实了邮费或传送费且正确标明地址后，将其投入信箱或以任何其他惯常通信手段交付传送；涉及票据时，应使用票据上注明的地址或另行商定的地址，在无此种地址时，应使用当时情况下为合理的地址；或

（A）to deposit in the mail or deliver for transmission by any other usual means of communication with postage or cost of transmission provided for and properly addressed and, in the case of an instrument, to an address specified thereon or otherwise agreed, or if there be none to any address reasonable under the circumstances;or

（B）以任何其他方式使记录或通知被收到，且不迟于在恰当发送时其本来应该到达的时间。

（B）in any other way cause to be received any record or notice within the time at which it would have arrived if properly sent.

（37）“签名”包括为采纳或接受一份书面文件而使用或采纳的任何符号。

（37）“Signed” includes using any symbol executed or adopted with present intention to adopt or accept a writing.

（38）“州”指美国的任何州、哥伦比亚特区、波多黎各、美属维尔京群岛和受美国管辖的任何地域或岛屿。

（38）“State” means a State of the United States, the District of Columbia, Puerto Rico, the United States Virgin Islands, or any territory or insular possession subject to the jurisdiction of the United States.

（39）“保人”包括保证人或其他次义务人。

（39）“Surety” includes a guarantor or other secondary obligor.

（40）“条款”指协议中涉及特定事项的任何部分。

（40）“Term” means a portion of an agreement that relates to a particular matter.

（41）“无授权签名”指未获得实际授权、默示授权或表见授权的签名。“无授权签名”包括伪造的签名。

（41）“Unauthorized signature” means a signature made without actual, implied, or apparent authority.The term includes a forgery.

（42）“仓单”指从事有偿货物存储业务的人所出具的所有权凭证。

（42）“Warehouse receipt” means a document of title issued by a person engaged in the business of storing goods for hire.

（43）“书写”包括打印、打字或以任何其他方法有意作出可见形式。“书面”具有与之相应的含义。

（43）“Writing” includes printing, typewriting, or any other intentional reduction to tangible form. “Written” has a corresponding meaning.

第 1.202 条　通知；知道

§ 1.202. Notice; Knowledge.

（a）除（f）款另有规定外，在下列情况下，一个人被视为得到一项事实的“通知”：

（a）Subject to Subsection（f）, a person has“notice” of a fact if the person:

（1）该人实际知道该事实；

（1）has actual knowledge of it;

（2）该人已收到该事实的通知；或

（2）has received a notice or notification of it;or

（3）该人根据当时知道的所有事实和情况，有理由知道该事实的存在。

（3）from all the facts and circumstances known to the person at the time in question, has reason to know that it exists.

（b）“知道”指实际知道。

（b）“Knowledge” means actual knowledge. “Knows” has a corresponding meaning.

（c）“发现”“得知”或具有类似含义的词语，指知道而不是有理由知道。

（c）“Discover,” “learn,” or words of similar import refer to knowledge rather than to reason to know.

（d）一个人在通知另一人时，只要采取了正常情况下为使该另一人获得通知所合理需要的步骤，即属于已“通知”该另一人，无论该另一人是否实际得知该通知。

（d）A person “notifies” or “gives” a notice or notification to another person by taking such steps as may be reasonably required to inform the other person in ordinary course, whether or not the other person actually comes to know of it.

（e）除（f）款另有规定外，一个人被视为在下列时间“收到”通知：

（e）Subject to Subsection（f）, a person “receives” a notice or notification when:

（1）该人注意到该通知的时间；或

（1）it comes to that person's attention;or

（2）该通知被适当送达的时间，即该通知以当时情况下合理的方式，被送至该人订立合同的营业地，或送至该人表明用于接收此类通信的其他地点。

（2）it is duly delivered in a form reasonable under the circumstances at the place of business through which the contract was made or at another location held out by that person as the place for receipt of such communications.

（f）如果一个组织内从事一项交易的个人，注意到该组织收到的涉及该交易的通知，则该通知从被注意到的时间起生效；无论如何，该通知从该组织行使适当勤勉时，该人本应注意到该通知的时间起生效。如果一个组织具有合理的日常制度，使从事该交易的人能够得到重要情况的通知，且该组织合理遵守了这些制度，该组织即行使了适当勤勉。适当勤勉不要求为该组织工作的任何个人去传送信息，除非该传送是该人日常职责的一部分；或该人有理由知道该交易，并知道该信息对该交易有重大影响。

（f）Notice, knowledge, or a notice or notification received by an organization is effective for a particular transaction from the time it is brought to the attention of the individual conducting that transaction and, in any event, from the time it would have been brought to the individual's attention if the organization had exercised due diligence. An organization exercises due diligence if it maintains reasonable routines for communicating significant information to the person conducting the transaction and there is reasonable compliance with the routines. Due diligence does not require an individual acting for the organization to communicate information unless the communication is part of the individual's regular duties or the individual has reason to know of the transaction and that the transaction would be materially affected by the information.

第 1.203 条　租赁与担保权益的区别

§ 1.203. Lease Distinguished from Security Interest.

（a）采用租赁形式的交易，所设立的是租赁还是担保权益，需要根据交易的事实确定。

（a）Whether a transaction in the form of a lease creates a lease or security interest is determined by the facts of each case.

（b）在采用租赁形式的交易中，如果承租方为取得占有

（b）A transaction in the form of a lease creates a security interest if the consideration

和使用货物的权利向出租方支付的对价，是租赁期内一直存续且承租方无权终止的义务，且同时存在下列情况，该交易即属于设立担保权益：

（1）租赁的原始期限等于或大于货物的剩余经济寿命期；

（2）承租方有义务在货物的剩余经济寿命期内续租，或有义务成为货物的所有权人；

（3）在遵守租赁协议的情况下，承租方有权选择不支付额外对价或支付象征性额外对价，即可在货物的剩余经济寿命期内续租；或

（4）在遵守租赁协议的情况下，承租方有权选择不支付额外对价或支付象征性额外对价，即可成为货物的所有权人。

（c）采用租赁形式的交易，并不仅因下列情况而成为设立担保权益的交易：

（1）为取得占有和使用货物的权利，承租方有义务向出租方支付的对价，其现值基本等于或大于达成租赁时货物的公平市场价值；

（2）承租方承担货物的损失风险；

（3）承租方同意支付与货

that the lessee is to pay the lessor for the right to possession and use of the goods is an obligation for the term of the lease and is not subject to termination by the lessee, and:

（1）the original term of the lease is equal to or greater than the remaining economic life of the goods;

（2）the lessee is bound to renew the lease for the remaining economic life of the goods or is bound to become the owner of the goods;

（3）the lessee has an option to renew the lease for the remaining economic life of the goods for no additional consideration or for nominal additional consideration upon compliance with the lease agreement;or

（4）the lessee has an option to become the owner of the goods for no additional consideration or for nominal additional consideration upon compliance with the lease agreement.

（c）A transaction in the form of a lease does not create a security interest merely because:

（1）the present value of the consideration the lessee is obligated to pay the lessor for the right to possession and use of the goods is substantially equal to or is greater than the fair market value of the goods at the time the lease is entered into;

（2）the lessee assumes risk of loss of the goods;

（3）the lessee agrees to pay, with respect

物有关的税务、保险、申报、记录或登记的费用，或服务或维修的费用；

to the goods, taxes, insurance, filing, recording, or registration fees, or service or maintenance costs;

（4）承租方有权选择续租或成为货物的所有权人；

（4）the lessee has an option to renew the lease or to become the owner of the goods;

（5）承租方有权选择以固定的租金续租，且租金等于或大于在行使选择权时，在续租期内使用货物而可合理预期的公平市场租金；或

（5）the lessee has an option to renew the lease for a fixed rent that is equal to or greater than the reasonably predictable fair market rent for the use of the goods for the term of the renewal at the time the option is to be performed;or

（6）承租方有权选择在支付固定价格后成为货物的所有权人，且价格等于或大于在行使选择权当时，可合理预期的货物的公平市场价值。

（6）the lessee has an option to become the owner of the goods for a fixed price that is equal to or greater than the reasonably predictable fair market value of the goods at the time the option is to be performed.

（d）如果额外对价低于在承租方不行使选择权时，其履行租赁协议之可合理预期的成本，该额外对价即为象征性对价。在下列情况下，额外对价不属于象征性对价：

（d）Additional consideration is nominal if it is less than the lessee's reasonably predictable cost of performing under the lease agreement if the option is not exercised. Additional consideration is not nominal if:

（1）在给予承租方续租选择权的当时，已说明应在行使选择权的当时确定租金，且租金应为续租期内使用货物的公平市场租金；或

（1）when the option to renew the lease is granted to the lessee, the rent is stated to be the fair market rent for the use of the goods for the term of the renewal determined at the time the option is to be performed;or

（2）在给予承租方成为货物所有权人之选择权的当时，已说明应在行使选择权的当时确定价格，且价格应为货物的公平市场价值。

（2）when the option to become the owner of the goods is granted to the lessee, the price is stated to be the fair market value of the goods determined at the timc the option is to be performed.

（e）"货物的剩余经济寿命

（e）The "remaining economic life of

期”，以及“可合理预期”的公平市场租金、公平市场价值或履行租赁协议的成本，必须根据达成交易当时的事实和客观情况来确定。

the goods” and “reasonably predictable” fair market rent, fair market value, or cost of performing under the lease agreement must be determined with reference to the facts and circumstances at the time the transaction is entered into.

第 1.204 条　价值

§ 1.204. Value.

除第 3 篇、第 4 篇和第 5 篇另有规定外，如果一个人为取得权利做出下列行为，即属于通过支付价值取得该权利：

Except as otherwise provided in Articles 3, 4, and 5, a person gives value for rights if the person acquires them:

（1）作为取得该权利的交换，就提供信贷承担约束性义务，或提供即时可用的信贷，无论信贷是否已被使用，也无论在收款遇到困难时是否享有倒账权；

（1）in return for a binding commitment to extend credit or for the extension of immediately available credit, whether or not drawn upon and whether or not a charge-back is provided for in the event of difficulties in collection;

（2）将该权利作为现存索赔的担保，或用来全部或部分偿付该索赔；

（2）as security for, or in total or partial satisfaction of, a preexisting claim;

（3）为取得该权利而根据前存购买合同接受交付；或

（3）by accepting delivery under a preexisting contract for purchase;or

（4）作为取得该权利的交换，支付任何足以支持简式合同的对价。

（4）in return for any consideration sufficient to support a simple contract.

第 1.205 条　合理时间；及时

§ 1.205. Reasonable Time; Seasonableness.

（a）作出本法所要求之行为的时间是否合理，应根据行为的性质、目的和情况确定。

（a）Whether a time for taking an action required by this Act is reasonable depends on the nature, purpose, and circumstances of the action.

（b）如果行为在约定的时间或之前作出，或如果对时间

（b）An action is taken seasonably if it is taken at or within the time agreed or, if no time

无约定，行为在合理时间内作出，即为及时。

is agreed, at or within a reasonable time.

第 1.206 条 假定

如果本法就一项事实作出“假定”，或规定一项事实“假定”存在，则事实审的审理人必须认定该事实存在，除非并直至有证据显示，应该认定该事实不存在。

§ 1.206. Presumptions.

Whenever this Act creates a “presumption” with respect to a fact, or provides that a fact is “presumed,” the trier of fact must find the existence of the fact unless and until evidence is introduced that supports a finding of its nonexistence.

第3章 地域效力和一般原则

PART 3. TERRITORIAL APPLICABILITY AND GENERAL RULES

第 1.301 条 本法的地域效力；当事方选择适用法的权力

（a）除本条下述另有规定外，如果一项交易既与本州有合理联系，也与另一州或他国有合理联系，当事方可以选择适用本州的法律，也可以选择适用该另一州或他国的法律，用于约束他们之间的权利和义务。如果当事方未作选择，本法适用于与本州有适当联系的交易。

（b）当本法下列任何条款规定了适用法时，应适用该条款；相反之协议，只在所规定之法律（包括冲突法）允许的范围内才有效：

§ 1.301. Territorial Application of the Act; Parties’ Power to Choose Applicable Law.

（a）Except as provided hereafter in this section, when a transaction bears a reasonable relation to this state and also to another state or nation the parties may agree that the law either of this state or of such other state or nation shall govern their rights and duties.Failing such agreement this Act applies to transactions bearing an appropriate relation to this state.

（b）one of the following provisions of this Act specifies the applicable law, that provision governs and a contrary agreement is effective only to the extent permitted by the law（including the conflict of laws rules）so specified:

·债权人对已售货物的权利 第 2.402 条

·Rights of creditors against sold goods. Section 2.402.

·《租赁》篇的适用范围 第 2A.105 条和第 2A.106 条

·Applicability of the Article on Leases. Sections 2A.105 and 2A.106.

·《银行存款和收款》篇的适用范围 第 4.102 条

·Applicability of the Article on Bank Deposits and Collections. Section 4.102.

·《资金转账》篇中的适用法 第 4A.507 条

·Governing law in the Article on Funds Transfers.Section 4A.507.

·《信用证》篇 第 5.116 条

·Letters of Credit.Section 5.116.

·《投资证券》篇的适用范围 第 8.110 条

·Applicability of the Article on Investment Securities.Section 8.110.

·规定担保权益和农业留置权之完善方式、完善或不完善的效力，以及优先顺序的法律 第 9.301 条至第 9.307 条

·Law governing perfection, the effect of perfection or nonperfection,and the priority of security interests and agricultural liens. Sections 9.301-9.307.

第 1.302 条 通过协议加以改变

§ 1.302. Variation by Agreement.

（a）除（b）款或本法其他条款另有规定外，本法条款的效力可以通过协议加以改变。

（a）Except as otherwise provided in Subsection（b）or elsewhere in this Act, the effect of provisions of this Act may be varied by agreement.

（b）本法规定的善意、勤勉、合理和谨慎的义务，不得通过协议加以排除，但当事方可以通过协议，制定履行这些义务的衡量标准，只要所制定的标准不是明显不合理。当本法要求一项行为在合理时间内作出时，可以通过协议规定一个时间，只要该时间不是明显不合理。

（b）The obligations of good faith, diligence, reasonableness, and care prescribed by this Act may not be disclaimed by agreement.The parties, by agreement, may determine the standards by which the performance of those obligations is to be measured if those standards are not manifestly unreasonable.Whenever this Act requires an action to be taken within a reasonable time, a time that is not manifestly unreasonable may be fixed by agreement.

（c）本法某些条款包含“除

（c）The presence in certain provisions

另有协议外”或具有类似含义的用语，但这并不意味着其他条款的效力不能通过本条所述的协议加以改变。

of this Act of the phrase “unless otherwise agreed,” or words of similar import, does not imply that the effect of other provisions may not be varied by agreement under this section.

第 1.303 条　履约过程、交易过程和行业惯例

§ 1.303. Course of Performance, Course of Dealing, and Usage of Trade.

（a）“履约过程”指特定交易当事方之间的下列系列行为：

（a）A “course of performance” is a sequence of conduct between the parties to a particular transaction that exists if:

（1）当事方有关该交易之协议包含一方多次发生的履约；并且

（1）the agreement of the parties with respect to the transaction involves repeated occasions for performance by a party;and

（2）另一方知道该履约的性质，并有机会予以反对，但接受了该履约，或默认了该履约而未提出反对。

（2）the other party, with knowledge of the nature of the performance and opportunity for objection to it, accepts the performance or acquiesces in it without objection.

（b）“交易过程”指特定交易当事方之间在先前交易中的系列行为，且从合理的角度，该系列行为应被视为已构成共同理解基础，用于解释他们的表达和其他行为。

（b）A course of dealing is a sequence of conduct concerning previous transactions between the parties to a particular transaction that is fairly to be regarded as establishing a common basis of understanding for interpreting their expressions and other conduct.

（c）“行业惯例”指在一个地方、一种行业或一类贸易中普遍遵守的交易做法或方法，以致有理由期待其在目前的交易中也会得到遵守。行业惯例是否存在以及适用范围，应作为事实问题加以证明。如果能够证明某种惯例已载入行业规范或类似记录，则该记录的解释属于法律问题。

（c）A “usage of trade” is any practice or method of dealing having such regularity of observance in a place, vocation, or trade as to justify an expectation that it will be observed with respect to the transaction in question.The existence and scope of such a usage must be proved as facts.If it is established that such a usage is embodied in a trade code or similar record, the interpretation of the record is a question of law.

（d）当事方之间的履约过

（d）A course of performance or course

程或交易过程，或当事方所从事之行业或贸易中的行业惯例，或当事方知道或应该知道的行业惯例，可用于澄清当事方协议的含义，并可能会使协议的某些条款产生特定含义，还可能会对协议的条款起到补充或限制作用。如果协议项下的部分履约发生在某个地方，则对于该部分履约，可以按上述规定使用该地适用的行业惯例。

of dealing between the parties or usage of trade in the vocation or trade in which they are engaged or of which they are or should be aware is relevant in ascertaining the meaning of the parties'agreement, may give particular meaning to specific terms of the agreement, and may supplement or qualify the terms of the agreement.A usage of trade applicable in the place in which part of the performance under the agreement is to occur may be so utilized as to that part of the performance.

（e）除（f）款另有规定外，在合理的情况下，必须将协议的明示条款与适用的履约过程、交易过程或行业惯例作出互不冲突的解释。如果此种解释不合理，则：

（e）Except as otherwise provided in Subsection（f）, the express terms of an agreement and any applicable course of performance, course of dealing, or usage of trade must be construed whenever reasonable as consistent with each other.If such a construction is unreasonable:

（1）明示条款的效力优于履约过程、交易过程和行业惯例；

（1）express terms prevail over course of performance, course of dealing, and usage of trade;

（2）履约过程的效力优于交易过程和行业惯例；以及

（2）course of performance prevails over course of dealing and usage of trade;and

（3）交易过程的效力优于行业惯例。

（3）course of dealing prevails over usage of trade.

（f）除第2.209条另有规定外，如果任何条款与履约过程不一致，则履约过程可用于证明该条款已被放弃或修改。

（f）Subject to Section 2.209, a course of performance is relevant to show a waiver or modification of any term inconsistent with the course of performance.

（g）一方为证明相关行业惯例而提供的证据，只有在已通知过另一方，使法院认为足以避免不公正地使另一方感到

（g）Evidence of a relevant usage of trade offered by one party is not admissible unless that party has given the other party notice that the court finds sufficient to prevent unfair

意外时，才可被接受。

surprise to the other party.

第 1.304 条 善意的义务

§ 1.304. Obligation of Good Faith.

任何人在履行和强制履行本法项下的任何合同或义务时，均有义务以善意进行。

Every contract or duty within this Act imposes an obligation of good faith in its performance and enforcement.

第 1.305 条 灵活提供救济

§ 1.305. Remedies to Be Liberally Administered.

（a）必须灵活提供本法规定的救济，以使受损方尽可能地达到另一方充分履行义务时受损方本应达到的状态；但是，除本法或其他法律原则另有具体规定外，受损方无权取得间接损失或特殊损失赔偿，也无权取得惩罚性赔偿。

（a）The remedies provided by this Act must be liberally administered to the end that the aggrieved party may be put in as good a position as if the other party had fully performed but neither consequential or special damages nor penal damages may be had except as specifically provided in this Act or by other rule of law.

（b）本法设定的任何权利或义务，均可通过诉讼强制履行，除非设定此种权利或义务的条款另有不同的和限制性的规定。

（b）Any right or obligation declared by this Act is enforceable by action unless the provision declaring it specifies a different and limited effect.

第 1.306 条 违约发生后放弃索赔或权利

§ 1.306. Waiver or Renunciation of Claim or Right After Breach.

只要受损方在业经认证的记录中作出同意，即可在没有对价的情况下，就其所追究的违约，全部或部分放弃相关的索赔或权利。

A claim or right arising out of an alleged breach may be discharged in whole or in part without consideration by agreement of the aggrieved party in an authenticated record.

第 1.307 条 第三方文件构成表面证据

§ 1.307. Prima Facie Evidence by Third-Party Documents.

格式适当并显示为提单、保险单或保险凭证、正式过磅单或检验单、领事发票，以及其他任何经合同授权或要求而

A document in due form purporting to be a bill of lading, policy or certificate of insurance, official weigher's or inspector's certificate, consular invoice, or any other document

由第三方出具的单据，构成其本身之可靠性和真实性的表面证据，并构成第三方在单据中所陈述之事实的表面证据。

authorized or required by the contract to be issued by a third party is prima facie evidence of its own authenticity and genuineness and of the facts stated in the document by the third party.

第 1.308 条　保留权利的履约或接受履约

§ 1.308. Performance or Acceptance Under Reservation of Rights.

（a）明确保留权利的一方，即使以另一方要求或提供的方式履约，或承诺履约，或接受履约，亦不因此损害其保留的权利。“不受损害”“保留异议”或类似词句，足以构成上述保留。

（a）A party that with explicit reservation of rights performs or promises performance or assents to performance in a manner demanded or offered by the other party does not thereby prejudice the rights reserved.Such words as “without prejudice,” “under protest,” or the like are sufficient.

（b）上述（a）款不适用于和解协议。

（b）Subsection（a）does not apply to an accord and satisfaction.

第 1.309 条　任意提前的选择权

§ 1.309. Option to Accelerate at Will.

如果条款规定，一方或其权益继承人可以“任意”或在“认为自己不安全”时，或在类似含义词句规定的情况下，要求另一方提前付款或履约，或要求提供担保物或增加担保物，则该条款的含义为，只有在前者善意地相信另一方付款或履约的前景存在危险时，才有权力提出此种要求。证明缺乏此种善意的举证责任，由被行使该权力的当事方承担。

A term providing that one party or that party’s successor in interest may accelerate payment or performance or require collateral or additional collateral “at will” or when the party “deems itself insecure,” or words of similar import, means that the party has power to do so only if that party in good faith believes that the prospect of payment or performance is impaired.The burden of establishing lack of good faith is on the party against which the power has been exercised.

第 1.310 条　债务的降位

§ 1.310. Subordinated Obligations.

在承担一项债务时，可以规定该债务系降位债务，即该

An obligation may be issued as subordinated to performance of another

债务的清偿顺序低于承债人的另一项债务。债权人也可通过与承债人或与承债人的其他债权人订立协议，对前者就一项债务取得履约的权利作出降位。降位不构成可以对抗共同债务人或被降位之债权人的担保权益。

obligation of the person obligated, or a creditor may subordinate its right to performance of an obligation by agreement with either the personobligated or another creditor of the person obligated.Subordination does not create a security interest as against either the common debtor or a subordinated creditor.

词汇索引

保人	surety	第 1.201 条（b）（39）
被告	defendant	第 1.201 条（b）（14）
仓单	warehouse receipt	第 1.201 条（b）（42）
持票人	bearer	第 1.201 条（b）（5）
代表人	representative	第 1.201 条（b）（33）
担保权益	security interest	第 1.201 条（b）（35）
当事方	party	第 1.201 条（b）（26）
发送	send	第 1.201 条（b）（36）
发现	discover	第 1.202 条（c）
分行	branch	第 1.201 条（b）（7）
购买	purchase	第 1.201 条（b）（29）
购买人	purchaser	第 1.201 条（b）（30）
过错	fault	第 1.201 条（b）（17）
行业惯例	usage of trade	第 1.303 条（c）
合同	contract	第 1.201 条（b）（12）
记录	record	第 1.201 条（b）（31）
假定	presumption	第 1.206 条
价值	value	第 1.204 条
交付	delivery	第 1.201 条（b）（15）
交易过程	course of dealing	第 1.303 条（b）
金钱	money	第 1.201 条（b）（24）
救济	remedy	第 1.201 条（b）（32）
举证责任	burden of establishing	第 1.201 条（b）（8）

续表

履约过程	course of performance	第 1.303 条（a）
破产	insolvent	第 1.201 条（b）（23）
破产程序	insolvency proceeding	第 1.201 条（b）（22）
签名	signed	第 1.201 条（b）（37）
权利	right	第 1.201 条（b）（34）
人	person	第 1.201 条（b）（27）
善意	good faith	第 1.201 条（b）（20）
收到	receipt	第 1.202 条（e）
受损方	aggrieved party	第 1.201 条（b）（2）
书写	writing	第 1.201 条（b）（43）
诉讼	action	第 1.201 条（b）（1）
所有权凭证	document of title	第 1.201 条（b）（16）
提单	bill of lading	第 1.201 条（b）（6）
条款	term	第 1.201 条（b）（40）
通知	notice	第 1.202 条（a）
无授权签名	unauthorized signature	第 1.201 条（b）（41）
现值	present value	第 1.201 条（b）（28）
消费者	consumer	第 1.201 条（b）（11）
协议	agreement	第 1.201 条（b）（3）
醒目	conspicuous	第 1.201 条（b）（10）
银行	bank	第 1.201 条（b）（4）
债权人	creditor	第 1.201 条（b）（13）
真实	genuine	第 1.201 条（b）（19）
正常业务中的买方	buyer in ordinary course of business	第 1.201 条（b）（9）
知道	knowledge	第 1.202 条（b）
执票人	holder	第 1.201 条（b）（21）
种类物	fungible goods	第 1.201 条（b）（18）
州	state	第 1.201 条（b）（38）
组织	organization	第 1.201 条（b）（25）

第2篇 买 卖

ARTICLE 2. SALES

第1章 简称、通用释义和适用范围

PART 1. SHORT TITLE, GENERAL CONSTRUCTION AND SUBJECT MATTER

第 2.101 条 简称

本篇被引用时可称为《统一商法典——买卖》。

第 2.102 条 适用范围；排除在本篇之外的某些担保交易和其他交易

除上下文另有所指外，本篇适用于货物交易；本篇不适用于意图作为担保交易，而仅是采用无条件销售合同形式或即时出售形式的交易，也不削弱或废除涉及向消费者、农业生产者或其他特定种类买方出售货物的任何法律。

第 2.103 条 定义和定义索引

（a）除上下文另有所指外，在本篇中：

（1）“买方”指买进货物或订立买进货物合同的人。

§ 2.101. Short Title.

This Article may be cited as Uniform Commercial Code—Sales.

§ 2.102. Scope; Certain Security and Other Transactions Excluded from This Article.

Unless the context otherwise requires, this Article applies to transactions in goods; it does not apply to any transaction which although in the form of an unconditional contract to sell or present sale is intended to operate only as a security transaction nor does this Article impair or repeal any statute regulating sales to consumers, farmers or other specified classes of buyers.

§ 2.103. Definitions and Index of Definitions.

（a）In this Article unless the context otherwise requires

（1）“Buyer” means a person who buys or contracts to buy goods.

（2）[保留]

（3）“收到”货物，指取得货物的实际占有。

（4）“卖方”指出售货物或订立出售货物合同的人。

（b）适用于本篇或本篇特定章的其他定义及其所在位置：

“接受”　第 2.606 条

“银行信用证”　第 2.325 条

“商人之间”　第 2.104 条

“解除”　第 2.106 条（d）款

“商业单位”　第 2.105 条

“保兑信用证”　第 2.325 条

“符合合同”　第 2.106 条

“买卖合同”　第 2.106 条

“补进”　第 2.712 条

“委托”　第 2.403 条

“融资机构”　第 2.104 条

“待定货物”　第 2.105 条

“货物”　第 2.105 条

“特定化”　第 2.501 条

“分期交货合同”　第 2.612 条

“信用证”　第 2.325 条

“一批”　第 2.105 条

“商人”　第 2.104 条

“海外”　第 2.323 条

“处于卖方地位的人”　第 2.707 条

“即时出售”　第 2.106 条

“买卖”　第 2.106 条

“试用”　第 2.326 条

“试销”　第 2.326 条

（2）[Reserved]

（3）“Receipt” of goods means taking physical possession of them.

（4）“Seller” means a person who sells or contracts to sell goods.

（b）Other definitions applying to this Article or to specific parts thereof, and the sections in which they appear are:

“Acceptance”. Section 2.606.

“Banker's credit”. Section 2.325.

“Between merchants”. Section 2.104.

“Cancellation”. Section 2.106（d）.

“Commercial unit”. Section 2.105.

“Confirmed credit”. Section 2.325.

“Conforming to contract”. Section 2.106.

“Contract for sale”. Section 2.106.

“Cover”. Section 2.712.

“Entrusting”. Section 2.403.

“Financing agency”. Section 2.104.

“Future goods”. Section 2.105.

“Goods”. Section 2.105.

“Identification”. Section 2.501.

“Installment contract”. Section 2.612.

“Letter of credit”. Section 2.325.

“Lot”. Section 2.105.

“Merchant”. Section 2.104.

“Overseas”. Section 2.323.

“Person in position of seller”. Section 2.707.

“Present sale”. Section 2.106.

“Sale”. Section 2.106.

“Sale on approval”. Section 2.326.

“Sale or return”. Section 2.326.

“终止” 第2.106条

（c）其他各篇中适用于本篇的定义：

“支票” 第3.104条

“收货人” 第7.102条

“发货人” 第7.102条

“消费品” 第9.102条

“控制” 第7.106条

“拒付” 第3.502条

“汇票” 第3.104条

（d）此外，第1篇中的通用定义和解释原则适用于本篇通篇。

“Termination”. Section 2.106.

（c）The following definitions in other Articles apply to this Article:

“Check”. Section 3.104.

“Consignee”. Section 7.102.

“Consignor”. Section 7.102.

“Consumer goods”. Section 9.102.

“Control”. Section 7.106.

“Dishonor”. Section 3.502.

“Draft”. Section 3.104.

（d）In addition Article 1 contains general definitions and principles of construction and interpretation applicable throughout this Article.

第2.104条 定义：“商人”；“商人之间”；“融资机构”

§2.104. Definitions: “Merchant”; “Between Merchants”; “Financing Agency”.

（a）“商人”指从事某类货物交易的人，或因其职业而显示对交易所涉及的做法或货物具有专门知识或技能的人，或因雇佣前述职业人作为代理人、经纪人或其他中间人而可被视为具有前述专门知识或技能的人。

（a）“Merchant” means a person who deals in goods of the kind or otherwise by his occupation holds himself out as having knowledge or skill peculiar to the practices or goods involved in the transaction or to whom such knowledge or skill may be attributed by his employment of an agent or broker or other intermediary who by his occupation holds himself out as having such knowledge or skill.

（b）“融资机构”指下列银行、金融公司或其他人：其在正常业务中，以货物或所有权凭证为依据提供贷款，或根据与卖方或买方达成的安排，以正常方式参与支付或收取买卖合同项下应付或应收的款项，

（b）“Financing agency” means a bank, finance company or other person who in the ordinary course of business makes advances against goods or documents of title or who by arrangement with either the seller or the buyer intervenes in ordinary course to make or collect payment due or claimed under the contract for

例如购买或支付卖方的汇票，或以汇票为依据提供贷款，或单纯收取汇票用于收款，而无论所有权凭证是否跟随或依附汇票。涉及就货物处于卖方地位和买方地位的人时（第2.707条），“融资机构”还包括以类似方式介入该等人之间的银行或其他人。

sale, as by purchasing or paying the seller's draft or making advances against it or by merely taking it for collection whether or not documents of title accompany or are associated with the draft. "Financing agency" includes also a bank or other person who similarly intervenes between persons who are in the position of seller and buyer in respect to the goods (Section 2.707).

（c）“商人之间”指在任何交易中，当事双方均可被视为对该交易拥有商人的知识或技能。

(c) "Between merchants" means in any transaction with respect to which both parties are chargeable with the knowledge or skill of merchants.

第2.105条 定义：可转让性；“货物”；“待定”货物；“一批”；“商业单位”

§ 2.105. Definitions:Transferability; "Goods"; "Future" Goods; "Lot"; "Commercial Unit".

（a）“货物”指在特定于买卖合同项下时可以移动的所有物品（包括特别制造的货物），但不包括用于支付价款的金钱，也不包括投资证券（第8篇）或诉权物。“货物”还包括待出生的动物幼仔和生长中的农作物，以及某些附着于不动产但已特定化的物品，即第2.107条所描述的尚待与不动产分离的货物。

(a) "Goods" means all things (including specially manufactured goods) which are movable at the time of identification to the contract for sale other than the money in which the price is to be paid, investment securities (Article 8) and things in action. "Goods" also includes the unborn young of animals and growing crops and other identified things attached to realty as described in the section on goods to be severed from realty (Section 2.107).

（b）货物必须现实存在并已特定化，其中的权益才能发生转移。不是现实存在并已特定化的货物，属于“待定”货物。对待定货物或其中任何权益试图作出的即时出售，效力

(b) Goods must be both existing and identified before any interest in them can pass.Goods which are not both existing and identified are "future" goods.A purported present sale of future goods or of any interest therein operates as a contract to sell.

上相当于订立出售合同。

（c）对现实存在并已特定化的货物，可以仅出售其中的部分权益。

（c）There may be a salc of a part interest in existing identified goods.

（d）已特定化的一份种类物，即使总量尚未确定，其中未与整份货物分离的任何份额，应被视为已足够特定，可以用于出售。该份货物中任何约定的比例，或任何以约定的数字、重量或其他标准计算的数量，可在卖方对该份货物所拥有之权益的范围内出售给买方，而买方因此成为共同所有权人。

（d）An undivided share in an identified bulk of fungible goods is sufficiently identified to be sold although the quantity of the bulk is not determined.Any agreed proportion of such a bulk or any quantity thereof agreed upon by number, weight or other measure may to the extent of the seller's interest in the bulk be sold to the buyer who then becomes an owner in common.

（e）“一批”指构成单独一次出售或交货的一宗或一件物品，无论其是否足以履行合同。

（e）“Lot” means a parcel or a single article which is the subject matter of a separate sale or delivery, whether or not it is sufficient to perform the contract.

（f）“商业单位”指在商业惯例中作为单一整体销售的货物单位，即如果将此单位分割，将严重损害货物的特性、市场价值或使用价值。一个商业单位可以是一件物品（如一台机器），或一组物品（如一套家具或一套尺寸不同的物品），或一定数量（如一包、一罗或一车），也可以是在使用中或在有关市场上被视作单一整体的任何其他单位。

（f）“Commercial unit” means such a unit of goods as by commercial usage is a single whole for purposes of sale and division of which materially impairs its character or value on the market or in use.A commercial unit may be a single article（as a machine）or a set of articles（as a suite of furniture or an assortment of sizes）or a quantity（as a bale, gross, or carload）or any other unit treated in use or in the relevant market as a single whole.

第 2.106 条 定义:“合同”;“协议”;“买卖合同”;“买卖”;“即时出售”;“符合”合同;“终止”;“解除”

§ 2.106.Definitions: “Contract”; “Agreement”; “Contract for Sale”; “Sale”; “Present Sale”; “Conforming” to Contract; “Termination”; “Cancellation”.

(a) 在本篇中,除上下文另有所指外,“合同”与“协议”仅限于与货物即时出售或未来出售有关的合同与协议。“买卖合同”既包括货物的即时出售,也包括在未来某一时间出售货物的合同。“买卖”指将所有权从卖方转移至买方,用于换取价款(第 2.401 条)。“即时出售”指订立合同的同时,买卖即告完成。

(a) In this Article unless the context otherwise requires “contract” and “agreement” are limited to those relating to the present or future sale of goods. “Contract for sale” includes both a present sale of goods and a contract to sell goods at a future time.A “sale” consists in the passing of title from the seller to the buyer for a price (Section 2.401).A “present sale” means a sale which is accomplished by the making of the contract.

(b) 货物或行为,包括履约中的任何部分,如果符合合同规定的义务,即为“符合”合同。

(b) Goods or conduct including any part of a performance are “conforming” or conform to the contract when they are in accordance with the obligations under the contract.

(c) 如果任何一方根据协议或法律赋予的权力,在另一方没有违约的情况下结束合同,合同即告“终止”。在“终止”之后,双方尚待履行的所有义务均被解除,但基于之前违约或履约而产生的权利继续存在。

(c) “Termination” occurs when either party pursuant to a power created by agreement or law puts an end to the contract otherwise than for its breach.On “termination” all obligations which are still executory on both sides are discharged but any right based on prior breach or performance survives.

(d) 如果任何一方因另一方违约而结束合同,合同即告“解除”。解除的效力与“终止”相同,但解除合同的一方,还就另一方违反整体合同或违反尚未履行的部分,保留所有救济。

(d) “Cancellation” occurs when either party puts an end to the contract for breach by the other and its effect is the same as that of “termination” except that the cancelling party also retains any remedy for breach of the whole contract or any unperformed balance.

第2.107条　尚待与不动产分离的货物：登记

（a）出售尚待与不动产分离的矿物或类似物质（包括石油和天然气）或一项结构或其材料的合同，属于本篇范围内的货物买卖合同，只要与不动产的分离系由卖方进行；但在分离之前，卖方试图对上述货物作出的即时出售，如果不能有效构成土地权益的转让，则效力上只相当于出售合同。

（b）如果合同系出售生长中的农作物（但不包括土地），或（a）款以外的附着于不动产但分离后不至于严重损坏不动产的物品，或待砍伐树木，则无论分离系由买方还是卖方进行，该合同均属于本篇的货物买卖合同，即使在订立合同时，该货物仍为不动产的组成部分。同时，当事方可以在分离之前，通过特定化完成即时出售。

（c）第三方根据不动产登记法享有的权利，优于本条各款的效力，但买卖合同可以作为转让土地权益的文件进行签署和登记。此时，对于买卖合同项下之买方的权利，该登记构成对第三方的通知。

§ 2.107. Goods to Be Severed From Realty:Recording.

(a) A contract for the sale of minerals or the like (including oil and gas) or a structure or its materials to be removed from realty is a contract for the sale of goods within this Article if they are to be severed by the seller but until severance a purported present sale thereof which is not effective as a transfer of an interest in land is effective only as a contract to sell.

(b) A contract for the sale apart from the land of growing crops or other things attached to realty and capable of severance without material harm thereto but not described in Subsection (a) or of timber to be cut is a contract for the sale of goods within this Article whether the subject matter is to be severed by the buyer or by the seller even though it forms part of the realty at the time of contracting, and the parties can by identification effect a present sale before severance.

(c) The provisions of this section are subject to any third party rights provided by the law relating to realty records, and the contract for sale may be executed and recorded as a document transferring an interest in land and shall then constitute notice to third parties of the buyer's rights under the contract for sale.

第2章　合同的形式、订立和变更

PART 2. FORM, FORMATION AND READJUSTMENT OF CONTRACT

第 2.201 条　形式要求；反欺诈法

（a）除本条另有规定外，价款达到或超过五百美元的货物买卖合同，只有存在足以表明当事方已达成买卖合同的书面文件，且被申请强制履行的当事方或其授权代理人或经纪人已在该书面文件上签名，才可通过诉讼或抗辩强制履行。一份书面文件，即使漏写或错写任何已约定的条款，也并非不足以表明合同的达成；但在本款意义上，合同只能在不超出该书面文件标明的货物数量的范围内强制履行。

（b）在商人之间，如果一方为确认合同，发出足以约束自己的书面文件，且另一方在合理时间内收到，并有理由知道其内容，此时，如果该另一方未在收到该书面文件后十日内，以书面通知拒绝其内容，该书面文件在对抗该另一方时即被视为满足了（a）款的要求。

（c）不符合（a）款要求但在其他方面有效的合同，在下列情况下可以强制履行：

（1）货物系专为买方制造，且不适合卖方在正常业务中向

§ 2.201. Formal Requirements; Statute of Frauds.

（a）Except as otherwise provided in this section a contract for the sale of goods for the price of $500 or more is not enforceable by way of action or defense unless there is some writing sufficient to indicate that a contract for sale has been made between the parties and signed by the party against whom enforcement is sought or by his authorized agent or broker. A writing is not insufficientbecause it omits or incorrectly states a term agreed upon but the contract is not enforceable under this paragraph beyond the quantity of goods shown in such writing.

（b）Between merchants if within a reasonable time a writing in confirmation of the contract and sufficient against the sender is received and the party receiving it has reason to know its contents, it satisfies the requirements of Subsection（a）against such party unless written notice of objection to its contents is given within ten days after it is received.

（c）A contract which does not satisfy the requirements of Subsection（a）but which is valid in other respects is enforceable

（1）if the goods are to be specially manufactured for the buyer and are not suitable

他人出售，且卖方在收到毁约通知之前，并在客观情况合理表明货物确系用于买方的状况下，已实质上开始货物的制造，或已就货物承担了采购义务；或

for sale to others in the ordinary course of the seller's business and the seller, before notice of repudiation is received and under circumstances which reasonably indicate that the goods are for the buyer, has made either a substantial beginning of their manufacture or commitments for their procurement;or

（2）被申请强制履行的一方，以答辩或作证承认，或在法庭上以其他方式承认，已订立买卖合同；但本款项下的强制履行，不超过该方所承认的货物数量；或

（2）if the party against whom enforcement is sought admits in his pleading, testimony or otherwise in court that a contract for sale was made, but the contract is not enforceable under this provision beyond the quantity of goods admitted;or

（3）对于强制履行所涉及的货物，货款已支付且已被接受，或货物已收到且已被接受（第2.606条）。

（3）with respect to goods for which payment has been made and accepted or which have been received and accepted（Section 2.606）.

第2.202条　最终书面表示：口头证据或外部证据

§2.202. Final Written Expression:Parol or Extrinsic Evidence.

当事方在确认性备忘录中同意的条款，或当事方以其他方式记录在书面文件中作为当事方协议之最终表示的条款，不得以任何之前达成的协议或同时达成的口头协议作为证据加以否认，但可以用下列内容加以解释或补充：

Terms with respect to which the confirmatory memoranda of the parties agree or which are otherwise set forth in a writing intended by the parties as a final expression of their agreement with respect to such terms as are included therein may not be contradicted by evidence of any prior agreement or of a contemporaneous oral agreement but may be explained or supplemented

（1）履约过程、交易过程或行业惯例（第1.303条）；以及

（1）by course of performance, course of dealing, or usage of trade（Section 1.303）;and

（2）与上述条款相和谐的补充条款证据，除非法院认定，

（2）by evidence of consistent additional terms unless the court finds the writing to have

当事方的意图是将上述书面文件作为协议条款之完整和排他的表述。

been intended also as a complete and exclusive statement of the terms of the agreement.

第 2.203 条　蜡印无效

证明买卖合同的书面文件，或证明买进或出售货物之要约的书面文件，即使加盖蜡印，亦不构成蜡封文书，有关蜡封文书的法律亦不适用于此种合同或要约。

§ 2.203. Seals Inoperative.

The affixing of a seal to a writing evidencing a contract for sale or an offer to buy or sell goods does not constitute the writing a sealed instrument and the law with respect to sealed instruments does not apply to such a contract or offer.

第 2.204 条　合同订立的一般规定

（a）货物买卖合同可以通过足以表明当事方协议的任何方式订立，包括双方承认合同之存在的行为。

（b）足以构成买卖合同的协议，即使达成的时间不确定，亦可成立。

（c）即使买卖合同的一项或多项条款存在空缺，只要当事方有意订立合同，且存在比较确定的方法用以提供适当救济，合同即不因缺乏确定性而不能成立。

§ 2.204. Formation in General.

（a）A contract for sale of goods may be made in any manner sufficient to show agreement, including conduct by both parties which recognizes the existence of such a contract.

（b）An agreement sufficient to constitute a contract for sale may be found even though the moment of its making is undetermined.

（c）Even though one or more terms are left open a contract for sale does not fail for indefiniteness if the parties have intended to make a contract and there is a reasonably certain basis for giving an appropriate remedy.

第 2.205 条　不可撤销的要约

如果商人在签名的书面文件中发出买进或出售货物的要约，且要约条款保证要约将保持有效，则在要约规定的有效时间内，或如果未规定时间，

§ 2.205. Firm Offers.

An offer by a merchant to buy or sell goods in a signed writing which by its terms gives assurance that it will be held open is not revocable, for lack of consideration, during the time stated or if no time is stated for a

则在合理时间内，即使缺乏对价，要约亦不可被撤销；但是，在任何情况下，要约不可撤销的期限都不超过三个月。如果此种保证条款载于受要约人提供的表格上，要约人必须在该条款处另加签名。

reasonable time, but in no event may such period of irrevocability exceed three months; but any such term of assurance on a form supplied by the offeree must be separately signed by the offeror.

第 2.206 条　订立合同的要约与承诺

§ 2.206.Offer and Acceptance in Formation of Contract.

（a）除语言或客观情况毫无疑义地另有所指外

（a）Unless otherwise unambiguously indicated by the language or circumstances

（1）订立合同的要约应被解释为，邀请另一方使用当时情况下为合理的任何方式和媒介作出承诺；

（1）an offer to make a contract shall be construed as inviting acceptance in any manner and by any medium reasonable in the circumstances;

（2）买进货物的订单或其他要约，如果要求迅速或立刻发运货物，即应被解释为邀请另一方以下列方式作出承诺：迅速作出发运货物的许诺，或迅速或立刻发运符合或不符合要约的货物。但是，如果发运的货物不符合要约，且卖方及时通知买方该货物仅为买方提供方便，则卖方的发货不构成承诺。

（2）an order or other offer to buy goods for prompt or current shipment shall be construed as inviting acceptance either by a prompt promise to ship or by the prompt or current shipment of conforming or non-conforming goods, but such a shipment of non-conforming goods does not constitute an acceptance if the seller seasonably notifies the buyer that the shipment is offered only as an accommodation to the buyer.

（b）即使开始作出被要求的履约属于作出承诺的合理方式，但要约人只要在合理时间内未收到关于该承诺的通知，即可认为要约未在有效时间内得到承诺而失效。

（b）Where the beginning of a requested performance is a reasonable mode of acceptance an offeror who is not notified of acceptance within a reasonable time may treat the offer as having lapsed before acceptance.

第 2.207 条 承诺或确认中的补充条款

（a）确定且及时的承诺表示，或合理时间内发送的书面确认，即使与要约条款或与已同意的条款相比，包含不同条款或补充条款，亦构成承诺，除非其明确规定，以要约人同意这些不同条款或补充条款作为承诺生效的条件。

（b）补充条款应被解释为对合同进行补充的建议。在商人之间，这些条款构成合同的组成部分，除非：

（1）要约明确规定，承诺限于要约条款；

（2）补充条款严重改变了要约；或

（3）已对补充条款作出过拒绝通知，或在收到补充条款通知后的合理时间内作出了拒绝通知。

（c）双方承认合同存在的行为，足以使买卖合同成立，即使双方的书面文件本不足以证明合同的成立。此时，该特定合同的条款，系当事方在书面文件中同意的条款，再加上根据本法任何其他规定而进入合同的填补条款。

§ 2.207. Additional Terms in Acceptance or Confirmation.

（a）A definite and seasonable expression of acceptance or a written confirmation which is sent within a reasonable time operates as an acceptance even though it states terms additional to or different from those offered or agreed upon, unless acceptance is expressly made conditional on assent to the additional or different terms.

（b）The additional terms are to be construed as proposals for addition to the contract.Between merchants such terms become part of the contract unless:

（1）the offer expressly limits acceptance to the terms of the offer;

（2）they materially alter it; or

（3）notification of objection to them has already been given or is given within a reasonable time after notice of them is received.

（c）Conduct by both parties which recognizes the existence of a contract is sufficient to establish a contract for sale although the writings of the parties do not otherwise establish a contract.In such case the terms of the particular contract consist of those terms on which the writings of the parties agree, together with any supplementary terms incorporated under any other provisions of this Act.

第 2.208 条 ［保留］

第 2.209 条 修改、取消和弃权

（a）修改本篇项下合同的协议，即使不存在对价，亦可具有约束力。

（b）如果已签署的协议规定，必须签署书面文件才能修改或取消该协议，则该协议不得用其他方法修改或取消；但除在商人之间外，如果此种规定载于商人一方提供的表格上，另一方必须在此规定处另加签名。

（c）如果修改后的合同属于本篇反欺诈条款（第 2.201 条）范围内的合同，则必须遵守该条的规定。

（d）意图作出修改或取消的行为，即使不满足（b）款或（c）款的要求，仍可构成弃权。

（e）一方作出影响合同尚未履行之部分的弃权后，可以撤回弃权，但应使另一方收到合理通知，说明另一方应严格履行弃权所涉及的条款。但是，如果另一方依赖该弃权已严重改变了处境，致使该撤回导致不公平，则不得撤回。

第 2.210 条 委托履约；转让权利

（a）一方可以委托他人代

§ 2.208. [Reserved]

§ 2.209. Modification, Rescission and Waiver.

（a）An agreement modifying a contract within this Article needs no consideration to be binding.

（b）A signed agreement which excludes modification or rescission except by a signed writing cannot be otherwise modified or rescinded, but except as between merchants such a requirement on a form supplied by the merchant must be separately signed by the other party.

（c）The requirements of the statute of frauds section of this Article（Section 2.201）must be satisfied if the contract as modified is within its provisions.

（d）Although an attempt at modification or rescission does not satisfy the requirements of Subsection（b）or（c）it can operate as a waiver.

（e）A party who has made a waiver affecting an executory portion of the contract may retract the waiver by reasonable notification received by the other party that strict performance will be required of any term waived, unless the retraction would be unjust in view of a material change of position in reliance on the waiver.

§ 2.210. Delegation of Performance; Assignment of Rights.

（a）A party may perform his duty through

为履行义务，除非当事方另有协议，或除非另一方有重大理由，需要其原始许诺人履行或控制合同所要求的活动。当事方委托履约，并不解除自己的履约义务或违约责任。

a delegate unless otherwise agreed or unless the other party has a substantial interest in having his original promisor perform or control the acts required by the contract.No delegation of performance relieves the party delegating of any duty to perform or any liability for breach.

（b）除另有协议外，卖方或买方的全部权利均可被转让，除非此种转让将严重改变另一方的义务，或严重增加另一方合同项下的负担或风险，或严重损害另一方获得回报履约的机会。基于另一方违反整体合同而产生的索赔权，或转让人在适当履行自己全部义务后获得的权利，可以被转让，即使协议有不同规定。

（b）Unless otherwise agreed all rights of either seller or buyer can be assigned except where the assignment would materially change the duty of the other party, or increase materially the burden or risk imposed on him by his contract, or impair materially his chance of obtaining return performance.A right to damages for breach of the whole contract or a right arising out of the assignor's due performance of his entire obligation can be assigned despite agreement otherwise.

（c）就卖方在合同项下的权益，设立、附着、完善或强制履行担保权益，不属于（b）款所述的严重改变买方义务、严重增加买方合同项下负担或风险，或严重损害买方获得回报履约机会的转让，除非强制履行实际造成卖方的重要履约被委托给他人；此时，仅在委托履约范围内构成该种转让。即使如此，担保权益的设立、附着、完善或强制履行仍然有效，只是：（i）如果委托履约给买方造成损失，则对于买方无法合理避免的那部分损失，卖方应承担赔偿责任；并且（ii）有

（c）The creation, attachment, perfection, or enforcement of a security interest in the seller's interest under a contract is not a transfer that materially changes the duty of or increases materially the burden or risk imposed on the buyer or impairs materially the buyer's chance of obtaining return performance within the purview of Subsection（b）unless, and then only to the extent that, enforcement actually results in a delegation of material performance of the seller.Even in that event, the creation, attachment, perfection, and enforcement of the security interest remain effective, but（i）the seller is liable to the buyer for damages caused by the delegation to the extent that the damages could not reasonably be prevented by the buyer,

管辖权的法院可以提供其他适当救济，包括解除买卖合同，或禁止担保权益强制履行的实施或完成。

and（ii）a court having jurisdiction may grant other appropriate relief, including cancellation of the contract for sale or an injunction against enforcement of the security interest or consummation of the enforcement.

（d）除客观情况另有所指外，禁止转让“合同”，应被解释为仅禁止将转让人的履约义务委托给受让人。

（d）Unless the circumstances indicate the contrary a prohibition of assignment of “the contract” is to be construed as barring only the delegation to the assignee of the assignor’s performance.

（e）转让“合同”，或转让“我在合同中的所有权利”，或以类似的概括语言作出的转让，是权利的转让；并且，除语言或客观情况（如为提供担保而作的转让）另有所指外，该转让也是转让人履约义务的委托。受让人接受委托后，即允诺履行该义务。该允诺可由转让人或原始合同的另一方强制履行。

（e）An assignment of “the contract” or of “all my rights under the contract” or an assignment in similar general terms is an assignment of rights and unless the language or the circumstances（as in an assignment for security）indicate the contrary, it is a delegation of performance of the duties of the assignor and its acceptance by the assignee constitutes a promise by him to perform those duties.This promise is enforceable by either the assignor or the other party to the original contract.

（f）如果转让构成委托履约，另一方可将其作为失去安全的合理理由，并可在不损害自己对抗转让人之权利的情况下，要求受让人提供履约保证（第 2.609 条）。

（f）The other party may treat any assignment which delegates performance as creating reasonable grounds for insecurity and may without prejudice to his rights against the assignor demand assurances from the assignee（Section 2.609）.

第3章　一般义务与合同的解释

PART 3. GENERAL OBLIGATION AND CONSTRUCTION OF CONTRACT

第 2.301 条　当事方的一般义务

卖方的义务是根据合同作出转让和交付；买方的义务是根据合同作出接受和付款。

第 2.302 条　显失公平的合同或条款

（a）如果法院认定，作为法律问题，合同或其任何条款在订立时显失公平，法院可以拒绝强制履行该合同，或仅强制履行显失公平条款以外的部分，或限制显失公平条款的适用以避免显失公平的后果。

（b）如果当事方主张，或如果法院认为，合同或其任何条款可能属于显失公平，当事方应被给予合理机会，就合同或条款的商业背景、目的和作用提供证明，帮助法院作出决定。

第 2.303 条　风险的承担或分担

如果本篇规定，在当事方之间，“除另有协议外”，一方承担一项风险或负担，则当事方通过协议，不仅可以规定另一方承担该风险或负担，也可

§ 2.301. General Obligations of Parties.

The obligation of the seller is to transfer and deliver and that of the buyer is to accept and pay in accordance with the contract.

§ 2.302. Unconscionable Contract or Clause.

（a）If the court as a matter of law finds the contract or any clause of the contract to have been unconscionable at the time it was made the court may refuse to enforce the contract, or it may enforce the remainder of the contract without the unconscionable clause, or it may so limit the application of any unconscionable clause as to avoid any unconscionable result.

（b）When it is claimed or appears to the court that the contract or any clause thereof may be unconscionable the parties shall be afforded a reasonable opportunity to present evidence as to its commercial setting, purpose and effect to aid the court in making the determination.

§ 2.303. Allocation or Division of Risks.

Where this Article allocates a risk or a burden as between the parties “unless otherwise agreed”, the agreement may not only shift the allocation but may also divide the risk or burden.

以规定当事方分担该风险或负担。

第 2.304 条 价款以金钱、货物、不动产或其他形式支付

§ 2.304. Price Payable in Money, Goods, Realty, or Otherwise.

（a）价款可以用金钱或其他形式支付。如果用货物支付全部或部分价款，则每一方均为自己即将转让之货物的卖方。

（a）The price can be made payable in money or otherwise.If it is payable in whole or in part in goods each party is a seller of the goods which he is to transfer.

（b）即使使用不动产权益支付全部或部分价款，货物的转让和卖方对货物的义务亦受本篇约束，但不动产权益的转让及其转让人的相应义务，不由本篇规定。

（b）Even though all or part of the price is payable in an interest in realty the transfer of the goods and the seller's obligations with reference to them are subject to this Article, but not the transfer of the interest in realty or the transferor's obligations in connection therewith.

第 2.305 条 价格条款存在空缺

§ 2.305. Open Price Term.

（a）即使价格未定，只要当事方有意在此种情况下订立买卖合同，合同亦可成立。此时，价格应为交付时的合理价格，只要：

（a）The parties if they so intend can conclude a contract for sale even though the price is not settled.In such a case the price is a reasonable price at the time for delivery if

（1）当事方对价格未作任何规定；或

（1）nothing is said as to price;or

（2）价格留待当事方商定而当事方未能商定；或

（2）the price is left to be agreed by the parties and they fail to agree;or

（3）价格的确定，应以第三人或第三方机构设立或记录的某个约定市场或其他标准为根据，而此种设立或记录未能进行。

（3）the price is to be fixed in terms of some agreed market or other standard as set or recorded by a third person or agency and it is not so set or recorded.

（b）如果价格应由卖方或买方单方确定，其必须以善意

（b）A price to be fixed by the seller or by the buyer means a price for him to fix in good

确定价格。

faith.

（c）如果价格不是通过当事方协议确定，而是通过其他方式确定，且由于一方过错致使价格未能确定，另一方可以认为合同已被解除，也可以自行确定一个合理价格。

（c）When a price left to be fixed otherwise than by agreement of the parties fails to be fixed through fault of one party the other may at his option treat the contract as cancelled or himself fix a reasonable price.

（d）但是，如果当事方无意在未确定或未商定价格的情况下受到约束，则只要未能确定或未能商定价格，合同即不成立。此时，买方必须退回已收到的货物，如果无法退回，必须支付货物交付时的合理价值；而卖方必须退回买方预付的任何价款。

（d）Where, howcver, the parties intend not to be bound unless the price be fixed or agreed and it is not fixed or agreed there is no contract.In such a case the buyer must return any goods already received or if unable so to do must pay their reasonable value at the time of delivery and the seller must return any portion of the price paid on account.

第2.306条　产出、需求和独营

§2.306. Output, Requirements and Exclusive Dealings.

（a）如果以卖方的产出量或买方的需求量作为计算数量的条款，则该条款指善意作为时的实际产出量或实际需求量。但是，提供的产出或索要的需求，与已作出的预估相比，或如果无此预估，与正常的或以前可比的产出量或需求量相比，不得有不合理的差距。

（a）A term which measures the quantity by the output of the seller or the requirements of the buyer means such actual output or requirements as may occur in good faith, except that no quantity unreasonably disproportionate to any stated estimate or in the absence of a stated estimate to any normal or otherwise comparable prior output or requirements may be tendered or demanded.

（b）如果存在合法协议，规定卖方或买方独营某种货物，则除另有协议外，卖方有义务尽最大努力提供该货物，买方有义务尽最大努力推销该货物。

（b）A lawful agreement by either the seller or the buyer for exclusive dealing in the kind of goods concerned imposes unless otherwise agreed an obligation by the seller to use best efforts to supply the goods and by the buyer to use best efforts to promote their sale.

第 2.307 条　整批交付或分批交付

除另有协议外，买卖合同所要求的全部货物，必须整批提示交付，且只有作出此种提示，价款才到支付时间。但是，如果客观情况使任何一方有权提出分批交付，则在价款可按比例计算时，卖方可以要求就每批货物取得相应价款。

§ 2.307. Delivery in Single Lot or Several Lots.

Unless otherwise agreed all goods called for by a contract for sale must be tendered in a single delivery and payment is due only on such tender but where the circumstances give either party the right to make or demand delivery in lots the price if it can be apportioned may be demanded for each lot.

第 2.308 条　未规定交货地点

除另有协议外，

（1）货物的交付地点为卖方的营业地；如果无营业地，则为卖方的住所地；但是

（2）如果合同出售的是已特定化的货物，且当事方在订立合同时已知货物在其他地点，则该其他地点为货物的交付地点；并且

（3）所有权凭证可以通过惯常银行渠道交付。

§ 2.308. Absence of Specified Place for Delivery.

Unless otherwise agreed

（1）the place for delivery of goods is the seller's place of business or if he has none his residence;but

（2）in a contract for sale of identified goods which to the knowledge of the parties at the time of contracting are in some other place, that place is the place for their delivery;and

（3）documents of title may be delivered through customary banking channels.

第 2.309 条　未规定具体时间；终止通知

（a）发运或交付的时间，或合同规定的其他行为的时间，如果本篇未作规定，也不存在协议，即应为合理时间。

（b）规定持续履行但未规定终止时间的合同，在合理期限内有效；但除另有协议外，任何一方均可随时终止合同。

§ 2.309. Absence of Specific Time Provisions; Notice of Termination.

（a）The time for shipment or delivery or any other action under a contract if not provided in this Article or agreed upon shall be a reasonable time.

（b）Where the contract provides for successive performances but is indefinite in duration it is valid for a reasonable time but unless otherwise agreed may be terminated at any time by either party.

（c）一方终止合同，除根据约定原因作出外，必须使另一方收到合理通知。免除此种通知的协议如果导致显失公平，即属无效。

（c）Termination of a contract by one party except on the happening of an agreed event requires that reasonable notification be received by the other party and an agreement dispensing with notification is invalid if its operation would be unconscionable.

第 2.310 条 未规定付款时间或信用开始时间；有权作出保留权利的发运

§ 2.310. Open Time for Payment or Running of Credit;Authority to Ship Under Reservation.

除另有协议外，

（1）价款应在买方预定收到货物的时间和地点支付，即使发运地同时为交付地；并且

（2）如果卖方被授权发送货物，其可以作出保留权利的发运，并可以提示交付所有权凭证。买方可以在货物到达后先行检验，然后再支付价款，除非此种检验与合同条款不符（第 2.513 条）；并且

（3）如果交付已得到授权，且应通过交付所有权凭证进行[上述（2）款规定的情况除外]，则无论预定收货地点为何处，均应在以下时间和地点付款：

（A）在买方预定收到实体凭证交付的时间和地点；或

（B）在买方预定收到电子凭证交付的时间，并在卖方的营业地，或如果没有营业地，

Unless otherwise agreed

（1）payment is due at the time and place at which the buyer is to receive the goods even though the place of shipment is the place of delivery;and

（2）if the seller is authorized to send the goods he may ship them under reservation, and may tender the documents of title, but the buyer may inspect the goods after their arrival before payment is due unless such inspection is inconsistent with the terms of the contract（Section 2.513）;and

（3）if delivery is authorized and made by way of documents of title otherwise than by Subdivision（2）then payment is due regardless of where the goods are to be received:

（A）at the time and place at which the buyer is to receive delivery of the tangible documents;or

（B）at the time the buyer is to receive delivery of the electronic documents and at the seller's place of business or if none, the

在卖方的住所地；并且

（4）如果卖方被要求或被授权凭信用发运货物，则信用期从发运时起计。但是，如果错后填写发货单的日期，或延迟送出发货单，则信用期的开始应相应推迟。

第 2.311 条　履约中的选择权与合作

（a）如果买卖协议在其他方面具有充分确定性［第 2.204 条（c）款］，足以构成合同，则即使某些履约细节被留待任何一方随后选定，合同亦不会因此无效。此种选择必须以善意作出，且必须具有商业合理性。

（b）除另有协议外，货物的花色规格由买方选择；且除第 2.319 条（a）（3）款和（c）款另有规定外，发运的规格或安排由卖方选择。

（c）如果此种选择对另一方的履约有重大影响，却未能及时作出选择，或如果一方的合作对另一方的约定履约为必要，却未能及时提供合作，则该另一方除享有所有其他救济外：

（1）对于因此导致的自己延迟履约，即被免除责任；并且

seller's residence;and

（4）where the sellcr is required or authorized to ship the goods on credit the credit period runs from the time of shipment but post-dating the invoice or delaying its dispatch will correspondingly delay the starting of the credit period.

§ 2.311. Options and Cooperation Respecting Performance.

（a）An agreement for sale which is otherwise sufficiently definite（Subsection（c）of Section 2.204）to be a contract is not made invalid by the fact that it leaves particulars of performance to be specified by one of the parties.Any such specification must be made in good faith and within limits set by commercial reasonableness.

（b）Unless otherwise agreed specifications relating to assortment of the goods are at the buyer's option and except as otherwise provided in Subsections（a）（3）and（c）of Section 2.319 specifications or arrangements relating to shipment are at the seller's option.

（c）Where such specification would materially affect the other party's performance but is not seasonably made or where one party's cooperation is necessary to the agreed performance of the other but is not seasonably forthcoming, the other party in addition to all other remedies

（1）is excused for any resulting delay in his own performance;and

（2）可以选择以任何合理方式继续履约，也可以选择在自己履约的重要部分已完成的情况下，把另一方未能作出选择或未能提供合作的行为，视为未能交付或未能接受货物的违约。

（2）may also either proceed to perform in any reasonable manner or after the time for a material part of his own performance treat the failure to specify or to cooperate as a breach by failure to deliver or accept the goods.

第 2.312 条 担保所有权；担保不存在侵权；买方不得侵权的义务

§ 2.312. Warranty of Title and Against Infringement; Buyer's Obligation Against Infringement.

（a）除（b）款另有规定外，买卖合同中包含卖方的下列担保：

（a）Subject to Subsection（b）there is in a contract for sale a warranty by the seller that

（1）所转让的所有权系属完好，且转让系属正当；并且

（1）the title conveyed shall be good, and its transfer rightful;and

（2）货物在交付时，不存在买方在订立合同时不知道的任何担保权益，或其他留置权或他项权。

（2）the goods shall be delivered free from any security interest or other lien or encumbrance of which the buyer at the time of contracting has no knowledge.

（b）要排除或修改（a）款规定的担保，必须通过具体的语言或客观情况，使买方有理由知道，出售货物的人不声称拥有所有权，或只试图出售自己或第三人可能拥有的那部分权利或所有权。

（b）A warranty under Subsection（a）will be excluded or modified only by specific language or by circumstances which give the buyer reason to know that the person selling does not claim title in himself or that he is purporting to sell only such right or title as he or a third person may have.

（c）除另有协议外，卖方如果是惯常从事该类货物交易的商人，即担保所交付的货物不受任何第三人以侵权或类似原因提出的正当索赔。但是，如果买方向卖方提供货物规格，且卖方因遵从该规格受到侵权

（c）Unless otherwise agreed a seller who is a merchant regularly dealing in goods of the kind warrants that the goods shall be delivered free of the rightful claim of any third person by way of infringement or the like but a buyer who furnishes specifications to the seller must hold the seller harmless against any such

索赔，买方必须保证卖方不受损失。

claim which arises out of compliance with the specifications.

第 2.313 条 通过确认、许诺、描述或样品作出的明示担保

§ 2.313. Express Warranties by Affirmation, Promise, Description, Sample.

（a）卖方通过下列方式作出明示担保：

（a）Express warranties by the seller are created as follows:

（1）如果卖方就货物向买方确认的事实或作出的许诺构成交易之基础的一部分，卖方即明示担保，货物将符合此种确认或许诺。

（1）Any affirmation of fact or promise made by the seller to the buyer which relates to the goods and becomes part of the basis of the bargain creates an express warranty that the goods shall conform to the affirmation or promise.

（2）如果对货物的任何描述构成交易之基础的一部分，卖方即明示担保，货物将符合此种描述。

（2）Any description of the goods which is made part of the basis of the bargain creates an express warranty that the goods shall conform to the description.

（3）如果任何样品或模型构成交易之基础的一部分，卖方即明示担保，全部货物都将符合此种样品或模型。

（3）Any sample or model which is made part of the basis of the bargain creates an express warranty that the whole of the goods shall conform to the sample or model.

（b）明示担保的产生，不取决于卖方是否使用“担保”或“保证”这类正式用语，也不取决于卖方是否具有提供担保的具体意图。但是，卖方仅确认货物的价值，或仅表明自己对货物的看法或赞扬，并不构成担保。

（b）It is not necessary to the creation of an express warranty that the seller use formal words such as “warrant” or “guarantee” or that he have a specific intention to make a warranty, but an affirmation merely of the value of the goods or a statement purporting to be merely the seller’s opinion or commendation of the goods does not create a warranty.

第 2.314 条 默示担保：商销性；行业惯例

§ 2.314. Implied Warranty: Merchantability; Usage of Trade.

（a）如果货物买卖合同的卖方是该类货物的商人，合同

（a）Unless excluded or modified（Section 2.316）, a warranty that the goods shall be

即包含一项默示担保，即货物具有商销性，除非该担保被排除或修改（第2.316条）。在本条中，为收取价值而提供在店堂或其他地点消费的食品或饮料，亦属买卖。

merchantable is implied in a contract for their sale if the seller is a merchant with respect to goods of that kind.Under this section the serving for value of food or drink to be consumed either on the premises or elsewhere is a sale.

（b）货物至少达到下列标准才具有商销性：

（b）Goods to be merchantable must be at least such as

（1）根据合同的描述，货物可以不受异议地得到本行业认可；并且

（1）pass without objection in the trade under the contract description;and

（2）涉及种类物时，货物在描述范围内具有良好平均品质；并且

（2）in the case of fungible goods, are of fair average quality within the description;and

（3）货物适合其使用的通常用途；并且

（3）are fit for the ordinary purposes for which such goods are used;and

（4）货物在每个单位内部以及全体相关单位之间，种类、质量及数量均匀，差异在协议允许的范围内；并且

（4）run, within the variations permitted by the agreement, of even kind, quality and quantity within each unit and among all units involved;and

（5）当协议有要求时，货物按要求妥善地置入容器、加以包装并贴上标签；并且

（5）are adequately contained, packaged, and labeled as the agreement may require;and

（6）当容器或标签上载有许诺或对事实的确认时，货物符合此种许诺或确认。

（6）conform to the promises or affirmations of fact made on the container or label if any.

（c）交易过程或行业惯例可以引起其他默示担保，除非该担保被排除或修改（第2.316条）。

（c）Unless excluded or modified（Section 2.316）other implied warranties may arise from course of dealing or usage of trade.

第2.315条 默示担保：适用于特定用途

§ 2.315. Implied Warranty:Fitness for Particular Purpose.

如果在订立合同时卖方有

Where the seller at the time of contracting

理由知道，货物系用于某种特定用途，且买方依赖卖方的技能或判断来选择或提供适合的货物，卖方即默示担保，货物将适用于该用途，除非该担保根据下条被排除或修改。

has reason to know any particular purpose for which the goods are required and that thc buyer is relying on the seller's skill or judgment to select or furnish suitable goods, there is unless excluded or modified under the next section an implied warranty that the goods shall be fit for such purpose.

第 2.316 条　排除或修改担保

§ 2.316. Exclusion or Modification of Warranties.

（a）引起明示担保的词句或行为，与具有否认或限制该担保之倾向的词句或行为，在合理的情况下，应作出互不矛盾的解释；但是，除本篇有关口头证据和外部证据的条款另有规定外（第 2.202 条），在此种解释不合理时，否认或限制无效。

（a）Words or conduct relevant to the creation of an express warranty and words or conduct tending to negate or limit warranty shall be construed wherever reasonable as consistent with each other;but subject to the provisions of this Article on parol or extrinsic evidence（Section 2.202）negation or limitation is inoperative to the extent that such construction is unreasonable.

（b）除（c）款另有规定外，要排除或修改有关商销性的默示担保或其任何部分，用语必须提及商销性；如果使用书面形式，书写必须醒目。要排除或修改有关适用性的默示担保，必须使用书面形式，且书写必须醒目。要排除有关适用性的所有默示担保，可以使用诸如“不存在超出此处描述的任何其他担保”一类的词句。

（b）Subject to Subsection（c）, to exclude or modify the implied warranty of merchantability or any part of it the language must mention merchantability and in case of a writing must be conspicuous, and to exclude or modify any implied warranty of fitness the exclusion must be by a writing and conspicuous.Language to exclude all implied warranties of fitness is sufficient if it states, for example, that “There are no warranties which extend beyond the description on the face hereof.”

（c）即使有（b）款的规定，

（c）Notwithstanding Subsection（b）

（1）除客观情况另有所指外，使用诸如“依现状”或“残

（1）unless the circumstances indicate otherwise, all implied warranties are excluded

次品”这类用语，或其他根据通常理解可使买方注意到排除担保且明确不存在默示担保的用语，即可排除所有默示担保；并且

by expressions like “as is”, “with all faults” or other language which in common understanding calls the buyer's attention to the exclusion of warranties and makes plain that there is no implied warranty;and

（2）如果买方在订立合同前，按照自己希望的详细程度检验了货物或其样品或模型，或拒绝检验货物，则对货物中通过检验在当时情况下本可发现的瑕疵，不存在默示担保；并且

（2）when the buyer before entering into the contract has examined the goods or the sample or model as fully as he desired or has refused to examine the goods there is no implied warranty with regard to defects which an examination ought in the circumstances to have revealed to him;and

（3）交易过程、履约过程或行业惯例也可以排除或修改默示担保。

（3）an implied warranty can also be excluded or modified by course of dealing or course of performance or usage of trade.

（d）可以根据本篇关于约定或限制损害赔偿的条款，以及关于通过合同修改救济的条款（第 2.718 条和第 2.719 条），对违反担保的救济加以限制。

（d）Remedies for breach of warranty can be limited in accordance with the provisions of this Article on liquidation or limitation of damages and on contractual modification of remedy（Sections 2.718 and 2.719）.

（e）有关商销性和适用性的默示担保，不适用于由血库或组织库或器官库所提供的人类血液、血浆或其他人体组织或器官。为本法目的，此种血液、血浆或其他组织或器官，不属于可以买卖或易货的商品，而应被视为医疗服务。

（e）The implied warranties of merchantability and fitness shall not be applicable to the furnishing of human blood, blood plasma, or other human tissue or organs from a blood bank or reservoir of such other tissues or organs.Such blood, blood plasma or tissue or organs shall not for the purpose of this Act be considered commodities subject to sale or barter, but shall be considered as medical services.

（f）有关商销性和适用性的默示担保，不适用于动物或其待出生幼仔的买卖或易货。

（f）The implied warranties of merchantability and fitness do not apply to the sale or barter of livestock or its unborn young.

第 2.317 条　明示担保或默示担保的叠加和冲突

各种担保，无论为明示或默示，均应被解释为互不矛盾，且效力叠加。如果此种解释不合理，应根据当事方的意图确定哪项担保为主。当事方的意图，应根据下列原则确定：

（1）精确规格或技术规格，排除不一致的样品或模型，或一般性文字描述。

（2）现存批量货物中抽出的样品，排除不一致的一般性文字描述。

（3）明示担保排除不一致的默示担保，但适用于特定用途的默示担保除外。

§ 2.317. Cumulation and Conflict of Warranties Express or Implied.

Warranties whether express or implied shall be construed as consistent with each other and as cumulative, but if such construction is unreasonable the intention of the parties shall determine which warranty is dominant.In ascertaining that intention the following rules apply:

（1）Exact or technical specifications displace an inconsistent sample or model or general language of description.

（2）A sample from an existing bulk displaces inconsistent general language of description.

（3）Express warranties displace inconsistent implied warranties other than an implied warranty of fitness for a particular purpose.

第 2.318 条　本篇对质量担保之第三方受益人问题及合同关系之必要性问题不作规定

对于下列问题，即向买方作出的有关质量的明示担保或默示担保是否可使买方以外的人受益，以及买方（或买方所获担保的其他受益人）是否可就货物质量瑕疵起诉除直接卖方以外的第三方，本篇不作规定。此类问题留给法院决定。

§ 2.318. Article Neutral on Question of Third Party Beneficiaries of Warranties of Quality and on Need for Privity of Contract.

This Article does not provide whether anyone other than a buyer may take advantage of an express or implied warranty of quality made to the buyer or whether the buyer or anyone entitled to take advantage of a warranty made to the buyer may sue a third party other than the immediate seller for deficiencies in the quality of the goods.These matters are left to the courts for their determination.

第 2.319 条　“运输工具上交货”条款；“船边交货”条款

（a）除另有协议外，在指

§ 2.319. F.O.B. and F.A.S. Terms.

（a）Unless otherwise agreed the term

定地点的“运输工具上交货”条款，即使仅用于所报的价格，仍构成包含下列内容的交付条款：

F.O.B.（which means “free on board”）at a named place, even though used only in connection with the stated price, is a delivery term under which

（1）如果使用发运地“运输工具上交货”条款，卖方必须按本篇规定的方式在该地发运货物（第 2.504 条），并承担将货物交给承运人占有的费用和风险；或

（1）when the term is F.O.B. the place of shipment, the seller must at that place ship the goods in the manner provided in this Article（Section 2.504）and bear the expense and risk of putting them into the possession of the carrier;or

（2）如果使用目的地“运输工具上交货”条款，卖方必须自行承担费用和风险，将货物运输到该地，并在该地按本篇规定的方式提示交付（第 2.503 条）；

（2）when the term is F.O.B. the place of destination, the seller must at his own expense and risk transport the goods to that place and there tender delivery of them in the manner provided in this Article（Section 2.503）；

（3）无论使用（1）款或（2）款所述的条款，如果其另外附有“船舶”“汽车”或其他运输工具字样，则卖方必须另外自行承担费用和风险，将货物装上相应的运输工具。如果使用“船舶运输工具上交货”条款，买方必须提供船舶的名称；在适用的情况下，卖方必须遵守本篇有关提单格式的条款（第 2.323 条）。

（3）when under either Subdivision（1）or（2）the term is also F.O.B. vessel, car or other vehicle, the seller must in addition at his own expense and risk load the goods on board.If the term is F.O.B. vessel the buyer must name the vessel and in an appropriate case the seller must comply with the provisions of this Article on the form of bill of lading（Section 2.323）.

（b）除另有协议外，指定港“船边交货”条款，即使仅用于所报的价格，仍构成交付条款，其中，卖方必须：

（b）Unless otherwise agreed the term F.A.S. vessel（which means “free alongside”）at a named port, even though used only in connection with the stated price, is a delivery term under which the seller must

（1）自行承担费用和风险，

（1）at his own expense and risk deliver

将货物以该港口惯常的方式运至船边，或运至买方指定或提供的码头；并且

the goods alongside the vessel in the manner usual in that port or on a dock designated and provided by the buyer;and

（2）取得货物收据并向买方提示交付该收据，且必须使承运人有义务凭该收据换发提单。

（2）obtain and tender a receipt for the goods in exchange for which the carrier is under a duty to issue a bill of lading.

（c）除涉及（a）（1）款或（3）款或（b）款所述情况时另有协议外，买方必须及时提供交付所需的指示，包括涉及"船边交货"条款或"运输工具上交货"条款时，说明船舶的装运舶位；在适用的情况下，还包括船舶的名称和航行日期。卖方如果未得到所需的指示，可以认为未获得本篇规定的合作（第 2.311 条）。卖方还可选择以任何合理方式移动货物，作为交付或发运的准备。

（c）Unless otherwise agreed in any case falling within Subsection（a）（1）or（3）or Subsection（b）the buyer must seasonably give any needed instructions for making delivery, including when the term is F.A.S. or F.O.B. the loading berth of the vessel and in an appropriate case its name and sailing date.The seller may treat the failure of needed instructions as a failure of cooperation under this Article（Section 2.311）. He may also at his option move the goods in any reasonable manner preparatory to delivery or shipment.

（d）在使用"船舶运输工具上交货"条款或"船边交货"条款时，除另有协议外，卖方一旦提示交付所需单据，买方就必须付款；卖方不得提示交付货物用于代替单据，买方也不得作此要求。

（d）Under the term F.O.B. vessel or F.A.S. unless otherwise agreed the buyer must make payment against tender of the required documents and the seller may not tender nor the buyer demand delivery of the goods in substitution for the documents.

第 2.320 条 "成本加保险费运费"条款；"成本加运费"条款

§ 2.320. C.I.F. and C. & F. Terms.

（a）"成本加保险费运费"条款，指在一个总体价格中包含了货物价格和将货物运达指

（a）The term C.I.F. means that the price includes in a lump sum the cost of the goods and the insurance and freight to the named

定目的地的保险费和运费。“成本加运费”条款，指在一个总体价格中包含了货物价格和将货物运达指定目的地的运费。

destination.The term C. & F. or C.F. means that the price so includes cost and freight to the named destination.

（b）除另有协议外，目的地“成本加保险费运费”条款或其他相等条款，即使仅用于所报的价格和目的地，仍要求卖方自行承担费用和风险完成下列：

（b）Unless otherwise agreed and even though used only in connection with the stated price and destination, the term C.I.F. destination or its equivalent requires the seller at his own expense and risk to

（1）在发运港将货物交给承运人占有，并取得将货物全程运至指定目的地的流通提单；并且

（1）put the goods into the possession of a carrier at the port for shipment and obtain a negotiable bill or bills of lading covering the entire transportation to the named destination;and

（2）将货物装上运输工具，并从承运人取得证明运费已付或已落实的收据（可包括在提单内）；并且

（2）load the goods and obtain a receipt from the carrier（which may be contained in the bill of lading）showing that the freight has been paid or provided for;and

（3）取得保险单或保险凭证（包括任何战争险），且类型和条款为发运港当时所通行，金额为惯常数额，货币为合同货币，涉及之货物为提单所覆盖的货物，损失赔偿的受款人为买方的指定人或其他相关人；但在含有战争险时，卖方可将此种保险的费用加计在货物价格内；并且

（3）obtain a policy or certificate of insurance, including any war risk insurance, of a kind and on terms then current at the port of shipment in the usual amount, in the currency of the contract, shown to cover the same goods covered by the bill of lading and providing for payment of loss to the order of the buyer or for the account of whom it may concern;but the seller may add to the price the amount of the premium for any such war risk insurance;and

（4）准备发货单，并取得所有为发运货物所必需的或合同所规定的其他单据；并且

（4）prepare an invoice of the goods and procure any other documents required to effect shipment or to comply with the contract;and

（5）以商业式迅捷送出并提示所有单据，且单据格式必

（5）forward and tender with commercial promptness all the documents in due form and

须适当，并附有为完善买方之权利所必要的任何背书。

with any indorsement necessary to perfect the buyer's rights.

（c）除另有协议外，"成本加运费"条款或其他相等条款，除不存在保险义务外，其他方面与"成本加保险费运费"条款的效力相同，且卖方应承担的义务和风险也相同。

（c）Unless otherwise agreed the term C. & F. or its equivalent has the same effect and imposes upon the seller the same obligations and risks as a C.I.F. term except the obligation as to insurance.

（d）在使用"成本加保险费运费"条款或"成本加运费"条款时，除另有协议外，卖方一旦提示交付所需的单据，买方就必须付款。卖方不得提示交付货物用于代替单据，买方也不得作此要求。

（d）Under the term C.I.F. or C. & F. unless otherwise agreed the buyer must make payment against tender of the required documents and the seller may not tender nor the buyer demand delivery of the goods in substitution for the documents.

第 2.321 条 "成本加保险费运费"条款或"成本加运费"条款："到货净重"；"货到付款"；担保到货品质

§ 2.321. C.I.F. or C. & F.: "Net Landed Weights"; "Payment on Arrival"; Warranty of Condition on Arrival.

当合同使用"成本加保险费运费"条款或"成本加运费"条款时：

Under a contract containing a term C.I.F. or C. & F.

（a）如果价格是根据"到货净重""交付后的重量""产出"数量或质量，或类似标准计算或调整时，除另有协议外，卖方必须合理估算价格。在提示合同规定的单据后，应支付的价格为此种估算价格。价格的最终调整完成后，结算必须以商业式迅捷完成。

（a）Where the price is based on or is to be adjusted according to "net landed weights", "delivered weights", "out turn" quantity or quality or the like, unless otherwise agreed the seller must reasonably estimate the price. The payment due on tender of the documents called for by the contract is the amount so estimated, but after final adjustment of the price a settlement must be made with commercial promptness.

（b）上述（a）款所述的协议，

（b）An agreement described in Subsection

或对到达货物之质量或状况的任何担保，使卖方对货物在运输途中出现的正常变质、减损或类似问题承担风险，但不影响货物特定于买卖合同项下的时间或地点，不影响交付的时间或地点，也不影响损失风险的转移。

(a) or any warranty of quality or condition of the goods on arrival places upon the seller the risk of ordinary deterioration, shrinkage and the like in transportation but has no effect on the place or time of identification to the contract for sale or delivery or on the passing of the risk of loss.

（c）除另有协议外，如果合同规定货到之时或之后付款，卖方必须允许在付款前对货物进行任何可行的初步检验；但如果货物已灭失，则交付单据和付款的时间，为货物本应到达的时间。

（c）Unless otherwise agreed where the contract provides for payment on or after arrival of the goods the seller must before payment allow such preliminary inspection as is feasible; but if the goods are lost delivery of the documents and payment are due when the goods should have arrived.

第 2.322 条 “目的港船上交货”条款

§ 2.322. Delivery “Ex-Ship”.

（a）除另有协议外，“目的港船上交货”条款（指装运船）或其他相等用语的交货条款，不要求使用特定船舶，而只要求装运货物的船舶到达指定目的港内惯常卸载该类货物的地方进行交付。

（a）Unless otherwise agreed a term for delivery of goods “ex-ship”（which means from the carrying vessel）or in equivalent language is not restricted to a particular ship and requires delivery from a ship which has reached a place at the named port of destination where goods of the kind are usually discharged.

（b）除另有协议外，此种条款表示：

（b）Under such a term unless otherwise agreed

（1）卖方必须解除因货物运输产生的所有留置权，并向买方提供一份指令，即承运人有义务据此承担交货义务的指令；并且

（1）the seller must discharge all liens arising out of the carriage and furnish the buyer with a direction which puts the carrier under a duty to deliver the goods;and

（2）在货物脱离船舶吊钩前或以其他适当方式卸载前，

（2）the risk of loss does not pass to the buyer until the goods leave the ship’s tackle or

损失风险不转移至买方。

第 2.323 条　海外运输所需的提单格式；“海外”

（a）如果合同涉及海外运输，并使用“成本加保险费运费”条款或“成本加运费”条款或“船舶运输工具上交货”条款，则除另有协议外，卖方必须取得标明货物已装上船舶的流通提单；在使用“成本加保险费运费”条款或“成本加运费”条款时，可以只取得货物已收待运的流通提单。

（b）涉及（a）款规定的情况时，如果一套提单出具时为一套几份，则除另有协议外，只要单据非属寄自国外，买方可以要求交付全套提单；否则，只须提示交付提单中的任何一份。即使协议明确要求提供全套提单：

（1）适当提示的单独一份提单，在本篇关于补救不适当交付之条款的范围内［第 2.508 条（a）款］，属于可以接受的提示；并且

（2）即使提出交付全套提单的要求，但如果单据系从国外寄来，提示交付不成套提单的一方，在提供买方以善意认为充分的赔偿保证书后，可以要求取得付款。

（c）如果水路运输或航空

are otherwise properly unloaded.

§ 2.323. Form of Bill of Lading Required in Overseas Shipment; “Overseas”.

（a）Where the contract contemplates overseas shipment and contains a term C.I.F. or C. & F. or F.O.B. vessel, the seller unless otherwise agreed must obtain a negotiable bill of lading stating that the goods have been loaded on board or, in the case of a term C.I.F. or C. & F., received for shipment.

（b）Where in a case within Subsection（a）a bill of lading has been issued in a set of parts, unless otherwise agreed if the documents are not to be sent from abroad the buyer may demand tender of the full set; otherwise only one part of the bill of lading need be tendered. Even if the agreement expressly requires a full set

（1）due tender of a single part is acceptable within the provisions of this Article on cure of improper delivery（Subsection（a）of Section 2.508）;and

（2）even though the full set is demanded, if the documents are sent from abroad the person tendering an incomplete set may nevertheless require payment upon furnishing an indemnity which the buyer in good faith deems adequate.

（c）A shipment by water or by air or

运输，或规定此种运输方式的合同，根据行业惯例或协议，应适用国际深水贸易的商业、金融或运输惯例，即具有“海外”性质。

a contract contemplating such shipment is “overseas” insofar as by usage of trade or agreement it is subject to the commercial, financing or shipping practices characteristic of international deep water commerce.

第 2.324 条 “货到成交”条款

§ 2.324. “No Arrival, No Sale” Term.

除另有协议外，“货到成交”条款或具有类似含义的条款指：

Under a term “no arrival, no sale” or terms of like meaning, unless otherwise agreed,

（1）卖方必须将符合合同的货物适当地发运，并在货物以任何方式到达时，作出提示交付；但是，卖方对货物能否到达不承担责任，除非未到达系由卖方造成。

（1）the seller must properly ship conforming goods and if they arrive by any means he must tender them on arrival but he assumes no obligation that the goods will arrive unless he has caused the non-arrival;and

（2）如果非因卖方过错，货物遭受部分灭失，或变质至不符合合同的程度，或到达时间迟于合同规定的时间，买方可按已特定化的货物发生灭失采取行动（第 2.613 条）。

（2）where without fault of the seller the goods are in part lost or have so deteriorated as no longer to conform to the contract or arrive after the contract time, the buyer may proceed as if there had been casualty to identified goods（Section 2.613）.

第 2.325 条 “信用证”条款；“保兑信用证”

§ 2.325. “Letter of Credit” Term; “Confirmed Credit”.

（a）买方未及时提供已商定的信用证，属于违反买卖合同。

（a）Failure of the buyer seasonably to furnish an agreed letter of credit is a breach of the contract for sale.

（b）买方向卖方交付适当的信用证后，买方的付款义务暂时中止。如果信用证被拒付，卖方可在及时通知买方后，要求买方直接付款。

（b）The delivery to seller of a proper letter of credit suspends the buyer's obligation to pay.If the letter of credit is dishonored, the seller may on seasonable notification to the buyer require payment directly from him.

（c）除另有协议外，买卖合同中的“信用证”或“银行

（c）Unless otherwise agreed the term “letter of credit” or “banker's credit” in a

信用证”条款，指信誉良好的金融机构出具的不可撤销的信用证；涉及海外运输时，该金融机构应有良好的国际信誉。“保兑信用证”条款，指该金融机构还必须就该信用证承担直接义务，且该机构应在卖方所在的金融市场从事业务。

contract for sale means an irrevocable credit issued by a financing agency of good repute and, where the shipment is overseas, of good international repute.The term “confirmed credit” means that the credit must also carry the direct obligation of such an agency which does business in the seller’s financial market.

第 2.326 条　试用和试销；债权人的权利

§ 2.326. Sale on Approval and Sale or Return;Rights of Creditors.

（a）除另有协议外，如果已交付的货物在符合合同的情况下亦可由买方退还给卖方，此种交易：

（1）在货物主要供使用而交付时，称为“试用”；以及

（2）在货物主要供转售而交付时，称为“试销”。

（b）作为试用而持有的货物在被接受前，不受买方债权人的追索；作为试销而持有的货物，在买方占有期间，可受此种追索。

（c）买卖合同中任何“试销”的退还条款，均应被视为本篇反欺诈法范围内（第 2.201 条）的独立买卖合同，并在本篇关于口头证据或外部证据之条款的范围内（第 2.202 条），被视为与合同的销售性质相矛盾。

（a）Unless otherwise agreed, if delivered goods may be returned by the buyer even though they conform to the contract, the transaction is

（1）a “sale on approval” if the goods are delivered primarily for use, and

（2）a “sale or return” if the goods are delivered primarily for resale.

（b）Goods held on approval are not subject to the claims of the buyer’s creditors until acceptance; goods held on sale or return are subject to such claims while in the buyer’s possession.

（c）Any “or return” term of a contract for sale is to be treated as a separate contract for sale within the statute of frauds section of this Article（Section 2.201）and as contradicting the sale aspect of the contract within the provisions of this Article on parol or extrinsic evidence（Section 2.202）.

第 2.327 条　试用和试销的特殊规定

§ 2.327. Special Incidents of Sale on Approval and Sale or Return.

（a）除另有协议外，在采

（a）Under a sale on approval unless

用试用方式时：

（1）即使货物已特定于合同项下，在买方接受货物前，风险和所有权不转移至买方；并且

（2）以符合试用目的的方式使用货物，不构成接受；但未能将退货的决定及时通知卖方，则构成接受。如果货物符合合同，则对部分货物的接受，即构成对全部货物的接受；并且

（3）就退货的决定作出适当通知后，卖方承担退还货物的风险和费用，但商人买方必须遵从任何合理指示。

（b）除另有协议外，在采用试销方式时：

（1）只要货物实质上保持了原状，就可以退还全部或任何商业单位的货物，但退货必须及时；并且

（2）买方承担退货的风险和费用。

otherwise agreed

（1）although the goods are identified to the contract the risk of loss and the title do not pass to the buyer until acceptance;and

（2）use of the goods consistent with the purpose of trial is not acceptance but failure seasonably to notify the seller of election to return the goods is acceptance, and if the goods conform to the contract acceptance of any part is acceptance of the whole;and

（3）after due notification of election to return, the return is at the seller's risk and expense but a merchant buyer must follow any reasonable instructions.

（b）Under a sale or return unless otherwise agreed

（1）the option to return extends to the whole or any commercial unit of the goods while in substantially their original condition, but must be exercised seasonably;and

（2）the return is at the buyer's risk and expense.

第 2.328 条　拍卖

（a）在拍卖中，如果货物被分成几批推出，则每批货物构成独立买卖。

（b）拍卖时，拍卖人以敲木槌或其他习惯方式宣布成交时，拍卖即告完成。如果木槌正在下敲以接受一个出价的同时，又有人另出价，则拍卖人

§ 2.328. Sale by Auction.

（a）In a sale by auction if goods are put up in lots each lot is the subject of a separate sale.

（b）A sale by auction is complete when the auctioneer so announces by the fall of the hammer or in other customary manner.Where a bid is made while the hammer is falling in acceptance of a prior bid the auctioneer may in

有权决定是重开竞叫，还是按木槌下敲前的那个出价出售货物。

his discretion reopen the bidding or declare the goods sold under the bid on which the hammer was falling.

（c）拍卖均为有保留拍卖，除非在推出货物时，明确规定为无保留。在有保留拍卖中，拍卖人有权在宣布成交前的任何时间撤回货物。在无保留拍卖中，拍卖人就一件或一批货物邀请出价后，即不能将货物撤回，除非在合理时间内无人出价。无论是有保留拍卖还是无保留拍卖，出价人在拍卖人宣布成交前的任何时间，均可撤回其出价，但此种撤回不使前一出价恢复效力。

（c）Such a sale is with reserve unless the goods are in explicit terms put up without reserve.In an auction with reserve the auctioneer may withdraw the goods at any time until he announces completion of the sale.In an auction without reserve, after the auctioneer calls for bids on an article or lot, that article or lot cannot be withdrawn unless no bid is made within a reasonable time.In either case a bidder may retract his bid until the auctioneer's announcement of completion of the sale, but a bidder's retraction does not revive any previous bid.

（d）如果未事先声明保留卖方的出价权，则只要拍卖人在知情的情况下接受代表卖方作出的出价，或只要卖方作出或指使作出出价，买方即有权决定是撤销该次出售，还是以拍卖完成前最后一个善意出价买进货物。本款不适用于法院强制出售中的出价。

（d）If the auctioneer knowingly receives a bid on the seller's behalf or the seller makes or procures such a bid, and notice has not been given that liberty for such bidding is reserved, the buyer may at his option avoid the sale or take the goods at the price of the last good faith bid prior to the completion of the sale.This subsection shall not apply to any bid at a forced sale.

第4章　所有权、债权人和善意购买人

PART 4. TITLE, CREDITORS AND GOOD FAITH PURCHASERS

第 2.401 条　所有权的转移；保留权利作为担保；本条的有限适用

§ 2.401. Passing of Title; Reservation for Security;Limited Application of This Section.

本篇有关卖方、买方、购

Each provision of this Article with regard

买人或其他第三方之权利、义务和救济的任何条款，在适用时均不考虑货物所有权问题，除非有关条款提及所有权。涉及本篇其他条款未规定的情况时，如果所有权问题至关重要，则应适用下列原则：

to the rights, obligations and remedies of the seller, the buyer, purchasers or other third parties applies irrespective of title to the goods except where the provision refers to such title. Insofar as situations are not covered by the other provisions of this Article and matters concerning title become material the following rules apply:

（a）在货物特定于买卖合同项下之前，货物的所有权不可能发生转移（第 2.501 条）；并且，除另有明确协议外，货物特定化使买方获得本法限定的特殊财产权。卖方在货物已发运给或交付给买方后所保留的对货物的所有权（财产权），效力上只相当于保留担保权益。除上述条款和《担保交易》篇（第 9 篇）另有规定外，货物所有权可按当事方明确同意的方式和条件从卖方转移至买方。

（a）Title to goods cannot pass under a contract for sale prior to their identification to the contract（Section 2.501）, and unless otherwise explicitly agreed the buyer acquires by their identification a special property as limited by this Act.Any retention or reservation by the seller of the title（property）in goods shipped or delivered to the buyer is limited in effect to a reservation of asecurity interest. Subject to these provisions and to the provisions of the Article on Secured Transactions（Article 9）, title to goods passes from the seller to the buyer in any manner and on any conditions explicitly agreed on by the parties.

（b）除另有明确协议外，货物所有权在卖方完成实际交付货物之义务的时间和地点转移至买方，即使卖方保留了担保权益，或即使所有权凭证将于另时另地交付；特别是，即使存在以提单保留担保权益的情况：

（b）Unless otherwise explicitly agreed title passes to the buyer at the time and place at which the seller completes his performance with reference to the physical delivery of the goods, despite any reservation of a security interest and even though a document of title is to be delivered at a different time or place;and in particular and despite any reservation of a security interest by the bill of lading

（1）当合同要求或授权卖方将货物发送给买方，但并未

（1）if the contract requires or authorizes the seller to send the goods to the buyer

要求卖方在目的地交付货物时，所有权在发运的时间和地点转移至买方；但是

（2）当合同规定在目的地交付时，则在目的地作出提示交付的时间，所有权发生转移。

（c）除另有明确协议外，如果货物不再移动即可交付：

（1）当卖方应交付实体所有权凭证时，所有权在卖方交付此种凭证的时间和地点转移；当卖方应交付电子所有权凭证时，所有权在卖方交付凭证的时间转移；或

（2）如果在合同订立时货物已特定化，且无须交付单据，则所有权在合同订立的时间和地点转移。

（d）当买方无论有无正当理由拒绝接收或拒绝保留货物时，或当买方正当撤销接受时，货物所有权重新转移至卖方。此种重新转移系由法律规定，不构成一次“买卖”。

第 2.402 条　卖方债权人对已售货物的权利

（a）除（b）款和（c）款另有规定外，卖方的无担保债权人对已特定于买卖合同项下之货物的权利，受制于买方根据本篇规定追索货物的权利（第 2.502 条及第 2.716 条）。

but does not require him to deliver them at destination, title passes to the buyer at the time and place of shipment;but

（2）if the contract requires delivery at destination, title passes on tender there.

（c）Unless otherwise explicitly agreed where delivery is to be made without moving the goods,

（1）if the seller is to deliver a tangible document of title, title passes at the time when and the place where he delivers such documents and if the seller is to deliver an electronic document of title, title passes when the seller delivers the document;or

（2）if the goods are at the time of contracting already identified and no documents are to be delivered, title passes at the time and place of contracting.

（d）A rejection or other refusal by the buyer to receive or retain the goods, whether or not justified, or a justified revocation of acceptance revests title to the goods in the seller.Such revesting occurs by operation of law and is not a“sale”.

§ 2.402. Rights of Seller's Creditors Against Sold Goods.

（a）Except as provided in Subsections（b）and（c）, rights of unsecured creditors of the seller with respect to goods which have been identified to a contract for sale are subject to the buyer's rights to recover the goods under this Article（Sections 2.502 and 2.716）.

（b）如果根据货物所在州的法律，相对于卖方的任何债权人，卖方继续占有货物的行为构成欺诈，则该债权人可将货物的出售或特定于买卖合同项下视为无效；但是，如果卖方为商人，则在货物出售或特定化后商业上合理的时间内，卖方在营业过程中以善意继续占有货物，不属于欺诈。

（b）A creditor of the seller may treat a sale or an identification of goods to a contract for sale as void if as against him a retention of possession by the seller is fraudulent under any rule of law of the state where the goods are situated, except that retention of possession in good faith and current course of trade by a merchant-seller for a commercially reasonable time after a sale or identification is not fraudulent.

（c）涉及下列情况时，本篇任何部分均不应被视为削弱卖方债权人的权利：

（c）Nothing in this Article shall be deemed to impair the rights of creditors of the seller

（1）该权利系根据《担保交易》篇（第9篇）取得；或

（1）under the provisions of the Article on Secured Transactions（Article 9）;or

（2）货物特定于合同项下或交付货物，不是用于目前的营业过程，而是用于清偿前存金钱债务、担保债务或类似债务，或是为此种债务设立担保权益；并且，根据货物所在州的任何法律，此种特定化或交付，在本篇以外，构成欺诈性转让或可撤销的优惠清偿。

（2）where identification to the contract or delivery is made not in current course of trade but in satisfaction of or as security for a pre-existing claim for money, security or the like and is made under circumstances which under any rule of law of the state where the goods are situated would apart from this Article constitute the transaction a fraudulent transfer or voidable preference.

第2.403条 转让的权力；善意购买货物；“委托”

§ 2.403. Power to Transfer; Good Faith Purchase of Goods; “Entrusting”.

（a）货物购买人取得的，是转让人拥有的或有权力转让的全部所有权；但是，有限权益的购买人，取得的只是所购权益范围内的权利。拥有可撤销所有权的人，有权力向支付了价值的善意购买人转让完好

（a）A purchaser of goods acquires all title which his transferor had or had power to transfer except that a purchaser of a limited interest acquires rights only to the extent of the interest purchased.Aperson with voidable title has power to transfer a good title to a good faith purchaser for value.When goods have

的所有权。购买人通过购买交易取得货物的交付后，即取得此种权力，即使：

（1）对于购买人的真实身份，转让人受到欺骗；或

（2）交付系为换取支票，但支票随后被拒付；或

（3）交易被约定作为“现金买卖”；或

（4）交付系通过欺诈取得，且该欺诈构成刑法中的盗窃罪。

（b）如果将货物委托给从事该类货物交易的商人占有，该商人即有权力将委托人的全部权利，转让给正常业务中的买方。

（c）“委托”包括交付货物和默认对货物的占有，无论在此种交付或默认的当事方之间设立了何种条件，也无论取得此种委托的方式，或占有人对货物的处分，是否构成刑法中的盗窃罪。

（d）货物其他购买人的权利，以及留置权债权人的权利，受《担保交易》篇（第9篇）和《所有权凭证》篇（第7篇）的约束。

been delivered under a transaction of purchase the purchaser has such power even though

（1）the transferor was deceived as to the identity of the purchaser, or

（2）the delivery was in exchange for a check which is later dishonored, or

（3）it was agreed that the transaction was to be a“cash sale”, or

（4）the delivery was procured through fraud punishable as larcenous under the criminal law.

（b）Any entrusting of possession of goods to a merchant who deals in goods of that kind gives him power to transfer all rights of the entruster to a buyer in ordinary course of business.

（c）“Entrusting” includes any delivery and any acquiescence in retention of possession regardless of any condition expressed between the parties to the delivery or acquiescence and regardless of whether the procurement of the entrusting or the possessor's disposition of the goods have been such as to be larcenous under the criminal law.

（d）The rights of other purchasers of goods and of lien creditors are governed by the Articles on Secured Transactions（Article 9）and Documents of Title（Article 7）.

第5章 履 约

PART 5. PERFORMANCE

第 2.501 条 对货物的保险利益；货物特定化的方式

（a）对于现实存在的货物，在其发生特定化并因此成为合同所指的货物后，买方即对货物取得特殊财产权和保险利益，即使特定化的货物不符合合同，致使买方有权退回或拒收。上述特定化可根据当事方的明确协议，在任何时间以任何方式发生；如果没有明确协议，则：

（1）当合同出售的是合同订立时现实存在且特定的货物时，特定化在合同订立时发生；

（2）当合同出售的是（3）款以外的待定货物时，特定化在卖方将货物发运、标记或以其他方式确定于合同项下时发生；

（3）当合同出售的是合同订立后十二个月内出生的动物幼仔，或合同订立后十二个月内或下一个自然收获季（以迟者计算）收获的农作物时，特定化在农作物播种或以其他方式开始生长时发生，或在动物怀胎时发生。

（b）卖方只要仍保留对货物的所有权或担保权益，即对货物拥有保险利益。当特定化

§ 2.501. Insurable Interest in Goods; Manner of Identification of Goods.

（a）The buyer obtains a special property and an insurable interest in goods by identification of existing goods as goods to which the contract rcfcrs even though the goods so identified are non-conforming and he has an option to return or reject them.Such identification can be made at any time and in any manner explicitly agreed to by the parties.In the absence of explicit agreement identification occurs

（1）when the contract is made if it is for the sale of goods already existing and identified;

（2）if the contract is for the sale of future goods other than those described in Subdivision（3）, when goods are shipped, marked or otherwise designated by the seller as goods to which the contract refers;

（3）when the crops are planted or otherwise become growing crops or the young are conceived if the contract is for the sale of unborn young to be born within twelve months after contracting or for the sale of crops to be harvested within twelve months or the next normal harvest season after contracting whichever is longer.

（b）The seller retains an insurable interest in goods so long as title to or any security interest in the goods remains in him and where

由卖方单方作出时，卖方可在自己违约或破产前，或在通知买方特定化已不可更改前，用其他货物替换已特定化的货物。

the identification is by the seller alone he may until default or insolvency or notification to the buyer that the identification is final substitute other goods for those identified.

（c）本条任何部分均不削弱其他法律所承认的保险利益。

（c）Nothing in this section impairs any insurable interest recognized under any other statute or rule of law.

第2.502条　卖方毁约、未能交付或破产时买方对货物的权利

§ 2.502. Buyer's Right to Goods on Seller's Repudiation, Failure to Deliver, or Insolvency.

（a）除（b）款和（c）款另有规定外，如果买方根据上条取得了货物的特殊财产权，且已支付了部分或全部价款，且对任何未付价款作出提示付款并保持该提示，则在下列情况下，即使货物尚未发运，买方亦可向卖方追索货物：

（a）Subject to Subsections（b）and（c）and even though the goods have not been shipped a buyer who has paid a part or all of the price of goods in which he has a special property under the provisions of the immediately preceding section may on making and keeping good a tender of any unpaid portion of their price recover them from the seller if:

（1）卖方毁约或未能按合同规定交付，只要货物系为个人、家庭或家用目的购买；或

（1）in the case of goods bought for personal, family, or household purposes, the seller repudiates or fails to deliver as required by the contract;or

（2）无论如何，卖方在收到价款的第一笔付款后十日内破产。

（2）in all cases, the seller becomes insolvent within ten days after receipt of the first installment on their price.

（b）买方取得货物的特殊财产权后，根据（a）（1）款追索货物的权利即开始存在，即使卖方尚未出现毁约或未能交付。

（b）The buyer's right to recover the goods under Subsection（a）（1）vests upon acquisition of a special property, even if the seller had not then repudiated or failed to deliver.

（c）如果买方作出特定化，并因此取得特殊财产权，则只

（c）If the identification creating his special property has been made by the buyer he

有当货物符合买卖合同时，买方才享有追索货物的权利。

acquires the right to recover the goods only if they conform to the contract for sale.

第 2.503 条 卖方提示交付的方式

§ 2.503. Manner of Seller's Tender of Delivery.

（a）为作出提示交付，卖方应将符合合同的货物置于并保持于买方处置之下，并给买方必要的合理通知，使其能够取得交付。提示交付的方式、时间和地点应符合协议和本篇的规定；特别是：

（a）Tender of delivery requires that the seller put and hold conforming goods at the buyer's disposition and give the buyer any notification reasonably necessary to enable him to take delivery.The manner, time and place for tender are determined by the agreement and this Article, and in particular

（1）提示交付必须在合理钟点作出；并且，如果提示交付的是货物，必须留出合理的提货期间，使买方能够取得货物的占有；但是

（1）tender must be at a reasonable hour, and if it is of goods they must be kept available for the period reasonably necessary to enable the buyer to take possession;but

（2）除另有协议外，买方应提供接收货物所需的合理设备。

（2）unless otherwise agreed the buyer must furnish facilities reasonably suited to the receipt of the goods.

（b）如果属于下条所述的发运，卖方的提示交付应符合该条的规定。

（b）Where the case is within the next section respecting shipment tender requires that the seller comply with its provisions.

（c）如果卖方被要求在特定目的地交付，提示交付应符合（a）款的规定；在适当情况下，还应提示交付本条（d）款和（e）款所述的单据。

（c）Where the seller is required to deliver at a particular destination tender requires that he comply with Subsection（a）and also in any appropriate case tender documents as described in Subsections（d）and（e）of this section.

（d）如果货物由货物保管人占有，且不再移动即可交付，则：

（d）Where goods are in the possession of a bailee and are to be delivered without being moved

（1）为作出提示交付，卖方应提示交付覆盖货物的流通所有权凭证，或取得货物保管

（1）tender requires that the seller either tender a negotiable document of title covering such goods or procure acknowledgment by the

人的确认，即承认买方有权占有货物；但是

（2）向买方提示交付不可流通所有权凭证，或提示交付给货物保管人发出的书面交货指示，亦足以构成提示交付，除非被买方及时拒绝。在货物保管人收到有关买方权利的通知后，买方的权利即可对抗货物保管人和所有第三方，但货物损失的风险，以及货物保管人拒付不可流通所有权凭证或拒绝服从卖方指示的风险，在买方有合理时间提示该凭证或指示之前，仍由卖方承担。如果货物保管人拒付凭证或拒绝服从指示，卖方的提示交付即告失效。

bailee of the buyer's right to possession of the goods;but

（2）tender to the buyer of a non-negotiable document of title or of a written direction to the bailee to deliver is sufficient tender unless the buyer seasonably objects, and receipt by the bailee of notification of the buyer's rights fixes those rights as against the bailee and all third persons;but risk of loss of the goods and of any failure by the bailee to honor the non-negotiable document of title or to obey the direction remains on the seller until the buyer has had a reasonable time to present the document or direction, and a refusal by the bailee to honor the document or to obey the direction defeats the tender.

（e）如果合同要求卖方交付单据：

（e）Where the contract requires the seller to deliver documents

（1）卖方必须按正确格式提示交付合同要求的全部单据，但本篇涉及成套提单时另有规定的除外［第 2.323 条（b）款］；并且

（1）he must tender all such documents in correct form, except as provided in this Article with respect to bills of lading in a set（Subsection（b）of Section 2.323）;and

（2）通过惯常银行渠道作出的提示交付，足以构成提示交付。如果伴随单据的汇票被拒付，即构成买方对提示交付的不接受或拒收。

（2）tender through customary banking channels is sufficient and dishonor of a draft accompanying or associated with the documents constitutes non-acceptance or rejection.

第 2.504 条　卖方发运货物

§ 2.504. Shipment by Seller.

如果卖方被要求或被授权将货物发送给买方，但合同并

Where the seller is required or authorized to send the goods to the buyer and the contract

未要求卖方在特定目的地交付货物，则除另有协议外，卖方必须：

does not require him to deliver them at a particular destination, then unless otherwise agreed he must

（1）根据货物的性质和其他客观情况，将货物交给适当的承运人占有，并订立适当的运输合同；并且

（1）put the goods in the possession of such a carrier and make such a contract for their transportation as may be reasonable having regard to the nature of the goods and other circumstances of the case;and

（2）取得格式适当并使买方有权占有货物的任何必要单据，或协议或行业惯例另行要求的任何单据，并迅即向买方交付或提示交付此种单据；并且

（2）obtain and promptly deliver or tender in due form any document necessary to enable the buyer to obtain possession of the goods or otherwise required by the agreement or by usage of trade;and

（3）将发运迅即通知买方。

（3）promptly notify the buyer of the shipment.

如果未能按（3）款要求通知买方，或未能按（1）款要求订立适当的合同，则只有在造成重大延迟或损失时，才构成拒收的理由。

Failure to notify the buyer under Subdivision（3）or to make a proper contract under Subdivision（1）is a ground for rejection only if material delay or loss ensues.

第 2.505 条　卖方保留权利的发运

§ 2.505. Seller's Shipment Under Reservation.

（a）如果卖方在发运时或发运前已将货物特定于合同项下：

（a）Where the seller has identified goods to the contract by or before shipment:

（1）卖方无论是取得向自己的指定人交货还是取得向其他人交货的流通提单，均保留对货物的担保权益。卖方取得向金融机构的指定人或买方的指定人交货的流通提单，只另外表明卖方的预期，即该权益

（1）his procurement of a negotiable bill of lading to his own order or otherwise reserves in him a security interest in the goods. His procurement of the bill to the order of a financing agency or of the buyer indicates in addition only the seller's expectation of transferring that interest to the person named.

将被转让给该机构或买方。

（2）向卖方或卖方指定人交货的不可流通提单，意味着卖方将货物作为担保而保持占有，但除涉及附条件交付外［第2.507条（b）款］，以买方为收货人的不可流通提单，即使由卖方占有或控制，亦不构成保留担保权益。

（b）如果卖方在保留担保权益的情况下发运货物违反了买卖合同，卖方订立的运输合同即不属于上条所述的适当合同，但这并不削弱因发运和货物特定于合同项下而使买方取得的权利，也不削弱卖方作为流通所有权凭证执票人的权力。

（2）a non-negotiable bill of lading to himself or his nominee reserves possession of the goods as security but except in a case of conditional delivery（Subsection（b）of Section 2.507）a non-negotiable bill of lading naming the buyer as consignee reserves no security interest even though the seller retains possession or control of the bill of lading.

（b）When shipment by the seller with reservation of a security interest is in violation of the contract for sale it constitutes an improper contract for transportation within the preceding section but impairs neither the rights given to the buyer by shipment and identification of the goods to the contract nor the seller's powers as a holder of a negotiable document of title.

第2.506条 融资机构的权利

§ 2.506. Rights of Financing Agency.

（a）涉及用于货物发运的汇票时，如果融资机构支付该汇票，或支付价值购买该汇票，则在付款或购买的范围内，融资机构除取得自己在汇票项下的权利，以及用于担保汇票之所有权凭证项下的权利外，还取得发运人对货物的全部权利，包括阻止交付的权利，以及发运人要求买方兑付汇票的权利。

（b）如果融资机构根据对买方承担的义务，或根据买方提供的授权，善意兑付或购买

（a）A financing agency by paying or purchasing for value a draft which relates to a shipment of goods acquires to the extent of the payment or purchase and in addition to its own rights under the draft and any document of title securing it any rights of the shipper in the goods including the right to stop delivery and the shipper's right to have the draft honored by the buyer.

（b）The right to reimbursement of a financing agency which has in good faith honored or purchased the draft under

了汇票，则即使以后发现任何相关单据存在瑕疵，只要单据当时表面正常，融资机构获得偿付的权利即不受削弱。

commitment to or authority from the buyer is not impaired by subsequent discovery of defects with reference to any relevant document which was apparently regular.

第2.507条 卖方提示交付的效力；附条件交付

§ 2.507. Effect of Seller's Tender; Delivery on Condition.

（a）提示交付是买方履行接受货物之义务的条件，且除另有协议外，也是买方就货物履行付款义务的条件。提示交付使卖方有权要求买方根据合同接受货物和作出付款。

（a）Tender of delivery is a condition to the buyer's duty to accept the goods and, unless otherwise agreed, to his duty to pay for them.Tender entitles the seller to acceptance of the goods and to payment according to the contract.

（b）卖方向买方交付货物或所有权凭证后，如果付款期已到且卖方已提出付款要求，则在对抗卖方时，买方保留和处置货物的权利，以买方支付到期款项为前提条件。

（b）Where payment is due and demanded on the delivery to the buyer of goods or documents of title, his right as against the seller to retain or dispose of them is conditional upon his making the payment due.

第2.508条 卖方对不适当提示交付或交付的补救；替换货物

§ 2.508. Cure by Seller of Improper Tender or Delivery; Replacement.

（a）如果卖方的提示交付或交付因不符合合同而被拒收，但履约时间还未过期，卖方可将其准备进行补救的意图及时通知买方，然后可在合同规定的时间内，作出符合合同的交付。

（a）Where any tender or delivery by the seller is rejected because non-conforming and the time for performance has not yet expired, the seller may seasonably notify the buyer of his intention to cure and may then within the contract time make a conforming delivery.

（b）如果提示交付不符合合同，但卖方原有合理理由相信，经过或不经过金钱调整，买方本可接受该交付，此时，如果买方拒收，卖方应获得额

（b）Where the buyer rejects a non-conforming tender which the seller had reasonable grounds to believe would be acceptable with or without money allowance the seller may if he seasonably notifies the buyer

外的合理时间，以便重新作出符合合同的交付，但卖方必须及时将此通知买方。

have a further reasonable time to substitute a conforming tender.

第 2.509 条　不存在违约时损失风险的承担

§ 2.509. Risk of Loss in the Absence of Breach.

（a）当合同要求或授权卖方通过承运人发运货物时：

（1）如果合同未规定卖方在特定目的地交付货物，则在卖方将货物适当交付给承运人时，损失风险即转移至买方，即使在发运时保留了权利（第 2.505 条）；但是

（2）如果合同规定卖方在特定目的地交付货物，且在货物到达目的地但仍由承运人占有期间，卖方作出了适当提示交付，则只要卖方的此种适当提示能够使买方取得交付，损失风险即于该时转移至买方。

（a）Where the contract requires or authorizes the seller to ship the goods by carrier

（1）if it does not require him to deliver them at a particular destination, the risk of loss passes to the buyer when the goods are duly delivered to the carrier even though the shipment is under reservation（Section 2.505）;but

（2）if it does require him to deliver them at a particular destination and the goods are there duly tendered while in the possession of the carrier, the risk of loss passes to the buyer when the goods are there duly so tendered as to enable the buyer to take delivery.

（b）如果货物由货物保管人持有，且不再移动即可交付，则损失风险在下列时间转移至买方：

（1）买方取得覆盖货物之流通所有权凭证之占有或控制的时间；或

（2）货物保管人确认买方有权占有货物的时间；或

（3）根据第 2.503 条（d）（2）款，买方取得不可流通所有权凭证或其他书面交货指示之占

（b）Where the goods are held by a bailee to be delivered without being moved, the risk of loss passes to the buyer

（1）on the buyer's receipt of possession or control of a negotiable document of title covering the goods;or

（2）on acknowledgment by the bailee of the buyer's right to possession of the goods;or

（3）after the buyer's receipt of possession or control of a non-negotiable document of title or other written direction to deliver, as provided

有或控制之后。

in Subsection（d）（2）of Section 2.503.

（c）涉及（a）款或（b）款以外的任何情况时，如果卖方是商人，损失风险在买方收到货物时转移至买方；否则，损失风险在提示交付时转移至买方。

（c）In any case not within Subsection（a）or（b）, the risk of loss passes to the buyer on his receipt of the goods if the seller is a merchant; otherwise the risk passes to the buyer on tender of delivery.

（d）本条的规定，受制于当事方协议中的相反规定，以及本篇有关试用的条款（第 2.327 条）和存在违约时损失风险之承担的条款（第 2.510 条）。

（d）The provisions of this section are subject to contrary agreement of the parties and to the provisions of this Article on sale on approval（Section 2.327）and on effect of breach on risk of loss（Section 2.510）.

第 2.510 条　存在违约时损失风险的承担

§ 2.510. Effect of Breach on Risk of Loss.

（a）如果提示交付或交付的货物不符合合同，致使买方有权拒收，则在卖方作出补救或在买方接受货物前，损失风险仍由卖方承担。

（a）Where a tender or delivery of goods so fails to conform to the contract as to give a right of rejection the risk of their loss remains on the seller until cure or acceptance.

（b）买方如果正当撤销对货物的接受，可就自己有效保险覆盖不足的部分，视损失风险从开始即一直由卖方承担。

（b）Where the buyer rightfully revokes acceptance he may to the extent of any deficiency in his effective insurance coverage treat the risk of loss as having rested on the seller from the beginning.

（c）涉及已特定于买卖合同项下的符合合同的货物时，如果买方在货物风险转移给买方之前毁弃合同或以其他方式违约，卖方可就自己有效保险覆盖不足的部分，视损失风险在商业上合理的时间内由买方承担。

（c）Where the buyer as to conforming goods already identified to the contract for sale repudiates or is otherwise in breach before risk of their loss has passed to him, the seller may to the extent of any deficiency in his effective insurance coverage treat the risk of loss as resting on the buyer for a commercially reasonable time.

第 2.511 条　买方提示付款；以支票付款

（a）除另有协议外，提示付款是卖方履行提示交付和完成交付之义务的条件。

（b）使用正常业务中通行的任何方法或方式作出提示付款，均属适当，除非卖方要求以法定货币付款，并合理给予必要的延长时间用于筹措货币。

（c）除本法在涉及票据对义务之影响时另有规定外（第 3.802 条），支票付款属于有条件付款。如果支票经适当提示后被拒付，在当事方之间，付款即告无效。

§ 2.511. Tender of Payment by Buyer; Payment by Check.

（a）Unless otherwise agreed tender of payment is a condition to the seller's duty to tender and complete any delivery.

（b）Tender of payment is sufficient when made by any means or in any manner current in the ordinary course of business unless the seller demands payment in legal tender and gives any extension of time reasonably necessary to procure it.

（c）Subject to the provisions of this Act on the effect of an instrument on an obligation（Section 3.802）, payment by check is conditional and is defeated as between the parties by dishonor of the check on due presentment.

第 2.512 条　买方在检验货物前付款

（a）如果合同规定在检验货物前付款，则即使货物不符合合同，买方的此种付款义务亦不被免除，除非：

（1）不符之处未经检验即已显露；或

（2）虽然已提示交付所需的单据，但当时的客观情况使法院有理由根据本法发出停止兑付的禁令［第 5.109 条（b）款］。

（b）根据（a）款作出的付款，不构成对货物的接受，也不削弱买方检验货物或得到任何救

§ 2.512. Payment by Buyer Before Inspection.

（a）Where the contract requires payment before inspection non-conformity of the goods does not excuse the buyer from so making payment unless

（1）the non-conformity appears without inspection;or

（2）despite tender of the required documents circumstances would justify injunction against honor under this Act（Section 5.109（b））.

（b）Payment pursuant to Subsection（a）does not constitute an acceptance of goods or impair the buyer's right to inspect or any of his

济的权利。

remedies.

第 2.513 条 买方检验货物的权利

§ 2.513. Buyer's Right to Inspection of Goods.

(a)除另有协议外，且除(c)款另有规定外，如果已提示交付或交付货物，或如果货物已特定于买卖合同项下，则买方有权在付款或接受货物之前，在任何合理时间和地点以任何合理方式检验货物。如果卖方被要求或被授权将货物发送给买方，检验货物可在货物到达之后进行。

(a) Unless otherwise agreed and subject to Subsection (c), where goods are tendered or delivered or identified to the contract for sale, the buyer has a right before payment or acceptance to inspect them at any reasonable place and time and in any reasonable manner. When the seller is required or authorized to send the goods to the buyer, the inspection may be after their arrival.

(b)检验货物的费用必须由买方承担，但在货物不符合合同且被拒收时，买方可向卖方索赔检验费。

(b) Expenses of inspection must be borne by the buyer but may be recovered from the seller if the goods do not conform and are rejected.

(c)除另有协议外，且除本篇涉及“成本加保险费运费”合同时另有规定外[第 2.321 条(c)款]，当合同存在下列规定时，买方无权在支付价款前检验货物：

(c) Unless otherwise agreed and subject to the provisions of this Article on C.I.F. contracts (Subsection (c) of Section 2.321), the buyer is not entitled to inspect the goods before payment of the price when the contract provides

(1)合同规定按“交货付现”条款或类似条款作出交付；或

(1) for delivery "C.O.D." or on other like terms;or

(2)合同规定在交付所有权凭证时付款，除非合同还规定，只有在有机会检验货物后，付款才到期。

(2) for payment against documents of title, except where such payment is due only after the goods are to become available for inspection.

(d)当事方选择的检验货物的地点或方法，被假定具有排他性；但除另有明确协议外，

(d) A place or method of inspection fixed by the parties is presumed to be exclusive but unless otherwise expressly agreed it does

此种选择不推迟特定化的时间，也不改变交付的地点或损失风险转移的地点。如果遵守此种选择成为不可能，应按本条规定的方式检验货物，除非当事方的明确意图是，所选择的地点或方法系必要条件，缺少该条件后，合同即告失效。

not postpone identification or shift the place for delivery or for passing the risk of loss.If compliance becomes impossible, inspection shall be as provided in thissection unless the place or method fixed was clearly intended as an indispensable condition failure of which avoids the contract.

第 2.514 条　承兑交单；付款交单

§ 2.514. When Documents Deliverable on Acceptance; When on Payment.

除另有协议外，如果汇票系提示后三日以后付款，则应在承兑汇票时，将汇票出立时规定的单据交付给受票人；否则，只在付款时交付单据。

Unless otherwise agreed documents against which a draft is drawn are to be delivered to the drawee on acceptance of the draft if it is payable more than three days after presentment; otherwise, only on payment.

第 2.515 条　货物存在争议时保存证据

§ 2.515. Preserving Evidence of Goods in Dispute.

为便于处理索赔和争议：

In furtherance of the adjustment of any claim or dispute

（1）任何一方为澄清事实和保留证据，均有权在向另一方作出合理通知后，对货物（包括处于另一方占有或控制下的货物）进行检验、试验和取样；并且

（1）either party on reasonable notification to the other and for the purpose of ascertaining the facts and preserving evidence has the right to inspect, test and sample the goods including such of them as may be in the possession or control of the other;and

（2）当事方可以同意由第三方进行检验和评估，以确定货物是否符合合同，或确定货物的状况；当事方还可以同意检验和评估的结果在随后进行的诉讼或理赔中对当事方有约束力。

（2）the parties may agree to a third party inspection or survey to determine the conformity or condition of the goods and may agree that the findings shall be binding upon them in any subsequent litigation or adjustment.

第6章 违约、毁约和免责

PART 6. BREACH, REPUDIATION AND EXCUSE

第 2.601 条 交付不当时买方的权利

除涉及分期交货合同的违约时本篇另有规定外（第 2.612 条），以及除根据通过合同限制救济的条款另有协议外（第 2.718 条和第 2.719 条），当货物或提示交付在任何方面不符合合同时，买方可以：

（1）拒收全部；或

（2）接受全部；或

（3）接受任何商业单位，但拒收其余。

第 2.602 条 正当拒收的方式和效力

（a）拒收货物必须在交付或提示交付后的合理时间内作出。如果买方未能及时通知卖方，拒收无效。

（b）除涉及被拒收之货物的后述两条另有规定外（第 2.603 条和第 2.604 条）：

（1）拒收后，买方对货物的任何商业单位行使所有权的行为，均构成对卖方的不当行为；并且

（2）如果买方在拒收货物前已实际占有货物，且根据本篇规定不对货物享有担保权益［第 2.711 条（c）款］，买方即

§ 2.601. Buyer's Rights on Improper Delivery.

Subject to the provisions of this Article on breach in installment contracts（Section 2.612） and unless otherwise agreed under the sections on contractual limitations of remedy（Sections 2.718 and 2.719）, if the goods or the tender of delivery fail in any respect to conform to the contract, the buyer may

（1）reject the whole;or

（2）accept the whole;or

（3）accept any commercial unit or units and reject the rest.

§ 2.602. Manner and Effect of Rightful Rejection.

（a）Rejection of goods must be within a reasonable time after their delivery or tender. It is ineffective unless the buyer seasonably notifies the seller.

（b）Subject to the provisions of the two following sections on rejected goods（Sections 2.603 and 2.604），

（1）after rejection any exercise of ownership by the buyer with respect to any commercial unit is wrongful as against the seller;and

（2）if the buyer has before rejection taken physical possession of goods in which he does not have a security interest under the provisions of this Article（Subsection（c）of Section

有义务在拒收后合理持有和照管货物，并使货物服从卖方处置，直至卖方有充分时间将货物运走；但是

（3）对于被正当拒收的货物，买方无其他进一步的义务。

（c）卖方对于被错误拒收之货物的权利，受本篇有关卖方一般救济之条款的约束（第2.703条）。

第2.603条 商人买方对被正当拒收之货物的义务

（a）除买方持有担保权益外［第2.711条（c）款］，当卖方在拒收地市场没有代理人或营业场所时，商人买方在拒收其占有或控制的货物后，有义务遵从卖方有关货物的合理指示；如果未收到合理指示，且货物易腐或价值可能迅速降低，买方有义务作出合理努力，代表卖方将货物出售。如果卖方被要求支付处置费用，但在收到要求后未迅即作出支付，卖方的指示即属不合理。

（b）买方如果根据（a）款出售货物，即有权就照管和出售货物的合理费用，从卖方或从售货收益中获得补偿；如果该费用未包括销售佣金，买方还有权获得金额为行业通常标准的佣金；如果无此标准，则

2.711）, he is under a duty after rejection to hold them with reasonable care at the seller's disposition for a time sufficient to permit the seller to remove them;but

（3）the buyer has no further obligations with regard to goods rightfully rejected.

（c）The seller's rights with respect to goods wrongfully rejected are governed by the provisions of this Article on seller's remedies in general（Section 2.703）.

§ 2.603. Merchant Buyer's Duties as to Rightfully Rejected Goods.

（a）Subject to any security interest in the buyer（Subsection（c）of Section 2.711）, when the seller has no agent or place of business at the market of rejection a merchant buyer is under a duty after rejection of goods in his possession or control to follow any reasonable instructions received from the seller with respect to the goods and in the absence of such instructions to make reasonable efforts to sell them for the seller's account if they are perishable or threaten to decline in value speedily.Instructions are not reasonable if on demand indemnity for expenses is not forthcoming.

（b）When the buyer sells goods under Subsection（a）, he is entitled to reimbursement from the seller or out of the proceeds for reasonable expenses of caring for and selling them, and if the expenses include no selling commission then to such commission as is usual in the trade or if there is none to a

应为合理金额，但不得超过总收益的10%。

（c）买方根据本条作为时，只承担善意的义务。根据本条作出的善意作为，不构成对货物的接受或侵占，也不构成损害赔偿诉讼的理由。

reasonable sum not exceeding ten per cent on the gross proceeds.

(c) In complying with this section the buyer is held only to good faith and good faith conduct hereunder is neither acceptance nor conversion nor the basis of an action for damages.

第2.604条 买方处置被正当拒收之货物的选择权

除上条对易腐货物另有规定外，如果在作出拒收通知后的合理时间内卖方未给予指示，买方可代表卖方将被拒收的货物存入仓库，或将货物运回给卖方，或代表卖方出售货物，并有权为此种处置取得上条规定的补偿。买方的此种行为不构成对货物的接受或侵占。

§ 2.604. Buyer's Options as to Salvage of Rightfully Rejected Goods.

Subject to the provisions of the immediately preceding section on perishables if the seller gives no instructions within a reasonable time after notification of rejection the buyer may store the rejected goods for the seller's account or reship them to him or resell them for the seller's account with reimbursement as provided in the preceding section.Such action is not acceptance or conversion.

第2.605条 未作出具体说明构成买方放弃异议

（a）如果买方未说明导致拒收的具体瑕疵，且该瑕疵经合理检验可以确定，则在下列情况下，买方无权以此种未说明的瑕疵为理由作出拒收或证明违约：

（1）假设及时说明瑕疵，卖方本可作出补救；或

（2）在商人之间，在拒收后卖方已书面要求买方就其依据的全部瑕疵作出完整的最终的书面说明。

§ 2.605. Waiver of Buyer's Objections by Failure to Particularize.

(a) The buyer's failure to state in connection with rejection a particular defect which is ascertainable by reasonable inspection precludes him from relying on the unstated defect to justify rejection or to establish breach

(1) where the seller could have cured it if stated seasonably;or

(2) between merchants when the seller has after rejection made a request in writing for a full and final written statement of all defects on which the buyer proposes to rely.

（b）如果在未保留权利的情况下基于单据作出付款，随后即无权以单据表面可以看出的瑕疵为理由收回付款。

（b）Payment against documents made without reservation of rights precludes recovery of the payment for defects apparent in the documents.

第 2.606 条　接受货物的方式

§ 2.606. What Constitutes Acceptance of Goods.

（a）下列情况代表货物已被接受：

（a）Acceptance of goods occurs when the buyer

（1）买方在有合理机会检验货物后，向卖方表示货物符合合同，或表示尽管货物不符合合同，买方仍将收取或保留货物；或

（1）after a reasonable opportunity to inspect the goods signifies to the seller that the goods are conforming or that he will take or retain them in spite of their non-conformity; or

（2）买方未能作出有效拒收［第 2.602 条（a）款］；但是，此种接受只有在买方有合理机会检验货物后才能发生；或

（2）fails to make an effective rejection（Subsection（a）of Section 2.602），but such acceptance does not occur until the buyer has had a reasonable opportunity to inspect them;or

（3）买方作出任何与卖方对货物之所有权相抵触的行为；但是，如果该行为属于对卖方的不当行为，则只有卖方确认该行为构成接受，该行为才构成对货物的接受。

（3）does any act inconsistent with the seller's ownership;but if such act is wrongful as against the seller it is an acceptance only if ratified by him.

（b）接受任何商业单位中的任何部分，构成对该商业单位整体的接受。

（b）Acceptance of a part of any commercial unit is acceptance of that entire unit.

第 2.607 条　接受的效力；违约通知；作出接受后的违约举证责任；向责任人通知索赔或诉讼

§ 2.607. Effect of Acceptance; Notice of Breach; Burden of Establishing Breach After Acceptance; Notice of Claim or Litigation to Person Answerable Over.

（a）买方必须按合同规定的价格，就已被接受的货物作出付款。

（a）The buyer must pay at the contract rate for any goods accepted.

（b）买方接受货物后，不能再拒收已被接受的货物；并且，如果在作出接受时即知道货物不符合合同，即不得以该不符为理由撤销接受，除非作出接受系基于合理假设，即该不符将会得到及时补救。但是，接受货物之行为本身，不削弱本篇就不符合合同提供的任何其他救济。

（b）Acceptance of goods by the buyer precludes rejection of the goods accepted and if made with knowledge of a non-conformity cannot be revoked because of it unless the acceptance was on the reasonable assumption that the non-conformity would be seasonably cured but acceptance does not of itself impair any other remedy provided by this Article for non-conformity.

（c）提示交付被接受后：

（c）Where a tender has been accepted

（1）买方应在发现或应该发现任何违约后的合理时间内，将违约通知卖方，否则无权得到任何救济；并且

（1）the buyer must within a reasonable time after he discovers or should have discovered any breach notify the seller of breach or be barred from any remedy;and

（2）如果索赔系因侵权或类似原因［第2.312条（c）款］，且买方因该违约被诉，则买方必须在收到诉讼通知后的合理时间内通知卖方，否则无权就诉讼中判定的责任取得任何救济。

（2）if the claim is one for infringement or the like（Subsection（c）of Section 2.312）and the buyer is sued as a result of such a breach he must so notify the seller within a reasonable time after he receives notice of the litigation or be barred from any remedy over for liability established by the litigation.

（d）对于已被接受的货物，证明货物存在违约的举证责任由买方承担。

（d）The burden is on the buyer to establish any breach with respect to the goods accepted.

（e）如果买方被诉违反担保或违反其他义务，而卖方应对此种违约承担责任：

（e）Where the buyer is sued for breach of a warranty or other obligation for which his seller is answerable over

（1）买方可将诉讼书面通知卖方。如果通知中说明，卖方可前来应诉，且如果卖方不应诉，则在买方对抗卖方的诉讼中，卖方应就两次诉讼中共同面临的事

（1）he may give his seller written notice of the litigation.If the notice states that the seller may come in and defend and that if the seller does not do so he will be bound in any action against him by his buyer by

实，受到此次诉讼对该事实之确认的约束。此时，卖方如果在及时收到该通知后未前来应诉，即应按上述所言受到约束。

any determination of fact common to the two litigations, then unless the seller after seasonable receipt of the notice does come in and defend he is so bound.

（2）如果索赔系因侵权或类似原因［第 2.312 条（c）款］，原始卖方可书面要求买方将诉讼（包括和解权）的控制移交给卖方，并可说明，买方如果不这样做，将无权就此得到任何救济。此时，如果卖方还同意承担全部费用并执行任何不利判决，买方在及时收到此种要求后，即应将诉讼的控制移交给卖方，否则即按上述所言无权获得救济。

（2）if the claim is one for infringement or the like（Subsection（c）of Section 2.312）the original seller may demand in writing that his buyer turn over to him control of the litigation including settlement or else be barred from any remedy over and if he also agrees to bear all expense and to satisfy any adverse judgment, then unless the buyer after seasonable receipt of the demand does turn over control the buyer is so barred.

（f）上述（c）款、（d）款和（e）款的规定，亦适用于买方不使卖方因侵权或类似原因受到损失的义务［第 2.312 条（c）款］。

（f）The provisions of Subsections（c）,（d）and（e）apply to any obligation of a buyer to hold the seller harmless against infringement or the like（Subsection（c）of Section 2.312）.

第 2.608 条　全部或部分撤销接受

§ 2.608. Revocation of Acceptance in Whole or in Part.

（a）如果已被接受的一批或一个商业单位的货物不符合合同，致使其对买方的价值严重降低，买方可以撤销接受，只要原来作出的接受系因：

（a）The buyer may revoke his acceptance of a lot or commercial unit whose non-conformity substantially impairs its value to him if he has accepted it

（1）有合理理由假定不符合合同之处将得到补救，但未得到及时补救；或

（1）on the reasonable assumption that its non-conformity would be cured and it has not been seasonably cured;or

（2）未发现该不符；但在此种情况下，该接受必须是合

（2）without discovery of such non-conformity if his acceptance was reasonably

理地基于，在作出接受前难以发现该不符，或卖方曾作出过保证。

induced either by the difficulty of discovery before acceptance or by the seller's assurances.

（b）撤销接受必须在买方发现或应该发现撤销理由后的合理时间内作出，并在货物状况发生重大改变前作出，除非该改变系因货物自身瑕疵造成。在买方通知卖方之前，买方的撤销不发生效力。

（b）Revocation of acceptance must occur within a reasonable time after the buyer discovers or should have discovered the ground for it and before any substantial change in condition of the goods which is not caused by their own defects.It is not effective until the buyer notifies the seller of it.

（c）买方作出上述撤销后，对货物拥有与其拒收货物时同样的权利和义务。

（c）A buyer who so revokes has the same rights and duties with regard to the goods involved as if he had rejected them.

第 2.609 条 就履约获得充分保证的权利

§ 2.609. Right to Adequate Assurance of Performance.

（a）买卖合同的每一方都预期另一方正常履约，而另一方则有义务不破坏此种预期。一方如果有合理理由担心另一方不能正常履约，可书面要求另一方提供正常履约的充分保证。不安全的一方在收到此种保证之前，只要商业上合理，即可针对另一方尚未履约的部分，暂停履行自己相应部分的义务。

（a）A contract for sale imposes an obligation on each party that the other's expectation of receiving due performance will not be impaired.When reasonable grounds for insecurity arise with respect to the performance of either party the other may in writing demand adequate assurance of due performance and until he receives such assurance may if commercially reasonable suspend any performance for which he has not already received the agreed return.

（b）在商人之间，不安全的理由是否合理，以及所提供的保证是否充分，必须根据商业标准确定。

（b）Between merchants the reasonableness of grounds for insecurity and the adequacy of any assurance offered shall be determined according to commercial standards.

（c）即使已接受任何不适当的交付或付款，亦不损害受损方要求对未来履约提供充分

（c）Acceptance of any improper delivery or payment does not prejudice the aggrieved party's right to demand adequate assurance of

保证的权利。

future performance.

（d）一方收到有正当理由的要求后，如果未能在最长不超过三十日的合理时间内，根据该案当时的情况提供充分的履约保证，即构成毁弃合同。

（d）After receipt of a justified demand failure to provide within a reasonable time not exceeding thirty days such assurance of due performance as is adequate under the circumstances of the particular case is a repudiation of the contract.

第 2.610 条　预前毁约

§ 2.610. Anticipatory Repudiation.

如果一方在一项履约到期前毁弃合同，且失去该履约将严重损害合同对另一方的价值，受损方可以：

When either party repudiates the contract with respect to a performance not yet due the loss of which will substantially impair the value of the contract to the other, the aggrieved party may

（1）在商业上合理的时间内，等待毁约方履行合同义务；或

（1）for a commercially reasonable time await performance by the repudiating party;or

（2）寻求任何违约救济（第 2.703 条或第 2.711 条），即使其已通知毁约方将等待后者履约，且已催促后者撤回毁约；以及

（2）resort to any remedy for breach（Section 2.703 or Section 2.711）, even though he has notified the repudiating party that he would await the latter's performance and has urged retraction;and

（3）在上述任何一种情况下，均可停止自己的履约，或根据本篇关于另一方违约时卖方仍可将货物特定于合同项下的规定或挽救半成品货物的规定（第 2.704 条），采取相应行动。

（3）in either case suspend his own performance or proceed in accordance with the provisions of this Article on the seller's right to identify goods to the contract notwithstanding breach or to salvage unfinished goods（Section 2.704）.

第 2.611 条　撤回预前毁约

§ 2.611. Retraction of Anticipatory Repudiation.

（a）毁约方在下一项履约到期前，可以撤回毁约，除非受损方在毁约发生后已解除合

（a）Until the repudiating party's next performance is due he can retract his repudiation unless the aggrieved party has since

同，或已严重改变处境，或已用其他方式表明其认为毁约已不可撤回。

the repudiation cancelled or materially changed his position or otherwise indicated that he considers the repudiation final.

（b）撤回毁约可以使用任何方式，只要可以清楚地向受损方表明毁约方准备履约的意愿，但毁约方必须提供根据本篇规定而正当索要的保证（第2.609条）。

（b）Retraction may be by any method which clearly indicates to the aggrieved party that the repudiating party intends to perform, but must include any assurance justifiably demanded under the provisions of this Article（Section 2.609）.

（c）撤回毁约使毁约方重新享有合同权利，但如果此种毁约造成受损方延迟履约，受损方应获得相应免责。

（c）Retraction reinstates the repudiating party's rights under the contract with due excuse and allowance to the aggrieved party for any delay occasioned by the repudiation.

第2.612条 "分期交货合同"；违约

§ 2.612. "Installment Contract"; Breach.

（a）"分期交货合同"指要求或授权分期交付货物且分期接受的合同，即使合同包括"每次交付构成一项独立合同"或相等条款。

（a）An "installment contract" is one which requires or authorizes the delivery of goods in separate lots to be separately accepted, even though the contract contains a clause "each delivery is a separate contract" or its equivalent.

（b）如果任何一期交付不符合合同，致使该期交付的价值严重降低且无法补救，或该不符系所需单据存在瑕疵，买方可以拒收该期交付；但是，如果该不符不属于（c）款所述的情况，且卖方作出进行补救的充分保证，买方即必须接受该期交付。

（b）The buyer may reject any installment which is non-conforming if the non-conformity substantially impairs the value of that installment and cannot be cured or if the non-conformity is a defect in the required documents;but if the non-conformity does not fall within Subsection（c）and the seller gives adequate assurance of its cure the buyer must accept that installment.

（c）如果一期或多期交付不符合合同或存在其他违约，致使整体合同的价值严重降低，

（c）Whenever non-conformity or default with respect to one or more installments substantially impairs the value of the whole

即构成违反整体合同。但是，如果受损方接受了不符合合同的一期交付且未能及时通知解除合同，或只对以前各期交付提起诉讼，或仍要求就未来各期交付继续履约，合同即恢复有效。

contract there is a breach of the whole.But the aggrieved party reinstates the contract if he accepts a non-conforming installment without seasonably notifying of cancellation or if he brings an action with respect only to past installments or demands performance as to future installments.

第 2.613 条　特定化的货物遭受损失

§ 2.613. Casualty to Identified Goods.

如果履行合同所需的货物在订立合同时系属特定，且在风险转移至买方之前，或在适当情况下，当合同采用“货到成交”条款时（第 2.324 条），货物非因任何一方过错而遭受损失，则：

Where the contract requires for its performance goods identified when the contract is made, and the goods suffer casualty without fault of either party before the risk of loss passes to the buyer, or in a proper case under a “no arrival, no sale” term（Section 2.324）then

（1）当货物全部损失时，合同失效；以及

（1）if the loss is total the contract is avoided;and

（2）当货物部分损失时，或当货物状况恶化至不符合合同的程度时，买方可以要求检验货物，并可以选择视合同为失效；也可以选择接受货物，并根据货物恶化情况或数量减少情况相应调整合同价格，但没有对抗卖方的进一步权利。

（2）if the loss is partial or the goods have so deteriorated as no longer to conform to the contract the buyer may nevertheless demand inspection and at his option either treat the contract as avoided or accept the goods with due allowance from the contract price for the deterioration or the deficiency in quantity but without further right against the seller.

第 2.614 条　替代履约

§ 2.614. Substituted Performance.

（a）如果非因任何一方过错，双方约定的停泊、装货或卸货设施无法使用，或约定种类的承运人无法获得，或由于其他原因致使约定的交付方式在商业上确实难以履行，此时，

（a）Where without fault of either party the agreed berthing, loading, or unloading facilities fail or an agreed type of carrier becomes unavailable or the agreed manner of delivery otherwise becomes commercially impracticable but a commercially reasonable substitute is

如果存在商业上合理的替代履约方式，双方必须提示使用和接受该方式。

available, such substitute performance must be tendered and accepted.

（b）如果由于本国或外国政府法令，约定的付款方法或方式无法实现，则在买方另行提供商业上基本相等的付款方法或方式之前，卖方可以中止或阻止交付。如果货物已经交付，买方按法令规定的付款方法或方式付款后，即被解除义务，除非该法令具有歧视、迫害或掠夺性质。

（b）If the agreed means or manner of payment fails because of domestic or foreign governmental regulation, the seller may withhold or stop delivery unless the buyer provides a means or manner of payment which is commercially a substantial equivalent.If delivery has already been taken, payment by the means or in the manner provided by the regulation discharges the buyer's obligation unless the regulation is discriminatory, oppressive or predatory.

第 2.615 条　失去预想条件时的免责

§ 2.615. Excuse by Failure of Presupposed Conditions.

除卖方已承担了进一步的义务外，且除有关替代履约的上条另有规定外：

（1）如果发生了订立合同时作为基本假设认为不会发生的意外情况，或如果卖方以善意遵守了外国或本国政府的法令（无论该法令以后是否被证实无效），致使卖方确实难以按约定方式履约，则即使发生延迟交付，或部分或全部未能交付，只要卖方遵守了（2）款和（3）款的规定，即不构成对买卖合同义务的违反。

（2）如果（1）款提到的情况仅部分地影响了卖方履约的能力，卖方必须把生产和交付

Except so far as a seller may have assumed a greater obligation and subject to the preceding section on substituted performance:

（1）Delay in delivery or non-delivery in whole or in part by a seller who complies with Subdivisions（2）and（3）is not a breach of his duty under a contract for sale if performance as agreed has been made impracticable by the occurrence of a contingency the non-occurrence of which was a basic assumption on which the contract was made or by compliance in good faith with any applicable foreign or domestic governmental regulation or order whether or not it later proves to be invalid.

（2）Where the causes mentioned in Subdivision（1）affect only a part of the seller's capacity to perform, he must allocate

能力在各位客户之间进行分配，但可以决定把那些当时不存在合同关系但经常联系的客户以及自己今后的生产需求也考虑在内。卖方的此种分配可以使用任何公平合理的方式。

（3）卖方必须将延迟交付或无法交付的情况及时通知买方。如果需要根据（2）款进行分配，卖方必须通知买方其有可能获得的预估数额。

production and deliveries among his customers but may at his option include regular customers not then under contract as well as his own requirements for further manufacture.He may so allocate in any manner which is fair and reasonable.

（3）The seller must notify the buyer seasonably that there will be delay or non-delivery and, when allocation is required under Subdivision（2）, of the estimated quota thus made available for the buyer.

第 2.616 条　免责通知后的程序

§ 2.616. Procedure on Notice Claiming Excuse.

（a）如果买方收到通知，即根据上条所述的合理理由，将出现严重或无限期延迟，或将作出分配，买方可书面通知卖方，就所涉及的货物，或如果根据本篇有关违反分期交货合同的规定（第 2.612 条），预期的短缺将导致整体合同的价值严重降低时，则就全部货物：

（1）终止合同，从而解除合同的任何未履行部分；或

（2）修改合同，即同意收取所分配的替代数额。

（b）如果在收到卖方上述通知后，买方未能在不超过三十日的合理时间内按上述方式修改合同，则合同在受影响之那部分交付的范围内，即告失效。

（a）Where the buyer receives notification of a material or indefinite delay or an allocation justified under the preceding section he may by written notification to the seller as to any delivery concerned, and where the prospective deficiency substantially impairs the value of the whole contract under the provisions of this Article relating to breach of installment contracts（Section 2.612）, then also as to the whole,

（1）terminate and thereby discharge any unexecuted portion of the contract;or

（2）modify the contract by agreeing to take his available quota in substitution.

（b）If after receipt of such notification from the seller the buyer fails so to modify the contract within a reasonable time not exceeding thirty days the contract lapses with respect to any deliveries affected.

（c）本条的规定不得通过协议加以排除，除非卖方已根据上条承担了进一步的义务。

（c）The provisions of this section may not be negated by agreement except insofar as the seller has assumed a greater obligation under the preceding section.

第7章 救 济

PART 7. REMEDIES

第 2.701 条 违反从属合同的救济不受削弱

涉及从属于买卖合同的任何义务或许诺时，其违约救济不因本篇的规定受到削弱。

§ 2.701. Remedies for Breach of Collateral Contracts Not Impaired.

Remedies for breach of any obligation or promise collateral or ancillary to a contract for sale are not impaired by the provisions of this Article.

第 2.702 条 卖方发现买方破产时的救济

（a）卖方如果发现买方破产，可以拒绝作出交付，除非买方支付现款，并付清到当时为止根据合同已交付之全部货物的价款；卖方还可以根据本篇规定阻止交付（第 2.705 条）。

（b）卖方如果发现买方在破产的情况下以信用方式收到货物，则只要在买方收到货物后十日内提出要求，即可收回货物；但如果买方在交货前三个月内，以书面形式向卖方作出了有清偿能力的不实陈述，则上述十日期限不适用。除本款的上述规定外，卖方无权以买方曾作出过有清偿能力或有付款意图的不实陈述为理由收回货物，无论该陈述系属欺诈

§ 2.702. Seller's Remedies on Discovery of Buyer's Insolvency.

（a）Where the seller discovers the buyer to be insolvent he may refuse delivery except for cash including payment for all goods theretofore delivered under the contract, and stop delivery under this Article（Section 2.705）.

（b）Where the seller discovers that the buyer has received goods on credit while insolvent he may reclaim the goods upon demand made within ten days after the receipt, but if misrepresentation of solvency has been made to the particular seller in writing within three months before delivery the ten day limitation does not apply.Except as provided in this subsection the seller may not base a right to reclaim goods on the buyer's fraudulent or innocent misrepresentation of solvency or of intent to pay.

还是无意。

（c）卖方根据（b）款收回货物的权利，受制于本篇项下正常业务中之买方或其他善意购买人或留置权债权人的权利（第 2.403 条）。卖方成功收回货物后，即丧失有关该货物的所有其他救济。

（c）The seller's right to reclaim under Subsection（b）is subject to the rights of a buyer in ordinary course or other good faith purchaser or lien creditor under this Article（Section 2.403）. Successful reclamation of goods excludes all other remedies with respect to them.

第 2.703 条　卖方救济的一般规定

§ 2.703. Seller's Remedies in General.

如果买方对货物错误拒收或错误撤销接受，或未能在交付之时或之前支付到期款项，或部分或全部毁弃合同，则针对直接受到影响的货物，或在违反整体合同的情况下（第 2.612 条），针对所有尚未交付的货物，受损害卖方可以：

（1）中止交付相关货物；

（2）根据后述规定，阻止货物保管人作出交付（第 2.705 条）；

（3）根据下条规定，对尚未特定于合同项下的货物采取行动；

（4）根据后述规定，转售货物并取得损害赔偿（第 2.706 条）；

（5）就拒收取得损害赔偿（第 2.708 条），或在适当情况下，取得价款（第 2.709 条）；

（6）解除合同。

Where the buyer wrongfully rejects or revokes acceptance of goods or fails to make a payment due on or before delivery or repudiates with respect to a part or the whole, then with respect to any goods directly affected and, if the breach is of the whole contract（Section 2.612）, then also with respect to the whole undelivered balance, the aggrieved seller may

（1）withhold delivery of such goods;

（2）stop delivery by any bailee as hereafter provided（Section 2.705）;

（3）proceed under the next section respecting goods still unidentified to the contract;

（4）resell and recover damages as hereafter provided（Section 2.706）;

（5）recover damages for non-acceptance（Section 2.708）or in a proper case the price（Section 2.709）;

（6）cancel.

第 2.704 条 违约后卖方将货物特定于合同项下的权利；卖方挽救半成品货物的权利

（a）上条中的受损害卖方可以：

（1）将尚未特定于合同项下的符合合同的货物特定于合同项下，只要卖方在得知违约时占有或控制货物；

（2）将明确显示用于该特定合同的货物视为转售的货物，即使货物尚属半成品。

（b）如果货物为半成品，受损害卖方基于合理的商业判断，并出于避免损失和有效兑现的目的，可以完成制造并将货物全部特定于合同项下，或可以停止制造并把现有半成品处理出售，或可以使用任何其他合理方式处置货物。

第 2.705 条 卖方就运输中或其他情况下的货物阻止交付

（a）如果卖方发现买方破产（第 2.702 条），且货物当时由承运人或其他货物保管人占有，卖方可以阻止其向买方交付货物。如果买方毁约或未能在交付前支付到期款项，或如果有其他原因使卖方有权中止交付或收回货物，卖方可就整车或整机的货物，或就大批量

§ 2.704. Seller's Right to Identify Goods to the Contract Notwithstanding Breach or to Salvage Unfinished Goods.

（a）An aggrieved seller under the preceding section may

（1）identify to the contract conforming goods not already identified if at the time he learned of the breach they are in his possession or control;

（2）treat as the subject of resale goods which have demonstrably been intended for the particular contract even though those goods are unfinished.

（b）Where the goods are unfinished an aggrieved seller may in the exercise of reasonable commercial judgment for the purposes of avoiding loss and of effective realization either complete the manufacture and wholly identify the goods to the contract or cease manufacture and resell for scrap or salvage value or proceed in any other reasonable manner.

§ 2.705. Seller's Stoppage of Delivery in Transit or Otherwise.

（a）The seller may stop delivery of goods in the possession of a carrier or other bailee when he discovers the buyer to be insolvent（Section 2.702）and may stop delivery of carload, truckload, planeload or larger shipments of express or freight when the buyer repudiates or fails to make a payment due before delivery or if for any other reason the seller has a right to withhold or reclaim the

快递运输的货物，阻止承运人或其他货物保管人向买方作出交付。

goods.

（b）卖方只能在下列情况发生之前针对上述买方阻止货物的交付：

（b）As against such buyer the seller may stop delivery until

（1）买方收到货物；或

（1）receipt of the goods by the buyer;or

（2）任何货物保管人（承运人除外）向买方确认，货物系为买方持有；或

（2）acknowledgment to the buyer by any bailee of the goods except a carrier that the bailee holds the goods for the buyer;or

（3）转船承运人或兼为承储人的承运人向买方作出此种确认；或

（3）such acknowledgment to the buyer by a carrier by reshipment or as a warehouse;or

（4）覆盖货物的流通所有权凭证被流通至买方。

（4）negotiation to the buyer of any negotiable document of title covering the goods.

（c）

（c）

（1）为阻止交付，卖方必须适当通知货物保管人，使其通过行使合理勤勉，可以防止货物的交付。

（1）To stop delivery the seller must so notify as to enable the bailee by reasonable diligence to prevent delivery of the goods.

（2）收到此种通知后，货物保管人必须根据卖方的指示持有和交付货物，但卖方应承担货物保管人因此产生的费用和损失。

（2）After such notification the bailee must hold and deliver the goods according to the directions of the seller but the seller is liable to the bailee for any ensuing charges or damages.

（3）如果已就货物出具流通所有权凭证，则在凭证的占有或控制被交出之前，货物保管人没有义务服从阻止交付的通知。

（3）If a negotiable document of title has been issued for goods the bailee is not obliged to obey a notification to stop until surrender of possession or control of the document.

（4）出具不可流通提单的承运人，没有义务服从除发货

（4）A carrier who has issued a non-negotiable bill of lading is not obliged to obey

人以外的任何人作出的阻止交付的通知。

第 2.706 条　卖方转售或订立转售合同

（a）卖方只要遵守有关卖方救济的第 2.703 条规定的条件，即可转售有关的货物，或转售尚未交付的剩余货物。只要转售以善意和商业上合理的方式进行，卖方即有权就转售价格与合同价格的差额取得赔偿，再加上本篇允许的任何附带损失（第 2.710 条），但须减去因买方违约致使卖方节省的费用。

（b）除（c）款另有规定外，且除另有协议外，转售可以公开进行或私下进行，并可以订立一个或多个买卖合同，也可以将货物特定于卖方任何现有合同的项下。货物出售可以整体或分批进行，可以在任何时间和地点以任何条件进行。但是，出售活动的各个方面，包括方法、方式、时间、地点和条件，都必须商业上合理。必须合理证明转售与被违反之合同的联系，但并不要求在违约发生前货物已经存在，或已经部分或全部特定于合同项下。

（c）如果转售是私下进行，卖方必须将转售的意图向买方作合理的通知。

a notification to stop received from a person other than the consignor.

§ 2.706. Seller's Resale Including Contract for Resale.

（a）Under the conditions stated in Section 2.703 on seller's remedies, the seller may resell the goods concerned or the undelivered balance thereof.Where the resale is made in good faith and in a commercially reasonable manner the seller may recover the difference between the resale priceand the contract price together with any incidental damages allowed under the provisions of this Article（Section 2.710）, but less expenses saved in consequence of the buyer's breach.

（b）Except as otherwise provided in Subsection（c）or unless otherwise agreed resale may be at public or private sale including sale by way of one or more contracts to sell or of identification to an existing contract of the seller.Sale may be as a unit or in parcels and at any time and place and on any terms but every aspect of the sale including the method, manner, time, place and terms must be commercially reasonable.The resale must be reasonably identified as referring to the broken contract, but it is not necessary that the goods be in existence or that any or all of them have been identified to the contract before the breach.

（c）Where the resale is at private sale the seller must give the buyer reasonable notification of his intention to resell.

（d）如果转售是公开进行：

（1）只有已特定化的货物可以出售，除非对于该类货物存在公开出售待定货物的公认市场；并且

（2）转售必须在公开出售的惯常地点或市场进行，只要存在可以合理使用的此种地点或市场；并且，除非货物易腐或价值可能迅速降低，卖方必须将转售的时间和地点向买方作出合理通知；并且

（3）如果前来购买货物的人不能见到货物，出售通知中必须说明货物的存放地点，并向可能的竞购人提供合理的检验货物的机会；并且

（4）卖方也可以买进。

（e）即使卖方未能遵守本条的一项或多项要求，购买人在转售中以善意买进货物后，即不受制于原始买方的任何权利。

（f）卖方没有义务向买方交出转售的利润。处于卖方地位的人（第 2.707 条），或作出正当拒收或正当撤销接受的买方，必须交出超出其担保权益的部分［如下述第 2.711 条（c）款所定义］。

（d）Where the resale is at public sale

（1）only identified goods can be sold except where there is a recognized market for a public sale of futures in goods of the kind;and

（2）it must be made at a usual place or market for public sale if one is reasonably available and except in the case of goods which are perishable or threaten to decline in value speedily the seller must give the buyer reasonable notice of the time and place of the resale;and

（3）if the goods are not to be within the view of those attending the sale the notification of sale must state the place where the goods are located and provide for their reasonable inspection by prospective bidders;and

（4）the seller may buy.

（e）A purchaser who buys in good faith at a resale takes the goods free of any rights of the original buyer even though the seller fails to comply with one or more of the requirements of this section.

（f）The seller is not accountable to the buyer for any profit made on any resale. A person in the position of a seller（Section 2.707）or a buyer who has rightfully rejected or justifiably revoked acceptance must account for any excess over the amount of his security interest, as hereinafter defined（Subsection（c）of Section 2.711）.

第 2.707 条 “处于卖方地位的人”

（a）在代理人对抗被代理人时，“处于卖方地位的人”包括代表被代理人支付了货物的价款或承担了付款责任的代理人。“处于卖方地位的人”也包括以其他方式对货物拥有担保权益或其他类似于卖方权利的任何人。

（b）处于卖方地位的人，可以根据本篇规定中止或阻止交付（第 2.705 条）、转售货物（第 2.706 条）和取得附带损失的赔偿（第 2.710 条）。

§ 2.707. “Person in the Position of a Seller”.

(a) A “person in the position of a seller” includes as against a principal an agent who has paid or become responsible for the price of goods on behalf of his principal or anyone who otherwise holds a security interest or other right in goods similar to that of a seller.

(b) A person in the position of a seller may as provided in this Article withhold or stop delivery (Section 2.705) and resell (Section 2.706) and recover incidental damages (Section 2.710).

第 2.708 条 买方不接受交付或毁约时卖方损失的计算

（a）除（b）款和本篇涉及市场价格证明的条款另有规定外（第 2.723 条），买方拒收或毁约所造成的损失，是提示交付之时之地的市场价格与未支付之合同价格的差价，加上本篇规定的任何附带损失（第 2.710 条），减去因买方违约致使卖方节省的费用。

（b）如果按（a）款计算的损害赔偿，不能使卖方处于合同履行时卖方本应达到的状态，那么，损害赔偿应为买方充分履行合同时卖方本应得到的利润（包括计入合理的间接运营

§ 2.708. Seller's Damages for Non-Acceptance or Repudiation.

(a) Subject to Subsection (b) and to the provisions of this Article with respect to proof of market price (Section 2.723), the measure of damages for non-acceptance or repudiation by the buyer is the difference between the market price at the time and place for tender and the unpaid contract price together with any incidental damages provided in this Article (Section 2.710), but less expenses saved in consequence of the buyer's breach.

(b) If the measure of damages provided in Subsection (a) is inadequate to put the seller in as good a position as performance would have done then the measure of damages is the profit (including reasonable overhead) which the seller would have made from full performance

费用），加上本篇规定的任何附带损失（第 2.710 条），再加上适当计算的合理费用，减去适当计算的收款或转售收益。

by the buyer, together with any incidental damages provided in this Article（Section 2.710）, due allowance for costs reasonably incurred and due credit for payments or proceeds of resale.

第 2.709 条　价款诉讼

（a）如果买方未能支付到期价款，卖方可以要求取得下列价款，以及下条规定的附带损失：

（1）已被接受之货物的价款，或在损失风险转移至买方后商业上合理的时间内灭失或损坏之符合合同的货物的价款；以及

（2）已特定于合同项下之货物的价款，只要卖方经过合理努力后未能以合理价格将货物转售，或情况合理表明此种努力没有意义。

（b）卖方为价款提起诉讼时，必须为买方持有已特定于合同项下但仍由卖方控制的货物；但如果遇有转售机会，卖方可在法院判决得到执行前的任何时间将货物转售。转售的净收入必须作为买方收入，且买方在按法院判决付款后，有权取得任何尚未转售的货物。

（c）如果买方错误拒收或错误撤销接受货物，或未能支付到期款项，或毁弃合同（第 2.610 条），则卖方即使无权根

§ 2.709. Action for the Price.

（a）When the buyer fails to pay the price as it becomes due the seller may recover, together with any incidental damages under the next section, the price

（1）of goods accepted or of conforming goods lost or damaged within a commercially reasonable time after risk of their loss has passed to the buyer;and

（2）of goods identified to the contract if the seller is unable after reasonable effort to resell them at a reasonable price or the circumstances reasonably indicate that such effort will be unavailing.

（b）Where the seller sues for the price he must hold for the buyer any goods which have been identified to the contract and are still in his control except that if resale becomes possible he may resell them at any time prior to the collection of the judgment.The net proceeds of any such resale must be credited to the buyer and payment of the judgment entitles him to any goods not resold.

（c）After the buyer has wrongfully rejected or revoked acceptance of the goods or has failed to make a payment due or has repudiated（Section 2.610）, a seller who is

据本条取得价款，仍可根据上条就拒收取得损害赔偿。

held not entitled to the price under this section shall nevertheless be awarded damages for nonacceptance under the preceding section.

第 2.710 条 卖方的附带损失

§ 2.710. Seller's Incidental Damages.

受损害卖方的附带损失包括，为阻止货物交付，为买方违约后运输、照管和存放货物，以及为退还货物和转售货物，卖方所支出的任何商业上合理的收费、费用和佣金，以及买方违约引起的其他费用。

Incidental damages to an aggrieved seller include any commercially reasonable charges, expenses or commissions incurred in stopping delivery, in the transportation, care and custody of goods after the buyer's breach, in connection with return or resale of the goods or otherwise resulting from the breach.

第 2.711 条 买方救济的一般规定；买方对被拒收之货物的担保权益

§ 2.711. Buyer's Remedies in General; Buyer's Security Interest in Rejected Goods.

（a）如果卖方未能交付或作出毁约，或如果买方正当拒收或正当撤销接受，买方可就所涉及的货物解除合同；或如果违约涉及整体合同（第 2.612 条），买方可就全部货物解除合同。同时，买方无论是否已解除合同，除可以收回已支付的价款外，还可以：

（1）“补进”货物，并根据下条就所有受影响的货物取得损害赔偿，无论货物是否已特定于合同项下；或

（2）根据本篇规定，就未能交付取得损害赔偿（第 2.713 条）。

（b）如果卖方未能交付或作出毁约，买方还可以：

（a）Where the seller fails to make delivery or repudiates or the buyer rightfully rejects or justifiably revokes acceptance then with respect to any goods involved, and with respect to the whole if the breach goes to the whole contract （Section 2.612）, the buyer may cancel and whether or not he has done so may in addition to recovering so much of the price as has been paid

（1）“cover” and have damages under the next section as to all the goods affected whether or not they have been identified to the contract;or

（2）recover damages for non-delivery as provided in this Article（Section 2.713）.

（b）Where the seller fails to deliver or repudiates the buyer may also

（1）当货物已特定化时，根据本篇规定追索货物（第2.502条）；或

（2）在适当情况下，根据本篇规定获得实际履行，或取回货物（第2.716条）。

（c）买方正当拒收或正当撤销接受后，就其已支付的价款，并就检验、接收、运输、保管和存储货物的任何合理费用，对其占有或控制的货物享有担保权益，并可使用与受损害卖方相同的方法持有和转售该货物（第2.706条）。

（1）if the goods have been identified recover them as provided in this Article（Section 2.502）;or

（2）in a proper case obtain specific performance or replevy the goods as provided in this Article（Section 2.716）.

（c）On rightful rejection or justifiable revocation of acceptance a buyer has a security interest in goods in his possession or control for any payments made on their price and any expenses reasonably incurred in their inspection, receipt, transportation, care and custody and may hold such goods and resell them in like manner as an aggrieved seller（Section 2.706）.

第2.712条 "补进"；买方获取替代货物

（a）发生上条所述的违约后，买方可以"补进"货物，即以善意和合理方式，购买或订立合同购买本应由卖方提供的货物，但不得有不合理的延迟。

（b）买方有权从卖方取得损害赔偿，即补进成本与合同价格的差额，加上后述定义的附带损失或间接损失（第2.715条），减去因卖方违约致使买方节省的费用。

（c）买方未能按本条规定补进货物，不妨碍其获得任何其他救济。

§ 2.712. "Cover";Buyer's Procurement of Substitute Goods.

（a）After a breach within the preceding section the buyer may "cover" by making in good faith and without unreasonable delay any reasonable purchase of or contract to purchase goods in substitution for those due from the seller.

（b）The buyer may recover from the seller as damages the difference between the cost of cover and the contract price together with any incidental or consequential damages as hereinafter defined（Section 2.715）, but less expenses saved in consequence of the seller's breach.

（c）Failure of the buyer to effect cover within this section does not bar him from any other remedy.

第 2.713 条　卖方未能交付或作出毁约时买方损失的计算

（a）除本篇涉及市场价格证明的条款另有规定外（第 2.723 条），卖方未能交付或作出毁约所造成的损失，是买方得知违约时的市场价格与合同价格的差额，加上本篇规定的任何附带损失和间接损失（第 2.715 条），减去因卖方违约致使买方节省的费用。

（b）市场价格应为提示交付地的市场价格；如果涉及货物到达后的拒收或撤销接受，则为货物到达地的市场价格。

第 2.714 条　已被接受的货物存在违约时买方损失的计算

（a）如果买方已接受货物并通知了卖方［第 2.607 条（c）款］，买方可就不符合合同的提示交付取得损害赔偿，即按任何合理方式计算的卖方之违约在正常情况下给买方造成的损失。

（b）违反担保所造成的损失，是在接受货物的时间和地点，被接受之货物的价值与货物符合担保时本应具有的价值的差额，除非存在其他特殊情况，显示损失金额实际不同于此。

（c）在适当情况下，买方

§ 2.713. Buyer's Damages for Non-Delivery or Repudiation.

(a) Subject to the provisions of this Article with respect to proof of market price (Section 2.723), the measure of damages for non-delivery or repudiation by the seller is the difference between the market price at the time when the buyer learned of the breach and the contract price together with any incidental and consequential damages provided in this Article (Section 2.715), but less expenses saved in consequence of the seller's breach.

(b) Market price is to be determined as of the place for tender or, in cases of rejection after arrival or revocation of acceptance, as of the place of arrival.

§ 2.714. Buyer's Damages for Breach in Regard to Accepted Goods.

(a) Where the buyer has accepted goods and given notification (Subsection (c) of Section 2.607) he may recover as damages for any non-conformity of tender the loss resulting in the ordinary course of events from the seller's breach as determined in any manner which is reasonable.

(b) The measure of damages for breach of warranty is the difference at the time and place of acceptance between the value of the goods accepted and the value they would have had if they had been as warranted, unless special circumstances show proximate damages of a different amount.

(c) In a proper case any incidental and

还可就下条规定的附带损失和间接损失取得赔偿。

consequential damages under the next section may also be recovered.

第 2.715 条 买方的附带损失和间接损失

§ 2.715. Buyer's Incidental and Consequential Damages.

（a）卖方违约造成的附带损失包括：为检验、接收、运输、照管和存储被正当拒收的货物而支出的合理费用，因补进货物而发生的任何商业上合理的收费、费用或佣金，以及因延迟或其他违约而附带引起的任何合理费用。

（a）Incidental damages resulting from the seller's breach include expenses reasonably incurred in inspection, receipt, transportation and care and custody of goods rightfully rejected, any commercially reasonable charges, expenses or commissions in connection with effecting cover and any other reasonable expense incident to the delay or other breach.

（b）卖方违约造成的间接损失包括：

（b）Consequential damages resulting from the seller's breach include

（1）因未能满足买方通常的或特殊的要求和需要所造成的损失，只要在订立合同时卖方有理由知道该要求和需要，且该损失无法通过补进货物或其他方法合理避免；以及

（1）any loss resulting from general or particular requirements and needs of which the seller at the time of contracting had reason to know and which could not reasonably be prevented by cover or otherwise;and

（2）主要因违反担保而对人身或财产造成的损害。

（2）injury to person or property proximately resulting from any breach of warranty.

第 2.716 条 买方获得实际履行或取回货物的权利

§ 2.716. Buyer's Right to Specific Performance or Replevin.

（a）如果货物具有独特性，或如果有其他适当原因，法院可以判决实际履行。

（a）Specific performance may be decreed where the goods are unique or in other proper circumstances.

（b）有关实际履行的判决，可以同时包含其他条款和条件，如价款支付、损害赔偿或法院认为公平的其他补救措施。

（b）The decree for specific performance may include such terms and conditions as to payment of the price, damages, or other relief as the court may deem just.

（c）如果买方经过合理努

（c）The buyer has a right of replevin

力无法就货物完成补进，或客观情况合理表明此种努力没有意义，或如果货物在保留权利的情况下发运但买方已偿付或已提示偿付该担保权益，则对于已特定于合同项下的货物，买方有权取回。涉及为个人、家庭或家用目的而购买的货物时，买方在取得货物的特殊财产权后，即有权取回货物，即使卖方当时尚未发生毁约或未能交付。

for goods identified to the contract if after reasonable effort he is unable to effect cover for such goods or the circumstances reasonably indicate that such effort will be unavailing or if the goods have been shipped under reservation and satisfaction of the security interest in them has been made or tendered.In the case of goods bought for personal, family, or household purposes, the buyer's right of replevin vests upon acquisition of a special property, even if the seller had not then repudiated or failed to deliver.

第 2.717 条　从价款中扣除损害赔偿

§ 2.717. Deduction of Damages from the Price.

买方可从同一合同中任何尚未支付的价款中，针对卖方对合同的任何违反，扣除部分或全部损害赔偿，但买方应事先将此种意图通知卖方。

The buyer on notifying the seller of his intention to do so may deduct all or any part of the damages resulting from any breach of the contract from any part of the price still due under the same contract.

第 2.718 条　约定或限制损害赔偿；预付款

§ 2.718. Liquidation or Limitation of Damages;Deposits.

（a）可以通过协议对任何一方违约时的损害赔偿金额进行约定，但相对于预期或实际的违约损失、证明损失的难度，以及通过其他方法取得充分救济的不方便或不现实程度，所约定的金额必须合理。金额高至不合理的条款，应被视为惩罚而无效。

（a）Damages for breach by either party may be liquidated in the agreement but only at an amount which is reasonable in the light of the anticipated or actual harm caused by the breach, the difficulties of proof of loss, and the inconvenience or non-feasibility of otherwise obtaining an adequate remedy.A term fixing unreasonably large liquidated damages is void as a penalty.

（b）如果买方违约致使卖方正当中止交付货物，买方有权收回其付款金额超出下列金

（b）Where the seller justifiably withholds delivery of goods because of the buyer's breach, the buyer is entitled to restitution of

额的部分：

（1）涉及（a）款所述的约定损害赔偿时，卖方根据协议条款有权得到的金额；或

（2）如果无此种条款，则为买方在合同项下全部履约义务价值的 20% 或为 500 美元，以金额低者为准。

（c）如果卖方能够证明下列情况，则买方根据（b）款收回付款的权利，应被相应抵销：

（1）根据（a）款以外的本篇其他条款，卖方有权取得的损害赔偿；以及

（2）买方从合同中直接或间接获益的金额或价值。

（d）如果以货物作为付款，则卖方所收到之货物的合理价值或转售收益，应作为（b）款规定的买方付款。但是，如果卖方收到的货物系作为部分履约，且在转售前得到买方违约的通知，则卖方的转售必须遵守本篇规定的受损害卖方进行转售的条件（第 2.706 条）。

any amount by which the sum of his payments exceeds

（1）the amount to which the seller is entitled by virtue of terms liquidating the seller's damages in accordance with Subsection（a）, or

（2）in the absence of such terms, twenty percent of the value of the total performance for which the buyer is obligated under the contract or $500, whichever is smaller.

（c）The buyer's right to restitution under Subsection（b）is subject to offset to the extent that the seller establishes

（1）a right to recover damages under the provisions of this Article other than Subsection（a）, and

（2）the amount or value of any benefits received by the buyer directly or indirectly by reason of the contract.

（d）Where a seller has received payment in goods their reasonable value or the proceeds of their resale shall be treated as payments for the purposes of Subsection（b）; but if the seller has notice of the buyer's breach before reselling goods received in part performance, his resale is subject to the conditions laid down in this Article on resale by an aggrieved seller（Section 2.706）.

第 2.719 条　通过合同修改或限制救济

（a）除本条（b）款和（c）款另有规定外，且除有关约定或限制损害赔偿的上条另有规

§ 2.719. Contractual Modification or Limitation of Remedy.

（a）Subject to the provisions of Subsections（b）and（c）of this section and of the preceding section on liquidation and

定外；

（1）可以通过协议约定救济，作为本篇规定之救济的补充或替代，也可以通过协议限制或改变本篇规定的损害赔偿。例如，可以把买方的救济限制为退回货物和收回价款，或限制为修理或调换不符合合同的货物或零件；并且

（2）所提供的任何一项救济均供自行选用，除非该项救济被明确约定具有排他性；此时，该救济为唯一的救济。

（b）如果客观情况致使一项排他的或有限的救济无法实现其根本目的，可以根据本法规定获得救济。

（c）可以限制或排除对间接损失的赔偿，除非此种限制或排除显失公平。涉及消费品时，对人身伤害的间接损失的赔偿作出限制，构成显失公平的表面证据；但对商业损失的限制，不构成此种证据。

第 2.720 条 "解除"或"撤销"合同对前存违约之索赔的影响

除另有明确的相反意图外，"解除"或"撤销"合同或类似表示，不应被解释为放弃或解除就前存违约取得损害赔偿的权利。

limitation of damages,

（1）the agreement may provide for remedies in addition to or in substitution for those provided in this Article and may limit or alter the measure of damages recoverable under this Article, as by limiting the buyer's remedies to return of the goods and repayment of the price or to repair and replacement of non-conforming goods or parts;and

（2）resort to a remedy as provided is optional unless the remedy is expressly agreed to be exclusive, in which case it is the sole remedy.

（b）Where circumstances cause an exclusive or limited remedy to fail of its essential purpose, remedy may be had as provided in this Act.

（c）Consequential damages may be limited or excluded unless the limitation or exclusion is unconscionable.Limitation of consequential damages for injury to the person in the case of consumer goods is prima facie unconscionable but limitation of damages where the loss is commercial is not.

§ 2.720. Effect of "Cancellation" or "Rescission" on Claims for Antecedent Breach.

Unless the contrary intention clearly appears, expressions of "cancellation" or "rescission" of the contract or the like shall not be construed as a renunciation or discharge of any claim in damages for an antecedent breach.

第 2.721 条　针对欺诈的救济

本篇针对非欺诈违约提供的全部救济，均可作为针对重大不实陈述或欺诈的救济。撤销买卖合同或要求撤销合同，或拒收或退回货物，均不排除或妨碍寻求损害赔偿或其他救济。

§ 2.721. Remedies for Fraud.

Remedies for material misrepresentation or fraud include all remedies available under this Article for non-fraudulent breach.Neither rescission or a claim for rescission of the contract for sale nor rejection or return of the goods shall bar or be deemed inconsistent with a claim for damages or other remedy.

第 2.722 条　第三方对货物造成损害时有权提起诉讼的人

如果第三方对已特定于买卖合同项下的货物，作出有损合同任何当事方的可被诉行为：

（1）买卖合同的任何当事方，只要对货物拥有所有权，或担保权益，或特殊财产权，或保险利益，即有权对该第三方提起诉讼。如果货物已被毁坏或被侵占，根据买卖合同承担了损失风险的当事方，或在损害发生后相对于另一方承担了此种风险的当事方，亦有权提起诉讼；

（2）如果作为原告的当事方，在损害发生时相对于买卖合同的另一方，并不承担货物损失的风险，且他们也未就损害赔偿的处置作出安排，则该原告当事方，除涉及自己利益时，只是作为合同另一方的受托人提起诉讼或达成和解；

§ 2.722. Who Can Sue Third Parties for Injury to Goods.

Where a third party so deals with goods which have been identified to a contract for sale as to cause actionable injury to a party to that contract

（1）a right of action against the third party is in either party to the contract for sale who has title to or a security interest or a special property or an insurable interest in the goods; and if the goods have been destroyed or converted a right of action is also in the party who either bore the risk of loss under the contract for sale or has since the injury assumed that risk as against the other;

（2）if at the time of the injury the party plaintiff did not bear the risk of loss as against the other party to the contract for sale and there is no arrangement between them for disposition of the recovery, his suit or settlement is, subject to his own interest, as a fiduciary for the other party to the contract;

（3）任何一方经另一方同意，均可为任何有关人的利益提起诉讼。

（3）either party may with the consent of the other sue for the benefit of whom it may concern.

第 2.723 条　市场价格的确定：时间和地点

§ 2.723. Proof of Market Price:Time and Place.

（a）如果就预前毁约提起诉讼，且在法院审理开始时，部分或全部货物的履约期限尚未超过，则在需要按市场价格确定损害赔偿时（第 2.708 条或第 2.713 条），应按受损方得知毁约时该货物的通行价格计算。

（a）If an action based on anticipatory repudiation comes to trial before the time for performance with respect to some or all of the goods, any damages based on market price（Section 2.708 or Section 2.713）shall be determined according to the price of such goods prevailing at the time when the aggrieved party learned of the repudiation.

（b）在证明本篇所述之时间或地点的通行价格时，如果一时难以获得其证据，则可使用相关的通行价格，即在该时间之前或之后合理期间内的价格，或根据商业判断或行业惯例，可作为合理替代之其他地点的价格，但此时应适当考虑将货物运进或运出该地的费用。

（b）If evidence of a price prevailing at the times or places described in this Article is not readily available the price prevailing within any reasonable time before or after the time described or atany other place which in commercial judgment or under usage of trade would serve as a reasonable substitute for the one described may be used, making any proper allowance for the cost of transporting the goods to or from such other place.

（c）如果一方提出的相关价格证明，是本篇所述时间和地点以外的通行价格，则只有在该方已通知另一方，且法院认为通知系属充分，不致构成对另一方不公正的意外时，法院才可接受该证明。

（c）Evidence of a relevant price prevailing at a time or place other than the one described in this Article offered by one party is not admissible unless and until he has given the other party such notice as the court finds sufficient to prevent unfair surprise.

第 2.724 条　可接受的市场牌价

§ 2.724. Admissibility of Market Quotations.

如果任何货物在任何公认

Whenever the prevailing price or value

的商品市场上惯常进行买卖，则在确定该货物的通行价格或价值时，正式出版物、贸易杂志、公开发行之报纸或杂志中的报告，只要属于该市场的报告，均可作为证明被法院接受。此种报告制备的具体情况，可影响其证明力度，但不影响其可接受性。

of any goods regularly bought and sold in any established commodity market is in issue, reports in official publications or trade journals or in newspapers or periodicals of general circulation published as the reports of such market shall be admissible in evidence.The circumstances of the preparation of such a report may be shown to affect its weight but not its admissibility.

第 2.725 条　买卖合同的诉讼时效

§ 2.725. Statute of Limitations in Contracts for Sale.

（a）有关违反买卖合同的诉讼，必须在诉讼原因发生后四年内提起。当事方可在原始协议中将此期限缩短至不少于一年，但不得将其延长。

（a）An action for breach of any contract for sale must be commenced within four years after the cause of action has accrued.By the original agreement the parties may reduce the period of limitation to not less than one year but may not extend it.

（b）诉讼原因在出现违约时发生，即使受损方并不知道该违约。违反担保的发生时间，为提示交付的时间。但是，如果一项担保明确延及货物的未来使用性能，且只有使用后才有可能发现违约，则诉讼原因在发现或应该发现违约时发生。

（b）A cause of action accrues when the breach occurs, regardless of the aggrieved party's lack of knowledge of the breach. A breach of warranty occurs when tender of delivery is made, except that where a warranty explicitly extends to future performance of the goods and discovery of the breach must await the time of such performance the cause of action accrues when the breach is or should have been discovered.

（c）如果诉讼在（a）款限制的时间内提起，且该诉讼终止后，尚有可能就同一违约再次提起诉讼以取得其他救济，则该另一诉讼可在上述限制的时效期满后提起，但必须在第

（c）Where an action commenced within the time limited by Subsection（a）is so terminated as to leave available a remedy by another action for the same breach such other action may be commenced after the expiration of the time limited and within six

一次诉讼终止后六个月内提起。如果第一次诉讼系自愿终止，或系因未能参诉或疏于参诉而被驳回，则不能再次提起诉讼。

months after the termination of the first action unless the termination resulted from voluntary discontinuance or from dismissal for failure or neglect to prosecute.

（d）本条不改变有关时效计算的法律，也不适用于本法生效前发生的诉讼原因。

（d）This section does not alter the law on tolling of the statute of limitations nor does it apply to causes of action which have accrued before this Act becomes effective.

词汇索引

续表

买卖	sale	第 2.103 条（a）
买卖合同	contract for sale	第 2.106 条（a）
卖方	seller	第 2.103 条（a）（4）
明示担保	express warranties	第 2.313 条
目的港船上交货	ex-ship	第 2.322 条
侵权	infringement	第 2.312 条
融资机构	financing agency	第 2.104 条（b）
商人	merchant	第 2.104 条（a）
商人之间	between merchants	第 2.104 条（c）
商销性	merchantability	第 2.314 条
商业单位	commercial unit	第 2.105 条（f）
实际履行	specific performance	第 2.716 条
试销	sale or return	第 2.326 条（a）（2）
试用	sale on approval	第 2.326 条（a）（1）
收到	receipt	第 2.103 条（a）（3）
特定化	identification	第 2.501 条
提示交付	tender of delivery	第 2.503 条
委托	entrusting	第 2.403 条
显失公平	unconscionable	第 2.302 条
信用证	letter of credit	第 2.325 条（c）
要约	offer	第 2.206 条
一批	lot	第 2.105 条（e）
银行信用证	banker’ s credit	第 2.325 条（c）
预前毁约	anticipatory repudiation	第 2.610 条
运输工具上交货	F.O.B.	第 2.319 条
终止	termination	第 2.106 条（c）
阻止交付	stoppage of delivery	第 2.705 条

第2A篇　租　赁

ARTICLE 2A. LEASES

第1章　总　则

PART 1. GENERAL PROVISIONS

第 2A.101 条　简称

本篇被引用时可称为《统一商法典——租赁》。

第 2A.102 条　适用范围

本篇适用于设立货物租赁的任何交易，无论交易采用何种形式。本篇不适用于设立不动产权益或不动产租赁的交易，但第 2A.309 条所述的不动产附着物租赁除外。

第 2A.103 条　定义和定义索引

（a）在本篇中，除上下文另有所指外：

（1）“正常业务中的买方”指以善意买进货物的人，且其不知道该销售侵犯了第三方对货物的所有权、担保权益或租赁权益，并以正常方式向从事该类货物销售的卖方（典当商除外）买进。“买进”可以支付现金，也可以使用其他财产交

§ 2A.101. Short Title.

This Article shall be known and may be cited as the Uniform Commercial Code—Leases.

§ 2A.102. Scope.

This Article applies to any transaction, regardless of form, that creates a lease of goods. This Article does not apply to a transaction that creates an interest in or lease of real estate, except to the extent that provision is made for leases of fixtures by Section 2A.309.

§ 2A.103. Definitions and Index of Definitions.

（a）In this Article unless the context otherwise requires:

（1）“Buyer in the ordinary course of business” means a person who in good faith and without knowledge that the sale to him or her is in violation of the ownership rights or security interest or leasehold interest of a third party in the goods buys in the ordinary course from a person in the business of selling goods of that kind but does not include a

换，或利用有担保或无担保的信贷，也包括根据前存买卖合同取得货物或所有权凭证，但不包括整体转让，也不包括为担保金钱债务或为全部或部分清偿金钱债务所作的转让。

pawnbroker. "Buying" may be for cash or by exchange of other property or on secured or unsecured credit and includes acquiring goods or documents of title under a preexisting contract for sale but does not include a transfer in bulk or as security for or in total or partial satisfaction of a money debt.

（2）如果任何一方因另一方违约而结束租赁合同，合同即告"解除"。

（2）"Cancellation" occurs when either party puts an end to the lease contract for default by the other party.

（3）"商业单位"指在商业惯例中作为单一整体用于租赁的货物单位，即如果将此单位分割，将严重损害货物的特性、市场价值或使用价值。一个商业单位可以是一件物品（如一台机器），或一组物品（如一套家具或一系列机器），或一定数量（如一罗或一车），也可以是在使用中或在有关市场上被视作单一整体的任何其他单位。

（3）"Commercial unit" means a unit of goods as by commercial usage is a single whole for purposes of lease and division of which materially impairs its character or value on the market or in use.A commercial unit may be a single article, as a machine, or a set of articles, as a suite of furniture or a line of machinery, or a quantity, as a gross or carload, or any other unit treated in use or in the relevant market as a single whole.

（4）如果租赁合同项下的货物或履约符合租赁合同规定的义务，即为"符合"合同。

（4）"Conforming" goods or performance under a lease contract means performance or goods that are in accordance with the obligations under the lease contract.

（5）"消费者租赁"指惯常从事租赁或销售业务的出租方向个人承租方提供的租赁，且承租方的租赁主要用于个人、家庭或家用目的，且租赁合同项下的付款总额不超过两万五千美元（为续租或购买之

（5）"Consumer lease" means a lease that a lessor regularly engaged in the business of leasing or selling makes to a lessee who is an individual and who takes under the lease primarily for a personal, family, or household purpose, if the total payments to be made under the lease contract, excluding payments for

选择权支付的费用除外）。

options to renew or buy, do not exceed $25,000.

（6）“过错”指不当行为、疏漏或违约。

（6）“Fault” means a wrongful act, omission, breach, or default.

（7）“融资租赁”指下列租赁：

（7）“Finance lease” means a lease with respect to which:

（A）出租方不挑选、制造或供应货物；

（A）the lessor does not select, manufacture, or supply the goods;

（B）出租方系为租赁目的取得货物或取得货物的占有权和使用权；并且

（B）the lessor acquires the goods or the right to possession and use of the goods in connection with the lease;and

（C）存在下列情况之一：

（C）one of the following occurs:

（i）承租方在签订租赁合同前，收到了出租方据以取得货物或货物占有权和使用权之合同的副本；

（i）the lessee receives a copy of the contract by which the lessor acquired the goods or the right to possession and use of the goods before signing the lease contract;

（ii）承租方对出租方据以取得货物或货物占有权和使用权之合同的批准，是租赁合同生效的前提条件；

（ii）the lessee's approval of the contract by which the lessor acquired the goods or the right to possession and use of the goods is a condition to effectiveness of the lease contract;

（iii）承租方在签订租赁合同前，对于提供货物之人向出租方就货物所规定的下列条件，收到了准确和完整的说明：承诺和担保，以及对担保的排除；对救济的限制或修改，或对损害赔偿金额的约定。前述条件也可以来自第三方，如货物的制造商。前述条件可以包含在出租方据以取得货物或货物占有权和使用权的合同之内，也可以基于该合同另行提供；或

（iii）the lessee, before signing the lease contract, receives an accurate and complete statement designating the promises and warranties, and any disclaimers of warranties, limitations or modifications of remedies, or liquidated damages, including those of a third party, such as the manufacturer of the goods, provided to the lessor by the person supplying the goods in connection with or as part of the contract by which the lessor acquired the goods or the right to possession and use of the goods;or

（iv）除消费者租赁外，在承租方签订租赁合同前，出租

（iv）if the lease is not a consumer lease, the lessor, before the lessee signs the lease

方以书面形式向承租方：（a）说明了向出租方提供货物之人的真实身份，除非系承租方挑选了该人，并指示出租方从该人取得货物或货物占有权和使用权；（b）说明了承租方根据本篇，有权受益于提供货物之人就货物所作的承诺和担保，无论该承诺和担保是来自于提供货物的人还是第三方，也无论其是基于出租方据以取得货物或货物占有权和使用权之合同本身，还是基于该合同另行提供；并且（c）说明了承租方可以联系向出租方提供货物之人，并从该人获得该承诺和担保的准确和完整的说明，包括对承诺和担保的排除和限制，或对救济的排除和限制。

contract, informs the lessee in writing (a) of the identity of the person supplying the goods to the lessor, unless the lessee has selected that person and directed the lessor to acquire the goods or the right to possession and use of the goods from that person, (b) that the lessee is entitled under this Article to the promises and warranties, including those of any third party, provided to the lessor by the person supplying the goods in connection with or as part of the contract by which the lessor acquired the goods or the right to possession and use of the goods, and (c) that the lessee may communicate with the person supplying the goods to the lessor and receive an accurate and complete statement of those promises and warranties, including any disclaimers and limitations of them or of remedies.

（8）"货物"指在特定于租赁合同项下时可以移动的所有物品，也指不动产附着物（第2A.309条），但不包括金钱、单据、票据、应收款、动产契据或一般无形财产，也不包括开采前的矿物或类似物质，如石油和天然气。"货物"还包括待出生的动物幼仔。

(8) "Goods" means all things that are moveable at the time of identification to the lease contract, or are fixtures (Section 2A.309), but the term does not include money, documents, instruments, accounts, chattel paper, general intangibles, or minerals or the like, including oil and gas, before extraction. The term also includes the unborn young of animals.

（9）"分期租赁合同"指要求或授权分期交付货物且分期接受的租赁合同，即使合同包括"每次交付构成一项独立租赁"或相等条款。

(9) "Installment lease contract" means a lease contract that authorizes or requires the delivery of goods in separate lots to be separately accepted, even though the lease contract contains the clause "each delivery is a

separate lease" or its equivalent.

（10）"租赁"指将货物在一定时间内的占有权和使用权进行转让，用于换取对价。买卖（包括试用或试销）以及保留或设立担保权益，不属于租赁。除上下文明确另有所指外，"租赁"包括分租。

(10) "Lease" means a transfer of the right to possession and use of goods for a term in return for consideration, but a sale, including a sale on approval or a sale or return, or retention or creation of a security interest is not a lease. Unless the context clearly indicates otherwise, the term includes a sublease.

（11）"租赁协议"指出租方和承租方就租赁达成的实际约定。该约定应通过双方使用的语言确定，或通过其他客观情况（包括本篇规定的交易过程、行业惯例或履约过程）推定。除上下文明确另有所指外，"租赁协议"包括分租协议。

(11) "Lease agreement" means the bargain, with respect to the lease, of the lessor and the lessee in fact as found in their language or by implication from other circumstances including course of dealing or usage of trade or course of performance as provided by this Article.Unless the context clearly indicates otherwise, the term includes a sublease agreement.

（12）"租赁合同"指基于当事方租赁协议而产生的，并受本篇和其他适用法调整的全部法律义务。除上下文明确另有所指外，"租赁合同"包括分租合同。

(12) "Lease contract" means the total legal obligation that results from the lease agreement as affected by this Article and any other applicable rules of law.Unless the context clearly indicates otherwise, the term includes a sublease contract.

（13）"租赁权益"指出租方或承租方在租赁合同项下的权益。

(13) "Leasehold interest" means the interest of the lessor or the lessee under a lease contract.

（14）"承租方"指通过租赁取得货物占有权和使用权的人。除上下文明确另有所指外，"承租方"包括分租承租方。

(14) "Lessee" means a person who acquires the right to possession and use of goods under a lease.Unless the context clearly indicates otherwise, the term includes a sublessee.

（15）"正常业务中的承租方"指以善意承租货物的人，

(15) "Lessee in ordinary course of business" means a person who in good faith

且其不知道该租赁侵犯了第三方对货物的所有权、担保权益或租赁权益，并以正常方式向从事该类货物销售或租赁的人（典当商除外）租赁货物。“租赁”可以支付现金，也可以使用其他财产交换，或利用有担保或无担保的信贷，也包括根据前存租赁合同取得货物或所有权凭证，但不包括整体转让，也不包括为担保金钱债务或为全部或部分清偿金钱债务所作的转让。

and without knowledge that the lease to him or her is in violation of the ownership rights or security interest or leasehold interest of a third party in the goods, leases in ordinary course from a person in the business of selling or leasing goods of that kind but does not include a pawnbroker. “Leasing” may be for cash or by exchange of other property or on secured or unsecured credit and includes acquiring goods or documents of title under a preexisting lease contract but does not include a transfer in bulk or as security for or in total or partial satisfaction of a money debt.

（16）“出租方”指通过租赁而转让货物占有权和使用权的人。除上下文明确另有所指外，“出租方”包括分租出租方。

（16）“Lessor” means a person who transfers the right to possession and use of goods under a lease.Unless the context clearly indicates otherwise, the term includes a sublessor.

（17）“出租方残余权益”指在租赁合同到期、终止或解除之后，出租方对货物拥有的权益。

（17）“Lessor’s residual interest” means the lessor’s interest in the goods after the expiration, termination, or cancellation of the lease contract.

（18）“留置权”指对货物拥有的抵押权或其他权益，用于担保债务的支付或义务的履行，但“留置权”不包括担保权益。

（18）“Lien” means a charge against or interest in goods to secure payment of a debt or performance of an obligation, but the term does not include a security interest.

（19）“一批”指构成单独一次租赁或交付的一宗或一件物品，无论其是否足以履行租赁合同。

（19）“Lot” means a parcel or a single article that is the subject matter of a separate lease or delivery, whether or not it is sufficient to perform the lease contract.

（20）“商人承租方”指对于租赁所涉及的货物种类，承

（20）“Merchant lessee” means a lessee that is a merchant with respect to goods of the

租方系属商人。

kind subject to the lease.

（21）“现值”指将一笔或多笔应在未来支付的款项，按照一定利率折现到某个特定日期时的金额。该利率可以由当事方商定，只要在达成交易的当时，所商定的利率不是明显不合理；或如果不存在商定利率，则利率应为，根据达成交易当时的事实和客观情况，商业上系属合理的利率。

（21）“Present value” means the amount as of a date certain of one or more sums payable in the future, discounted to the date certain.The discount is determined by the interest rate specified by the parties if the rate was not manifestly unreasonable at the time the transaction was entered into;otherwise, the discount is determined by a commercially reasonable rate that takes into account the facts and circumstances of each case at the time the transaction was entered into.

（22）“购买”指通过下列方式取得：买卖、租赁、不动产抵押、设立担保权益、质押、赠予，或任何其他在货物中设立权益的自愿交易。

（22）“Purchase” includes taking by sale, lease, mortgage, security interest, pledge, gift, or any other voluntary transaction creating an interest in goods.

（23）“分租”指在租赁中，出租方用于出租的货物，系该出租方原以承租方身份从一项现存租赁中取得该货物的占有权和使用权。

（23）“Sublease” means a lease of goods the right to possession and use of which was acquired by the lessor as a lessee under an existing lease.

（24）“供应商”指出租方从其买进或租赁用于融资租赁之货物的人。

（24）“Supplier” means a person from whom a lessor buys or leases goods to be leased under a finance lease.

（25）“供应合同”指出租方据以买进或租赁用于租赁之货物的合同。

（25）“Supply contract” means a contract under which a lessor buys or leases goods to be leased.

（26）如果任何一方根据协议或法律赋予的权力，在另一方没有违约的情况下结束租赁合同，合同即告“终止”。

（26）“Termination” occurs when either party pursuant to a power created by agreement or law puts an end to the lease contract otherwise than for default.

（b）适用于本篇的其他定

（b）Other definitions applying to this

义及其所在位置：

Article and the sections in which they appear are:

"添附物" 第2A.310条（a）款

"Accessions". Section 2A.310（a）.

"建设抵押权" 第2A.309条（a）（4）款

"Construction mortgage". Section 2A.309（a）（4）.

"不动产他项权" 第2A.309条（a）（5）款

"Encumbrance". Section 2A.309（a）（5）.

"不动产附着物" 第2A.309条（a）（1）款

"Fixtures". Section 2A.309（a）（1）.

"不动产附着物登记" 第2A.309条（a）（2）款

"Fixture filing". Section 2A.309（a）（2）.

"价款租赁" 第2A.309条（a）（3）款

"Purchase money lease". Section 2A.309（a）（3）.

（c）其他各篇中适用于本篇的定义：

（c）The following definitions in other Articles apply to this Article:

"应收款" 第9.102条（a）（2）款

"Account". Section 9.102（a）（2）.

"商人之间" 第2.104条（c）款

"Between merchants". Section 2.104（c）.

"买方" 第2.103条（a）（1）款

"Buyer". Section 2.103（a）（1）.

"动产契据" 第9.102条（a）（11）款

"Chattel paper". Section 9.102（a）（11）.

"消费品" 第9.102条（a）（23）款

"Consumer goods". Section 9.102（a）（23）.

"凭证" 第9.102条（a）（30）款

"Document". Section 9.102（a）（30）.

"委托" 第2.403条（c）款

"Entrusting". Section 2.403（c）.

"一般无形财产" 第9.102条（a）（42）款

"General intangible". Section 9.102（a）（42）.

"票据" 第9.102条（a）

"Instrument". Section 9.102（a）（47）.

（47）款

“商人” 第2.104条（a）款

“Merchant”. Section 2.104（a）.

“不动产抵押权” 第9.102条（a）（55）款

“Mortgage”. Section 9.102（a）（55）.

“根据承诺” 第9.102条（a）（69）款

“Pursuant to commitment”. Section 9.102（a）（69）.

“收到” 第2.103条(a)(3)款

“Receipt”. Section 2.103（a）（3）.

“买卖” 第2.106条（a）款

“Sale”. Section 2.106（a）.

“试用” 第2.326条

“Sale on approval”. Section 2.326.

“试销” 第2.326条

“Sale or return”. Section 2.326.

“卖方” 第2.103条(a)(4)款

“Seller”. Section 2.103（a）（4）.

（d）此外，第1篇中的通用定义和解释原则适用于本篇通篇。

（d）In addition Article 1 contains general definitions and principles of construction and interpretation applicable throughout this Article.

第2A.104条 受其他法律约束的租赁

§ 2A.104. Leases Subject to Other Laws.

（a）一项租赁即使受本篇约束，亦同时受下列适用法的约束：

（a）A lease, although subject to this Article, is also subject to any applicable:

（1）本州有关产权证书的法律；

（1）certificate of title statute of this state;

（2）另一州有关产权证书的法律（第2A.105条）；或

（2）certificate of title statute of another jurisdiction（Section 2A.105）;or

（3）本州的消费者法，包括判例法和制定法。

（3）consumer law of this state, both decisional and statutory.

（b）如果本篇与（a）款所列的法律存在冲突，应以该等法律为准，但是，第2A.105

（b）In case of conflict between this Article, other than Sections 2A.105, 2A.304（c）and 2A.305（c）, and any statute or law

条、第 2A.304 条（c）款和第 2A.305 条（c）款除外。

（c）如果未能遵守任何适用法，仅产生该适用法规定的后果。

referred to in Subsection（a）, the statute or law controls.

（c）Failure to comply with any applicable statute has only the effect specified therein.

第 2A.105 条 涉及产权证书覆盖的货物时本篇的地域效力

§ 2A.105. Territorial Application of Article to Goods Covered by Certificate of Title.

除第 2A.304 条（c）款和第 2A.305 条(c)款另有规定外，如果货物的产权证书系根据本州或另一州法律颁发，则该产权证书是否遵守了产权证书法，以及遵守或未遵守的后果，应根据产权证书颁发州的法律(包括其冲突法）确定，直至（以先发生者为准）：

（1）产权证书被交出；或

（2）货物被移出产权证书颁发州四个月之后；并且，在此之后，直至另一州颁发新的产权证书。

Subject to the provisions of Sections 2A.304（c）and 2A.305（c）, with respect to goods covered by a certificate of title issued under a statute of this state or of another jurisdiction, compliance and the effect of compliance or noncompliance with a certificate of title statute are governed by the law（including the conflict of laws rules）of the jurisdiction issuing the certificate until the earlier of:

（1）surrender of the certificate;or

（2）four months after the goods are removed from that jurisdiction and thereafter until a new certificate of title is issued by another jurisdiction.

第 2A.106 条 消费者租赁之当事方选择适用法和司法机构的权力受到限制

§ 2A.106. Limitation on Power of Parties to Consumer Lease to Choose Applicable Law and Judicial Forum.

(a) 对于消费者租赁之当事方选择的适用法，如果该法所属的州不是承租方的居住州，即租赁协议产生强制履行力之时或之后三十日内承租方的居住州，也不是货物的预计使用州，则当事方的选择不可

(a) If the law chosen by the parties to a consumer lease is that of a jurisdiction other than a jurisdiction in which the lessee resides at the time the lease agreement becomes enforceable or within 30 days thereafter or in which the goods are to be used, the choice is not enforceable.

强制履行。

（b）对于消费者租赁之当事方选择的司法机构，如果该机构所在的州不是承租方实际签署租赁协议的所在州，或诉讼开始时承租方的居住州，或租赁合同产生强制履行力时承租方的居住州，或承租方实际使用货物的所在州，则当事方的选择不可强制履行。

（b）If the judicial forum chosen by the parties to a consumer lease is a forum located in a jurisdiction other than the jurisdiction in which the lessee in fact signed the lease agreement, resides at the commencement of the action, or resided at the time the lease contract became enforceable or in which the goods are in fact used by the lessee, the choice is not enforceable.

第 2A.107 条　违约发生后放弃索赔或权利

只要受损方签署并交付书面弃权文件，即可在没有对价的情况下，就其所追究的违约或违反担保，全部或部分放弃相关的索赔或权利。

§ 2A.107. Waiver or Renunciation of Claim or Right After Default.

A claim or right arising out of an alleged default or breach of warranty may be discharged in whole or in part without consideration by a written waiver or renunciation signed and delivered by the aggrieved party.

第 2A.108 条　显失公平

（a）如果法院认定，作为法律问题，租赁合同或其任何条款在订立时显失公平，法院可以拒绝强制履行该租赁合同，或仅强制履行租赁合同显失公平条款以外的部分，或限制显失公平条款的适用以避免显失公平的后果。

§ 2A.108. Unconscionability.

（a）If the court as a matter of law finds a lease contract or any clause of a lease contract to have been unconscionable at the time it was made, the court may refuse to enforce the lease contract, or it may enforce the remainder of the lease contract without the unconscionable clause, or it may so limit the application of any unconscionable clause as to avoid any unconscionable result.

（b）涉及消费者租赁时，如果法院认定，作为法律问题，租赁合同或其任何条款受到显失公平之行为的诱导，或在追取租赁合同欠款的过程中存在显失公平的行为，法院可以提

（b）With respect to a consumer lease, if the court as a matter of law finds that a lease contract or any clause of a lease contract has been induced by unconscionable conduct or that unconscionable conduct has occurred in the collection of a claim arising from a lease

供适当救助。

（c）在认定存在（a）款或（b）款所述的显失公平之前，法院应该自行提出或根据当事人要求，给当事方以合理机会，就租赁合同或其条款，或相关行为的背景、目的和作用，提供证明。

（d）当承租方在诉讼中指控消费者租赁存在显失公平时：

（1）如果法院认定存在（a）款或（b）款所述的显失公平，法院应判定向承租方支付合理的律师费；

（2）如果法院认定不存在显失公平，且提出显失公平指控的承租方在知道其指控缺乏根据的情况下，仍然起诉或不放弃诉讼，法院应判定该承租方向受到显失公平指控的一方支付合理的律师费；并且

（3）在确定律师费的金额时，指控方根据（a）款或（b）款获得的赔偿金额，不具有决定性的影响。

第 2A.109 条 任意提前的选择权

（a）如果条款规定，一方或其权益继承人可以“任意”或在“认为自己不安全”时，或在类似含义词句规定的情况

contract, the court may grant appropriate relief.

（c）Before making a finding of unconscionability under Subsection（a）or（b）, the court, on its own motion or that of a party, shall afford the parties a reasonable opportunity to present evidence as to the setting, purpose, and effect of the lease contract or clause thereof or of the conduct.

（d）In an action in which the lessee claims unconscionability with respect to a consumer lease:

（1）if the court finds unconscionability under Subsection（a）or（b）, the court shall award reasonable attorney's fees to the lessee;

（2）if the court does not find unconscionability and the lessee claiming unconscionability has brought or maintained an action he or she knew to be groundless, the court shall award reasonable attorney's fees to the party against whom the claim is made;and

（3）in determining attorney's fees, the amount of the recovery on behalf of the claimant under Subsections（a）and（b）is not controlling.

§ 2A.109. Option to Accelerate at Will.

（a）A term providing that one party or the party's successor in interest may accelerate payment or performance or require collateral or additional collateral "at will" or "when the

下，要求另一方提前付款或履约，或要求提供担保物或增加担保物，则该条款必须被解释为，只有在前者善意地相信另一方付款或履约的前景存在危险时，才有权力提出此种要求。

party deems himself or herself insecure" or in words of similar import must be construed to mean that the party has power to do so only if the party in good faith believes that the prospect of payment or performance is impaired.

（b）涉及消费者租赁时，证明存在（a）款所述善意的举证责任，由行使该权力的当事方承担；在其他情况下，证明缺乏此种善意的举证责任，由被行使该权力的当事方承担。

（b）With respect to a consumer lease, the burden of establishing good faith under Subsection（a）is on the party who exercises the power; otherwise the burden of establishing lack of good faith is on the party against whom the power has been exercised.

第2章　租赁合同的订立和解释

PART 2. FORMATION AND CONSTRUCTION OF LEASE CONTRACT

第 2A.201 条　反欺诈法

§ 2A.201. Statute of Frauds.

（a）只有在下列情况下，租赁合同才可通过诉讼或抗辩强制履行：

（a）A lease contract is not enforceable by way of action or defense unless:

（1）租赁合同项下应支付的全部款项（不包括续租或购买之选择权的费用）不超过1000 美元；或

（1）the total payments to be made under the lease contract, excluding payments for options to renew or buy, are less than $1,000; or

（2）存在被申请强制履行之当事方或其授权代理人签名的书面文件，且该文件足以表明当事方已达成租赁合同，并足以描述所租赁的货物和租赁期限。

（2）there is a writing, signed by the party against whom enforcement is sought or by that party's authorized agent, sufficient to indicate that a lease contract has been made between the parties and to describe the goods leased and the lease term.

（b）对所租赁的货物或租赁期限的描述，无论是否具体，

（b）Any description of leased goods or of the lease term is sufficient and satisfies

只要合理指明了所描述的内容，即为充分，并满足（a）（2）款的要求。

Subsection（a）（2）, whether or not it is specific, if it reasonably identifies what is described.

（c）一份书面文件，即使漏写或错写任何已约定的条款，也并非不足以表明合同的达成，但在（a）（2）款意义上，租赁合同只能在不超出该书面文件标明的租赁期限和货物数量的范围内强制履行。

（c）A writing is not insufficient because it omits or incorrectly states a term agreed upon, but the lease contract is not enforceable under Subsection（a）（2）beyond the lease term and the quantity of goods shown in the writing.

（d）不符合（a）款要求但在其他方面有效的租赁合同，在下列情况下可以强制履行：

（d）A lease contract that does not satisfy the requirements of Subsection（a）, but which is valid in other respects, is enforceable:

（1）货物系专为承租方制造或取得，且不适合出租方在正常业务中向他人出租或出售，且出租方在收到毁约通知之前，并在客观情况合理表明货物确系用于承租方的状况下，已实质上开始货物的制造，或已就货物承担了采购义务；

（1）if the goods are to be specially manufactured or obtained for the lessee and are not suitable for lease or sale to others in the ordinary course of the lessor's business, and the lessor, before notice of repudiation is received and under circumstances that reasonably indicate that the goods are for the lessee, has made either a substantial beginning of their manufacture or commitments for their procurement;

（2）被申请强制履行的一方，以答辩或作证承认，或在法庭上以其他形式承认，已订立租赁合同；但本款项下的强制履行，不超过该方所承认的货物数量；

（2）if the party against whom enforcement is sought admits in that party's pleading, testimony or otherwise in court that a lease contract was made, but the lease contract is not enforceable under this provision beyond the quantity of goods admitted;

（3）承租方已收到并已接受货物；或

（3）with respect to goods that have been received and accepted by the lessee;or

（4）根据禁止自相矛盾、信赖损失或不当得利的一般原

（4）if the lease contract would otherwise be enforceable under general principles of

则，租赁合同本应予以强制履行。

equitable estoppel, detrimental reliance or unjust enrichment.

（e）上述（d）款所述之租赁合同的租赁期限：

（e）The lease term under a lease contract referred to in Subsection（d）is:

（1）当被申请强制履行的当事方或其授权代理人已在包含租赁期限的书面文件上签名时，应为该书面文件规定的期限；

（1）if there is a writing signed by the party against whom enforcement is sought or by that party's authorized agent specifying the lease term, the term so specified;

（2）当被申请强制履行的当事方以答辩或作证承认了租赁期限，或在法庭上以其他方式承认了租赁期限时，应为其承认的期限；或

（2）if the party against whom enforcement is sought admits in that party's pleading, testimony, or otherwise in court a lease term, the term so admitted;or

（3）应为合理租赁期限。

（3）a reasonable lease term.

第 2A.202 条　最终书面表示：口头证据或外部证据

§ 2A.202. Final Written Expression:Parol or Extrinsic Evidence.

当事方在确认性备忘录中同意的条款，或当事方以其他方式记录在书面文件中作为当事方协议之最终表示的条款，不得以任何之前达成的协议或同时达成的口头协议作为证据加以否认，但可以用下列内容加以解释或补充：

Terms with respect to which the confirmatory memoranda of the parties agree or which are otherwise set forth in a writing intended by the parties as a final expression of their agreement with respect to such terms as are included therein may not be contradicted by evidence of a prior agreement or of a contemporaneous oral agreement but may be explained or supplemented:

（1）交易过程、行业惯例或履约过程；以及

（1）by course of dealing or usage of trade or by course of performance; and

（2）与上述条款相和谐的补充条款证据，除非法院认定，当事方的意图是将上述书面文件作为协议条款之完整和排他的表述。

（2）by evidence of consistent additional terms unless the court finds the writing to have been intended also as a complete and exclusive statement of the terms of the agreement.

第 2A.203 条 蜡印无效

证明租赁合同的书面文件，或证明有关签订租赁合同之要约的书面文件，即使加盖蜡印，亦不构成蜡封文书，有关蜡封文书的法律亦不适用于此种租赁合同或要约。

§ 2A.203. Seals Inoperative.

The affixing of a seal to a writing evidencing a lease contract or an offer to enter into a lease contract does not render the writing a sealed instrument and the law with respect to sealed instruments does not apply to the lease contract or offer.

第 2A.204 条 合同订立的一般规定

（a）租赁合同可以通过足以表明当事方协议的任何方式订立，包括双方承认租赁合同之存在的行为。

（b）足以构成租赁合同的协议，即使达成的时间不确定，亦可成立。

（c）即使租赁合同的一项或多项条款存在空缺，只要当事方有意订立租赁合同，且存在比较确定的方法用以提供适当救济，合同即不因缺乏确定性而不能成立。

§ 2A.204. Formation in General.

（a）A lease contract may be made in any manner sufficient to show agreement, including conduct by both parties which recognizes the existence of a lease contract.

（b）An agreement sufficient to constitute a lease contract may be found although the moment of its making is undetermined.

（c）Although one or more terms are left open, a lease contract does not fail for indefiniteness if the parties have intended to make a lease contract and there is a reasonably certain basis for giving an appropriate remedy.

第 2A.205 条 不可撤销的要约

如果商人在签名的书面文件中向另一人发出出租或承租货物的要约，且要约条款保证要约将保持有效，则在要约规定的有效时间内，或如果未规定时间，则在合理时间内，即使缺乏对价，要约亦不可被撤销；但是，在任何情况下，要约不可撤销的期限都不超过三

§ 2A.205. Firm Offers.

An offer by a merchant to lease goods to or from another person in a signed writing that by its terms gives assurance it will be held open is not revocable, for lack of consideration, during the time stated or, if no time is stated, for a reasonable time, but in no event may the period of irrevocability exceed three months. Any such term of assurance on a form supplied by the offeree must be separately signed by the

个月。如果此种保证条款载于受要约人提供的表格上，要约人必须在该条款处另加签名。

offeror.

第 2A.206 条 订立租赁合同的要约与承诺

§ 2A.206. Offer and Acceptance in Formation of Lease Contract.

（a）除语言或客观情况毫无疑义地另有所指外，订立租赁合同的要约必须被解释为，邀请另一方使用当时情况下合理的任何方式和媒介作出承诺。

（a）Unless otherwise unambiguously indicated by the language or circumstances, an offer to make a lease contract must be construed as inviting acceptance in any manner and by any medium reasonable in the circumstances.

（b）即使开始作出被要求的履约属于作出承诺的合理方式，但要约人只要在合理时间内未收到关于该承诺的通知，即可认为要约未在有效时间内得到承诺而失效。

（b）If the beginning of a requested performance is a reasonable method of acceptance, an offeror who is not notified of acceptance within a reasonable time may treat the offer as having lapsed before acceptance.

第 2A.207 条 ［保留］

§ 2A.207.［Reserved］

第 2A.208 条 修改、取消和弃权

§ 2A.208. Modification, Rescission and Waiver.

（a）修改租赁合同的协议，即使不存在对价，亦可具有约束力。

（a）An agreement modifying a lease contract needs no consideration to be binding.

（b）如果已签署的租赁协议规定，必须签署书面文件才能修改或取消该协议，则该协议不得用其他方法修改或取消；但除在商人之间外，如果此种规定载于商人一方提供的表格上，另一方必须在此规定处另加签名。

（b）A signed lease agreement that excludes modification or rescission except by a signed writing may not be otherwise modified or rescinded, but, except as between merchants, such a requirement on a form supplied by a merchant must be separately signed by the other party.

（c）意图作出修改或取消的行为，即使不满足（b）款的

（c）Although an attempt at modification or rescission does not satisfy the requirements

要求，仍可构成弃权。

（d）一方作出影响租赁合同尚未履行之部分的弃权后，可以撤回弃权，但应使另一方收到合理通知，说明另一方应严格履行弃权所涉及的条款。但是，如果另一方依赖该弃权已严重改变了处境，致使该撤回导致不公平，则不得撤回。

of Subsection（b）, it may operate as a waiver.

（d）A party who has made a waiver affecting an executory portion of a lease contract may retract the waiver by reasonable notification received by the other party that strict performance will be required of any term waived, unless a retraction would be unjust in view of a material change of position in reliance on the waiver.

第 2A.209 条　融资租赁中承租方作为供应合同的受益人

§ 2A.209. Lessee Under Finance Lease as Beneficiary of Supply Contract.

（a）供应商在供应合同中向出租方作出的承诺，以及全部的明示担保和默示担保，包括第三方提供的担保，无论其来自供应合同本身，还是根据供应合同另行提供，受益权均延及承租方；但是，承租方享有的权利，不超出承租方在供应合同所涉及之融资租赁项下的租赁权益，并受制于担保条款和供应合同条款，也受制于所有相关抗辩和索赔。

（a）The benefit of a supplier's promises to the lessor under the supply contract and of all warranties, whether express or implied, including those of any third party provided in connection with or as part of the supply contract, extends to the lessee to the extent of the lessee's leasehold interest under a finance lease related to the supply contract, but is subject to the terms of the warranty and of the supply contract and all defenses or claims arising therefrom.

（b）尽管承租方就各项担保及供应商的承诺享有受益权［第 2A.209 条（a）款］，但该权利：

（b）The extension of the benefit of a supplier's promises and of warranties to the lessee（Section 2A.209（a））does not:

（1）不修改供应合同当事方的权利和义务，无论其来自该合同还是其他来源；并且

（1）modify the rights and obligations of the parties to the supply contract, whether arising therefrom or otherwise;or

（2）不使承租方对供应合同承担任何义务或责任。

（2）impose any duty or liability under the supply contract on the lessee.

（c）供应商和出租方对供

（c）Any modification or rescission of the

应合同作出的修改或撤销，在供应商和承租方之间亦具有效力，除非在修改或撤销之前，供应商已得到通知，即承租方已基于该供应合同达成了融资租赁。如果该修改或撤销在供应商和承租方之间具有效力，则出租方应被视为，除向承租方承担租赁合同项下的义务外，还应按修改或撤销之前承租方有权受益的内容，向承租方承担原有的各项担保及供应商原本对出租方作出的承诺。

supply contract by the supplier and the lessor is effective between the supplier and the lessee unless, before the modification or rescission, the supplier has received notice that the lessee has entered into a finance lease related to the supply contract.If the modification or rescission is effective between the supplier and the lessee, the lessor is deemed to have assumed, in addition to the obligations of the lessor to the lessee under the lease contract,promises of the supplier to the lessor and warranties that were so modified or rescinded as they existed and were available to the lessee before modification or rescission.

（d）承租方除了根据（a）款受益于各项担保及供应商的承诺，还保留其根据承租方与供应商之间的协议或根据其他法律而可能享有的对抗供应商的全部权利。

（d）In addition to the extension of the benefit of the supplier's promises and of warranties to the lessee under Subsection（a）, the lessee retains all rights that the lessee may have against the supplier which arise from an agreement between the lessee and the supplier or under other law.

第 2A.210 条　明示担保

（a）出租方通过下列方式作出明示担保：

（1）如果出租方就货物向承租方确认的事实或作出的许诺构成交易之基础的一部分，出租方即明示担保，货物将符合此种确认或许诺。

（2）如果对货物的任何描述构成交易之基础的一部分，出租方即明示担保，货物将符

§ 2A.210. Express Warranties.

（a）Express warranties by the lessor are created as follows:

（1）Any affirmation of fact or promise made by the lessor to the lessee that relates to the goods and becomes part of the basis of the bargain creates an express warranty that the goods will conform to the affirmation or promise.

（2）Any description of the goods which is made part of the basis of the bargain creates an express warranty that the goods will conform to

合此种描述。

（3）如果任何样品或模型构成交易之基础的一部分，出租方即明示担保，全部货物都将符合此种样品或模型。

（b）明示担保的产生，不取决于出租方是否使用“担保”或“保证”这类正式用语，也不取决于出租方是否具有提供担保的具体意图。但是，出租方仅确认货物的价值，或仅表明自己对货物的看法或赞扬，并不构成担保。

the description.

（3）Any sample or model that is made part of the basis of the bargain creates an express warranty that the whole of the goods will conform to the sample or model.

（b）It is not necessary to the creation of an express warranty that the lessor use formal words, such as “warrant” or “guarantee,” or that the lessor have a specific intention to make a warranty, but an affirmation merely of the value of the goods or a statement purporting to be merely the lessor’s opinion or commendation of the goods does not create a warranty.

第 2A.211 条 担保不造成干扰和不存在侵权；承租方不得侵权的义务

（a）租赁合同包含一项担保，即在租赁期限内，不因出租方的行为或疏漏，导致他人对货物持有索赔或权益（侵权或类似原因引起的索赔除外），以致干扰承租方享用其租赁权益。

（b）除融资租赁外，如果对于租赁合同涉及的货物，出租方是惯常从事该类货物交易的商人，租赁合同即包含一项担保，即所交付的货物不受任何人以侵权或类似原因提出的正当索赔。

（c）如果承租方向出租方或供应商提供货物规格，且出

§ 2A.211. Warranties Against Interference and Against Infringement;Lessee’s Obligation Against Infringement.

（a）There is in a lease contract a warranty that for the lease term no person holds a claim to or interest in the goods that arose from an act or omission of the lessor other than a claim by way of infringement or the like, which will interfere with the lessee’s enjoyment of its leasehold interest.

（b）Except in a finance lease there is in a lease contract by a lessor who is a merchant regularly dealing in goods of the kind a warranty that the goods are delivered free of the rightful claim of any person by way of infringement or the like.

（c）A lessee who furnishes specifications to a lessor or a supplier shall hold the lessor

租方或供应商因遵从该规格受到侵权索赔或类似索赔，承租方必须保证出租方和供应商不受损失。

and the supplier harmless against a claim by way of infringement or the like that arises out of compliance with the specifications.

第 2A.212 条　商销性的默示担保

§ 2A.212. Implied Warranty of Merchantability.

（a）除融资租赁外，如果租赁合同的出租方是该类货物的商人，合同即包含一项默示担保，即货物具有商销性。

（b）货物至少达到下列标准才具有商销性：

（1）根据租赁协议的描述，货物可以不受异议地得到本行业认可；

（2）涉及种类物时，货物在描述范围内具有良好平均品质；

（3）货物适合该类货物使用的通常用途；

（4）货物在每个单位内部以及全体相关单位之间，种类、质量及数量均匀，差异在租赁协议允许的范围内；

（5）当租赁协议有要求时，货物按要求妥善地置入容器、加以包装并贴上标签；并且

（6）当容器或标签上载有许诺或对事实的确认时，货物符合此种许诺或确认。

（c）交易过程或行业惯例可以引起其他默示担保。

（a）Except in a finance lease, a warranty that the goods will be merchantable is implied in a lease contract if the lessor is a merchant with respect to goods of that kind.

（b）Goods to be merchantable must be at least such as:

（1）pass without objection in the trade under the description in the lease agreement;

（2）in the case of fungible goods, are of fair average quality within the description;

（3）are fit for the ordinary purposes for which goods of that type are used;

（4）run, within the variation permitted by the lease agreement, of even kind, quality, and quantity within each unit and among all units involved;

（5）are adequately contained, packaged, and labeled as the lease agreement may require;and

（6）conform to any promises or affirmations of fact made on the container or label.

（c）Other implied warranties may arise from course of dealing or usage of trade.

第 2A.213 条 适用于特定用途的默示担保

除融资租赁外，如果在订立租赁合同时出租方有理由知道，货物系用于某种特定用途，且承租方依赖出租方的技能或判断来选择或提供适合的货物，租赁合同即包含一项默示担保，即货物将适用于该用途。

§ 2A.213. Implied Warranty of Fitness for Particular Purpose.

Except in a finance lease, if the lessor at the time the lease contract is made has reason to know of any particular purpose for which the goods are required and that the lessee is relying on the lessor's skill or judgment to select or furnish suitable goods, there is in the lease contract an implied warranty that the goods will be fit for that purpose.

第 2A.214 条 排除或修改担保

（a）引起明示担保的词句或行为，与具有否认或限制该担保之倾向的词句或行为，在合理的情况下，必须作出互不矛盾的解释；但是，除本篇有关口头证据和外部证据的条款另有规定外（第 2A.202 条），在此种解释不合理时，否认或限制无效。

（b）除（c）款另有规定外，要排除或修改有关商销性的默示担保或其任何部分，用语必须提及"商销性"，且必须使用醒目书写的书面形式。除（c）款另有规定外，要排除或修改有关适用性的默示担保，必须使用醒目书写的书面形式。要排除有关适用性的所有默示担保，只要使用醒目书写的书面形式，并使用诸如"不担保货物适用于特定用途"等说明，

§ 2A.214. Exclusion or Modification of Warranties.

（a）Words or conduct relevant to the creation of an express warranty and words or conduct tending to negate or limit a warranty must be construed whenever reasonable, as consistent with each other;but, subject to the provisions of Section 2A.202 on parol or extrinsic evidence, negation or limitation is inoperative to the extent that the construction is unreasonable.

（b）Subject to Subsection（c）, to exclude or modify the implied warranty of merchantability or any part of it the language must mention "merchantability," be by a writing, and be conspicuous.Subject to Subsection（c）, to exclude or modify an implied warranty of fitness the exclusion must be by a writing and be conspicuous.Language to exclude all implied warranties of fitness is sufficient if it is in writing, is conspicuous and states, for example, "There is no warranty that the goods will be fit for a particular purpose."

即为充分。

（c）除（d）款另有规定外，即使有（b）款的规定：

（1）除客观情况另有所指外，使用诸如“依现状”或“残次品”这类用语，或其他根据通常理解可使承租方注意到排除担保且明确不存在默示担保的用语，即可排除所有默示担保，但必须使用醒目书写的书面形式；

（2）如果承租方在订立租赁合同前，按照自己希望的详细程度检验了货物或其样品或模型，或拒绝检验货物，则对货物中存在的通过检验在当时情况下本可发现的瑕疵，不存在默示担保；并且

（3）交易过程、履约过程或行业惯例也可以排除或修改默示担保。

（d）要排除或修改有关不造成干扰和不存在侵权之担保或其任何部分（第 2A.211 条），用语必须具体，且必须采用醒目书写的书面形式，除非根据客观情况，包括履约过程、交易过程或行业惯例，承租方有理由知道，货物的租赁受制于他人的索赔或权益。

（c）Notwithstanding Subsection（b）, but subject to Subsection（d）:

（1）unless the circumstances indicate otherwise, all implied warranties are excluded by expressions like "as is," or "with all faults," or by other language that in common understanding calls the lessee's attention to the exclusion of warranties and makes plain that there is no implied warranty, if in writing and conspicuous;

（2）if the lessee before entering into the lease contract has examined the goods or the sample or model as fully as desired or has refused to examine the goods, there is no implied warranty with regard to defects that an examination ought in the circumstances to have revealed;and

（3）an implied warranty also may be excluded or modified by course of dealing, course of performance, or usage of trade.

（d）To exclude or modify a warranty against interference or against infringement（Section 2A.211）or any part of it, the language must be specific, be by a writing, and be conspicuous, unless the circumstances, including course of performance, course of dealing, or usage of trade, give the lessee reason to know that the goods are being leased subject to a claim or interest of any person.

第 2A.215 条　明示担保或默示担保的叠加和冲突

各种担保，无论明示或默

§ 2A.215. Accumulation and Conflict of Warranties Express or Implied.

Warranties, whether express or implied,

示，均必须被解释为互不矛盾，且效力叠加。如果此种解释不合理，应根据当事方的意图确定哪项担保为主。当事方的意图，应根据下列原则确定：

（1）精确规格或技术规格，排除不一致的样品或模型，或一般性文字描述；

（2）现存批量货物中抽出的样品，排除不一致的一般性文字描述；以及

（3）明示担保排除不一致的默示担保，但适用于特定用途的默示担保除外。

must be construed as consistent with each other and as cumulative, but if that construction is unreasonable, the intention of the parties determines which warranty is dominant.In ascertaining that intention the following rules apply:

（1）exact or technical specifications displace an inconsistent sample or model or general language of description;

（2）a sample from an existing bulk displaces inconsistent general language of description;and

（3）express warranties displace inconsistent implied warranties other than an implied warranty of fitness for a particular purpose.

第 2A.216 条 明示担保和默示担保的第三方受益人

对于下列问题，即向承租方作出的有关质量的明示担保或默示担保是否可使承租方以外的人受益，以及承租方（或承租方所获担保的其他受益人）是否可就货物质量瑕疵起诉除直接出租方以外的第三方，或起诉融资租赁中的供应商，本篇不作规定。此类问题留给法院决定。

§ 2A.216. Third-Party Beneficiaries of Express and Implied Warranties.

This Article does not provide whether anyone other than a lessee may take advantage of an express or implied warranty of quality made to the lessee or whether the lessee or anyone entitled to take advantage of a warranty made to the lessee may sue a third party other than the immediate lessor, or the supplier in a finance lease, for deficiencies in the quality of the goods.These matters are left to the courts for their determination.

第 2A.217 条 特定化

可以根据当事方的明确协议，在任何时间以任何方式将货物特定为租赁合同项下的货物。在没有明确协议的情况下：

§ 2A.217. Identification.

Identification of goods as goods to which a lease contract refers may be made at any time and in any manner explicitly agreed to by the parties.In the absence of explicit agreement, identification occurs:

（1）如果租赁合同租赁的是合同订立时现实存在且特定的货物，则特定化在租赁合同订立时发生；

（1）when the lease contract is made if the lease contract is for a lease of goods that are existing and identified;

（2）如果租赁合同租赁的不是合同订立时现实存在且特定的货物，则特定化在出租方将货物发运、标记或以其他方式确定于租赁合同项下时发生；或

（2）when the goods are shipped, marked, or otherwise designated by the lessor as goods to which the lease contract refers, if the lease contract is for a lease of goods that are not existing and identified;or

（3）如果租赁合同租赁的是动物的待出生幼仔，则特定化在动物怀胎时发生。

（3）when the young are conceived, if the lease contract is for a lease of the unborn young of animals.

第 2A.218 条　保险和理赔款

§ 2A.218. Insurance and Proceeds.

（a）现实存在的货物被特定于租赁合同项下后，承租方即对货物取得保险利益，即使特定化的货物不符合合同，致使承租方可以拒收。

（a）A lessee obtains an insurable interest when existing goods are identified to the lease contract even though the goods identified are nonconforming and the lessee has an option to reject them.

（b）如果出租方对货物作出的特定化，是承租方取得保险利益的唯一原因，则出租方可在自己违约或破产前，或在通知承租方特定化已不可改变前，用其他货物替换已特定化的货物。

（b）If a lessee has an insurable interest only by reason of the lessor's identification of the goods, the lessor, until default or insolvency or notification to the lessee that identification is final, may substitute other goods for those identified.

（c）即使承租方根据（a）款和（b）款享有保险利益，在租赁合同存续期间，出租方亦持有保险利益。

（c）Notwithstanding a lessee's insurable interest under Subsections（a）and（b）, the lessor retains an insurable interest during the existence of the lease contract.

（d）本条任何部分均不削

（d）Nothing in this section impairs any

弱其他法律承认的保险利益。

insurable interest recognized under any other statute or rule of law.

（e）当事方可以通过协议，规定一方或多方有义务获取覆盖货物的保险并支付保费，也可以规定保险理赔款的受益人。

（e）The parties by agreement may determine that one or more parties have an obligation to obtain and pay for insurance covering the goods and by agreement may determine the beneficiary of the proceeds of the insurance.

第 2A.219 条 损失风险

§ 2A.219. Risk of Loss.

（a）除融资租赁外，损失风险由出租方承担，不转移至承租方。在融资租赁中，损失风险转移至承租方。

（a）Except in the case of a finance lease, risk of loss is retained by the lessor and does not pass to the lessee.In the case of a finance lease, risk of loss passes to the lessee.

（b）除本篇有关违约对风险转移之影响的条款另有规定外（第 2A.220 条），如果损失风险应转移至承租方，但未规定转移时间，则应适用下列原则：

（b）Subject to the provisions of this Article on the effect of default on risk of loss（Section 2A.220）, if risk of loss is to pass to the lessee and the time of passage is not stated, the following rules apply:

（1）当租赁合同要求或授权通过承运人发运货物时：

（1）If the lease contract requires or authorizes the goods to be shipped by carrier:

（A）如果租赁合同未规定在特定目的地作出交付，则在货物被适当交付给承运人时，损失风险转移至承租方；但是

（A）and it does not require delivery at a particular destination, the risk of loss passes to the lessee when the goods are duly delivered to the carrier;but

（B）如果租赁合同规定在特定目的地作出交付，且在货物到达目的地但仍由承运人占有期间，在该地作出了适当提示交付，则只要就货物在该地作出的适当提示，能够使承租方取得交付，损失风险即于该时转移至承租方。

（B）if it does require delivery at a particular destination and the goods are there duly tendered while in the possession of the carrier, the risk of loss passes to the lessee when the goods are there duly so tendered as to enable the lessee to take delivery.

（2）如果货物由货物保管人持有，且不再移动即可交付，则只要货物保管人确认承租方有权占有货物，损失风险即于该时转移至承租方。

（3）涉及（1）款和（2）款以外的情况时，如果承租方是商人，损失风险在提示交付时转移至承租方；否则，损失风险在承租方收到货物时转移。

（2）If the goods are held by a bailee to be delivered without being moved, the risk of loss passes to the lessee on acknowledgement by the bailee of the lessee's right to possession of the goods.

（3）In any case not within Subdivision（1）or（2）, the risk of loss passes to the lessee on tender of delivery if the lessee is a merchant; otherwise the risk of loss passes to the lessee on the lessee's receipt of the goods.

第 2A.220 条　违约对损失风险的影响

§ 2A.220. Effect of Default on Risk of Loss.

（a）当损失风险应转移至承租方，但未规定转移的时间时：

（1）如果提示交付或交付的货物不符合租赁合同，致使承租方有权拒收，则在违约被补救或货物被接受前，损失风险仍由出租方承担；或在涉及融资租赁时，由供应商承担。

（2）承租方如果正当撤销对货物的接受，可就自己有效保险覆盖不足的部分，视损失风险从开始即一直由出租方承担。

（b）无论损失风险是否应转移至承租方，在涉及已特定于租赁合同项下并符合合同的货物时，如果承租方毁弃租赁合同或以其他方式违约，则出租方或融资租赁中的供应商，可就自己有效保险覆盖不足的

（a）Where risk of loss is to pass to the lessee and the time of passage is not stated:

（1）if a tender or delivery of goods so fails to conform to the lease contract as to give a right of rejection, the risk of their loss remains with the lessor, or, in the case of a finance lease, the supplier, until cure or acceptance;or

（2）if the lessee rightfully revokes acceptance, the lessee, to the extent of any deficiency in the lessee's effective insurance coverage, may treat the risk of loss as having remained with the lessor from the beginning.

（b）Whether or not risk of loss is to pass to the lessee, if the lessee as to conforming goods already identified to a lease contract repudiates or is otherwise in default under the lease contract, the lessor, or, in the case of a finance lease, the supplier, to the extent of any deficiency in the lessor's or the supplier's

部分，视损失风险在商业上合理的时间内由承租方承担。

effective insurance coverage may treat the risk of loss as resting on the lessee for a commercially reasonable time.

第 2A.221 条 特定化的货物遭受损失

§ 2A.221. Casualty to Identified Goods.

如果履行租赁合同所需的货物在订立合同时系属特定，且货物在交付之前，非因承租方、出租方或供应商任何一方的过错而遭受损失，或货物在损失风险根据租赁协议或根据第 2A.219 条转移至承租方之前遭受损失，则：

If a lease contract requires goods identified when the lease contract is made, and the goods suffer casualty without fault of the lessee, the lessor or the supplier before delivery, or the goods suffer casualty before risk of loss passes to the lessee under the lease agreement or Section 2A.219:

（1）当货物全部损失时，租赁合同失效；以及

（2）当货物部分损失时，或当货物状况恶化至不符合租赁合同的程度时，承租方可以要求检验货物，并可以选择视租赁合同为失效；且除融资租赁（不包括消费者租赁）外，也可以选择接受货物，并根据货物恶化情况或数量减少情况，相应调整租赁剩余期间的租金，但没有对抗出租方的进一步权利。

（1）if the loss is total, the lease contract is avoided;and

（2）if the loss is partial or the goods have so deteriorated as to no longer conform to the lease contract, the lessee may nevertheless demand inspection and at the lessee's option either treat the lease contract as avoided or, except in a finance lease that is not a consumer lease, accept the goods with due allowance from the rent payable for the balance of the lease term for the deterioration or the deficiency in quantity but without further right against the lessor.

第3章 租赁合同的效力

PART 3. EFFECT OF LEASE CONTRACT

第 2A.301 条 租赁合同的强制履行力

§ 2A.301. Enforceability of Lease Contract.

除本篇另有规定外，在当

Except as otherwise provided in this

事方之间，以及在对抗货物购买人和当事方债权人时，租赁合同的效力根据其条款确定，并可按合同条款强制履行。

Article, a lease contract is effective and enforceable according to its terms between the parties, against purchasers of the goods and against creditors of the parties.

第 2A.302 条　货物的所有权和占有

§ 2A.302. Title to and Possession of Goods.

除本篇另有规定外，无论是出租方还是第三方拥有货物所有权，也无论是出租方还是承租方或第三方占有货物，本篇的全部条款均适用，即使根据相关法律，对货物的占有或不占有构成欺诈。

Except as otherwise provided in this Article, each provision of this Article applies whether the lessor or a third party has title to the goods, and whether the lessor, the lessee, or a third party has possession of the goods, notwithstanding any statute or rule of law that possession or the absence of possession is fraudulent.

第 2A.303 条　租赁合同项下当事方权益的可转让性；货物中出租方残余权益的可转让性；委托履约；权利转让

§ 2A.303. Alienability of Party's Interest Under Lease Contract or of Lessor's Residual Interest in Goods; Delegation of Performance;Transfer of Rights.

（a）在本条中，“设立担保权益”包括租赁合同的出售，只要根据第 9.109 条（a）（3）款，该出售受本法第 9 篇《担保交易》篇的约束。

（a）As used in this section, “creation of a security interest” includes the sale of a lease contract that is subject to Article 9 of this Act, Secured Transactions, by reason of Section 9.109（a）（3）.

（b）除第 9.407 条（c）款另有规定外，如果租赁协议的条款：（1）在涉及租赁合同项下当事方之权益或货物中之出租方残余权益时，禁止该权益的自愿或非自愿转让，包括通过买卖、分租、设立或强制履行担保权益、查封、扣押或其他司法程序进行的转让；或（2）规定该转让构成违约，此时，

（b）Except as provided in Section 9.407（c）, a provision in a lease agreement which（1）prohibits the voluntary or involuntary transfer, including a transfer by sale, sublease, creation or enforcement of a security interest, or attachment, levy, or other judicial process, of an interest of a party under the lease contract or of the lessor's residual interest in the goods, or（2）makes such a transfer an event of default, gives rise to the rights and remedies provided

该条款将引发（d）款提供的权利和救济，但该转让在其他方面仍然有效，即使该转让被协议禁止，或构成租赁协议项下的违约。

in Subsection（d）, but a transfer that is prohibited or is an event of default under the lease agreement is otherwise effective.

（c）如果租赁协议的条款：（1）在涉及一方违反整体租赁合同后另一方寻求损害赔偿之权利或一方适当履行自己全部义务后要求另一方付款之权利时，禁止该权利的转让，或（2）规定该转让构成违约，此时，该条款不可强制履行，且该转让不属于（d）款所述的转让，即该转让不会严重损害租赁合同另一方获得回报履约的机会，或严重改变其义务，或严重增加其负担或风险。

（c）A provision in a lease agreement which（1）prohibits a transfer of a right to damages for default with respect to the whole lease contract or of a right to payment arising out of the transferor's due performance of the transferor's entire obligation, or（2）makes such a transfer an event of default, is not enforceable, and such a transfer is not a transfer that materially impairs the prospect of obtaining return performance by, materially changes the duty of, or materially increases the burden or risk imposed on, the other party to the lease contract within the purview of Subsection（d）.

（d）除第9.407条（c）款另有规定外：

（d）Subject to Section 9.407（c）:

（1）如果发生转让，且根据租赁协议该转让构成违约，则租赁合同中未作出转让的一方，享有第2A.501条（b）款提供的权利和救济，除非其已就该违约放弃权利或通过其他方式表示同意；并且

（1）if a transfer is made which is made an event of default under a lease agreement, the party to the lease contract not making the transfer, unless that party waives the default or otherwise agrees, has the rights and remedies described in Section 2A.501（b）;and

（2）如果（1）款不适用且转让已发生，且该转让：（A）被租赁协议禁止，或（B）严重损害租赁合同另一方获得回报履约的机会，或严重改变其义务，或严重增加其负担或风险，

（2）if Subdivision（1）is not applicable and if a transfer is made that（A）is prohibited under a lease agreement or（B）materially impairs the prospect of obtaining return performance by, materially changes the duty of, or materially increases the burden of

此时，除非未作出转让的一方于任何时间在租赁合同中或通过其他方式同意该转让，否则，除合同另有限制外：（i）转让方应向未作转让的一方，就转让给后者造成的损失承担赔偿责任，但只限于未作转让的一方不能合理防止的损失，并且（ii）拥有管辖权的法院可以提供其他适当救助，包括解除租赁合同或禁止转让。

risk imposed on, the other party to the lease contract, unless the party not making the transfer agrees at any time to the transfer in the lease contract or otherwise, then, except as limited by contract, (i) the transferor is liable to the party not making the transfer for damages caused by the transfer to the extent that the damages could not reasonably be prevented by the party not making the transfer and (ii) a court having jurisdiction may grant other appropriate relief, including cancellation of the lease contract or an injunction against the transfer.

（e）转让“租赁”，或转让“我在租赁项下的全部权利”，或以类似的概括语言作出的转让，是权利的转让；并且，除语言或客观情况（如为提供担保而作的转让）另有所指外，该转让也是转让人履约义务的委托。受让人接受委托后，即允诺履行该义务。该允诺可由转让人或租赁合同的另一方强制履行。

(e) A transfer of "the lease" or of "all my rights under the lease," or a transfer in similar general terms, is a transfer of rights and, unless the language or the circumstances, as in a transfer for security, indicate the contrary, the transfer is a delegation of duties by the transferor to the transferee.Acceptance by the transferee constitutes a promise by the transferee to perform those duties.This promise is enforceable by either the transferor or the other party to the lease contract.

（f）除出租方和承租方另有协议外，委托履约不解除转让人对另一方的履约义务或违约责任。

(f) Unless otherwise agreed by the lessor and the lessee, a delegation of performance does not relieve the transferor as against the other party of any duty to perform or of any liability for default.

（g）在消费者租赁中，如果要禁止当事方转让租赁合同项下的权益，或规定转让构成违约，用语必须具体，且必须

(g) In a consumer lease, to prohibit the transfer of an interest of a party under the lease contract or to make a transfer an event of default, the language must be specific, by a

采用醒目书写的书面形式。

writing, and conspicuous.

第2A.304条 出租方随后另行出租货物

§ 2A.304. Subsequent Lease of Goods by Lessor.

(a) 除本篇第2A.303条另有规定外，如果现有租赁合同的出租方，将货物另行出租给后手承租方，则该后手承租方取得的，是出租方拥有的或有权力转让的货物租赁权益，但不超出所转让的租赁权益；并且，除(b)款或第2A.527条(d)款另有规定外，后手承租方取得的权益，受制于现有租赁合同。拥有可撤销所有权的出租方，有权力向善意支付了价值的后手承租方转让完好的租赁权益，但不超出前句所述的范围。出租方通过购买交易取得货物的交付后，即取得此种权力，即使：

(a) Subject to Section 2A.303 of this Article, a subsequent lessee from a lessor of goods under an existing lease contract obtains, to the extent of the leasehold interest transferred, the leasehold interest in the goods that the lessor had or had power to transfer, and except as provided by Subsection (b) or Section 2A.527 (d) takes subject to the existing lease contract.A lessor with voidable title has power to transfer a good leasehold interest to a good faith subsequent lessee for value, but only to the extent set forth in the preceding sentence.If goods have been delivered under a transaction of purchase, the lessor has that power even though:

(1) 对于出租方的真实身份，出租方的转让人受到欺骗；

(1) the lessor's transferor was deceived as to the identity of the lessor;

(2) 交付系为换取支票，但支票随后被拒付；

(2) the delivery was in exchange for a check which is later dishonored;

(3) 交易被约定作为“现金买卖”；或

(3) it was agreed that the transaction was to be a "cash sale";or

(4) 交付系通过欺诈取得，且该欺诈构成刑法中的盗窃罪。

(4) the delivery was procured through fraud punishable as larcenous under the criminal law.

(b) 如果现有承租方将货物委托给经营该类货物的商人出租方，且后手承租方在正常业务中从出租方取得该货物，

(b) A subsequent lessee in the ordinary course of business from a lessor who is a merchant dealing in goods of that kind to whom the goods were entrusted by the existing

且上述委托发生在后手承租方之权益取得可对抗出租方之强制履行力之前，则在所转让的租赁权益的范围内，后手承租方取得出租方以及现有承租方对货物的全部权利，且不受制于现有租赁合同。

lessee of that lessor before the interest of the subsequent lessee became enforceable against that lessor obtains, to the extent of the leasehold interest transferred, all of that lessor's and the existing lessee's rights to the goods, and takes free of the existing lease contract.

（c）如果现有租赁合同项下的货物，由根据本州或另一州法律颁发的产权证书覆盖，则后手承租方从出租方取得该货物后，所取得的权利不超出本条及产权证书颁发州法律提供的权利。

（c）A subsequent lessee from the lessor of goods that are subject to an existing lease contract and are covered by a certificate of title issued under a statute of this state or of another jurisdiction takes no greater rights than those provided both by this section and by the certificate of title statute.

第 2A.305 条　承租方出售或分租货物

§ 2A.305. Sale or Sublease of Goods by Lessee.

（a）除第 2A.303 条另有规定外，如果现有租赁合同的承租方，将货物出售给买方，或分租给分租承租方，则该买方或分租承租方取得的，是承租方拥有的或有权力转让的货物租赁权益，但不超出所转让的租赁权益；并且，除（b）款或第 2A.511 条另有规定外，买方或分租承租方取得的权益，受制于现有租赁合同。拥有可撤销租赁权益的承租方，有权力向善意支付了价值的买方或分租承租方转让完好的租赁权益，但不超出前句所述的范围。承租方通过租赁交易取得货物的交付后，即取得此种

（a）Subject to the provisions of Section 2A.303, a buyer or sublessee from the lessee of goods under an existing lease contract obtains, to the extent of the interest transferred, the leasehold interest in the goods that the lessee had or had power to transfer, and except as provided by Subsection（b）and Section 2A.511, takes subject to the existing lease contract.A lessee with a voidable leasehold interest has power to transfer a good leasehold interest to a good faith buyer for value or a good faith sublessee for value, but only to the extent set forth in the preceding sentence.When goods have been delivered under a transaction of lease the lessee has that power even though:

权力，即使：

（1）对于承租方的真实身份，出租方受到欺骗；

（2）交付系为换取支票，但支票随后被拒付；或

（3）交付系通过欺诈取得，且该欺诈构成刑法中的盗窃罪。

（1）the lessor was deceived as to the identity of the lessee;

（2）the delivery was in exchange for a check which is later dishonored;or

（3）the delivery was procured through fraud punishable as larcenous under the criminal law.

（b）如果出租方将货物委托给经营该类货物的商人承租方，且正常业务中的买方或分租承租方从承租方取得该货物，则在所转让的权益范围内，买方或分租承租方取得出租方和承租方对货物的全部权利，且不受制于现有租赁合同。

（b）A buyer in the ordinary course of business or a sublessee in the ordinary course of business from a lessee who is a merchant dealing in goods of that kind to whom the goods were entrusted by the lessor obtains, to the extent of the interest transferred, all of the lessor's and lessee's rights to the goods, and takes free of the existing lease contract.

（c）如果现有租赁合同项下的货物，被根据本州或另一州法律颁发的产权证书覆盖，则买方或分租承租方从承租方取得该货物后，所取得的权利不超出本条及产权证书颁发州法律提供的权利。

（c）A buyer or sublessee from the lessee of goods that are subject to an existing lease contract and are covered by a certificate of title issued under a statute of this state or of another jurisdiction takes no greater rights than those provided both by this section and by the certificate of title statute.

第 2A.306 条 某些依法自动产生之留置权的优先权

如果任何人在正常业务中就租赁合同项下的货物提供服务或材料，且根据法律就该服务或材料对其占有的货物持有留置权，则在对抗出租方或承租方在租赁合同项下或本篇项下的权益时，该人的留置权享有优先权，除非设立该留置权

§ 2A.306. Priority of Certain Liens Arising by Operation of Law.

If a person in the ordinary course of the person's business furnishes services or materials with respect to goods subject to a lease contract, a lien upon those goods in the possession of that person given by statute or rule of law for those materials or services takes priority over any interest of the lessor or lessee under the lease contract or this Article unless

的法律另有不同规定。

the lien is created by statute and the statute provides otherwise or unless the lien is created by rule of law and the rule of law provides otherwise.

第2A.307条　某些权益的优先权：查封或扣押货物产生的留置权；货物中的担保权益；对货物的其他主张权

§ 2A.307. Priority of Liens Arising by Attachment or Levy on, Security Interests in, and Other Claims to Goods.

（a）除第2A.306条另有规定外，承租方之债权人从承租方取得的权利，受制于租赁合同。

（a）Except as otherwise provided in Section 2A.306, a creditor of a lessee takes subject to the lease contract.

（b）除（c）款及第2A.306条和第2A.308条另有规定外，出租方之债权人从出租方取得的权利，受制于租赁合同，除非在租赁合同取得强制履行力之前，债权人对货物的留置权已经发生附着。

（b）Except as otherwise provided in Subsection（c）and Sections 2A.306 and 2A.308, a creditor of a lessor takes subject to the lease contract unless the creditor holds a lien that attached to the goods before the lease contract became enforceable.

（c）除第9.317条、第9.321条和第9.323条另有规定外，承租方取得的租赁权益，受制于出租方之债权人持有的担保权益。

（c）Except as otherwise provided in Sections 9.317, 9.321, and 9.323, a lessee takes a leasehold interest subject to a security interest held by a creditor of the lessor.

第2A.308条　债权人的特别权利

§ 2A.308. Special Rights of Creditors.

（a）如果出租方保留对租赁合同项下之货物的占有，且根据任何法律，该占有构成对出租方之任何债权人的欺诈，或导致租赁合同失效，则出租方的该债权人可将该租赁合同视为无效。但是，出租方在租

（a）A creditor of a lessor in possession of goods subject to a lease contract may treat the lease contract as void if as against the creditor retention of possession by the lessor is fraudulent or voids the lease contract under any statute or rule of law, but retention of possession in good faith and current course

赁合同取得强制履行力后商业上合理的时间内，在业务过程中善意保留对货物的占有，不构成欺诈，亦不使租赁合同失效。

of trade by the lessor for a commercially reasonable time after the lease contract becomes enforceable is not fraudulent and does not void the lease contract.

（b）如果根据租赁合同的订立情况，本篇以外的任何法律视该交易为欺诈性转让或可撤销的优惠清偿，则出租方之债权人的权利，不受本篇的削弱。

（b）Nothing in this Article impairs the rights of creditors of a lessor if the lease contract is made under circumstances which under any statute or rule of law apart from this Article would constitute the transaction a fraudulent transfer or voidable preference.

（c）在货物出售或特定于买卖合同之后，如果卖方保留对货物的占有，且根据任何法律，该占有构成对卖方之任何债权人的欺诈，则该债权人可将该出售视为无效，或将该特定化视为无效。但是，如果买方作为出租方而卖方作为承租方签订租赁合同，且该出售或特定化系用于该租赁合同，且卖方系根据租赁合同保留对货物的占有，则只要买方以善意通过支付价值买进该货物，卖方的占有即不构成欺诈。

（c）A creditor of a seller may treat a sale or an identification of goods to a contract for sale as void if as against the creditor retention of possession by the seller is fraudulent under any statute or rule of law, but retention of possession of the goods pursuant to a lease contract entered into by the seller as lessee and the buyer as lessor in connection with the sale or identification of the goods is not fraudulent if the buyer bought for value and in good faith.

第 2A.309 条 货物成为不动产附着物后出租方和承租方的权利

§ 2A.309. Lessor's and Lessee's Rights When Goods Become Fixtures.

（a）在本条中：

（a）In this section:

（1）如果货物与特定不动产发生紧密联系，致使货物权益受不动产法的约束，该货物即属于“不动产附着物”；

（1）goods are “fixtures” when they become so related to particular real estate that an interest in them arises under real estate law;

（2）“不动产附着物登记”指在登记或记录不动产抵押的营业处，就已经属于或即将成为不动产附着物且符合第9.502条（a）款和（b）款要求的货物，对覆盖该货物的融资声明作出登记；

（2）a “fixture filing” is the filing, in the office where a record of a mortgage on the real estate would be filed or recorded, of a financing statement covering goods that are or are to become fixtures and conforming to the requirements of Sections 9.502（a）and（b）;

（3）除非在租赁协议取得强制履行力之前，承租方已经占有或使用货物，或有权占有或使用货物，否则，租赁即属于“价款租赁”；

（3）a lease is a “purchase money lease” unless the lessee has possession or use of the goods or the right to possession or use of the goods before the lease agreement is enforceable;

（4）如果为在土地上进行改善性建设而承担债务（包括土地购置成本），则用于担保该债务的不动产抵押权，即属于“建设抵押权”，但登记文件必须如此注明；以及

（4）a mortgage is a “construction mortgage” to the extent it secures an obligation incurred for the construction of an improvement on land including the acquisition cost of the land, if the recorded writing so indicates;and

（5）“不动产他项权”包括不动产抵押权和其他不动产留置权，以及不动产上除所有权外的所有其他权利。

（5）“encumbrance” includes real estate mortgages and other liens on real estate and all other rights in real estate that are not ownership interests.

（b）在本篇中，租赁的货物可以是不动产附着物；如果租赁的货物随后成为不动产附着物，租赁亦可继续。但是，在本篇中，普通建筑材料被用于土地上的改善性建设后，不可再用于租赁。

（b）Under this Article a lease may be of goods that are fixtures or may continue in goods that become fixtures, but no lease exists under this Article of ordinary building materials incorporated into an improvement on land.

（c）本篇不禁止根据不动产法而租赁不动产附着物。

（c）This Article does not prevent the creation of a lease of fixtures pursuant to real estate law.

（d）不动产附着物之出租

（d）The perfected interest of a lessor of

方拥有的已完善的权益，优于不动产他项权人或不动产所有权人的冲突权益，只要：

fixtures has priority over a conflicting interest of an encumbrancer or owner of the real estate if:

（1）租赁属于价款租赁，且该他项权人或所有权人的冲突权益在货物成为不动产附着物之前产生，且覆盖货物的不动产附着物登记在货物成为不动产附着物之前或其后十日内作出，且承租方对不动产持有注册权益或占有不动产；或

（1）the lease is a purchase money lease, the conflicting interest of the encumbrancer or owner arises before the goods become fixtures, a fixture filing covering the fixtures is filed or recorded before the goods become fixtures or within 10 days thereafter, and the lessee has an interest of record in the real estate or is in possession of the real estate;or

（2）在该他项权人或所有权人的权益获得注册之前，出租方的权益通过不动产附着物登记获得完善，且出租方的权益优于该他项权人或所有权人的前手所有权人的任何冲突权益，且承租方对不动产持有注册权益或占有不动产。

（2）the interest of the lessor is perfected by a fixture filing before the interest of the encumbrancer or owner is of record, the lessor's interest has priority over any conflicting interest of a predecessor in title of the encumbrancer or owner, and the lessee has an interest of record in the real estate or is in possession of the real estate.

（e）不动产附着物之出租方的权益，无论是否获得完善，均优于不动产他项权人或不动产所有权人的冲突权益，只要：

（e）The interest of a lessor of fixtures, whether or not perfected, has priority over the conflicting interest of an encumbrancer or owner of the real estate if:

（1）不动产附着物系方便拆移的工厂机器或办公机器，或方便拆移且并非主要用于（或租赁之后主要用于）不动产经营的设备，或方便拆移且属于消费者租赁项下之家用电器的替换货物；同时，在货物成为不动产附着物之前，租赁合同取得强制履行力；或

（1）the fixtures are readily removable factory or office machines, readily removable equipment that is not primarily used or leased for use in the operation of the real estate, or readily removable replacements of domestic appliances that are goods subject to a consumer lease, and before the goods become fixtures the lease contract is enforceable;or

（2）冲突权益系在租赁合同取得强制履行力之后，通过法律程序或衡平程序取得的不动产留置权；或

（2）the conflicting interest is a lien on the real estatc obtained by legal or equitable proceedings after the lease contract is enforceable;or

（3）不动产他项权人或不动产所有权人已书面同意该租赁，或已放弃将该货物作为不动产附着物而主张权益；或

（3）the encumbrancer or owner has consented in writing to the lease or has disclaimed an interest in the goods as fixtures;or

（4）相对于该他项权人或所有权人，承租方有权拆移货物。如果承租方拆移的权利终止，出租方权益的优先权在合理时间内仍继续存在。

（4）the lessee has a right to remove the goods as against the encumbrancer or owner. If the lessee's right to remove terminates, the priority of the interest of the lessor continues for a reasonable time.

（f）除（d）款和（e）款另有规定外，尽管有（d）（1）款的规定，如果货物在建设完成之前成为不动产附着物，则只要在货物成为不动产附着物之前对建设抵押权作出登记，不动产附着物出租方的权益，包括出租方残余权益，即次于建设抵押中不动产他项权人的冲突权益。如果任何不动产他项权人因对建设抵押提供再融资而取得不动产抵押权，则其持有的冲突权益，与前述建设抵押中不动产他项权人的权益，享有同等优先权。

（f）Notwithstanding Subsection（d）（1）but otherwise subject to Subsections（d）and（e）, the interest of a lessor of fixtures, including the lessor's residual interest, is subordinate to the conflicting interest of an encumbrancer of the real estate under a construction mortgage recorded before the goods become fixtures if the goods become fixtures before the completion of the construction.To the extent given to refinance a construction mortgage, the conflicting interest of an encumbrancer of the real estate under a mortgage has this priority to the same extent as the encumbrancer of the real estate under the construction mortgage.

（g）涉及上述各款以外的情况时，不动产附着物出租方的权益，包括出租方残余权益，在对抗不动产他项权人或不动产所有权人（承租方除外）的

（g）In cases not within the preceding subsections, priority between the interest of a lessor of fixtures, including the lessor's residual interest, and the conflicting interest of an encumbrancer or owner of the real estate

冲突权益时，两者之间的优先顺序，应根据不动产冲突权益的优先顺序规则来确定。

who is not the lessee is determined by the priority rules governing conflicting interests in real estate.

（h）如果不动产附着物出租方的权益，包括出租方残余权益，优于全部不动产所有权人和不动产他项权人的任何冲突权益，则出租方或承租方：（1）除租赁协议和本篇另有规定外，在租赁协议出现违约、到期、终止或解除时，或（2）在需要强制履行出租方或承租方在本篇项下的其他权利和救济时，可以从不动产上拆移货物，且不受制于任何不动产所有权人和不动产他项权人的任何冲突权益。但是，如果不动产所有权人或不动产他项权人（承租方除外）未同意承担拆移所造成的物理损伤的维修费，出租方或承租方必须向其提供补偿。补偿无须包括货物拆移之后不动产价值的降低，或替换被拆移货物所需的成本。在拆移货物的人就履行补偿义务提供充分保证之前，有权获得补偿的人可以拒绝货物的拆移。

（h）If the interest of a lessor of fixtures, including the lessor's residual interest, has priority over all conflicting interests of all owners and encumbrancers of the real estate, the lessor or the lessee may（1）on default, expiration, termination, or cancellation of the lease agreement but subject to the lease agreement and this Article, or（2）if necessary to enforce other rights and remedies of the lessor or lessee under this Article, remove the goods from the real estate, free and clear of all conflicting interests of all owners and encumbrancers of the real estate, but the lessor or lessee must reimburse any encumbrancer or owner of the real estate who is not the lessee and who has not otherwise agreed for the cost of repair of any physical injury, but not for any diminution in value of the real estate caused by the absence of the goods removed or by any necessity of replacing them.A person entitled to reimbursement may refuse permission to remove until the party seeking removal gives adequate security for the performance of this obligation.

（i）即使租赁协议不属于设立担保权益，只要所租赁的货物根据第9篇已经属于或即将成为不动产附着物，不动产附着物的出租方即可使用融资

（i）Even though the lease agreement does not create a security interest, the interest of a lessor of fixtures, including the lessor's residual interest, is perfected by filing a financing statement as a fixture filing for

声明对所租赁的货物进行不动产附着物登记，使自己的权益（包括出租方残余权益）获得完善。

leased goods that are or are to become fixtures in accordance with the relevant provisions of Article 9.

第2A.310条 货物成为添附物后出租方和承租方的权利

§ 2A.310. Lessor's and Lessee's Rights When Goods Become Accessions.

（a）货物被安装或固定在其他货物上之后，即成为“添附物”。

（a）Goods are “accessions” when they are installed in or affixed to other goods.

（b）添附物中的出租方残余权益，或在涉及货物成为添附物之前订立的租赁合同时，出租方或承租方在租赁合同项下的权益，除（d）款另有规定外，优于任何对货物整体的权益。

（b）The lessor's residual interest in the accessions and the interest of a lessor or a lessee under a lease contract entered into before the goods became accessions are superior to all interests in the whole except as stated in Subsection（d）.

（c）添附物中的出租方残余权益，或在涉及货物成为添附物之时或之后订立的租赁合同时，出租方或承租方在租赁合同项下的权益，除（d）款另有规定外，优于任何后手取得的对货物整体的权益，但次于在租赁合同订立时已经存在的对货物整体的权益，除非货物整体权益的持有人已书面同意该租赁，或已放弃将该货物作为货物整体的一部分而主张权益。

（c）The lessor's residual interest in the accessions and the interest of a lessor or a lessee under a lease contract entered into at the time or after the goods became accessions are superior to all subsequently acquired interests in the whole except as stated in Subsection（d）but are subordinate to interests in the whole existing at the time the lease contract was made unless the holders of such interests in the whole have in writing consented to the lease or disclaimed an interest in the goods as part of the whole.

（d）上述（b）款或（c）款所述的添附物中的出租方残余权益，或出租方或承租方在租赁合同项下的权益，次于下列人的权益：

（d）The lessor's residual interest in the accessions and the interest of a lessor or a lessee under a lease contract described by Subsection（b）or（c）are subordinate to the interest of:

（1）正常业务中的买方或正常业务中的承租方，只要其在货物成为添附物之后取得对货物整体的权益；或

（1）a buyer in the ordinary course of business or a lessee in the ordinary course of business of any interest in the whole acquired after the goods became accessions;or

（2）债权人，只要其在租赁合同订立前，完善了对货物整体的担保权益，但条件是，债权人随后提供的贷款，系在不了解租赁合同之存在的情况下作出。

（2）a creditor with a security interest in the whole perfected before the lease contract was made to the extent that the creditor makes subsequent advances without knowledge of the lease contract.

（e）如果根据（b）款或（c）款，以及根据（d）款，添附物之出租方或承租方的权益，优于任何对货物整体的权益，则出租方或承租方:（1）除租赁合同和本篇另有规定外，在租赁合同出现另一方违约、到期、终止或解除时，或（2）在需要强制履行出租方或承租方在本篇项下的其他权利和救济时，可以从货物整体上拆移货物，且不受制于任何对货物整体的权益。但是，如果任何对货物整体持有权益的人（承租方除外）未同意承担拆移所造成的物理损伤的维修费，拆移方必须向该权益人提供补偿。补偿无须包括货物拆移之后货物整体的价值的降低，或替换被拆移货物所需的成本。在拆移货物的人就履行补偿义务提供充分保证之前，有权获得补偿的人可以拒绝货物的拆移。

（e）When under Subsections（b）or（c）and（d）a lessor or a lessee of accessions holds an interest that is superior to all interests in the whole, the lessor or the lessee may（1）on default, expiration, termination, or cancellation of the lease contract by the other party but subject to the provisions of the lease contract and this Article, or（2）if necessary to enforce the lessor's or lessee's other rights and remedies under this Article, remove the goods from the whole, free and clear of all interests in the whole, but the party must reimburse any holder of an interest in the whole who is not the lessee and who has not otherwise agreed for the cost of repair of any physical injury but not for any diminution in value of the whole caused by the absence of the goods removed or by any necessity for replacing them.A person entitled to reimbursement may refuse permission to remove until the party seeking removal gives adequate security for the performance of this obligation.

第4章　租赁合同的履行：毁约、替代和免责

PART 4. PERFORMANCE OF LEASE CONTRACT:REPUDIATED, SUBSTITUTED AND EXCUSED

第 2A.401 条　不安全：履约的充分保证

（a）租赁合同的每一方都预期另一方正常履约，而另一方则有义务不破坏此种预期。

（b）一方如果有合理理由担心另一方不能正常履约，可书面要求另一方提供正常履约的充分保证。不安全的一方在收到此种保证之前，只要商业上合理，即可针对另一方尚未履约的部分，暂停履行自己相应部分的义务。

（c）不安全的一方提出要求后，如果另一方未能在收到要求后不超过三十日的合理时间内，根据该案当时的情况提供充分的履约保证，即构成毁弃租赁合同。

（d）在商人之间，不安全的理由是否合理，以及所提供的保证是否充分，必须根据商业标准确定。

（e）即使已接受任何不符合合同的交付或付款，亦不损

§ 2A.401. Insecurity:Adequate Assurance of Performance.

（a）A lease contract imposes an obligation on each party that the other's expectation of receiving due performance will not be impaired.

（b）If reasonable grounds for insecurity arise with respect to the performance of either party, the insecure party may demand in writing adequate assurance of due performance.Until the insecure party receives that assurance, if commercially reasonable, the insecure party may suspend any performance for which the party has not already received the agreed return.

（c）A repudiation of the lease contract occurs if assurance of due performance adequate under the circumstances of the particular case is not provided to the insecure party within a reasonable time, not to exceed 30 days after receipt of a demand by the other party.

（d）Between merchants, the reasonableness of grounds for insecurity and the adequacy of any assurance offered must be determined according to commercial standards.

（e）Acceptance of any nonconforming delivery or payment does not prejudice the

害受损方要求对未来履约提供充分保证的权利。

aggrieved party's right to demand adequate assurance of future performance.

第 2A.402 条 预前毁约

§ 2A.402. Anticipatory Repudiation.

如果一方在一项履约到期前毁弃租赁合同，且失去该履约将严重损害租赁合同对另一方的价值，受损方可以：

If either party repudiates a lease contract with respect to a performance not yet due under the lease contract, the loss of which performance will substantially impair the value of the lease contract to the other, the aggrieved party may:

（1）在商业上合理的时间内，等待毁约方撤回毁约并履约；

（1）for a commercially reasonable time, await retraction of repudiation and performance by the repudiating party;

（2）根据第 2A.401 条提出要求，并等待就未来履约收到在该案当时情况下系属充分的保证；或

（2）make demand pursuant to Section 2A.401 and await assurance of future performance adequate under the circumstances of the particular case;or

（3）根据租赁合同或本篇，就该违约行使任何权利或寻求任何救济，即使受损方已通知毁约方将等待后者的履约和保证，并已催促毁约方撤回毁约。此外，受损方无论是否寻求任何上述救济，均可暂停自己的履约，或如果受损方是出租方，还可根据本篇关于另一方违约时出租方仍可将货物特定于租赁合同项下的规定或挽救半成品货物的规定（第 2A.524 条），采取相应行动。

（3）resort to any right or remedy on default under the lease contract or this Article, even though the aggrieved party has notified the repudiating party that the aggrieved party would await the repudiating party's performance and assurance and has urged retraction.In addition, whether or not the aggrieved party is pursuing one of the foregoing remedies, the aggrieved party may suspend performance or, if the aggrieved party is the lessor, proceed in accordance with the provisions of this Article on the lessor's right to identify goods to the lease contract notwithstanding default or to salvage unfinished goods（Section 2A.524）.

第 2A.403 条 撤回预前毁约

§ 2A.403. Retraction of Anticipatory Repudiation.

（a）毁约方在下一项履约

（a）Until the repudiating party's next

到期前，可以撤回毁约，除非受损方在毁约发生后已解除租赁合同，或已严重改变处境，或已用其他方式表明其认为毁约已不可撤回。

performance is due, the repudiating party can retract the repudiation unless, since the repudiation, the aggrieved party has canceled the lease contract or materially changed the aggrieved party's position or otherwise indicated that the aggrieved party considers the repudiation final.

（b）撤回毁约可以使用任何方式，只要可以清楚地向受损方表明毁约方准备履约的意愿，并提供根据第 2A.401 条索要的任何保证。

（b）Retraction may be by any method that clearly indicates to the aggrieved party that the repudiating party intends to perform under the lease contract and includes any assurance demanded under Section 2A.401.

（c）撤回毁约使毁约方重新享有租赁合同的权利，但如果此种毁约造成受损方延迟履约，受损方应获得相应免责。

（c）Retraction reinstates a repudiating party's rights under a lease contract with due excuse and allowance to the aggrieved party for any delay occasioned by the repudiation.

第 2A.404 条　替代履约

§ 2A.404. Substituted Performance.

（a）如果非因出租方、承租方和供应商过错，约定的停泊、装货或卸货设施无法使用，或约定种类的承运人无法获得，或由于其他原因致使约定的交付方式在商业上确实难以履行，此时，如果存在商业上合理的替代履约方式，各方必须提示使用和接受该方式。

（a）If without fault of the lessee, the lessor and the supplier, the agreed berthing, loading, or unloading facilities fail or the agreed type of carrier becomes unavailable or the agreed manner of delivery otherwise becomes commercially impracticable, but a commercially reasonable substitute is available, the substitute performance must be tendered and accepted.

（b）如果由于本国或外国政府法令，约定的付款方法或方式无法实现，则：

（b）If the agreed means or manner of payment fails because of domestic or foreign governmental regulation:

（1）在承租方另行提供商业上基本相等的付款方法或方式之前，出租方可以中止或阻止交付，或致使供应商中止或

（1）the lessor may withhold or stop delivery or cause the supplier to withhold or stop delivery unless the lessee provides a means or manner of payment that is commercially a

阻止交付；而

（2）如果货物已经交付，承租方按法令规定的方式或方法付款后，即被解除义务，除非该法令具有歧视、迫害或掠夺性质。

第 2A.405 条　免除履约

除第 2A.404 条对替代履约另有规定外，应适用下列原则：

（1）如果发生了订立租赁合同时作为基本假设认为不会发生的意外情况，或如果善意遵守了外国或本国政府的法令（无论该法令以后是否被证实无效），致使出租方或供应商确实难以按约定方式履约，则即使发生延迟交付，或部分或全部未能交付，只要出租方或供应商遵守了（2）款和（3）款的规定，即不构成对租赁合同的违反。

（2）如果（1）款提到的情况仅部分地影响了出租方或供应商履约的能力，出租方或供应商必须把生产和交付能力在各位客户之间进行分配，但可以决定把那些当时不存在买卖合同或租赁合同关系但经常有联系的客户以及自己今后的生产需求也考虑在内。出租方或供应商的此种分配可以使用任何公平合理的方式。

substantial equivalent;and

（2）if delivery has already been taken, payment by the means or in the manner provided by the regulation discharges the lessee’s obligation unless the regulation is discriminatory, oppressive, or predatory.

§ 2A.405. Excused Performance.

Subject to Section 2A.404 on substituted performance, the following rules apply:

（1）Delay in delivery or nondelivery in whole or in part by a lessor or a supplier who complies with Subdivisions（2）and（3）is not a default under the lease contract if performance as agreed has been made impracticable by the occurrence of a contingency the nonoccurrence of which was a basic assumption on which the lease contract was made or by compliance in good faith with any applicable foreign or domestic governmental regulation or order, whether or not the regulation or order later proves to be invalid.

（2）If the causes mentioned in Subdivision（1）affect only part of the lessor’s or the supplier’s capacity to perform, the lessor or supplier shall allocate production and deliveries among the lessor’s or supplier’s customers but at the lessor’s or supplier’s option may include regular customers not then under contract for sale or lease as well as the lessor’s or supplier’s own requirements for further manufacture.The lessor or supplier may so allocate in any manner that is fair and reasonable.

（3）出租方应将延迟交付或无法交付的情况及时通知承租方。涉及融资租赁时，供应商应及时通知出租方和承租方（如果已知）。如果需要根据（2）款进行分配，通知应包括承租方可能获得的预估数额。

（3）The lessor seasonably shall notify the lessee and in the case of a finance lease the supplier seasonably shall notify the lessor and the lessee, if known, that there will be delay or nondelivery and, if allocation is required under Subdivision（2）, of the estimated quota made available for the lessee.

第 2A.406 条 免除履约后的程序

§ 2A.406. Procedure on Excused Performance.

（a）如果承租方收到通知，即根据第 2A.405 条所述的合理理由，将出现严重或无限期延迟，或将作出分配，承租方可书面通知出租方，就所涉及的货物，或如果是分期租赁合同且整体租赁合同的价值将严重降低（第 2A.510 条），则就全部货物：

（a）If the lessee receives notification of a material or indefinite delay or an allocation justified under Section 2A.405, the lessee may by written notification to the lessor as to any goods involved, and with respect to all of the goods if under an installment lease contract the value of the whole lease contract is substantially impaired（Section 2A.510）:

（1）终止租赁合同［第 2A.505 条（b）款］；或

（1）terminate the lease contract（Section 2A.505（b））;or

（2）修改租赁合同，即接受所分配的替代数额，同时根据短缺情况，相应调整剩余租期应支付的租金，但没有对抗出租方的进一步权利；但是，融资租赁（不包括消费者租赁）除外。

（2）except in a finance lease that is not a consumer lease, modify the lease contract by accepting the available quota in substitution, with due allowance from the rent payable for the balance of the lease term for the deficiency but without further right against the lessor.

（b）如果在收到出租方根据第 2A.405 条作出的通知后，承租方未能在不超过三十日的合理时间内修改租赁协议，租赁合同在受影响的那部分交付的范围内，即告失效。

（b）If, after receipt of a notification from the lessor under Section 2A.405, the lessee fails to modify the lease agreement within a reasonable time not exceeding 30 days, the lease contract lapses with respect to any deliveries affected.

第 2A.407 条 不可撤销的承诺：融资租赁

（a）涉及融资租赁时（不包括消费者租赁），如果租赁协议的条款规定，承租方在租赁合同项下的承诺，在承租方接受货物后即成为不可撤销和独立存在的承诺，则该条款具有强制履行力。

（b）根据（a）款成为不可撤销和独立存在之承诺：

（1）在当事方之间系属有效并可强制履行；对第三方（包括当事方的受让人）亦属有效，并可由该第三方强制履行，或针对该第三方强制履行；并且

（2）如果承诺的受益方未作出同意，不得解除、终止、修改、毁弃、免除或替换该承诺。

§ 2A.407. Irrevocable Promises: Finance Leases.

（a）In the case of a finance lease that is not a consumer lease, a term in the lease agreement that provides that the lessee's promises under the lease contract become irrevocable and independent upon the lessee's acceptance of the goods is enforceable.

（b）A promise that has become irrevocable and independent under Subsection（a）:

（1）is effective and enforceable between the parties, and by or against third parties including assignees of the parties;and

（2）is not subject to cancellation, termination, modification, repudiation, excuse, or substitution without the consent of the party to whom the promise runs.

第5章 违 约

PART 5. DEFAULT

第 2A.501 条 违约：程序

（a）出租方或承租方是否违反租赁合同，应根据租赁协议和本篇确定。

（b）如果出租方或承租方违反租赁合同，寻求强制履行的一方享有本篇提供的权利和救济，且除本篇另有限制外，还享有租赁协议提供的权利和救济。

§ 2A.501. Default:Procedure.

（a）Whether the lessor or the lessee is in default under a lease contract is determined by the lease agreement and this Article.

（b）If the lessor or the lessee is in default under the lease contract, the party seeking enforcement has rights and remedies as provided in this Article and, except as limited by this Article, as provided in the lease agreement.

（c）如果出租方或承租方违反租赁合同，寻求强制履行的一方可以就索赔取得法院判决，也可以根据本篇规定，以自助方式，或通过任何可用的司法或非司法程序，包括行政程序、仲裁或类似方法，强制履行租赁合同。

（c）If the lessor or the lessee is in default under the lease contract, the party seeking enforcement may reduce the party's claim to judgment or otherwise enforce the lease contract by self-help or any available judicial procedure or nonjudicial procedure, including administrative proceeding, arbitration, or the like, in accordance with this Article.

（d）除第 1.305 条（a）款或本篇或租赁协议另有规定外，上述（b）款或（c）款所述的权利和救济可以叠加。

（d）Except as otherwise provided by Section 1.305（a）or this Article or the lease agreement, the rights and remedies referred to in Subsections（b）and（c）are cumulative.

（e）如果租赁协议同时包含不动产和货物，则寻求强制履行的一方，可以根据本章就货物采取行动，也可以根据其他适用法，基于其对不动产享有的权利和救济，同时就不动产和货物采取行动。在后一种情况下，本章不再适用。

（e）If the lease agreement covers both real property and goods, the party seeking enforcement may proceed under this Part as to the goods, or under other applicable law as to both the real property and the goods in accordance with that party's rights and remedies in respect of the real property, in which case this Part does not apply.

第 2A.502 条　违约后的通知

§ 2A.502. Notice After Default.

除本篇或租赁协议另有规定外，出租方或承租方违反租赁合同后，无权要求租赁协议的另一方发出违约通知或强制履行通知。

Except as provided by this Article or the lease agreement, the lessor or lessee in default under the lease contract is not entitled to notice of default or notice of enforcement from the other party to the lease agreement.

第 2A.503 条　权利和救济的修改或削弱

§ 2A.503. Modification or Impairment of Rights and Remedies.

（a）除本篇另有规定外，租赁协议可以包含违约时的权利和救济，用于补充或代替本篇提供的权利和救济；租赁协

（a）Except as otherwise provided in this Article, the lease agreement may include rights and remedies for default in addition to or in substitution for those provided by this Article

议也可以限制或改变本篇提供的损害赔偿金额。

（b）本篇或租赁协议提供的任何一项救济，均供自行选用，除非该项救济被明确约定具有排他性。如果客观情况致使一项排他的或有限的救济无法实现其根本目的，或如果排他救济条款显失公平，则可以根据本篇规定获得救济。

（c）可以根据第 2A.504 条的规定，约定间接损失的赔偿金额，或以其他方式限制、改变或排除间接损失的赔偿，除非该限制、改变或排除显失公平。涉及消费品时，对人身伤害的间接损失赔偿作出约定、限制、改变或排除，构成显失公平的表面证据；但涉及商业损失时，作出此种约定、限制、改变或排除，不构成显失公平的表面证据。

（d）如果出租方或承租方违反从属于租赁合同的任何义务或许诺，因该违约产生的权利和救济，不受本篇的削弱。

第 2A.504 条　约定损害赔偿

（a）对于违约或任何其他行为或疏漏所造成的损失，包括预期税务优惠的损失或减少，或出租方残余权益的损失或损害，租赁协议可以约定违约方

and may limit or alter the measure of damages recoverable under this Article.

（b）Resort to a remedy provided under this Article or in the lease agreement is optional unless the remedy is expressly agreed to be exclusive.If circumstances cause an exclusive or limited remedy to fail its essential purpose, or provision for an exclusive remedy is unconscionable, remedy may be had as provided by this Article.

（c）Consequential damages may be liquidated under Section 2A.504 or otherwise be limited, altered, or excluded unless the limitation, alteration, or exclusion is unconscionable.Liquidation, limitation, alteration, or exclusion of consequential damages for injury to the person in the case of consumer goods is prima facie unconscionable, but liquidation, limitation, alteration, or exclusion of damages where the loss is commercial is not prima facie unconscionable.

（d）Rights and remedies on default by the lessor or the lessee with respect to an obligation or promise collateral or ancillary to the lease contract are not impaired by this Article.

§ 2A.504. Liquidation of Damages.

（a）Damages payable by either party for default or any other act or omission, including indemnity for loss or diminution of anticipated tax benefits or loss or damage to lessor’s residual interest, may be liquidated in

应支付的损害赔偿金额，但相对于当时预期的因违约或其他行为或疏漏所造成的损失，约定的金额或计算方法必须合理。在消费者租赁中，如果相对于实际损失，约定的损害赔偿金额高至不合理，该条款即属于惩罚，不可强制履行。

the lease agreement but only at an amount or by a formula that is reasonable in light of the then anticipated harm caused by the default or other act or omission.In a consumer lease, a term fixing liquidated damages that are unreasonably large in light of the actual harm is unenforceable as a penalty.

（b）如果租赁协议约定了损害赔偿金额，但该条款不符合（a）款规定，或该条款属于客观情况致使其根本目的无法实现的排他或有限救济，则可根据本篇规定获得救济。

（b）If the lease agreement provides for liquidation of damages, and such provision does not comply with Subsection（a）or such provision is an exclusive or limited remedy that circumstances cause to fail of its essential purpose, remedy may be had as provided in this Article.

（c）如果承租方违约或破产，致使出租方正当中止交付或阻止交付货物（第 2A.525 条或第 2A.526 条），承租方有权收回其付款金额超出下列金额的部分：

（c）If the lessor justifiably withholds or stops delivery of goods because of the lessee's default or insolvency（Section 2A.525 or 2A.526）, the lessee is entitled to restitution of any amount by which the sum of the lessee's payments exceeds:

（1）涉及（a）款所述的约定损害赔偿时，出租方根据协议条款有权得到的金额；或

（1）the amount to which the lessor is entitled by virtue of terms liquidating the lessor's damages in accordance with Subsection（a）;or

（2）如果无此种条款，则为承租方在剩余租期内有义务支付之租金总额当时现值的 20%；或在涉及消费者租赁时，为该金额或者五百美元，以金额低者为准。

（2）in the absence of those terms, 20 percent of the then present value of the total rent the lessee was obligated to pay for the balance of the lease term, or, in the case of a consumer lease, the lesser of such amount or $500.

（d）如果出租方能够证明下列情况，则承租方根据（c）

（d）A lessee's right to restitution under Subsection（c）is subject to offset to the extent

款收回付款的权利，应被相应抵销：

（1）根据（a）款以外的本篇其他条款，出租方有权取得的损害赔偿；以及

（2）承租方从租赁合同中直接或间接获益的金额或价值。

the lessor establishes:

（1） a right to recover damages under the provisions of this Article other than Subsection （a） ;and

（2） the amount or value of any benefits received by the lessee directly or indirectly by reason of the lease contract.

第 2A.505 条 解除和终止；解除、终止、取消或欺诈对权利和救济的影响

§ 2A.505. Cancellation and Termination and Effect of Cancellation, Termination, Rescission, or Fraud on Rights and Remedies.

（a）租赁合同解除后，双方尚待履行的所有义务均被解除，但基于之前违约或履约而产生的权利继续存在。同时，解除合同的一方，还就另一方违反整体租赁合同或违反尚未履行的部分，保留所有救济。

（b）租赁合同终止后，双方尚待履行的所有义务均被解除，但基于之前违约或履约而产生的权利继续存在。

（c）除另有明确的相反意图外，“解除”或“撤销”租赁合同或类似表示，不应被解释为放弃或解除就前存违约取得损害赔偿的权利。

（d）本篇针对违约提供的全部权利和救济，均可作为针对重大不实陈述或欺诈的权利和救济。

（a） On cancellation of the lease contract, all obligations that are still executory on both sides are discharged, but any right based on prior default or performance survives, and the canceling party also retains any remedy for default of the whole lease contract or any unperformed balance.

（b） On termination of the lease contract, all obligations that are still executory on both sides are discharged but any right based on a prior default or performance survives.

（c） Unless the contrary intention clearly appears, expressions of “cancellation,” “rescission,” or the like of the lease contract may not be construed as a renunciation or discharge of any claim in damages for an antecedent default.

（d） Rights and remedies for material misrepresentation or fraud include all rights and remedies available under this Article for default.

（e）撤销租赁合同或要求撤销租赁合同，或拒收或退回货物，均不排除或妨碍寻求损害赔偿或其他权利或救济。

（e）Neither rescission nor a claim for rescission of the lease contract nor rejection or return of the goods may bar or be deemed inconsistent with a claim for damages or other right or remedy.

第 2A.506 条　诉讼时效

§ 2A.506. Statute of Limitations.

（a）有关违反租赁合同的诉讼，包括有关违反担保或赔偿承诺的诉讼，必须在诉讼原因发生后四年内提起。当事方在原始租赁合同中不得延长此种诉讼时效，但如果不涉及消费者租赁，可将时效缩短至不少于一年。

（a）An action for default under a lease contract, including breach of warranty or indemnity, must be commenced within four years after the cause of action accrued.By the original lease contract the parties may not expand such period of limitation but, except in the case of a consumer lease, may reduce the period of limitation to not less than one year.

（b）涉及违约或违反担保的行为或疏漏时，诉讼原因在受损方发现或应该发现该行为或疏漏时发生。寻求赔偿的诉讼原因在下列时间发生：

（b）A cause of action for default accrues when the act or omission on which the default or breach of warranty is based is or should have been discovered by the aggrieved party.A cause of action for indemnity accrues:

（1）如果赔偿系基于行为或疏漏的责任，则在受偿方发现或应该发现引起赔偿义务的行为或疏漏时发生；或

（1）in the case of an indemnity against liability, when the act or omission on which the claim for indemnity is based is or should have been discovered by the indemnified party;or

（2）如果赔偿系基于造成的损失或损害，则在受偿方为该损失或损害支出付款时发生。

（2）in the case of an indemnity against loss or damage, when the person indemnified makes payment thereof.

（c）如果诉讼在（a）款限制的时间内提起，且该诉讼终止后，尚有可能就同一违约、违反担保或赔偿承诺而再次提起诉讼以取得其他救济，则该另一诉讼可在上述限制的时效期满后提起，但必须在第一次

（c）If an action commenced within the time limited by Subsection（a）is so terminated as to leave available a remedy by another action for the same default or breach of warranty or indemnity, the other action may be commenced after the expiration of the time limited and within six months after the termination of the

诉讼终止后六个月内提起。如果第一次诉讼系自愿终止，或系因未能参诉或疏于参诉而被驳回，则不能再次提起诉讼。

first action unless the termination resulted from voluntary discontinuance or from dismissal for failure or neglect to prosecute.

（d）本条不改变有关时效计算的法律，也不适用于本篇生效前发生的诉讼原因。

（d）This section does not alter the law on tolling of the statute of limitations nor does it apply to causes of action that have accrued before this Article becomes effective.

第 2A.507 条 证明市场租金

§ 2A.507. Proof of Market Rent.

（a）如果需要根据市场租金计算损害赔偿（第 2A.519 条或第 2A.528 条），则市场租金应为：为使用相关货物，在相当于原始租赁协议剩余租期的租赁期内，并在第 2A.519 条和第 2A.528 条规定的时间，所需要支付的通行租金。

（a）Damages based on market rent（Section 2A.519 or 2A.528）are determined according to the rent for the use of the goods concerned for a lease term identical to the remaining lease term of the original lease agreement and prevailing at the times specified in Sections 2A.519 and 2A.528.

（b）如果一时难以获得证据，证明在相当于原始租赁协议剩余租期的租赁期内，并在本篇规定的时间或地点，使用相关货物所需要支付的通行租金，则可以使用另外相关的通行租金，即在该时间之前或之后合理期间内的租金，或根据商业判断或行业惯例，可以作为合理替代之其他地点或其他租赁期的租金，但此时应根据差别之处适当调整租金，包括适当考虑将货物运进或运出该地的费用。

（b）If evidence of rent for the use of the goods concerned for a lease term identical to the remaining lease term of the original lease agreement and prevailing at the times or places described in this Article is not readily available, the rent prevailing within any reasonable time before or after the time described or at any other place or for a different lease term which in commercial judgment or under usage of trade would serve as a reasonable substitute for the one described may be used, making any proper allowance for the difference, including the cost of transporting the goods to or from the other place.

（c）如果一方提出的相关

（c）Evidence of a relevant rent prevailing

租金证明，是本篇所述时间、地点或租期以外的通行租金，则只有在该方已通知另一方，且法院认为通知系属充分，不致构成对另一方不公正的意外时，法院才可接受该证明。

at a time or place or for a lease term other than the one described in this Article offered by one party is not admissible unless and until the party has given the other party notice the court finds sufficient to prevent unfair surprise.

（d）如果任何货物在任何公认的商品市场上惯常进行租赁，则在确定该货物的通行租金或价值时，正式出版物、贸易杂志、公开发行之报纸或杂志中的报告，只要属于该市场的报告，均可作为证明被法院接受。此种报告制备的具体情况，可影响其证明力度，但不影响其可接受性。

（d）If the prevailing rent or value of any goods regularly leased in any established market is in issue, reports in official publications or trade journals or in newspapers or periodicals of general circulation published as the reports of that market are admissible in evidence.The circumstances of the preparation of the report may be shown to affect its weight but not its admissibility.

第 2A.508 条　承租方的救济

§ 2A.508. Lessee's Remedies.

（a）如果出租方未能交付符合租赁合同的货物（第 2A.509 条）或毁弃租赁合同（第 2A.402 条），或如果承租方正当拒收货物（第 2A.509 条）或正当撤销对货物的接受（第 2A.517 条），则对所涉及的货物，或如果是分期租赁合同，且整体租赁合同的价值严重降低（第 2A.510 条），则对全部货物，出租方被视为违反租赁合同。此时，承租方可以：

（a）If a lessor fails to deliver the goods in conformity to the lease contract（Section 2A.509）or repudiates the lease contract（Section 2A.402）, or a lessee rightfully rejects the goods（Section 2A.509）or justifiably revokes acceptance of the goods（Section 2A.517）, then with respect to any goods involved, and with respect to all of the goods if under an installment lease contract and the value of the whole lease contract is substantially impaired（Section 2A.510）, the lessor is in default under the lease contract and the lessee may:

（1）解除租赁合同［第 2A.505 条（a）款］；

（1）cancel the lease contract（Section 2A.505（a））;

（2）收回已支付之租金和保证金中根据当时情况有理由收回的部分；

（2）recover so much of the rent and security as has been paid and is just under the circumstances;

（3）补进货物，并就受影响的所有货物取得损害赔偿，无论该货物是否已特定于租赁合同项下（第2A.518条和第2A.520条），或就未能交付取得损害赔偿（第2A.519条和第2A.520条）；或

（3）cover and recover damages as to all goods affected whether or not they have been identified to the lease contract（Sections 2A.518 and 2A.520）, or recover damages for nondelivery（Sections 2A.519 and 2A.520）;or

（4）行使租赁合同提供的任何其他权利，或寻求租赁合同提供的任何其他救济。

（4）exercise any other rights or pursue any other remedies provided in the lease contract.

（b）如果出租方未能交付符合租赁合同的货物，或毁弃租赁合同，承租方还可以：

（b）If a lessor fails to deliver the goods in conformity to the lease contract or repudiates the lease contract, the lessee may also:

（1）追索货物（第2A.522条），只要货物已特定化；或

（1）if the goods have been identified, recover them（Section 2A.522）;or

（2）在适当情况下，就货物取得实际履行、取回、暂扣或类似救济（第2A.521条）。

（2）in a proper case, obtain specific performance, replevin, detinue, sequestration, claim and delivery, or the like for the goods（Section 2A.521）.

（c）如果出租方以其他方式违反租赁合同，承租方可以根据租赁合同的规定和第2A.519条（c）款的规定，行使权利和寻求救济，包括租赁合同中可能包含的解除租赁的权利。

（c）If a lessor is otherwise in default under a lease contract, the lessee may exercise the rights and pursue the remedies provided in the lease contract, which may include a right to cancel the lease, and in Section 2A.519（c）.

（d）如果出租方违反担保，无论是明示担保还是默示担保，承租方均可取得损害赔偿［第2A.519条（d）款］。

（d）If a lessor has breached a warranty, whether express or implied, the lessee may recover damages（Section 2A.519（d））.

（e）承租方对货物正当拒

（e）On rightful rejection or justifiable

收或正当撤销接受后，如果仍占有或控制货物，则针对已支付的租金和保证金，以及为货物之检验、接收、运输、管理和保存所支出的费用，对货物享有担保权益。承租方可留持货物，并在遵守第2A.527条（e）款的条件下，以善意和商业上合理的方式处置货物。

（f）除第2A.407条另有规定外，承租方可从同一租赁合同中尚未支付的任何租金中，针对出租方对租赁合同的任何违反，扣除部分或全部的损害赔偿，但承租方应事先将此种意图通知出租方。

revocation of acceptance, a lessee has a security interest in goods in the lessee's possession or control for any rent and security that has been paid and any expenses reasonably incurred in their inspection, receipt, transportation, and care and custody and may hold those goods and dispose of them in good faith and in a commercially reasonable manner, subject to Section 2A.527（e）.

（f）Subject to the provisions of Section 2A.407, a lessee, on notifying the lessor of the lessee's intention to do so, may deduct all or part of the damages resulting from any default under the lease contract from any part of the rent still due under the same lease contract.

第2A.509条　不当交付时承租方的权利；正当拒收

§ 2A.509. Lessee's Rights on Improper Delivery;Rightful Rejection.

（a）除第2A.510条对分期租赁合同的违约另有规定外，如果货物、提示交付或交付在任何方面不符合租赁合同，承租方可以拒收，但也可以接受交付，或接受任何商业单位而拒收货物的其余部分。

（b）承租方拒收货物，必须在货物提示交付或交付后的合理时间内作出，并及时通知出租方，否则拒收无效。

（a）Subject to the provisions of Section 2A.510 on default in installment lease contracts, if the goods or the tender or delivery fail in any respect to conform to the lease contract, the lessee may reject or accept the goods or accept any commercial unit or units and reject the rest of the goods.

（b）Rejection of goods is ineffective unless it is within a reasonable time after tender or delivery of the goods and the lessee seasonably notifies the lessor.

第2A.510条　分期租赁合同：拒收和违约

§ 2A.510. Installment Lease Contracts: Rejection and Default.

（a）涉及分期租赁合同时，如果任何一期交付不符合合同，

（a）Under an installment lease contract a lessee may reject any delivery

致使该期交付的价值严重降低且无法补救，或该不符系所需单据存在瑕疵，承租方可以拒收该期交付；但是，如果该不符不属于（b）款所述情况，且出租方或供应商作出进行补救的充分保证，承租方即必须接受该期交付。

that is nonconforming if the nonconformity substantially impairs the value of that delivery and cannot be cured or the nonconformity is a defect in the required documents; but if the nonconformity does not fall within Subsection (b) and the lessor or the supplier gives adequate assurance of its cure, the lessee must accept the delivery.

（b）如果一期或多期交付不符合合同或存在违约，致使分期租赁合同的整体价值严重降低，该不符或违约即构成对整体合同的违反。但是，如果受损方接受了不符合合同的一期交付且未能及时通知解除合同，或只对以前各期交付提起诉讼，或仍要求就未来各期交付继续履约，受损方即恢复分期租赁合同的整体效力。

（b）Whenever nonconformity or default with respect to one or more deliveries substantially impairs the value of the installment lease contract as a whole there is a default with respect to the whole.But the aggrieved party reinstates the installment lease contract as a whole if the aggrieved party accepts a nonconforming delivery without seasonably notifying of cancellation or brings an action with respect only to past deliveries or demands performance as to future deliveries.

第 2A.511 条　商人承租方对被正当拒收之货物的义务

§ 2A.511. Merchant Lessee's Duties as to Rightfully Rejected Goods.

除承租方持有担保权益外［第 2A.508 条（e）款］，当出租方或供应商在拒收地市场没有代理人或营业场所时，商人承租方在拒收其占有或控制的货物后，应遵从出租方或供应商有关货物的合理指示；如果未收到合理指示，且货物价值可能迅速降低，商人承租方有义务作出合理努力，代表出租方将货物出售、出租或作其他处置。如果承租方要求收到处

Subject to any security interest of a lessee（Section 2A.508（e））, if a lessor or a supplier has no agent or place of business at the market of rejection, a merchant lessee, after rejection of goods in the lessee's possession or control, shall follow any reasonable instructions received from the lessor or the supplier with respect to the goods.In the absence of those instructions, a merchant lessee shall make reasonable efforts to sell, lease, or otherwise dispose of the goods for the lessor's account if they threaten to decline in value speedily.

置费用，但该要求未得到迅即满足，出租方或供应商的指示即属不合理。

Instructions are not reasonable if on demand indemnity for expenses is not forthcoming.

第 2A.512 条 承租方对被正当拒收之货物的义务

§ 2A.512. Lessee's Duties as to Rightfully Rejected Goods.

（a）除对价值可能迅速降低的货物另有规定外（第 2A.511 条），且除承租方持有担保权益外［第 2A.508 条（e）款］：

（a）Except as otherwise provided with respect to goods that threaten to decline in value speedily（Section 2A.511）and subject to any security interest of a lessee（Section 2A.508（e））:

（1）承租方在拒收其占有或控制的货物后，应及时作出拒收通知，并在之后一段合理时间内，合理谨慎地持有货物，并遵从出租方或供应商的处置；

（1）the lessee, after rejection of goods in the lessee's possession, shall hold them with reasonable care at the lessor's or the supplier's disposition for a reasonable time after the lessee's seasonable notification of rejection;

（2）如果在作出拒收通知后的合理时间内，出租方或供应商未给予指示，承租方可代表出租方或供应商将被拒收的货物存入仓库，或将货物运回给出租方或供应商，或代表出租方或供应商处置货物，并根据（d）款规定获得费用补偿；但是

（2）if the lessor or the supplier gives no instructions within a reasonable time after notification of rejection, the lessee may store the rejected goods for the lessor's or the supplier's account or ship them to the lessor or the supplier or dispose of them for the lessor's or the supplier's account with reimbursement in the manner provided by Subsection（d）;but

（3）对于被正当拒收的货物，承租方无进一步的义务。

（3）the lessee has no further obligations with regard to goods rightfully rejected.

（b）承租方根据（a）款采取的行动，不构成对货物的接受或侵占。

（b）Action by the lessee pursuant to Subsection（a）is not acceptance or conversion.

（c）商人承租方（第 2A.511 条）或任何其他承租方如果处置货物，有权就照管和处置货物

（c）If a merchant lessee（Section 2A.511）or any other lessee disposes of goods, the lessee is entitled to reimbursement either from the

的合理费用，从出租方或供应商获得补偿，或从处置收益中扣除。如果该费用未包括处置佣金，还有权获得行业惯常佣金，或如果无此种惯常佣金，则可获得合理佣金，但不超过总收益的10%。

lessor or the supplier or out of the proceeds for reasonable expenses of caring for and disposing of the goods and, if the expenses include no disposition commission, to such commission as is usual in the trade, or if there is none, to a reasonable sum not exceeding 10 percent of the gross proceeds.

（d）承租方根据本条或第2A.511条作为时，只承担善意的义务。据此作出的善意作为，不构成对货物的接受或侵占，也不构成损害赔偿诉讼的理由。

（d）In complying with this section or Section 2A.511, the lessee is held only to good faith.Good faith conduct hereunder is neither acceptance or conversion nor the basis of an action for damages.

（e）即使承租方未能遵守本篇的一项或多项要求，购买人根据本条或第2A.511条以善意从承租方购买货物后，即不受制于出租方或供应商的任何权利。

（e）A purchaser who purchases in good faith from a lessee pursuant to this section or Section 2A.511 takes the goods free of any rights of the lessor and the supplier even though the lessee fails to comply with one or more of the requirements of this Article.

第2A.513条　出租方对不当提示交付或交付的补救；替换货物

§ 2A.513. Cure by Lessor of Improper Tender or Delivery; Replacement.

（a）如果出租方或供应商的提示交付或交付因不符合合同而被拒收，但履约时间还未过期，出租方或供应商可将其准备进行补救的意图及时通知承租方，然后可在租赁合同规定的时间内，作出符合合同的交付。

（a）If any tender or delivery by the lessor or the supplier is rejected because nonconforming and the time for performance has not yet expired, the lessor or the supplier may seasonably notify the lessee of the lessor's or the supplier's intention to cure and may then make a conforming delivery within the time provided by the lease contract.

（b）如果承租方拒收不符合合同的提示交付，但出租方或供应商原有合理理由相信，经过或不经过金钱调整，承租

（b）If the lessee rejects a nonconforming tender that the lessor or the supplier had reasonable grounds to believe would be acceptable with or without money allowance,

方本可接受该提示交付，此时，出租方或供应商应获得额外的合理时间，以便重新作出符合合同的替换提示交付，但出租方或供应商应及时将此通知承租方。

the lessor or the supplier may have a further reasonable time to substitute a conforming tender if the lessor or supplier seasonably notifies the lessee.

第 2A.514 条 承租方放弃异议

§ 2A.514. Waiver of Lessee's Objections.

（a）如果承租方在拒收货物时未能具体说明瑕疵，且该瑕疵经合理检验可以确定，则在下列情况下，承租方无权以该瑕疵为理由作出拒收或证明违约：

（a）In rejecting goods, a lessee's failure to state a particular defect that is ascertainable by reasonable inspection precludes the lessee from relying on the defect to justify rejection or to establish default:

（1）假设及时说明瑕疵，出租方或供应商本可作出补救（第 2A.513 条）；或

（1）if, stated seasonably, the lessor or the supplier could have cured it（Section 2A.513）;or

（2）在商人之间，出租方或供应商在拒收后已书面要求承租方就其依据的全部瑕疵作出完整的最终的书面说明。

（2）between merchants if the lessor or the supplier after rejection has made a request in writing for a full and final written statement of all defects on which the lessee proposes to rely.

（b）承租方如果在未保留权利的情况下基于单据支付了租金或其他对价，随后即无权以单据表面可以看出的瑕疵为理由收回付款。

（b）A lessee's failure to reserve rights when paying rent or other consideration against documents precludes recovery of the payment for defects apparent in the documents.

第 2A.515 条 接受货物

§ 2A.515. Acceptance of Goods.

（a）如果在承租方有合理机会检验货物后发生下列情况，即构成承租方对货物的接受：

（a）Acceptance of goods occurs after the lessee has had a reasonable opportunity to inspect the goods and:

（1）承租方向出租方或供应商表示，或以其对待货物的

（1）the lessee signifies or acts with respect to the goods in a manner that signifies

方式向出租方或供应商表示，货物符合合同，或尽管存在不符，承租方仍将收取或保留货物；或

to the lessor or the supplier that the goods are conforming or that the lessee will take or retain them in spite of their nonconformity;or

（2）承租方未能对货物作出有效拒收［第2A.509条（b）款］。

（2）the lessee fails to make an effective rejection of the goods（Section 2A.509（b））.

（b）接受任何商业单位中的任何部分，构成对该商业单位整体的接受。

（b）Acceptance of a part of any commercial unit is acceptance of that entire unit.

第2A.516条　接受货物的效力；违约通知；作出接受后的违约举证责任；向责任人通知索赔或诉讼

§ 2A.516. Effect of Acceptance of Goods; Notice of Default;Burden of Establishing Default After Acceptance; Notice of Claim or Litigation to Person Answerable Over.

（a）承租方必须按租赁合同的规定，就已被接受的货物支付租金，但可就被正当拒收之货物或未交付之货物作相应扣除。

（a）A lessee must pay rent for any goods accepted in accordance with the lease contract, with due allowance for goods rightfully rejected or not delivered.

（b）承租方接受货物后，不能再拒收已被接受的货物。涉及融资租赁（不包括消费者租赁）时，如果在作出接受时即知道存在不符合合同之处，即不得以该不符为理由撤销接受。在所有其他情况下，如果在作出接受时即知道存在不符，即不得以该不符为理由撤销接受，除非作出接受系基于合理假设，即该不符将会得到及时补救。但是，接受货物之行为本身，不削弱本篇或租赁协议就不符合合同提供的任何其他救济。

（b）A lessee's acceptance of goods precludes rejection of the goods accepted. In the case of a finance lease that is not a consumer lease, if made with knowledge of a nonconformity, acceptance cannot be revoked because of it.In any other case, if made with knowledge of anonconformity, acceptance cannot be revoked because of it unless the acceptance was on the reasonable assumption that the nonconformity would be seasonably cured.Acceptance does not of itself impair any other remedy provided by this Article or the lease agreement for nonconformity.

（c）提示交付被接受后：

（1）承租方应在发现或应该发现任何违约后的合理时间内，将违约通知出租方和供应商（如有），否则在对抗未得到通知的当事方时无权获得救济；

（2）承租方应在收到侵权或类似原因（第2A.211条）之诉讼通知后的合理时间内通知出租方，否则即无权就诉讼中判定的责任从出租方取得救济；并且

（3）承租方承担违约的举证责任。

（d）如果承租方被诉违反担保或其他义务，而出租方或供应商应对此种违约承担责任，则应适用下列原则：

（1）承租方可将诉讼以书面形式通知出租方或供应商，或同时通知两者。如果通知中说明，被通知人可前来应诉，且如果被通知人不应诉，则在承租方对抗该人的诉讼中，该人应就两次诉讼中共同面临的事实，受到此次诉讼对该事实之确认的约束，此时，被通知人如果在及时收到该通知后未前来应诉，即应按上述所言受到约束。

（2）如果索赔系因侵权或类似原因（第2A.211条），出租方或供应商可书面要求承租方将诉讼（包括和解）的控制

(c) If a tender has been accepted:

(1) within a reasonable time after the lessee discovers or should have discovered any default, the lessee shall notify the lessor and supplier, if any, or be barred from any remedy against the party not notified;

(2) within a reasonable time after the lessee receives notice of litigation for infringement or the like (Section 2A.211) the lessee shall notify the lessor or be barred from any remedy over for liability established by the litigation;and

(3) the burden is on the lessee to establish any default.

(d) If a lessee is sued for breach of a warranty or other obligation for which a lessor or a supplier is answerable over, the following apply:

(1) The lessee may give the lessor or the supplier, or both, written notice of the litigation. If the notice states that the person notified may come in and defend and that if the person notified does not do so that person will be bound in any action against that person by the lessee by any determination of fact common to both litigations, then unless the person notified after seasonable receipt of the notice does come in and defend that person is so bound.

(2) The lessor or the supplier may demand in writing that the lessee turn over control of the litigation including settlement if the claim is one for infringement or the like

移交给出租方或供应商，否则承租方即无权获得任何救济。如果该要求说明，出租方或供应商同意承担全部费用，并同意执行任何不利判决，此时，承租方除非在及时收到该要求后移交控制，否则即按上述所言无权获得救济。

（Section 2A.211）or else be barred from any remedy over.If the demand states that the lessor or the supplier agrees to bear all expense and to satisfy any adverse judgment, then unless the lessee after seasonable receipt of the demand does turn over control the lessee is so barred.

（e）上述（c）款和（d）款的规定，亦适用于承租方不使出租方或供应商因侵权或类似原因受到损失的义务（第2A.211条）。

（e）Subsections（c）and（d）apply to any obligation of a lessee to hold the lessor or the supplier harmless against infringement or the like（Section 2A.211）.

（f）上述（c）款不适用于消费者租赁。

（f）Subsection（c）shall not apply to a consumer lease.

第2A.517条 撤销对货物的接受

§ 2A.517. Revocation of Acceptance of Goods.

（a）如果已被接受的一批或一个商业单位的货物不符合合同，致使其对承租方的价值严重降低，承租方可以撤销接受，只要原来作出的接受系因：

（a）A lessee may revoke acceptance of a lot or commercial unit whose nonconformity substantially impairs its value to the lessee if the lessee has accepted it:

（1）有合理理由假定不符合合同之处将得到补救，但未得到及时补救；融资租赁（不包括消费者租赁）除外；或

（1）except in the case of a finance lease that is not a consumer lease, on the reasonable assumption that its nonconformity would be cured and it has not been seasonably cured;or

（2）未发现该不符；但在此种情况下，该接受必须是合理地基于出租方曾作出过保证，或在涉及融资租赁（不包括消费者租赁）以外的情况时，合理地基于在作出接受前难以发现该不符。

（2）without discovery of the nonconformity if the lessee's acceptance was reasonably induced either by the lessor's assurances or, except in the case of a finance lease that is not a consumer lease, by the difficulty of discovery before acceptance.

（b）如果出租方违反租赁合同，致使一批或一个商业单位的货物对承租方的价值严重降低，承租方可就该一批或一个商业单位撤销接受。

（b）A lessee may revoke acceptance of a lot or commercial unit if the lessor defaults under the lease contract and the default substantially impairs the value of that lot or commercial unit to the lessee.

（c）如果租赁协议中有相应规定，则在出租方发生其他违约时，承租方亦可就一批或一个商业单位的货物撤销接受。

（c）If the lease agreement so provides, the lessee may revoke acceptance of a lot or commercial unit because of other defaults by the lessor.

（d）撤销接受必须在承租方发现或应该发现撤销理由后的合理时间内作出，并在货物状况发生重大改变前作出，除非该改变系因货物不符合合同引起。在承租方通知出租方之前，撤销不发生效力。

（d）Revocation of acceptance must occur within a reasonable time after the lessee discovers or should have discovered the ground for it and before any substantial change in condition of the goods which is not caused by the nonconformity.Revocation is not effective until the lessee notifies the lessor.

（e）承租方作出上述撤销后，对相关货物拥有与其拒收货物时同样的权利和义务。

（e）A lessee who so revokes has the same rights and duties with regard to the goods involved as if the lessee had rejected them.

第 2A.518 条　补进；替代货物

§ 2A.518. Cover; Substitute Goods.

（a）出租方发生第 2A.508 条（a）款所述类型的对租赁合同的违约后，承租方可以补进，即购买或租赁货物，或订立合同购买或租赁货物，用于代替出租方本应交付的货物。如果当事方有约定，则出租方发生其他类型的违约后，承租方也可以补进。

（a）After default by a lessor under the lease contract of the type described by Section 2A.508（a）, or, if agreed, after other default by the lessor, the lessee may cover by making any purchase or lease of or contract to purchase or lease goods in substitution for those due from the lessor.

（b）除涉及通过租赁协议约定损害赔偿金额时另有规定外（第 2A.504 条），且除根

（b）Except as otherwise provided with respect to damages liquidated in the lease agreement（Section 2A.504）or otherwise

据当事方协议对损害赔偿金额另有认定外（第1.302条和第2A.503条），如果承租方的补进，系通过订立与原始租赁协议实质上相同的租赁协议，且新租赁协议系以善意和商业上合理的方式订立，承租方即可从出租方获得下列损害赔偿：（1）以新租赁协议开始日为准计算的租金现值，减去原始租赁协议按同样日期计算的全部租金现值；在计算租金现值时，新租赁协议的租赁期应等于原始租赁协议的剩余租赁期，并且（2）加上任何附带损失或间接损失，但减去因出租方违约致使承租方节省的费用。

determined pursuant to agreement of the parties (Sections 1.302 and 2A.503), if a lessee's cover is by a lease agreement substantially similar to the original lease agreement and the new lease agreement is made in good faith and in a commercially reasonable manner, the lessee may recover from the lessor as damages (1) the present value, as of the date of the commencement of the term of the new lease agreement, of the rent under the new lease agreement applicable to that period of the new lease term which is comparable to the then remaining term of the original lease agreement minus the present value as of the same date of the total rent for the then remaining lease term of the original lease agreement, and (2) any incidental or consequential damages, less expenses saved as a consequence of the lessor's default.

（c）如果承租方通过订立租赁协议补进，但该协议由于任何原因未达到（b）款要求，不能享受该款待遇，或如果补进系通过购买或其他方法作出，则承租方可以如同未作出补进一样，从出租方取得赔偿。此时，应适用第2A.519条。

(c) If the lessee's cover is by lease agreement that for any reason does not qualify for treatment under Subsection (b) or is by purchase or otherwise, the lessee may recover from the lessor as if the lessee had elected not to cover and Section 2A.519 governs.

第2A.519条 未能交付、毁约、违约以及被接受之货物违反担保时承租方损失的计算

§ 2A.519. Lessee's Damages for Nondelivery, Repudiation, Default, and Breach of Warranty in Regard to Accepted Goods.

（a）除涉及通过租赁协议约定损害赔偿金额时另有规定

(a) Except as otherwise provided with respect to damages liquidated in the lease

外（第2A.504条），且除根据当事方协议对损害赔偿金额另有认定外（第1.302条和第2A.503条），如果承租方选择不补进，或选择订立租赁协议补进，但该协议由于任何原因未达到第2A.518条（b）款的要求，不能享受该款待遇，或选择购买或其他方法，此时，对于出租方未能交付或毁约，或对于承租方拒收或撤销接受，计算承租方损害赔偿金额的方法为，以违约日为准的市场租金现值，减去原始租赁协议剩余期限内原始租金在该日的现值，加上附带损失和间接损失，减去因出租方违约致使承租方节省的费用。

agreement（Section 2A.504）or otherwise determined pursuant to agreement of the parties（Sections 1.302 and 2A.503）, if a lessee elects not to cover or a lessee elects to cover and the cover is by lease agreement that for any reason does not qualify for treatment under Section 2A.518（b）or is by purchase or otherwise, the measure of damages for nondelivery or repudiation by the lessor or for rejection or revocation of acceptance by the lessee is the present value, as of the date of the default, of the then market rent minus the present value as of the same date of the original rent, computed for the remaining lease term of the original lease agreement, together with incidental and consequential damages, less expenses saved in consequence of the lessor's default.

（b）市场租金应按提示交付地的租金确定；或在涉及货物到达后的拒收或撤销接受时，按到达地的租金确定。

（b）Market rent is to be determined as of the place for tender or, in cases of rejection after arrival or revocation of acceptance, as of the place of arrival.

（c）除另有约定外，如果承租方已接受货物并作出通知［第2A.516条（c）款］，则对于不符合合同的提示交付或交付，或出租方的其他违约，损害赔偿金额应为按任何合理方式计算的，出租方之违约在正常情况下给承租方造成的损失，加上附带损失和间接损失，减去因出租方违约致使承租方节省的费用。

（c）Except as otherwise agreed, if the lessee has accepted goods and given notification（Section 2A.516（c））, the measure of damages for nonconforming tender or delivery or other default by a lessor is the loss resulting in the ordinary course of events from the lessor's default as determined in any manner that is reasonable together with incidental and consequential damages, less expenses saved in consequence of the lessor's default.

（d）除另有约定外，违反担保的损害赔偿金额，在没有特殊情况显示其他的实际金额时，应为在接受货物的当时当地，按现值计算，被接受之货物的使用价值与货物符合担保时在租赁期本应具有之价值的差额，加上附带损失和间接损失，减去因出租方违约或违反担保致使承租方节省的费用。

（d）Except as otherwise agreed, the measure of damages for breach of warranty is the present value at the time and place of acceptance of the difference between the value of the use of the goods accepted and the value if they had been as warranted for the lease term, unless special circumstances show proximate damages of a different amount, together with incidental and consequential damages, less expenses saved in consequence of the lessor's default or breach of warranty.

第 2A.520 条　承租方的附带损失和间接损失

§ 2A.520. Lessee's Incidental and Consequential Damages.

（a）出租方违约造成的附带损失，在涉及被正当拒收和被正当撤销接受的货物时，包括为检验、接收、运输或保管货物而合理支出的费用，任何商业上合理的收费，作出补进时支出的费用和佣金，以及因违约而附带引起的任何合理费用。

（a）Incidental damages resulting from a lessor's default include expenses reasonably incurred in inspection, receipt, transportation, and care and custody of goods rightfully rejected or goods the acceptance of which is justifiably revoked, any commercially reasonable charges, expenses or commissions in connection with effecting cover, and any other reasonable expense incident to the default.

（b）出租方违约造成的间接损失包括：

（b）Consequential damages resulting from a lessor's default include:

（1）因未能满足任何通常的或特殊的要求和需求而造成的损失，只要在订立合同时出租方有理由知道该要求和需求，且该损失无法通过补进货物或其他方法合理避免；以及

（1）any loss resulting from general or particular requirements and needs of which the lessor at the time of contracting had reason to know and which could not reasonably be prevented by cover or otherwise;and

（2）主要因违反担保而对人身或财产造成的损害。

（2）injury to person or property proximately resulting from any breach of warranty.

第2A.521条 承租方获得实际履行、取回货物及其他救济的权利

（a）如果货物具有独特性，或如果有其他适当原因，法院可以判决实际履行。

（b）有关实际履行的判决，可以同时包含其他条款和条件，如租金支付、损害赔偿或法院认为公平的其他补救措施。

（c）如果承租方经过合理努力无法就货物完成补进，或如果客观情况合理表明此种努力没有意义，则对于已特定于租赁合同项下的货物，承租方享有取回、暂扣或类似权利。

§ 2A.521. Lessee's Right to Specific Performance, Replevin, and Other Remedies.

(a) Specific performance may be decreed if the goods are unique or in other proper circumstances.

(b) A decree for specific performance may include the terms and conditions as to payment of the rent, damages, or other relief that the court deems just.

(c) A lessee has a right of replevin, detinue, sequestration, claim and delivery, or the like for goods identified to the lease contract if after reasonable effort the lessee is unable to effect cover for those goods or the circumstances reasonably indicate that the effort will be unavailing.

第2A.522条 出租方破产时承租方对货物的权利

（a）除（b）款另有规定外，如果货物已特定于租赁合同项下（第2A.217条），且承租方已支付了部分或全部租金和保证金，同时对租赁合同项下任何尚未支付的租金和保证金作出并保持提示支付，则只要出租方在收到第一笔租金和保证金后十日内破产，承租方即可从出租方追索已特定化的货物，即使货物尚未发运。

（b）只有在货物符合合同时，承租方才有权追索已特定于租赁合同项下的货物。

§ 2A.522. Lessee's Right to Goods on Lessor's Insolvency.

(a) Subject to Subsection (b) and even though the goods have not been shipped, a lessee who has paid a part or all of the rent and security for goods identified to a lease contract (Section 2A.217) on making and keeping good a tender of any unpaid portion of the rent and security due under the lease contract may recover the goods identified from the lessor if the lessor becomes insolvent within 10 days after receipt of the first installment of rent and security.

(b) A lessee acquires the right to recover goods identified to a lease contract only if they conform to the lease contract.

第 2A.523 条 出租方的救济

（a）如果承租方对货物错误拒收或错误撤销接受，或未能支付到期款项，或部分或全部毁弃合同，则就所涉及的货物，或如果是分期租赁合同，且整体租赁合同的价值严重降低（第 2A.510 条），则就全部货物，承租方的行为构成对租赁合同的违反；此时，出租方可以：

（1）解除租赁合同［第 2A.505 条（a）款］；

（2）就尚未特定于租赁合同项下的货物采取行动（第 2A.524 条）；

（3）中止交付货物，并就已经交付的货物取得占有（第 2A.525 条）；

（4）阻止货物保管人交付货物（第 2A.526 条）；

（5）处置货物并取得损害赔偿（第 2A.527 条），或留持货物并取得损害赔偿（第 2A.528 条），或在适当情况下，索赔租金（第 2A.529 条）；或

（6）行使租赁合同提供的任何其他权利，或寻求租赁合同提供的任何其他救济。

（b）出租方如果未充分行使（a）款项下其有权行使的权利，或未充分获得（a）款项下

§ 2A.523. Lessor's Remedies.

（a）If a lessee wrongfully rejects or revokes acceptance of goods or fails to make a payment when due or repudiates with respect to a part or the whole, then, with respect to any goods involved, and with respect to all of the goods if under an installment lease contract, the value of the whole lease contract is substantially impaired（Section 2A.510）, the lessee is in default under the lease contract and the lessor may:

（1）cancel the lease contract（Section 2A.505（a））;

（2）proceed respecting goods not identified to the lease contract（Section 2A.524）;

（3）withhold delivery of the goods and take possession of goods previously delivered（Section 2A.525）;

（4）stop delivery of the goods by any bailee（Section 2A.526）;

（5）dispose of the goods and recover damages（Section 2A.527）, or retain the goods and recover damages（Section 2A.528）, or in a proper case recover rent（Section 2A.529）;or

（6）exercise any other rights or pursue any other remedies provided in the lease contract.

（b）If a lessor does not fully exercise a right or obtain a remedy to which the lessor is entitled under Subsection（a）, the lessor

其有权获得的救济，则可从承租方获得下列赔偿：以任何合理方式计算的，承租方违约在正常情况下给出租方造成的损失，加上附带损失，减去因承租方违约致使出租方节省的费用。

may recover the loss resulting in the ordinary course of events from the lessee's default as determined in any reasonable manner, together with incidental damages, less expenses saved in consequence of the lessee's default.

（c）如果承租方以其他方式违反租赁合同，出租方可以根据租赁合同行使权利和寻求救济，包括解除租赁的权利。此外，除租赁合同另有规定外：

（c）If a lessee is otherwise in default under a lease contract, the lessor may exercise the rights and pursue the remedies provided in the lease contract, which may include a right to cancel the lease.In addition, unless otherwise provided in the lease contract:

（1）如果违约严重损害租赁合同对出租方的价值，出租方可以根据（a）款或（b）款行使权利或寻求救济；或

（1）if the default substantially impairs the value of the lease contract to the lessor, the lessor may exercise the rights and pursue the remedies provided by Subsection（a）or（b）;or

（2）如果违约未严重损害租赁合同对出租方的价值，出租方可以根据（b）款取得损害赔偿。

（2）if the default does not substantially impair the value of the lease contract to the lessor, the lessor may recover as provided by Subsection（b）.

第 2A.524 条　出租方将货物特定于租赁合同项下的权利

§ 2A.524. Lessor's Right to Identify Goods to Lease Contract.

（a）受到第 2A.523 条（a）款所述损害的出租方可以：

（a）A lessor aggrieved under Section 2A.523（a）may:

（1）将符合合同但尚未特定于租赁合同项下的货物特定化，只要在出租方得知违约时，出租方或供应商占有或控制货物；并且

（1）identify to the lease contract conforming goods not already identified, if at the time the lessor learned of the default they were in the lessor's or the supplier's possession or control;and

（2）将明确显示用于该特定租赁合同的货物予以处置［第 2A.527 条（a）款］，即使货物尚属半成品。

（2）dispose of goods（Section 2A.527（a））that demonstrably have been intended for the particular lease contract even though those goods are unfinished.

（b）如果货物为半成品，受损害出租方或供应商基于合理的商业判断，并出于避免损失和有效兑现的目的，可以完成制造并将货物全部特定于租赁合同项下，也可以停止制造并将货物作为处理品进行出租、出售或作其他处置，也可以采取任何其他合理行动。

（b）If the goods are unfinished, in the exercise of reasonable commercial judgment for the purposes of avoiding loss and of effective realization, an aggrieved lessor or the supplier may either complete manufacture and wholly identify the goods to the lease contract or cease manufacture and lease, sell, or otherwise dispose of the goods for scrap or salvage value or proceed in any other reasonable manner.

第 2A.525 条 出租方占有货物的权利

§ 2A.525. Lessor's Right to Possession of Goods.

（a）出租方如果发现承租方破产，可以拒绝交付货物。

（a）If a lessor discovers the lessee to be insolvent, the lessor may refuse to deliver the goods.

（b）如果承租方对租赁合同作出第 2A.523 条（a）款或（c）（1）款所述类型的违约，出租方有权取得货物的占有；如果系其他违约，出租方在双方有约定时，亦可占有货物。如果租赁合同有相应规定，出租方可要求承租方集齐货物，在出租方指定但对双方都合理的方便地点，使出租方能够取得货物。出租方可在不拆移货物的情况下，使正在经营或业务中使用的货物失去使用性能，并可在承租方的场地处置货物（第 2A.527 条）。

（b）After a default by the lessee under the lease contract of the type described by Section 2A.523（a）or（c）（1）or, if agreed, after other default by the lessee, the lessor has the right to take possession of the goods.If the lease contract so provides, the lessor may require the lessee to assemble the goods and make them available to the lessor at a place to be designated by the lessor which is reasonably convenient to both parties.Without removal, the lessor may render unusable any goods employed in trade or business, and may dispose of goods on the lessee's premises（Section 2A.527）.

（c）只要能够和平进行，出租方可不通过司法程序而采取（b）款的行动；否则，出租方可以提起诉讼。

（c）The lessor may proceed under Subsection（b）without judicial process if that can be done without breach of the peace or the lessor may proceed by action.

第 2A.526 条　出租方就运输中或其他情况下的货物阻止交付

（a）如果出租方发现承租方破产，且货物当时由承运人或其他货物保管人占有，出租方可以阻止其交付货物。如果承租方毁约或未能在交付前支付到期款项（包括租金、保证金和租赁合同项下的其他付款），或如果出租方因其他理由有权中止交付或取得货物占有，出租方均可就整车、整机或大宗快递的货物阻止交付。

（b）在行使（a）款的救济时，出租方只能在下列情况发生之前阻止交付：

（1）承租方收到货物；

（2）任何货物保管人（承运人除外）向承租方确认，货物系为承租方持有；或

（3）转船承运人或兼为承储人的承运人向承租方作出此种确认。

（c）

（1）为阻止交付，出租方必须适当通知货物保管人，使其可以通过行使合理勤勉，来防止货物的交付。

（2）收到此种通知后，货物保管人必须根据出租方的指示持有和交付货物，但出租方应承担货物保管人因此产生的

§ 2A.526. Lessor's Stoppage of Delivery in Transit or Otherwise.

（a）A lessor may stop delivery of goods in the possession of a carrier or other bailee if the lessor discovers the lessee to be insolvent and may stop delivery of carload, truckload, planeload, or larger shipments of express or freight if the lessee repudiates or fails to make a payment due before delivery, whether for rent, security or otherwise under the lease contract, or for any other reason the lessor has a right to withhold or take possession of the goods.

（b）In pursuing its remedies under Subsection（a）, the lessor may stop delivery until:

（1）receipt of the goods by the lessee;

（2）acknowledgement to the lessee by any bailee of the goods, except a carrier, that the bailee holds the goods for the lessee;or

（3）such an acknowledgement to the lessee by a carrier via reshipment or as a warehouse.

（c）

（1）To stop delivery, a lessor shall so notify as to enable the bailee by reasonable diligence to prevent delivery of the goods.

（2）After notification, the bailee shall hold and deliver the goods according to the directions of the lessor, but the lessor is liable to the bailee for any ensuing charges or

费用和损失。

（3）出具不可流通提单的承运人，没有义务服从除发货人以外的任何人作出的阻止交付的通知。

damages.

（3）A carrier who has issued a nonnegotiable bill of lading is not obligated to obey a notification to stop received from a person other than the consignor.

第 2A.527 条　出租方处置货物的权利

§ 2A.527. Lessor's Rights to Dispose of Goods.

（a）如果承租方对租赁合同作出第 2A.523 条（a）款或（c）（1）款所述类型的违约，或如果出租方拒绝交付，或如果出租方取得货物的占有（第 2A.525 条或第 2A.526 条），出租方即可通过出租、出售或其他方式，处置货物或其尚未交付的任何部分；如果承租方发生其他违约，出租方在当事方有约定时，亦可采取上述行动。

（a）After a default by a lessee under the lease contract of the type described in Section 2A.523（a）or（c）（1）or after the lessor refuses to deliver or takes possession of goods（Section 2A.525 or 2A.526）, or, if agreed, after other default by a lessee, the lessor may dispose of the goods concerned or the undelivered balance thereof by lease, sale or otherwise.

（b）除涉及通过租赁协议约定损害赔偿金额时另有规定外（第 2A.504 条），且除根据当事方协议对损害赔偿金额另有认定外（第 1.302 条及第 2A.503 条），如果处置系通过订立与原始租赁协议实质上相同的租赁协议，且新租赁协议系以善意和商业上合理的方式订立，出租方即可从承租方获得下列损害赔偿：（1）以新租赁协议租期开始日为准，之前已经发生但尚未支付的租金，（2）原始租赁协议剩余期限租金总额在该日的现值，减去新

（b）Except as otherwise provided with respect to damages liquidated in the lease agreement（Section 2A.504）or otherwise determined pursuant to agreement of the parties（Sections 1.302 and 2A.503）, if the disposition is by lease agreement substantially similar to the original lease agreement and the new lease agreement is made in good faith and in a commercially reasonable manner, the lessor may recover from the lessee as damages（1）accrued and unpaid rent as of the date of the commencement of the term of the new lease agreement,（2）the present value, as of the same date, of the total rent for the then remaining lease term of the original lease

租赁协议相当于原始租赁协议剩余期限之租金在该日的现值，以及（3）第2A.530条允许的任何附带损失，但减去因承租方违约致使出租方节省的费用。

agreement minus the present value, as of the same date, of the rent under the new lease agreement applicable to that period of the new lease term which is comparable to the then remaining term of the original lease agreement, and（3）any incidental damages allowed under Section 2A.530, less expenses saved in consequence of the lessee's default.

（c）如果出租方的处置系通过订立租赁协议，但该协议由于任何原因不能享受（b）款的待遇，或如果出租方的处置系通过出售或其他方式，则出租方可以如同未选择处置货物那样，从承租方取得赔偿。此时，应适用第2A.528条。

（c）If the lessor's disposition is by lease agreement that for any reason does not qualify for treatment under Subsection（b）, or is by sale or otherwise, the lessor may recover from the lessee as if the lessor had elected not to dispose of the goods and Section 2A.528 governs.

（d）即使出租方在根据本条作出处置时未能遵守本篇的一项或多项规定，从出租方购买或租赁货物的后手买方或承租方，只要以善意支付价值，在取得货物后即不受制于原始租赁合同或原始承租方的任何权利。

（d）A subsequent buyer or lessee who buys or leases from the lessor in good faith for value as a result of a disposition under this section takes the goods free of the original lease contract and any rights of the original lessee even though the lessor fails to comply with one or more of the requirements of this Article.

（e）出租方没有义务向承租方交出处置的利润。但是，正当拒收或正当撤销接受的承租方，应将超出承租方担保权益的部分交给出租方［第2A.508条（e）款］。

（e）The lessor is not accountable to the lessee for any profit made on any disposition.A lessee who has rightfully rejected or justifiably revoked acceptance shall account to the lessor for any excess over the amount of the lessee's security interest（Section 2A.508（e））.

第2A.528条　不接受交付、不付款、毁约或出现其他违约时出租方损失的计算

§ 2A.528. Lessor's Damages for Nonacceptance, Failure to Pay, Repudiation, or Other Default.

（a）除涉及通过租赁协议

（a）Except as otherwise provided with

约定损害赔偿金额时另有规定外（第 2A.504 条），且除根据当事方协议对损害赔偿金额另有认定外（第 1.302 条及第 2A.503 条），如果出租方选择保留货物，或如果出租方的处置系通过租赁协议，但该协议由于任何原因不能享受第 2A.527 条（b）款的待遇，或如果处置系通过出售或其他方式，此时，在承租方的违约系第 2A.523 条（a）款或（c）（1）款所述类型时，或在承租方的违约系其他类型但当事方对下列赔偿有协议时，出租方有权从承租方获得下列赔偿：（i）如果承租方从未占有过货物，则为违约日之前已发生但尚未支付的租金；如果承租方已占有货物，则为出租方收回货物日之前的上述租金；如果承租方在该收回之前已向出租方提示归还货物，则为提示日之前的上述租金，（ii）原始租赁协议剩余租期内的租金总额［按（i）款所述截止日计算的现值］，减去货物所在地同样租期的市场租金（按同日计算的现值），以及（iii）第 2A.530 条允许的任何附带损失，但减去因承租方违约致使出租方节省的费用。

respect to damages liquidated in the lease agreement（Section 2A.504）or otherwise determined pursuant to agreement of the parties（Sections 1.302 and 2A.503）, if a lessor elects to retain the goods or a lessor elects to dispose of the goods and the disposition is by lease agreement that for any reason does not qualify for treatment under Section 2A.527（b）or is by sale or otherwise, the lessor may recover from the lessee as damages for a default of the type described in Section 2A.523（a）or（c）（1）, or, if agreed, for other default of the lessee,（i）accrued and unpaid rent as of the date of default if the lessee has never taken possession of the goods, or, if the lessee has taken possession of the goods, as of the date the lessor repossesses the goods or an earlier date on which the lessee makes a tender of the goods to the lessor,（ii）the present value as of the date determined under clause（i）of the total rent for the then remaining lease term of the original lease agreement minus the present value as of the same date of the market rent at the place where the goods are located computed for the same lease term, and（iii）any incidental damages allowed under Section 2A.530, less expenses saved in consequence of the lessee's default.

（b）如果按（a）款计算的损害赔偿，不能使出租方处于

（b）If the measure of damages provided in Subsection（a）is inadequate to put a lessor in

合同履行时其本应达到的状态，那么，损害赔偿应为承租方充分履行合同时，出租方本应得到之利润（包括计入合理的间接运营费用）的现值，加上第2A.530条允许的附带损失，再加上适当计算的合理费用，减去适当计算的收款或处置收益。

as good a position as performance would have, the measure of damages is the present value of the profit, including reasonable overhead, the lessor would have made from full performance by the lessee, together with any incidental damages allowed under Section 2A.530, due allowance for costs reasonably incurred and due credit for payments or proceeds of disposition.

第2A.529条　出租方的租金诉讼

§ 2A.529. Lessor's Action for the Rent.

（a）如果承租方对租赁合同作出第2A.523条(a)款或(c)(1)款所述类型的违约，或如果违约系其他类型但当事方对下列赔偿有约定，则出租方在遵守（b）款的条件下，可从承租方取得下列赔偿：

（a）After default by the lessee under the lease contract of the type described in Section 2A.523（a）or（c）（1）, or, if agreed, after other default by the lessee, if the lessor complies with Subsection（b）, the lessor may recover from the lessee as damages:

（1）涉及承租方已接受且出租方尚未收回或承租方尚未提出归还的货物时，或涉及损失风险转移至承租方后商业上合理的一段时间内灭失或受损的符合合同的货物时（第2A.219条），出租方可以取得：(i）出租方获得胜诉判决之日前，已发生但尚未支付的租金，(ii）租赁协议剩余租期内之租金以同日为准计算的现值，以及（iii）第2A.530条允许的附带损失，减去因承租方违约致使出租方节省的费用；以及

（1）for goods accepted by the lessee and not repossessed by or tendered to the lessor, and for conforming goods lost or damaged within a commercially reasonable time after risk of loss passes to the lessee（Section 2A.219）,（i）accrued and unpaid rent as of the date of entry of judgment in favor of the lessor,（ii）the present value as of the same date of the rent for the then remaining lease term of the lease agreement, and（iii）any incidental damages allowed under Section 2A.530, less expenses saved in consequence of the lessee's default;and

（2）涉及已特定于租赁合同项下的货物时，如果出租方

（2）for goods identified to the lease contract if the lessor is unable after reasonable

在作出合理努力后未能以合理价格处置货物，或情况合理表明此种努力没有意义，出租方可以取得：(i) 出租方获得胜诉判决之日前，已发生但尚未支付的租金，(ii) 租赁协议剩余租期内之租金以同日为准计算的现值，以及 (iii) 第2A.530条允许的附带损失，减去因承租方违约致使出租方节省的费用。

effort to dispose of them at a reasonable price or the circumstances reasonably indicate that effort will be unavailing, (i) accrued and unpaid rent as of the date of entry of judgment in favor of the lessor, (ii) the present value as of the same date of the rent for the then remaining lease term of the lease agreement, and (iii) any incidental damages allowed under Section 2A.530, less expenses saved in consequence of the lessee's default.

(b) 除本条 (c) 款另有规定外，出租方应在租赁协议剩余租期内，为承租方持有已特定于租赁合同项下但由出租方控制的货物。

(b) Except as provided by Subsection (c) of this section, the lessor shall hold for the lessee for the remaining lease term of the lease agreement any goods that have been identified to the lease contract and are in the lessor's control.

(c) 出租方可在法院根据 (a) 款作出的损害赔偿判决得到执行前的任何时间处置货物。如果处置时租赁协议尚有剩余租期，则对于出租方可从承租方取得的损害赔偿，应适用第2A.527条或第2A.528条；并且，如果判决金额超出第2A.527条或第2A.528条规定的赔偿，出租方应就超出部分予以返还。

(c) The lessor may dispose of the goods at any time before collection of the judgment for damages obtained pursuant to Subsection (a). If the disposition is before the end of the remaining lease term of the lease agreement, the lessor's recovery against the lessee for damages is governed by Section 2A.527 or 2A.528, and the lessor will cause an appropriate credit to be provided against any judgment for damages to the extent that the amount of the judgment exceeds the recovery available pursuant to Section 2A.527 or 2A.528.

(d) 承租方在支付了根据 (a) 款作出的损害赔偿判决后，有权在租赁协议剩余期限内，根据租赁协议的规定，使用和占有尚未被处置的货物。

(d) Payment of the judgment for damages obtained pursuant to Subsection (a) entitles the lessee to the use and possession of the goods not then disposed of for the remaining lease term of and in accordance with the lease agreement.

（e）如果承租方对货物错误拒收或错误撤销接受，或未能支付到期租金，或发生毁约（第 2A.402 条），则即使出租方无权根据本条获得租金，其仍有权根据第 2A.527 条或第 2A.528 条，就不接受货物取得损害赔偿。

（e）After a lessee has wrongfully rejected or revoked acceptance of goods, has failed to pay rent then due, or has repudiated（Section 2A.402）, a lessor who is held not entitled to rent under this section must nevertheless be awarded damages for nonacceptance under Section 2A.527 or 2A.528.

第 2A.530 条　出租方的附带损失

§ 2A.530. Lessor's Incidental Damages.

受损害出租方的附带损失，包括为阻止货物交付，为承租方违约后运输、照管和存储货物，为退还货物或处置货物而支出的任何商业上合理的收费、支出或佣金，以及违约造成的其他费用。

Incidental damages to an aggrieved lessor include any commercially reasonable charges, expenses, or commissions incurred in stopping delivery, in the transportation, care and custody of goods after the lessee's default, in connection with return or disposition of the goods, or otherwise resulting from the default.

第 2A.531 条　第三方对货物造成损害时的起诉权

§ 2A.531. Standing to Sue Third Parties for Injury to Goods.

（a）如果第三方对已特定于租赁合同项下的货物，作出有损租赁合同任何当事方的可被诉行为：

（1）出租方有权起诉该第三方；并且

（2）承租方也有权起诉该第三方，只要承租方：

（A）对货物持有担保权益；

（B）对货物持有保险利益；

（C）承担租赁合同项下的损失风险，或在损害发生后相对于出租方承担了该风险，且

（a）If a third party so deals with goods that have been identified to a lease contract as to cause actionable injury to a party to the lease contract:

（1）the lessor has a right of action against the third party;and

（2）the lessee also has a right of action against the third party if the lessee:

（A）has a security interest in the goods;

（B）has an insurable interest in the goods;

（C）bears the risk of loss under the lease contract or has since the injury assumed that risk as against the lessor and the goods have

货物已被侵占或已被毁坏。

been converted or destroyed.

（b）如果作为原告的当事方在损害发生时相对于租赁合同的另一方并不承担损失风险，且他们也未就损害赔偿的处置作出安排，则该原告当事方只是作为租赁合同另一方的受托人提起诉讼或达成和解，但涉及该原告自己利益时除外。

(b) If at the time of the injury the party plaintiff did not bear the risk of loss as against the other party to the lease contract and there is no arrangement between them for disposition of the recovery, the party's suit or settlement, subject to the party's own interest, is as a fiduciary for the other party to the lease contract.

（c）任何一方经另一方同意，均可为任何有关人的利益提起诉讼。

(c) Either party with the consent of the other may sue for the benefit of whom it may concern.

第 2A.532 条　出租方对残余权益的权利

§ 2A.532. Lessor's Rights to Residual Interest.

除本篇或其他法律允许的任何其他赔偿外，如果承租方违约，并对出租方在货物中的残余权益造成任何损失或损害，出租方可就该损失或损害从承租方取得充分赔偿。

In addition to any other recovery permitted by this Article or other law, the lessor may recover from the lessee an amount that will fully compensate the lessor for any loss of or damage to the lessor's residual interest in the goods caused by the default of the lessee.

词汇索引

不动产附着物	fixtures	第 2A.309 条（a）（1）
不动产附着物登记	fixture filing	第 2A.309 条（a）（2）
不动产他项权	encumbrance	第 2A.309 条（a）（5）
承租方	lessee	第 2A.103 条（a）（14）
出租方	lessor	第 2A.103 条（a）（16）
出租方残余权益	lessor' s residual interest	第 2A.103 条（a）（17）
分期租赁合同	installment lease contract	第 2A.103 条（a）（9）
分租	sublease	第 2A.103 条（a）（23）
符合	conforming	第 2A.103 条（a）（4）
供应合同	supply contract	第 2A.103 条（a）（25）
供应商	supplier	第 2A.103 条（a）（24）
购买	purchase	第 2A.103 条（a）（22）
过错	fault	第 2A.103 条（a）（6）
货物	goods	第 2A.103 条（a）（8）
价款租赁	purchase money lease	第 2A.309 条（a）（3）
建设抵押权	construction mortgage	第 2A.309 条（a）（4）
解除	cancellation	第 2A.103 条（a）（2）
留置权	lien	第 2A.103 条（a）（18）

续表

融资租赁	finance lease	第 2A.103 条（a）（7）
商人承租方	merchant lessee	第 2A.103 条（a）（20）
商业单位	commercial unit	第 2A.103 条（a）（3）
添附物	accessions	第 2A.310 条（a）
现值	present value	第 2A.103 条（a）（21）
消费者租赁	consumer lease	第 2A.103 条（a）（5）
一批	lot	第 2A.103 条（a）（19）
正常业务中的承租方	lessee in ordinary course of business	第 2A.103 条（a）（15）
正常业务中的买方	buyer in the ordinary course of business	第 2A.103 条（a）（1）
终止	termination	第 2A.103 条（a）（26）
租赁	lease	第 2A.103 条（a）（10）
租赁合同	lease contract	第 2A.103 条（a）（12）
租赁权益	leasehold interest	第 2A.103 条（a）（13）
租赁协议	lease agreement	第 2A.103 条（a）（11）

第3篇　流通票据

ARTICLE 3. NEGOTIABLE INSTRUMENTS

第1章　总则和定义

PART 1. GENERAL PROVISIONS AND DEFINITIONS

第 3.101 条　简称

本篇被引用时可称为《统一商法典——流通票据》。

第 3.102 条　适用范围

（a）本篇适用于流通票据。本篇不适用于金钱、第 4A 篇管辖的支付命令或第 8 篇管辖的证券。

（b）如果本篇与第 4 篇或第 9 篇存在冲突，以第 4 篇和第 9 篇为准。

（c）如果联邦储备系统管理委员会条例及联邦储备银行规则与本篇任何条款存在冲突，则对于冲突部分，前者取代本篇的冲突条款。

第 3.103 条　定义

（a）在本篇中：

（1）“承兑人”指已承兑汇票的受票人。

（2）“消费者账户”指个人

§ 3.101. Short Title.

This Article may be cited as Uniform Commercial Code—Negotiable Instruments.

§ 3.102. Subject Matter.

（a）This Article applies to negotiable instruments.It does not apply to money, to payment orders governed by Article 4A, or to securities governed by Article 8.

（b）If there is conflict between this Article and Article 4 or 9, Articles 4 and 9 govern.

（c）Regulations of the Board of Governors of the Federal Reserve System and operating circulars of the Federal Reserve Banks supersede any inconsistent provision of this Article to the extent of the inconsistency.

§ 3.103. Definitions.

（a）In this Article:

（1）“Acceptor” means a drawee who has accepted a draft.

（2）“Consumer account” means an

主要为个人、家庭或家用目的设立的账户。

account established by an individual primarily for personal, family, or household purposes.

（3）“消费者交易”指个人主要为个人、家庭或家用目的而承担义务的交易。

（3）“Consumer transaction” means a transaction in which an individual incurs an obligation primarily for personal, family, or household purposes.

（4）“受票人”指汇票中被命令付款的人。

（4）“Drawee” means a person ordered in a draft to make payment.

（5）“出票人”指汇票中作为付款命令人签名的人，或汇票中显示为付款命令人的人。

（5）“Drawer” means a person who signs or is identified in a draft as a person ordering payment.

（6）[保留]

（6）[Reserved]

（7）“制票人”指本票中作为付款许诺人签名的人，或本票中显示为付款许诺人的人。

（7）“Maker” means a person who signs or is identified in a note as a person undertaking to pay.

（8）“命令”指书面付款指令，并由发出指令的人签名。可以将指令发给任何人，包括指令人本人；可以发给一人，也可以发给多人，但该多人只能系连带关系或任选关系，不得系先后关系。付款授权不是命令，除非拥有付款授权的人另外获得付款指令。

（8）“Order” means a written instruction to pay money signed by the person giving the instruction.The instruction may be addressed to any person, including the person giving the instruction, or to one or more persons jointly or in the alternative but not in succession.An authorization to pay is not an order unless the person authorized to pay is also instructed to pay.

（9）对于从事商业的人，“正常谨慎”指遵守该人所在地通行的并适用于该人商业领域的合理商业准则。如果任何银行以自动化方式处理任何票据的收款或付款，合理商业准则不要求该银行检验该票据，只要省略该检验并不违反该银行自己制定的规则，且只要该银行

（9）“Ordinary care” in the case of a person engaged in business means observance of reasonable commercial standards, prevailing in the area in which the person is located, with respect to the business in which the person is engaged.In the case of a bank that takes an instrument for processing for collection or payment by automated means, reasonable commercial standards do not require the bank

的规则并未不合理地偏离本篇或第4篇未予禁止的一般银行惯例。

to examine the instrument if the failure to examine does not violate the bank's prescribed procedures and the bank's procedures do not vary unreasonably from general banking usage not disapproved by this Article or Article 4.

（10）"当事方"指票据的当事方。

（10）"Party" means a party to an instrument.

（11）涉及票据时，"主义务人"指受融通方，或指次义务人有权根据本篇对其进行追索的任何其他的票据当事方。

（11）"Principal obligor," with respect to an instrument, means the accommodated party or any other party to the instrument against whom a secondary obligor has recourse under this Article.

（12）"承诺"指书面付款许诺，并由作出许诺的人签名。义务人对义务的承认不是付款承诺，除非义务人另外作出付款许诺。

（12）"Promise" means a written undertaking to pay money signed by the person undertaking to pay.An acknowledgment of an obligation by the obligor is not a promise unless the obligor also undertakes to pay the obligation.

（13）涉及一项事实时，"证明"指完成该事实的举证责任[第1.201条（b）（8）款]。

（13）"Prove" with respect to a fact means to meet the burden of establishing the fact（Section 1.201（b）（8））.

（14）[保留]

（14）[Reserved]

（15）"汇付人"指从票据立票人购买票据的人，只要票据应向该购买人以外的其他特定人付款。

（15）"Remitter" means a person who purchases an instrument from its issuer if the instrument is payable to an identified person other than the purchaser.

（16）"远程制作的票证"指由付款银行以外第三方制作的票证，其显示已获得票证出票人的授权，从出票人的银行账户支取款项，但其所显示的出票人的签名，不是出票人的手写签名。

（16）"Remotely-created item" means an item that is created by a third party, other than the payor bank, under the purported authority of the drawer of the item for the purpose of charging the drawer's account with a bank and that does not bear a handwritten signature purporting to be the signature of the drawer.

（17）涉及票据时，“次义务人”指（A）背书人或融通方，（B）承担第3.414条（d）款所述义务的出票人，或（C）票据的任何其他当事方，只要其根据第3.116条（b）款，有权对票据的另一当事方进行追索。

（17）“Secondary obligor,” with respect to an instrument, means（A）an indorser or an accommodation party,（B）a drawer having the obligation described in Section 3.414（d）, or（C）any other party to the instrument that has recourse against another party to the instrument pursuant to Section 3.116（b）.

（b）适用于本篇的其他定义及其所在位置：

（b）Other definitions applying to this Article and the sections in which they appear are:

“承兑” 第3.409条	“Acceptance” Section 3.409.
“受融通方” 第3.419条	“Accommodated party” Section 3.419.
“融通方” 第3.419条	“Accommodation party” Section 3.419.
“涂改” 第3.407条	“Alteration” Section 3.407.
“异常背书” 第3.205条	“Anomalous indorsement” Section 3.205.
“空白背书” 第3.205条	“Blank indorsement” Section 3.205.
“银行本票” 第3.104条	“Cashier’s check” Section 3.104.
“存款凭证” 第3.104条	“Certificate of deposit” Section 3.104.
“保兑支票” 第3.409条	“Certified check” Section 3.409.
“支票” 第3.104条	“Check” Section 3.104.
“对价” 第3.303条	“Consideration” Section 3.303.
“第三方汇票” 第3.104条	“Demand draft” Section 3.104.
“汇票” 第3.104条	“Draft” Section 3.104.
“正当执票人” 第3.302条	“Holder in due course” Section 3.302.
“不完整票据” 第3.115条	“Incomplete instrument” Section 3.115.
“背书” 第3.204条	“Indorsement” Section 3.204.
“背书人” 第3.204条	“Indorser” Section 3.204.
“票据” 第3.104条	“Instrument” Section 3.104.
“出立” 第3.105条	“Issue” Section 3.105.
“立票人” 第3.105条	“Issuer” Section 3.105.
“流通票据” 第3.104条	“Negotiable instrument” Section 3.104.
“流通” 第3.201条	“Negotiation” Section 3.201.

“本票” 第 3.104 条

“Note” Section 3.104.

“定时付款” 第 3.108 条

“Payable at a definite time” Section 3.108.

“即时付款” 第 3.108 条

“Payable on demand” Section 3.108.

“凭票付款” 第 3.109 条

“Payable to bearer” Section 3.109.

“凭令付款” 第 3.109 条

“Payable to order” Section 3.109.

“付款” 第 3.602 条

“Payment” Section 3.602.

“有权强制履行”的人 第 3.301 条

“Person entitled to enforce” Section 3.301.

“提示” 第 3.501 条

“Presentment” Section 3.501.

“再取得” 第 3.207 条

“Reacquisition” Section 3.207.

“记名背书” 第 3.205 条

“Special indorsement” Section 3.205.

“银行支票” 第 3.104 条

“Teller's check” Section 3.104.

“票据转让” 第 3.203 条

“Transfer of instrument” Section 3.203.

“旅行支票” 第 3.104 条

“Traveler's check” Section 3.104.

“价值” 第 3.303 条

“Value” Section 3.303.

（c）其他各篇中适用于本篇的定义：

（c）The following definitions in other Articles apply to this Article:

“账户” 第 4.104 条

“Account” Section 4.104

“银行营业日” 第 4.104 条

“Banking day” Section 4.104.

“票证清算行” 第 4.104 条

“Clearing house” Section 4.104.

“收款银行” 第 4.105 条

“Collecting bank” Section 4.105.

“存款银行” 第 4.105 条

“Depositary bank” Section 4.105.

“跟单汇票” 第 4.104 条

“Documentary draft” Section 4.104.

“中间银行” 第 4.105 条

“Intermediary bank” Section 4.105.

“票证” 第 4.104 条

“Item” Section 4.104.

“付款银行” 第 4.105 条

“Payor bank” Section 4.105.

“暂停对外付款” 第 4.104 条

“Suspends payments” Section 4.104.

（d）此外，第 1 篇中的通用定义和解释原则适用于本篇通篇。

（d）In addition, Article 1 contains general definitions and principles of construction and interpretation applicable throughout this Article.

第 3.104 条 流通票据

§ 3.104. Negotiable Instrument.

（a）除（c）款和（d）款

（a）Except as provided in Subsections（c）

另有规定外，“流通票据”指无条件支付确定金额款项的付款承诺或付款命令，无论其是否对利息或其他费用予以说明，只要该承诺或命令：

and（d），“negotiable instrument” means an unconditional promise or order to pay a fixed amount of money, with or without interest or other charges described in the promise or order, if it:

（1）在出立时或在首次被执票人占有时，规定凭票付款，或凭令付款；

（1）is payable to bearer or to order at the time it is issued or first comes into possession of a holder;

（2）规定即时付款，或定时付款；并且

（2）is payable on demand or at a definite time;and

（3）除付款以外，不包含付款承诺人或付款命令人就其他行为作出的许诺或指令；但是，该承诺或命令可以包含下列：

（3）does not state any other undertaking or instruction by the person promising or ordering payment to do any act in addition to the payment of money, but the promise or order may contain:

（A）许诺或授权提供、维持或保护担保物，用于担保付款；

（A）an undertaking or power to give, maintain, or protect collateral to secure payment;

（B）对执票人给予授权或权力，允许其在诉讼中承认败诉，或允许其兑现或处置担保物；或

（B）an authorization or power to the holder to confess judgment or realize on or dispose of collateral;or

（C）放弃任何旨在向义务人提供优惠或保护之法律所规定的待遇。

（C）a waiver of the benefit of any law intended for the advantage or protection of an obligor.

（b）“票据”指流通票据。

（b）“Instrument” means a negotiable instrument.

（c）一项命令如果满足（a）款中除（1）款外的全部条件，且在其他方面符合（f）款对“支票”的定义，即为流通票据，同时也是支票。

（c）An order that meets all of the requirements of Subsection（a），except Subdivision（1），and otherwise falls within the definition of “check” in Subsection（f）is a negotiable instrument and a check.

（d）如果承诺或除支票外

（d）A promise or order other than a check

的命令，在出立时或在首次被执票人占有时包含醒目说明（无论使用何种用语），即该承诺或命令不可流通，或不属于本篇管辖的票据，则该承诺或命令即不属于票据。

is not an instrument if, at the time it is issued or first comes into possession of a holder, it contains a conspicuous statement, however expressed, to the effect that the promise or order is not negotiable or is not an instrument governed by this Article.

（e）一项票据，如果系承诺，即为“本票”；如果系命令，即为“汇票”。如果一项票据同时满足“本票”和“汇票”的定义，则有权强制履行该票据的人，可将其视为任何一者。

（e）An instrument is a “note” if it is a promise and is a “draft” if it is an order.If an instrument falls within the definition of both “note” and “draft,” a person entitled to enforce the instrument may treat it as either.

（f）“支票”指（i）以银行为受票人的即时付款的汇票，但不包括跟单汇票，或（ii）银行本票或银行支票。即使票据的票面使用其他形容用语，如“现金汇票”，该票据也可以是支票。

（f）“Check” means（i）a draft, other than a documentary draft, payable on demand and drawn on a bank or（ii）a cashier’s check or teller’s check.An instrument may be a check even though it is described on its face by another term, such as “money order.”

（g）“银行本票”指出票人和受票人为同一银行（或同一银行之不同分行）的汇票。

（g）“Cashier’s check” means a draft with respect to which the drawer and drawee are the same bank or branches of the same bank.

（h）“银行支票”指银行作为出票人的下列汇票：

（1）受票人为另一银行；或

（2）在另一银行付款，或通过另一银行付款。

（h）“Teller’s check” means a draft drawn by a bank:

（1）on another bank;or

（2）payable at or through a bank.

（i）“旅行支票”指下列票据：

（1）即时付款；

（2）以银行为受票人，或

（i）“Traveler’s check” means an instrument that:

（1）is payable on demand;

（2）is drawn on or payable at or through a

在银行付款，或通过银行付款；

（3）标注有“旅行支票”或实质类似的用语；以及

（4）作为付款条件，要求票据上留有签名样本的人作出副签。

（j）“存款凭证”指载有银行确认和承诺的票据，即确认银行已收到一定金额的款项，并承诺将偿还该金额的款项。存款凭证是银行的本票。

（k）“第三方汇票”指下列书面文件：不载有第4.104条(a)(5)款所定义之客户的签名，而是由第三方声称基于该客户的授权制作，用于支取该客户的银行账户。第三方汇票不包括由第3.307条所定义之诚信受托人出立的支票。第三方汇票可以包含下列任何部分或全部特征：

（1）以印刷或打字形式，显示客户的名字和账号；

（2）注明客户已就该汇票提供授权；以及

（3）标注“无须签名”“授权见存档”“签名见存档”或具有类似含义的用语。

第3.105条 票据的出立

（a）“出立”指制票人或出票人为向任何人提供对票据的权利，首次将票据交付给执票

bank;

（3）is designated by the term “traveler’s check” or by a substantially similar term;and

（4）requires, as a condition to payment, a countersignature by a person whose specimen signature appears on the instrument.

（j）“Certificate of deposit” means an instrument containing an acknowledgment by a bank that a sum of money has been received by the bank and a promise by the bank to repay the sum of money.A certificate of deposit is a note of the bank.

（k）“Demand draft” means a writing that is not signed by a customer, as defined in Section 4.104（a）（5）, and that is created by a third party under the purported authority of the customer for the purpose of charging the customer’s account with a bank.A demand draft does not include a check drawn by a fiduciary, as defined in Section 3.307.A demand draft may contain any or all of the following:

（1）the customer’s printed or typewritten name or account number;

（2）a notation that the customer authorized the draft; and

（3）the statement “No signature required,” “Authorization on file,” “Signature on file,” or words to that effect.

§ 3.105. Issue of Instrument.

（a）“Issue” means the first delivery of an instrument by the maker or drawer, whether to a holder or nonholder, for the purpose of giving

人或非执票人。

rights on the instrument to any person.

（b）未出立的票据，或未出立且不完整但被添补完整的票据，亦对制票人或出票人具有约束力；但是，未出立之事实构成抗辩。附条件出立或为特殊目的出立的票据，亦对制票人或出票人具有约束力，但是，该条件或该特殊目的未获满足之事实构成抗辩。

（b）An unissucd instrument, or an unissued incomplete instrument that is completed, is binding on the maker or drawer, but nonissuance is a defense.An instrument that is conditionally issued or is issued for a special purpose is binding on the maker or drawer, but failure of the condition or special purpose to be fulfilled is a defense.

（c）"立票人"包括票据的制票人和出票人，并适用于已出立的票据和未出立的票据。

（c）"Issuer" applies to issued and unissued instruments and means a maker or drawer of an instrument.

第 3.106 条　无条件承诺或命令

§ 3.106. Unconditional Promise or Order.

（a）除本条另有规定外，为第 3.104 条（a）款目的，只要不存在下列情况，承诺或命令即属于无条件承诺或命令：（i）付款附有明确的条件，（ii）承诺或命令受另一项记录的制约或管辖，或（iii）与承诺或命令有关的权利和义务，记载于另一项记录中。但是，提及另一项记录，其本身不使承诺或命令成为附条件承诺或命令。

（a）Except as provided in this section, for the purposes of Section 3.104（a）, a promise or order is unconditional unless it states（i）an express condition to payment,（ii）that the promise or order is subject to or governed by another record, or（iii）that rights or obligations with respect to the promise or order are stated in another record.A reference to another record does not of itself make the promise or order conditional.

（b）承诺或命令不因下列情况被视为附有条件：（i）提及的另一项记录说明了有关担保物、提前付款或提前履约的权利，或（ii）付款被限于使用特定资金或来源。

（b）A promise or order is not made conditional（i）by a reference to another record for a statement of rights with respect to collateral, prepayment, or acceleration, or（ii）because payment is limited to resort to a particular fund or source.

（c）如果承诺或命令规定，

（c）If a promise or order requires, as a

作为付款条件，在承诺或命令上留有签名样本的人需要作出副签，此时，该承诺或命令不因该规定成为第3.104条（a）款所述的附条件承诺或命令。票据上留有签名样本的人未能作出副签，构成立票人义务的抗辩，但不妨碍票据的受让人成为票据的执票人。

condition to payment, a countersignature by a person whose specimen signature appears on the promise or order, the condition does not make the promise or order conditional for the purposes of Section 3.104（a）.If the person whose specimen signature appears on an instrument fails to countersign the instrument, the failure to countersign is a defense to the obligation of the issuer, but the failure does not prevent a transferee of the instrument from becoming a holder of the instrument.

（d）即使承诺或命令在出立时，或在首次被执票人占有时，根据适用法的要求包含一项说明，即如果立票人有权向原始受款人主张索赔或抗辩，则执票人或受让人的权利将受制于立票人的该权利，此时，该承诺或命令不因包含该说明而成为第3.104条（a）款所述的附条件承诺或命令；但是，如果该承诺或命令系票据，则该票据不可能存在正当执票人。

（d）If a promise or order at the time it is issued or first comes into possession of a holder contains a statement, required by applicable statutory or administrative law, to the effect that the rights of a holder or transferee are subject to claims or defenses that the issuer could assert against the original payee, the promise or order is not thereby made conditional for the purposes of Section 3.104（a）;but if the promise or order is an instrument, there cannot be a holder in due course of the instrument.

第3.107条　以外国货币支付的票据

如果票据规定以一定金额的外国货币支付，则除该票据另有规定外，该票据可以用该外国货币支付，也可以按票据支付当天付款地银行提供的现汇汇率，购买同等金额的美元作出支付。

§ 3.107. Instrument Payable in Foreign Money.

Unless the instrument otherwise provides, an instrument that states the amount payable in foreign money may be paid in the foreign money or in an equivalent amount in dollars calculated by using the current bank offered spot rate at the place of payment for the purchase of dollars on the day on which the instrument is paid.

第3.108条 即时付款；定时付款

（a）下列承诺或命令为"即时付款"：

（1）规定收到要求后或见到票据后即时付款，或以其他方式规定，根据执票人的意愿付款；或

（2）未规定付款时间。

（b）如果承诺或命令应在见票后或承兑后一个确定期限到期时付款，或在一个或多个确定日期付款，或在一个或多个时间付款且该时间在承诺或命令出立时即可简单确定，则该承诺或命令即为"定时付款"，即使该承诺或命令受制于下列权利：

（1）提前付款的权利；

（2）要求对方提前履约的权利；

（3）执票人作出延期的权利；或

（4）制票人或承兑人延期至另一个确定时间的权利；或在发生规定的行为或事件之时或之后，自动延期至另一个确定时间的权利。

（c）如果票据规定在确定日期付款，但同时规定，如果在该确定日期之前提出要求，应即时付款，则在该确定日期之前，票据属于即时付款；但

§ 3.108. Payable on Demand or at Definite Time.

（a）A promise or order is "payable on demand" if it:

（1）states that it is payable on demand or at sight, or otherwise indicates that it is payable at the will of the holder;or

（2）does not state any time of payment.

（b）A promise or order is "payable at a definite time" if it is payable on elapse of a definite period of time after sight or acceptance or at a fixed date or dates or at a time or times readily ascertainable at the time the promise or order is issued, subject to rights of:

（1）prepayment;

（2）acceleration;

（3）extension at the option of the holder;or

（4）extension to a further definite time at the option of the maker or acceptor or automatically on or after a specified act or event.

（c）If an instrument, payable at a fixed date, is also payable on demand made before the fixed date, the instrument is payable on demand until the fixed date and, if demand for payment is not made before that date, becomes

是，如果在该确定日期之前未提出付款要求，则票据在该确定日期到期时，成为定时付款。

payable at a definite time on the fixed date.

第 3.109 条　凭票付款；凭令付款

§ 3.109. Payable to Bearer or to Order.

（a）下列承诺或命令属于凭票付款：

（1）注明支付给持票人或支付给持票人的指定人，或以其他方式表明，占有承诺或命令的人有权获得付款；

（2）未注明受款人；或

（3）注明支付给“现金”或支付给“现金”的指定人，或以其他方式表明，无须向任何特定人付款。

（a）A promise or order is payable to bearer if it:

（1）states that it is payable to bearer or to the order of bearer or otherwise indicates that the person in possession of the promise or order is entitled to payment;

（2）does not state a payee;or

（3）states that it is payable to or to the order of cash or otherwise indicates that it is not payable to an identified person.

（b）如果承诺或命令不属于凭票付款，则在下列情况下属于凭令付款：（i）支付给特定人的指定人，或（ii）支付给特定人或其指定人。如果承诺或命令规定支付给特定人的指定人，即等于支付给该特定人。

（b）A promise or order that is not payable to bearer is payable to order if it is payable（i）to the order of an identified person, or（ii）to an identified person or order.A promise or order that is payable to order is payable to the identified person.

（c）根据第 3.205 条（a）款对凭票付款的票据作出记名背书后，该票据可以成为向特定人付款的凭令付款的票据。根据第 3.205 条（b）款对向特定人付款的票据作出空白背书后，该票据可以成为凭票付款的票据。

（c）An instrument payable to bearer may become payable to an identified person if it is specially indorsed pursuant to Section 3.205（a）.An instrument payable to an identified person may become payable to bearer if it is indorsed in blank pursuant to Section 3.205(b).

第3.110条 确定票据向谁付款

（a）票据初始时应向何人付款，应根据下列人的意图决定：作为票据立票人签名的人，或以票据立票人名字签名的人，或代表票据立票人签名的人，而无论前述签名人是否拥有授权。票据应向该签名人意指的人付款，即使票据上显示的名字或其他识别方式，并不归属于该签名人意指的人。如果以票据立票人名字签名或代表立票人签名的人为多人，且并非所有签名人均意指同一人为受款人，则票据应向任何一个或多个签名人所意指的任何一人付款。

（b）如果票据立票人的签名以自动方式生成，例如使用支票打印机生成，则该票据的受款人，应根据提供受款人名字或识别方式之人的意图决定，无论该提供人是否拥有如此操作的授权。

（c）可以使用任何方式指定有权获得票据付款的人，包括名字、识别号码、办公室或账号。在确定票据的执票人时，应适用下列原则：

（1）如果票据应向一个账户付款，且该账户仅用数字识

§ 3.110. Identification of Person to Whom Instrument is Payable.

（a）The person to whom an instrument is initially payable is determined by the intent of the person, whether or not authorized, signing as, or in the name or behalf of, the issuer of the instrument.The instrument is payable to the person intended by the signer even if that person is identified in the instrument by a name or other identification that is not that of the intended person.If more than one person signs in the name or behalf of the issuer of an instrument and all the signers do not intend the same person as payee, the instrument is payable to any person intended by one or more of the signers.

（b）If the signature of the issuer of an instrument is made by automated means, such as a check-writing machine, the payee of the instrument is determined by the intent of the person who supplied the name or identification of the payee, whether or not authorized to do so.

（c）A person to whom an instrument is payable may be identified in any way, including by name, identifying number, office, or account number.For the purpose of determining the holder of an instrument, the following rules apply:

（1）If an instrument is payable to an account and the account is identified only by

别，则该账户应向其付款的人，即为票据应向其付款的人。如果票据应向一个账户付款，但该账户同时使用数字和一个人的名字识别，则具有该名字的人，即为票据应向其付款的人，无论该人是否系使用该数字识别之账户的所有权人。

number, the instrument is payable to the person to whom the account is payable.If an instrument is payable to an account identified by number and by the name of a person, the instrument is payable to the named person, whether or not that person is the owner of the account identified by number.

（2）如果票据：

（2）If an instrument is payable to:

（A）应向信托或遗产付款，或应向被称为信托或遗产之受托人或代表人的人付款，则票据应向其付款的人，为该信托或遗产的受托人或代表人，或他们的继任人，无论受益人或遗产的名字是否同时被列明；

（A）a trust, an estate, or a person described as trustee or representative of a trust or estate, the instrument is payable to the trustee, the representative, or a successor of either, whether or not the beneficiary or estate is also named;

（B）应向被称为特定人之代理人或类似代表人的人付款，则票据应向其付款的人，为被代表人、代表人或代表人的继任人；

（B）a person described as agent or similar representative of a named or identified person, the instrument is payable to the represented person, the representative, or a successor of the representative;

（C）应向非为法律实体的基金或组织付款，则票据应向其付款的人，为该基金或组织之成员的代表人；或

（C）a fund or organization that is not a legal entity, the instrument is payable to a representative of the members of the fund or organization;or

（D）应向办公室或被称为执掌该办公室的特定人付款，则票据应向其付款的人，为该特定人、该办公室的执掌人或该执掌人的继任人。

（D）an office or to a person described as holding an office, the instrument is payable to the named person, the incumbent of the office, or a successor to the incumbent.

（d）如果票据应向两人或多人任选付款，则票据应向其

（d）If an instrument is payable to two or more persons alternatively, it is payable to any

付款的人，为他们中的任何一人，且票据可由他们之中占有票据的任何一人或全体人作出流通、解除义务或强制履行。如果票据应向两人或多人付款，但不得任选，则票据应向其付款的人，为他们全体人，并只可由他们全体人共同作出流通、解除义务或强制履行。如果票据应向两人或多人付款，但不明确是否可以任选，则该票据属于可以任选。

of them and may be negotiated, discharged, or enforced by any or all of them in possession of the instrument.If an instrument is payable to two or more persons not alternatively, it is payable to all of them and may be negotiated, discharged, or enforced only by all of them.If an instrument payable to two or more persons is ambiguous as to whether it is payable to the persons alternatively, the instrument is payable to the persons alternatively.

第 3.111 条　付款地点

除第 4 篇对票证另有规定外，票据应在其注明的付款地点付款。如果未注明付款地点，票据在其注明的受票人或制票人地址付款。如果未注明此种地址，付款地点为受票人或制票人的营业地。如果受票人或制票人拥有一个以上的营业地，则有权强制履行票据的人，可以选择受票人或制票人的任何一个营业地。如果受票人或制票人没有营业地，付款地点为受票人或制票人的住所。

§ 3.111. Place of Payment.

Except as otherwise provided for items in Article 4, an instrument is payable at the place of payment stated in the instrument.If no place of payment is stated, an instrument is payable at the address of the drawee or maker stated in the instrument.If no address is stated, the place of payment is the place of business of the drawee or maker.If a drawee or maker has more than one place of business, the place of payment is any place of business of the drawee or maker chosen by the person entitled to enforce the instrument.If the drawee or maker has no place of business, the place of payment is the residence of the drawee or maker.

第 3.112 条　利息

（a）除票据中另有规定外：

（1）票据的付款不计利息；以及

（2）对于支付利息的票据，

§ 3.112. Interest.

（a）Unless otherwise provided in the instrument:

（1）an instrument is not payable with interest;and

（2）interest on an interest-bearing

利息从票据日期开始计算。

（b）票据对利息的说明，可以使用固定或浮动的金额，也可以使用固定或浮动的利率。票据对金额或利率的说明或描述，可以采用任何方式，并可以规定引用票据票面以外的信息。如果票据规定支付利息，但利息的金额无法从票据的描述中计算得出，则利率应为，在利息首次发生的时间，票据付款地法院判案使用的利率。

instrument is payable from the date of the instrument.

（b）Interest may be stated in an instrument as a fixed or variable amount of money or it may be expressed as a fixed or variable rate or rates.The amount or rate of interest may be stated or described in the instrument in any manner and may require reference to information not contained in the instrument.If an instrument provides for interest, but the amount of interest payable cannot be ascertained from the description, interest is payable at the judgment rate in effect at the place of payment of the instrument and at the time interest first accrues.

第 3.113 条 票据日期

（a）票据日期可以错前填写或错后填写。如果票据应在票据日期之后的确定期限付款，则票据日期决定付款日期。除第 4.401 条（c）款另有规定外，对于即时付款的票据，不得在票据日期之前要求付款。

（b）如果票据未载明日期，则出立日期为票据日期；如果票据尚未出立，则执票人首次占有票据的日期为票据日期。

§ 3.113. Date of Instrument.

（a）An instrument may be antedated or postdated.The date stated determines the time of payment if the instrument is payable at a fixed period after date.Except as provided in Section 4.401（c）, an instrument payable on demand is not payable before the date of the instrument.

（b）If an instrument is undated, its date is the date of its issue or, in the case of an unissued instrument, the date it first comes into possession of a holder.

第 3.114 条 票据的冲突条款

如果票据包含冲突条款，则打字条款优于印刷条款，手写条款优于打字条款和印刷条款，大写数字优于阿拉伯数字。

§ 3.114. Contradictory Terms of Instrument.

If an instrument contains contradictory terms, typewritten terms prevail over printed terms, handwritten terms prevail over both, and words prevail over numbers.

第 3.115 条 不完整票据

（a）“不完整票据”指已签名的书面文件（无论是否已由签名人出立），且文件签名时的状况显示，其内容尚不完整，但签名人当时的意图是通过添加文字或数字使其完整。

（b）除（c）款另有规定外，如果不完整票据属于第 3.104 条所述的票据，则在尚未添补完整时，可按现有条款强制履行；在添补完整后，可按添补完整后的条款强制履行。如果不完整票据不属于第 3.104 条所述的票据，但在添补完整后满足了第 3.104 条的规定，则票据可按添补完整后的条款强制履行。

（c）如果在不完整票据上添加文字或数字的行为未得到签名人的授权，即构成第 3.407 条所述的对不完整票据的涂改。

（d）如果任何人主张，在不完整票据上添加文字或数字的行为未得到签名人的授权，则主张缺乏授权的人应承担举证责任。

§ 3.115. Incomplete Instrument.

（a）“Incomplete instrument” means a signed writing, whether or not issued by the signer, the contents of which show at the time of signing that it is incomplete but that the signer intended it to be completed by the addition of words or numbers.

（b）Subject to Subsection（c）, if an incomplete instrument is an instrument under Section 3.104, it may be enforced according to its terms if it is not completed, or according to its terms as augmented bycompletion.If an incomplete instrument is not an instrument under Section 3.104, but, after completion, the requirements of Section 3.104 are met, the instrument may be enforced according to its terms as augmented by completion.

（c）If words or numbers are added to an incomplete instrument without authority of the signer, there is an alteration of the incomplete instrument under Section 3.407.

（d）The burden of establishing that words or numbers were added to an incomplete instrument without authority of the signer is on the person asserting the lack of authority.

第 3.116 条 连带责任；份额

（a）除票据另有规定外，对票据承担相同责任的两个或多个制票人、出票人、承兑人、以共同受款人身份背书的背书

§ 3.116. Joint and Several Liability; Contribution.

（a）Except as otherwise provided in the instrument, two or more persons who have the same liability on an instrument as makers, drawers, acceptors, indorsers who indorse as

人或异常背书人，应根据该两人或多人签名时的身份，对票据承担连带责任。

（b）除第3.419条（e）款另有规定外，或除受影响之当事方另有协议外，承担连带责任的一方在支付票据后，可以根据适用法，向承担同样连带责任的任何其他方追索该其他方应承担的份额。

joint payees, or anomalous indorsers are jointly and severally liable in the capacity in which they sign.

(b)Except as provided in Section 3.419(e) or by agreement of the affected parties, a party having joint and several liability who pays the instrument is entitled to receive from any party having the same joint and several liability contribution in accordance with applicable law.

第3.117条 影响票据的其他协议

除相关适用法对于同时达成或之前达成之协议作为证据的效力另有排除外，义务人可与有权强制履行票据的人另行订立协议，用以修改、补充或免除票据任何当事方支付票据的义务，只要该协议系出立票据或承担义务的基础，或只要出立票据或承担义务系与该协议同为一项交易的组成部分。如果该义务被本条所述的协议修改、补充或免除，则该协议即构成该义务的抗辩。

§ 3.117. Other Agreements Affecting Instrument.

Subject to applicable law regarding exclusion of proof of contemporaneous or previous agreements, the obligation of a party to an instrument to pay the instrument may be modified, supplemented, or nullified by a separate agreement of the obligor and a person entitled to enforce the instrument, if the instrument is issued or the obligation is incurred in reliance on the agreement or as part of the same transaction giving rise to the agreement.To the extent an obligation is modified, supplemented, or nullified by an agreement under this section, the agreement is a defense to the obligation.

第3.118条 诉讼时效

（a）除（e）款另有规定外，涉及定时付款的本票时，强制履行当事方之本票支付义务的诉讼，必须在本票注明的到期日后六年内提起；如果到期日被提前，则必须在被提前后的

§ 3.118. Statute of Limitations.

(a) Except as provided in Subsection (e), an action to enforce the obligation of a party to pay a note payable at a definite time must be commenced within six years after the due date or dates stated in the note or, if a due date is accelerated, within six years after the

到期日后六年内提起。

（b）除（d）款或（e）款另有规定外，涉及即时付款的本票时，如果已对制票人提出付款要求，则强制履行当事方之本票支付义务的诉讼，必须在提出要求后六年内提起。如果未曾对制票人提出过付款要求，且本票的本金和利息连续十年未曾支付，则不得再就本票提起强制履行的诉讼。

（c）除（d）款另有规定外，涉及未承兑的汇票时，强制履行汇票当事方之汇票支付义务的诉讼，必须在汇票被拒付后三年内提起，或在汇票日期后十年内提起，以先发生者为准。

（d）涉及保兑支票的承兑人时，或涉及银行支票、银行本票或旅行支票的立票人时，强制履行该人义务的诉讼，必须在对承兑人或立票人（以适用者为准）提出付款要求后三年内提起。

（e）涉及存款凭证时，强制履行当事方之票据支付义务的诉讼，必须在对制票人提出付款要求后六年内提起。但是，如果票据载有到期日，且制票人没有义务在该日之前付款，则只有在已提出过付款要求，且该到期日已到期时，才开始计算上述六年期限。

accelerated due date.

（b）Except as provided in Subsection（d）or（e）, if demand for payment is made to the maker of a note payable on demand, an action to enforce the obligation of a party to pay the note must be commenced within six years after the demand.If no demand for payment is made to the maker, an action to enforce the note is barred if neither principal nor interest on the note has been paid for a continuous period of 10 years.

（c）Except as provided in Subsection（d）, an action to enforce the obligation of a party to an unaccepted draft to pay the draft must be commenced within three years after dishonor of the draft or 10 years after the date of the draft, whichever period expires first.

（d）An action to enforce the obligation of the acceptor of a certified check or the issuer of a teller’s check, cashier’s check, or traveler’s check must be commenced within three years after demand for payment is made to the acceptor or issuer, as the case may be.

（e）An action to enforce the obligation of a party to a certificate of deposit to pay the instrument must be commenced within six years after demand for payment is made to the maker, but if the instrument states a due date and the maker is not required to pay before that date, the six-year period begins when a demand for payment is in effect and the due date has passed.

（f）涉及已承兑的汇票时（保兑支票除外），强制履行当事方之支付义务的诉讼，必须在下列期限内提起：

（f）An action to enforce the obligation of a party to pay an accepted draft, other than a certified check, must be commenced:

（1）如果承兑人有义务定时付款，则在汇票或承兑注明的到期日后六年内；或

（1）within six years after the due date or dates stated in the draft or acceptance if the obligation of the acceptor is payable at a definite time;or

（2）如果承兑人有义务即时付款，则在承兑日后六年内。

（2）within six years after the date of the acceptance if the obligation of the acceptor is payable on demand.

（g）除涉及赔偿责任或份额责任时受其他法律管辖外，有关下列事项的诉讼，必须在诉讼原因产生后三年内提起：

（g）Unless governed by other law regarding claims for indemnity or contribution, the following actions must be commenced within three years after the cause of action accrues:

（1）侵占票据、侵占收到的款项或类似的侵占；

（1）an action for conversion of an instrument, an action for money had and received, or like action based on conversion;

（2）违反担保；或

（2）an action for breach of warranty;or

（3）源于本篇但不受本条管辖的债务、义务或权利的强制履行。

（3）an action to enforce an obligation, duty, or right arising under this Article and not governed by this section.

第 3.119 条　通知第三方有权应诉

§ 3.119. Notice of Right to Defend Action.

涉及违反义务的诉讼时，如果根据本篇或第 4 篇，第三人应对该义务承担责任，则被告可向该第三人以记录形式发送诉讼通知，而该被通知人也可将类似通知再发给对义务承担责任的其他人。如果通知说明：（i）被通知人可前来应诉，

In an action for breach of an obligation for which a third person is answerable over pursuant to this Article or Article 4, the defendant may give the third person notice of the litigation in a record, and the person notified may then give similar notice to any other person who is answerable over.If the notice states（i）that the person notified may

并且（ii）如果未能前来应诉，在未来由通知人提起的诉讼中，被通知人应就两次诉讼共同面临的事实，受到此次诉讼对该事实之确认的约束，此时，被通知人除非在及时收到通知后前来应诉，否则就要按通知所言受到约束。

come in and defend, and (ii) that failure to do so will bind the person notified in an action later brought by the person giving the notice as to any determination of fact common to the two litigations, the person notified is so bound unless after seasonable receipt of the notice the person notified does come in and defend.

第2章 流通、转让和背书

PART 2. NEGOTIATION, TRANSFER, AND INDORSEMENT

第3.201条 流通

（a）"流通"指任何人（立票人除外）自愿或非自愿地将票据的占有转让给另一人，并使其因此成为票据的执票人。

（b）除汇付人作出的流通外，如果票据应向特定人付款，则必须转让票据的占有，并由执票人作出背书，才能构成流通。如果票据属于凭票付款，则仅转让占有，即可构成流通。

§ 3.201. Negotiation.

(a) "Negotiation" means a transfer of possession, whether voluntary or involuntary, of an instrument by a person other than the issuer to a person who thereby becomes its holder.

(b) Except for negotiation by a remitter, if an instrument is payable to an identified person, negotiation requires transfer of possession of the instrument and its indorsement by the holder.If an instrument is payable to bearer, it may be negotiated by transfer of possession alone.

第3.202条 可撤销的流通

（a）流通即使以下列方式取得，亦属有效：

（1）从未成年人、越权公司或无行为能力人处取得；

（2）以欺诈、胁迫或误解方式取得；或

（3）以违反义务的方式取

§ 3.202. Negotiation Subject to Rescission.

(a) Negotiation is effective even if obtained:

(1) from an infant, a corporation exceeding its powers, or a person without capacity;

(2) by fraud, duress, or mistake;or

(3) in breach of duty or as part of an illegal

得，或在非法交易中取得。

（b）在其他法律允许的范围内，流通可以被撤销或受制于其他救济，但此种救济不能对抗后手正当执票人，也不能对抗以善意支付了票据且对导致撤销或其他救济之事实不了解的其他人。

transaction.

（b）To the extent permitted by other law, negotiation may be rescinded or may be subject to other remedies, but those remedies may not be asserted against a subsequent holder in due course or aperson paying the instrument in good faith and without knowledge of facts that are a basis for rescission or other remedy.

第 3.203 条 票据转让；转让后取得的权利

§ 3.203. Transfer of Instrument; Rights Acquired by Transfer.

（a）如果任何人（立票人除外）交付票据，且目的在于使取得交付的人有权强制履行票据，票据即被转让。

（a）An instrument is transferred when it is delivered by a person other than its issuer for the purpose of giving to the person receiving delivery the right to enforce the instrument.

（b）票据的转让，无论是否构成流通，均使受让人取得转让人所拥有的强制履行票据的任何权利，包括正当执票人的权利。但是，受让人如果参与涉及票据的欺诈或非法活动，则即使直接或间接地从正当执票人处取得票据转让，亦不能取得正当执票人的权利。

（b）Transfer of an instrument, whether or not the transfer is a negotiation, vests in the transferee any right of the transferor to enforce the instrument, including any right as a holder in due course.The transferee cannot acquire rights of a holder in due course by a transfer, directly or indirectly, from a holder in due course if the transferee engaged in fraud or illegality affecting the instrument.

（c）除另有约定外，如果通过支付价值取得票据转让，但转让人未作背书，致使受让人未能成为执票人，则受让人有权要求转让人以实际履行的方式作出无限制背书；但是，在作出背书之前，票据不发生流通。

（c）Unless otherwise agreed, if an instrument is transferred for value and the transferee does not become a holder because of lack of indorsement by the transferor, the transferee has a specifically enforceable right to the unqualified indorsement of the transferor, but negotiation of the instrument does not occur until the indorsement is made.

（d）如果转让人意图转让

（d）If a transferor purports to transfer

少于整体票据的权利，则票据不发生流通，且受让人不能取得本篇项下的任何权利，而只能作为部分权益的受让人取得权利。

less than the entire instrument, negotiation of the instrument does not occur.The transferee obtains no rights under this Article and has only the rights of a partial assignee.

第 3.204 条　背书

§ 3.204. Indorsement.

（a）"背书"指在票据上作出的伴有或不伴有其他文字的签名（不包括以制票人、出票人或承兑人身份作出的签名），且目的在于：（i）将票据进行流通，（ii）对票据的付款作出限制，或（iii）使背书人对票据承担责任。但是，无论签名人具有何种目的，签名及其伴随文字均构成背书，除非伴随文字、票据条款、签名位置或其他客观情况毫无疑义地表明，签名系为背书以外目的。在确定签名是否在票据上作出时，固定在票据上的纸张，亦为票据的组成部分。

（a）"Indorsement" means a signature, other than that of a signer as maker, drawer, or acceptor, that alone or accompanied by other words is made on an instrument for the purpose of（i）negotiating the instrument,（ii）restricting payment of the instrument, or（iii）incurring indorser's liability on the instrument, but regardless of the intent of the signer, a signature and its accompanying words is an indorsement unless the accompanying words, terms of the instrument, place of the signature, or other circumstances unambiguously indicate that the signature was made for a purpose other than indorsement.For the purpose of determining whether a signature is made on an instrument, a paper affixed to the instrument is a part of the instrument.

（b）"背书人"指作出背书的人。

（b）"Indorser" means a person who makes an indorsement.

（c）在确定票据的受让人是否为执票人时，用于转让票据中担保权益的背书，具有无限制背书的效力。

（c）For the purpose of determining whether the transferee of an instrument is a holder, an indorsement that transfers a security interest in the instrument is effective as an unqualified indorsement of the instrument.

（d）如果票据应向执票人付款，但票据上注明的该执票人的名字，实际上不是该执票

（d）If an instrument is payable to a holder under a name that is not the name of the holder, indorsement may be made by the holder in the

人的名字，则该执票人在背书时，可以使用票据上注明的名字，也可以使用自己的名字，或同时使用两者。但是，支付票据的人，或支付价值取得票据用于收款的人，有权要求该执票人同时签署该两个名字。

name stated in the instrument or in the holder's name or both, but signature in both names may be required by a person paying or taking the instrument for value or collection.

第 3.205 条 记名背书；空白背书；异常背书

（a）如果背书系由票据（无论票据是向特定人付款，还是凭票付款）的执票人作出，则只要该背书将任何特定人指定为票据应向其付款的人，该背书即为“记名背书”。票据被记名背书后，即成为凭令付款的票据，并仅可由背书指定的特定人作出背书而流通。第 3.110 条所述的原则，适用于记名背书。

（b）如果票据的执票人作出背书，但该背书不属于记名背书，则该背书即为“空白背书”。票据被空白背书后，即成为凭票付款的票据，并在下一次被记名背书前，可以仅凭转让票据的占有而流通。

（c）如果空白背书仅由签名构成，执票人可在背书人签名的上方添加文字，指定票据应向其付款的特定人，从而将空白背书转为记名背书。

§ 3.205. Special Indorsement; Blank Indorsement; Anomalous Indorsement.

（a）If an indorsement is made by the holder of an instrument, whether payable to an identified person or payable to bearer, and the indorsement identifies a person to whom it makes the instrument payable, it is a "special indorsement". When specially indorsed, an instrument becomes payable to the identified person and may be negotiated only by the indorsement of that person.The principles stated in Section 3.110 apply to special indorsements.

（b）If an indorsement is made by the holder of an instrument and it is not a special indorsement, it is a "blank indorsement". When indorsed in blank, an instrument becomes payable to bearer and may be negotiated by transfer of possession alone until specially indorsed.

（c）The holder may convert a blank indorsement that consists only of a signature into a special indorsement by writing, above the signature of the indorser, words identifying the person to whom the instrument is made payable.

（d）如果作出背书的人不是票据的执票人，该背书即为“异常背书”。异常背书不影响票据流通的方式。

（d）“Anomalous indorsement” means an indorsement made by a person who is not the holder of the instrument.An anomalous indorsement does not affect the manner in which the instrument may be negotiated.

第 3.206 条 限制性背书

§ 3.206. Restrictive Indorsement.

（a）即使背书规定只能向特定人付款，或以其他方式禁止票据的进一步转让或流通，该背书也不具有阻止票据进一步转让或流通的效力。

（a）An indorsement limiting payment to a particular person or otherwise prohibiting further transfer or negotiation of the instrument is not effective to prevent further transfer or negotiation of the instrument.

（b）即使背书对被背书人获得付款的权利规定了条件，被背书人强制履行票据的权利亦不受影响。支付票据的人，或通过支付价值取得或为收款目的取得票据的人，可以无视该条件，且该人的权利和义务不受该条件是否得到满足的影响。

（b）An indorsement stating a condition to the right of the indorsee to receive payment does not affect the right of the indorsee to enforce the instrument.A person paying the instrument or taking it for value or collection may disregard the condition, and the rights and liabilities of that person are not affected by whether the condition has been fulfilled.

（c）如果票据（i）载有第 4.201 条（b）款所述的背书，或（ii）载有空白背书，或载有给特定银行的背书，注明“用于存款”或“用于收款”，或说明票据系通过银行进行收款，用于该背书人或特定账户，则应适用下列原则：

（c）If an instrument bears an indorsement（i）described in Section 4.201（b）, or（ii）in blank or to a particular bank using the words “for deposit” or “for collection,” or other words indicating a purpose of having the instrument collected by a bank for the indorser or for a particular account, the following rules apply:

（1）如果任何人（银行除外）购买载有此种背书的票据，但背书人未收到为票据支付的金额，且该金额也未用于背书规定的目的，购买人即属于侵占

（1）a person, other than a bank, who purchases the instrument when so indorsed converts the instrument unless the amount paid for the instrument is received by the indorser or applied consistently with the indorsement;

票据；

（2）如果存款银行购买载有此种背书的票据，或为收款目的取得该票据，但背书人未收到银行为票据支付的金额，且该金额也未用于背书规定的目的，存款银行即属于侵占票据；

（2）a depositary bank that purchases the instrument or takes it for collection when so indorsed converts the instrument unless the amount paid by the bank with respect to the instrument is received by the indorser or applied consistently with the indorsement;

（3）如果付款银行同时系存款银行，或如果付款银行在柜台上从任何人（收款银行除外）取得票据，用于柜台上的即时付款，但背书人未收到票据的收益，且该收益也未用于背书规定的目的，付款银行即属于侵占票据；以及

（3）a payor bank that is also the depositary bank or that takes the instrument for immediate payment over the counter from a person other than a collecting bank converts the instrument unless the proceeds of the instrument are received by the indorser or applied consistently with the indorsement;and

（4）除（3）款另有规定外，付款银行或中间银行可以无视该背书，并且，即使背书人未收到票据的收益，或该收益未用于背书规定的目的，该等银行亦不承担责任。

（4）except as otherwise provided in Subdivision（3）, a payor bank or intermediary bank may disregard the indorsement and is not liable if the proceeds of the instrument are not received by the indorser or applied consistently with the indorsement.

（d）除涉及（c）款所述的背书外，如果票据的背书伴有文字，说明应向其付款的被背书人，是为背书人或另一人之利益作为的代理人、受托人或其他诚信受托人，则应适用下列原则：

（d）Except for an indorsement covered by Subsection（c）, if an instrument bears an indorsement using words to the effect that payment is to be made to the indorsee as agent, trustee, or other fiduciary for the benefit of the indorser or another person, the following rules apply:

（1）除非存在第3.307条所述的有关违反信托义务的通知，否则，从被背书人处购买票据的人，或为收款或付款目

（1）unless there is notice of breach of fiduciary duty as provided in Section 3.307, a person who purchases the instrument from the indorsee or takes the instrument from the

的从被背书人处取得票据的人，可将付款的收益或票据付款的价值支付给被背书人，而无须考虑被背书人是否违反了其对背书人的信托义务；并且

indorsee for collection or payment may pay the proceeds of payment or the value given for the instrument to the indorsee without regard to whether the indorsee violates a fiduciary duty to the indorser;and

（2）票据的后手受让人，或支付票据的人，只要不知道诚信受托人以违反信托义务的方式处理票据或其收益，即不应被视为收到通知，亦不在其他方面受背书所载之限制的影响。

（2）a subsequent transferee of the instrument or person who pays the instrument is neither given notice nor otherwise affected by the restriction in the indorsement unless the transferee or payor knows that the fiduciary dealt with the instrument or its proceeds in breach of fiduciary duty.

（e）票据即使载有本条适用的背书，亦不妨碍票据购买人成为票据的正当执票人，除非购买人系（c）款所述的侵占人，或如（d）款所述对违反信托义务已得到通知或已有了解。

（e）The presence on an instrument of an indorsement to which this section applies does not prevent a purchaser of the instrument from becoming a holder in due course of the instrument unless the purchaser is a converter under Subsection（c）or has notice or knowledge of breach of fiduciary duty as stated in Subsection（d）.

（f）在强制履行当事方之票据支付义务的诉讼中，如果付款将违反本条所适用的背书，且付款不被本条允许，义务人即被视为持有抗辩。

（f）In an action to enforce the obligation of a party to pay the instrument, the obligor has a defense if payment would violate an indorsement to which this section applies and the payment is not permitted by this section.

第 3.207 条　再取得

§ 3.207. Reacquisition.

如果票据通过流通或其他方式，被转让给曾经的执票人，即属于票据的再取得。曾经的执票人如果再取得票据，可将其在首次成为票据执票人之后产生的背书全部取消。如果取消此种背书后，票据应向再取得人付款，

Reacquisition of an instrument occurs if it is transferred to a former holder, by negotiation or otherwise.A former holder who reacquires the instrument may cancel indorsements made after the reacquirer first became a holder of the instrument.If the cancellation causes the instrument to be payable to the reacquirer or

或成为凭票付款，则该再取得人可将票据进行流通。如果任何背书人的背书被取消，该背书人即被解除义务，且该解除可以有效对抗后手执票人。

to bearer, the reacquirer may negotiate the instrument.An indorser whose indorsement is canceled is discharged, and the discharge is effective against any subsequent holder.

第3章 票据的强制履行

PART 3. ENFORCEMENT OF INSTRUMENTS

第 3.301 条 有权强制履行票据的人

“有权强制履行”票据的人指（i）票据的执票人，（ii）占有票据且享有执票人权利的非执票人，或（iii）不占有票据但根据第 3.309 条或第 3.418 条（d）款有权强制履行票据的人。一个人即使不是票据的所有权人，或即使不当占有票据，仍有可能成为有权强制履行票据的人。

§ 3.301. Person Entitled to Enforce Instrument.

“Person entitled to enforce” an instrument means（i）the holder of the instrument,（ii）a nonholder in possession of the instrument who has the rights of a holder, or（iii）a person not in possession of the instrument who is entitled to enforce the instrument pursuant to Section 3.309 or 3.418（d）.A person may be a person entitled to enforce the instrument even though the person is not the owner of the instrument or is in wrongful possession of the instrument.

第 3.302 条 正当执票人

（a）除（c）款和第 3.106 条（d）款另有规定外，“正当执票人”指下列情况下的票据执票人：

（1）票据在出立或流通给执票人时，不存在导致票据真实性存疑的伪造迹象、涂改迹象或其他不正常或不完整之处；并且

（2）执票人以下列方式取得票据：

§ 3.302. Holder in Due Course.

（a）Subject to Subsection（c）and Section 3.106（d）,“holder in due course” means the holder of an instrument if:

（1）the instrument when issued or negotiated to the holder does not bear such apparent evidence of forgery or alteration or is not otherwise so irregular or incomplete as to call into question its authenticity;and

（2）the holder took the instrument:

（A）支付了价值；

（B）以善意作为；

（C）未得到票据已经过期或曾被拒付的通知；也未得到通知，即作为票据同一系列的另一票据，存在未得到补救的付款违约；

（D）未得到票据存在无授权签名或涂改的通知；

（E）未得到票据存在第3.306条所述之索赔的通知；以及

（F）未得到任何当事方持有第3.305条（a）款所述之抗辩或扣减权的通知。

（b）当事方已被解除义务（破产程序中的解除义务除外）的通知，不构成（a）款所述的抗辩通知，但是，如果任何人在得到该解除义务通知后成为正当执票人，该解除义务可以有效对抗该执票人。对任何文件进行公共申报或登记，其本身不构成票据存在抗辩、扣减权或票据索赔的通知。

（c）以下列方式取得票据的人，不能获得正当执票人的权利，除非其转让人或前手权益人拥有正当执票人的权利：

（1）在司法程序中取得票据，或在执行程序、破产程序或债权人出售或类似程序中通过购买取得票据；

（A）for value;

（B）in good faith;

（C）without notice that the instrument is overdue or has been dishonored or that there is an uncured default with respect to payment of another instrument issued as part of the same series;

（D）without notice that the instrument contains an unauthorized signature or has been altered;

（E）without notice of any claim to the instrument described in Section 3.306;and

（F）without notice that any party has a defense or claim in recoupment described in Section 3.305（a）.

（b）Notice of discharge of a party, other than discharge in an insolvency proceeding, is not notice of a defense under Subsection（a）, but discharge is effective against a person who became a holder indue course with notice of the discharge.Public filing or recording of a document does not of itself constitute notice of a defense, claim in recoupment, or claim to the instrument.

（c）Except to the extent a transferor or predecessor in interest has rights as a holder in due course, a person does not acquire rights of a holder in due course of an instrument taken:

（1）by legal process or by purchase in an execution, bankruptcy, or creditor's sale or similar proceeding;

（2）在转让人的非正常业务过程中的整体转让中，通过购买取得票据；或

（2）by purchase as part of a bulk transaction not in ordinary course of business of the transferor;or

（3）作为遗产或其他组织之权益继承人取得票据。

（3）as the successor in interest to an estate or other organization.

（d）如果根据第3.303条（a）（1）款，票据的对价是履约承诺，且履约已部分完成，则票据的执票人可以主张正当执票人的权利，但不超过票据项下付款的相应比例，即已完成之履约的价值除以承诺之履约的价值的比例。

（d）If, under Section 3.303（a）（1）, the promise of performance that is the consideration for an instrument has been partially performed, the holder may assert rights as a holder in due course of the instrument only to the fraction of the amount payable under the instrument equal to the value of the partial performance divided by the value of the promised performance.

（e）如果（i）有权强制履行票据的人对票据仅拥有担保权益，且（ii）有义务支付票据的人持有抗辩、扣减权或票据索赔，可以对抗提供担保权益的人，此时，有权强制履行票据的人在主张正当执票人的权利时，仅限于在强制履行当时，不超出票据项下未偿担保债务的金额。

（e）If（i）the person entitled to enforce an instrument has only a security interest in the instrument, and（ii）the person obliged to pay the instrument has a defense, claim in recoupment, or claim to the instrument that may be asserted against the person who granted the security interest, the person entitled to enforce the instrument may assert rights as a holder in due course only to an amount payable under the instrument that, at the time of enforcement of the instrument, does not exceed the amount of the unpaid obligation secured.

（f）一项通知，其收到的时间和方式，必须留有据以作为的合理机会，方为有效通知。

（f）To be effective, notice must be received at a time and in a manner that gives a reasonable opportunity to act on it.

（g）如果任何法律对在特定种类之交易中取得正当执票人地位的条件作出限制，则该法律优于本条。

（g）This section is subject to any law limiting status as a holder in due course in particular classes of transactions.

第 3.303 条 价值和对价

（a）在下列情况下，票据的出立或转让被视为取得价值：

（1）票据的出立或转让系用于换取履约承诺，但已履行的承诺方可构成价值；

（2）受让人对票据取得担保权益或其他留置权，但司法程序中取得的留置权除外；

（3）票据的出立或转让系用于偿付对任何人的前存索赔，或为该索赔设立担保权益，无论该索赔是否已到支付日期；

（4）票据的出立或转让系用于换取流通票据；或

（5）票据的出立或转让系用于换取票据取得人向第三方承担的不可撤销义务。

（b）“对价”指足以支持简式合同的对价。如果票据的出立不存在对价，票据的出票人或制票人即持有抗辩。如果票据的出立系用于换取履约承诺，但所承诺的履约已到期而未履行，立票人即持有抗辩。如果票据的出立根据（a）款被视为取得价值，则票据的出立亦被视为存在对价。

§ 3.303. Value and Consideration.

（a）An instrument is issued or transferred for value if:

（1）the instrument is issued or transferred for a promise of performance, to the extent the promise has been performed;

（2）the transferee acquires a security interest or other lien in the instrument other than a lien obtained by judicial proceeding;

（3）the instrument is issued or transferred as payment of, or as security for, an antecedent claim against any person, whether or not the claim is due;

（4）the instrument is issued or transferred in exchange for a negotiable instrument;or

（5）the instrument is issued or transferred in exchange for the incurring of an irrevocable obligation to a third party by the person taking the instrument.

（b）“Consideration” means any consideration sufficient to support a simple contract.The drawer or maker of an instrument has a defense if the instrument is issued without consideration. If an instrument is issued for a promise of performance, the issuer has a defense to the extent performance of the promise is due and the promise has not been performed.If an instrument is issued for value as stated in Subsection（a）, the instrument is also issued for consideration.

第 3.304 条 过期票据

（a）即时付款的票据，在

§ 3.304. Overdue Instrument.

（a）An instrument payable on demand

下列最早时间开始时，成为过期票据：

（1）正常提出付款要求当日的下一日；

（2）当票据是支票时，从支票日期起超过 90 天；或

（3）当票据不是支票时，根据票据的性质和行业惯例，从票据日期起已超过该案具体情况下的合理时间。

becomes overdue at the earliest of the following times:

（1）on the day after the day demand for payment is duly made;

（2）if the instrument is a check, 90 days after its date;or

（3）if the instrument is not a check, when the instrument has been outstanding for a period of time after its date that is unreasonably long under the circumstances of the particular case in light of the nature of the instrument and usage of the trade.

（b）定时付款的票据，应适用下列原则：

（1）如果本金应分期支付，且到期日未被提前，则只要票据任何一笔分期付款因违约未能支付，票据即属过期，且在违约被纠正前，票据一直属于过期；

（2）如果本金不属于分期支付，且到期日未被提前，则票据在到期日的下一日过期；以及

（3）如果本金的到期日被提前，则在被提前后的到期日的下一日，票据过期。

（b）With respect to an instrument payable at a definite time the following rules apply:

（1）if the principal is payable in installments and a due date has not been accelerated, the instrument becomes overdue on default under the instrument for nonpayment of an installment, and the instrument remains overdue until the default is cured;

（2）if the principal is not payable in installments and the due date has not been accelerated, the instrument becomes overdue on the day after the due date;and

（3）if a due date with respect to principal has been accelerated, the instrument becomes overdue on the day after the accelerated due date.

（c）除本金的到期日被提前外，如果利息的支付存在违约，但本金的支付不存在违约，则票据不属于过期。

（c）Unless the due date of principal has been accelerated, an instrument does not become overdue if there is default in payment of interest but no default in payment of principal.

第 3.305 条　抗辩和扣减权

（a）除本条另有规定外，对当事方之票据支付义务进行强制履行的权利，受制于下列抗辩或扣减权：

（1）义务人基于下列理由的抗辩：

（A）义务人系未成年人，只要该情况可以构成简式合同项下的抗辩；

（B）存在胁迫、缺乏法定行为能力或非法交易，且根据其他法律，该情况导致义务人的义务无效；

（C）义务人受到欺诈，在既不了解也无合理机会了解票据之性质或关键条款的情况下，被诱导签署票据；或

（D）义务人的义务在破产程序中被解除。

（2）义务人根据本篇其他条款持有的抗辩；或义务人在简式合同项下可以使用的其他抗辩，即假设有权强制履行票据的人在强制履行简式合同项下的收款权利时，义务人本可使用的抗辩；以及

（3）义务人持有的可对抗票据原始受款人的扣减权，只要该权利与票据产生于同一交易；但是，义务人对抗票据受让人的权利主张，只能用于扣减在提起诉讼时票据项下的未

§ 3.305. Defenses and Claims in Recoupment.

（a）Except as otherwise provided in this section, the right to enforce the obligation of a party to pay an instrument is subject to the following:

（1）a defense of the obligor based on:

（A）infancy of the obligor to the extent it is a defense to a simple contract;

（B）duress, lack of legal capacity, or illegality of the transaction that, under other law, nullifies the obligation of the obligor;

（C）fraud that induced the obligor to sign the instrument with neither knowledge nor reasonable opportunity to learn of its character or its essential terms;or

（D）discharge of the obligor in insolvency proceedings;

（2）a defense of the obligor stated in another section of this Article or a defense of the obligor that would be available if the person entitled to enforce the instrument were enforcing a right to payment under a simple contract;and

（3）a claim in recoupment of the obligor against the original payee of the instrument if the claim arose from the transaction that gave rise to the instrument;but the claim of the obligor may be asserted against a transferee of the instrument only to reduce the amount

偿金额。

(b)正当执票人强制履行当事方之票据支付义务的权利，受制于(a)(1)款所述之义务人的抗辩，但不受制于(a)(2)款所述之义务人的抗辩，也不受制于(a)(3)款所述的针对任何人的扣减权，但针对执票人的扣减权除外。

(c)除(d)款另有规定外，在强制履行当事方之票据支付义务的诉讼中，义务人在对抗有权强制履行票据的人时，不得引用其他人的抗辩、扣减权或票据索赔(第3.306条)；但是，如果该他人加入诉讼，并自行对有权强制履行票据的人提出票据索赔，则义务人亦可提出该主张。如果寻求强制履行票据的人不拥有正当执票人的权利，且义务人能够证明，票据系遗失或被盗票据，则义务人无义务支付票据。

(d)在强制履行融通方之票据支付义务的诉讼中，融通方在对抗有权强制履行票据的人时，可以主张(a)款所述的抗辩或扣减权，只要受融通方有权对强制履行票据的人主张该抗辩或扣减权，但下列抗辩

owing on the instrument at the time the action is brought.

(b) The right of a holder in due course to enforce the obligation of a party to pay the instrument is subject to defenses of the obligor stated in Subsection (a)(1), but is not subject to defenses of the obligor stated in Subsection (a)(2) or claims in recoupment stated in Subsection (a)(3) against a person other than the holder.

(c) Except as provided in Subsection (d), in an action to enforce the obligation of a party to pay the instrument, the obligor may not assert against the person entitled to enforce the instrument a defense, claim in recoupment, or claim to the instrument (Section 3.306) of another person, but the other person's claim to the instrument may be asserted by the obligor if the other person is joined in the action and personally asserts the claim against the person entitled to enforce the instrument.An obligor is not obliged to pay the instrument if the person seeking enforcement of the instrument does not have rights of a holder in due course and the obligor proves that the instrument is a lost or stolen instrument.

(d) In an action to enforce the obligation of an accommodation party to pay an instrument, the accommodation party may assert against the person entitled to enforce the instrument any defense or claim in recoupment under Subsection (a) that the accommodated party could assert against the person entitled to

除外：破产程序中的解除义务、未成年人行为以及缺乏法定行为能力。

（e）在消费者交易中，如果本篇以外的其他法律规定，票据应包含一项说明，即执票人或受让人的权利受制于立票人可向原始受款人主张的索赔或抗辩，但票据实际未包含此种说明，此时：

（1）票据的效力，与票据包含此种说明时的效力相同；

（2）立票人可向执票人或受让人主张的全部索赔和抗辩，与票据包含此种说明时相同；并且

（3）在确定可向执票人或受让人索赔的程度时，票据被视为已包含此种说明。

如果票据包含该说明，或根据本款被视为包含该说明，则根据该说明对立票人承担责任的执票人或受让人，只要不是货物或服务的卖方，即有权就执票人或受让人承担的源于立票人对卖方之索赔或抗辩的责任，从卖方获得充分补偿，再加上合理的律师费。本条关于补偿的明确规定，不影响执票人或受让人根据任何规则、书面合同、司法判决或其他法律而享有的补偿、代位或追索

enforce the instrument, except the defenses of discharge in insolvency proceedings, infancy, and lack of legal capacity.

（e）In a consumer transaction, if law other than this Article requires that an instrument include a statement to the effect that the rights of a holder or transferee are subject to a claim or defense that the issuer could assert against the original payee, and the instrument does not include such a statement:

（1）the instrument has the same effect as if the instrument included such a statement;

（2）the issuer may assert against the holder or transferee all claims and defenses that would have been available if the instrument included such a statement;and

（3）the extent to which claims may be asserted against the holder or transferee is determined as if the instrument included such a statement.

If an instrument includes or is deemed to include a statement under this subsection, a holder or transferee who is liable under the statement to the issuer, but who is not the seller of the goods or services, shall be entitled to full indemnity from the seller for any liability under the statement incurred by the holder or transferee that results from the issuer's claims or defenses against the seller, plus reasonable attorney's fees.The provision in this section for express indemnity does not affect any right of indemnity, subrogation, or recovery to which a holder or transferee may be entitled under

权利。如果执票人或受让人自己作出可被诉的不当行为，且该行为与声明项下的衍生责任无关，则执票人或受让人不能根据本条，就其对立票人直接承担的责任，从卖方取得补偿。

any rule, written contract, judicial decision, or other statute.This section is not intended to provide a holder or transferee indemnity from the seller with respect to the holder or transferee's direct liability to the issuer for the holder or transferee's own actionable misconduct unrelated to derivative liability under the statement.

（f）如果本法以外的其他法律为消费者交易制定了不同规则，则本法受制于该法。

（f）This section is subject to law other than this Article that establishes a different rule for consumer transactions.

第 3.306 条　票据索赔

§ 3.306. Claims to an Instrument.

取得票据的人，如果不拥有正当执票人的权利，即受制于票据上或其收益上存在的财产权或占有权，包括撤销流通及收回票据或其收益的权利。拥有正当执票人权利的人，取得票据后，不受制于上述权利。

A person taking an instrument, other than a person having rights of a holder in due course, is subject to a claim of a property or possessory right in the instrument or its proceeds, including a claim to rescind a negotiation and to recover the instrument or its proceeds.A person having rights of a holder in due course takes free of the claim to the instrument.

第 3.307 条　违反信托义务的通知

§ 3.307. Notice of Breach of Fiduciary Duty.

（a）在本条中：

（1）“诚信受托人”指代理人、受托人、合伙人、公司执行官或董事，或对票据负有信托义务的其他代表人。

（2）“被代表人”指被代理人、受益人、合伙、公司，或（1）款所述义务的其他受益人。

（b）如果（i）任何人通过支付价值，或为付款或收款，

（a）In this section:

（1）“Fiduciary” means an agent, trustee, partner, corporate officer or director, or other representative owing a fiduciary duty with respect to an instrument.

（2）“Represented person” means the principal, beneficiary, partnership, corporation, or other person to whom the duty stated in Subdivision（1）is owed.

（b）If（i）an instrument is taken from a fiduciary for payment or collection or for value,

从诚信受托人取得票据，（ii）该取得人知道诚信受托人的信托身份，并且（iii）被代表人声称诚信受托人的交易违反了信托义务，并因此对票据或其收益提出权利主张，此时，应适用下列原则：

（ii）the taker has knowledge of the fiduciary status of the fiduciary, and（iii）the represented person makes a claim to the instrument or its proceeds on the basis that the transaction of the fiduciary is a breach of fiduciary duty, the following rules apply:

（1）诚信受托人违反信托义务的通知，即构成被代表人提出权利主张的通知；

（1）notice of breach of fiduciary duty by the fiduciary is notice of the claim of the represented person;

（2）如果票据应向被代表人付款，或基于诚信受托人的身份应向诚信受托人付款，则在下列情况下，票据的取得人被视为收到违反信托义务之通知：

（2）in the case of an instrument payable to the represented person or the fiduciary as such, the taker has notice of the breach of fiduciary duty if the instrument is:

（A）该取得人知道，票据系用于支付诚信受托人的个人债务，或为该债务设立担保；

（A）taken in payment of or as security for a debt known by the taker to be the personal debt of the fiduciary;

（B）该取得人知道，票据交易系用于诚信受托人的个人利益；或

（B）taken in a transaction known by the taker to be for the personal benefit of the fiduciary;or

（C）票据存入的账户，不是诚信受托人基于信托身份设立的账户，也不是被代表人的账户；

（C）deposited to an account other than an account of the fiduciary, as such, or an account of the represented person;

（3）如果出立票据的人系被代表人，或系以诚信受托人身份而作为的诚信受托人，则即使票据向诚信受托人个人付款，其本身亦不构成违反信托义务的通知，除非票据的取得人知道存在对信托义务的违反；

（3）if an instrument is issued by the represented person or the fiduciary as such, and made payable to the fiduciary personally, the taker does not have notice of the breach of fiduciary duty unless the taker knows of the breach of fiduciary duty;and

并且

（4）如果出立票据的人系被代表人，或系以诚信受托人身份而作为的诚信受托人，且受款人为票据的取得人，则在下列情况下，取得人被视为收到违反信托义务的通知：

（4）if an instrument is issued by the represented person or the fiduciary as such, to the taker as payee, the taker has notice of the breach of fiduciary duty if the instrument is:

（A）该取得人知道，票据系用于支付诚信受托人的个人债务，或为该债务设立担保；

（A）taken in payment of or as security for a debt known by the taker to be the personal debt of the fiduciary;

（B）该取得人知道，票据交易系用于诚信受托人的个人利益；或

（B）taken in a transaction known by the taker to be for the personal benefit of the fiduciary;or

（C）票据存入的账户，不是诚信受托人基于信托身份设立的账户，也不是被代表人的账户。

（C）deposited to an account other than an account of the fiduciary, as such, or an account of the represented person.

第 3.308 条　签名及正当执票人地位的证明

§ 3.308. Proof of Signatures and Status as Holder in Due Course.

（a）在票据诉讼的采证阶段，票据上的每一个签名，除在诉答程序中被特别否认外，均应被采纳为系属真实和业经授权。如果任何签名的有效性在诉答程序中被否认，主张该签名为有效的人应承担举证责任，但签名应被假定系属真实并业经授权；但是，如果诉讼系为强制履行该争议签名人的责任，但在审理签名的有效性时，该签名人已死亡或已失去行为能力，则不应作出上述假定。在强制履行票据的诉讼中，

（a）In an action with respect to an instrument, the authenticity of, and authority to make, each signature on the instrument are admitted unless specifically denied in the pleadings.If the validity of a signature is denied in the pleadings, the burden of establishing validity is on the person claiming validity, but the signature is presumed to be authentic and authorized unless the action is to enforce the liability of the purported signer and the signer is dead or incompetent at the time of trial of the issue of validity of the signaturc.If an action to enforce the instrument is brought against a person as the undisclosed principal of

如果原告认为，被告系隐名被代理人，而作为票据当事方在票据上签名的人，系该被代理人的代表人，则原告应承担举证责任，证明被告应作为第3.402条（a）款所述的被代表人而承担票据责任。

a person who signed the instrument as a party to the instrument, the plaintiff has the burden of establishing that the defendant is liable on the instrument as a represented person under Section 3.402（a）.

（b）如果签名的有效性得到采纳或证明，且（a）款的规定得到遵守，则只要原告出示票据，并证明其根据第3.301条有权强制履行票据，原告即有权获得付款，除非被告证明其拥有抗辩或扣减权。如果被告证明存在抗辩或扣减权，原告获得付款的权利，即受制于该抗辩或扣减权，除非原告证明，其拥有正当执票人的权利，因此不受制于该抗辩或扣减权。

（b）If the validity of signatures is admitted or proved and there is compliance with Subsection（a）, a plaintiff producing the instrument is entitled to payment if the plaintiff proves entitlement to enforce the instrument under Section 3.301, unless the defendant proves a defense or claim in recoupment.If a defense or claim in recoupment is proved, the right to payment of the plaintiff is subject to the defense or claim, except to the extent the plaintiff proves that the plaintiff has rights of a holder in due course that are not subject to the defense or claim.

第3.309条　遗失、损毁或被盗票据的强制履行

§ 3.309. Enforcement of Lost, Destroyed, or Stolen Instrument.

（a）在下列情况下，一个人即使不占有票据，亦有权强制履行票据：

（a）A person who is not in possession of an instrument is entitled to enforce the instrument if:

（1）寻求强制履行的该人：

（1）the person seeking to enforce the instrument:

（A）在失去票据占有的当时，有权强制履行票据；或

（A）was entitled to enforce the instrument when loss of possession occurred;or

（B）直接或间接从另一人处取得票据的所有权，而该另一人在失去票据占有的当时，有权强制履行票据；

（B）has directly or indirectly acquired ownership of the instrument from a person who was entitled to enforce the instrument when loss of possession occurred;

（2）失去票据的占有，非因该人作出转让，亦非因发生合法扣押；并且

（2）the loss of possession was not the result of a transfer by the person or a lawful seizure;and

（3）该人无法合理获得票据的占有，系因票据已损毁、已无法找到或已被任何人非法占有且该占有人处于未知、无法找到或无法送达诉讼通知的状态。

（3）the person cannot reasonably obtain possession of the instrument because the instrument was destroyed, its whereabouts cannot be determined, or it is in the wrongful possession of an unknown person or a person that cannot be found or is not amenable to service of process.

（b）根据（a）款寻求强制履行票据的人，必须证明票据的条款，并证明其强制履行票据的权利。如果能够作出此种证明，则应适用第3.308条，视该人已出示票据。对于寻求强制履行票据的人，法院在作出支持判决之前，必须首先认定，被要求付款的人已获得充分保护，不会在另一人寻求强制履行票据时受到损失。法院可以采用任何合理方式提供此种充分保护。

（b）A person seeking enforcement of an instrument under Subsection（a）must prove the terms of the instrument and the person's right to enforce the instrument.If that proof is made, Section 3.308 applies to the case as if the person seeking enforcement had produced the instrument.The court may not enter judgment in favor of the person seeking enforcement unless it finds that the person required to pay the instrument is adequately protected against loss that might occur by reason of a claim by another person to enforce the instrument. Adequate protection may be provided by any reasonable means.

第3.310条 票据对基础义务的影响

§ 3.310. Effect of Instrument on Obligation for Which Taken.

（a）除另有协议外，如果收取保兑支票、银行本票或银行支票系用于一项基础义务的解除，则其对于解除该义务的效力，相当于收取等同于票据金额的金钱，用于该义务的解除。该义务的解除不影响义务

（a）Unless otherwise agreed, if a certified check, cashier's check, or teller's check is taken for an obligation, the obligation is discharged to the same extent discharge would result if an amount of money equal to the amount of the instrument were taken in payment of the obligation.Discharge of the

人作为票据背书人的责任。

obligation does not affect any liability that the obligor may have as an indorser of the instrument.

（b）除另有协议外，且除（a）款另有规定外，如果收取本票或未保兑支票用于一项基础义务的解除，则该义务暂时中止，且其对于解除该义务的效力，相当于在适用下列原则的条件下，收取等同于票据金额的金钱，用于该义务的解除：

（b）Unless otherwise agreed and except as provided in Subsection（a）, if a note or an uncertified check is taken for an obligation, the obligation is suspended to the same extent the obligation would be discharged if an amount of money equal to the amount of the instrument were taken, and the following rules apply:

（1）涉及未保兑支票时，该义务的暂时中止延续至支票被拒付、被支付或被保兑。在支票得到支付或保兑后，该义务在支票金额的范围内被解除。

（1）In the case of an uncertified check, suspension of the obligation continues until dishonor of the check or until it is paid or certified.Payment or certification of the check results in discharge of the obligation to the extent of the amount of the check.

（2）涉及本票时，义务的暂时中止延续至本票被拒付或被支付。在本票得到支付后，该义务在支付金额的范围内被解除。

（2）In the case of a note, suspension of the obligation continues until dishonor of the note or until it is paid.Payment of the note results in discharge of the obligation to the extent of the payment.

（3）除（4）款另有规定外，如果支票或本票被拒付，且基础义务的权利人是有权强制履行票据的人，则该权利人可以强制履行该票据，也可以强制履行该义务。涉及由该义务人流通给该权利人的第三人票据时，只要解除该义务人的票据义务，即同时解除该义务人的该基础义务。

（3）Except as provided in Subdivision（4）, if the check or note is dishonored and the obligee of the obligation for which the instrument was taken is the person entitled to enforce the instrument, the obligee may enforce either the instrument or the obligation. In the case of an instrument of a third person that is negotiated to the obligee by the obligor, discharge of the obligor on the instrument also discharges the obligation.

（4）如果有权强制履行票

（4）If the person entitled to enforce

据的人不是基础义务的权利人，则在该基础义务暂时中止期间，该义务的权利人不得强制履行该义务。如果该权利人是有权强制履行票据的人，但因票据遗失、被盗或损毁而不再占有票据，则在票据应付金额的范围内，该权利人不得强制履行该基础义务，且在该范围内，该权利人对抗义务人的权利，亦仅限于强制履行票据。

（c）如果为解除一项基础义务而收取的票据不是（a）款或（b）款所述的票据，则：

（1）当银行作为制票人或承兑人对票据承担责任时，票据的效力如（a）款所述；或

（2）在所有其他情况下，票据的效力如（b）款所述。

第 3.311 条 使用票据作出和解

（a）如果任何人被索赔，但该人能够证明下列，则应适用（b）款至（d）款：

（1）被索赔人以善意向索赔人提示了票据，作为对索赔的充分清偿；

（2）不存在关于索赔金额的约定，或索赔金额存在正当争议；并且

（3）索赔人取得了票据的付款。

（b）除应适用（c）款的情

the instrument taken for an obligation is a person other than the obligee, the obligee may not enforce the obligation to the extent the obligation is suspended.If the obligee is the person entitled to enforce the instrument but no longer has possession of it because it was lost, stolen, or destroyed, the obligation may not be enforced to the extent of the amount payable on the instrument, and to that extent the obligee's rights against the obligor are limited to enforcement of the instrument.

（c）If an instrument other than one described in Subsection（a）or（b）is taken for an obligation, the effect is:

（1）that stated in Subsection（a）if the instrument is one for which a bank is liable as maker or acceptor;or

（2）that stated in Subsection（b）in any other case.

§ 3.311. Accord and Satisfaction by Use of Instrument.

（a）Subsections（b）-（d）apply if a person against whom a claim is asserted proves that:

（1）that person in good faith tendered an instrument to the claimant as full satisfaction of the claim;

（2）the amount of the claim was unliquidated or subject to a bona fide dispute;and

（3）the claimant obtained payment of the instrument.

（b）Unless Subsection（c）applies, the

况外，只要被索赔人能够证明，票据或伴随票据的书面通信包含醒目说明，即该票据是对索赔的充分清偿，该索赔即被视为得到清偿。

claim is discharged if the person against whom the claim is asserted proves that the instrument or an accompanying written communication contained a conspicuous statement to the effect that the instrument was tendered as full satisfaction of the claim.

（c）除（d）款另有规定外，如果存在下列任何一种情况，索赔即不被视为根据（b）款得到清偿：

（c）Subject to Subsection（d）, a claim is not discharged under Subsection（b）if either of the following applies:

（1）索赔人系一个组织，且能够证明：

（1）The claimant, if an organization, proves that:

（A）在票据提示前的一段合理时间内，索赔人向被索赔人发送了醒目说明，即应将有关争议债务的通信，包括用于债务充分清偿而提示的票据，发送至指定的人、办事处或地点；并且

（A）within a reasonable time before the tender, the claimant sent a conspicuous statement to the person against whom the claim is asserted that communications concerning disputed debts, including an instrument tendered as full satisfaction of a debt, are to be sent to a designated person, office, or place;and

（B）该指定的人、办事处或地点未收到票据或伴随票据的通信。

（B）the instrument or accompanying communication was not received by that designated person, office, or place.

（2）无论是否系一个组织，索赔人能够证明，在票据付款后 90 日内，索赔人向被索赔人曾提示返还票据金额。但是，如果索赔人系一个组织，且发送了符合（1）（A）款所述的说明，则本款不适用。

（2）The claimant, whether or not an organization, proves that within 90 days after payment of the instrument, the claimant tendered repayment of the amount of the instrument to the person against whom the claim is asserted.This subdivision does not apply if the claimant is an organization that sent a statement complying with Subdivision（1）（A）.

（d）如果被索赔人能够证明，在索赔人发起票据收款前

（d）A claim is discharged if the person against whom the claim is asserted proves

的合理时间内，索赔人已知道，或对争议债务直接负责的索赔人之代理人已知道，票据的提示系用于对索赔的充分清偿，则索赔即被视为得到清偿。

that within a reasonable time before collection of the instrument was initiated, the claimant, or an agent of the claimant having direct responsibility with respect to the disputed obligation, knew that the instrument was tendered in full satisfaction of the claim.

第3.312条 遗失、损毁或被盗的银行本票、银行支票或保兑支票

§ 3.312. Lost, Destroyed, or Stolen Cashier's Check, Teller's Check, or Certified Check.

（a）在本条中：

（a）In this section:

（1）"支票"指银行本票、银行支票或保兑支票。

（1）"Check" means a cashier's check, teller's check, or certified check.

（2）涉及已遗失、损毁或被盗的银行本票、银行支票或保兑支票时，"主张人"指主张有权获得支票金额的人。

（2）"Claimant" means a person who claims the right to receive the amount of a cashier's check, teller's check, or certified check that was lost, destroyed, or stolen.

（3）"报失声明"指在同意接受伪证罪责任的条件下，以记录形式作出的声明，其中说明：

（3）"Declaration of loss" means a statement, made in a record under penalty of perjury, to the effect that:

（A）声明人失去支票的占有；

（A）the declarer lost possession of a check;

（B）涉及保兑支票时，声明人系支票的出票人或受款人；涉及银行本票或银行支票时，声明人系支票的汇付人或受款人；

（B）the declarer is the drawer or payee of the check, in the case of a certified check, or the remitter or payee of the check, in the case of a cashier's check or teller's check;

（C）失去支票的占有，非因声明人的转让，亦非因合法扣押；以及

（C）the loss of possession was not the result of a transfer by the declarer or a lawful seizure;and

（D）声明人无法合理取得支票的占有，系因支票已损毁、已无法找到，或已被任何人非

（D）the declarer cannot reasonably obtain possession of the check because the check was destroyed, its whereabouts cannot be

法占有且该人处于未知、无法找到或无法送达诉讼通知的状态。

determined, or it is in the wrongful possession of an unknown person or a person that cannot be found or is not amenable to service of process.

（4）“承债银行”指银行本票或银行支票的立票人，或保兑支票的承兑人。

（4）“Obligated bank” means the issuer of a cashier’s check or teller’s check or the acceptor of a certified check.

（b）主张人就支票金额提出权利主张时，可向承债银行发送通信，合理描述支票的特征，并要求支付支票金额，只要（i）主张人系保兑支票的出票人或受款人，或系银行本票或银行支票的汇付人或受款人，（ii）通信中包含或附有主张人就支票作出的报失声明，（iii）基于银行收到该通信的时间和方式，银行有合理时间在支付支票前，根据该通信据以作为，以及（iv）在承债银行提出要求时，主张人提供了合理的身份证明。报失声明的提交，构成一项保证，即担保声明中的陈述系属真实。如果所提出的权利主张符合本款规定，则应适用下列原则：

（b）A claimant may assert a claim to the amount of a check by a communication to the obligated bank describing the check with reasonable certainty and requesting payment of the amount of the check, if（i）the claimant is the drawer or payee of a certified check or the remitter or payee of a cashier’s check or teller’s check,（ii）the communication contains or is accompanied by a declaration of loss of the claimant with respect to the check,（iii）the communication is received at a time and in a manner affording the bank a reasonable time to act on it before the check is paid, and（iv）the claimant provides reasonable identification if requested by the obligated bank.Delivery of a declaration of loss is a warranty of the truth of the statements made in the declaration. If a claim is asserted in compliance with this subsection, the following rules apply:

（1）在下列较晚时间，该权利主张取得强制履行力：（i）提出权利主张的时间，或（ii）涉及银行本票或银行支票时，从支票日期次日起第九十天；涉及保兑支票时，从承兑日期次

（1）The claim becomes enforceable at the later of（i）the time the claim is asserted, or（ii）the 90th day following the date of the check, in the case of a cashier’s check or teller’s check, or the 90th day following the date of the acceptance, in the case of a certified check.

日起第九十天。

（2）在该权利主张取得强制履行力之前，该权利主张没有法律效力，因此，承债银行可以支付支票，或在涉及银行支票时，可以允许受票人支付支票。在向有权强制履行支票的人付款之后，承债银行对支票的全部义务即被解除。

（2）Until the claim becomes enforceable, it has no legal effect and the obligated bank may pay the check or, in the case of a teller's check, may permit the drawee to pay the check. Payment to a person entitled to enforce the check discharges all liability of the obligated bank with respect to the check.

（3）如果在支票被提示付款前，该权利主张取得强制履行力，则承债银行无义务支付支票。

（3）If the claim becomes enforceable before the check is presented for payment, the obligated bank is not obliged to pay the check.

（4）在该权利主张取得强制履行力时，承债银行即有义务向主张人支付支票金额，只要之前未曾向有权强制履行支票的人付款。除第 4.302 条（a）（1）款另有规定外，向主张人付款之后，承债银行对支票的全部义务即被解除。

（4）When the claim becomes enforceable, the obligated bank becomes obliged to pay the amount of the check to the claimant if payment of the check has not been made to a person entitled to enforce the check.Subject to Section 4.302（a）（1）, payment to the claimant discharges all liability of the obligated bank with respect to the check.

（c）如果承债银行根据（b）（4）款向主张人支付支票金额，但享有正当执票人权利的人出示支票并要求付款，则主张人有义务：

（c）If the obligated bank pays the amount of a check to a claimant under Subsection（b）（4）and the check is presented for payment by a person having rights of a holder in due course, the claimant is obliged to:

（1）当支票已被支付时，向承债银行退回付款；或

（1）refund the payment to the obligated bank if the check is paid;or

（2）当支票已被拒付时，向拥有正当执票人权利的人支付支票金额。

（2）pay the amount of the check to the person having rights of a holder in due course if the check is dishonored.

（d）如果主张人有权根据（b）款提出权利主张，同时系

（d）If a claimant has the right to assert a claim under Subsection（b）and is also a person

有权强制履行已遗失、损毁或被盗之银行本票、银行支票或保兑支票的人，则该主张人就支票主张权利时，可以根据本条主张，也可以根据第 3.309 条主张。

who is entitled to enforce a cashier's check, teller's check, or certified check that is lost, destroyed, or stolen, the claimant may assert rights with respect to the check under either this section or Section 3.309.

第4章　当事方的责任

PART 4. LIABILITY OF PARTIES

第 3.401 条　签名

（a）只有在下列情况下，一个人才对票据承担责任：

（1）该人在票据上签名；或

（2）该人的代理人或代表人在票据上签名，且根据第 3.402 条，该签名对被代表人有约束力。

（b）签名可以通过下列方式作出：（i）手写或使用工具或机器打印，并且（ii）使用任何名字，包括商号或别名，或使用或采纳任何字词、标识或符号，只要在使用或采纳的当时，行为人的意图是对书面文件进行认证。

§ 3.401. Signature.

（a）A person is not liable on an instrument unless the person:

（1）signed the instrument;or

（2）is represented by an agent or representative who signed the instrument and the signature is binding on the represented person under Section 3.402.

（b）A signature may be made（i）manually or by means of a device or machine, and（ii）by the use of any name, including a trade or assumed name, or by a word, mark, or symbol executed or adopted by a person with present intention to authenticate a writing.

第 3.402 条　代表人的签名

（a）如果在票据上签名的人，系代表人或自视为代表人，且在签名时使用被代表人的名字，或使用签名人自己的名字，此时，该签名对被代表人的约束力，相当于该签名签署在简式合同上时被代表人所受的约

§ 3.402. Signature by Representative.

（a）If a person acting, or purporting to act, as a representative signs an instrument by signing either the name of the represented person or the name of the signer, the represented person is bound by the signature to the same extent the represented person would be bound if the signature were on a simple contract.If the

束。如果被代表人受该签名的约束，则代表人的签名即属于“被代表人的授权签名”，且被代表人即对票据承担责任，无论票据上是否指明了该被代表人。

represented person is bound, the signature of the representative is the “authorized signature of the represented person” and the represented person is liable on the instrument, whether or not identified in the instrument.

（b）如果代表人在票据上签署代表人的名字，且该签名属于被代表人的授权签名，则应适用下列原则：

（b）If a representative signs the name of the representative to an instrument and the signature is an authorized signature of the represented person, the following rules apply:

（1）如果签名的格式毫无疑义地表明，签名系代表被代表人作出，且票据上指明了被代表人，则代表人不对票据承担责任。

（1）If the form of the signature shows unambiguously that the signature is made on behalf of the represented person who is identified in the instrument, the representative is not liable on the instrument.

（2）除（c）款另有规定外，如果正当执票人在取得票据时未得到通知，即代表人无意对票据承担责任，则在下列情况下，代表人应对票据承担责任：（i）签名的格式并非毫无疑义地表明，签名系以代表人的身份作出，或（ii）票据上未指明被代表人。涉及任何其他人时，除非代表人能够证明，各个原始当事方无意让代表人承担票据责任，否则，代表人即对票据承担责任。

（2）Subject to Subsection（c）, the representative is liable on the instrument to a holder in due course that took the instrument without notice that the representative was not intended to be liable on the instrument if（i）the form of the signature does not show unambiguously that the signature is made in a representative capacity, or（ii）the represented person is not identified in the instrument.With respect to any other person, the representative is liable on the instrument unless the representative proves that the original parties did not intend the representative to be liable on the instrument.

（c）如果代表人作为支票的出票人签署代表人的名字，但未注明其代表人的身份，则只要该支票所支取的账户属于

（c）If a representative signs the name of the representative as drawer of a check without indication of the representative status and the check is payable from an account of

支票上注明的被代表人，且该签名属于被代表人的授权签名，签名人即不对支票承担责任。

the represented person who is identified on the check, the signer is not liable on the check if the signature is an authorized signature of the represented person.

第 3.403 条 无授权签名

§ 3.403. Unauthorized Signature.

（a）除本篇或第 4 篇另有规定外，无授权签名不具有效力；但是，为保护以善意支付票据的人，或通过支付价值取得票据的人，无授权签名构成签名人自己的有效签名。为本篇任何目的，无授权签名均可被事后批准。

（a）Unless otherwise provided in this Article or Article 4, an unauthorized signature is ineffective except as the signature of the unauthorized signer in favor of a person who in good faith pays the instrument or takes it for value.An unauthorized signature may be ratified for all purposes of this Article.

（b）如果一个组织的授权签名，由一人以上的签名构成，则缺少任何一个必要签名，该组织的签名即属于无授权签名。

（b）If the signature of more than one person is required to constitute the authorized signature of an organization, the signature of the organization is unauthorized if one of the required signatures is lacking.

（c）即使为本篇目的，本篇任何条款允许无授权签名具有效力，但对于作出无授权签名的人，其应承担的民事或刑事责任不受此种条款的影响。

（c）The civil or criminal liability of a person who makes an unauthorized signature is not affected by any provision of this Article that makes the unauthorized signature effective for the purposes of this Article.

第 3.404 条 冒名人；虚构受款人

§ 3.404. Impostors;Fictitious Payees.

（a）如果冒名人通过邮件或其他形式，冒充票据的受款人或受款人的授权代表人，诱使票据的立票人向冒名人出立票据，或向冒名人的合谋人出立票据，此时，如果任何人以该受款人的名字在票据上作出背书，则为保护以善意支付票

（a）If an impostor, by use of the mails or otherwise, induces the issuer of an instrument to issue the instrument to the impostor, or to a person acting in concert with the impostor, by impersonating the payee of the instrument or a person authorized to act for the payee, an indorsement of the instrument by any person in the name of the payee is effective as the

据的人，或为保护通过支付价值取得或为收款目的取得票据的人，该背书具有该受款人背书的效力。

indorsement of the payee in favor of a person who, in good faith, pays the instrument or takes it for value or for collection.

（b）如果（i）票据应向何人付款系由某人的意图决定［第3.110条（a）款或（b）款］，而该人无意让被注明为受款人的人对票据取得任何权益，或（ii）被注明为票据受款人的人系虚构的人，此时，在票据通过记名背书被流通之前，应适用下列原则：

（b）If（i）a person whose intent determines to whom an instrument is payable（Section 3.110（a）or（b））does not intend the person identified as payee to have any interest in the instrument, or（ii）the person identified as payee of an instrument is a fictitious person, the following rules apply until the instrument is negotiated by special indorsement:

（1）任何占有票据的人，均为票据的执票人。

（1）Any person in possession of the instrument is its holder.

（2）如果任何人以票据上被注明之受款人的名字作出背书，则为保护以善意支付票据的人，或为保护通过支付价值取得或为收款目的取得票据的人，该背书具有该受款人背书的效力。

（2）An indorsement by any person in the name of the payee stated in the instrument is effective as the indorsement of the payee in favor of a person who, in good faith, pays the instrument or takes it for value or for collection.

（c）为（a）款或（b）款目的，在下列情况下，背书被视为以受款人的名字作出：

（c）Under Subsection（a）or（b）, an indorsement is made in the name of a payee if:

（1）背书使用的名字，与受款人的名字基本相似；或

（1）it is made in a name substantially similar to that of the payee;or

（2）无论是否经过背书，票据被存入存款银行，且存入账户的名字，与受款人的名字基本相似。

（2）the instrument, whether or not indorsed, is deposited in a depositary bank to an account in a name substantially similar to that of the payee.

（d）涉及（a）款或（b）款适用的票据时，如果任何人

（d）With respect to an instrument to which Subsection（a）or（b）applies, if a

在支付票据时，或在通过支付价值取得或为收款目的取得票据时，未能行使正常谨慎，且该过失对票据之付款损失起到助推作用，则受到损失的人，可就未能行使正常谨慎所造成的那部分损失，从未能行使正常谨慎的人取得赔偿。

person paying the instrument or taking it for value or for collection fails to exercise ordinary care in paying or taking the instrument and that failure contributes to loss resulting from payment of the instrument, the person bearing the loss may recover from the person failing to exercise ordinary care to the extent the failure to exercise ordinary care contributed to the loss.

第 3.405 条　雇员作出欺诈背书时雇主的责任

（a）在本条中：

（1）“雇员”包括雇主使用的独立承包商，以及该独立承包商的雇员。

（2）“欺诈性背书”：

（A）涉及向雇主付款的票据时，指显示为雇主之背书的伪造背书；或

（B）涉及雇主系立票人且票据注明了受款人的票据时，指显示为该受款人之背书的伪造背书。

（3）涉及票据时，“职责”指作出下列行为的权限：（i）代表雇主在票据上签名或背书，（ii）就雇主收到的票据，进行账目处理、存入账户或作出其他处置，（iii）对票据进行准备或处置，以便使用雇主的名字出立票据，（iv）对于以雇主名字出立的票据，提供相关信息，以便确定票据受款人的名

§ 3.405. Employer’s Responsibility for Fraudulent Indorsement by Employee.

（a）In this section:

（1）“Employee” includes an independent contractor and employee of an independent contractor retained by the employer.

（2）“Fraudulent indorsement” means:

（A）in the case of an instrument payable to the employer, a forged indorsement purporting to be that of the employer;or

（B）in the case of an instrument with respect to which the employer is the issuer, a forged indorsement purporting to be that of the person identified as payee.

（3）“Responsibility” with respect to instruments means authority（i）to sign or indorse instruments on behalf of the employer,（ii）to process instruments received by the employer for bookkeeping purposes, for deposit to an account, or for other disposition,（iii）to prepare or process instruments for issue in the name of the employer,（iv）to supply information determining the names or addresses of payees of instruments to be issued

字或地址，（v）对于以雇主名字出立的票据，管控票据的处置，或（vi）以履行职责的身份，从事其他有关票据的行为。如果雇员的权限，仅限于可以接触处于储存、运输或寄送过程中的票据、空白票据表格或半成品票据表格，或发生类似接触，该权限不构成“职责”。

in the name of the employer,（v）to control the disposition of instruments to be issued in the name of the employer, or（vi）to act otherwise with respect to instruments in a responsible capacity. “Responsibility” does not include authority that merely allows an employee to have access to instruments or blank or incomplete instrument forms that are being stored or transported or are part of incoming or outgoing mail, or similar access.

（b）如果任何人以善意支付票据，或通过支付价值取得或为收款目的取得票据，则在确定该人之权利和义务时，只要雇主将票据的职责委托给雇员，则即使该雇员或其同谋人在票据上作出欺诈性背书，只要背书系以票据应向其付款之人的名字作出，该背书即具有该受款人背书的效力。如果任何人在支付票据时，或在通过支付价值取得或为收款目的取得票据时，未能行使正常谨慎，且该过失对欺诈造成的损失起到助推作用，则受到损失的人，可就未能行使正常谨慎所造成的那部分损失，从未能行使正常谨慎的人取得赔偿。

（b）For the purpose of determining the rights and liabilities of a person who, in good faith, pays an instrument or takes it for value or for collection, if an employer entrusted an employee with responsibility with respect to the instrument and the employee or a person acting in concert with the employee makes a fraudulent indorsement of the instrument, the indorsement is effective as the indorsement of the person to whom the instrument is payable if it is made in the name of that person.If the person paying the instrument or taking it for value or for collection fails to exercise ordinary care in paying or taking the instrument and that failure contributes to loss resulting from the fraud, the person bearing the loss may recover from the person failing to exercise ordinary care to the extent the failure to exercise ordinary care contributed to the loss.

（c）为（b）款目的，下列情况属于使用应向其付款之人的名字作出背书：

（c）Under Subsection（b）, an indorsement is made in the name of the person to whom an instrument is payable if:

（1）背书使用的名字，与

（1）it is made in a name substantially

该人的名字基本相似；或

（2）无论是否经过背书，票据被存入存款银行，且存入账户的名字，与该人的名字基本相似。

similar to the name of that person;or

（2）the instrument, whether or not indorsed, is deposited in a depositary bank to an account in a name substantially similar to the name of that person.

第 3.406 条 对票据之伪造签名或涂改起助推作用的疏忽

§ 3.406. Negligence Contributing to Forged Signature or Alteration of Instrument.

（a）如果任何人未能行使正常谨慎，且该过失对票据发生涂改或伪造签名起到重大助推作用，则在对抗以善意支付票据的人时，或在对抗通过支付价值取得或为收款目的取得票据的人时，未能行使正常谨慎的人即无权以票据存在涂改或伪造而主张权利。

（a）A person whose failure to exercise ordinary care substantially contributes to an alteration of an instrument or to the making of a forged signature on an instrument is precluded from asserting the alteration or the forgery against a person who, in good faith, pays the instrument or takes it for value or for collection.

（b）为（a）款目的，如果主张他人丧失主张权的人，自己在支付或取得票据时亦未能行使正常谨慎，且该过失对损失的发生亦起到助推作用，则丧失主张权的人，和主张他人丧失主张权的人，应按他们各自未能行使正常谨慎对损失发生的影响程度，分担损失。

（b）Under Subsection（a）, if the person asserting the preclusion fails to exercise ordinary care in paying or taking the instrument and that failure contributes to loss, the loss is allocated between the person precluded and the person asserting the preclusion according to the extent to which the failure of each to exercise ordinary care contributed to the loss.

（c）为（a）款目的，证明未能行使正常谨慎的举证责任，由主张他人丧失主张权的人承担。为（b）款目的，证明未能行使正常谨慎的举证责任，由丧失主张权的人承担。

（c）Under Subsection（a）, the burden of proving failure to exercise ordinary care is on the person asserting the preclusion.Under Subsection（b）, the burden of proving failure to exercise ordinary care is on the person precluded.

第 3.407 条 涂改

§ 3.407. Alteration.

（a）“涂改”指：

（a）“Alteration” means:

（1）未经授权在票据上作出的，意图在任何方面修改任何当事方义务的改动；或

（1）an unauthorized change in an instrument that purports to modify in any respect the obligation of a party;or

（2）未经授权在不完整票据上添补的，影响任何当事方义务的文字或数字，或其他改动。

（2）an unauthorized addition of words or numbers or other change to an incomplete instrument relating to the obligation of a party.

（b）除（c）款另有规定外，以欺诈方式作出的涂改，如果影响到任何当事方的义务，该当事方的义务即被解除，除非该当事方同意该涂改，或丧失对该涂改的主张权。任何其他涂改，均不解除当事方的义务，且票据可按原始条款强制履行。

（b）Except as provided in Subsection（c）, an alteration fraudulently made discharges a party whose obligation is affected by the alteration unless that party assents or is precluded from asserting the alteration.No other alteration discharges a party, and the instrument may be enforced according to its original terms.

（c）如果票据存在欺诈性涂改，但付款银行或受票人支付了票据，或任何人以善意通过支付价值取得了票据，且未得到票据存在涂改的通知，其即有权按下列条款强制履行有关该票据的权利：

（c）A payor bank or drawee paying a fraudulently altered instrument or a person taking it for value, in good faith and without notice of the alteration, may enforce rights with respect to the instrument:

（1）按票据的原始条款；或

（1）according to its original terms;or

（2）涉及不完整票据通过无授权涂改被添补完整时，按添补完整后的条款。

（2）in the case of an incomplete instrument altered by unauthorized completion, according to its terms as completed.

第 3.408 条　受票人不对未承兑的汇票承担责任

§ 3.408. Drawee Not Liable on Unaccepted Draft.

支票或其他汇票本身，不构成受票人手中可用于支付该票据之资金的转让。受票人在承兑支票或其他汇票前，不对票据承担责任。

A check or other draft does not of itself operate as an assignment of funds in the hands of the drawee available for its payment, and the drawee is not liable on the instrument until the drawee accepts it.

第 3.409 条 汇票的承兑；保兑支票

（a）“承兑”指受票人以签名方式，同意在汇票被提示时支付汇票。该同意必须写在汇票上，并可仅由受票人的签名构成。承兑可在任何时间作出，并在作出下列行为的时间生效：根据相关指示作出通知；或交付已承兑的汇票，以使任何人基于该承兑取得权利。

（b）汇票即使未经出票人签名，或在其他方面不完整，或已过期，或已被拒付，仍可被承兑。

（c）如果汇票应于见票后一个确定期间后付款，但承兑人未写承兑日期，则执票人可以善意地填上一个日期，使承兑变为完整。

（d）“保兑支票”指已由受票银行承兑的支票。承兑可以按（a）款所述的方式作出，也可以在支票上写明支票已获保兑。支票的受票人没有义务对支票作出保兑，且拒绝作出保兑不构成对支票的拒付。

§ 3.409. Acceptance of Draft; Certified Check.

(a) "Acceptance" means the drawee's signed agreement to pay a draft as presented. It must be written on the draft and may consist of the drawee's signature alone.Acceptance may be made at any time and becomes effective when notification pursuant to instructions is given or the accepted draft is delivered for the purpose of giving rights on the acceptance to any person.

(b) A draft may be accepted although it has not been signed by the drawer, is otherwise incomplete, is overdue, or has been dishonored.

(c) If a draft is payable at a fixed period after sight and the acceptor fails to date the acceptance, the holder may complete the acceptance by supplying a date in good faith.

(d) "Certified check" means a check accepted by the bank on which it is drawn. Acceptance may be made as stated in Subsection (a) or by a writing on the check that indicates that the check is certified.The drawee of a check has no obligation to certify the check, and refusal to certify is not dishonor of the check.

第 3.410 条 改变汇票的承兑

（a）如果受票人所作之承兑的条款，与所提示之汇票的条款不同，执票人可以拒绝该

§ 3.410. Acceptance Varying Draft.

(a) If the terms of a drawee's acceptance vary from the terms of the draft as presented, the holder may refuse the acceptance and treat

承兑，并视汇票已被拒付。此时，受票人可以撤销该承兑。

（b）规定在位于美国的任何特定银行或地点支付汇票的承兑，不应被视为对汇票条款作出改变，除非承兑说明，只能在该银行或该地支付该汇票。

（c）如果执票人对改变汇票条款的承兑表示同意，则每一个未明确同意此种改变的出票人和背书人即被解除义务。

the draft as dishonored.In that case, the drawee may cancel the acceptance.

（b）The terms of a draft are not varied by an acceptance to pay at a particular bank or place in the United States, unless the acceptance states that the draft is to be paid only at that bank or place.

（c）If the holder assents to an acceptance varying the terms of a draft, the obligation of each drawer and indorser that does not expressly assent to the acceptance is discharged.

第 3.411 条　拒绝支付银行本票、银行支票和保兑支票

§ 3.411. Refusal to Pay Cashier's Checks, Teller's Checks, and Certified Checks.

（a）在本条中，“承债银行”指保兑支票的承兑人；或指银行本票或银行支票的立票人，只要票据系从该立票人处购买。

（b）如果承债银行错误地：（i）拒绝支付银行本票或保兑支票，（ii）阻止支付银行支票，或（iii）拒绝支付被拒付的银行支票，此时，强制履行该票据的人，有权就该未能支付所造成的费用和利息损失取得赔偿，并且，如果承债银行在收到造成间接损失之情况的通知后，仍然拒绝支付，则该人还有权就间接损失取得赔偿。

（c）如果承债银行由于下列原因拒付，即无须赔偿（b）款所述的费用或间接损失：

（a）In this section, “obligated bank” means the acceptor of a certified check or the issuer of a cashier's check or teller's check bought from the issuer.

（b）If the obligated bank wrongfully（i）refuses to pay a cashier's check or certified check,（ii）stops payment of a teller's check, or（iii）refuses to pay a dishonored teller's check, the person asserting the right to enforce the check is entitled to compensation for expenses and loss of interest resulting from the nonpayment and may recover consequential damages if the obligated bank refuses to pay after receiving notice of particular circumstances giving rise to the damages.

（c）Expenses or consequential damages under Subsection（b）are not recoverable if the refusal of the obligated bank to pay occurs because:

（1）承债银行已暂停对外付款；

（1）the obligated bank suspends payments;

（2）承债银行有合理理由相信，其拥有索赔或抗辩，可以对抗有权强制履行票据的人；

（2）the obligated bank asserts a claim or defense of the bank that it has reasonable grounds to believe is available against the person entitled to enforce the instrument;

（3）承债银行有合理理由怀疑，要求取得付款的人是否系有权强制履行票据的人；或

（3）the obligated bank has a reasonable doubt whether the person demanding payment is the person entitled to enforce the instrument;or

（4）付款被法律禁止。

（4）payment is prohibited by law.

第 3.412 条　本票或银行本票立票人的义务

本票或银行本票的立票人，或以出票人为付款人之其他汇票的立票人，有义务按下列条款支付票据：（i）按票据出立时的条款支付；或如果票据未出立，按票据首次被执票人占有时的条款支付，或（ii）如果立票人签署了不完整票据，则在第 3.115 条和第 3.407 条所述的限度内，按票据被添补完整后的条款支付。此项义务的受益人，是有权强制履行票据的人，或根据第 3.415 条支付了票据的背书人。

§ 3.412. Obligation of Issuer of Note or Cashier's Check.

The issuer of a note or cashier's check or other draft drawn on the drawer is obliged to pay the instrument（i）according to its terms at the time it was issued or, if not issued, at the time it first came into possession of a holder, or（ii）if the issuer signed an incomplete instrument, according to its terms when completed, to the extent stated in Sections 3.115 and 3.407.The obligation is owed to a person entitled to enforce the instrument or to an indorser who paid the instrument under Section 3.415.

第 3.413 条　承兑人的义务

（a）汇票的承兑人有义务按下列条款支付票据：（i）按汇票承兑时的条款支付，即使承兑规定按"原始出票"条款支付汇票，或使用了类似用语，

§ 3.413. Obligation of Acceptor.

（a）The acceptor of a draft is obliged to pay the draft（i）according to its terms at the time it was accepted, even though the acceptance states that the draft is payable "as originally drawn" or equivalent terms,（ii）if

（ii）如果承兑改变了汇票条款，则按改变后的汇票条款支付，或（iii）如果承兑的是不完整票据，则在第3.115条和第3.407条所述的限度内，按汇票被添补完整后的条款支付。此项义务的受益人，是有权强制履行汇票的人，或出票人，或根据第3.414条或第3.415条支付了汇票的背书人。

the acceptance varies the terms of the draft, according to the terms of the draft as varied, or (iii) if the acceptance is of a draft that is an incomplete instrument, according to its terms when completed, to the extent stated in Sections 3.115 and 3.407.The obligation is owed to a person entitled to enforce the draft or to the drawer or an indorser who paid the draft under Section 3.414 or 3.415.

（b）如果对支票的保兑或对汇票的承兑，规定了保兑或承兑的金额，则该金额即为承兑人的义务。在下列情况下，承兑人的义务，为正当执票人取得票据时的票据金额：

(b) If the certification of a check or other acceptance of a draft states the amount certified or accepted, the obligation of the acceptor is that amount.The obligation of the acceptor is the amount of the instrument at the time it was taken by the holder in due course if:

（1）保兑或承兑未规定金额；

(1) the certification or acceptance does not state an amount;

（2）票据金额随后被提高；并且

(2) the amount of the instrument is subsequently raised;and

（3）票据再随后被流通给正当执票人。

(3) the instrument is then negotiated to a holder in due course.

第3.414条 出票人的义务

§ 3.414. Obligation of Drawer.

（a）本条不适用于银行本票或其他以出票人为付款人的汇票。

(a) This section does not apply to cashier's checks or other drafts drawn on the drawer.

（b）如果未承兑的汇票被拒付，出票人有义务按下列条款支付汇票：（i）按汇票出立时的条款支付；或如果未出立，按汇票首次被执票人占有时的条款支付，或（ii）如果出票人签署了不完整票据，则在第

(b) If an unaccepted draft is dishonored, the drawer is obliged to pay the draft (i) according to its terms at the time it was issued or, if not issued, at the time it first came into possession of a holder, or (ii) if the drawer signed an incomplete instrument, according to its ter a s when completed, to the extent stated in

3.115 条和第 3.407 条所述的限度内，按汇票被添补完整后的条款支付。此项义务的受益人，是有权强制履行汇票的人，或根据第 3.415 条支付了汇票的背书人。

Sections 3.115 and 3.407.The obligation is owed to a person entitled to enforce the draft or to an indorser who paid the draft under Section 3.415.

（c）如果汇票被银行承兑，无论承兑在何时或由何人取得，出票人即被解除义务。

（c）If a draft is accepted by a bank, the drawer is discharged, regardless of when or by whom acceptance was obtained.

（d）如果汇票被承兑，但承兑人不是银行，则在承兑人拒付汇票时，出票人支付汇票的义务，等同于第 3.415 条（a）款和（c）款所述之背书人的义务。

（d）If a draft is accepted and the acceptor is not a bank, the obligation of the drawer to pay the draft if the draft is dishonored by the acceptor is the same as the obligation of an indorser under Sections 3.415（a）and（c）.

（e）如果汇票注明以“无追索权”方式出立，或以其他方式排除出票人支付汇票的义务，则当汇票非系支票时，出票人不承担（b）款的义务，但当汇票系支票时，对（b）款义务的排除无效。

（e)If a draft states that it is drawn “without recourse” or otherwise disclaims liability of the drawer to pay the draft, the drawer is not liable under Subsection（b）to pay the draft if the draft is not a check.A disclaimer of the liability stated in Subsection（b）is not effective if the draft is a check.

（f）如果（i）支票从票面日期之后超过 30 日未被提示付款，也未被交付给存款银行用于收款，（ii）受票人在该 30 日期限后暂停对外付款，且未支付该支票，并且（iii）由于该暂停对外付款，出票人对受票人掌管的用于该支票付款的资金失去控制，此时，只要出票人把控制受票人使用该资金的权利，转让给有权强制履行支

（f）If（i）a check is not presented for payment or given to a depositary bank for collection within 30 days after its date,（ii）the drawee suspends payments after expiration of the 30-day period without paying the check, and（iii）because of the suspension of payments, the drawer is deprived of funds maintained with the drawee to cover payment of the check, the drawer to the extent deprived of funds may discharge its obligation to pay the check by assigning to the person entitled to enforce

票的人，出票人即在失去控制之资金的限度内，被解除支付支票的义务。

the check the rights of the drawer against the drawee with respect to the funds.

第3.415条　背书人的义务

（a）除（b）款、（c）款、（d）款和（e）款或第3.419条（d）款另有规定外，如果票据被拒付，背书人有义务按下列条款支付票据的到期金额：（i）按票据背书时的条款支付，或（ii）如果背书人系对不完整票据作出背书，则在第3.115条和第3.407条所述的限度内，按票据被添补完整后的条款支付。背书人此项义务的受益人，是有权强制履行票据的人，或根据本条支付了票据的后手背书人。

（b）如果背书注明以“无追索权”方式作出，或以其他方式排除了背书人支付票据的义务，则背书人不承担（a）款规定的支付票据的义务。

（c）如果第3.503条要求就票据拒付作出通知，但并未向背书人作出符合该条要求的拒付通知，则背书人在（a）款项下的义务即被解除。

（d）如果汇票在背书后被银行承兑，则背书人在（a）款项下的义务即被解除。

（e）如果支票的背书人承担（a）款规定的义务，但支票在背书之后，超过30天未被提

§ 3.415. Obligation of Indorser.

（a）Subject to Subsections（b），（c），（d），and（e）and to Section 3.419（d），if an instrument is dishonored, an indorser is obliged to pay the amount due on the instrument（i）according to the terms of the instrument at the time it was indorsed, or（ii）if the indorser indorsed an incomplete instrument, according to its terms when completed, to the extent stated in Sections 3.115 and 3.407.The obligation of the indorser is owed to a person entitled to enforce the instrument or to a subsequent indorser who paid the instrument under this section.

（b）If an indorsement states that it is made“without recourse”or otherwise disclaims liability of the indorser, the indorser is not liable under Subsection（a）to pay the instrument.

（c）If notice of dishonor of an instrument is required by Section 3.503 and notice of dishonor complying with that section is not given to an indorser, the liability of the indorser under Subsection（a）is discharged.

（d）If a draft is accepted by a bank after an indorsement is made, the liability of the indorser under Subsection（a）is discharged.

（e）If an indorser of a check is liable under Subsection（a）and the check is not presented for payment, or given to a depositary

示付款或交付给存款银行用于收款，则背书人在（a）款项下的义务即被解除。

第3.416条 转让时的担保

（a）为取得对价而转让票据的人，向受让人担保，并且，如果转让系以背书方式作出，则同时向任何后手受让人担保：

（1）担保人系有权强制履行票据的人；

（2）票据上所有的签名均属真实并业经授权；

（3）票据不存在涂改；

（4）票据不受制于任何当事方持有的可对抗担保人的抗辩或扣减权；

（5）担保人不知道任何针对制票人或承兑人提起的破产程序；或如果票据为未承兑的汇票，针对出票人提起的破产程序；以及

（6）涉及远程制作的票证时，票证支取账户的持有人，已授权按票证显示的金额出立票证。

（b）如果获得上述（a）款担保的人以善意取得票据，则在担保人违反担保时，前者可就违反担保所造成的损失，从担保人取得不超过票据金额的损害赔偿，再加上违反担保造成的费用及利息损失。

bank for collection, within 30 days after the day the indorsement was made, the liability of the indorser under Subsection (a) is discharged.

§ 3.416. Transfer Warranties.

(a) A person who transfers an instrument for consideration warrants to the transferee and, if the transfer is by indorsement, to any subsequent transferee that:

(1) the warrantor is a person entitled to enforce the instrument;

(2) all signatures on the instrument are authentic and authorized;

(3) the instrument has not been altered;

(4) the instrument is not subject to a defense or claim in recoupment of any party that can be asserted against the warrantor;

(5) the warrantor has no knowledge of any insolvency proceeding commenced with respect to the maker or acceptor or, in the case of an unaccepted draft, the drawer;and

(6) with respect to a remotely-created item, that the person on whose account the item is drawn authorized the issuance of the item in the amount for which the item is drawn.

(b) A person to whom the warranties under Subsection (a) are made and who took the instrument in good faith may recover from the warrantor as damages for breach of warranty an amount equal to the loss suffered as a result of the breach, but not more than the amount of the instrument plus expenses and loss of interest incurred as a result of the breach.

（c）涉及支票时，上述（a）款所述的担保不得被排除。索赔人应在有理由知道违反担保并有理由知道担保人的真实身份后三十日内，将违反担保的索赔通知发送给担保人，否则，就延迟发出通知所造成的那部分损失，担保人在（b）款项下的义务即被解除。

（c）The warranties stated in Subsection（a）cannot be disclaimed with respect to checks. Unless notice of a claim for breach of warranty is given to the warrantor within 30 days after the claimant has reason to know of the breach and the identity of the warrantor, the liability of the warrantor under Subsection（b）is discharged to the extent of any loss caused by the delay in giving notice of the claim.

（d）索赔人有理由知道违反担保的时间，即为本条所述的违反担保之诉讼理由的产生时间。

（d）A cause of action for breach of warranty under this section accrues when the claimant has reason to know of the breach.

（e）涉及特定票证时，如果（1）受让人（包括收款银行）就违反担保主张（a）（6）款所述的索赔，但是，（2）根据适用法（包括适用的冲突法原则），在该受让人自己是转让人时，其本来不会作出本质上类似于（a）（6）款所述的担保，此时，该受让人即不被视为从任何转让人收到（a）（6）款所述的担保。

（e）If as to a particular item（1）a transferee（including a collecting bank）asserts a claim for breach of the warranty in Subsection（a）（6）, but（2）under applicable law（including the applicable choice-of-law principles）that transferee would not make a warranty substantially similar to the warranty in Subsection（a）（6）if such transferee were a transferor, then that transferee would not receive the warranty in Subsection（a）（6）from any transferor.

第 3.417 条 提示时的担保

§ 3.417. Presentment Warranties.

（a）如果未承兑的汇票被提示给受票人，要求其付款或承兑，且受票人支付或承兑了汇票，则（i）取得付款或承兑的人，在提示之时，以及（ii）汇票的前手转让人，在转让之时，向以善意支付或承兑汇票的受

（a）If an unaccepted draft is presented to the drawee for payment or acceptance and the drawee pays or accepts the draft,（i）the person obtaining payment or acceptance, at the time of presentment, and（ii）a previous transferor of the draft, at the time of transfer, warrant to the drawee making payment or accepting the draft

票人担保：

in good faith that:

（1）担保人系有权强制履行汇票的人，或有权代表该人取得汇票的付款或承兑，或在转让汇票时拥有该权利；

（1）the warrantor is, or was, at the time the warrantor transferred the draft, a person entitled to enforce the draft or authorized to obtain payment or acceptance of the draft on behalf of a person entitled to enforce the draft;

（2）汇票不存在涂改；

（2）the draft has not been altered;

（3）担保人不知道汇票出票人的签名未经授权；以及

（3）the warrantor has no knowledge that the signature of the drawer of the draft is unauthorized;and

（4）涉及远程制作的票证时，票证支取账户的持有人，已授权按票证显示的金额出立票证。

（4）with respect to a remotely-created item, that the person on whose account the item is drawn authorized the issuance of the item in the amount for which the item is drawn.

（b）如果担保人违反担保，作出付款的受票人可就其支付的金额从担保人取得赔偿，但应减去受票人因付款而从出票人收到的或有权收到的金额。此外，受票人有权就违反担保造成的费用和利息损失取得赔偿。受票人即使在付款时未能行使正常谨慎，其根据本款取得赔偿的权利亦不受影响。如果受票人承兑汇票，则违反担保构成承兑人义务的抗辩。承兑人如果为汇票作出付款，可就任何担保人的违反担保，从担保人取得本款所述的赔偿。

（b）A drawee making payment may recover from any warrantor damages for breach of warranty equal to the amount paid by the drawee less the amount the drawee received or is entitled to receive from the drawer because of the payment.In addition, the drawee is entitled to compensation for expenses and loss of interest resulting from the breach.The right of the drawee to recover damages under this subsection is not affected by any failure of the drawee to exercise ordinary care in making payment.If the drawee accepts the draft, breach of warranty is a defense to the obligation of the acceptor.If the acceptor makes payment with respect to the draft, the acceptor is entitled to recover from any warrantor for breach of warranty the amounts stated in this subsection.

（c）如果汇票存在无授权背书或涂改，且受票人因此根

（c）If a drawee asserts a claim for breach of warranty under Subsection（a）based on an

据（a）款提出违反担保的索赔，则担保人可以通过证明下列进行抗辩：根据第3.404条或第3.405条，该背书系属有效；或根据第3.406条或4.406条，出票人无权针对受票人就该无授权背书或涂改主张权利。

unauthorized indorsement of the draft or an alteration of the draft, the warrantor may defend by proving that the indorsement is effective under Section 3.404 or 3.405 or the drawer is precluded under Section 3.406 or 4.406 from asserting against the drawee the unauthorized indorsement or alteration.

（d）如果（i）被拒付的汇票被提示给出票人或背书人要求付款，或（ii）任何其他票据被提示给有义务支付票据的当事方要求付款，并且（iii）付款被收到，此时，应适用下列原则：

（d）If（i）a dishonored draft is presented for payment to the drawer or an indorser, or（ii）any other instrument is presented for payment to a party obliged to pay the instrument, and（iii）payment is received, the following rules apply:

（1）取得付款的人以及票据的前手转让人，向善意付款的人担保，担保人系有权强制履行票据的人，或有权代表该人取得付款，或在转让票据时拥有该权利。

（1）The person obtaining payment and a prior transferor of the instrument warrant to the person making payment in good faith that the warrantor is, or was, at the time the warrantor transferred the instrument, a person entitled to enforce the instrument or authorized to obtain payment on behalf of a person entitled to enforce the instrument.

（2）如果担保人违反担保，作出付款的人可就其支付的金额从担保人取得赔偿，再加上违约造成的费用和利息损失。

（2）The person making payment may recover from any warrantor for breach of warranty an amount equal to the amount paid plus expenses and loss of interest resulting from the breach.

（e）涉及支票时，（a）款和（d）款所述的担保不得被排除。索赔人应在有理由知道违反担保并有理由知道担保人真实身份后三十日内，向担保人发送违反担保的索赔通知，否

（e）The warranties stated in Subsections（a）and（d）cannot be disclaimed with respect to checks.Unless notice of a claim for breach of warranty is given to the warrantor within 30 days after the claimant has reason to know of the breach and the identity of the warrantor,

则，就延迟发出通知造成的那部分损失，担保人在（b）款或（d）款项下的义务即被解除。

the liability of the warrantor under Subsection (b) or (d) is discharged to the extent of any loss caused by the delay in giving notice of the claim.

（f）本条所述的违反担保的诉讼理由，在索赔人有理由知道违反担保时产生。

(f) A cause of action for breach of warranty under this section accrues when the claimant has reason to know of the breach.

（g）涉及特定票证时，如果（1）受让人（包括收款银行）就违反担保主张（a）（4）款所述的索赔，但是，（2）根据适用法（包括适用的冲突法原则），该受让人在自己是转让人时，其本来不会作出本质上类似于（a）（4）款所述的担保，此时，该受让人即不被视为从任何转让人收到（a）（4）款所述的担保。

(g) If as to a particular item (1) a transferee (including a collecting bank) asserts a claim for breach of the warranty in Subsection (a) (4), but (2) under applicable law (including the applicable choice-of-law principles) that transferee would not make a warranty substantially similar to the warranty in Subsection (a) (4) if such transferee were a transferor, then that transferee would not receive the warranty in Subsection (a) (4) from any transferor.

第3.418条　基于误解的付款或承兑

§ 3.418. Payment or Acceptance by Mistake.

（a）除（c）款另有规定外，如果汇票的受票人支付或承兑了汇票，但支付或承兑系基于下列误解：（i）不知道存在根据第4.403条针对汇票付款作出的停付，或（ii）不知道汇票出票人的签名未经授权，此时，受票人可从付款的接收人或获益人追回所付的汇票金额，或在涉及承兑时，可取消承兑。受票人即使在付款或承兑时未能行使正常谨慎，其在本款项下的权利亦不受影响。

(a) Except as provided in Subsection (c), if the drawee of a draft pays or accepts the draft and the drawee acted on the mistaken belief that (i) payment of the draft had not been stopped pursuant to Section 4.403, or (ii) the signature of the drawer of the draft was authorized, the drawee may recover the amount of the draft from the person to whom or for whose benefit payment was made or, in the case of acceptance, may revoke the acceptance. Rights of the drawee under this subsection are not affected by failure of the drawee to exercise ordinary care in paying or accepting the draft.

（b）除（c）款另有规定外，如果基于误解而支付或承兑了票据，且属于（a）款以外的情况，则作出付款或承兑的人，可在有关误解或返还之法律允许的范围内：

（b）Except as provided in Subsection（c），if an instrument has been paid or accepted by mistake and the case is not covered by Subsection（a），the person paying or accepting may, to the extent permitted by the law governing mistake and restitution:

（1）从付款的接收人或获益人收回付款；或

（1）recover the payment from the person to whom or for whose benefit payment was made;or

（2）在涉及承兑时，取消承兑。

（2）in the case of acceptance, revoke the acceptance.

（c）对于以善意支付价值取得票据的人，或因善意依赖付款或承兑而改变处境的人，不得针对该人主张（a）款或（b）款的救济。本款不限制第3.417条或第4.407条提供的救济。

（c）The remedies provided by Subsection（a）or（b）may not be asserted against a person who took the instrument in good faith and for value or who in good faith changed position in reliance on the payment or acceptance.This subsection does not limit remedies provided by Section 3.417 or 4.407.

（d）即使有第4.215条的规定，如果基于误解支付或承兑了汇票，但付款人或承兑人根据（a）款或（b）款收回了付款或取消了承兑，则票据不应被视为已付款或已承兑，而应被视为已被拒付；因此，被收回付款的人，被视为有权强制履行被拒付票据的人，并享有该人的权利。

（d）Notwithstanding Section 4.215, if an instrument is paid or accepted by mistake and the payor or acceptor recovers payment or revokes acceptance under Subsection（a）or（b），the instrument is deemed not to have been paid or accepted and is treated as dishonored, and the person from whom payment is recovered has rights as a person entitled to enforce the dishonored instrument.

第3.419条 用于融通而签署的票据

§ 3.419. Instruments Signed for Accommodation.

（a）如果为票据出立而支付的价值，系以票据的一个当事方为受益方（“受融通方”），

（a）If an instrument is issued for value given for the benefit of a party to the instrument（“accommodated party”）and another party to

而票据的另一当事方（“融通方”）在票据上签名时，意图在于对票据承担责任，但并不直接受益于为票据支付的价值，则该融通方对票据的签署，即属于“用于融通”。

the instrument（“accommodation party”）signs the instrument for the purpose of incurring liability on the instrument without being a direct beneficiary of the value given for the instrument, the instrument is signed by the accommodation party “for accommodation.”

（b）融通方可以作为制票人、出票人、承兑人或背书人在票据上签名。除（d）款另有规定外，融通方有义务根据其签名的身份支付票据。无论反欺诈法如何规定，也无论融通方是否就融通获得对价，均可强制履行融通方的义务。

（b）An accommodation party may sign the instrument as maker, drawer, acceptor, or indorser.Subject to Subsection（d）, the accommodation party is obliged to pay the instrument in the capacity in which the accommodation party signs.The obligation of an accommodation party may be enforced notwithstanding any statute of frauds and whether or not the accommodation party receives consideration for the accommodation.

（c）票据上的任何签名，如果属于异常背书，或如果伴有文字，说明签名人系作为保证人签名，用于担保票据另一当事方的义务，签名人即应被假定为融通方，并应认为存在通知，即对票据的签署系用于融通。除第 3.605 条另有规定外，有权强制履行融通方之票据支付义务的人，即使在取得票据时已得到通知，即融通方对票据的签署系用于融通，融通方支付票据的义务亦不受影响。

（c）A person signing an instrument is presumed to be an accommodation party and there is notice that the instrument is signed for accommodation if the signature is an anomalous indorsement or is accompanied by words indicating that the signer is acting as surety or guarantor with respect to the obligation of another party to the instrument.Except as provided in Section 3.605, the obligation of an accommodation party to pay the instrument is not affected by the fact that the person enforcing the obligation had notice when the instrument was taken by that person that the accommodation party signed the instrument for accommodation.

（d）如果票据当事方的签名伴有文字，毫无疑义地表明

（d）If the signature of a party to an instrument is accompanied by words indicating

该签名人就另一当事方的义务保证完成收款，但不保证该另一当事方作出付款，此时只有在下列情况下，签名人才有义务向有权强制履行票据的人支付票据的到期金额：

（1）针对该另一当事方的法院判决未能获得执行；

（2）该另一当事方已破产或处于破产程序中；

（3）无法向该另一当事方送达起诉通知；或

（4）存在其他情况，显示无法从该另一当事方取得付款。

（e）如果票据当事方的签名伴有文字，说明该当事方对付款作出保证，或如果签名人作为融通方以其他方式在票据上签名，但该方式并非毫无疑义地表明，签名人的意图是保证收款，而不保证付款，此时，签名人向有权强制履行票据的人支付票据到期金额的义务，等同于受融通方的支付义务，而该权利人亦无须首先向受融通方追索。

（f）支付了票据的融通方，有权从受融通方获得补偿，并有权对受融通方强制履行票据。在适当情况下，融通方可以通过司法程序要求受融通方履行票据义务。支付了票据的受融

unambiguously that the party is guaranteeing collection rather than payment of the obligation of another party to the instrument, the signer is obliged to pay the amount due on the instrument to a person entitled to enforce the instrument only if:

（1）execution of judgment against the other party has been returned unsatisfied;

（2）the other party is insolvent or in an insolvency proceeding;

（3）the other party cannot be served with process;or

（4）it is otherwise apparent that payment cannot be obtained from the other party.

（e）If the signature of a party to an instrument is accompanied by words indicating that the party guarantees payment or the signer signs the instrument as an accommodation party in some other manner that does not unambiguously indicate an intention to guarantee collection rather than payment, the signer is obliged to pay the amount due on the instrument to a person entitled to enforce the instrument in the same circumstances as the accommodated party would be obliged, without prior resort to the accommodated party by the person entitled to enforce the instrument.

（f）An accommodation party who pays the instrument is entitled to reimbursement from the accommodated party and is entitled to enforce the instrument against the accommodated party. In proper circumstances, an accommodation party may obtain relief that requires the

通方，无权对融通方进行追索，也无权要求融通方分担付款。

accommodated party to perform its obligations on the instrument.An accommodated party that pays the instrument has no right of recourse against, and is not entitled to contribution from, an accommodation party.

第 3.420 条　侵占票据

§ 3.420. Conversion of Instrument.

（a）适用于动产侵占的法律，也适用于票据。此外，如果通过转让从无权强制履行票据的人取得票据，且该转让不属于流通，或如果银行代表任何人就票据作出付款或取得付款，但该人无权强制履行票据或取得付款，此等情况亦构成对票据的侵占。下列人无权就票据的侵占提起诉讼：

（a）The law applicable to conversion of personal property applies to instruments.An instrument is also converted if it is taken by transfer, other than a negotiation, from a person not entitled to enforce the instrument or a bank makes or obtains payment with respect to the instrument for a person not entitled to enforce the instrument or receive payment.An action for conversion of an instrument may not be brought by:

（1）票据的立票人或承兑人；或

（1）the issuer or acceptor of the instrument; or

（2）票据的受款人或被背书人，只要其未收到票据的交付，无论是直接交付，还是其代理人或共同受款人取得的交付。

（2）a payee or indorsee who did not receive delivery of the instrument either directly or through delivery to an agent or a co-payee.

（b）根据（a）款提起的诉讼，责任限度被假定为票据的应付金额，且赔偿金额不得超过原告的票据权益金额。

（b）In an action under Subsection（a）, the measure of liability is presumed to be the amount payable on the instrument, but recovery may not exceed the amount of the plaintiff's interest in the instrument.

（c）如果任何代表人（存款银行除外）以善意处理票据或其收益，但其所代表的人不是有权强制履行票据的人，则该代表人对有权强制履行票据

（c）A representative, other than a depositary bank, who has in good faith dealt with an instrument or its proceeds on behalf of one who was not the person entitled to enforce the instrument is not liable in conversion to that

的人承担的侵占责任，不超过该代表人尚未付出的收益金额。

person beyond the amount of any proceeds that it has not paid out.

第5章 拒 付

PART 5. DISHONOR

第3.501条 提示

（a）“提示”指有权强制履行票据的人提出的下列要求，也包括代表该人提出的下列要求：

（1）向受票人或有义务支付票据的人提出的票据付款要求，或对于在银行支付的本票或已承兑的汇票，向银行提出的票据付款要求；或

（2）向受票人提出的汇票承兑要求。

（b）下列原则受制于第4篇、当事方协议、清算行规则及类似规则：

（1）提示可在票据付款地点作出；如果票据应在位于美国的银行付款，则提示必须在票据付款地点作出。提示可用任何商业上合理的方式作出，包括口头、书面或电子形式。提示在下列时间生效：

（A）被提示人收到付款或承兑要求的时间；以及

（B）如果制票人、承兑人、

§ 3.501. Presentment.

（a）“Presentment” means a demand made by or on behalf of a person entitled to enforce an instrument to:

（1）pay the instrument made to the drawee or a party obliged to pay the instrument or, in the case of a note or accepted draft payable at a bank, to the bank;or

（2）accept a draft made to the drawee.

（b）The following rules are subject to Article 4, agreement of the parties, and clearing-house rules and the like:

（1）Presentment may be made at the place of payment of the instrument and must be made at the place of payment if the instrument is payable at a bank in the United States. Presentment may be made by any commercially reasonable means, including an oral, written, or electronic communication.Presentment is effective:

（A）when the demand for payment or acceptance is received by the person to whom presentment is made;and

（B）if made to any one of two or more

受票人或其他付款人不止一人，向其中任何一人作出提示的时间。

makers, acceptors, drawees, or other payors.

（2）如果被提示人提出要求，提示人必须：

（2）On demand of the person to whom presentment is made, the person making presentment must:

（A）出示票据；

（A）exhibit the instrument;

（B）提供合理的身份证明；如果代表另一人作出提示，还必须提供合理的授权证明；以及

（B）give reasonable identification and, if presentment is made on behalf of another person, reasonable evidence of authority to do so;and

（C）就收到的付款在票据上签名确认；或如果款已付清，则交出票据。

（C）sign a receipt on the instrument for any payment made or surrender the instrument if full payment is made.

（3）收到提示的当事方，可以作出下列行为而不构成对票据的拒付：

（3）Without dishonoring the instrument, the party to whom presentment is made may:

（A）在缺乏必要背书时，退回票据；或

（A）return the instrument for lack of a necessary indorsement;or

（B）在提示未能遵守票据条款、当事方协议或其他适用法时，拒绝付款或承兑。

（B）refuse payment or acceptance for failure of the presentment to comply with the terms of the instrument, an agreement of the parties, or other applicable law or rule.

（4）如果收到提示的当事方，就接收和处理被提示付款或承兑的票据，设立了不早于下午两点的截止时间，则对于截止时间之后收到的提示，该当事方可将其视为提示日后下一个营业日作出的提示。

（4）The party to whom presentment is made may treat presentment as occurring on the next business day after the day of presentment if the party to whom presentment is made has established a cutoff hour not earlier than 2 p.m. for the receipt and processing of instruments presented for payment or acceptance and presentment is made after the cutoff hour.

第 3.502 条　拒付

§ 3.502. Dishonor.

（a）下列原则适用于本票

（a）Dishonor of a note is governed by the

的拒付：

following rules:

（1）对于即时付款的本票，如果向制票人作出正常提示后，本票未在提示日获得付款，即属于拒付。

（1）If the note is payable on demand, the note is dishonored if presentment is duly made to the maker and the note is not paid on the day of presentment.

（2）如果本票不是即时付款，且系在银行付款或通过银行付款，或如果本票条款要求作出提示，则只要作出正常提示后，本票未在付款日或提示日（以晚者为准）获得付款，即属于拒付。

（2）If the note is not payable on demand and is payable at or through a bank or the terms of the note require presentment, the note is dishonored if presentment is duly made and the note is not paid on the day it becomes payable or the day of presentment, whichever is later.

（3）如果本票不是即时付款，且（2）款不适用，则只要本票未在付款日获得付款，即属于拒付。

（3）If the note is not payable on demand and Subdivision（2）does not apply, the note is dishonored if it is not paid on the day it becomes payable.

（b）下列原则适用于未承兑的汇票（跟单汇票除外）的拒付：

（b）Dishonor of an unaccepted draft other than a documentary draft is governed by the following rules:

（1）如果支票被正常提示给付款银行要求付款，但未要求在柜台立即付款，则只要付款银行及时退回支票，或根据第4.301条或第4.302条及时发出拒付通知或未付通知，或根据第4.302条对支票金额承担责任，即属于拒付。

（1）If a check is duly presented for payment to the payor bank otherwise than for immediate payment over the counter, the check is dishonored if the payor bank makes timely return of the check or sends timely notice of dishonor or nonpayment under Section 4.301 or 4.302, or becomes accountable for the amount of the check under Section 4.302.

（2）如果汇票属于即时付款，且（1）款不适用，则只要向受票人作出正常付款提示后，汇票未在提示日获得付款，即属于拒付。

（2）If a draft is payable on demand and Subdivision（1）does not apply, the draft is dishonored if presentment for payment is duly made to the drawee and the draft is not paid on the day of presentment.

（3）如果汇票应在汇票上

（3）If a draft is payable on a date stated in

注明的日期付款，下列情况构成对该汇票的拒付：

（A）向受票人作出正常付款提示后，汇票未在付款日或提示日（以晚者为准）获得付款；或

（B）在汇票付款日之前作出正常承兑提示后，汇票未在提示日获得承兑。

（4）如果汇票应在见票后或承兑后的一段时间届满时付款，则只要作出正常承兑提示后，汇票未在提示日获得承兑，即属于拒付。

（c）涉及未承兑的跟单汇票时，应根据（b）（2）款、（3）款和（4）款所述的原则，确定是否存在拒付；但是，付款或承兑可从上述各款要求的付款日或承兑日的下一日起，延至受票人第三个营业日结束之前；在这个时间内，不属于拒付。

（d）下列原则适用于已承兑的汇票的拒付：

（1）对于即时付款的汇票，只要向承兑人作出正常付款提示后，汇票未在当天获得付款，即属于拒付。

（2）如果汇票不是即时付款，只要向承兑人作出正常付款提示后，汇票未在付款日或提示日（以晚者为准）获得付款，

the draft, the draft is dishonored if:

（A）presentment for payment is duly made to the drawee and payment is not made on the day the draft becomes payable or the day of presentment, whichever is later;or

（B）presentment for acceptance is duly made before the day the draft becomes payable and the draft is not accepted on the day of presentment.

（4）If a draft is payable on elapse of a period of time after sight or acceptance, the draft is dishonored if presentment for acceptance is duly made and the draft is not accepted on the day of presentment.

（c）Dishonor of an unaccepted documentary draft occurs according to the rules stated in Subsections（b）（2）,（3）, and（4）, except that payment or acceptance may be delayed without dishonor until not later than the close of the third business day of the drawee following the day on which payment or acceptance is required by those subdivisions.

（d）Dishonor of an accepted draft is governed by the following rules:

（1）If the draft is payable on demand, the draft is dishonored if presentment for payment is duly made to the acceptor and the draft is not paid on the day of presentment.

（2）If the draft is not payable on demand, the draft is dishonored if presentment for payment is duly made to the acceptor and payment is not made on the day it becomes

即属于拒付。

payable or the day of presentment, whichever is later.

（e）在所有其他情况下，如果本条规定只有作出提示后才有可能发生拒付，但提示被第3.504条所免除，则票据即使未作出提示，只要未获得正常承兑或付款，即属于拒付。

（e）In any case in which presentment is otherwise required for dishonor under this section and presentment is excused under Section 3.504, dishonor occurs without presentment if the instrument is not duly accepted or paid.

（f）如果汇票由于未获得及时承兑被视为拒付，但有权获得承兑的人同意将承兑延迟，则从作出承兑时起，汇票被视为从未发生过拒付。

（f）If a draft is dishonored because timely acceptance of the draft was not made and the person entitled to demand acceptance consents to a late acceptance, from the time of acceptance the draft is treated as never having been dishonored.

第3.503条　拒付通知

§ 3.503. Notice of Dishonor.

（a）在满足下列条件之前，不得强制履行背书人在第3.415条（a）款项下的义务，以及出票人在第3.414条（d）款项下的义务：

（a）The obligation of an indorser stated in Section 3.415（a）and the obligation of a drawer stated in Section 3.414（d）may not be enforced unless:

（1）已向背书人或出票人作出符合本条规定的票据拒付通知；或

（1）the indorser or drawer is given notice of dishonor of the instrument complying with this section;or

（2）根据第3.504条（b）款，拒付通知被免除。

（2）notice of dishonor is excused under Section 3.504（b）.

（b）拒付通知可由任何人作出，并可使用任何商业上合理的方式，包括口头、书面或电子形式。如果拒付通知合理指明票据，并说明票据已被拒付，或说明票据未获得付款或承兑，通知即为充分。将银行用于收款的票据退回，亦构成

（b）Notice of dishonor may be given by any person;may be given by any commercially reasonable means, including an oral, written, or electronic communication;and is sufficient if it reasonably identifies the instrument and indicates that the instrument has been dishonored or has not been paid or accepted. Return of an instrument given to a bank for

充分的拒付通知。

（c）除第3.504条（c）款另有规定外，涉及收款银行收到的用于收款的票据时：（i）该收款银行在收到票据拒付通知后，应在收到通知之银行营业日的下一个银行营业日午夜之前，发出拒付通知，或（ii）任何其他人在收到拒付通知后，应从收到通知之次日起30日内，发出拒付通知。涉及任何其他票据时，拒付通知必须从拒付发生之次日起三十日内发出。

collection is sufficient notice of dishonor.

（c）Subject to Section 3.504（c）, with respect to an instrument taken for collection by a collecting bank, notice of dishonor must be given（i）by the bank before midnight of the next banking day following the banking day on which the bank receives notice of dishonor of the instrument, or（ii）by any other person within 30 days following the day on which the person receives notice of dishonor.With respect to any other instrument, notice of dishonor must be given within 30 days following the day on which dishonor occurs.

第3.504条　提示和拒付通知的免除

§ 3.504. Excused Presentment and Notice of Dishonor.

（a）票据的付款提示或承兑提示，在下列情况下被免除：

（1）有权提示票据的人，经过合理努力后无法作出提示；

（2）制票人或承兑人已就票据支付义务毁约，或已死亡，或已进入破产程序；

（3）根据票据条款，无须提示即可强制履行背书人或出票人的义务；

（4）被强制履行义务的出票人或背书人，已放弃对提示的要求，或已因其他原因，无理由期待或无权要求票据获得付款或承兑；或

（5）出票人曾指示受票人

（a）Presentment for payment or acceptance of an instrument is excused if:

（1）the person entitled to present the instrument cannot with reasonable diligence make presentment;

（2）the maker or acceptor has repudiated an obligation to pay the instrument or is dead or in insolvency proceedings;

（3）by the terms of the instrument presentment is not necessary to enforce the obligation of indorsers or the drawer;

（4）the drawer or indorser whose obligation is being enforced has waived presentment or otherwise has no reason to expect or right to require that the instrument be paid or accepted;or

（5）the drawer instructed the drawee not

不得支付或承兑汇票，或受票人不对出票人承担支付汇票的义务。

to pay or accept the draft or the drawee was not obligated to the drawer to pay the draft.

（b）拒付通知在下列情况下被免除：（i）根据票据条款，无须作出拒付通知即可强制履行当事方之支付票据的义务；或（ii）被强制履行义务的当事方，放弃了对拒付通知的要求。放弃对提示的要求，即同时构成对拒付通知的放弃。

（b）Notice of dishonor is excused if（i）by the terms of the instrument notice of dishonor is not necessary to enforce the obligation of a party to pay the instrument, or（ii）the party whose obligation is being enforced waived notice of dishonor.A waiver of presentment is also a waiver of notice of dishonor.

（c）如果延迟作出拒付通知，但延迟系由于超出通知人控制的因素引起，且通知人在延迟原因消失后尽了合理努力，通知人即无须对该延迟承担责任。

（c）Delay in giving notice of dishonor is excused if the delay was caused by circumstances beyond the control of the person giving the notice and the person giving the notice exercised reasonable diligence after the cause of the delay ceased to operate.

第 3.505 条 拒付的证明

§ 3.505. Evidence of Dishonor.

（a）下列证据属于可采纳的证据，并构成假定，即其中所述的拒付和拒付通知系属存在：

（a）The following are admissible as evidence and create a presumption of dishonor and of any notice of dishonor stated:

（1）下列（b）款所述的格式正常并注明为拒付书的文件；

（1）a document regular in form as provided in Subsection（b）that purports to be a protest;

（2）票据上或伴随票据的印章或文字，显示来自于受票人、付款银行或提示银行，并说明承兑或付款已被拒绝；但是，说明了拒绝理由，但该理由不属于拒付的印章或文字除外；

（2）a purported stamp or writing of the drawee, payor bank, or presenting bank on or accompanying the instrument stating that acceptance or payment has been refused unless reasons for the refusal are stated and the reasons are not consistent with dishonor;

（3）受票人、付款银行或

（3）a book or record of the drawee, payor

收款银行在日常业务中保存的显示拒付的账目或记录，即使缺乏可以确认录入人的证据。

bank, or collecting bank that is kept in the usual course of business and that shows dishonor, even if there is no evidence of who made the entry.

（b）拒付书是下列人出具的拒付证书：美国的领事或副领事、公证员或根据拒付发生地法律有权记录证言的其他人。该人可根据其认为可以接受的信息出具拒付书。拒付书必须指明票据，并确认已作出提示，或如果未作出提示，确认未提示的原因，然后确认票据由于未付款或未承兑而被视为拒付。拒付书还可以确认，拒付通知已发给某些或全部当事方。

（b）A protest is a certificate of dishonor made by a United States consul or vice consul, or a notary public or other person authorized to administer oaths by the law of the place where dishonor occurs.It may be made on information satisfactory to that person.The protest must identify the instrument and certify either that presentment has been made or, if not made, the reason why it was not made, and that the instrument has been dishonored by nonacceptance or nonpayment.The protest may also certify that notice of dishonor has been given to some or all parties.

第3.506条　支付工具之执票人的手续费

§ 3.506. Processing Fee by Holder of Payment Device.

（a）为本条目的，“支付工具”指任何支票、票证、纸质或电子形式的付款，或作为付款媒介的其他支付工具。

（a）For purposes of this section, “payment device” means any check, item, paper or electronic payment, or other payment device used as a medium for payment.

（b）如果付款人对支付工具作出拒付，并将支付工具退回给执票人，则执票人，或执票人的受让人、代理人或代表人，或受执票人委托就被拒付之支付工具票面价值收款的其他人，可向出票人或背书人收取不超过30美元的合理手续费。

（b）On return of a payment device to the holder following dishonor of the payment device by a payor, the holder, the holder’s assignee, agent, or representative, or any other person retained by the holder to seek collection of the face value of the dishonored payment device may charge the drawer or indorser a reasonable processing fee of not more than $30.

第6章　解除义务和付款

PART 6. DISCHARGE AND PAYMENT

第 3.601 条　解除义务；解除义务的效力

§ 3.601. Discharge and Effect of Discharge.

（a）当事方支付票据的义务，可以根据本篇规定被解除，也可以通过对该当事方作出的行为或与该当事方达成的协议被解除，只要该行为或协议足以解除简式合同项下支付金钱的义务。

（a）The obligation of a party to pay the instrument is discharged as stated in this Article or by an act or agreement with the party that would discharge an obligation to pay money under a simple contract.

（b）如果任何人在取得正当执票人的权利时，未得到解除义务的通知，则任何当事方的义务解除，对该人不具效力。

（b）Discharge of the obligation of a party is not effective against a person acquiring rights of a holder in due course of the instrument without notice of the discharge.

第 3.602 条　付款

§ 3.602. Payment.

（a）除（e）款另有规定外，如果承担票据支付义务的当事方或其代表人，向有权强制履行票据的人作出付款，票据即被视为获得付款。

（a）Subject to Subsection（e）, an instrument is paid to the extent payment is made by or on behalf of a party obliged to pay the instrument, and to a person entitled to enforce the instrument.

（b）除（e）款另有规定外，如果承担本票支付义务的当事方或其代表人，向曾经有权强制履行本票的人作出付款，本票即被视为获得付款，只要在付款当时，有支付义务的当事方未得到充分通知，即本票已被转让，因此付款本应向受让人作出。通知必须经转让人或受让人签名，合理指明被转让的本票，并提供用于随后付款

（b）Subject to Subsection（e）, a note is paid to the extent payment is made by or on behalf of a party obliged to pay the note to a person that formerly was entitled to enforce the note only if at the time of the payment the party obliged to pay has not received adequate notification that the note has been transferred and that payment is to be made to the transferee. A notification is adequate only if it is signed by the transferor or the transferee, reasonably identifies the transferred note, and provides an

的地址，方为充分。受让人在收到要求时，应及时提供本票已被转让的合理证明。如果受让人未能满足该要求，则为（c）款目的，向曾经有权强制履行本票的人作出的付款系属有效，即使有义务支付本票的人，已收到了本款所述的通知。

address at which payments subsequently are to be made.Upon request, a transferee shall seasonably furnish reasonable proof that the note has been transferred.Unless the transferee complies with the request, a payment to the person that formerly was entitled to enforce the note is effective for purposes of Subsection（c）even if the party obliged to pay the note has received a notification under this subsection.

（c）除（e）款另有规定外，如果承担票据支付义务的当事方作出（a）款和（b）款所述的付款，其付款义务即被解除，即使其在支付票据时，知道另一人根据第 3.306 条对票据持有索赔。

（c）Subject to Subsection（e），to the extent of a payment under Subsections（a）and（b），the obligation of the party obliged to pay the instrument is discharged even though payment is made with knowledge of a claim to the instrument under Section 3.306 by another person.

（d）除（e）款另有规定外，受让人或直接或间接从受让人取得票据权利的任何当事方，包括享有正当执票人权利的此种当事方，对于在本票被转让给受让人之后但在有义务支付本票的当事方收到有关转让的充分通知之前作出的（b）款所述的付款，被视为得到该付款的通知。

（d）Subject to Subsection（e），a transferee, or any party that has acquired rights in the instrument directly or indirectly from a transferee, including any such party that has rights as a holder in due course, is deemed to have notice of any payment that is made under Subsection（b）after the date that the note is transferred to the transferee but before the party obliged to pay the note receives adequate notification of the transfer.

（e）如果存在下列情况，当事方支付票据的义务不能根据（a）款至（d）款得到解除：

（e）The obligation of a party to pay the instrument is not discharged under Subsections（a）through（d）if:

（1）第 3.306 条所述的票据索赔可对收到付款的当事方强制履行，同时：

（1）a claim to the instrument under Section 3.306 is enforceable against the party receiving payment and:

（A）付款人在作出付款时

（A）payment is made with knowledge

知道，有管辖权的法院已发出禁令或类似命令，禁止该付款；或

by the payor that payment is prohibited by injunction or similar process of a court of competent jurisdiction;or

（B）涉及银行本票、银行支票或保兑支票以外的票据时，作出付款的当事方从对票据持有索赔的人接受了赔偿保证，即如果有权强制履行票据的人未能得到付款，该索赔人将赔偿所产生的损失；或

（B）in the case of an instrument other than a cashier's check, teller's check, or certified check, the party making payment accepted, from the person having a claim to the instrument, indemnity against loss resulting from refusal to pay the person entitled to enforce the instrument;or

（2）作出付款的人知道票据系被盗票据，且知道获得付款的人系不当占有票据。

（2）the person making payment knows that the instrument is a stolen instrument and pays a person it knows is in wrongful possession of the instrument.

（f）在本条中，涉及非书面记录时，如果该记录以电子符号、声音或程序体现，"签名"指该记录的附件或指与该记录有逻辑联系的其他表达，只要该附件或表达当时的目的是采纳或接受该记录。

（f）As used in this section, "signed," with respect to a record that is not a writing, includes the attachment to or logical association with the record of an electronic symbol, sound, or process with the present intent to adopt or accept the record.

第 3.603 条　付款表示

§ 3.603. Tender of Payment.

（a）如果向有权强制履行票据的人作出履行票据支付义务的表示，则该表示的效力，应根据适用于简式合同项下付款表示的相关法律原则确定。

（a）If tender of payment of an obligation to pay an instrument is made to a person entitled to enforce the instrument, the effect of tender is governed by principles of law applicable to tender of payment under a simple contract.

（b）如果向有权强制履行票据的人作出履行票据支付义务的表示，但该表示被拒绝，则在表示支付之金额的限度内，对相关付款义务拥有追索权之

（b）If tender of payment of an obligation to pay an instrument is made to a person entitled to enforce the instrument and the tender is refused, there is discharge, to the extent of the amount of the tender, of the obligation of

背书人和融通方的义务即被解除。

an indorser or accommodation party having a right of recourse with respect to the obligation to which the tender relates.

（c）如果向有权强制履行票据的人作出支付票据到期金额的表示，则对于到期日之后相关金额的利息，义务人的义务即被解除。如果票据需要提示，且义务人有能力并已准备好于到期日在票据注明的任何一个付款地点付款，该义务人即被视为已向有权强制履行票据的人作出在到期日付款的表示。

（c）If tender of payment of an amount due on an instrument is made to a person entitled to enforce the instrument, the obligation of the obligor to pay interest after the due date on the amount tendered is discharged.If presentment is required with respect to an instrument and the obligor is able and ready to pay on the due date at every place of payment stated in the instrument, the obligor is deemed to have made tender of payment on the due date to the person entitled to enforce the instrument.

第 3.604 条　注销或弃权引起的义务解除

§ 3.604. Discharge by Cancellation or Renunciation.

（a）无论是否存在对价，有权强制履行票据的人，均可通过下列方式，解除任何当事方的票据支付义务：

（a）A person entitled to enforce an instrument, with or without consideration, may discharge the obligation of a party to pay the instrument:

（1）通过有意的自愿行为作出解除，例如把票据交回该当事方，销毁、剪缺或注销票据，取消或划掉该当事方的签名，或在票据上加注解除义务的文字；或

（1）by an intentional voluntary act, such as surrender of the instrument to the party, destruction, mutilation, or cancellation of the instrument, cancellation or striking out of the party's signature, or the addition of words to the instrument indicating discharge;or

（2）在签名的记录中同意不起诉该当事方，或以其他方式放弃对抗该当事方的权利。

（2）by agreeing not to sue or otherwise renouncing rights against the party by a signed record.

（b）任何当事方从任何背书取得的地位或权利，不受根据（a）款取消或划掉该背书的影响。

（b）Cancellation or striking out of an indorsement pursuant to Subsection（a）does not affect the status and rights of a party derived from the indorsement.

（c）在本条中，涉及非书面记录时，如果该记录以电子符号、声音或程序体现，“签名”指该记录的附件或指与该记录有逻辑联系的其他表达，只要该附件或表达当时的目的是采纳或接受该记录。

（c）In this section, “signed,” with respect to a record that is not a writing, includes the attachment to or logical association with the record of an electronic symbol, sound, or process with the present intent to adopt or accept the record.

第 3.605 条　次义务人的义务解除

§ 3.605. Discharge of Secondary Obligors.

（a）如果有权强制履行票据的人，全部或部分解除了主义务人的义务，且相对于主义务人的义务，票据的另一当事方为次义务人，则应适用下列原则：

（a）If a person entitled to enforce an instrument releases the obligation of a principal obligor in whole or in part, and another party to the instrument is a secondary obligor with respect to the obligation of that principal obligor, the following rules apply:

（1）如果次义务人已作出付款，主义务人基于该付款对次义务人承担的义务不受影响。但是，除非解除义务的条款保留了次义务人的追索权，否则，在解除条款的范围内，主义务人在本篇项下对次义务人的任何其他义务均被解除。

（1）Any obligations of the principal obligor to the secondary obligor with respect to any previous payment by the secondary obligor are not affected.Unless the terms of the release preserve the secondary obligor’s recourse, the principal obligor is discharged, to the extent of the release, from any other duties to the secondary obligor under this Article.

（2）除非解除条款规定，有权强制履行票据的人，保留对次义务人强制履行票据的权利，否则，次义务人将和主义务人在同等程度上被解除票据的任何尚未履行的义务。如果票据是支票，且次义务人基于背书对支票承担责任，则无论解除义务使用何种语言或基于何种情况，次义务人的义务均

（2）Unless the terms of the release provide that the person entitled to enforce the instrument retains the right to enforce the instrument against the secondary obligor, the secondary obligor is discharged to the same extent as the principal obligor from any unperformed portion of its obligation on the instrument.If the instrument is a check and the obligation of the secondary obligor is based on an indorsement of the check, the secondary

被解除。

obligor is discharged without regard to the language or circumstances of the discharge or other release.

（3）如果次义务人未根据（2）款被解除义务，则在为该解除所支付之对价的价值的限度内，并在该解除对次义务人所造成之损失的范围内，次义务人被解除义务。

（3）If the secondary obligor is not discharged under Subdivision（2）, the secondary obligor is discharged to the extent of the value of the consideration for the release, and to the extent that the release would otherwise cause the secondary obligor a loss.

（b）如果有权强制履行票据的人，就票据到期的一笔或多笔付款，给主义务人一段时间的延期，且相对于主义务人的义务，票据的另一当事方为次义务人，则应适用下列原则：

（b）If a person entitled to enforce an instrument grants a principal obligor an extension of the time at which one or more payments are due on the instrument and another party to the instrument is a secondary obligor with respect to the obligation of that principal obligor, the following rules apply:

（1）如果次义务人已作出付款，主义务人基于该付款对次义务人承担的义务不受影响。但是，除非延期的条款保留了次义务人的追索权，否则，主义务人在本篇项下对次义务人的任何其他义务，其履行时间均被相应延期。

（1）Any obligations of the principal obligor to the secondary obligor with respect to any previous payment by the secondary obligor are not affected.Unless the terms of the extension preserve the secondary obligor's recourse, the extension correspondingly extends the time for performance of any other duties owed to the secondary obligor by the principal obligor under this Article.

（2）如果延期给次义务人造成其他损失，则在损失的限度内，次义务人被解除义务。

（2）The secondary obligor is discharged to the extent that the extension would otherwise cause the secondary obligor a loss.

（3）如果次义务人未根据（2）款被解除义务，则对于未被解除的义务，次义务人可按付款时间未曾被延期一样，向有权强制履行票据的人履行义

（3）To the extent that the secondary obligor is not discharged under Subdivision（2）, the secondary obligor may perform its obligations to a person entitled to enforce the instrument as if the time for payment had

务；或者，次义务人可认为其履行义务的时间也被相应延期，除非延期条款规定，有权强制履行票据的人保留权利，可按付款时间未曾被延期一样，对次义务人强制履行票据。

not been extended or, unless the terms of the extension provide that the person entitled to enforce the instrument retains the right to enforce the instrument against the secondary obligor as if the time for payment had not been extended, treat the time for performance of its obligations as having been extended correspondingly.

（c）无论是否存在对价，如果有权强制履行票据的人，同意修改主义务人的义务，但并非全部或部分解除义务，亦非延长到期日，且相对于主义务人的义务，票据的另一当事方为次义务人，则应适用下列原则：

（c）If a person entitled to enforce an instrument agrees, with or without consideration, to a modification of the obligation of a principal obligor other than a complete or partial release or an extension of the due date and another party to the instrument is a secondary obligor with respect to the obligation of that principal obligor, the following rules apply:

（1）如果次义务人已作出付款，主义务人基于该付款对次义务人承担的义务不受影响。主义务人在本篇项下对次义务人的任何其他义务，均被相应修改。

（1）Any obligations of the principal obligor to the secondary obligor with respect to any previous payment by the secondary obligor are not affected.The modification correspondingly modifies any other duties owed to the secondary obligor by the principal obligor under this Article.

（2）如果修改给次义务人造成其他损失，则在损失的限度内，次义务人尚未履行的任何义务即被解除。

（2）The secondary obligor is discharged from any unperformed portion of its obligation to the extent that the modification would otherwise cause the secondary obligor a loss.

（3）如果次义务人未根据（2）款被解除义务，则对于未被解除的义务，次义务人可按修改未曾发生一样履行其票据义务，但也可认为其票据义务已被相应修改。

（3）To the extent that the secondary obligor is not discharged under Subdivision（2）, the secondary obligor may satisfy its obligation on the instrument as if the modification had not occurred, or treat its obligation on the instrument as having been modified correspondingly.

（d）如果主义务人的义务由担保物中的权益担保，且票据另一当事方为该义务的次义务人，且有权强制履行票据的人损害了担保物中之权益的价值，则在所造成之损害的限度内，次义务人的义务即被解除。如果权益的价值降至低于次义务人的追索权金额，或如果权益价值的降低导致追索权金额进一步高于权益的价值，则在受影响的限度内，担保物中之权益的价值被视为受到损害。为本款目的，对担保物中之权益价值的损害，包括下列行为：未能就担保物中之权益取得或维持其完善或登记；将担保物释放，但未能取得相等价值的替代担保物，或未能相应减少基础义务的金额；未能履行根据第 9 篇或其他法律，对义务人或其他次义务人承担的义务，维持担保物的价值；以及，在处置担保物中之权益或以其他方式强制履行担保物中之权益时，未能遵守相关法律。

（d）If the obligation of a principal obligor is secured by an interest in collateral, another party to the instrument is a secondary obligor with respect to that obligation, and a person entitled to enforce the instrument impairs the value of the interest in collateral, the obligation of the secondary obligor is discharged to the extent of the impairment.The value of an interest in collateral is impaired to the extent the value of the interest is reduced to an amount less than the amount of the recourse of the secondary obligor, or the reduction in value of the interest causes an increase in the amount by which the amount of the recourse exceeds the value of the interest.For purposes of this subsection, impairing the value of an interest in collateral includes failure to obtain or maintain perfection or recordation of the interest in collateral, release of collateral without substitution of collateral of equal value or equivalent reduction of the underlying obligation, failure to perform a duty to preserve the value of collateral owed, under Article 9 or other law, to a debtor or other person secondarily liable, and failure to comply with applicable law in disposing of or otherwise enforcing the interest in collateral.

（e）除非有权强制履行票据的人知道次义务人为次义务人，或根据第 3.419 条（c）款得到票据签名系用于融通的通知，否则，次义务人即不能根

（e）A secondary obligor is not discharged under Subsection（a）（3），（b），（c），or（d）unless the person entitled to enforce the instrument knows that the person is a secondary obligor or has notice under Section

据（a）（3）款、（b）款、（c）款或（d）款被解除义务。

3.419（c）that the instrument was signed for accommodation.

（f）在下列情况下，次义务人不能根据本条被解除义务：次义务人对构成解除义务的事件或行为给予同意；票据或当事方另外的协议特别规定，放弃本条项下的义务解除；票据或该协议概括规定，当事方放弃基于担保或基于担保物损害所拥有的抗辩。除客观情况另有显示外，如果一项行为会导致本条所述的义务解除，则主义务人对该行为的同意，即构成次义务人对该行为的同意，只要次义务人控制主义务人，或在与有权强制履行票据的人进行交往时，代表主义务人。

（f）A secondary obligor is not discharged under this section if the secondary obligor consents to the event or conduct that is the basis of the discharge, or the instrument or a separate agreement of the party provides for waiver of discharge under this section specifically or by general language indicating that parties waive defenses based on suretyship or impairment of collateral.Unless the circumstances indicate otherwise, consent by the principal obligor to an act that would lead to a discharge under this section constitutes consent to that act by the secondary obligor if the secondary obligor controls the principal obligor or deals with the person entitled to enforce the instrument on behalf of the principal obligor.

（g）如果解除义务或延期的条款规定，有权强制履行票据的人，保留对次义务人强制履行票据的权利，则该义务解除或延期，即保留次义务人的追索权。次义务人的追索权，如同该义务解除或延期未发生一样，继续存在。

（g）A release or extension preserves a secondary obligor's recourse if the terms of the release or extension provide that the person entitled to enforce the instrument retains the right to enforce the instrument against the secondary obligor.The recourse of the secondary obligor continues as though the release or extension had not been granted.

（h）除（i）款另有规定外，次义务人如果根据本条主张义务解除，即应承担举证责任，证明发生了所声称的对次义务人的损害行为，并同时证明该行为所造成的损失或损害。

（h）Except as otherwise provided in Subsection（i）, a secondary obligor asserting discharge under this section has the burden of persuasion both with respect to the occurrence of the acts alleged to harm the secondary obligor and loss or prejudice caused by those acts.

（i）如果次义务人能够证明因追索权受到损害而受到损失，且该案的客观情况表明，损失的金额无法合理计算，或计算所需的事实无法获得，此时应假定，损害追索权之行为所造成的损失或损害，等于次义务人的对票据承担的义务。此时，证明损失小于该金额的举证责任，由有权强制履行票据的人承担。

(i) If the secondary obligor demonstrates prejudice caused by an impairment of its recourse, and the circumstances of the case indicate that the amount of loss is not reasonably susceptible of calculation or requires proof of facts that are not ascertainable, it is presumed that the act impairing recourse caused a loss or impairment equal to the liability of the secondary obligor on the instrument.In that event, the burden of persuasion as to any lesser amount of the loss is on the person entitled to enforce the instrument.

词汇索引

保兑支票	certified check	第 3.409 条（d）
背书	indorsement	第 3.204 条（a）
背书人	indorser	第 3.204 条（b）
本票	note	第 3.104 条（e）
不完整票据	incomplete instrument	第 3.115 条（a）
承兑	acceptance	第 3.409 条（a）
承兑人	acceptor	第 3.103 条（a）（1）
承诺	promise	第 3.103 条（a）（12）
出立	issue	第 3.105 条（a）
出票人	drawer	第 3.103 条（a）（5）
次义务人	secondary obligor	第 3.103 条（a）（17）
存款凭证	certificate of deposit	第 3.104 条（j）
当事方	party	第 3.103 条（a）（10）
定时付款	payable at a definite time	第 3.108 条（b）
对价	consideration	第 3.303 条（b）
付款	payment	第 3.602 条（a）
汇付人	remitter	第 3.103 条（a）（15）
汇票	draft	第 3.104 条（e）
第三方汇票	demand draft	第 3.104 条（k）
即时付款	payable on demand	第 3.108 条（a）
记名背书	special indorsement	第 3.205 条（a）
价值	value	第 3.303 条
拒付	dishonor	第 3.502 条

续表

空白背书	blank indorsement	第 3.205 条（b）
立票人	issuer	第 3.105 条（c）
流通	negotiation	第 3.201 条（a）
流通票据	negotiable instrument	第 3.104 条（a）
旅行支票	traveler's check	第 3.104 条（i）
命令	order	第 3.103 条（a）（8）
票据	instrument	第 3.104 条（b）
票据转让	transfer of instrument	第 3.203 条（b）
凭令付款	payable to order	第 3.109 条（b）
凭票付款	payable to bearer	第 3.109 条（a）
融通方	accommodation party	第 3.419 条（a）
受票人	drawee	第 3.103 条（a）（4）
受融通方	accommodated party	第 3.419 条（a）
提示	presentment	第 3.501 条（a）
涂改	alteration	第 3.407 条（a）
限制性背书	restrictive indorsement	第 3.206 条
消费者交易	consumer transaction	第 3.103 条（a）（3）
消费者账户	consumer account	第 3.103 条（a）（2）
异常背书	anomalous indorsement	第 3.205 条（d）
银行本票	cashier's check	第 3.104 条（g）
银行支票	teller's check	第 3.104 条（h）
有权强制履行的人	person entitled to enforce	第 3.301 条
远程制作的票证	remotely-created item	第 3.103 条（a）（16）
再取得	reacquisition	第 3.207 条
正常谨慎	ordinary care	第 3.103 条（a）（9）
正当执票人	holder in due course	第 3.302 条（a）
证明	prove	第 3.103 条（a）（13）
支票	check	第 3.104 条（f）
制票人	maker	第 3.103 条（a）（7）
主义务人	principal obligor	第 3.103 条（a）（11）

第4篇 银行存款和收款

ARTICLE 4. BANK DEPOSITS AND COLLECTIONS

第1章 总则和定义

PART 1. GENERAL PROVISIONS AND DEFINITIONS

第 4.101 条 简称

本篇被引用时可称为《统一商法典——银行存款和收款》。

第 4.102 条 适用范围

（a）如果本篇范围内的票证同时也在第 3 篇和第 8 篇范围之内，则在相关范围内，该票证亦受第 3 篇和第 8 篇的约束。如果存在冲突，本篇优于第 3 篇，第 8 篇优于本篇。

（b）银行在处理票证的提示、付款或收款时，银行之作为或不作为的责任，应适用银行所在州的法律。涉及银行之分行或独立营业厅的作为或不作为时，或涉及在分行或独立营业厅发生的作为或不作为时，银行的责任应适用该分行或独立营业厅所在州的法律。

§ 4.101. Short Title.

This Article may be cited as Uniform Commercial Code—Bank Deposits and Collections.

§ 4.102. Applicability.

（a）To the extent that items within this Article are also within Articles 3 and 8, they are subject to those Articles.If there is conflict, this Article governs Article 3, but Article 8 governs this Article.

（b）The liability of a bank for action or non-action with respect to an item handled by it for purposes of presentment, payment, or collection is governed by the law of the place where the bank is located.In the case of action or non-action by or at a branch or separate office of a bank, its liability is governed by the law of the place where the branch or separate office is located.

（c）即使有第 1.301 条的规定，在涉及银行与消费者账户持有人之间的存款合同时，只要接受存款合同的银行分行或独立营业厅位于本州，即应适用本州的法律。为本款目的，“消费者账户持有人”指主要为个人、家庭或家用目的持有存款账户的个人，但以职业身份为他人持有账户的个人除外。

（c）Notwithstanding Section 1.301, the laws of this state govern a deposit contract between a bank and a consumer account holder if the branch or separate office of the bank that accepts the deposit contract is located in this state.For purposes of this subsection, “consumer account holder” means a natural person who holds a deposit account primarily for personal, family, or household purposes but does not include a natural person who holds an account for another in a professional capacity.

第 4.103 条　通过协议加以改变；损失的计算；构成正常谨慎的行为

§ 4.103. Variation by Agreement; Measure of Damages;Action Constituting Ordinary Care.

（a）可以通过协议改变本篇条款的效力；但是，协议的当事方不得排除银行因缺乏善意或未能行使正常谨慎而应承担的责任，也不得为缺乏善意或未能行使正常谨慎限制损害赔偿金额。但是，当事方可以通过协议，确定衡量银行责任的标准，只要该标准不是明显不合理。

（a）The effect of the provisions of this Article may be varied by agreement, but the parties to the agreement cannot disclaim a bank’s responsibility for its lack of good faith or failure to exercise ordinary care or limit the measure of damages for the lack or failure.However, the parties may determine by agreement the standards by which the bank’s responsibility is to be measured if those standards are not manifestly unreasonable.

（b）联邦储备条例或实施细则、票证清算行规则或类似规则，具有（a）款所述之协议的效力，无论该等规则是否得到对相关票证拥有权益之全部当事方的特别同意。

（b）Federal Reserve regulations and operating circulars, clearing-house rules, and the like have the effect of agreements under Subsection（a）, whether or not specifically assented to by all parties interested in items handled.

（c）任何作为或不作为，只要被本篇允许，或符合联邦储备条例或实施细则，即属于

（c）Action or non-action approved by this Article or pursuant to Federal Reserve regulations or operating circulars is the exercise

行使了正常谨慎。任何作为或不作为，在没有特别指示的情况下，只要符合票证清算行规则或类似规则，或符合本篇不禁止的银行一般惯例，即构成行使正常谨慎的表面证据。

of ordinary care and, in the absence of special instructions, action or non-action consistent with clearing-house rules and the like or with a general banking usage not disapproved by this Article, is prima facie the exercise of ordinary care.

（d）即使本篇规定或认可某些程序，该规定或认可并不构成对具体情况下可能为合理的其他程序的否定。

（d）The specification or approval of certain procedures by this Article is not disapproval of other procedures that may be reasonable under the circumstances.

（e）处理票证时未能行使正常谨慎所造成的损失，为票证金额减去行使正常谨慎亦无法实现的金额；如果存在恶意，还包括主要因该恶意而使当事方受到的任何其他损失。

（e）The measure of damages for failure to exercise ordinary care in handling an item is the amount of the item reduced by an amount that could not have been realized by the exercise of ordinary care.If there is also bad faith, it includes any other damages the party suffered as a proximate consequence.

第 4.104 条　定义和定义索引

§ 4.104. Definitions and Index of Definitions.

（a）除上下文另有所指外，在本篇中：

（a）In this Article, unless the context otherwise requires:

（1）“账户”指在银行设立的任何存款账户或信贷账户，包括活期账户、定期账户、储蓄账户、存折账户、信贷合作社支票账户或类似账户，但不包括由存款凭证代表的账户。

（1）“Account” means any deposit or credit account with a bank, including a demand, time, savings, passbook, share draft, or like account, other than an account evidenced by a certificate of deposit.

（2）“下午”指一天中从正午到午夜的这段时间。

（2）“Afternoon” means the period of a day between noon and midnight.

（3）“银行营业日”指一天中银行对公众开放并处理几乎全部银行业务项目的这段时间。

（3）“Banking day” means the part of a day on which a bank is open to the public for carrying on substantially all of its banking functions.

（4）“票证清算行”指日常从事票证清算的银行联合会或其他付款人。

（4）“Clearing house” means an association of banks or other payors regularly clearing items.

（5）“客户”指在银行设立账户的人，或银行同意代其进行票证收款的人，也包括在其他银行设立账户的银行。

（5）“Customer” means a person having an account with a bank or for whom a bank has agreed to collect items, including a bank that maintains an account at another bank.

（6）“跟单汇票”指下列汇票：汇票在提示承兑或提示付款后，受票人或其他付款人需要先收到特定文件、票式证券（第 8.102 条）或无票证券的指示（第 8.102 条），或其他凭证、声明或类似材料，才能承兑或支付汇票。

（6）“Documentary draft” means a draft to be presented for acceptance or payment if specified documents, certificated securities（Section 8.102）or instructions for uncertificated securities（Section 8.102）, or other certificates, statements, or the like are to be received by the drawee or other payor before acceptance or payment of the draft.

（7）“汇票”指第 3.104 条所定义的汇票；或指不属于票据但构成命令的票证。

（7）“Draft” means a draft as defined in Section 3.104 or an item, other than an instrument, that is an order.

（8）“受票人”指汇票中被命令付款的人。

（8）“Drawee” means a person ordered in a draft to make payment.

（9）“票证”指银行出于收款或付款目的所处理的票据，或支付金钱的承诺或命令，但不包括受第 4A 篇约束的支付命令，也不包括信用卡或借记卡的记账凭单。

（9）“Item” means an instrument or a promise or order to pay money handled by a bank for collection or payment.The term does not include a payment order governed by Article 4A or a credit or debit card slip.

（10）涉及银行时，如果在任何银行营业日，银行收到有关票证或通知，或就有关行为开始计算时间（以迟者为准），则该日之下一个银行营业日的午夜，即为“午夜截止期”。

（10）“Midnight deadline” with respect to a bank is midnight on its next banking day following the banking day on which it receives the relevant item or notice or from which the time for taking action commences to run, whichever is later.

（11）“结算”指通过下列

（11）“Settle” means to pay in cash, by

方式作出支付：支付现金、通过票证清算行结算、作出借记或贷记、进行汇付，或以其他约定的方式支付。结算可以是临时的，也可以是最终的。

clearing-house settlement, in a charge or credit or by remittance, or otherwise as agreed.A settlement may be either provisional or final.

（12）涉及银行时，“暂停对外付款”指银行被主管当局关闭，或被政府官员接管，或在日常业务中停止或拒绝付款。

（12）“Suspends payments” with respect to a bank means that it has been closed by order of the supervisory authorities, that a public officer has been appointed to take it over, or that it ceases or refuses to make payments in the ordinary course of business.

（b）适用于本篇的其他定义及其所在位置：

“电子提示协议”　第 4.110 条

“银行”　第 4.105 条

“收款银行”　第 4.105 条

“存款银行”　第 4.105 条

“中间银行”　第 4.105 条

“付款银行”　第 4.105 条

“提示通知”　第 4.110 条

（b）Other definitions applying to this Article and the sections in which they appear are:

“Agreement for electronic presentment” Section 4.110.

“Bank” Section 4.105.

“Collecting bank” Section 4.105.

“Depositary bank” Section 4.105.

“Intermediary bank” Section 4.105.

“Payor bank” Section 4.105.

“Presentment notice” Section 4.110.

（c）其他各篇中的下列定义适用于本篇：

“承兑”　第 3.409 条

“涂改”　第 3.407 条

“银行本票”　第 3.104 条

“存款凭证”　第 3.104 条

“保兑支票”　第 3.409 条

“支票”　第 3.104 条

“正当执票人”　第 3.302 条

“票据”　第 3.104 条

“拒付通知”　第 3.503 条

（c）The following definitions in other Articles apply to this Article:

“Acceptance” Section 3.409.

“Alteration” Section 3.407.

“Cashier's check” Section 3.104.

“Certificate of deposit” Section 3.104.

“Certified check” Section 3.409.

“Check” Section 3.104.

“Holder in due course” Section 3.302.

“Instrument” Section 3.104.

“Notice of dishonor” Section 3.503.

"命令" 第3.103条

"正常谨慎" 第3.103条

"有权强制履行"的人 第3.301条

"提示" 第3.501条

"承诺" 第3.103条

"证明" 第3.103条

"记录" 第1.201条

"远程制作的票证" 第3.103条

"银行支票" 第3.104条

"无授权签名" 第3.403条

（d）此外，第1篇中的通用定义和解释原则适用于本篇通篇。

"Order" Section 3.103.

"Ordinary care" Section 3.103.

"Person entitled to enforce" Section 3.301.

"Presentment" Section 3.501.

"Promise" Section 3.103.

"Prove" Section 3.103.

"Record" Section 1.201.

"Remotely-created item" Section 3.103.

"Teller's check" Section 3.104.

"Unauthorized signature" Section 3.403.

（d）In addition, Article 1 contains general definitions and principles of construction and interpretation applicable throughout this Article.

第4.105条 "银行"；"存款银行"；"中间银行"；"收款银行"；"付款银行"；"提示银行"

§ 4.105. "Bank"; "Depositary Bank"; "Intermediary Bank"; "Collecting Bank"; "Payor Bank"; "Presenting Bank".

在本篇中：

（1）"银行"指从事银行业务的人，包括储蓄银行、储贷协会、信贷合作社或信托公司。

（2）"存款银行"指首个取得票证的银行，即使其亦为付款银行，除非票证系在柜台提示，用于即时付款。

（3）"付款银行"指汇票的受票人银行。

（4）"中间银行"指在收款

In this Article:

（1）"Bank" means a person engaged in the business of banking, including a savings bank, savings and loan association, credit union, or trust company.

（2）"Depositary bank" means the first bank to take an item even though it is also the payor bank, unless the item is presented for immediate payment over the counter.

（3）"Payor bank" means a bank that is the drawee of a draft.

（4）"Intermediary bank" means a bank

过程中取得票证转让的银行，但不包括存款银行和付款银行。

（5）“收款银行”指为收款而处理票证的银行，但不包括付款银行。

（6）“提示银行”指提示票证的银行，但不包括付款银行。

第 4.106 条　通过银行支付或在银行支付；收款银行

（a）如果票证标明，应“通过”票证上指明的银行付款，则该票证即：

（1）指定该银行为收款银行，但其本身并不授权该银行支付票证；并且

（2）只能由该银行或通过该银行作出付款提示。

（b）如果票证标明，应“在”票证上指明的银行付款，则该票证即相当于以该银行为受票人的汇票。

（c）如果汇票指定的受票人不是银行，且无法判断汇票上标注的一家银行是共同受票人还是收款银行，此时，该银行为收款银行。

第 4.107 条　银行的独立营业厅

涉及本篇或第 3 篇允许采取的行为或规定必须给出的通知或命令时，为确定采取行为或给出通知或命令的最迟时间，或确定其发生州或目的州，银

to which an item is transferred in course of collection except the depositary or payor bank.

（5）“Collecting bank” means a bank handling an item for collection except the payor bank.

（6）“Presenting bank” means a bank presenting an item except a payor bank.

§ 4.106. Payable Through or Payable at Bank; Collecting Bank.

（a）If an item states that it is “payable through” a bank identified in the item, the item:

（1）designates the bank as a collecting bank and does not by itself authorize the bank to pay the item;and

（2）may be presented for payment only by or through the bank.

（b）If an item states that it is “payable at” a bank identified in the item, the item is equivalent to a draft drawn on the bank.

（c）If a draft names a nonbank drawee and it is unclear whether a bank named in the draft is a co-drawee or a collecting bank, the bank is a collecting bank.

§ 4.107. Separate Office of a Bank.

A branch or separate office of a bank is a separate bank for the purpose of computing the time within which and determining the place at or to which action may be taken or notices or orders must be given under this Article and

行的分行或独立营业厅被视为独立的银行。

under Article 3.

第 4.108 条　收到票证的时间

§ 4.108. Time of Receipt of Items.

（a）为留出时间处理票证、核对收支并作出必要入账以确定当日账目，银行可将钱款和票证之受理业务的截止时间，以及进行项目入账的截止时间，定为下午两点或更晚的一个时间。

（a）For the purpose of allowing time to process items, prove balances, and make the necessary entries on its books to determine its position for the day, a bank may fix an afternoon hour of two P.M. or later as a cutoff hour for the handling of money and items and the making of entries on its books.

（b）在任何一天的上述截止时间之后或银行营业日结束之后收到的票证或存款，可被视为在下一个银行营业日开始时收到。

（b）An item or deposit of money received on any day after a cutoff hour so fixed or after the close of the banking day may be treated as being received at the opening of the next banking day.

第 4.109 条　延迟

§ 4.109. Delays.

（a）除另有指示外，当票证指明的付款人不是银行时，只要收款银行系为取得票证付款而善意作出努力，则无论是否得到有关人的批准，收款银行均可放弃、修改或延长本法所规定或允许的时间限制，但最多不超过额外的两个银行营业日。收款银行的此种行为，不解除出票人或背书人的义务，也不使收款银行对其转让人或任何前手当事方承担责任。

（a）Unless otherwise instructed, a collecting bank in a good faith effort to secure payment of a specific item drawn on a payor other than a bank, and with or without the approval of any person involved, may waive, modify, or extend time limits imposed or permitted by this Act for a period not exceeding two additional banking days without discharge of drawers or indorsers or liability to its transferor or a prior party.

（b）在下列情况下，即使收款银行或付款银行出现延迟，超出了本法或其他指示所规定或允许的时间，银行亦无须承

（b）Delay by a collecting bank or payor bank beyond time limits prescribed or permitted by this Act or by instructions is excused if:

担责任：

（1）延迟系因通信或计算机设备故障、其他银行暂停对外付款、战争、紧急情况、设备故障，或其他超出银行控制的原因引起；并且

（2）银行行使了当时情况下所需的勤勉。

第 4.110 条　电子提示

（a）“电子提示协议”指涉及票证提示的协议、票证清算行规则、联邦储备条例或实施细则，只要其允许通过传送票证的图像或描述信息（“提示通知”）作出提示，而无须交付票证本身。该协议可以规定票证的保留、提示、付款和拒付程序，以及协议项下之票证的其他事项。

（b）对于提示协议项下的票证，收到提示通知即被视为作出提示。

（c）如果通过提示通知作出提示，则本篇在提到“票证”或“支票”时，即指提示通知，除非上下文另有所指。

第 4.111 条　诉讼时效

强制履行本篇项下之债务、义务或权利的诉讼，必须在诉讼原因产生后三年内提起。

（1）the delay is caused by interruption of communication or computer facilities, suspension of payments by another bank, war, emergency conditions, failure of equipment, or other circumstances beyond the control of the bank;and

（2）the bank exercises such diligence as the circumstances require.

§ 4.110. Electronic Presentment.

（a）“Agreement for electronic presentment” means an agreement, clearing-house rule, or Federal Reserve regulation or operating circular providing that presentment of an item may be made by transmission of an image of an item or information describing the item（“presentment notice”）rather than delivery of the item itself. The agreement may provide for procedures governing retention, presentment, payment, dishonor, and other matters concerning items subject to the agreement.

（b）Presentment of an item under an agreement for presentment is made when the presentment notice is received.

（c）If presentment is made by presentment notice, a reference to “item” or “check” in this Article means the presentment notice unless the context otherwise indicates.

§ 4.111. Statute of Limitations.

An action to enforce an obligation, duty, or right arising under this Article must be commenced within three years after the cause of action accrues.

第 4.112 条 按票面金额支付支票

（a）除第 3 篇或本篇另有规定外，作为受票人的付款银行对于所收到的支票，只要所支取的账户有足够余额，即应按支票的票面金额付款，无论受款人是否在该银行持有账户。

（b）本条不禁止银行在结算支票之前，以商业上合理的方式核实受款人的真实身份。

（c）在法律提供的任何救济之外，本州银行委员会主席应与财务委员会协调，确保付款银行遵守本条的要求。

§ 4.112. Payment of Check at Par.

（a）Except as otherwise provided by Article 3 or this Article, a payor bank shall pay a check drawn on it against an account with a sufficient balance at par without regard to whether the payee holds an account at the bank.

（b）This section does not prohibit a bank from requiring commercially reasonable verification of the payee's identity before settlement of the check.

（c）In addition to any remedy provided by law, the banking commissioner, in coordination with the Finance Commission of Texas, shall ensure that payor banks comply with the requirements of this section.

第2章 票证收款：存款银行和收款银行

PART 2. COLLECTION OF ITEMS:DEPOSITARY AND COLLECTING BANKS

第 4.201 条 收款银行的代理身份及信贷的临时性；本篇的适用范围；载有“向任何银行付款”背书的票证

（a）除另有明确表示的相反意图外，在收款银行对票证作出的结算成为最终结算之前，就所涉及的票证，银行是票证所有权人的代理人或再代理人，且对票证的任何结算均属临时结算。无论背书为何种形式，

§ 4.201. Status of Collecting Bank as Agent and Provisional Status of Credits; Applicability of Article;Item Indorsed “Pay Any Bank”.

（a）Unless a contrary intent clearly appears and before the time that a settlement given by a collecting bank for an item is or becomes final, the bank, with respect to the item, is an agent or sub-agent of the owner of the item and any settlement given for the item is provisional.This provision applies

或是否存在背书，也无论给予票证的信贷是否有权即时提用，或是否事实上已被提用，上述原则均适用。但是，票证所有权人所继续拥有的所有权，以及该所有权人对票证收益享有的任何权利，均受制于收款银行的权利，例如银行因票证尚有未偿贷款而享有的权利，以及银行的扣减权或抵销权。如果票证在提示、付款、收款或退回的过程中经由多个银行处理，则即使当事方的行为明确证实，其中某个银行已购买了票证并成为其所有权人，本篇的有关条款仍然适用。

regardless of the form of indorsement or lack of indorsement and even though credit given for the item is subject to immediate withdrawal as of right or is in fact withdrawn;but the continuance of ownership of an item by its owner and any rights of the owner to proceeds of the item are subject to rights of a collecting bank, such as those resulting from outstanding advances on the item and rights of recoupment or setoff.If an item is handled by banks for purposes of presentment, payment, collection, or return, the relevant provisions of this Article apply even though action of the parties clearly establishes that a particular bank has purchased the item and is the owner of it.

（b）如果票证的背书载有“向任何银行付款”或类似词句，则在下列情况发生之前，只有银行能够取得执票人的权利：

（1）票证被交还给发起收款的客户；或

（2）票证由银行通过记名背书转让给非系银行的人。

（b）After an item has been indorsed with the words “pay any bank” or the like, only a bank may acquire the rights of a holder until the item has been:

（1）returned to the customer initiating collection;or

（2）specially indorsed by a bank to a person who is not a bank.

第 4.202 条　收款或退回时的责任；作为的及时性

§ 4.202. Responsibility for Collection or Return; When Action Timely.

（a）收款银行从事下列行为时，必须行使正常谨慎：

（1）提示票证，或寄送票证用于提示；

（2）在得知票证未获付款或未获承兑后，寄送拒付通知或未付通知，或将票证（跟单

（a）A collecting bank must exercise ordinary care in:

（1）presenting an item or sending it for presentment;

（2）sending notice of dishonor or non-payment or returning an item other than a documentary draft to the bank’s transferor

汇票除外）退回给银行的转让人；

after learning that the item has not been paid or accepted, as thc case may be;

（3）在银行收到最终结算后，为票证作出结算；以及

（3）settling for an item when the bank receives final settlement;and

（4）在发现收款过程中的任何损失或延迟后，在合理时间内通知银行的转让人。

（4）notifying its transferor of any loss or delay in transit within a reasonable time after discovery thereof.

（b）如果收款银行在收到票证、通知或结算后，在其午夜截止期前作出适当行为，即属于行使了（a）款所述的正常谨慎。如果作出适当行为的时间超过了上述期限但仍在合理限度内，也有可能属于行使了正常谨慎，但银行应对行为的及时性承担举证责任。

（b）A collecting bank exercises ordinary care under Subsection（a）by taking proper action before its midnight deadline following receipt of an item, notice, or settlement.Taking proper action within a reasonably longer time may constitute the exercise of ordinary care, but the bank has the burden of establishing timeliness.

（c）除（a）（1）款另有规定外，银行不对另一银行或另一人的破产、疏忽、不当行为、错误或违约承担责任，也不对转送中或其他人占有中之票证的遗失或损毁承担责任。

（c）Subject to Subsection（a）（1），a bank is not liable for the insolvency, neglect, misconduct, mistake, or default of another bank or person or for loss or destruction of an item in the possession of others or in transit.

第 4.203 条　指示的效力

除第 3 篇涉及侵占票据（第 3.420 条）和限制性背书（第 3.206 条）时另有规定外，只有收款银行之转让人向银行发出的指示，才对银行有效，或构成对银行的通知。收款银行如果根据此种指示作为，或根据与银行之转让人的协议作为，即不对前手当事方承担责任。

§ 4.203. Effect of Instructions.

Subject to Article 3 concerning conversion of instruments（Section 3.420）and restrictive indorsements（Section 3.206），only a collecting bank’s transferor can give instructions that affect the bank or constitute notice to it, and a collecting bank is not liable to prior parties for any action taken pursuant to the instructions or in accordance with any agreement with its transferor.

第4.204条 发送和提示的方式；直接发送至付款银行

（a）收款银行在发送票证时，应在考虑到相关指示、票证性质、手中该种票证的数量、相关收款费用，以及自己或他人在提示该种票证时惯常采用的方式后，以合理迅捷的方式发送票证。

（b）收款银行可以：

（1）将票证直接发送至付款银行；

（2）在得到其转让人授权后，将票证发送至非银行付款人；以及

（3）在联邦储备条例或实施细则、票证清算行规则或类似规则给予授权的情况下，将票证（跟单汇票除外）发送至非银行付款人。

（c）提示银行可在付款银行或其他付款人所要求的提示地点作出提示。

§ 4.204. Methods of Sending and Presenting; Sending Directly to Payor Bank.

（a）A collecting bank shall send items by a reasonably prompt method, taking into consideration relevant instructions, the nature of the item, the number of those items on hand, the cost of collection involved, and the method generally used by it or others to present those items.

（b）A collecting bank may send:

（1）an item directly to the payor bank;

（2）an item to a non-bank payor if authorized by its transferor;and

（3）an item other than a documentary draft to a non-bank payor, if authorized by Federal Reserve regulation or operating circular, clearing-house rule, or the like.

（c）Presentment may be made by a presenting bank at a place where the payor bank or other payor has requested that presentment be made.

第4.205条 存款银行作为无背书票证的执票人

如果客户将票证交给存款银行用于收款，则：

（1）存款银行在收到用于收款的票证时，即成为该票证的执票人，无论客户是否为票证作出背书，只要客户在交付票证时，其自己是票证的执

§ 4.205. Depository Bank Holder of Unindorsed Item.

If a customer delivers an item to a depositary bank for collection, the depositary bank:

（1）becomes a holder of the item at the time it receives the item for collection if the customer at the time of delivery was a holder of the item, whether or not the customer indorses the item, and, if the bank satisfies the other

票人；并且，银行如果满足第3.302条的其他要求，即成为正当执票人；并且

requirements of Section 3.302, the bank is a holder in due course;and

（2）存款银行向收款银行、付款银行或其他付款人，以及出票人担保，票证金额已支付给客户，或已存入客户的账户。

（2）warrants to collecting banks, the payor bank or other payor, and the drawer that the amount of the item was paid to the customer or deposited to the customer's account.

第4.206条　银行间的转让

§ 4.206. Transfer Between Banks.

任何约定的方法，只要能够指明转让人银行，即足以使票证再度向另一银行转让。

Any agreed method that identifies the transferor bank is sufficient for the item's further transfer to another bank.

第4.207条　转让时的担保

§ 4.207. Transfer Warranties.

（a）客户或收款银行如果转让票证，并收到结算或其他对价，即对受让人和任何后手收款银行担保：

（a）A customer or collecting bank that transfers an item and receives a settlement or other consideration warrants to the transferee and to any subsequent collecting bank that:

（1）担保人系有权强制履行票证的人；

（1）the warrantor is a person entitled to enforce the item;

（2）票证上全部签名均属真实并业经授权；

（2）all signatures on the item are authentic and authorized;

（3）票证不存在涂改；

（3）the item has not been altered;

（4）票证不受制于任何当事方持有的可对抗担保人的抗辩或扣减权［第3.305条（a）款］；

（4）the item is not subject to a defense or claim in recoupment（Section 3.305（a））of any party that can be asserted against the warrantor;

（5）担保人不知道任何针对制票人或承兑人的已开始的破产程序；或在涉及未承兑的汇票时，针对出票人的破产程序；以及

（5）the warrantor has no knowledge of any insolvency proceeding commenced with respect to the maker or acceptor or, in the case of an unaccepted draft, the drawer;and

（6）涉及远程制作的票证时，票证支取账户的持有人已授权按票证显示的金额出立票证。

（6）with respect to a remotely-created item, that the person on whose account the item is drawn authorized the issuance of the item in the amount for which the item is drawn.

（b）如果票证被拒付，转让票证并收到结算或其他对价的客户或收款银行，有义务按下列条款支付票证的到期金额：（i）按票证转让时的条款支付，或（ii）如果转让的是不完整票证，则根据第3.115条和第3.407条的规定，按被添补完整的票证条款支付。转让人此项义务的受益人，是受让人和以善意取得票证的任何后手收款银行。转让人不得在背书时，通过使用“无追索权”用语或以其他方式，排除其在本款项下的义务。

（b）If an item is dishonored, a customer or collecting bank transferring the item and receiving settlement or other consideration is obliged to pay the amount due on the item（i）according to the terms of the item at the time it was transferred, or（ii）if the transfer was of an incomplete item, according to its terms when completed as stated in Sections 3.115 and 3.407.The obligation of a transferor is owed to the transferee and to any subsequent collecting bank that takes the item in good faith.A transferor cannot disclaim its obligation under this subsection by an indorsement stating that it is made“without recourse”or otherwise disclaiming liability.

（c）任何人如果获得（a）款项下的担保，并善意取得票证，即可在担保人违反担保时，就违反担保所造成的损失，从担保人取得相当于损失金额但最多不超过票证金额的赔偿，再加上违反担保所造成的费用和利息损失。

（c）A person to whom the warranties under Subsection（a）are made and who took the item in good faith may recover from the warrantor as damages for breach of warranty an amount equal to the loss suffered as a result of the breach, but not more than the amount of the item plus expenses and loss of interest incurred as a result of the breach.

（d）涉及支票时，不得排除（a）款所述的担保。出现违反担保时，索赔人应在有理由知道该违约以及担保人的真实身份后，在30天内发出索赔通知，否则，对于延迟发出索赔通知所造成的那部分损失，担保人不承担责任。

（d）The warranties stated in Subsection（a）cannot be disclaimed with respect to checks. Unless notice of a claim for breach of warranty is given to the warrantor within 30 days after the claimant has reason to know of the breach and the identity of the warrantor, the warrantor is discharged to the extent of any loss caused by the delay in giving notice of the claim.

（e）本条项下违反担保的

（e）A cause of action for breach of

诉讼理由，在索赔人有理由知道违反担保时产生。

（f）如果根据适用的冲突法原则，转让人或收款银行不提供（a）（6）款项下的担保，则在该转让人是受让人时，其也不能获得该担保，且该受让人的任何前手收款银行亦不能获得该担保。

warranty under this section accrues when the claimant has reason to know of the breach.

（f）If the warranty under Subsection（a）（6）is not given by a transferor or collecting bank under applicable conflict of law rules, the warranty is not given to that transferor when that transferor is a transferee or to any prior collecting bank of that transferee.

第 4.208 条　提示时的担保

（a）如果未承兑的汇票被提示给受票人，要求付款或承兑，且该受票人支付或承兑了该汇票，则（i）获得付款或承兑的人在提示时，以及（ii）汇票的前手转让人在转让时，向善意支付或承兑汇票的受票人担保：

（1）担保人系有权强制履行汇票的人，或有权代表该人取得汇票的付款或承兑，或在转让汇票时拥有该权利；

（2）汇票不存在涂改；

（3）担保人不知道显示为汇票出票人之签名系无授权签名；并且

（4）涉及远程制作的票证时，票证支取账户的持有人已授权按票证显示的金额出立票证。

（b）如果出现违反担保，作出付款的受票人可从担保人

§ 4.208. Presentment Warranties.

（a）If an unaccepted draft is presented to the drawee for payment or acceptance and the drawee pays or accepts the draft,（i）the person obtaining payment or acceptance, at the time of presentment, and（ii）a previous transferor of the draft, at the time of transfer, warrant to the drawee that pays or accepts the draft in good faith that:

（1）the warrantor is, or was, at the time the warrantor transferred the draft, a person entitled to enforce the draft or authorized to obtain payment or acceptance of the draft on behalf of a person entitled to enforce the draft;

（2）the draft has not been altered;

（3）the warrantor has no knowledge that the signature of the purported drawer of the draft is unauthorized;and

（4）with respect to any remotely-created item, that the person on whose account the item is drawn authorized the issuance of the item in the amount for which the item is drawn.

（b）A drawee making payment may recover from a warrantor damages for breach

取得相当于受票人支付金额的损害赔偿，但应减去受票人因该付款而从出票人收到的或有权收到的金额。此外，受票人有权就违约所造成的费用和利息损失取得赔偿。受票人即使在付款时未能行使正常谨慎，其根据本款取得赔偿的权利亦不受影响。如果受票人承兑汇票，则违反担保构成承兑人义务的抗辩。如果承兑人为汇票作出付款，在出现违反担保时，承兑人有权从担保人获得本款规定的损害赔偿。

of warranty equal to the amount paid by the drawee less the amount the drawee received or is entitled to receive from the drawer because of the payment.In addition, the drawee is entitled to compensation for expenses and loss of interest resulting from the breach.The right of the drawee to recover damages under this subsection is not affected by any failure of the drawee to exercise ordinary care in making payment.If the drawee accepts the draft, breach of warranty is a defense to the obligation of the acceptor.If the acceptor makes payment with respect to the draft, the acceptor is entitled to recover from a warrantor for breach of warranty the amounts stated in this subsection.

（c）如果受票人基于汇票存在无授权背书或涂改而根据（a）款提出违反担保的索赔，则只要担保人能够证明，根据第 3.404 条或第 3.405 条，背书系属有效，或根据第 3.406 条或第 4.406 条，出票人无权以该无授权背书或涂改对抗受票人，担保人即可将其作为抗辩。

（c）If a drawee asserts a claim for breach of warranty under Subsection（a）based on an unauthorized indorsement of the draft or an alteration of the draft, the warrantor may defend by proving that the indorsement is effective under Section 3.404 or 3.405 or the drawer is precluded under Section 3.406 or 4.406 from asserting against the drawee the unauthorized indorsement or alteration.

（d）如果（i）被拒付的汇票被提示给出票人或背书人付款，或（ii）其他票证被提示给有义务支付票证的当事方付款，且票证获得付款，则取得付款的人，以及票证的前手转让人，向善意作出付款的人担保，担保人系有权强制履行票证的人，或有权代表该人取得付款，或

（d）If（i）a dishonored draft is presented for payment to the drawer or an indorser, or（ii）any other item is presented for payment to a party obliged to pay the item, and the item is paid, the person obtaining payment and a prior transferor of the item warrant to the person making payment in good faith that the warrantor is, or was, at the time the warrantor transferred the item, a person entitled to enforce

在转让票证时拥有该权利。如果担保人违反担保，付款人可从担保人取得相当于支付金额的损害赔偿，再加上违约所造成的费用和利息损失。

the item or authorized to obtain payment on behalf of a person entitled to enforce the item. The person making payment may recover from any warrantor for breach of warranty an amount equal to the amount paid plus expenses and loss of interest resulting from the breach.

（e）涉及支票时，不得排除（a）款和（d）款所述的担保。在出现违反担保时，索赔人应在有理由知道该违约以及担保人的真实身份后，在三十天内发出索赔通知，否则，对于延迟发出索赔通知所造成的那部分损失，担保人不承担责任。

（e）The warranties stated in Subsections（a）and（d）cannot be disclaimed with respect to checks.Unless notice of a claim for breach of warranty is given to the warrantor within 30 days after the claimant has reason to know of the breach and the identity of the warrantor, the warrantor is discharged to the extent of any loss caused by the delay in giving notice of the claim.

（f）本条项下违反担保的诉讼理由，在索赔人有理由知道违反担保时产生。

（f）A cause of action for breach of warranty under this section accrues when the claimant has reason to know of the breach.

（g）涉及特定票证时，如果:（i）受让人（包括收款银行）根据（a）（4）款就违反担保提出索赔，但是，（ii）根据适用法（包括适用的冲突法原则），在该受让人自己是转让人时，其本来不会作出实质上类似于（a）（4）款所述的担保，则该受让人即不被视为从任何转让人收到（a）（4）款所述的担保。

（g）If as to a particular item（i）a transferee（including a collecting bank）asserts a claim for breach of the warranty under Subsection（a）（4）, but（ii）under applicable law（including the applicable choice-of-law principles）that transferee would not make a warranty substantially similar to the warranty in Subsection（a）（4）if such transferee were a transferor, then that transferee would not receive the warranty in Subsection（a）（4）from any transferor.

第 4.209 条　录入和保存时的担保

§ 4.209. Encoding and Retention Warranties.

（a）票证出立后，在票证上录入信息的人，或就票证录

（a）A person who encodes information on or with respect to an item after issue warrants

入信息的人，向任何后手收款银行担保，并向付款银行或其他付款人担保，信息的录入系属准确。如果信息由存款银行的客户录入，则银行同时作出该担保。

to any subsequent collecting bank and to the payor bank or other payor that the information is correctly encoded.If the customer of a depositary bank encodes, that bank also makes the warranty.

（b）承诺根据电子提示协议保存票证的人，向任何后手收款银行担保，并向付款银行或其他付款人担保，票证的保存和提示均符合该协议。如果保存票证的承诺由存款银行的客户作出，则银行同时作出该担保。

（b）A person who undertakes to retain an item pursuant to an agreement for electronic presentment warrants to any subsequent collecting bank and to the payor bank or other payor that retention and presentment of the item comply with the agreement.If a customer of a depositary bank undertakes to retain an item, that bank also makes this warranty.

（c）出现违反担保时，收到本条所述担保且善意取得票证的人，可就违反担保从担保人取得相当于损失金额的损害赔偿，再加上违约所造成的费用和利息损失。

（c）A person to whom warranties are made under this section and who took the item in good faith may recover from the warrantor as damages for breach of warranty an amount equal to the loss suffered as a result of the breach, plus expenses and loss of interest incurred as a result of the breach.

第 4.210 条　收款银行对票证、附属单据和收益的担保权益

§ 4.210. Security Interest of Collecting Bank in Items, Accompanying Documents and Proceeds.

（a）收款银行对票证和任何附属单据，或其中任何一项的收益，享有下列担保权益：

（a）A collecting bank has a security interest in an item and any accompanying documents or the proceeds of either:

（1）涉及存入账户的票证时，担保权益的限度为已被提取或使用的信贷；

（1）in case of an item deposited in an account, to the extent to which credit given for the item has been withdrawn or applied;

（2）涉及为票证提供有权随时提取的信贷时，担保权益的限度为已提供的信贷，无论

（2）in case of an item for which it has given credit available for withdrawal as of right, to the extent of the credit given, whether

该信贷是否已提取，也无论银行是否拥有倒账权；或

（3）如果银行为票证提供贷款或依据票证提供贷款，银行即享有上述担保权益。

（b）涉及多项同时收到的或根据同一协议出立的票证时，为该等票证提供的信贷，即使仅被部分地提取或使用，银行仍对全部票证、附属单据或其中任何一项的收益享有担保权益。为本条目的，首先提供的信贷被视为首先提取。

（c）收款银行收到票证的最终结算后，其对票证、附属单据及收益的担保权益即获兑现。只要银行未收到票证的最终结算，亦未因收款以外的原因放弃占有票证，或放弃占有或控制附属单据，担保权益即在相应限度内继续存在，并受第9篇的约束，只是：

（1）无须担保协议，该担保权益亦可具有强制履行力[第9.203条（b）（3）（A）款]；

（2）无须登记，该担保权益亦可获得完善；并且

（3）该担保权益优于票证、附属单据或收益中冲突的其他已完善担保权益。

第4.211条　银行何时通过支付价值成为正当执票人

在确定银行的正当执票人

or not the credit is drawn upon or there is a right of charge-back;or

（3）if it makes an advance on or against the item.

（b）If credit given for several items received at one time or pursuant to a single agreement is withdrawn or applied in part, the security interest remains upon all the items, any accompanying documents, or the proceeds of either.For the purpose of this section, credits first given are first withdrawn.

（c）Receipt by a collecting bank of a final settlement for an item is a realization on its security interest in the item, accompanying documents, and proceeds.So long as the bank does not receive final settlement for the item or give up possession of the item or possession or control of the accompanying documents for purposes other than collection, the security interest continues to that extent and is subject to Article 9, but:

（1）no security agreement is necessary to make the security interest enforceable（Section 9.203（b）（3）（A））；

（2）no filing is required to perfect the security interest;and

（3）the security interest has priority over conflicting perfected security interests in the item, accompanying documents, or proceeds.

§ 4.211. When Bank Gives Value for Purposes of Holder in Due Course.

For purposes of determining its status

地位时，如果银行对票证享有担保权益，则在该担保权益的限度内，银行被视为已支付价值，但银行必须在其他方面同时符合第 3.302 条对正当执票人的要求。

as a holder in due course, a bank has given value to the extent it has a security interest in an item, if the bank otherwise complies with the requirements of Section 3.302 on what constitutes a holder in due course.

第 4.212 条　以通知方式提示非由或非在或非通过银行付款的票证；出票人或背书人的责任

§ 4.212. Presentment by Notice of Item Not Payable by, Through or at a Bank; Liability of Drawer or Indorser.

（a）除另有指示外，收款银行为提示一项非由或非在或非通过银行付款的票证，可向承兑或付款的当事方发送构成通知的记录，说明银行持有待承兑或待付款的票证。通知必须及时发出，以便在提示到期之日或之前可以被收到；并且，对于承兑方或付款方根据第 3.501 条提出的任何要求，银行必须在得知要求后的下一个银行营业日结束之前予以满足。

（a）Unless otherwise instructed, a collecting bank may present an item not payable by, through, or at a bank by sending to the party to accept or pay a record providing notice that the bank holds the item for acceptance or payment.The notice must be sent in time to be received on or before the day when presentment is due, and the bank must meet any requirement of the party to accept or pay under Section 3.501 by the close of the bank's next banking day after it knows of the requirement.

（b）如果以通知方式作出提示，且在票证到期日后的下一日营业结束时，或在涉及即时票证时，在通知发送后的第三个银行营业日营业结束时，仍未收到付款或承兑，也未收到根据第 3.501 条提出的要求，提示银行即可认为票证已被拒付，并可通过向任何出票人或背书人通知该事实，从该出票人或背书人获得付款。

（b）If presentment is made by notice and payment, acceptance, or request for compliance with a requirement under Section 3.501 is not received by the close of business on the day after maturity or, in the case of demand items, by the close of business on the third banking day after notice was sent, the presenting bank may treat the item as dishonored and charge any drawer or indorser by sending it notice of the facts.

第 4.213 条　银行作出结算的方法和时间

（a）联邦储备条例或实施细则、票证清算行规则、类似规则或协议，可以规定银行作出结算的方法和时间。如果未规定，则：

（1）结算的方法为支付现金，或贷记在联邦储备银行的账户，或贷记收取结算的人所规定的账户；以及

（2）结算的时间为：

（A）如果提示结算以现金、银行本票或银行支票作出，则为发出或交付现金或银行本票或银行支票的时间；

（B）如果提示结算以贷记联邦储备银行账户作出，则为作出贷记的时间；

（C）如果提示结算以贷记或借记银行账户作出，则为作出贷记或借记的时间；或如果提示结算系通过对支取账户给予授权而作出，则为发出或交付授权的时间；或

（D）如果提示结算以资金转账作出，则为根据第 4A.406 条（a）款向收取结算的人作出付款的时间。

（b）如果提示结算不使用（a）款允许的方法，或如果结算的时间未在（a）款规定之内，

§ 4.213. Medium and Time of Settlement by Bank.

（a）With respect to settlement by a bank, the medium and time of settlement may be prescribed by Federal Reserve regulations or circulars, clearing-house rules, and the like or by agreement.In the absence of such a prescription:

（1）the medium of settlement is cash or credit to an account in a Federal Reserve bank of or specified by the person to receive settlement;and

（2）the time of settlement is:

（A）with respect to tender of settlement by cash, a cashier's check, or a teller's check, when the cash or check is sent or delivered;

（B）with respect to tender of settlement by credit to an account in a Federal Reserve bank, when the credit is made;

（C）with respect to tender of settlement by a credit or debit to an account in a bank, when the credit or debit is made or, in the case of tender of settlement by authority to charge an account, when the authority is sent or delivered;or

（D）with respect to tender of settlement by a funds transfer, when payment is made pursuant to Section 4A.406（a）to the person receiving settlement.

（b）If the tender of settlement is not by a medium authorized by Subsection（a）or the time of settlement is not fixed by Subsection

则只有在收取结算的人接受提示结算时，结算才发生。

(a), a settlement does not occur until the tender of settlement is accepted by the person receiving settlement.

（c）如果票证结算使用银行本票或银行支票，且收取结算之人在其午夜截止期之前：

(c) If settlement for an item is made by cashier's check or teller's check and the person receiving settlement, before its midnight deadline:

（1）提示或转发该本票或支票用于收款，则在该本票或支票获得最终支付时，结算成为最终结算；或

(1) presents or forwards the check for collection, settlement is final when the check is finally paid;or

（2）未能提示或转发该本票或支票用于收款，则在收取结算之人的午夜截止期到期时，结算成为最终结算。

(2) fails to present or forward the check for collection, settlement is final at the midnight deadline of the person receiving settlement.

（d）如果作出结算的银行在收取结算的银行持有账户，且票证结算系通过授权从该账户中支取，且该账户中存有可用于票证金额的资金，则在收取结算的银行完成支取时，结算成为最终结算。

(d) If settlement for an item is made by giving authority to charge the account of the bank giving settlement in the bank receiving settlement, settlement is final when the charge is made by the bank receiving settlement if there are funds available in the account for the amount of the item.

第 4.214 条　倒账权或退款权；收款银行的责任；票证的退回

§ 4.214. Right of Charge-Back or Refund;Liability of Collecting Bank;Return of Item.

（a）收款银行就票证与客户作出临时结算后，如果因拒付、银行暂停对外付款或其他原因，致使收款银行自己未能就票证收到最终结算，银行可以撤销已作出的结算，或就票证已给予客户账户的信贷金额，倒记客户账户，或从客户取得

(a) If a collecting bank has made provisional settlement with its customer for an item and fails by reason of dishonor, suspension of payments by a bank, or otherwise to receive settlement for the item that is or becomes final, the bank may revoke the settlement given by it, charge back the amount of any credit given for the item to its customer's account, or obtain refund from

退款，而无论自己是否能够退回票证，只要银行在得知相关事实后的午夜截止期前，或更长的合理时间内，退回票证或发出有关事实的通知。如果银行出现延迟，未能在其得知相关事实后的午夜截止期前，或更长的合理时间内，作出退回或通知，银行仍可撤销结算、倒记信贷或从客户取得退款，但应对延迟所造成的损失负责。撤销、倒记和取得退款的权利，在收款银行收到的票证结算成为最终结算时终止。

its customer, whether or not it is able to return the item, if by its midnight deadline or within a longer reasonable time after it learns the facts it returns the item or sends notification of the facts.If the return or notice is delayed beyond the bank's midnight deadline or a longer reasonable time after it learns the facts, the bank may revoke the settlement, charge back the credit, or obtain refund from its customers, but it is liable for any loss resulting from the delay.These rights to revoke, charge-back, and obtain refund terminate if and when a settlement for the item received by the bank is or becomes final.

（b）收款银行把票证发送给或交付给银行的客户或转让人，或根据其指示发送或交付，即属于退回票证。

（b）A collecting bank returns an item when it is sent or delivered to the bank's customer or transferor or pursuant to its instructions.

（c）存款银行如果同时为付款人，可按票证金额倒记其客户的账户，或根据有关付款银行退回已在自己账目中作出贷记之票证的规定（第 4.301 条）取得退款。

（c）A depositary bank that is also the payor may charge-back the amount of an item to its customer's account or obtain refund in accordance with the section governing return of an item received by a payor bank for credit on its books（Section 4.301）.

（d）倒账权不受下列因素的影响：

（d）The right to charge-back is not affected by:

（1）给予票证的信贷已被使用；或

（1）previous use of a credit given for the item;or

（2）任何银行未能就票证行使正常谨慎；但是，未能行使正常谨慎的银行仍须承担责任。

（2）failure by any bank to exercise ordinary care with respect to the item, but a bank so failing remains liable.

（e）未能作出倒账或未能

（e）A failure to charge-back or claim

要求退款，不影响银行对抗客户或任何其他当事方的其他权利。

refund does not affect other rights of the bank against the customer or any other party.

（f）涉及以外汇付款的票证时，如果所提供的信贷系与票证等值的美元，则倒账或退款的美元金额，应为有权作出倒账或取得退款的人，在了解到其无法以正常方式获得付款之日，按该外汇之银行即期汇率换算的美元金额。

（f）If credit is given in dollars as the equivalent of the value of an item payable in foreign money, the dollar amount of any charge-back or refund must be calculated on the basis of the bank-offered spot rate for the foreign money prevailing on the day when the person entitled to the charge-back or refund learns that it will not receive payment in ordinary course.

第 4.215 条　付款银行对票证的最终付款；临时借记和贷记成为最终的时间；某些信贷可供提取的时间

§ 4.215. Final Payment of Item by Payor Bank;When Provisional Debits and Credits Become Final;When Certain Credits Become Available for Withdrawal.

（a）付款银行首次作出下列任何一种行为时，付款银行即完成对票证的最终付款：

（a）An item is finally paid by a payor bank when the bank has first done any of the following:

（1）用现金支付票证；

（1）paid the item in cash;

（2）对票证作出结算，且不因任何法律、票证清算行规则或协议而拥有撤销结算的权利；或

（2）settled for the item without having a right to revoke the settlement under statute, clearing-house rule, or agreement;or

（3）对票证作出临时结算，且未能根据法律、票证清算行规则或协议允许的时间和方式撤销结算。

（3）made a provisional settlement for the item and failed to revoke the settlement in the time and manner permitted by statute, clearing-house rule, or agreement.

（b）如果票证的临时结算未能成为最终结算，票证即属于未获最终付款。

（b）If provisional settlement for an item does not become final, the item is not finally paid.

（c）如果提示银行和付款银行之间对票证的临时结算，系通过票证清算行作出，或通

（c）If provisional settlement for an item between the presenting and payor banks is made through a clearing house or by debits or credits

过借记或贷记它们之间的账户作出，则只要在提示银行和付款银行之间，或顺次在提示银行和连续的各前手收款银行之间，已就票证在账户中作出临时借记或贷记，该等记账即在付款银行最终支付票证后成为最终。

in an account between them, then to the extent that provisional debits or credits for the item are entered in accounts between the presenting and payor banks or between the presenting and successive prior collecting banks seriatim, they become final upon final payment of the item by the payor bank.

（d）在收款银行收到票证的最终结算后，银行即向客户承担票证金额的责任，且向客户账户提供的任何临时信贷均成为最终。

（d）If a collecting bank receives a settlement for an item that is or becomes final, the bank is accountable to its customer for the amount of the item, and any provisional credit given for the item in an account with its customer becomes final.

（e）除受制于（i）适用法对资金开始使用之时间的规定，以及（ii）银行将信贷用于抵偿客户债务的权利外，银行就票证给客户账户提供的信贷，在下列时间成为有权提取的信贷：

（1）如果银行已收到票证的临时结算，则在结算成为最终结算的时间，只要已有合理时间使银行收到退回的票证，但票证在该时间内未收到；或

（2）如果银行同时为存款银行和付款银行，且票证已获最终付款，则在银行收到票证后的第二个银行营业日开始的时间。

（e）Subject to（i）applicable law stating a time for availability of funds, and（ii）any right of the bank to apply the credit to an obligation of the customer, credit given by a bank for an item in a customer's account becomes available for withdrawal as of right if the bank:

（1）has received a provisional settlement for the item,—when the settlement becomes final and the bank has had a reasonable time to receive return of the item and the item has not been received within that time;or

（2）is both the depositary bank and the payor bank, and the item is finally paid,—at the opening of the bank's second banking day following receipt of the item.

（f）除受制于适用法对资金开始使用之时间的规定，以及银行将存款用于抵偿存款人

（f）Subject to applicable law stating a time for availability of funds and any right of a bank to apply a deposit to an obligation

债务的权利外，存入的款项可在下一个银行营业日开始时提取。

of the depositor, a deposit of money becomes available for withdrawal as of right at the opening of the bank's next banking day after receipt of the deposit.

第4.216条 破产和优先权

§ 4.216. Insolvency and Preference.

（a）如果占有或收到票证的付款银行或收款银行暂停对外付款，且票证未获最终付款，管理停业银行之接管人、受托人或代理人，必须将票证退回至提示银行，或停业银行的客户。

（a）If an item is in or comes into the possession of a payor or collecting bank that suspends payment and the item has not been finally paid, the item must be returned by the receiver, trustee, or agent in charge of the closed bank to the presenting bank or the closed bank's customer.

（b）如果付款银行对票证作出最终支付，且在未与其客户或提示银行就票证作出最终结算的情况下暂停对外付款，则票证的所有权人对付款银行享有优先索赔权。

（b）If a payor bank finally pays an item and suspends payments without making a settlement for the item with its customer or the presenting bank, which settlement is or becomes final, the owner of the item has a preferred claim against the payor bank.

（c）如果付款银行对票证作出临时结算后暂停对外付款，或收款银行对票证作出或接受临时结算后暂停对外付款，该暂停对外付款并不阻止或妨碍该结算成为最终结算，只要最终结算系因超过一定时间期限或系因发生某种情况而自动发生。

（c）If a payor bank gives or a collecting bank gives or receives a provisional settlement for an item and thereafter suspends payments, the suspension does not prevent or interfere with the settlement's becoming final if the finality occurs automatically upon the lapse of certain time or the happening of certain events.

（d）如果收款银行从后手当事方收到票证结算，且该结算成为最终结算，但收款银行在未与其客户就票证作出最终结算的情况下暂停对外付款，则票证的所有权人对收款银行

（d）If a collecting bank receives from subsequent parties settlement for an item, which settlement is or becomes final, and the bank suspends payments without making a settlement for the item with its customer, which settlement is or becomes final, the owner of the

享有优先索赔权。

item has a preferred claim against the collecting bank.

第3章 票证收款：付款银行

PART 3. COLLECTION OF ITEMS:PAYOR BANKS

第 4.301 条 延迟入账；通过退回票证收回付款；拒付的时间；付款银行退回票证

（a）如果对于所提示的即时票证（跟单汇票除外），付款银行在收到票证之银行营业日的午夜前作出结算，且结算非为柜台即时付款，则银行只要在作出最终付款之前并在午夜截止期之前作出下列行为，即有权撤销并收回结算：

（1）退回票证；

（2）退回票证的图像，只要被退回的人已签订协议，同意接受图像作为退回票证，且该图像系根据协议规定被退回；或

（3）当不存在可用于退还的票证时，发出构成拒付通知或停付通知的记录。

（b）如果付款银行收到即时票证，用于在自己账目上作出贷记，则银行只要按（a）款规定的时间和方式作为，即可退回票证或发出拒付通知，并可撤销任何已提供的信贷，或收回客户已提取的任何款项。

§ 4.301. Deferred Posting;Recovery of Payment by Return of Items;Time of Dishonor; Return of Items by Payor Bank.

（a）If a payor bank settles for a demand item other than a documentary draft presented otherwise than for immediate payment over the counter before midnight of the banking day of receipt, the payor bank may revoke the settlement and recover the settlement if, before it has made final payment and before its midnight deadline, it:

（1）returns the item;

（2）returns an image of the item, if the party to which the return is made has entered into an agreement to accept an image as a return of the item, and the image is returned in accordance with that agreement;or

（3）sends a record providing notice of dishonor or nonpayment if the item is unavailable for return.

（b）If a demand item is received by a payor bank for credit on its books, it may return the item or send notice of dishonor and may revoke any credit given or recover the amount thereof withdrawn by its customer, if it acts within the time limit and in the manner specified in Subsection（a）.

（c）除之前已发出拒付通知外，如果为拒付目的而根据本条退回票证或发出通知，则退回或通知的时间，即为票证的拒付时间。

（c）Unless previous notice of dishonor has been sent, an item is dishonored at the time when for purposes of dishonor it is returned or notice sent in accordance with this section.

（d）退回票证的发生时间如下：

（d）An item is returned:

（1）涉及通过票证清算行提示的票证时，退回票证的发生时间为：向提示银行或最后一个收款银行交付票证的时间，或向票证清算行交付票证的时间，或根据票证清算行规则发送或交付票证的时间；或

（1）as to an item presented through a clearing house, when it is delivered to the presenting or last collecting bank or to the clearing house or is sent or delivered in accordance with clearing-house rules;or

（2）在所有其他情况下，退回票证的发生时间为：向银行之客户或转让人发送或交付票证的时间，或根据客户或转让人指示发送或交付票证的时间。

（2）in all other cases, when it is sent or delivered to the bank's customer or transferor or pursuant to instructions.

第 4.302 条　付款银行延迟退回票证的责任

§ 4.302. Payor Bank's Responsibility for Late Return of Item.

（a）如果付款银行收到提示的票证：

（a）If an item is presented to and received by a payor bank, the bank is accountable for the amount of:

（1）无论票证是否属于正常可付，在下列情况下，银行均对即时票证（跟单汇票除外）的票证金额承担责任：银行在任何情况下均非兼为存款银行，且在收到票证之银行营业日的午夜过后，仍留持票证而未作出结算；或无论银行是否兼为存款银行，其在午夜截止期之

（1）a demand item, other than a documentary draft, whether properly payable or not, if the bank, in any case in which it is not also the depositary bank, retains the item beyond midnight of the banking day of receipt without settling for it or, whether or not it is also the depositary bank, does not pay or return the item or send notice of dishonor until after its midnight deadline;or

前未支付票证，亦未退回票证或发出拒付通知；或

（2）除非银行在票证允许的承兑或付款时间内，承兑或支付票证，或退回票证和附属单据，否则，银行即对任何其他正常可付票证的票证金额承担责任。

（2）any other properly payable item unless, within the time allowed for acceptance or payment of that item, the bank either accepts or pays the item or returns it and accompanying documents.

（b）付款银行根据（a）款承担的支付票证的责任，受制于下列：因违反提示担保（第4.208条）而产生的抗辩；有证据表明，寻求强制履行上述责任的人，系出于欺诈付款银行目的而提示或转让票证。

（b）The liability of a payor bank to pay an item pursuant to Subsection（a）is subject to defenses based on breach of a presentment warranty（Section 4.208）or proof that the person seeking enforcement of the liability presented or transferred the item for the purpose of defrauding the payor bank.

第4.303条　通知、停付命令、诉讼传票或账目抵销对票证产生影响的时间；票证支取或保兑的顺序

§ 4.303. When Items Subject to Notice, Stop-Payment Order, Legal Process, or Setoff;Order in Which Items May Be Charged or Certified.

（a）如果付款银行收到任何信息、通知、停付命令或诉讼传票，或作出任何账目抵销，但银行在收到信息、通知、停付命令或诉讼传票后，没有合理时间内据以作为，或银行所作的账目抵销，系在下列最早者发生之后，则该信息、通知、停付命令、诉讼传票或账目抵销，即被视为过迟，不能终止、中断或改变银行支付票证或就票证支取客户账户的权利或义务：

（a）Any knowledge, notice, or stop-payment order received by, legal process served upon, or setoff exercised by a payor bank comes too late to terminate, suspend, or modify the bank's right or duty to pay an item or to charge its customer's account for the item if the knowledge, notice, stop-payment order, or legal process is received or served and a reasonable time for the bank to act thereon expires or the setoff is exercised after the earliest of the following:

（1）银行承兑票证，或保

（1）the bank accepts or certifies the item;

兑票证；

（2）银行用现金支付票证；

（3）银行对票证作出结算，且不因任何法律、票证清算行规则或协议而拥有撤销结算的权利；

（4）根据第4.302条有关延迟退回票证时付款银行之责任的规定，银行对票证金额承担责任；或

（5）涉及支票时，银行收到支票之银行营业日后下一个银行营业日的截止时间已到，只要该截止时间不早于该下一个营业日开始后一小时且不晚于其营业结束的时间；或如果未规定截止时间，只要银行收到支票之银行营业日后下一个银行营业日的结束时间已到。

（b）除（a）款另有规定外，可按任何顺序承兑、支付或保兑票证，或按任何顺序就票证支取银行之客户指定的账户，并可在银行正常营业时间之前或之后作出。银行无义务确定在一天中收到票证的具体时间；并且，如果需要核实有关票证的任何信息、通知、停付命令或诉讼传票的效力、后果或优先权，则在核实期间，银行可留持票证金额而无须承担责任；银行亦可参与诉讼，以就该款项及其主张人进行确权。

（2）the bank pays the item in cash;

（3）the bank settles for the item without having a right to revoke the settlement under statute, clearing-house rule, or agreement;

（4）the bank becomes accountable for the amount of the item under Section 4.302 dealing with the payor bank's responsibility for late return of items;or

（5）with respect to checks, a cutoff hour not earlier than one hour after the opening of the next banking day after the banking day on which the bank received the check and not later than the close of that next banking day or, if no cutoff hour is fixed, the close of the next banking day after the banking day on which the bank received the check.

（b）Subject to Subsection（a）, items may be accepted, paid, certified, or charged to the indicated account of a bank's customer in any order and before or after the bank's regular banking hours.A bank is under no obligation to determine the time of day an item is received and without liability may withhold the amount thereof pending a determination of the effect, consequence or priority of any knowledge, notice, stop-payment order, or legal process concerning the same, or interplead such amount and the claimants thereto.

第4章 付款银行和客户的关系

PART 4. RELATIONSHIP BETWEEN PAYOR BANK AND ITS CUSTOMER

第 4.401 条 银行支取客户账户的条件

（a）如果票证属于可从客户账户支取的正常可付票证，银行即可就该票证支取该账户，即使此种支取将造成透支。票证只要得到客户的授权，且符合客户与银行之间的任何协议，即属于正常可付。

（b）涉及透支时，如果客户未在票证上签名，亦未受益于票证的收益，客户即不对透支的金额承担责任。

（c）银行可在支票日期之前作出付款，并就该支票支取客户账户，只要该支票在其他方面系该账户的正常可付票证，除非客户已通知银行，支票系错后填写日期，且合理描述了票证的细节。该通知的有效期限，为第 4.403 条（b）款所述的停付命令的有效期限，但收到通知的时间和方式，必须使银行有合理机会，在就支票采取第 4.303 条所述的行动之前，能够根据通知据以作为。如果银行收到有关错后填写日期的通知，但在通知所述日期之前

§ 4.401. When Bank May Charge Customer's Account.

（a）A bank may charge against the account of a customer an item that is properly payable from that account even though the charge creates an overdraft.An item is properly payable if it is authorized by the customer and is in accordance with any agreement between the customer and the bank.

（b）A customer is not liable for the amount of an overdraft if the customer neither signed the item nor benefited from the proceeds of the item.

（c）A bank may charge against the account of a customer a check that is otherwise properly payable from the account, even though payment was made before the date of the check, unless the customer has given notice to the bank of the postdating describing the check with reasonable certainty.The notice is effective for the period stated in Section 4.403（b）for stop-payment ordersand must be received at such time and in such manner as to afford the bank a reasonable opportunity to act on it before the bank takes any action with respect to the check described in Section 4.303.If a bank charges against the account of a customer a check before the date stated in the notice of postdating, the bank is

就支票支取了客户账户，银行即应对所造成的损失承担责任。损失可以包括第 4.402 条所述的后续票证受到拒付的损失。

liable for damages for the loss resulting from its act.The loss may include damages for dishonor of subsequent items under Section 4.402.

（d）善意支付执票人的银行，可以按下列条款支取客户的指定账户：

（d）A bank that in good faith makes payment to a holder may charge the indicated account of its customer according to:

（1）按受到涂改之票证的原始条款；或

（1）the original terms of the altered item;or

（2）按被添补完整之票证的条款，即使银行知道票证曾被添补完整，只要银行未得到存在不适当添补完整的通知。

（2）the terms of the completed item, even though the bank knows the item has been completed, unless the bank has notice that the completion was improper.

第 4.402 条　银行错误拒付时对客户的责任

§ 4.402. Bank's Liability to Customer for Wrongful Dishonor.

（a）除本篇另有规定外，如果付款银行拒付正常可付票证，即属于错误拒付；但是，如果票证将造成透支，银行可以拒付该票证，除非银行已同意支付透支的票证。

（a）Except as otherwise provided by this Article, a payor bank wrongfully dishonors an item if it dishonors an item that is properly payable, but a bank may dishonor an item that would create an overdraft unless it has agreed to pay the overdraft.

（b）付款银行对客户主要因错误拒付而受到的损失承担责任。责任限于可证明的实际损失，并可包括客户受到逮捕或起诉的损失，或其他间接损失。任何间接损失是否主要因错误拒付引起，属于事实问题，应根据当事案件的情况确定。

（b）A payor bank is liable to its customer for damages proximately caused by the wrongful dishonor of an item.Liability is limited to actual damages proved and may include damages for an arrest or prosecution of the customer or other consequential damages. Whether any consequential damages are proximately caused by the wrongful dishonor is a question of fact to be determined in each case.

（c）付款银行可以核实客户账户的余额，以便在可用资

（c）A payor bank's determination of the customer's account balance on which

金不足时作为拒付票证的理由。从付款银行收到票证时起至退回票证时止，或至发出通知以代替退回票证时止，银行可在该期间内的任何时间进行上述核实，且只须核实一次。如果付款银行选择随后再次核实余额，以重新评估银行的拒付决定，则该时间点的账户余额的资金充足度，对于以资金不足作为拒付理由是否构成错误拒付，具有决定意义。

a decision to dishonor for insufficiency of available funds is based may be made at any time between the time the item is received by the payor bank and the time that the payor bank returns the item or gives notice in lieu of return, and no more than one determination need be made.If, at the election of the payor bank, a subsequent balance determination is made for the purpose of reevaluating the bank's decision to dishonor the item, the account balance at that time is determinative of whether a dishonor for insufficiency of available funds is wrongful.

第 4.403 条　客户停止付款的权利；损失的举证责任

§ 4.403. Customer's Right to Stop Payment; Burden of Proof of Loss.

（a）对于任何支取客户账户的票证，客户可以向银行发出命令，停止该票证付款，或关闭该账户。如果一个以上的人对该账户拥有支取权，则其中任何一人均可发出此种命令。命令应以合理的明确性描述票证或账户，且收到命令的时间和方式，必须使银行有合理机会，在根据第 4.303 条对票证采取任何行动前，能够根据命令据以作为。即使支取该账户需要一个以上的人签名，其中任何一人均可停止付款或关闭账户。

（a）A customer or any person authorized to draw on the account if there is more than one person may stop payment of any item drawn on the customer's account or close the account by an order to the bank describing the item or account with reasonable certainty received at a time and in a manner that affords the bank a reasonable opportunity to act on it before any action by the bank with respect to the item described in Section 4.303.If the signature of more than one person is required to draw on an account, any of those persons may stop payment or close the account.

（b）停付命令的有效期为六个月。构成停付命令的记录，必须注明日期、业经认证并确

（b）A stop-payment order is effective for six months and is binding on the bank only if it is in a dated, authenticated record that describes

切描述票证，才对银行具有约束力。可以通过向银行发出业经认证的记录，以延续停付命令的有效期，每次延续六个月，但必须在停付命令有效期内发出延续命令。

the item with certainty.A stop-payment order may be renewed for additional six-month periods by an authenticated record given to the bank within a period during which the stop-payment order is effective.

（c）对于未能遵从停止付款或关闭账户的命令是否造成损失，以及损失的程度，客户应承担举证责任。在违反停付命令的情况下支付票证所造成的损失，可以包括第4.402条所述的后续票证受到拒付的损失。

（c）The burden of establishing the fact and amount of loss resulting from the payment of an item contrary to a stop-payment order or order to close an account is on the customer. The loss from payment of an item contrary to a stop-payment order may include damages for dishonor of subsequent items under Section 4.402.

第4.404条 银行无义务支付超过六个月的支票

§ 4.404. Bank Not Obligated to Pay Check More Than Six Months Old.

对于持有支票账户的客户，银行无义务支付超过票证日期六个月才提示的支票（保兑支票除外）；但是，如果银行善意支付了超期支票，银行有权支取客户账户。

A bank is under no obligation to a customer having a checking account to pay a check, other than a certified check, that is presented more than six months after its date, but it may charge its customer's account for a payment made thereafter in good faith.

第4.405条 客户死亡或丧失行为能力

§ 4.405. Death or Incompetence of Customer.

（a）如果付款银行或收款银行拥有授权，就票证作出承兑、付款或收款，或就收款的收益作出结算，且该授权在其他方面系属有效，则即使其中任何一个银行的客户，在其出立票证或在银行接受收款委托时，即已丧失行为能力，银行的授权亦不因此无效，只要银

（a）A payor or collecting bank's authority to accept, pay, or collect an item or to account for proceeds of its collection, if otherwise effective, is not rendered ineffective by the incompetence of a customer of either bank existing at the time the item is issued or its collection is undertaken if the bank does not know of an adjudication of incompetence.Neither death nor incompetence of a customer revokes the authority to accept,

行不知道无行为能力的法院裁决。即使客户死亡或丧失行为能力，在银行了解死亡事实或无行为能力法院裁决并有合理机会据以作为之前，银行作出承兑、付款、收款或处置的授权保持有效。

pay, collect, or account until the bank knows of the fact of death or of an adjudication of incompetence and has reasonable opportunity to act on it.

（b）即使已了解客户死亡的事实，银行仍可在客户死亡后十日内，支付或保兑死亡日或之前出立的支票，除非对账户主张权益的人发出停付命令。

（b）Even with knowledge, a bank may for 10 days after the date of death pay or certify checks drawn on or before that date unless ordered to stop payment by a person claiming an interest in the account.

第 4.406 条　客户有义务发现并报告无授权签名或涂改

§ 4.406. Customer's Duty to Discover and Report Unauthorized Signature or Alteration.

（a）只要银行向客户发送或提供账户报告单，显示账户内的票证支付情况，银行即应将已支付的票证退还给或提供给客户，或在账户报告单中提供充分的信息，使客户能合理辨别已支付的票证。如果账户报告单提供票证的序号、金额及支付日期，信息即为充分。银行如果不退还票证，即应在账户报告单上提供电话号码，使客户可以打电话要求退还票证，或获得（b）款所述的票证的清晰复印件。

（a）A bank that sends or makes available to a customer a statement of account showing payment of items for the account shall either return or make available to the customer the items paid or provide information in the statement of account sufficient to allow the customer reasonably to identify the items paid. The statement of account provides sufficient information if the item is described by item number, amount, and date of payment.If the bank does not return the items, it shall provide in the statement of account the telephone number that the customer may call to request an item or a legible copy of the items pursuant to Subsection（b）.

（b）如果票证未被退还给客户，留持票证的人应保存票证，或如果票证被销毁，应有

（b）If the items are not returned to the customer, the person retaining the items shall either retain the items or, if the items are

能力提供票证的清晰复印件，直至收到票证后超过七年。客户可向支付票证的银行索要票证，而银行必须在合理时间内提供票证，或在票证已被销毁或无法获得时，提供票证的清晰复印件。对于每一份给客户的账户报告单，银行只要收到要求，即应免费向客户提供至少两项票证或其清晰复印件。

destroyed, maintain the capacity to furnish legible copies of the items until the expiration of seven years after receipt of the items.A customer may request an item from the bank that paid the item, and that bank must provide in a reasonable time either the item or, if the item has been destroyed or is not otherwise obtainable, a legible copy of the item.A bank shall provide, on request and without charge to the customer, at least two items or a legible copy of the items with respect to each statement of account sent to the customer.

（c）如果银行根据（a）款发送或提供账户报告单或票证，客户必须合理迅捷地查验报告单和票证，以确定是否由于票证存在涂改，或是否由于显示为客户之签名或代表客户所作之签名未经授权，致使任何付款未经授权。如果根据所提供的报告单或票证，客户本应合理发现付款未经授权，客户必须将相关事实及时通知银行。

（c）If a bank sends or makes available a statement of account or items pursuant to Subsection（a）, the customer must exercise reasonable promptness in examining the statement or the items to determine whether any payment was not authorized because of an alteration of an item or because a purported signature by or on behalf of the customer was not authorized.If, based on the statement or items provided, the customer should reasonably have discovered the unauthorized payment, the customer must promptly notify the bank of the relevant facts.

（d）如果银行能够证明，客户在涉及某项票证时，未能遵守（c）款对客户规定的义务，则在对抗银行时，客户即无权主张：

（d）If the bank proves that the customer failed, with respect to an item, to comply with the duties imposed on the customer by Subsection（c）, the customer is precluded from asserting against the bank:

（1）票证上存在客户无授权签名或涂改，只要银行还能够证明，银行由于客户的该过

（1）the customer's unauthorized signature or any alteration on the item, if the bank also proves that it suffered a loss by reason of the

失而受到损失；以及

（2）在银行善意支付的任何其他票证上，存在同一不法行为人作出的客户无授权签名或涂改，只要银行的付款，系在银行收到客户有关无授权签名或涂改的通知之前，且在客户已有合理时间（最长不超过30天）查验票证或账户报告单并通知银行之后。

（e）如果（d）款适用，但客户能够证明，银行在支付票证时未能行使正常谨慎，而该过失对于损失的发生具有助推作用，则该损失应由无权追责之客户，与主张该无权追责之银行，根据客户未能遵守（c）款及银行未能行使正常谨慎各自造成的损失程度，按比例分担。如果客户能够证明，银行未善意支付票证，则（d）款所述的无权追责即不适用。

（f）无论客户或银行是否行使了谨慎，在报告单或票证提供给客户后［上述（a）款］，客户如果在一年内未能发现和报告票证的任何无授权签名或涂改，即无权对该银行主张该无授权签名或涂改。如果根据本款无权追责，则对于相应的无授权签名或涂改，银行即无权根据第4.208条就违反担保

failure;and

（2）the customer's unauthorized signature or alteration by the same wrongdoer on any other item paid in good faith by the bank if the payment was made before the bank received notice from the customer of the unauthorized signature or alteration and after the customer had been afforded areasonable period of time, not exceeding 30 days, in which to examine the item or statement of account and notify the bank.

（e）If Subsection（d）applies and the customer proves that the bank failed to exercise ordinary care in paying the item and that the failure contributed to loss, the loss is allocated between the customer precluded and the bank asserting the preclusion according to the extent to which the failure of the customer to comply with Subsection（c）and the failure of the bank to exercise ordinary care contributed to the loss.If the customer proves that the bank did not pay the item in good faith, the preclusion under Subsection（d）does not apply.

（f）Without regard to care or lack of care of either the customer or the bank, a customer who does not within one year after the statement or items are made available to the customer（Subsection（a））discover and report the customer's unauthorized signature on or any alteration on the item is precluded from asserting against the bank the unauthorized signature or alteration.If there is a preclusion under this subsection, the payor bank may not

取得赔偿。

recover for breach of warranty under Section 4.208 with respect to the unauthorized signature or alteration to which the preclusion applies.

第 4.407 条　付款银行不当付款后取得代位权

§ 4.407. Payor Bank's Right to Subrogation on Improper Payment.

如果付款银行支付了票证，但出票人或制票人之前已发出停付命令，或账户之前已被关闭，或出票人或制票人因其他理由有权对付款提出异议，则为防止不当得利，并只在避免银行因支付票证而遭受损失的必要限度内，付款银行就下列人的权利取得代位权：

If a payor bank has paid an item over the order of the drawer or maker to stop payment, or after an account has been closed, or otherwise under circumstances giving a basis for objection by the drawer or maker, to prevent unjust enrichment and only to the extent necessary to prevent loss to the bank by reason of its payment of the item, the payor bank is subrogated to the rights:

（1）正当执票人就票证拥有的对抗出票人或制票人的权利；

（1）of any holder in due course on the item against the drawer or maker;

（2）受款人或票证任何其他执票人就票证拥有的对抗出票人或制票人的权利，或因票证基础交易拥有的此种权利；以及

（2）of the payee or any other holder of the item against the drawer or maker either on the item or under the transaction out of which the item arose;and

（3）出票人或制票人因票证基础交易拥有的对抗受款人或票证任何其他执票人的权利。

（3）of the drawer or maker against the payee or any other holder of the item with respect to the transaction out of which the item arose.

第5章　跟单汇票的收款

PART 5. COLLECTION OF DOCUMENTARY DRAFTS

第 4.501 条　跟单汇票的处理；就提示作出发送的义务；向客户通知拒付的义务

§ 4.501. Handling of Documentary Drafts; Duty to Send for Presentment and to Notify Customer of Dishonor.

银行在取得用于收款的跟

A bank that takes a documentary draft for

单汇票后，应提示该汇票及附属单据，或将其发送用于提示，并在了解到汇票未获正常支付或承兑后，将该事实及时通知客户，即使银行已贴现或购买了汇票，或已提供了有权提取的信贷。

collection shall present or send the draft and accompanying documents for presentment and, upon learning that the draft has not been paid or accepted in due course, shall seasonably notify its customer of the fact even though it may have discounted or bought the draft or extended credit available for withdrawal as of right.

第 4.502 条 "到货"汇票的提示

§ 4.502. Presentment of "On Arrival" Drafts.

如果汇票或相关指示要求，提示应在"到达""货物到达"或类似情况下作出，则收款银行无须在其预估的货物合理到达时间之前作出提示。因货物未到引起的拒绝承兑或拒绝付款，不构成拒付；但是，银行必须将拒绝事实通知其转让人。银行在收到再次提示的指示前，或在得知货物到达前，无须再次提示。

If a draft or the relevant instructions require presentment "on arrival", "when goods arrive", or the like, the collecting bank need not present until in its judgment a reasonable time for arrival of the goods has expired. Refusal to pay or accept because the goods have not arrived is not dishonor; the bank must notify its transferor of the refusal but need not present the draft again until it is instructed to do so or learns of the arrival of the goods.

第 4.503 条 提示银行对单据和货物的责任；报告拒付原因；临时协调人

§ 4.503. Responsibility of Presenting Bank for Documents and Goods;Report of Reasons for Dishonor;Referee in Case of Need.

除另有指示外，且除第 5 篇另有规定外，提示跟单汇票的银行：

（1）必须在汇票获得承兑时向受票人交付单据，只要汇票系从承兑之时起三天之后付款；否则，只在获得付款时交付单据；以及

（2）发生拒付后，无论涉

Unless otherwise instructed and except as provided in Article 5, a bank presenting a documentary draft:

（1）must deliver the documents to the drawee on acceptance of the draft if it is payable more than three days after presentment;otherwise, only on payment;and

（2）upon dishonor, either in the case of

及承兑提示还是付款提示，均可向汇票中指定的临时协调人寻求指示并遵从该指示，或如果提示银行不打算利用该协调人的服务，银行必须以勤勉和善意辨清拒付的原因，必须向转让人通知该拒付，必须报告自己对拒付原因的调查结果，且必须要求给予指示。提示银行应遵从及时收到的任何合理指示，但除此之外，提示银行对单据所代表的货物不承担其他义务；并且，银行有权就遵从该指示的费用取得补偿，并有权就该费用取得预付或赔付。

presentment for acceptance or presentment for payment, may seek and follow instructions from any referee in case of need designated in the draft or, if the presenting bank does not choose to utilize the referee's services, it must use diligence and good faith to ascertain the reason for dishonor, must notify its transferor of the dishonor and of the results of its effort to ascertain the reasons therefor, and must request instructions.However, the presenting bank is under no obligation with respect to goods represented by the documents except to follow any reasonable instructions seasonably received;it has a right to reimbursement for any expense incurred in following instructions and to prepayment of or indemnity for those expenses.

第 4.504 条　提示银行处置货物的选择权；就费用取得担保权益

§ 4.504. Privilege of Presenting Bank to Deal With Goods; Security Interest for Expenses.

（a）在跟单汇票被拒付后，如果提示银行及时寻求指示，但在合理时间内未获得指示，银行可以存储、出售或以其他合理方式处置货物。

（a）A presenting bank that, following the dishonor of a documentary draft, has seasonably requested instructions but does not receive them within a reasonable time may store, sell, or otherwise deal with the goods in any reasonable manner.

（b）对于因（a）款所述之行为产生的合理费用，提示银行对货物或其收益享有留置权，并且，可以采用与未获付款之卖方的留置权同样的方式，对货物或其收益进行变现。

（b）For its reasonable expenses incurred by action under Subsection（a）the presenting bank has a lien upon the goods or their proceeds, which may be foreclosed in the same manner as an unpaid seller's lien.

词汇索引

存款银行	depositary bank	第 4.105 条（2）
电子提示协议	agreement for electronic presentment	第 4.110 条（a）
付款银行	payor bank	第 4.105 条（3）
跟单汇票	documentary draft	第 4.104 条（a）（6）
汇票	draft	第 4.104 条（a）（7）
结算	settle	第 4.104 条（a）（11）
客户	customer	第 4.104 条（a）（5）
票证	item	第 4.104 条（a）（9）
票证清算行	clearing house	第 4.104 条（a）（4）
收款银行	collecting bank	第 4.105 条（5）
受票人	drawee	第 4.104 条（a）（8）
提示通知	presentment notice	第 4.110 条（b）
午夜截止期	midnight deadline	第 4.104 条（a）（10）
下午	afternoon	第 4.104 条（a）（2）
银行	bank	第 4.105 条（1）
银行营业日	banking day	第 4.104 条（a）（3）
暂停对外付款	suspends payments	第 4.104 条（a）（12）
账户	account	第 4.104 条（a）（1）
中间银行	intermediary bank	第 4.105 条（4）

第4A篇　资金转账

ARTICLE 4A. FUNDS TRANSFERS

第1章　适用范围和定义

PART 1. SUBJECT MATTER AND DEFINITIONS

第4A.101条　简称

本篇被引用时可称为《统一商法典——资金转账》。

第4A.102条　适用范围

除第4A.108条另有规定外，本篇适用于第4A.104条定义的资金转账。

第4A.103条　支付命令：定义

（a）在本篇中：

（1）“支付命令”指发送人以口头、电子或书面形式发送给接收银行的指示，要求其向受益人支付或致使另一银行向受益人支付金额固定或金额可算的款项，但是：

（A）该指示除了说明向受益人付款的时间，不得包含其他付款条件；

（B）接收银行获得补偿的方式，必须是借记发送人账户，

§ 4A.101. Short Title.

This Article may be cited as Uniform Commercial Code—Funds Transfers.

§ 4A.102. Subject Matter.

Except as otherwise provided in Section 4A.108, this Article applies to funds transfers defined in Section 4A.104.

§ 4A.103. Payment Order—Definitions.

（a）In this Article:

（1）“Payment order” means an instruction of a sender to a receiving bank, transmitted orally, electronically, or in writing, to pay, or to cause another bank to pay, a fixed or determinable amount of money to a beneficiary if:

（A）the instruction does not state a condition of payment to the beneficiary other than the time of payment;

（B）the receiving bank is to be reimbursed by debiting an account of, or otherwise

或以其他方式从发送人获得付款；并且

receiving payment from, the sender;and

（C）发送人必须直接把指示发送给接收银行；或发送给代理人、资金转账系统或通信系统，再转发给接收银行。

（C）the instruction is transmitted by the sender directly to the receiving bank or to an agent, funds transfer system, or communication system for transmittal to the receiving bank.

（2）“受益人”指受益人银行应向其付款的人。

（2）“Beneficiary” means the person to be paid by the beneficiary's bank.

（3）“受益人银行”指支付命令中指定的，应根据支付命令贷记受益人在该银行所持账户的银行；或如果支付命令未规定向某个账户付款，则指支付命令中指定的，应以其他方式向受益人付款的银行。

（3）“Beneficiary's bank” means the bank identified in a payment order in which an account of the beneficiary is to be credited pursuant to the order or which otherwise is to make payment to the beneficiary if the order does not provide for payment to an account.

（4）“接收银行”指发送人向其发送指示的银行。

（4）“Receiving bank” means the bank to which the sender's instruction is addressed.

（5）“发送人”指向接收银行发送指示的人。

（5）“Sender” means the person giving the instruction to the receiving bank.

（b）如果一项指示符合（a）（1）款的规定，并要求向受益人作出一次以上的付款，则对于每一次付款，该指示都是单独的支付命令。

（b）If an instruction complying with Subsection（a）（1）is to make more than one payment to a beneficiary, the instruction is a separate payment order with respect to each payment.

（c）将支付命令发送给接收银行，即构成支付命令的出具。

（c）A payment order is issued when it is sent to the receiving bank.

第 4A.104 条　资金转账：定义

§ 4A.104. Funds Transfer—Definitions.

在本篇中：

In this Article:

（1）“资金转账”指一个系列交易，从发起人出具支付命令开始，目的在于向支付命令

（1）“Funds transfer” means the series of transactions, beginning with the originator's payment order, made for the purpose of making

的受益人付款。“资金转账”包括任何由发起人银行或中间银行出具的支付命令，只要其目的在于执行发起人的支付命令。如果受益人银行为了发起人之支付命令之受益人的利益，接受一项支付命令，资金转账即告完成。

payment to the beneficiary of the order. The term includes any payment order issued by the originator's bank or an intermediary bank intended to carry out theoriginator's payment order.A funds transfer is completed by acceptance by the beneficiary's bank of a payment order for the benefit of the beneficiary of the originator's payment order.

（2）“中间银行”指除发起人银行和受益人银行外的接收银行。

（2）“Intermediary bank” means a receiving bank other than the originator's bank or the beneficiary's bank.

（3）“发起人”指资金转账中首个支付命令的发送人。

（3）“Originator” means the sender of the first payment order in a funds transfer.

（4）“发起人银行”：

（4）“Originator's bank” means:

（A）当发起人不是银行时，指发起人向其出具支付命令的接收银行；或

（A）the receiving bank to which the payment order of the originator is issued if the originator is not a bank;or

（B）当发起人是银行时，指发起人。

（B）the originator if the originator is a bank.

第 4A.105 条 其他定义

§ 4A.105. Other Definitions.

（a）在本篇中：

（a）In this Article:

（1）“授权账户”指客户在银行持有的并由客户指定的存款账户，并在客户向银行出具支付命令后，作为付款的来源。如果客户未指定此种账户，则客户的任何账户均为授权账户，只要根据支付命令从该账户付款并不违反该账户的使用限制。

（1）“Authorized account” means a deposit account of a customer in a bank designated by the customer as a source of payment of payment orders issued by the customer to the bank.If a customer does not so designate an account, any account of the customer is an authorized account if payment of a payment order from that account is not inconsistent with a restriction on the use of that account.

（2）“银行”指从事银行业务的人，包括储蓄银行、储贷协会、信贷合作社和信托公司。

（2）“Bank” means a person engaged in the business of banking and includes a savings bank, savings and loan association, credit

为本篇目的，银行的分行或独立营业厅是独立的银行。

union, and trust company.A branch or separate office of a bank is a separate bank for purposes of this Article.

（3）“客户”指在银行持有账户的人，或银行同意从其接收支付命令的人。“客户”包括银行。

（3）“Customer” means a person, including a bank, having an account with a bank or from whom a bank has agreed to receive payment orders.

（4）接收银行的“资金转账营业日”指一天中接收银行公开营业的那段时间，在该期间可以接收、处理和发送支付命令，以及取消或修改支付命令。

（4）“Funds transfer business day” of a receiving bank means the part of a day during which the receiving bank is open for the receipt, processing, and transmittal of payment orders and cancellations and amendments of payment orders.

（5）“资金转账系统”指汇款转账系统、自动化票证清算行，或票证清算行或银行协会的其他通信系统，可用于将银行的支付命令发送到接收该命令的银行。

（5）“Funds transfer system” means a wire transfer network, automated clearinghouse, or other communication system of a clearinghouse or other association of banks through which a payment order by a bank may be transmitted to the bank to which the order is addressed.

（6）[保留]

（6）[Reserved]

（7）涉及一项事实时，“证明”指承担该事实的举证责任[第 1.201 条（b）（8）款]。

（7）“Prove” with respect to a fact means to meet the burden of establishing the fact（Section 1.201（b）（8））.

（b）适用于本篇的其他定义及其所在位置：

（b）Other definitions applying to this Article and the sections in which they appear are:

“接受” 第 4A.209 条
“受益人” 第 4A.103 条
“受益人银行” 第 4A.103 条
“已执行” 第 4A.301 条
“执行日” 第 4A.301 条
“资金转账” 第 4A.104 条

“Acceptance.” Section 4A.209.
“Beneficiary.” Section 4A.103.
“Beneficiary’s bank.” Section 4A.103.
“Executed.” Section 4A.301.
“Execution date.” Section 4A.301.
“Funds transfer.” Section 4A.104.

"资金转账系统规则"　第4A.501条

"中间银行"　第4A.104条

"发起人"　第4A.104条

"发起人银行"　第4A.104条

"受益人银行向受益人的付款"　第4A.405条

"发起人向受益人的付款"第4A.406条

"发送人向接收银行的付款"　第4A.403条

"付款日"　第4A.401条

"支付命令"　第4A.103条

"接收银行"　第4A.103条

"安全程序"　第4A.201条

"发送人"　第4A.103条

（c）第4篇中的下列定义适用于本篇：

"票证清算行"　第4.104条

"票证"　第4.104条

"暂停对外付款"　第4.104条

（d）此外，第1篇中的通用定义和解释原则适用于本篇通篇。

"Funds transfer system rule." Section 4A.501.

"Intermediary bank." Section 4A.104.

"Originator." Section 4A.104.

"Originator's bank." Section 4A.104.

"Payment by beneficiary's bank to beneficiary." Section 4A.405.

"Payment by originator to beneficiary." Section 4A.406.

"Payment by sender to receiving bank." Section 4A.403.

"Payment date." Section 4A.401.

"Payment order." Section 4A.103.

"Receiving bank." Section 4A.103.

"Security procedure." Section 4A.201.

"Sender." Section 4A.103.

(c) The following definitions in Article 4 apply to this Article:

"Clearinghouse." Section 4.104.

"Item." Section 4.104.

"Suspends payments." Section 4.104.

(d) In addition, Article 1 contains general definitions and principles of construction and interpretation applicable throughout this Article.

第4A.106条　收到支付命令的时间

（a）收到支付命令的时间，或收到取消或修改支付命令之通信的时间，应根据第1.202条有关通知收到时间的原则确定。接收银行可为资金转账营业日制定一个或多个截止时间，

§ 4A.106. Time Payment Order Is Received.

(a) The time of receipt of a payment order or communication cancelling or amending a payment order is determined by the rules applicable to receipt of a notice stated in Section 1.202.A receiving bank may fix a cutoff time or times on a funds transfer business

用于接收和处理支付命令，或接收或处理有关取消或修改支付命令的通信。可以为支付命令、取消或修改制定不同的截止时间，也可以为不同种类的支付命令、取消或修改制定不同的截止时间。可以将同一截止时间适用于所有发送人，也可以为不同的发送人或不同的支付命令种类，制定不同的截止时间。如果支付命令，或有关取消或修改支付命令的通信，在资金转账营业日结束之后收到，或在资金转账营业日的相关截止时间之后收到，接收银行可将该支付命令或通信视为在下一个资金转账营业日开始时收到。

day for the receipt and processing of payment orders and communications cancelling or amending payment orders.Different cutoff times may apply to payment orders, cancellations, or amendments, or to different categories of payment orders, cancellations, or amendments. A cutoff time may apply to senders generally or different cutoff times may apply to different senders or categories of payment orders.If a payment order or communication cancelling or amending a payment order is received after the close of a funds transfer business day or after the appropriate cutoff time on a funds transfer business day, the receiving bank may treat the payment order or communication as received at the opening of the next funds transfer business day.

（b）如果本篇涉及执行日或付款日，或涉及接收银行需要采取行动的行动日，但该日不是资金转账营业日，则应将下一个资金转账营业日视为该日，除非本篇有相反规定。

（b）If this Article refers to an execution date or payment date or states a day on which a receiving bank is required to take action, and the date or day does not fall on a funds transfer business day, the next day that is a funds transfer business day is treated as the date or day stated, unless the contrary is stated in this Article.

第 4A.107 条　联邦储备条例和实施细则

§ 4A.107. Federal Reserve Regulations and Operating Circulars.

如果本篇任何条款与联邦储备系统委员会条例或联邦储备银行实施细则存在冲突，则在冲突所涉及的范围内，应适用该条例或细则。

Regulations of the Board of Governors of the Federal Reserve System and operating circulars of the Federal Reserve Banks supersede any inconsistent provision of this Article to the extent of the inconsistency.

第 4A.108 条 排除由联邦法管辖的消费者交易

如果一项资金转账在任何方面受最新修订的《电子资金转账法》的约束，则本篇不适用于该资金转账。

§ 4A.108. Exclusion of Consumer Transactions Governed by Federal Law.

This Article does not apply to a funds transfer any part of which is governed by the Electronic Fund Transfer Act, as amended from time to time.

第2章 支付命令的出具和接受

PART 2. ISSUE AND ACCEPTANCE OF PAYMENT ORDER

第 4A.201 条 安全程序

“安全程序”指客户与接收银行通过协议为下列目的设立的程序：(i) 确认支付命令以及有关修改或取消支付命令的通信系来自客户，或 (ii) 发现支付命令或通信中的发送错误或内容错误。安全程序可能需要使用密码或其他代码、识别词语或数字、加密措施、回叫程序或类似保密设施。将支付命令或通信中的签名与客户的授权签名样本进行比对，其本身不构成安全程序。

§ 4A.201. Security Procedure.

“Security procedure” means a procedure established by an agreement between a customer and a receiving bank for the purpose of (i) verifying that a payment order or communication amending or cancelling a payment order is that of the customer, or (ii) detecting error in the transmission or the content of the payment order or communication.A security procedure may require the use of algorithms or other codes, identifying words or numbers, encryption, callback procedures, or similar security devices.Comparison of a signature on a payment order or communication with an authorized specimen signature of the customer is not by itself a security procedure.

第 4A.202 条 已授权和已核实的支付命令

(a) 如果任何人对一项支付命令作出授权，或根据代理法基于其他原因受该支付命令的约束，且支付命令显示该人系发送人，则接收银行收到的

§ 4A.202. Authorized and Verified Payment Orders.

(a) A payment order received by the receiving bank is the authorized order of the person identified as sender if that person authorized the order or is otherwise bound by it under the law of agency.

该支付命令，即构成该人的授权命令。

（b）如果银行与客户约定，对于以客户名字作为发送人出具给银行的支付命令，将使用安全程序予以核实，此时，只要接收银行收到的支付命令符合下列，即为客户的有效命令，无论命令是否业经授权：（i）作为防止无授权支付命令的安全措施，该安全程序系商业上合理的方法，并且（ii）银行能够证明，其以善意接受了支付命令，遵守了安全程序，并遵守了书面协议或客户指示中对接受以客户名字出具之支付命令的限制性规定。如果任何指示违反了与客户的书面协议，或该指示收到的时间与方式使银行没有合理机会在接受支付命令之前据以作为，银行即无须服从该指示。

（b）If a bank and its customer have agreed that the authenticity of payment orders issued to the bank in the name of the customer as sender will be verified pursuant to a security procedure, a payment order received by the receiving bank is effective as the order of the customer, whether or not authorized, if （i）the security procedure is a commercially reasonable method of providing security against unauthorized payment orders, and（ii）the bank proves that it accepted the payment order in good faith and in compliance with the security procedure and any written agreement or instruction of the customer restricting acceptance of payment orders issued in the name of the customer.The bank is not required to follow an instruction that violates a written agreement with the customer or notice of which is not received at a time and in a manner affording the bank a reasonable opportunity to act on it before the payment order is accepted.

（c）安全程序的商业合理性，属于法律问题，应根据下列因素确定：客户向银行表达的愿望、银行所知的客户情况（包括该客户通常出具给该银行之支付命令的金额、类型和频率）、提供给客户选用的其他安全程序，以及类似情况下其他客户和接收银行一般使用的安全程序。在下列情况下，安全

（c）Commercial reasonableness of a security procedure is a question of law to be determined by considering the wishes of the customer expressed to the bank, the circumstances of the customer known to the bank, including the size, type, and frequency of payment orders normally issued by the customer to the bank, alternative security procedures offered to the customer, and security procedures in general use by customers and receiving banks similarly

程序被视为商业上合理：

situated.A security procedure is deemed to be commercially reasonable if:

（1）安全程序系由客户选定，且银行在此之前提供了对客户商业上合理的安全程序，但被客户拒绝；并且

（1）the security procedure was chosen by the customer after the bank offered, and the customer refused, a security procedure that was commercially reasonable for the customer;and

（2）客户以书面明确同意，对于以其名字出具的支付命令，无论是否业经授权，只要银行在遵守客户选定之安全程序的情况下作出接受，该支付命令即对客户有约束力。

（2）the customer expressly agreed in writing to be bound by any payment order, whether or not authorized, issued in its name and accepted by the bank in compliance with the security procedure chosen by the customer.

（d）在本篇中，如果支付命令以客户的名字发送，“发送人”即包括该客户，只要该命令根据（a）款属于客户的授权命令，或根据（b）款属于客户的有效命令。

（d）The term “sender” in this Article includes the customer in whose name a payment order is issued if the order is the authorized order of the customer under Subsection（a）or it is effective as the order of the customer under Subsection（b）.

（e）本条适用于支付命令的修改或取消，且适用程度与支付命令相同。

（e）This section applies to amendments and cancellations of payment orders to the same extent it applies to payment orders.

（f）除本条及第4A.203条（a）（1）款另有规定外，本条或第4A.203条规定的权利和义务，不得通过协议加以改变。

（f）Except as provided in this section and in Section 4A.203（a）（1）, the rights and obligations arising under this section or Section 4A.203 may not be varied by agreement.

第4A.203条　某些已核实的支付命令不可强制履行

§ 4A.203. Unenforceability of Certain Verified Payment Orders.

（a）如果已被接受的支付命令指明发送人为客户，且根据第4A.202条（a）款，命令不属于客户的授权命令，但根据第4A.202条（b）款，属于客户的有效命令，则应适用下

（a）If an accepted payment order is not, under Section 4A.202（a）, an authorized order of a customer identified as sender, but is effective as an order of the customer pursuant to Section 4A.202（b）, the following rules apply:

列原则：

（1）接收银行可以通过明示书面协议，对银行的权限进行限制，即银行在何种程度上有权强制履行或保留支付命令的付款。

（2）如果客户能够证明，支付命令非由下列人直接或间接引起，则接收银行无权强制履行或保留该支付命令的付款：

（A）该人曾在任何时间接受委托，有义务代表客户就支付命令或安全程序采取行动；或

（B）该人曾接触过客户的发送设施；或曾获取到有助于破解安全程序的信息，无论该信息如何获取，也无论客户是否存在过错，只要该信息的获取，系通过客户控制的端口，且未得到接收银行的授权。信息包括任何接入设备、电脑软件或类似设施。

（b）本条适用于支付命令的修改，且适用程度与支付命令相同。

第4A.204条　付款的退还；客户报告无授权支付命令的义务

（a）如果接收银行接受了以客户名字作为发送人的支付命令，但该命令：(i) 根据第

（1）By express written agreement, the receiving bank may limit the extent to which it is entitled to enforce or retain payment of the payment order.

（2）The receiving bank is not entitled to enforce or retain payment of the payment order if the customer proves that the order was not caused, directly or indirectly, by a person:

（A）entrusted at any time with duties to act for the customer with respect to payment orders or the security procedure;or

（B）who obtained access to transmitting facilities of the customer or who obtained, from a source controlled by the customer and without authority of the receiving bank, information facilitating breach of the security procedure, regardless of how the information was obtained or whether the customer was at fault.Information includes any access device, computer software, or the like.

（b）This section applies to amendments of payment orders to the same extent it applies to payment orders.

§ 4A.204. Refund of Payment and Duty of Customer to Report With Respect to Unauthorized Payment Order.

（a）If a receiving bank accepts a payment order issued in the name of its customer as sender which is（i）not authorized and not

4A.202条，不能作为具有授权或具有效力的客户命令，或（ii）根据第4A.203条，不能对客户全部或部分地强制履行，此时，在银行无权强制履行付款的限度内，银行对于从客户就支付命令收到的付款，应予退还；同时，应就所退还的金额，从银行收到款项至退还款项这段时间，支付利息。但是，如果客户未能行使正常谨慎，即未能注意到该命令未经客户授权，且未能在收到银行通知，说明该命令已被接受或已就该命令借记客户账户后，在最长不超过90天的合理时间内，将相关事实通知银行，客户即无权就应被退还的款项，从银行获得利息。即使客户未能根据本条向银行作出通知，银行亦无权向客户索赔。

effective as the order of the customer under Section 4A.202, or（ii）not enforceable, in whole or in part, against the customer under Section 4A.203, the bank shall refund any payment of the payment order received from the customer to the extent the bank is not entitled to enforce payment and shall pay interest on the refundable amount calculated from the date the bank received payment to the date of the refund.However, the customer is not entitled to interest from the bank on the amount to be refunded if the customer fails to exercise ordinary care to determine that the order was not authorized by the customer and to notify the bank of the relevant facts within a reasonable time not exceeding 90 days after the date the customer received notification from the bank that the order was accepted or that the customer's account was debited with respect to the order.The bank is not entitled to any recovery from the customer on account of a failure by the customer to give notification as stated in this section.

（b）可以通过第1.302条（b）款所述的协议，确定（a）款项下的合理时间，但除此之外，接收银行在（a）款项下退还付款的义务，不得通过协议加以改变。

（b）Reasonable time under Subsection（a）may be fixed by agreement as stated in Section 1.302（b）, but the obligation of a receiving bank to refund payment as stated in Subsection（a）may not otherwise be varied by agreement.

第4A.205条　错误的支付命令

§ 4A.205. Erroneous Payment Orders.

（a）如果已被接受的支付命令系根据防错安全程序发送，

（a）If an accepted payment order was transmitted pursuant to a security procedure for

但该命令（i）错误地指定了非属发送人本意的付款受益人，（ii）错误地规定了大于发送人本意的付款金额，或（iii）错误地重复发送了发送人已经发送过的支付命令，则应适用下列原则：

the detection of error and the payment order（i）erroneously instructed payment to a beneficiary not intended by the sender,（ii）erroneously instructed payment in an amount greater than the amount intended by the sender, or（iii）was an erroneously transmitted duplicate of a payment order previously sent by the sender, the following rules apply:

（1）如果发送人能够证明，发送人或根据第4A.206条代表发送人作为的人遵守了安全程序，且在接收银行亦遵守该程序时该错误本可被发现，则在（2）款和（3）款规定的范围内，发送人没有义务为该命令付款。

（1）If the sender proves that the sender or a person acting on behalf of the sender pursuant to Section 4A.206 complied with the security procedure and that the error would have been detected if the receiving bank had also complied, the sender is not obliged to pay the order to the extent stated in Subdivisions（2）and（3）.

（2）如果资金转账已基于（a）（i）款或（a）（iii）款所述的错误支付命令完成，则发送人没有义务就该命令付款，但接收银行有权在有关误解和返还之法律允许的限度内，向受益人追索所支付的金额。

（2）If the funds transfer is completed on the basis of an erroneous payment order described in clause（i）or（iii）of Subsection（a）, the sender is not obliged to pay the order and the receiving bank is entitled to recover from the beneficiary any amount paid to the beneficiary to the extent allowed by the law governing mistake and restitution.

（3）如果资金转账已基于（a)(ii)款所述的支付命令完成，则对于受益人收到的超出发送人本意的金额部分，发送人没有义务就该命令付款。此时，接收银行有权在有关误解和返还之法律允许的限度内，向受益人追索所支付的额外金额。

（3）If the funds transfer is completed on the basis of a payment order described in clause（ii）of Subsection（a）, the sender is not obliged to pay the order to the extent the amount received by the beneficiary is greater than the amount intended by the sender.In that case, the receiving bank is entitled to recover from the beneficiary the excess amount received to the extent allowed by the law governing mistake and restitution.

（b）如果（i）上述（a）款所述的错误支付命令的发送人没有义务就该命令作出全部或部分付款，但是，（ii）发送人从接收银行收到通知，即银行已接受该命令，或已就该命令借记发送人账户，此时，发送人在收到银行通知后，即有义务行使正常谨慎，根据发送人可以获得的信息发现命令中的错误，并在最多不超过九十天的合理时间内，将相关事实通知银行。如果银行能够证明，发送人未履行该义务，且银行因此受到损失，则发送人应对银行承担赔偿责任，但责任的限度不超过发送人命令中的金额。

（b）If（i）the sender of an erroneous payment order described in Subsection（a）is not obliged to pay all or part of the order, and（ii）the sender receives notification from the receiving bank that the order was accepted by the bank or that the sender's account was debited with respect to the order, the sender has a duty to exercise ordinary care, on the basis of information available to the sender, to discover the error with respect to the order and to advise the bank of the relevant facts within a reasonable time, not exceeding 90 days, after the bank's notification was received by the sender.If the bank proves that the sender failed to perform that duty, the sender is liable to the bank for the loss the bank proves it incurred as a result of the failure, but the liability of the sender may not exceed the amount of the sender's order.

（c）本条适用于支付命令的修改，且适用程度与支付命令相同。

（c）This section applies to amendments to payment orders to the same extent it applies to payment orders.

第4A.206条　通过资金转账系统或其他通信系统发送支付命令

§ 4A.206. Transmission of Payment Order Through Funds Transfer or Other Communication System.

（a）如果通过资金转账系统或其他第三方通信系统向接收银行转发支付命令，则对于向该银行发送的支付命令，该系统被视为发送人的代理人。如果发送给该系统之支付命令的条款，与该系统发送给银行

（a）If a payment order addressed to a receiving bank is transmitted to a funds transfer system or other third-party communication system for transmittal to the bank, the system is deemed to be an agent of the sender for the purpose of transmitting the payment order to the bank.If there is a discrepancy between the

之支付命令的条款存在差异，则该系统发送的条款，被视为发送人支付命令的条款。本条不适用于联邦储备银行的资金转账系统。

terms of the payment order transmitted to the system and the terms of the payment order transmitted by the system to the bank, the terms of the payment order of the sender are those transmitted by the system.This section does not apply to a funds transfer system of the Federal Reserve Banks.

（b）本条适用于支付命令的取消与修改，且适用程度与支付命令相同。

（b）This section applies to cancellations and amendments of payment orders to the same extent it applies to payment orders.

第 4A.207 条　错误描述受益人

§ 4A.207. Misdescription of Beneficiary.

（a）除（b）款另有规定外，如果在受益人银行收到的支付命令中，受益人的名字、银行账户号码或其他识别信息，涉及不存在或无法识别的人或账户，则任何人均不享有该命令之受益人的权利，且该命令也不可能发生被接受的情况。

（a）Subject to Subsection（b），if, in a payment order received by the beneficiary's bank, the name, bank account number, or other identification of the beneficiary refers to a nonexistent or unidentifiable person or account, no person has rights as a beneficiary of the order and acceptance of the order cannot occur.

（b）如果在受益人银行收到的支付命令中，同时以名字和识别号码或银行账户号码指明受益人，但该名字和号码属于不同的人，则应适用下列原则：

（b）If a payment order received by the beneficiary's bank identifies the beneficiary both by name and by an identifying or bank account number and the name and number identify different persons, the following rules apply:

（1）除（c）款另有规定外，如果受益人银行不知道该名字和号码属于不同的人，或如果受益人银行以全自动方式处理该资金转账，则银行可以把号码作为识别受益人的适当方法。受益人银行无须确认该名字和

（1）Except as provided in Subsection（c），if the beneficiary's bank does not know that the name and number refer to different persons or if the funds transfer is processed by the beneficiary bank in a fully automated manner, it may rely on the number as the proper identification of the beneficiaryof the order.

号码是否属于同一人。

The beneficiary's bank need not determine whether the name and number refer to the same person.

（2）如果受益人银行向被指明名字的人付款，或如果代表受益人银行处理该资金转账的个人，知道该名字和号码属于不同的人，则从受益人银行收到付款的人，只有在其有权从资金转账的发起人获得付款时，才能享有受益人的权利，而任何其他人均不享有受益人的权利。如果任何人均不享有受益人的权利，则该命令不可能发生被接受的情况。

（2）If the beneficiary's bank pays the person identified by name or any individual processing the funds transfer on behalf of the beneficiary bank knows that the name and number identify different persons, no person has rights as beneficiary except the person paid by the beneficiary's bank if that person was entitled to receive payment from the originator of the funds transfer.If no person has rights as beneficiary, acceptance of the order cannot occur.

（c）如果（i）上述（b）款所述的支付命令已被接受，（ii）发起人的支付命令对受益人名字和号码的描述存在矛盾，并且（iii）受益人银行根据（b）（1）款允许的方式，向被指明号码的人付款，则应适用下列原则：

（c）If（i）a payment order described in Subsection（b）is accepted,（ii）the originator's payment order described the beneficiary inconsistently by name and number, and（iii）the beneficiary's bank pays the person identified by number as permitted by Subsection（b）（1）, the following rules apply:

（1）如果发起人是银行，则发起人有义务就该命令付款。

（1）If the originator is a bank, the originator is obliged to pay its order.

（2）如果发起人不是银行，且能够证明，以号码指明的人无权从发起人获得付款，则发起人没有义务就该命令付款，除非发起人银行能够证明，在发起人命令被接受前，发起人已得到通知，即在涉及发起人支付命令项下的付款时，受益

（2）If the originator is not a bank and proves that the person identified by number was not entitled to receive payment from the originator, the originator is not obliged to pay its order unless the originator's bank proves that the originator, before acceptance of the originator's order, had notice that payment of a payment order issued by the originator might

人银行可以根据识别号码或银行账户号码付款，即使该号码指明的人，与使用名字指明的受益人不同。要证明已得到通知，可以使用任何允许的证据。如果发起人银行能够证明，在支付命令被接受前，发起人签署过书面文件，其中注明了通知的相关信息，发起人银行即完成举证责任。

be made by the beneficiary's bank on the basis of an identifying or bank account number even if it identifies a person different from the named beneficiary.Proof of notice may be made by any admissible evidence.The originator's bank satisfies the burden of proof if it proves that the originator, before the payment order was accepted, signed a writing stating the information to which the notice relates.

（d）涉及（b）（1）款适用的情况时，如果受益人银行正当地向以号码识别的人作出付款，但该人无权从发起人获得付款，则可以在有关误解和返还之法律允许的范围内，根据下列原则从该人追回所付的金额：

（d）In a case governed by Subsection（b）（1）, if the beneficiary's bank rightfully pays the person identified by number and that person was not entitled to receive payment from the originator, the amount paid may be recovered from that person to the extent allowed by the law governing mistake and restitution as follows:

（1）如果根据（c）款，发起人有义务就支付命令付款，则发起人有权追回付款。

（1）If the originator is obliged to pay its payment order as stated in Subsection（c）, the originator has the right to recover.

（2）如果发起人不是银行，且没有义务就支付命令付款，则发起人银行有权追回付款。

（2）If the originator is not a bank and is not obliged to pay its payment order, the originator's bank has the right to recover.

第 4A.208 条　错误描述中间银行或受益人银行

§ 4A.208. Misdescription of Intermediary Bank or Beneficiary's Bank.

（a）本款适用于仅以识别号码识别中间银行或受益人银行的支付命令。

（a）This subsection applies to a payment order identifying an intermediary bank or the beneficiary's bank only by an identifying number.

（1）接收银行可以依赖该号码作为识别中间银行或受益人银行的适当方法，而无须确

（1）The receiving bank may rely on the number as the proper identification of the intermediary or beneficiary's bank and does

认该号码是否属于一个银行。

not need to determine whether the number identifies a bank.

（2）如果接收银行依赖该号码执行命令或试图执行命令，并因此受到损失或发生费用，发送人有义务补偿接收银行。

（2）The sender is obliged to compensate the receiving bank for any loss and expenses incurred by the receiving bank as a result of its reliance on the number in executing or attempting to execute the order.

（b）如果支付命令同时以名字和识别号码识别中间银行或受益人银行，但名字和号码属于不同的人，则应适用本款。

（b）This subsection applies to a payment order identifying an intermediary bank or the beneficiary's bank both by name and an identifying number if the name and number identify different persons.

（1）如果发送人是银行，则接收银行可以依赖该号码作为识别中间银行或受益人银行的适当方法，只要接收银行在执行发送人命令时，不知道名字和号码属于不同的人。接收银行无须确认该名字和号码是否属于同一人，或该号码是否属于一个银行。如果接收银行依赖该号码执行命令或试图执行命令，并因此受到损失或发生费用，发送人有义务补偿接收银行。

（1）If the sender is a bank, the receiving bank may rely on the number as the proper identification of the intermediary or beneficiary's bank if the receiving bank, when it executes the sender's order, does not know that the name and number identify different persons.The receiving bank need not determine whether the name and number refer to the same person or whether the number refersto a bank.The sender is obliged to compensate the receiving bank for any loss and expenses incurred by the receiving bank as a result of its reliance on the number in executing or attempting to execute the order.

（2）如果发送人不是银行，但接收银行能够证明，在支付命令被接受前，发送人已得到通知，即接收银行可能会依赖号码作为识别中间人银行或受益人银行的适当方法，即使该号码所识别的人不是该名字所识别的银行，此时，发送人和

（2）If the sender is not a bank and the receiving bank proves that the sender, before the payment order was accepted, had notice that the receiving bank might rely on the number as the proper identification of the intermediary or beneficiary's bank even if it identifics a person different from the bank identified by name, the rights and obligations of the sender and

接收银行的权利和义务，与发送人为银行时一样，受（b）(1）款的约束。要证明已得到通知，可以使用任何允许的证据。如果接收银行能够证明，在支付命令被接受前，发送人签署过书面文件，其中注明了通知的相关信息，接收银行即完成举证责任。

the receiving bank are governed by Subsection（b）（1）, as though the sender were a bank. Proof of notice may be made by any admissible evidence.The receiving bank satisfies the burden of proof if it proves that the sender, before the payment order was accepted, signed a writing stating the information to which the notice relates.

（3）无论发送人是否为银行，接收银行均可把名字作为识别中间银行或受益人银行的适当方法，只要接收银行在执行发送人命令时，不知道该名字和号码属于不同的人。接收银行无须确认该名字和号码是否属于同一人。

（3）Regardless of whether the sender is a bank, the receiving bank may rely on the name as the proper identification of the intermediary or beneficiary's bank if the receiving bank, at the time it executes the sender's order, does not know that the name and number identify different persons.The receiving bank need not determine whether the name and number refer to the same person.

（4）如果接收银行知道名字和号码属于不同的人，则无论是依赖名字还是依赖号码执行发送人的支付命令，均属于对第 4A.302 条（a）（1）款所述之义务的违反。

（4）If the receiving bank knows that the name and number identify different persons, reliance on either the name or the number in executing the sender's payment order is a breach of the obligation stated in Section 4A.302（a）（1）.

第 4A.209 条　接受支付命令

§ 4A.209. Acceptance of Payment Order.

（a）除（d）款另有规定外，只要接收银行（受益人银行除外）执行支付命令，即构成对命令的接受。

（a）Subject to Subsection（d）, a receiving bank other than the beneficiary's bank accepts a payment order when it executes the order.

（b）除（c）款和（d）款另有规定外，下列最早者发生的时间，系受益人银行接受支

（b）Subject to Subsections（c）and（d）, a beneficiary's bank accepts a payment order at the earliest of the following times:

付命令的时间：

（1）银行（i）根据第4A.405条（a）款或（b）款所述，向受益人付款的时间，或（ii）向受益人作出通知的时间，说明收到该命令，或已就该命令贷记受益人账户，除非通知还说明，银行准备拒绝该命令，或说明该命令项下的资金，在银行收到命令发送人付款之前不能提取或使用；

（1）when the bank（i）pays the beneficiary as stated in Section 4A.405（a）or（b），or（ii）notifies the beneficiary of receipt of the order or that the account of the beneficiary has been credited with respect to the order unless the notice indicates that the bank is rejecting the order or that funds with respect to the order may not be withdrawn or used until receipt of payment from the sender of the order;

（2）根据第4A.403条（a）（1）款或（2）款，银行收到发送人命令项下全部付款的时间；或

（2）when the bank receives payment of the entire amount of the sender's order pursuant to Section 4A.403（a）（1）or（2）;or

（3）支付命令之付款日后银行下一个资金转账营业日开始的时间，只要在那个时间，在发送人授权账户中，相对于发送人命令的金额，存在足额的可用信贷，或银行通过其他方式已从发送人收到充分付款；除非在那个时间之前，该命令已被拒绝，或（i）在那个时间之后一小时内被拒绝，或（ii）在付款日后发送人下一个营业日开始后一小时内被拒绝（如果此时间更晚）。如果发送人在付款日之后收到拒绝通知，且发送人的授权账户不产生利息，则银行有义务向发送人支付利息，即根据命令的金额，从付款日起至发送人收到通知或得

（3）the opening of the next funds transfer business day of the bank following the payment date of the order if, at that time, the amount of the sender's order is fully covered by a withdrawable credit balance in an authorized account of the sender or the bank has otherwise received full payment from the sender, unless the order was rejected before that time or is rejected within（i）one hour after that time, or（ii）one hour after the opening of the next business day of the sender following the payment date if that time is later.If notice of rejection is received by the sender after the payment date and the authorized account of the sender does not bear interest, the bank is obliged to pay interest to the sender on the amount of the order for the number of days elapsing after the payment date to the day the

知命令未被接受时止，按该期间的天数计算，包括得到通知的那天。如果在这个期间，可用信贷余额低于命令金额，应付的利息金额应相应减少。

sender receives notice or learns that the order was not accepted, counting that day as an elapsed day.If the withdrawable credit balance during that period falls below the amount of the order, the amount of interest payable is reduced accordingly.

（c）在接收银行收到支付命令之前，命令不可能发生被接受的情况。如果支付命令的受益人在接收银行没有账户，或账户已关闭，或法律不允许接收银行接受对受益人账户的贷记，则不可能发生（b）（2）款或（3）款所述的接受。

（c）Acceptance of a payment order cannot occur before the order is received by the receiving bank.Acceptance does not occur under Subsection（b）（2）or（3）if the beneficiary of the payment order does not have an account with the receiving bank, the account has been closed, or the receiving bank is not permitted by law to receive credits for the beneficiary's account.

（d）如果发起人银行同时系受益人银行，则向发起人银行出具的支付命令，在付款日之前不可能发生被接受的情况；当发起人银行不是受益人银行时，在执行日之前不可能发生被接受的情况。如果发起人银行在执行日之前执行发起人的支付命令，或在付款日之前向发起人支付命令的受益人付款，但支付命令随后根据第4A.211条（b）款被取消，银行可以在有关误解和返还之法律允许的限度内，从受益人收回受益人收到的付款。

（d）A payment order issued to the originator's bank cannot be accepted until the payment date if the bank is the beneficiary's bank, or the execution date if the bank is not the beneficiary's bank.If the originator's bank executes the originator's payment order before the execution date or pays the beneficiary of the originator's payment order before the payment date and the payment order is subsequently canceled pursuant to Section 4A.211（b）, the bank may recover from the beneficiary any payment received to the extent allowed by the law governing mistake and restitution.

第4A.210条　拒绝支付命令

§ 4A.210. Rejection of Payment Order.

（a）如果接收银行通过口

（a）A payment order is rejected by

头、电子或书面形式，就支付命令向发送人发送拒绝通知，即构成对该支付命令的拒绝。拒绝通知无须使用任何特定词语，而只要说明接收银行拒绝该命令，或不会执行或支付该命令，即属充分。如果拒绝通知的发送方式在当时情况下为合理，则拒绝在发出通知时生效。如果拒绝通知使用的方式不合理，则拒绝在收到通知时生效。如果发送人与接收银行的协议规定了对支付命令的拒绝方式，则：

（1）任何符合协议的方式均属合理；以及

（2）任何不符合协议的方式均属不合理，除非使用该不符方式并未造成通知收到之时间的显著延迟。

（b）如果在执行日当天，发送人的授权账户存在足以用于支付命令之付款的可用信贷余额，但接收银行（受益人银行除外）未能执行支付命令，则应适用本款。如果在执行日，发送人未就有关命令收到拒绝通知，且发送人的授权账户不产生利息，则银行有义务向发送人支付利息，即根据命令的金额，从执行日起至命令根据第4A.211条（d）款被取消之日止，或至发送人得到通知或

the receiving bank by a notice of rejection transmitted to the sender orally, electronically, or in writing.A notice of rejection need not use any particular words and is sufficient if it indicates that the receiving bank is rejecting the order or will not execute or pay the order. Rejection is effective when the notice is given if transmission is by a means that is reasonable under the circumstances.If notice of rejection is given by a means that is not reasonable, rejection is effective when the notice is received.If an agreement of the sender and receiving bank establishes the means to be used to reject a payment order:

（1）any means complying with the agreement is reasonable;and

（2）any means not complying is not reasonable unless no significant delay in receipt of the notice resulted from the use of the noncomplying means.

（b）This subsection applies if a receiving bank other than the beneficiary's bank fails to execute a payment order despite the existence on the execution date of a withdrawable credit balance in an authorized account of the sender sufficient to cover the order.If the sender does not receive notice of rejection of the order on the execution date and the authorized account of the sender does not bear interest, the bank is obliged to pay interest to the sender on the amount of the order for the number of days elapsing after the execution date to the earlier of the day the order is canceled pursuant to

得知命令不会被执行之日止（以较早日期为准），按该期间的天数计算，包括该期间的最后一天。如果在这个期间，可用信贷余额低于命令金额，应付的利息金额应相应减少。

Section 4A.211（d）or the day the sender receives notice or learns that the order was not executed, counting the final day of the period as an elapsed day.If the withdrawable credit balance during that period falls below the amount of the order, the amount of interest is reduced accordingly.

（c）如果接收银行暂停对外付款，则从银行暂停对外付款时起，所有已出具给该银行但尚未被接受的支付命令，均属被拒绝。

（c）If a receiving bank suspends payments, all unaccepted payment orders issued to it are deemed rejected at the time the bank suspends payments.

（d）支付命令被接受后，不得随后再被拒绝。支付命令被拒绝后，不得随后再被接受。

（d）Acceptance of a payment order precludes a later rejection of the order.Rejection of a payment order precludes a later acceptance of the order.

第 4A.211 条　取消和修改支付命令

§ 4A.211. Cancellation and Amendment of Payment Order.

（a）支付命令的发送人可以通过口头、电子或书面形式，将有关取消或修改该命令的通信，发送给接收银行。如果在发送人和接收银行之间存在有效的安全程序，则只有在根据安全程序对通信进行核实后，或在银行同意该取消或修改后，该通信才能有效取消或修改该命令。

（a）A communication of the sender of a payment order cancelling or amending the order may be transmitted to the receiving bank orally, electronically, or in writing.If a security procedure is in effect between the sender and the receiving bank, the communication is not effective to cancel or amend the order unless the communication is verified pursuant to the security procedure or the bank agrees to the cancellation or amendment.

（b）除（a）款另有规定外，发送人取消或修改支付命令的通信，只有在其收到的时间和方式使接收银行有合理机会在接受支付命令前根据该通信据

（b）Subject to Subsection（a）, a communication by the sender cancelling or amending a payment order is effective to cancel or amend the order if notice of the communication is received at a time and in a manner affording the

以作为时，该通信才能有效取消或修改该命令。

receiving bank a reasonable opportunity to act on the communication before the bank accepts the payment order.

（c）如果支付命令已被接受，则对该命令的取消或修改，只有在接收银行同意时，或在资金转账系统规则允许不经银行同意而作出取消或修改时，方为有效。

（c）After a payment order has been accepted, cancellation or amendment of the order is not effective unless the receiving bank agrees or a funds transfer system rule allows cancellation or amendment without agreement of the bank.

（1）如果支付命令已被接收银行（受益人银行除外）接受，则对该命令的取消或修改，只有在接收银行对自己的支付命令也相应取消或修改后，方为有效。

（1）With respect to a payment order accepted by a receiving bank other than the beneficiary's bank, cancellation or amendment is not effective unless a conforming cancellation or amendment of the payment order issued by the receiving bank is also made.

（2）如果支付命令已被受益人银行接受，则对该命令的取消或修改，只有在下列情况下，方为有效：该命令系为执行一项无授权支付命令；或该命令系发送人在资金转账中出现错误，致使所产生的支付命令：（i）构成发送人之前已经发送之命令的重复，（ii）向无权从发起人收到付款的受益人付款，或（iii）向受益人支付的金额，大于受益人有权从发起人收到的金额。如果该支付命令被取消或修改，受益人银行有权在有关误解和返还之法律允许的限度内，从受益人追回所付的金额。

（2）With respect to a payment order accepted by the beneficiary's bank, cancellation or amendment is not effective unless the order was issued in execution of an unauthorized payment order or because of a mistake by a sender in the funds transfer which resulted in the issuance of a payment order（i）that is a duplicate of a payment order previously issued by the sender,（ii）that orders payment to a beneficiary not entitled to receive payment from the originator, or（iii）that orders payment in an amount greater than the amount the beneficiary was entitled to receive from the originator.If the payment order is canceled or amended, the beneficiary's bank is entitled to recover from the beneficiary any amount paid to the beneficiary to the extent allowed by the law governing mistake and restitution.

（d）未被接受的支付命令，从该命令的执行日或付款日的次日起，在接收银行第五个资金转账营业日结束时，根据法律规定被自动取消。

（d）An unaccepted payment order is canceled by operation of law at the close of the fifth funds transfer business day of the receiving bank after the execution date or payment date of the order.

（e）已被取消的支付命令不可能再被接受。如果已被接受的支付命令被取消，该接受即失去法律效力，因此无人可以基于该接受拥有任何权利或义务。如果支付命令被修改，则从修改之时起，原始命令被取消；同时，修改后的新支付命令被出具。

（e）A canceled payment order cannot be accepted.If an accepted payment order is canceled, the acceptance is nullified and no person has any right or obligation based on the acceptance.Amendment of a payment order is deemed to be cancellation of the original order at the time of amendment and issue of a new payment order in the amended form at the same time.

（f）除当事方协议或资金转账系统规则另有规定外，如果接收银行在接受支付命令后同意发送人对命令的取消或修改，或如果资金转账系统规则规定，该取消或修改无须银行同意，且银行受到该规则约束，则无论该取消或修改是否有效，对于作出或试图作出取消或修改而给银行造成的损失和费用，包括合理的律师费，发送人应对银行承担责任。

（f）Unless otherwise provided in an agreement of the parties or in a funds transfer system rule, if the receiving bank, after accepting a payment order, agrees to cancellation or amendment of the order by the sender or is bound by a funds transfer system rule allowing cancellation or amendment without the bank's agreement, the sender, whether or not cancellation or amendment is effective, is liable to the bank for any loss and expenses, including reasonable attorney's fees, incurred by the bank as a result of the cancellation or amendment or attempted cancellation or amendment.

（g）即使支付命令的发送人死亡或失去法定行为能力，亦不导致命令的撤回，除非接收银行知道该死亡，或知道有管辖权之法院作出的无行为能

（g）A payment order is not revoked by the death or legal incapacity of the sender unless the receiving bank knows of the death or of an adjudication of incapacity by a court of competent jurisdiction and has reasonable

力裁定，且在接受该命令前有合理机会据以作为。

（h）如果资金转账系统规则与（c）（2）款存在冲突，则对于冲突部分，前者无效。

第 4A.212 条　接收银行对未被接受之支付命令的责任和义务

如果接收银行未接受一项支付命令，但根据明示协议其有义务接受该命令，则银行应根据协议或本篇规定，承担违反合同的责任。但是，除此之外，银行没有义务接受任何一项支付命令；并且，在作出接受前，也没有义务就支付命令采取或不采取任何行动，除非本篇或明示协议另有规定。因作出接受而承担的责任，也只有在该接受系根据第 4A.209 条作出时才产生，且仅限于本篇规定的责任。接收银行不是其所接受之支付命令之发送人或受益人的代理人，也不是资金转账中任何其他当事方的代理人；并且，银行对资金转账中的任何当事方，仅承担本篇或明示协议所规定的义务，而不承担任何其他义务。

opportunity to act before acceptance of the order.

（h）A funds transfer system rule is not effective to the extent it conflicts with Subsection（c）（2）.

§ 4A.212. Liability and Duty of Receiving Bank Regarding Unaccepted Payment Order.

If a receiving bank fails to accept a payment order that it is obliged by express agreement to accept, the bank is liable for breach of the agreement to the extent provided in the agreement or in this Article, but does not otherwise have any duty to accept a payment order or, before acceptance, to take any action, or refrain from taking action, with respect to the order except as provided in this Article or by express agreement.Liability based on acceptance arises only when acceptance occurs as stated in Section 4A.209, and liability is limited to that provided in this Article.A receiving bank is not the agent of the sender orbeneficiary of the payment order it accepts, or of any other party to the funds transfer, and the bank owes no duty to any party to the funds transfer except as provided in this Article or by express agreement.

第3章 接收银行执行发送人的支付命令

PART 3. EXECUTION OF SENDER'S PAYMENT ORDER BY RECEIVING BANK

第 4A.301 条 执行与执行日

（a）如果接收银行收到支付命令后，为了履行该命令而出具了自己的支付命令，即属于“已执行”收到的支付命令。受益人银行收到的支付命令可以被接受，但不可能被执行。

（b）为了执行发送人的支付命令，接收银行应在适当之日出具自己的支付命令。该出具日即为支付命令的“执行日”。执行日可以在发送人的指示中规定，但不得早于支付命令的收到日，并且，除非另有不同规定，应为支付命令的收到日。如果发送人在指示中规定了付款日，则执行日即为付款日；但是，如果为使受益人在付款日获得付款而需要先行作出执行，则执行日应为一个更早的合理之日。

§ 4A.301. Execution and Execution Date.

（a）A payment order is “executed” by the receiving bank when it issues a payment order intended to carry out the payment order received by the bank.A payment order received by the beneficiary's bank can be accepted but cannot be executed.

（b）“Execution date” of a payment order means the date on which the receiving bank may properly issue a payment order in execution of the sender's order.The execution date may be determined by instruction of the sender but cannot be earlier than the day the order is received and, unless otherwise determined, is the day the order is received.If the sender's instruction states a payment date, the execution date is the payment date or an earlier date on which execution is reasonably necessary to allow payment to the beneficiary on the payment date.

第 4A.302 条 接收银行执行支付命令时的义务

（a）除（b）款至（d）款另有规定外，如果接收银行根据第 4A.209 条（a）款接受了支付命令，则银行在执行该命令时，需承担如下义务：

§ 4A.302. Obligations of Receiving Bank in Execution of Payment Order.

（a）Except as provided in Subsections（b）through（d）, if the receiving bank accepts a payment order pursuant to Section 4A.209（a）, the bank has the following obligations in executing the order:

（1）接收银行有义务在执行日出具符合发送人命令的支付命令，并遵从发送人有关下列事项的指示：（i）完成资金转账所应使用的中间银行或资金转账系统，或（ii）资金转账中支付命令的传送方式。如果发起人银行向中间银行出具支付命令，则发起人银行有义务根据发起人的指示向中间银行作出指示。资金转账中的中间银行，在接受发送人的支付命令后，也同样受到发送人指示的约束。

（1）The receiving bank is obliged to issue, on the execution date, a payment order complying with the sender's order and to follow the sender's instructions concerning（i）any intermediary bank or funds transfer system to be used in carrying out the funds transfer, or（ii）the means by which payment orders are to be transmitted in the funds transfer.If the originator's bank issues a payment order to an intermediary bank, the originator's bank is obliged to instruct the intermediary bank according to the instruction of the originator. An intermediary bank in the funds transfer is similarly bound by an instruction given to it by the sender of the payment order it accepts.

（2）如果发送人的指示说明，资金转账应通过电话或电汇完成，或以其他方式说明，资金转账应以最快捷的方式完成，则接收银行有义务以可行的最快捷方式传送自己的支付命令，并向任何中间银行作出相应指示。如果发送人的指示说明了付款日，则接收银行有义务合理选择自己支付命令的发出时间和方式，以使受益人在付款日获得付款，或在其后尽可能快的时间内获得付款。

（2）If the sender's instruction states that the funds transfer is to be carried out telephonically or by wire transfer or otherwise indicates that the funds transfer is to be carried out by the most expeditious means, the receiving bank is obliged to transmit its payment order by the most expeditious available means and to instruct any intermediary bank accordingly.If a sender's instruction states a payment date, the receiving bank is obliged to transmit its payment order at a time and by means reasonably necessary to allow payment to the beneficiary on the payment date or as soon thereafter as is feasible.

（b）除另有指示外，接收银行在执行支付命令时，（i）可以使用任何资金转账系统，只要根据当时情况，使用该系统

（b）Unless otherwise instructed, a receiving bank executing a payment order may（i）use any funds transfer system if use of that system is reasonable in the circumstances, and

系属合理，并且（ii）可以向受益人银行出具支付命令；也可以向中间银行出具支付命令，以便通过该中间银行，迅捷地向受益人银行出具符合发送人命令的支付命令，但是，接收银行在选择中间银行时，应当行使正常谨慎。如果发送人指定了资金转账使用的资金转账系统，但接收银行善意地相信，缺乏可行的方法遵从该指示，或遵从该指示将不适当地延迟资金转账的完成，则接收银行无须遵从发送人的指示。

（ii）issue a payment order to the beneficiary's bank or to an intermediary bank through which a payment order conforming to the sender's order can expeditiously be issued to the beneficiary's bank if the receiving bank exercises ordinary care in the selection of the intermediary bank.A receiving bank is not required to follow an instruction of the sender designating a funds transfer system to be used in carrying out the funds transfer if the receiving bank, in good faith, determines that it is not feasible to follow the instruction or that following the instruction would unduly delay completion of the funds transfer.

（c）除涉及应适用（a）（2）款的情况外，且除接收银行获得不同指示外，接收银行为执行支付命令而出具自己的支付命令时，可以使用一等邮件或在当时情况下为合理的任何方式进行发送。如果接收银行得到指示，即在执行发送人命令时应使用特定方式发送自己的支付命令，则接收银行可以使用所要求的方式出具自己的支付命令，也可以使用同等速度的其他方式。

（c）Unless Subsection（a）（2）applies or the receiving bank is otherwise instructed, the bank may execute a payment order by transmitting its payment order by first class mail or by any means reasonable in the circumstances.If the receiving bank is instructed to execute the sender's order by transmitting its payment order by a particular means, the receiving bank may issue its payment order by the means stated or by any means as expeditious as the means stated.

（d）除发送人另有指示外，（i）接收银行不得为了收取服务费，而在自己出具之支付命令中，从发送人命令的金额中减去执行发送人命令所需的服务费或费用，并且（ii）接收银

（d）Unless instructed by the sender,（i）the receiving bank may not obtain payment of its charges for services and expenses in connection with the execution of the sender's order by issuing a payment order in an amount equal to the amount of the sender's order less the

行不得指示随后的接收银行按同样的金额收取后者所需的费用。

amount of the charges, and (ii) may not instruct a subsequent receiving bank to obtain payment of its charges in the same amount.

第 4A.303 条　错误执行支付命令

§ 4A.303. Erroneous Execution of Payment Order.

(a) 如果接收银行 (i) 在执行发送人的支付命令时，自己出具之支付命令的金额，大于发送人命令的金额，或 (ii) 为执行发送人的命令，自己已出具过支付命令，但之后又重复出具，此时，银行有权根据第 4A.402 条 (c) 款，按发送人命令的金额取得付款，只要该 (c) 款的其他要求也得到满足。银行有权在有关误解和返还之法律允许的限度内，从错误命令的受益人追回多付的金额。

(a) A receiving bank that (i) executes the payment order of the sender by issuing a payment order in an amount greater than the amount of the sender's order or (ii) issues a payment order in execution of the sender's order and then issues a duplicate order, is entitled to payment of the amount of the sender's order under Section 4A.402 (c) if that subsection is otherwise satisfied.The bank is entitled to recover from the beneficiary of the erroneous order the excess payment received to the extent allowed by the law governing mistake and restitution.

(b) 如果接收银行在执行发送人的支付命令时，自己出具之支付命令的金额，小于发送人命令的金额，则接收银行仍有权根据第 4A.402 条(c)款，按发送人命令的金额取得付款，只要 (i) 该 (c) 款的其他要求得到满足，并且 (ii) 银行纠正其错误，为发送人命令的受益人出具额外的支付命令。如果错误未得到纠正，则错误命令的出具者，仅在错误命令的范围内，有权就所接受的发送人命令，取得或保留命令发送

(b) A receiving bank that executes the payment order of the sender by issuing a payment order in an amount less than the amount of the sender's order is entitled to payment of the amount of the sender's order under Section 4A.402 (c) if (i) that subsection is otherwise satisfied and (ii) the bank corrects its mistake by issuing an additional payment order for the benefit of the beneficiary of the sender's order.If the error is not corrected, the issuer of the erroneous order is entitled to receive or retain payment from the sender of the order it accepted only to the extent of the amount of the erroneous order.This subsection does not apply

人的付款。但是，如果接收银行系遵从发送人的指示，在执行发送人的支付命令时，扣除了自己的服务费和费用，导致自己支付命令的金额相应小于发送人命令的金额，则本款不适用。

if the receiving bank executes the sender's payment order by issuing a payment order in an amount less than the amount of the sender's order for the purpose of obtaining payment of its charges for services and expenses pursuant to instruction of the sender.

（c）如果接收银行在执行发送人的支付命令时，自己出具之支付命令的受益人，不是发送人命令的受益人，且资金转账基于该错误获得完成，则支付命令被错误执行的发送人，以及资金转账中所有之前的发送人，均无义务就他们出具的支付命令付款。出具错误命令的人，有权在有关误解和返还之法律允许的限度内，从该命令的受益人追回其收到的付款。

（c）If a receiving bank executes the payment order of the sender by issuing a payment order to a beneficiary different from the beneficiary of the sender's order and the funds transfer is completed on the basis of that error, the sender of the payment order that was erroneously executed and all previous senders in the funds transfer are not obliged to pay the payment orders they issued.The issuer of the erroneous order is entitled to recover from the beneficiary of the order the payment received to the extent allowed by the law governing mistake and restitution.

第 4A.304 条 发送人报告错误执行之支付命令的义务

涉及第 4A.303 条所述的被错误执行的支付命令时，如果发送人得到接收银行的通知，即命令已被执行，或发送人的账户已因该命令被借记，发送人即有义务行使正常谨慎，根据发送人能够得到的信息，发现该命令被错误执行，并在发送人从银行得到通知后最长不超过 90 天的合理时间内，将相关事实通知银行。如果发送

§ 4A.304. Duty of Sender to Report Erroneously Executed Payment Order.

If the sender of a payment order that is erroneously executed as stated in Section 4A.303 receives notification from the receiving bank that the order was executed or that the sender's account was debited with respect to the order, the sender has a duty to exercise ordinary care to determine, on the basis of information available to the sender, that the order was erroneously executed and to notify the bank of the relevant facts within a reasonable time not exceeding 90 days after

人未能履行该义务，则对于根据第 4A.402 条（d）款银行应退还给发送人的任何金额，银行没有义务就其得知错误执行之前的这段时间支付利息。即使发送人未能履行本条所述的义务，银行亦无权向发送人索赔。

the notification from the bank was received by the sender.If the sender fails to perform that duty, the bank is not obliged to pay interest on any amount refundable to the sender under Section 4A.402（d）for the period before the bank learns of the execution error.The bank is not entitled to any recovery from the sender on account of a failure by the sender to perform the duty stated in this section.

第 4A.305 条 延迟执行、不当执行或未能执行支付命令的责任

§ 4A.305. Liability for Late or Improper Execution or Failure to Execute Payment Order.

（a）如果资金转账获得完成，但接收银行在执行支付命令时，违反了本篇第 4A.302 条的规定，并造成向受益人付款的延迟，则对于不当执行造成延迟的期间，银行有义务向发起人或资金转账受益人支付利息。除（c）款另有规定外，银行不对其他额外损失负责。

（a）If a funds transfer is completed but execution of a payment order by the receiving bank in breach of Section 4A.302 of this Article results in delay in payment to the beneficiary, the bank is obliged to pay interest to either the originator or the beneficiary of the funds transfer for the period of delay caused by the improper execution.Except as provided by Subsection（c）,additional damages are not recoverable.

（b）如果接收银行在执行支付命令时，违反了第 4A.302 条的规定，造成（i）资金转账未能完成，（ii）未能使用发起人指定的中间银行，或（iii）发出的支付命令不符合发起人支付命令的条款，此时，银行应就发起人在资金转账中的费用、附带费用及利息损失，向发起人承担责任，只要这些损失系因不当执行引起，且未包括在

（b）If execution of a payment order by a receiving bank in breach of Section 4A.302 results in（i）noncompletion of the funds transfer,（ii）failure to use an intermediary bank designated by the originator, or（iii）issuance of a payment order that does not comply with the terms of the payment order of the originator, the bank is liable to the originator for its expenses in the funds transfer and for incidental expenses and interest losses, to the extent not covered by Subsection

本条（a）款的范围内。除（c）款另有规定外，银行不对其他额外损失负责。

(a) of this section, resulting from the improper execution.Except as provided by Subsection (c), additional damages are not recoverable.

（c）除根据（a）款和（b）款规定可以获得的补偿外，还可以根据接收银行之书面明示协议的规定，就包括间接损失在内的损失取得赔偿。

(c) In addition to the amounts payable under Subsections (a) and (b), damages, including consequential damages, are recoverable to the extent provided in an express written agreement of the receiving bank.

（d）如果接收银行未能执行根据明示协议其有义务执行的支付命令，则银行应就未能执行而给发送人造成的交易费用、附带费用和利息损失，承担补偿责任。其他额外损失，包括间接损失，只有在银行的书面明示协议规定应予赔偿时，才应赔偿，而在其他情况下不予赔偿。

(d) If a receiving bank fails to execute a payment order it was obliged by express agreement to execute, the receiving bank is liable to the sender for its expenses in the transaction and for incidental expenses and interest losses resulting from the failure to execute.Additional damages, including consequential damages, are recoverable to the extent provided in an express written agreement of the receiving bank, but are not otherwise recoverable.

（e）如果曾根据（a）款或（b）款提出补偿要求，但被拒绝，则在随后提起的索赔诉讼中，可以索赔合理的律师费。如果索赔系基于违反（d）款项下的协议，但该协议未规定损害赔偿，则只要曾根据本条（d）款提出补偿要求，但被拒绝，即可在随后提起的赔偿诉讼中，索赔合理的律师费。

(e) Reasonable attorney's fees are recoverable if demand for compensation under Subsection (a) or (b) is made and refused before an action is brought on the claim.If a claim is made for breach of an agreement under Subsection (d) and the agreement does not provide for damages, reasonable attorney's fees are recoverable if demand for compensation under Subsection (d) of this section is made and refused before an action is brought on the claim.

（f）除本条另有规定外，接收银行在本条（a）款和（b）款项下的责任，不得通过协议

(f) Except as provided by this section, the liability of a receiving bank under Subsections (a) and (b) of this section may not be varied

加以改变。

by agreement.

第4章　付　款

PART 4. PAYMENT

第 4A.401 条　付款日

支付命令的“付款日”，指受益人银行应向受益人就支付命令的金额作出付款之日。付款日可以在发送人的指示中规定，但不能早于受益人银行收到命令的收到日，并且，除另有规定外，应为受益人银行收到命令的收到日。

§ 4A.401. Payment Date.

“Payment date” of a payment order means the day on which the amount of the order is payable to the beneficiary by the beneficiary’s bank. The payment date may be determined by instruction of the sender but cannot be earlier than the day the order is received by the beneficiary’s bank and, unless otherwise determined, is the day the order is received by the beneficiary’s bank.

第 4A.402 条　发送人向接收银行付款的义务

（a）本条受制于第 4A.205 条和第 4A.207 条。

（b）受益人银行接受向其出具的支付命令后，发送人即有义务就支付命令的金额向银行付款，但该付款只有在命令的付款日才到期。

（c）本款受制于（e）款和第 4A.303 条。接收银行（受益人银行除外）接受向其出具的支付命令后，发送人即有义务就支付命令的金额向银行付款，但该付款只有在发送人命令的执行日才到期。如果发送人的支付命令指示向受益人付款，但受益人银行未接受该支付命令，致使资金转账未能完

§ 4A.402. Obligation of Sender to Pay Receiving Bank.

（a）This section is subject to Sections 4A.205 and 4A.207.

（b）With respect to a payment order issued to the beneficiary’s bank, acceptance of the order by the bank obliges the sender to pay the bank the amount of the order, but payment is not due until the payment date of the order.

（c）This subsection is subject to Subsection (e) and to Section 4A.303. With respect to a payment order issued to a receiving bank other than the beneficiary’s bank, acceptance of the order by the receiving bank obliges the sender to pay the bank the amount of the sender’s order. Payment by the sender is not due until the execution date of the sender’s order. The obligation of that sender to pay its payment order is excused if the funds transfer is not

成，则发送人就其支付命令作出付款的义务即被免除。

completed by acceptance by thebeneficiary's bank of a payment order instructing payment to the beneficiary of that sender's payment order.

（d）如果发送人就其支付命令作出付款，但对于所支付之金额的部分或全部，其本来没有义务支付，则收到付款的银行，有义务就发送人没有义务支付的那一部分金额，退还付款。除第 4A.204 条和第 4A.304 条另有规定外，对于应退还的部分，应从发送人付款之日起支付利息。

（d）If the sender of a payment order pays the order and was not obliged to pay all or part of the amount paid, the bank receiving payment is obliged to refund payment to the extent the sender was not obliged to pay.Except as provided by Sections 4A.204 and 4A.304, interest is payable on the refundable amount from the date of payment.

（e）如果资金转账如（c）款所述未能完成，且中间银行有义务根据（d）款退回付款，但相关法律不允许退款，或银行因已暂停对外付款而无法退款，则资金转账的任何发送人，只要已根据第 4A.302 条（a）（1）款，遵从所得到的指示，通过该中间银行执行了资金转账的支付命令，即有权从其所接受之支付命令的发送人，获得付款或保留付款。在资金转账中，如果任何银行已支付该中间银行，则首个发出指示，要求通过该中间银行进行资金转账的发送人，即代位取得该支付银行的权利，有权得到（d）款所述的退款。

（e）If a funds transfer is not completed as provided by Subsection（c）and an intermediary bank is obliged to refund payment as provided by Subsection（d）but is unable to do so because not permitted by applicable law or because the bank suspends payments, a sender in the funds transfer that executed a payment order in compliance with an instruction, as provided by Section 4A.302（a）（1）, to route the funds transfer through that intermediary bank is entitled to receive or retain payment from the sender of the payment order that it accepted.The first sender in the funds transfer that issued an instruction requiring routing through that intermediary bank is subrogated to the right of the bank that paid the intermediary bank to a refund as stated in Subsection（d）.

（f）支付命令发送人根据

（f）The right of the sender of a payment

（c）款无义务就命令作出付款或根据（d）款有权得到退款的权利，不得通过协议加以改变。

order to be excused from the obligation to pay the order as stated in Subsection（c）or to receive a refund under Subsection（d）may not be varied by agreement.

第 4A.403 条 发送人向接收银行的付款

§ 4A.403. Payment by Sender to Receiving Bank.

（a）下列时间被视为发送人根据第 4A.402 条规定，履行向接收银行之付款义务的时间：

（a）Payment of the sender's obligation under Section 4A.402 to pay the receiving bank occurs as follows:

（1）如果发送人为银行，则付款时间为接收银行通过联邦储备银行或资金转账系统，收到该付款之最终结算的时间。

（1）If the sender is a bank, payment occurs when the receiving bank receives final settlement of the obligation through a Federal Reserve Bank or through a funds transfer system.

（2）如果发送人为银行，且发送人（i）贷记了接收银行在发送人的账户，或（ii）致使接收银行在另一家银行的账户被贷记，则付款时间为信贷被提取的时间，或如果未被提取，则为信贷可被提取且接收银行亦得知该事实之日的午夜。

（2）If the sender is a bank and the sender（i）credited an account of the receiving bank with the sender, or（ii）caused an account of the receiving bank in another bank to be credited, payment occurs when the credit is withdrawn or, if not withdrawn, at midnight of the day on which the credit is withdrawable and the receiving bank learns of that fact.

（3）如果接收银行借记发送人在接收银行的账户，则付款时间为作出借记的时间，但该账户中的可用信贷余额必须能够满足该借记。

（3）If the receiving bank debits an account of the sender with the receiving bank, payment occurs when the debit is made to the extent the debit is covered by a withdrawable credit balance in the account.

（b）如果发送人和接收银行均为某个资金转账系统的成员，且系统为成员各方互相抵销债务，则在根据该系统之规则完成清算时，接收银行被视为收到最终结算。对于通过资

（b）If the sender and receiving bank are members of a funds transfer system that nets obligations multilaterally among participants, the receiving bank receives final settlement when settlement is complete in accordance with the rules of the system.The obligation

金转账系统传送的任何支付命令，发送人就支付命令之金额作出付款的义务，可在该系统规则允许的限度内，与发送人有权从接收银行获得的付款金额进行抵销，即与该接收银行通过该资金转账系统传送给发送人的任何其他支付命令的金额进行抵销。每个发送人在该资金转账系统中对每个接收银行所欠债务的总体余额，可在该系统规则允许的限度内，用于抵销系统其他成员对发送人所欠债务的总体余额。总体余额应在行使了本款第二句所述的抵销权之后予以确定。

of the sender to pay the amount of a payment order transmitted through the funds transfer system may be satisfied, to the extent permitted by the rules of the system, by setting off and applying against the sender's obligation the right of the sender to receive payment from the receiving bank of the amount of any other payment order transmitted to the sender by the receiving bank through the funds transfer system.The aggregate balance of obligations owed by each sender to each receiving bank in the funds transfer system may be satisfied, to the extent permitted by the rules of the system, by setting off and applying against that balance the aggregate balance of obligations owed to the sender by other members of the system.The aggregate balance is determined after the right of setoff stated in the second sentence of this subsection has been exercised.

（c）如果两家银行互相发送支付命令，且双方同意，一家银行根据第 4A.402 条对另一家银行所欠的债务，应在每天（或其他期限）结束时进行结算，则应将一家银行的全部支付命令的欠付总额，与另一家银行的全部支付命令的欠付总额进行抵销。在所作抵销的范围内，一家银行被视为已向另一家银行作出付款。

（c）If two banks transmit payment orders to each other under an agreement that settlement of the obligations of each bank to the other under Section 4A.402 will be made at the end of the day or other period, the total amount owed with respect to all orders transmitted by one bank shall be setoff against the total amount owed with respect to all orders transmitted by the other bank.To the extent of the setoff, each bank has made payment to the other.

（d）涉及（a）款以外的情况时，发送人履行第 4A.402 条（b）款或（c）款项下付款义务

（d）In a case not covered by Subsection（a）, the time when payment of the sender's obligation under Section 4A.402（b）or（c）

的时间，应根据有关义务履行时间的适用法确定。

occurs is governed by applicable principles of law that determine when an obligation is satisfied.

第 4A.404 条　受益人银行向受益人付款并作出通知的义务

§ 4A.404. Obligation of Beneficiary's Bank to Pay and Give Notice to Beneficiary.

（a）除第 4A.211 条（e）款和第 4A.405 条（d）款和（e）款另有规定外，受益人银行接受支付命令后，即有义务向命令的受益人就支付命令的金额作出付款。付款在命令的付款日到期，但如果在付款日接受命令，且接受系在银行资金转账营业日结束后，则付款在下一个资金转账营业日到期。如果受益人提出付款要求，但银行拒绝付款，且银行已得到通知，即根据当时的具体情况，不付款会产生间接损失，则受益人可就拒绝付款的损失，在银行所得到之损失通知的限度内，从银行取得赔偿，除非银行能够证明，拒绝付款系因对受益人获得付款的权利存在合理怀疑。

（a）Subject to Sections 4A.211（e）and 4A.405（d）and（e）, if a beneficiary's bank accepts a payment order, the bank is obliged to pay the amount of the order to the beneficiary of the order.Payment is due on the payment date of the order, but if acceptance occurs on the payment date after the close of the funds transfer business day of the bank, payment is due on the next funds transfer business day.If the bank refuses to pay after demand by the beneficiary and receipt of notice of particular circumstances that will give rise to consequential damages as a result of nonpayment, the beneficiary may recover damages resulting from the refusal to pay to the extent the bank had notice of the damages, unless the bank proves that it did not pay because of a reasonable doubt concerning the right of the beneficiary to payment.

（b）如果受益人银行接受的支付命令，系指示向受益人的账户付款，银行有义务在付款日后下一个资金转账营业日午夜前，将收到命令的情况通知受益人。如果支付命令未指示向受益人的账户付款，则只

（b）If a payment order accepted by the beneficiary's bank instructs payment to an account of the beneficiary, the bank is obliged to notify the beneficiary of receipt of the order before midnight of the next funds transfer business day following the payment date.If the payment order does not instruct payment

有在命令要求作出通知时，银行才需要作出通知。作出通知，可使用一等邮件或当时情况下为合理的其他方式。如果银行未能作出必要的通知，银行有义务就支付命令的金额，从通知本应作出之日，至受益人得知银行收到支付命令之日，向受益人支付利息；但是，银行无义务支付其他赔偿。如果曾提出支付利息的要求，但被拒绝，则在随后提起的索赔诉讼中，可以要求赔偿合理的律师费。

to an account of the beneficiary, the bank is required to notify the beneficiary only if notice is required by the order.Notice may be given by first class mail or any other means reasonable in the circumstances.If the bank fails to give the required notice, the bank is obliged to pay interest to the beneficiary on the amount of the payment order from the day notice should have been given until the day the beneficiary learned of receipt of the payment order by the bank. No other damages are recoverable.Reasonable attorney's fees are recoverable if demand for interest is made and refused before an action is brought on the claim.

（c）受益人根据（a）款获得付款和损害赔偿的权利，不得通过协议或资金转账系统规则加以改变。受益人根据（b）款获得通知的权利，可以通过受益人协议或资金转账系统规则加以改变，只要在发起资金转账之前，受益人得到该规则的通知。

（c）The right of a beneficiary to receive payment and damages as stated in Subsection（a）may not be varied by agreement or a funds transfer system rule.The right of a beneficiary to be notified as stated in Subsection（b）may be varied by agreement of the beneficiary or by a funds transfer system rule if the beneficiary is notified of the rule before initiation of the funds transfer.

第 4A.405 条　受益人银行向受益人的付款

§ 4A.405. Payment by Beneficiary's Bank to Beneficiary.

（a）如果受益人银行贷记支付命令之受益人的账户，则在下列时间和下列程度内，受益人银行被视为履行了第 4A.404 条（a）款项下的付款义务：

（a）If the beneficiary's bank credits an account of the beneficiary of a payment order, payment of the bank's obligation under Section 4A.404（a）occurs when and to the extent:

（1）受益人收到其有权提用信贷的通知；

（1）the beneficiary is notified of the right to withdraw the credit;

（2）银行合法地将该信贷用于清偿受益人的债务；或

（3）银行以其他方式将命令项下的资金提供给受益人。

（2）the bank lawfully applies the credit to a debt of the beneficiary;or

（3）funds with respect to the order are otherwise made available to the beneficiary by the bank.

（b）如果受益人银行不贷记支付命令之受益人的账户，则受益人银行履行第4A.404条（a）款项下付款义务的时间，应根据有关义务履行时间的适用法确定。

（b）If the beneficiary's bank does not credit an account of the beneficiary of a payment order, the time when payment of the bank's obligation under Section 4A.404（a）occurs is governed by principles of law that determine when an obligation is satisfied.

（c）除（d）款和（e）款另有规定外，如果受益人银行向支付命令的受益人付款，但附有条件或得到受益人同意，即银行在自己就该命令未收到付款时，有权从受益人追回付款，此时，该付款条件或同意不可强制履行。

（c）Except as provided by Subsections（d）and（e）, if the beneficiary's bank pays the beneficiary of a payment order under a condition to payment or agreement of the beneficiary giving the bank the right to recover payment from the beneficiary if the bank does not receive payment of the order, the condition to payment or agreement is not enforceable.

（d）资金转账系统规则可以规定，通过该系统向资金转账受益人作出的付款，在受益人银行就所接受的支付命令收到付款前，付款具有临时性。根据该规则作出临时性付款的受益人银行，在下列条件下可从受益人获得退款：（i）规则规定，在发起资金转账前，应通知受益人和发起人双方，即该付款具有临时性，（ii）受益人、受益人银行和发起人银行均同意受该规则的约束，并且（iii）受益人银行未就所接受的

（d）A funds transfer system rule may provide that payments made to beneficiaries of funds transfers through the system are provisional until receipt of payment by the beneficiary's bank of the payment order it accepted.A beneficiary's bank that makes a payment that is provisional under the rule is entitled to refund from the beneficiary if（i）the rule requires that both the beneficiary and the originator be given notice of the provisional nature of the payment before the funds transfer is initiated,（ii）the beneficiary, the beneficiary's bank and the originator's bank agreed to be bound by the rule, and（iii）the

支付命令收到付款。只要受益人有义务向受益人银行退还已作出的付款，受益人银行对支付命令的接受亦被撤销；同时，第4A.406条所述的资金转账发起人向受益人作出的付款，亦被视为未曾发生。

beneficiary's bank did not receive payment of the payment order that it accepted.If the beneficiary is obliged to refund payment to the beneficiary's bank, acceptance of the payment order by the beneficiary's bank is nullified and no payment by the originator of the funds transfer to the beneficiary occurs under Section 4A.406.

（e）在资金转账中，如果任何支付命令系通过下列资金转账系统传送，本款即适用于该资金转账：（i）该系统在其成员中进行多边债务抵销，并且（ii）该系统成员之间存在损失分担协议，以便提供必要的资金，在一个或多个成员未履行清算义务时，使用该资金完成债务清算。如果该资金转账中的受益人银行接受了支付命令，但对于资金转账中的任何支付命令，该系统未能根据系统规则完成清算，则：

（e）This subsection applies to a funds transfer that includes a payment order transmitted over a funds transfer system that（i）nets obligations multilaterally among participants, and（ii）has in effect a loss-sharing agreement among participants for the purpose of providing funds necessary to complete settlement of the obligations of one or more participants that do not meet their settlement obligations.If the beneficiary's bank in the funds transfer accepts a payment order and the system fails to complete settlement pursuant to its rules with respect to any payment order in the funds transfer:

（1）受益人银行的接受即被撤销，且任何人均不因该接受取得任何权利或义务；

（1）the acceptance by the beneficiary's bank is nullified and no person has any right or obligation based on the acceptance;

（2）受益人银行有权从受益人追回付款；

（2）the beneficiary's bank is entitled to recover payment from the beneficiary;

（3）第4A.406条所述的发起人向受益人的付款被视为未曾发生；以及

（3）no payment by the originator to the beneficiary occurs under Section 4A.406;and

（4）除第4A.402条（e）款另有规定外，由于资金转账未能完成，资金转账中的每一个

（4）subject to Section 4A.402（e）, each sender in the funds transfer is excused from its obligation to pay its payment order under

发送人，均被解除第 4A.402 条（c）款项下的就自己的支付命令作出付款的义务。

Section 4A.402（c）because the funds transfer has not been completed.

第 4A.406 条　发起人向受益人的付款；基础义务的解除

§ 4A.406. Payment by Originator to Beneficiary; Discharge of Underlying Obligation.

（a）除第 4A.211 条（e）款和第 4A.405 条（d）款和（e）款另有规定外，资金转账的发起人，被视为在下列时间和按下列金额，向其支付命令的受益人作出付款：

（a）Subject to Sections 4A.211（e）and 4A.405（d）and（e）, the originator of a funds transfer pays the beneficiary of the originator's payment order:

（1）付款时间为受益人银行在资金转账中，为受益人利益而接受支付命令的时间；以及

（1）at the time a payment order for the benefit of the beneficiary is accepted by the beneficiary's bank in the funds transfer;and

（2）付款金额为受益人银行所接受之支付命令的金额，但不超过发起人命令中的金额。

（2）in an amount equal to the amount of the order accepted by the beneficiary's bank, but not more than the amount of the originator's order.

（b）如果（a）款项下的付款系为履行发起人的义务，则作出该付款后，该义务即被解除，相当于向受益人支付了同等金额的金钱后，该义务所得到的解除，除非（i）本条（a）款项下之付款采用的方法，被受益人有关该义务的合同所禁止，（ii）受益人收到通知，即受益人银行已收到该命令，且受益人在收到该通知后的合理时间内通知发起人，拒绝该付款，（iii）该命令项下的资金没

（b）If payment under Subsection（a）is made to satisfy an obligation, the obligation is discharged to the same extent discharge would result from payment to the beneficiary of the same amount in money, unless（i）the payment under Subsection（a）of this section was made by a means prohibited by the contract of the beneficiary with respect to the obligation,（ii）the beneficiary, within a reasonable time after receiving notice of receipt of the order by the beneficiary's bank, notified the originator of the beneficiary's refusal of the payment,（iii）funds with respect to the order were not

有被受益人取用，也未用于受益人的债务，并且（iv）受益人将会受到损失，而假设付款以符合合同的方法作出时，该损失本可合理避免。如果根据本条，发起人的付款不能导致其义务的解除，则发起人将代位取得受益人的权利，可以根据第 4A.404 条（a）款从受益人银行获得付款。

withdrawn by the beneficiary or applied to a debt of the beneficiary, and (iv) the beneficiary would suffer a loss that could reasonably have been avoided if payment had been made by a means complying with the contract.If payment by the originator does not result in discharge under this section, the originator is subrogated to the rights of the beneficiary to receive payment from the beneficiary's bank under Section 4A.404 (a).

（c）在确定一项义务是否根据（b）款得到解除时，如果受益人银行接受了支付命令，且命令的金额等于发起人支付命令的金额减去一个或多个接收银行在资金转账中的服务费的金额，则向受益人的付款金额，应被视为等于发起人支付命令的金额，除非在受益人提出要求后，发起人不向受益人支付所减去的那一部分服务费。

(c) For the purpose of determining whether discharge of an obligation occurs under Subsection (b), if the beneficiary's bank accepts a payment order in an amount equal to the amount of the originator's payment order less charges of one or more receiving banks in the funds transfer, payment to the beneficiary is deemed to be in the amount of the originator's order unless upon demand by the beneficiary the originator does not pay the beneficiary the amount of the deducted charges.

（d）资金转账中发起人或受益人在本条项下的权利，仅可通过发起人和受益人的协议加以改变。

(d) Rights of the originator or of the beneficiary of a funds transfer under this section may be varied only by agreement of the originator and the beneficiary.

第5章　其他规定

PART 5. MISCELLANEOUS PROVISIONS

第 4A.501 条　通过协议加以改变；资金转账系统规则的效力

§ 4A.501. Variation by Agreement and Effect of Funds Transfer System Rule.

（a）除本篇另有规定外，资

(a) Except as otherwise provided in this

金转账中当事方的权利和义务，可以通过受影响之当事方的协议加以改变。

Article, the rights and obligations of a party to a funds transfer may be varied by agreement of the affected party.

（b）“资金转账系统规则”指银行协会约束下列内容的规则：（i）通过协会之资金转账系统传送的支付命令，以及有关此种支付命令的权利和义务，或（ii）作为资金转账当事方之各银行之间的权利和义务，只要在该转账中，任何联邦储备银行作为中间银行向受益人银行发送支付命令。除本篇另有规定外，一项资金转账系统规则，如果涉及该系统之成员银行的权利和义务，则即使与本篇冲突并间接影响到资金转账中未同意该规则的另一方，该规则仍有可能具有效力。除约束成员银行外，一项资金转账系统规则，在第4A.404条（c）款、第4A.405条（d）款和第4A.507条（c）款所述的范围内，亦可约束使用该系统之其他当事方的权利和义务。

（b）“Funds transfer system rule” means a rule of an association of banks（i）governing transmission of payment orders by means of a funds transfer system of the association or rights and obligations with respect to those orders, or（ii）to the extent the rule governs rights and obligations between banks that are parties to a funds transfer in which a Federal Reserve Bank, acting as an intermediary bank, sends a payment order to the beneficiary’s bank.Except as otherwise provided in this Article, a funds transfer system rule governing rights and obligations between participating banks using the system may be effective even if the rule conflicts with this Article and indirectly affects another party to the funds transfer who does not consent to the rule.A funds transfer system rule may also govern rights and obligations of parties other than participating banks using the system to the extent stated in Sections 4A.404（c）, 4A.405（d）, and 4A.507（c）.

第4A.502条　向接收银行送达债权人查封书；受益人银行作出的抵销

§ 4A.502. Creditor Process Served on Receiving Bank; Setoff by Beneficiary’s Bank.

（a）在本条中，“债权人查封书”指债权人或其他索赔人发出或代表其发出的，对账户采取扣押、查封、留置或类似法律程序的通知。

（a）As used in this section, “creditor process” means levy, attachment, garnishment, notice of lien, sequestration, or similar process issued by or on behalf of a creditor or other claimant with respect to an account.

（b）本款适用于针对支付命令发送人之授权账户的债权人查封书，只要接收银行已收到该债权人查封书的送达。在确定债权人查封书所涉及的权利时，如果接收银行接受了支付命令，且未以其他形式收到该命令的付款，则该授权账户的余额，即被视为按支付命令的金额被相应扣减，除非债权人查封书的送达时间和方式，使银行在接受支付命令前，有合理机会据以作为。

（b）This subsection applies to creditor process with respect to an authorized account of the sender of a payment order if the creditor process is served on the receiving bank.For the purpose of determining rights with respect to the creditor process, if the receiving bank accepts the payment order, the balance in the authorized account is deemed to be reduced by the amount of the payment order to the extent the bank did not otherwise receive payment of the order, unless the creditor process is served at a time and in a manner affording the bank a reasonable opportunity to act on it before the bank accepts the payment order.

（c）如果受益人银行已收到支付命令，应向受益人在银行的账户付款，则应适用下列原则：

（c）If a beneficiary's bank has received a payment order for payment to the beneficiary's account in the bank the following rules apply:

（1）银行可以贷记受益人的账户，且贷记的金额，可以用于抵销受益人欠银行的债务，也可以在银行收到针对该账户的债权人查封书后，用来作相应支付。

（1）The bank may credit the beneficiary's account, and the amount credited may be set off against an obligation owed by the beneficiary to the bank or may be applied to satisfy creditor process served on the bank with respect to the account.

（2）银行可以贷记受益人的账户，同时允许提取所贷记的金额，除非银行已收到针对该账户的债权人查封书，且查封书收到的时间和方式，使银行有合理机会据以作为，阻止该提取。

（2）The bank may credit the beneficiary's account and allow withdrawal of the amount credited unless creditor process with respect to the account is served at a time and in a manner affording the bank a reasonable opportunity to act to prevent withdrawal.

（3）如果银行已收到针对受益人账户的债权人查封书，

（3）If creditor process with respect to the beneficiary's account has been served and the

且有合理机会据以作为，则银行不得拒绝相关支付命令，除非拒绝的原因与该查封书无关。

bank has had a reasonable opportunity to act on it, the bank may not reject the payment order except for a reason unrelated to the service of process.

（d）如果一项债权人查封书系针对发起人通过资金转账向受益人作出的一项付款，则该查封书仅可针对受益人银行对受益人所欠之债务，向该银行作出通知。收到债权人查封书的其他银行，没有义务就该查封书采取作为。

（d）Creditor process with respect to a payment by the originator to the beneficiary pursuant to a funds transfer may be served only on the beneficiary's bank with respect to the debt owed by that bank to the beneficiary.Any other bank served with the creditor process is not obliged to act with respect to the process.

第 4A.503 条　针对资金转账的禁止令

§ 4A.503. Injunction or Restraining Order With Respect to Funds Transfer.

如果存在正当原因且符合相关法律，法院可以（i）禁止任何人通过出具支付命令进行资金转账，（ii）禁止发起人银行执行发起人的支付命令，或（iii）禁止受益人银行向受益人交付资金，或禁止受益人提取资金。除上述之外，法院不得禁止任何人的下列行为：出具支付命令、就支付命令付款、接收支付命令的付款或就资金转账采取其他作为。

For proper cause and in compliance with applicable law, a court may restrain（i）a person from issuing a payment order to initiate a funds transfer,（ii）an originator's bank from executing the payment order of the originator, or（iii）the beneficiary's bank from releasing funds to the beneficiary or the beneficiary from withdrawing the funds.A court may not otherwise restrain a person from issuing a payment order, paying or receiving payment of a payment order, or otherwise acting with respect to a funds transfer.

第 4A.504 条　票证或支付命令支取账户的顺序；从账户提取款项的顺序

§ 4A.504. Order in Which Items and Payment Orders May Be Charged to Account; Order of Withdrawals From Account.

（a）如果接收银行从发送人收到一个以上的支付命令，或收到应从发送人账户支取的一个或多个支付命令和其他票

（a）If a receiving bank has received more than one payment order of the sender or one or more payment orders and other items that are payable from the sender's account, the bank

证，银行可以采用任何顺序，就不同命令和票证支取发送人的账户。

may charge the sender's account with respect to the various orders and items in any sequence.

（b）在确定账户中一项信贷是否已被账户持有人提取，或已用于支付账户持有人的债务时，先进入账户的信贷，被视为先提取或使用。

（b）In determining whether a credit to an account has been withdrawn by the holder of the account or applied to a debt of the holder of the account, credits first made to the account are first withdrawn or applied.

第 4A.505 条　无权反对借记客户账户

§ 4A.505. Preclusion of Objection to Debit of Customer's Account.

如果客户作为发送人，以自己的名字发出支付命令，且命令被接收银行接受，且接收银行已从客户收到付款，且客户已收到合理指明该命令的通知，此时，只要客户未在收到通知后的一年内，向银行发出反对该付款的通知，客户即无权对银行保留该付款提出异议。

If a receiving bank has received payment from its customer with respect to a payment order issued in the name of the customer as sender and accepted by the bank, and the customer received notification reasonably identifying the order, the customer is precluded from asserting that the bank is not entitled to retain the payment unless the customer notifies the bank of the customer's objection to the payment within one year after the notification was received by the customer.

第 4A.506 条　利率

§ 4A.506. Rate of Interest.

（a）如果根据本篇，接收银行对于出具给自己的支付命令有义务支付利息，则所应支付的利息金额，可以根据下列确定：(i）发送人与接收银行之间的协议，或（ii）资金转账系统规则，只要支付命令系通过资金转账系统传送。

（a）If, under this Article, a receiving bank is obliged to pay interest with respect to a payment order issued to the bank, the amount payable may be determined（i）by agreement of the sender and receiving bank, or（ii）by funds transfer system rule if the payment order is transmitted through a funds transfer system.

（b）如果不通过（a）款所述的协议或规则确定利息的金额，则金额应根据下列原则

（b）If the amount of interest is not determined by an agreement or rule as stated in Subsection（a）, the amount is calculated by

确定：以适用的联邦资金利率，乘以应计利息的金额，再乘以应计利息的天数。适用的联邦资金利率，为纽约联邦储备银行公布的联邦资金利率的平均值，即应计利息之每一天的公布利率的平均值，然后除以三百六十。如果任何一天不存在公布的联邦资金利率，则该天的利率应为下一个存在公布利率那天的利率。如果由于资金转账未完成，致使接受了支付命令的接收银行必须向命令发送人退还付款，但转账未完成并非出于银行的过错，则应付利息应按照接收银行之存款准备金的百分比，降低相同的百分点。

multiplying the applicable Federal Funds rate by the amount on which interest is payable, and then multiplying the product by the number of days for which interest is payable.The applicable Federal Funds rate is the average of the Federal Funds rates published by the Federal Reserve Bank of New York for each of the days for which interest is payable divided by 360.The Federal Funds rate for any day on which a published rate is not available is the same as the published rate for the next preceding day for which there is a published rate.If a receiving bank that accepted a payment order is required to refund payment to the sender of the order because the funds transfer was not completed, but the failure to complete was not due to any faultby the bank, the interest payable is reduced by a percentage equal to the reserve requirement on deposits of the receiving bank.

第 4A.507 条 法律选择

（a）除受影响之当事方另有协议或除涉及应适用（c）款的情况外，应适用下列原则：

（1）支付命令发送人与接收银行之间的权利和义务，由接收银行所在州的法律管辖。

（2）受益人银行与受益人之间的权利和义务，由受益人银行所在州的法律管辖。

（3）资金转账中发起人向

§ 4A.507. Choice of Law.

（a）The following rules apply unless the affected parties otherwise agree or Subsection（c）applies:

（1）The rights and obligations between the sender of a payment order and the receiving bank are governed by the law of the jurisdiction in which the receiving bank is located.

（2）The rights and obligations between the beneficiary's bank and the beneficiary are governed by the law of the jurisdiction in which the beneficiary's bank is located.

（3）The issue of when payment is made

受益人付款的时间问题，由受益人银行所在州的法律管辖。

pursuant to a funds transfer by the originator to the beneficiary is governed by the law of the jurisdiction in which the beneficiary's bank is located.

（b）如果（a）款各段中所述的当事方通过订立协议，选择了特定州的法律管辖他们之间的权利和义务，则在涉及该等权利和义务的解释时，亦应适用该州的法律，无论支付命令或资金转账是否与该州存在合理联系；在涉及该等权利和义务的有效性时，在本法第1.301条允许的限度内，亦应适用该州的法律。

（b）If the parties described by each subdivision of Subsection（a）have made an agreement selecting the law of a particular jurisdiction to govern rights and obligations between each other, the law of that jurisdiction governs those rights and obligations as to matters of construction and interpretation, whether or not the payment order or the funds transfer bears a reasonable relation to that jurisdiction, and as to validity, to the extent permitted by Section 1.301 of this code.

（c）一项资金转账系统规则，可以选择特定州的法律管辖下列问题：（i）涉及通过该系统传送或处理的支付命令时，成员银行之间的权利和义务，或（ii）资金转账中某些当事方或所有当事方的权利和义务，只要资金转账的任何一部分系通过该系统完成。根据（i）款选择的法律，对成员银行有约束力。根据（ii）款选择的法律，对发起人、其他发送人或接收银行具有约束力，只要在其出具或接受支付命令时，已得到资金转账可能使用该系统的通知，并得到该系统所选择之法律的通知。资金转账的受益人亦受所选择之法律的约束，只

（c）A funds transfer system rule may select the law of a particular jurisdiction to govern（i）rights and obligations between participating banks with respect to payment orders transmitted or processed through the system, or（ii）the rights and obligations of some or all parties to a funds transfer any part of which is carried out by means of the system. A choice of law made pursuant to clause（i）is binding on participating banks.A choice of law made pursuant to clause（ii）is binding on the originator, other sender, or a receiving bank having notice that the funds transfer system might be used in the funds transfer and of the choice of law by the system when the originator, other sender, or receiving bank issued or accepted a payment order.The beneficiary of a funds transfer is bound by the choice of law

要在发起资金转账时，受益人已得到资金转账可能使用该系统的通知，并得到该系统所选择之法律的通知。根据本（c）款选择的法律，亦可管辖解释问题，无论该法律是否与涉及的问题存在合理联系。

if, when the funds transfer is initiated, the beneficiary has notice that the funds transfer system might be used in the funds transfer and of the choice of law by the system.The law of a jurisdiction selected pursuant to this Subsection（c）may govern, as to matters of construction and interpretation, whether or not the law bears a reasonable relation to the matter in issue.

（d）如果（b）款项下的协议与（c）款项下的法律选择条款存在冲突，应适用（b）款项下的协议。

（d）In the event of inconsistency between an agreement under Subsection（b）and a choice-of-law rule under Subsection（c）, the agreement under Subsection（b）prevails.

（e）如果资金转账使用一个以上的资金转账系统，且各系统对法律的选择不一致，则应适用其中与相关问题有最重要联系的那个州的法律。

（e）If a funds transfer is made by use of more than one funds transfer system and there is inconsistency between choice-of-law rules of the systems, the matter in issue is governed by the law of the selected jurisdiction that has the most significant relationship to the matter in issue.

词汇索引

安全程序	security procedure	第 4A.201 条
接受	acceptance	第 4A.209 条
发起人	originator	第 4A.104 条（3）
发送人向接收银行的付款	payment by sender to receiving bank	第 4A.403 条
发起人向受益人的付款	payment by originator to beneficiary	第 4A.406 条
发起人银行	originator’s bank	第 4A.104 条（4）
发送人	sender	第 4A.103 条（a）（5）
付款日	payment date	第 4A.401 条
接收银行	receiving bank	第 4A.103 条（a）（4）
客户	customer	第 4A.105 条（a）（3）
受益人	beneficiary	第 4A.103 条（a）（2）
受益人银行	beneficiary’s bank	第 4A.103 条（a）（3）
受益人银行向受益人的付款	payment by benefiary’s bank to beneficiary	第 4A.405 条
授权账户	authorized account	第 4A.105 条（a）（1）
已执行	executed	第 4A.301 条
银行	bank	第 4A.105 条（a）（2）
证明	prove	第 4A.105 条（a）（7）
支付命令	payment order	第 4A.103 条（a）（1）
执行日	execution date	第 4A.301 条
中间银行	intermediary bank	第 4A.104 条（2）
资金转账	funds transfer	第 4A.104 条（1）
资金转账系统	funds transfer system	第 4A.105 条（a）（5）
资金转账系统规则	funds transfer system rule	第 4A.501 条（b）
资金转账营业日	funds transfer business day	第 4A.105 条（a）（4）

第5篇　信用证

ARTICLE 5. LETTERS OF CREDIT

第 5.101 条　简称

本篇被引用时可称为《统一商法典——信用证》。

第 5.102 条　定义

（a）在本篇中：

（1）“通知人”指基于开证人、保兑人或另一通知人的要求，就信用证已被开立、保兑或修改的情况，向受益人作出通知的人；也指要求另一通知人作出此种通知的人。

（2）“申请人”指就信用证的开立提出要求或承担支付责任的人。“申请人”也包括代表他人要求开证人开立信用证的人，但提出该要求的人必须对开证人承担补偿义务。

（3）“受益人”指根据信用证条款，有权就自己符合要求之提示获得兑付的人。“受益人”也包括可转让信用证项下之提款权被转让后的受让人。

§ 5.101. Short Title.

This Article may be cited as Uniform Commercial Code—Letters of Credit.

§ 5.102. Definitions.

（a）In this Article:

（1）“Adviser” means a person who, at the request of the issuer, a confirmer, or another adviser, notifies or requests another adviser to notify the beneficiary that a letter of credit has been issued, confirmed, or amended.

（2）“Applicant” means a person at whose request or for whose account a letter of credit is issued.The term includes a person who requests an issuer to issue a letter of credit on behalf of another if the person making the request undertakes an obligation to reimburse the issuer.

（3）“Beneficiary” means a person who under the terms of a letter of credit is entitled to have its complying presentation honored.The term includes a person to whom drawing rights have been transferred under a transferable letter of credit.

（4）“保兑人”指下述指定人：其基于开证人的要求或同意，承诺兑付另一人所开立之信用证的提示。

（4）“Confirmer” means a nominated person who undertakes, at the request or with the consent of the issuer, to honor a presentation under a letter of credit issued by another.

（5）信用证的“拒付”，指未能及时作出兑付，或未能及时作出信用证可能要求的中间环节行为，如汇票承兑。

（5）“Dishonor” of a letter of credit means failure timely to honor or to take an interim action, such as acceptance of a draft, that may be required by the letter of credit.

（6）“单据”指：汇票或其他指令、所有权凭证、投资证券、证书、发货单，或关于事实、法律、权利或意见的其他记录、说明或陈述，只要：（i）该材料之提示使用了信用证允许的书面形式或其他媒介；或者，除被信用证所禁止外，使用了第 5.108 条（e）款所述的标准做法；并且（ii）存在查验该材料是否符合信用证条款和条件的方法。单据不得为口头形式。

（6）“Document” means a draft or other demand, document of title, investment security, certificate, invoice, or other record, statement, or representation of fact, law, right, or opinion（i）that is presented in a written or other medium permitted by the letter of credit or, unless prohibited by the letter of credit, by the standard practice referred to in Section 5.108（e）;and（ii）that is capable of being examined for compliance with the terms and conditions of the letter of credit.A document may not be oral.

（7）“善意”指有关行为或交易中事实上的诚实。

（7）“Good faith” means honesty in fact in the conduct or transaction concerned.

（8）信用证的“兑付”，指履行开证人在信用证项下之作出付款或交付有价值之物品的义务。除信用证另有规定外，“兑付”：

（8）“Honor” of a letter of credit means performance of the issuer's undertaking in the letter of credit to pay or deliver an item of value.Unless the letter of credit otherwise provides, “honor” occurs:

（A）在付款时发生；

（A）upon payment;

（B）如果信用证要求作出承兑，则在对汇票作出承兑并于到期日作出付款时发生；或

（B）if the letter of credit provides for acceptance, upon acceptance of a draft and, at maturity, its payment;or

（C）如果信用证要求承担延后履行的义务，则在承担该义务并于到期日作出履行时发生。

（C）if the letter of credit provides for incurring a deferred obligation, upon incurring the obligation and, at maturity, its performance.

（9）“开证人”指开立信用证的银行或其他人，但不包括为个人、家庭或家用目的承担义务的个人。

（9）“Issuer” means a bank or other person that issues a letter of credit, but does not include an individual who makes an engagement for personal, family, or household purposes.

（10）“信用证”指满足第5.104条之条件的下列确定承诺：出于申请人的要求或担责，开证人向受益人承诺，通过作出付款或交付有价值之物品，对跟单提示予以兑付；或在开证人为金融机构时，开证人向自己承诺或由自身担责，承诺通过作出付款或交付有价值之物品，对跟单提示予以兑付。

（10）“Letter of credit” means a definite undertaking that satisfies the requirements of Section 5.104 by an issuer to a beneficiary at the request or for the account of an applicant or, in the case of a financial institution, to itself or for its own account, to honor a documentary presentation by payment or delivery of an item of value.

（11）“指定人”指开证人对其作出下列行为的人：

（A）指定或授权其就信用证作出付款、承兑或流通，或以其他方式支付价值；并且

（B）根据协议或习惯和做法，承诺对其给予补偿。

（11）“Nominated person” means a person whom the issuer:

（A）designates or authorizes to pay, accept, negotiate, or otherwise give value under a letter of credit;and

（B）undertakes by agreement or custom and practice to reimburse.

（12）“提示”指向开证人或指定人交付单据，用于取得信用证项下的兑付或价值交付。

（12）“Presentation” means delivery of a document to an issuer or nominated person for honor or giving of value under a letter of credit.

（13）“提示人”指以受益人或指定人身份作出提示的人，或代表该人作出提示的人。

（13）“Presenter” means a person making a presentation as or on bchalf of a beneficiary or nominated person.

（14）“记录”指记录在有

（14）“Record” means information that

形介质上的信息，或以电子或其他介质存储并能读取的信息。

is inscribed on a tangible medium or that is stored in an electronic or other medium and is retrievable in perceivable form.

（15）“受益人的继承人”指依法继承受益人几乎全部权利的人，包括对受益人作出兼并或整合的公司，也包括管理人、执行人、私人代表人、破产受托人、管理破产财产之债务人、清算人及破产接收人。

（15）“Successor of a beneficiary” means a person who succeeds to substantially all of the rights of a beneficiary by operation of law, including a corporation with or into which the beneficiary has been merged or consolidated, an administrator, an executor, a personal representative, a trustee in bankruptcy, a debtor in possession, a liquidator, and a receiver.

（b）本法其他各篇中适用于本篇的定义及其所在位置：

（b）Definitions in other Articles of this Act applying to this Article and the sections in which they appear are:

“承兑” 第 3.409 条

“价值” 第3.303 条和第4.211 条

“Accept” or “Acceptance”. Section 3.409.

“Value” . Sections 3.303 and 4.211.

（c）第 1 篇中包含的某些其他通用定义和解释原则适用于本篇通篇。

（c）Article 1 contains certain additional general definitions and principles of construction and interpretation applicable throughout this Article.

第 5.103 条　范围

§ 5.103. Scope.

（a）本篇适用于信用证，并适用于与信用证有关之交易所引起的某些权利和义务。

（a）This Article applies to letters of credit and to certain rights and obligations arising out of transactions involving letters of credit.

（b）涉及本篇不覆盖的情况或未规定的人时，本篇规定的任何原则，其本身并不要求、暗示或妨碍对该情况或该人适用相同或不同的原则。

（b）The statement of a rule in this Article does not by itself require, imply, or negate application of the same or a different rule to a situation not provided for, or to a person not specified, in this Article.

（c）除本款、（a）款和（d）款、第 5.102 条（a）（9）款和（10）款、第 5.106 条（d）款、第 5.110

（c）With the exception of this subsection, Subsections（a）and（d）, Sections 5.102（a）（9）and（10）, Section 5.106（d）, Section

条（c）款、第5.114条（d）款另有规定外，且除第1.302条和第5.117条(d)款另有禁止外，本篇的效力可以通过协议加以改变，或通过在承诺中陈述或引用的条款加以改变。如果协议或承诺的条款一般性地排除责任，或一般性地限制未履行义务时的救济，则该条款不足以改变本篇规定的义务。

5.110（c）, and Section 5.114（d）and except to the extent prohibited in Sections 1.302 and 5.117（d）, the effect of this Article may be varied by agreement or by a provision stated or incorporated by reference in an undertaking.A term in an agreement or undertaking generally excusing liability or generally limiting remedies for failure to perform obligations is not sufficient to vary obligations prescribed by this Article.

（d）即使一项合同或安排是信用证的起因或基础，开证人在信用证项下对受益人或指定人持有的权利和义务，亦不受该合同或安排之存在、履行或不履行的影响。此种合同或安排包括：开证人和申请人之间的，以及申请人和受益人之间的合同或安排。

（d）Rights and obligations of an issuer to a beneficiary or a nominated person under a letter of credit are independent of the existence, performance, or nonperformance of a contract or arrangement out of which the letter of credit arises or which underlies it, including contracts or arrangements between the issuer and the applicant and between the applicant and the beneficiary.

第5.104条　形式要求

§ 5.104. Formal Requirements.

可以使用任何形式开立信用证、保兑、通知、转让、修改或取消，只要该形式构成一项记录，且该记录：

A letter of credit, confirmation, advice, transfer, amendment, or cancellation may be issued in any form that is a record and is authenticated:

（1）通过签名得到认证；或

（1）by a signature;or

（2）根据当事方协议或第5.108条（e）款所述的标准做法得到认证。

（2）in accordance with the agreement of the parties or the standard practice referred to in Section 5.108（e）.

第5.105条　对价

§ 5.105. Consideration.

开立、修改、转让或取消信用证、通知或保兑，不需要对价。

Consideration is not required to issue, amend, transfer, or cancel a letter of credit, advice, or confirmation.

第5.106条　开立、修改、取消和期限

（a）只要开证人将信用证发送给或以其他形式传送给被要求就信用证作出通知的人，或发送给或传送给受益人，信用证即为开立，并可按其条款对开证人强制履行。信用证只有规定可以撤销时，才可被撤销。

（b）如果信用证在开立后被修改或取消，对于未同意该修改或取消的受益人、申请人、保兑人和开证人，其权利和义务不受该修改或取消的影响，除非信用证规定可以撤销，或规定开证人可不经此种同意而修改或取消信用证。

（c）如果信用证未注明到期日，也没有其他条款可以确定期限，则信用证从注明的开立日期起一年后失效，或如果未注明日期，从开立的日期起一年后失效。

（d）注明为永久有效的信用证，从注明的开立日期起五年后失效，或如果未注明日期，从开立的日期起五年后失效。

§ 5.106. Issuance, Amendment, Cancellation, and Duration.

（a）A letter of credit is issued and becomes enforceable according to its terms against the issuer when the issuer sends or otherwise transmits it to the person requested to advise or to the beneficiary.A letter of credit is revocable only if it so provides.

（b）After a letter of credit is issued, rights and obligations of a beneficiary, applicant, confirmer, and issuer are not affected by an amendment or cancellation to which that person has not consented except to the extent the letter of credit provides that it is revocable or that the issuer may amend or cancel the letter of credit without that consent.

（c）If there is no stated expiration date or other provision that determines its duration, a letter of credit expires one year after its stated date of issuance or, if no date is stated, after the date on which it is issued.

（d）A letter of credit that states that it is perpetual expires five years after its stated date of issuance or, if no date is stated, after the date on which it is issued.

第5.107条　保兑人；指定人；通知人

（a）保兑人对信用证承担直接义务，并在保兑范围内，持有开证人的权利和义务。保兑人亦对开证人持有权利和承

§ 5.107. Confirmer, Nominated Person, and Adviser.

（a）A confirmer is directly obligated on a letter of credit and has the rights and obligations of an issuer to the extent of its confirmation.The confirmer also has rights

担义务，即相当于开证人为申请人，而保兑人系出于开证人的要求或担责而开立信用证。

against and obligations to the issuer as if the issuer were an applicant and the confirmer had issued the letter of credit at the request and for the account of the issuer.

（b）指定人如果不是保兑人，即没有义务对提示作出兑付或以其他方式支付价值。

（b）A nominated person who is not a confirmer is not obligated to honor or otherwise give value for a presentation.

（c）被要求作出通知的人，可以拒绝担任通知人。通知人如果不是保兑人，则没有义务对提示作出兑付，也没有义务以其他方式支付价值。通知人向开证人和受益人承诺，对于通知人收到的信用证、保兑、修改或通知，将就其条款作出准确通知；同时，向受益人承诺，对于请求通知人作出通知的要求，将查验该要求的表见授权。即使作出的通知不准确，信用证、保兑或修改仍可按开立时的条款强制履行。

（c）A person requested to advise may decline to act as an adviser.An adviser that is not a confirmer is not obligated to honor or give value for a presentation.An adviser undertakes to the issuer and to the beneficiary accurately to advise the terms of the letter of credit, confirmation, amendment, or advice received by that person and undertakes to the beneficiary to check the apparent authenticity of the request to advise.Even if the advice is inaccurate, the letter of credit, confirmation, or amendment is enforceable as issued.

（d）涉及身为受让人之受益人时，向该受益人就信用证、保兑、修改或通知之条款作出通知的人，拥有（c）款项下之通知人的权利和义务。向该受益人所作通知的条款，可以不同于向身为转让人之受益人所作通知的条款，只要通知人收到的信用证、保兑、修改或通知允许此种不同。

（d）A person who notifies a transferee beneficiary of the terms of a letter of credit, confirmation, amendment, or advice has the rights and obligations of an adviser under Subsection（c）.The terms in the notice to the transferee beneficiary may differ from the terms in any notice to the transferor beneficiary to the extent permitted by the letter of credit, confirmation, amendment, or advice received by the person who so notifies.

第 5.108 条　开证人的权利和义务

（a）除第 5.109 条另有规定外，如果根据（e）款所述的标准做法能够确认，提示的外表情况显示，提示严格符合信用证的条款和条件，则开证人即应作出兑付。除第 5.113 条另有规定外，且除与申请人另有约定外，对于显示未达到上述条件的提示，开证人应予拒付。

（b）收到提示后，开证人应被给予合理时间作出下列行为，但至迟不得超过开证人收到单据后第七个工作日结束时：

（1）作出兑付；

（2）承兑汇票或承担延后履行的义务，只要信用证规定应从提示起七个工作日之后再完成兑付；或

（3）向提示人作出通知，说明提示存在瑕疵。

（c）除（d）款另有规定外，如果在涉及任何瑕疵时，开证人未能及时作出通知，或及时作出通知但未能说明瑕疵，开证人即不得以该瑕疵作为拒付的理由。

（d）即使开证人未能作出（b）款规定的通知，或未能在通知中提到欺诈、伪造或过期，亦不妨碍开证人将第 5.109 条

§ 5.108. Issuer's Rights and Obligations.

（a）Except as otherwise provided in Section 5.109, an issuer shall honor a presentation that, as determined by the standard practice referred to in Subsection（e）, appears on its face strictly to comply with the terms and conditions of the letter of credit.Except as otherwise provided in Section 5.113 and unless otherwise agreed with the applicant, an issuer shall dishonor a presentation that does not appear so to comply.

（b）An issuer has a reasonable time after presentation, but not beyond the end of the seventh business day of the issuer after the date of its receipt of documents:

（1）to honor;

（2）if the letter of credit provides for honor to be completed more than seven business days after presentation, to accept a draft or incur a deferred obligation;or

（3）to give notice to the presenter of discrepancies in the presentation.

（c）Except as otherwise provided in Subsection（d）, an issuer is precluded from asserting as a basis for dishonor any discrepancy if timely notice is not given or any discrepancy not stated in the notice if timely notice is given.

（d）Failure to give the notice specified in Subsection（b）or to mention fraud, forgery, or expiration in the notice does not preclude the issuer from asserting as a basis for dishonor

（a）款所述的欺诈或伪造，或将信用证在提示前即已过期的事实，作为拒付的理由。

fraud or forgery as described in Section 5.109（a）or expiration of the letter of credit before presentation.

（e）开证人应遵守惯常从事信用证开立之金融机构的标准做法。开证人是否遵守了该标准做法，属于解释问题，应由法院判定。法院应向当事方提供合理机会，用于提交有关标准做法的证据。

（e）An issuer shall observe standard practice of financial institutions that regularly issue letters of credit.Determination of the issuer's observance of the standard practice is a matter of interpretation for the court. The court shall offer the parties a reasonable opportunity to present evidence of the standard practice.

（f）开证人：

（f）An issuer is not responsible for:

（1）不对基础的合同、安排或交易之履行或未履行承担责任；

（1）the performance or nonperformance of the underlying contract, arrangement, or transaction;

（2）不对他人的行为或疏漏承担责任；以及

（2）an act or omission of others;or

（3）没有义务遵守或了解任何特定的行业惯例，但（e）款所述的标准做法除外。

（3）observance or knowledge of the usage of a particular trade other than the standard practice referred to in Subsection（e）.

（g）如果一项承诺构成第 5.102 条（a）（10）款项下的信用证，且包含非单据的条件，则开证人应无视该非单据条件，并应视承诺未注明该条件。

（g）If an undertaking constituting a letter of credit under Section 5.102（a）（10）contains nondocumentary conditions, an issuer shall disregard the nondocumentary conditions and treat them as if they were not stated.

（h）开证人在对提示作出拒付后，应归还单据；或在服从提示人处置的条件下留持单据，并将此告知提示人。

（h）An issuer that has dishonored a presentation shall return the documents or hold them at the disposal of, and send advice to that effect to, the presenter.

（i）开证人对提示作出本篇允许或要求的兑付后，即：

（i）An issuer that has honored a presentation as permitted or required by this Article:

（1）有权要求申请人以立即可用的资金作出补偿，且不晚于开证人支付资金的付款日；

（2）对于所取得的单据，不受受益人或提示人的索赔；

（3）不得根据第3.414条和第3.415条对汇票主张追索权；

（4）除第5.110条和第5.117条另有规定外，无权以误解为理由，追回所作出的付款或所支付的价值，只要该误解涉及单据不符或提交方式不符，且该不符从提示的表面即可看出；以及

（5）在其所完成之信用证履约的范围内，被解除义务，除非在开证人兑付的提示中，受益人的必要签名系属伪造。

第5.109条　欺诈与伪造

（a）当提示表面显示严格符合信用证的条款和条件时，即使某个必要单据存在伪造或严重欺诈，或即使兑付该提示将助推受益人对开证人或申请人的严重欺诈：

（1）只要下列人要求得到兑付，开证人仍应兑付该提示：

（A）善意支付了价值且未得到伪造或严重欺诈通知的指定人；

（B）善意兑付了自己之保

（1）is entitled to be reimbursed by the applicant in immediately available funds not later than the date of its payment of funds;

（2）takes the documents free of claims of the beneficiary or presenter;

（3）is precluded from asserting a right of recourse on a draft under Sections 3.414 and 3.415;

（4）except as otherwise provided in Sections 5.110 and 5.117, is precluded from restitution of money paid or other value given by mistake to the extent the mistake concerns discrepancies in the documents or tender that are apparent on the face of the presentation;and

（5）is discharged to the extent of its performance under the letter of credit unless the issuer honored a presentation in which a required signature of a beneficiary was forged.

§ 5.109. Fraud and Forgery.

（a）If a presentation is made that appears on its face strictly to comply with the terms and conditions of the letter of credit, but a required document is forged or materially fraudulent, or honor of the presentation would facilitate a material fraud by the beneficiary on the issuer or applicant:

（1）the issuer shall honor the presentation if honor is demanded by:

（A）a nominated person who has given value in good faith and without notice of forgery or material fraud;

（B）a confirmer who has honored its

兑的保兑人；

（C）信用证项下之汇票的正当执票人，只要汇票系在开证人或指定人作出承兑之后取得；或

（D）开证人或指定人的延后履行之义务的受让人，只要受让系在未得到伪造或严重欺诈之通知的情况下，通过支付价值，在开证人或指定人承担该义务之后取得；以及

（2）在所有其他情况下，开证人只要善意作为，即可选择兑付提示或拒付提示。

（b）如果申请人声称，某个必要单据存在伪造或严重欺诈，或兑付该提示将助推受益人对开证人或申请人的严重欺诈，则有适当管辖权的法院，可以暂时禁止或完全禁止开证人兑付提示，也可以提供对抗开证人或其他人的类似救济，但必须首先认定：

（1）适用于已承兑汇票或开证人延后履行之义务的法律，并不禁止该救济；

（2）可能受到该救济不利影响的受益人、开证人或指定人，已得到充分保护，不致在提供该救济后受到损失；

（3）本州法律对获得该救济所规定的全部条件，均已获得满足；并且

confirmation in good faith;

（C）a holder in due course of a draft drawn under the letter of credit that was taken after acceptance by the issuer or nominated person;or

（D）an assignee of the issuer's or nominated person's deferred obligation that was taken for value and without notice of forgery or material fraud after the obligation was incurred by the issuer or nominated person;and

（2）the issuer, acting in good faith, may honor or dishonor the presentation in any other case.

（b）If an applicant claims that a required document is forged or materially fraudulent or that honor of the presentation would facilitate a material fraud by the beneficiary on the issuer or applicant, a court of competent jurisdiction may temporarily or permanently enjoin the issuer from honoring a presentation or grant similar relief against the issuer or other persons only if the court finds that:

（1）the relief is not prohibited under the law applicable to an accepted draft or deferred obligation incurred by the issuer;

（2）a beneficiary, issuer, or nominated person who may be adversely affected is adequately protected against loss that it may suffer because the relief is granted;

（3）all of the conditions to entitle a person to the relief under the law of this state have been met;and

（4）根据向法院提交的信息，申请人就该伪造或严重欺诈提出的指控，成立的可能性大于不成立的可能性，且要求取得兑付的人没有资格获得（a）（1）款的保护。

（4）on the basis of the information submitted to the court, the applicant is more likely than not to succeed under its claim of forgery or material fraud and the person demanding honor does not qualify for protection under Subsection（a）（1）.

第 5.110 条　担保

§ 5.110. Warranties.

（a）如果受益人的提示获得兑付，受益人即：

（a）If its presentation is honored, the beneficiary warrants:

（1）向开证人、收到提示的其他人以及申请人担保，不存在第 5.109 条（a）款所述种类的欺诈或伪造；并且

（1）to the issuer, any other person to whom presentation is made, and the applicant that there is no fraud or forgery of the kind described in Section 5.109（a）;and

（2）向申请人担保，提款不违反申请人与受益人之间的任何协议，也不违反他们意图以信用证对其进行补充的任何其他协议。

（2）to the applicant that the drawing does not violate any agreement between the applicant and beneficiary or any other agreement intended by them to be augmented by the letter of credit.

（b）如果单据的提示或转让在第 3 篇、第 4 篇、第 7 篇和第 8 篇范围之内，且该各篇就该提示或转让规定了相应担保，则上述（a）款中的担保，为该各篇中之担保的补充。

（b）The warranties in Subsection（a）are in addition to warranties arising under Articles 3, 4, 7, and 8 because of the presentation or transfer of documents covered by any of those Articles.

（c）只有开证人兑付信用证后，上述（a）款中的担保才产生，即使协议或条款另有相反规定。

（c）Notwithstanding any agreement or term to the contrary, the warranties in Subsection（a）do not arise until the issuer honors the letter of credit.

第 5.111 条　救济

§ 5.111. Remedies.

（a）如果开证人错误拒付，或在提示之前就信用证项下的付款义务毁约，则受益人、继承人，或代表自己作出提示的

（a）If an issuer wrongfully dishonors or repudiates its obligation to pay money under a letter of credit before presentation, the beneficiary, successor, or nominated person

指定人，可以就拒付或毁约涉及的金额，从开证人获得赔偿。如果开证人在信用证项下的义务非系付款，索赔人可以获得实际履行，但亦可选择取得金钱赔偿，而赔偿金额为开证人之履约的价值。无论哪种情况，索赔人均可就附带损失取得赔偿，但无权就间接损失取得赔偿。对于开证人在本款项下可能需要承担的损失，索赔人无义务采取行动避免该损失。尽管索赔人无义务避免该损失，但是，如果其已实际避免了该损失，则索赔人从开证人取得的赔偿，应减去被避免的损失。开证人有义务证明被避免之损失的金额。如果发生毁约，索赔人无须提示单据。

presenting on its own behalf may recover from the issuer the amount that is the subject of the dishonor or repudiation.If the issuer's obligation under the letter of credit is not for the payment of money, the claimant may obtain specific performance or, at the claimant's election, recover an amount equal to the value of performance from the issuer.In either case, the claimant may also recover incidental but not consequential damages.The claimant is not obligated to take action to avoid damages that might be due from the issuer under this subsection.If, although not obligated to do so, the claimant avoids damages, the claimant's recovery from the issuer must be reduced by the amount ofdamages avoided.The issuer has the burden of proving the amount of damages avoided.In the case of repudiation the claimant need not present any document.

（b）如果开证人错误拒付信用证项下提示的汇票或请求，或在兑付汇票或请求时违反对申请人的义务，申请人可就该违约造成的损失取得赔偿，包括附带损失，但不包括间接损失，再减去因违约节省的金额。

（b）If an issuer wrongfully dishonors a draft or demand presented under a letter of credit or honors a draft or demand in breach of its obligation to the applicant, the applicant may recover damages resulting from the breach, including incidental but not consequential damages, less any amount saved as a result of the breach.

（c）如果通知人或指定人（保兑人除外）违反本篇规定的义务，或如果开证人违反（a）款或（b）款范围以外的义务，有权获得履约的人，可以就该违约造成的损失取得赔偿，包

（c）If an adviser or nominated person other than a confirmer breaches an obligation under this Article or an issuer breaches an obligation not covered in Subsection（a）or（b）, a person to whom the obligation is owed may recover damages resulting from the breach,

括附带损失，但不包括间接损失，再减去因违约节省的金额。在保兑的范围内，保兑人承担本款及（a）款和（b）款规定的开证人的责任。

including incidental but not consequential damages, less any amount saved as a result of the breach.To the extent of the confirmation, a confirmer has the liability of an issuer specified in this subsection and Subsections（a）and（b）.

（d）根据（a）款、（b）款或（c）款应当承担赔偿责任的开证人、指定人或通知人，还应支付从错误拒付之日期或其他适当日期起算的赔偿金额的利息。

（d）An issuer, nominated person, or adviser who is found liable under Subsection（a）,（b）, or（c）shall pay interest on the amount owed thereunder from the date of wrongful dishonor or other appropriate date.

（e）在根据本篇寻求救济的诉讼中，胜诉方可就合理的律师费及其他诉讼费取得赔偿。

（e）Reasonable attorney's fees and other expenses of litigation may be awarded to the prevailing party in an action in which a remedy is sought under this Article.

（f）对于当事方违反本篇义务而应支付的损害赔偿，可以通过协议或承诺，事先约定赔偿金额，但相对于预期的损失，所约定的金额或计算公式必须合理。

（f）Damages that would otherwise be payable by a party for breach of an obligation under this Article may be liquidated by agreement or undertaking, but only in an amount or by a formula that is reasonable in light of the harm anticipated.

第 5.112 条　信用证的转让

§ 5.112. Transfer of Letter of Credit.

（a）除第 5.113 条另有规定外，只要信用证未规定可以转让，受益人在信用证项下提取款项或以其他方式获得履约的权利，均属不可转让。

（a）Except as otherwise provided in Section 5.113, unless a letter of credit provides that it is transferable, the right of a beneficiary to draw or otherwise demand performance under a letter of credit may not be transferred.

（b）即使信用证规定可以转让，开证人在下列情况下，仍可拒绝承认或执行转让：

（b）Even if a letter of credit provides that it is transferable, the issuer may refuse to recognize or carry out a transfer if:

（1）转让将违反适用法；或

（1）the transfer would violate applicable law;or

（2）转让人或受让人未能

（2）the transferor or transferee has failed

遵守信用证规定的条件；或未能遵守开证人提出的其他转让条件，只要该条件在第5.108条（e）款所述的标准做法范围之内，或根据当时情况系属合理。

to comply with any requirement stated in the letter of credit or any other requirement relating to transfer imposed by the issuer which is within the standard practice referred to in Section 5.108（e）or is otherwise reasonable under the circumstances.

第5.113条 依法自动发生的转让

§ 5.113. Transfer by Operation of Law.

（a）受益人的继承人可以使用受益人的名字，对修改作出同意，签署并提示单据，以及接受付款或其他有价值的物品，而无须表明其继承人的身份。

（a）A successor of a beneficiary may consent to amendments, sign and present documents, and receive payment or other items of value in the name of the beneficiary without disclosing its status as a successor.

（b）受益人的继承人在表明其继承人的身份后，可以使用自己的名字，对修改作出同意，签署并提示单据，以及接受付款或其他有价值的物品。除（e）款另有规定外，如果受益人的继承人已表明其身份，开证人应承认其系完全取代被继承人的受益人；但是，对于依法自动发生的提款权的转让，如果第5.108条（e）款所述的标准做法规定了开证人承认该转让的条件，则应遵守该规定，或如果不存在此种标准做法，则应遵守足以保护开证人的其他合理程序。

（b）A successor of a beneficiary may consent to amendments, sign and present documents, and receive payment or other items of value in its own name as the disclosed successor of the beneficiary.Except as otherwise provided in Subsection（e）, an issuer shall recognize a disclosed successor of a beneficiary as beneficiary in full substitution for its predecessor upon compliance with the requirements for recognition by the issuer of a transfer of drawing rights by operation of law under the standard practice referred to in Section 5.108（e）or, in the absence of such a practice, compliance with other reasonable procedures sufficient to protect the issuer.

（c）如果任何人声称是受益人的继承人，开证人没有义务核实该人是否为受益人的继

（c）An issuer is not obliged to determine whether a purported successor is a successor of a beneficiary or whether the signature of a

承人，或该人的签名是否系属真实或业经授权。

（d）如果声称的继承人所作的提示，表面上符合（a）款或（b）款，则对该提示的兑付，即具有第5.108条（i）款规定的后果，即使声称的继承人实际不是受益人的继承人。如果单据上的签名使用了受益人的名字，或使用了已表明身份之继承人的名字，但签名人既不是受益人，也不是受益人的继承人，则该单据属于第5.109条所述的伪造单据。

（e）对于任何开证人，如果其获得补偿的权利未规定在（d）款或实质上类似的法律中，则该开证人，以及任何保兑人或指定人，可以拒绝承认（b）款项下的提示。

（f）如果在信用证开立之后，受益人改变名字，该受益人持有同于本条所述的受益人之继承人的权利和义务。

第5.114条　收益的转让

（a）在本条中，“信用证收益”指开证人或指定人根据信用证作出兑付或支付价值时，所支付或交付的现金、支票、已承兑汇票，或其他有价值的物品。“信用证收益”不包括受益人的提款权，或受益人所提示的单据。

purported successor is genuine or authorized.

（d）Honor of a purported successor's apparently complying presentation under Subsection（a）or（b）has the consequences specified in Section 5.108（i）even if the purported successor is not the successor of a beneficiary.Documents signed in the name of the beneficiary or of a disclosed successor by a person who is neither the beneficiary nor the successor of the beneficiary are forged documents for the purposes of Section 5.109.

（e）An issuer whose rights of reimbursement are not covered by Subsection（d）or substantially similar law and any confirmer or nominated person may decline to recognize a presentation under Subsection（b）.

（f）A beneficiary whose name is changed after the issuance of a letter of credit has the same rights and obligations as a successor of a beneficiary under this section.

§ 5.114. Assignment of Proceeds.

（a）In this section, “proceeds of a letter of credit” means the cash, check, accepted draft, or other item of value paid or delivered upon honor or giving of value by the issuer or any nominated person under the letter of credit. The term does not include a beneficiary's drawing rights or documents presented by the beneficiary.

（b）受益人可将其获取部分或全部信用证收益的权利予以转让。受益人亦可在提示前，以即时转让的方式，转让其获取收益的权利，但前提是受益人必须满足信用证的条款和条件。

（b）A beneficiary may assign its right to part or all of the proceeds of a letter of credit. The beneficiary may do so before presentation as a present assignment of its right to receive proceeds contingent upon its compliance with the terms and conditions of the letter of credit.

（c）开证人或指定人在对信用证收益的转让给予同意之前，无须承认该转让。

（c）An issuer or nominated person need not recognize an assignment of proceeds of a letter of credit until it consents to the assignment.

（d）开证人或指定人没有义务对信用证收益的转让给予或不给予同意，但如果受让人占有并出示信用证，且提示信用证是兑付的条件，则开证人或指定人不得不合理地拒绝给予同意。

（d）An issuer or nominated person has no obligation to give or withhold its consent to an assignment of proceeds of a letter of credit, but consent may not be unreasonably withheld if the assignee possesses and exhibits the letter of credit and presentation of the letter of credit is a condition to honor.

（e）指定人或身为信用证受让人之受益人的权利，独立于受益人对信用证收益的转让，并优于收益受让人对收益的权利。

（e）Rights of a transferee beneficiary or nominated person are independent of the beneficiary's assignment of the proceeds of a letter of credit and are superior to the assignee's right to the proceeds.

（f）本条所承认的收益受让人与开证人之间，收益受让人与身为信用证受让人之受益人之间，或收益受让人与指定人之间的权利，以及开证人或指定人向收益受让人或第三人作出的收益支付，均不影响收益受让人与任何其他人（不包括开证人、身为信用证受让人之受益人或指定人）之间的权利。涉及受益人对收益的权利时，在该

（f）Neither the rights recognized by this section between an assignee and an issuer, transferee beneficiary, or nominated person nor the issuer's or nominated person's payment of proceeds to an assignee or a third person affect the rights between the assignee and any person other than the issuer, transferee beneficiary, or nominated person. The mode of creating and perfecting a security interest in or granting an assignment of a beneficiary's rights to proceeds is governed by Article 9 or

权利上设立并完善担保权益的方式，或转让此种权利的方式，受第9篇或其他法律管辖。在对抗除开证人、身为信用证受让人之受益人，或指定人以外的其他人时，如果在受益人对收益之权利上设立担保权益或作出其他转让，则该担保权益或转让所引起的权利和义务，以及该担保权益或转让获得完善的方式，受第9篇或其他法律的管辖。

other law.Against persons other than the issuer, transferee beneficiary, or nominated person, the rights and obligations arising upon the creation of a security interest or other assignment of a beneficiary's right to proceeds and its perfection are governed by Article 9 or other law.

第5.115条　诉讼时效

强制履行本篇项下之权利或义务的诉讼，必须从相关信用证之失效日期起一年内提起，或从诉讼原因发生起一年内提起，以迟者为准。诉讼原因在违约时发生，即使受损方并不知道该违约。

§ 5.115. Statute of Limitations.

An action to enforce a right or obligation arising under this Article must be commenced within one year after the expiration date of the relevant letter of credit or one year after the cause of action accrues, whichever occurs later.A cause of action accrues when the breach occurs, regardless of the aggrieved party's lack of knowledge of the breach.

第5.116条　选择法律和诉讼地

（a）涉及开证人、指定人或通知人之行为或疏漏的责任时，当事方可以选择管辖该责任的法律。该选择可以通过相关当事方的协议作出，即通过第5.104条所述的由相关当事方签署或认证的包含当事方协议的记录作出；也可以通过开证人、指定人或通知人在信用证、保兑或其他承诺中的条款作出。所选择的法律无须与交

§ 5.116. Choice of Law and Forum.

(a) The liability of an issuer, nominated person, or adviser for action or omission is governed by the law of the jurisdiction chosen by an agreement in the form of a record signed or otherwise authenticated by the affected parties in the manner provided in Section 5.104 or by a provision in the person's letter of credit, confirmation, or other undertaking.The jurisdiction whose law is chosen need not bear any relation to the transaction.

易存在任何联系。

（b）除涉及应适用（a）款的情况外，开证人、指定人或通知人之行为或疏漏的责任，应由其所在州的法律管辖。该人的所在州，应为该人在承诺中注明的地址。如果注明的地址超过一个，该人的所在州应为作出承诺的州。在确定法律辖区、法律选择，以及分支机构间信用证的承认时，一个银行的各个分行在法律管辖上应被视为独立的实体，而银行的所在州，应为根据本款确定的相关分行的所在州。上述规定不适用于判决的强制履行。

（b）Unless Subsection（a）applies, the liability of an issuer, nominated person, or adviser for action or omission is governed by the law of the jurisdiction in which the person is located.The person is considered to be located at the address indicated in the person's undertaking.If more than one address is indicated, the person is considered to be located at the address from which the person's undertaking was issued.For the purpose of jurisdiction, choice of law, and recognition of interbranch letters of credit, but not enforcement of a judgment, all branches of a bank are considered separate juridical entities, and a bank is considered to be located at the place where its relevant branch is considered to be located under this subsection.

（c）除本款另有规定外，开证人、指定人或通知人的责任，应由信用证、保兑或其他承诺明确采纳的任何惯例或做法中的规则管辖，例如《跟单信用证统一惯例》。如果（i）根据（a）款或（b）款，开证人、指定人或通知人的责任应受本篇管辖，（ii）相关承诺采纳了该惯例或做法中的规则，以及（iii）本篇与适用于该承诺的该规则存在冲突，此时，应适用该规则，但第5.103条（c）款规定的不可加以改变的条款除外。

（c）Except as otherwise provided in this subsection, the liability of an issuer, nominated person, or adviser is governed by any rules of custom or practice, such as the Uniform Customs and Practice for Documentary Credits, to which the letter of credit, confirmation, or other undertaking is expressly made subject. If（i）this Article would govern the liability of an issuer, nominated person, or adviser under Subsection（a）or（b）,（ii）the relevant undertaking incorporates rules of custom or practice, and（iii）there is conflict between this Article and those rules as applied to that undertaking, those rules govern except to the extent of any conflict with the nonvariable provisions specified in Section 5.103（c）.

（d）如果本篇与第3篇、第4篇、第4A篇或第9篇存在冲突，应以本篇为准。

（d）If there is conflict between this Article and Article 3, 4, 4A, or 9, this Article governs.

（e）涉及因本篇项下之承诺所引起的争议时，上述（a）款有关适用法选择方法的规定，同样适用于对解决争议之诉讼所在州的选择，且对诉讼所在州的选择亦具有同样约束力。

（e）The forum for settling disputes arising out of an undertaking within this Article may be chosen in the manner and with the binding effect that governing law may be chosen in accordance with Subsection（a）.

第5.117条　开证人、申请人和指定人的代位

§ 5.117. Subrogation of Issuer, Applicant, and Nominated Person.

（a）开证人在兑付受益人的提示后，代位受益人的权利，即对于向受益人承担的基础义务，开证人相当于该义务的次义务人；并且，还代位申请人的权利，即对于向申请人承担的基础义务，开证人相当于该义务的次义务人。

（a）An issuer that honors a beneficiary's presentation is subrogated to the rights of the beneficiary to the same extent as if the issuer were a secondary obligor of the underlying obligation owed to the beneficiary and of the applicant to the same extent as if the issuer were the secondary obligor of the underlying obligation owed to the applicant.

（b）申请人在补偿开证人后，在对抗任何受益人、提示人或指定人时，代位开证人的权利，即对于向开证人承担的义务，申请人相当于该义务的次义务人；并且，还享有开证人拥有的代位权，可以代位（a）款所述受益人的权利。

（b）An applicant that reimburses an issuer is subrogated to the rights of the issuer against any beneficiary, presenter, or nominated person to the same extent as if the applicant were the secondary obligor of the obligations owed to the issuer and has the rights of subrogation of the issuer to the rights of the beneficiary stated in Subsection（a）.

（c）涉及根据信用证作出提示的汇票或指令时，指定人在付款或支付价值后，即代位下列权利：

（c）A nominated person who pays or gives value against a draft or demand presented under a letter of credit is subrogated to the rights of:

（1）开证人对抗申请人的权利，即对于申请人向开证人承担的义务，指定人相当于该义务的次义务人；

（2）受益人的权利，即对于向受益人承担的基础义务，指定人相当于该义务的次义务人；以及

（3）申请人的权利，即对于向申请人承担的基础义务，指定人相当于该义务的次义务人。

（d）即使任何协议或条款有相反规定，上述（a）款和（b）款所述的代位权，亦只有在开证人兑付信用证或以其他方式付款后才发生，且（c）款所述的权利，只有在指定人付款或以其他方式支付价值后才发生。在此之前，开证人、指定人和申请人不能根据本条获得现实或潜在的权利，用作索赔、抗辩或免责的理由。

第 5.118 条　开证人或指定人的担保权益

（a）开证人或指定人对提示作出兑付或支付价值后，即相应地对所提示的信用证项下的单据拥有担保权益。

（b）涉及（a）款所述的对单据的担保权益时，只要开证人或指定人尚未获得补偿，或

（1）the issuer against the applicant to the same extent as if the nominated person were a secondary obligor of the obligation owed to the issuer by the applicant;

（2）the beneficiary to the same extent as if the nominated person were a secondary obligor of the underlying obligation owed to the beneficiary;and

（3）the applicant to the same extent as if the nominated person were a secondary obligor of the underlying obligation owed to the applicant.

（d）Notwithstanding any agreement or term to the contrary, the rights of subrogation stated in Subsections（a）and（b）do not arise until the issuer honors the letter of credit or otherwise pays, and the rights in Subsection（c）do not arise until the nominated person pays or otherwise givesvalue.Until then, the issuer, the nominated person, and the applicant do not derive under this section present or prospective rights forming the basis of a claim, defense, or excuse.

§ 5.118. Security Interest of Issuer or Nominated Person.

（a）An issuer or nominated person has a security interest in a document presented under a letter of credit to the extent that the issuer or nominated person honors or gives value for the presentation.

（b）So long as and to the extent that an issuer or nominated person has not been reimbursed or has not otherwise recovered the

尚未以其他方式收回就该担保权益支付的价值，则在相应范围内，担保权益即继续存在，并受第9篇的约束，但是：

（1）无须担保协议，亦可使该担保权益具有第9.203条（b）（3）款项下的强制履行力；

（2）如果单据非以书面或其他有形介质作出提示，该担保权益即属于完善担保权益；并且

（3）如果单据以书面或其他有形介质作出提示，且该单据不是票式证券、动产契据、所有权凭证、票据或信用证，则只要债务人不占有该单据，该担保权益即属于完善担保权益，且优于单据中冲突的担保权益。

value given with respect to a security interest in a document under Subsection（a）, the security interest continues and is subject to Article 9, but:

（1）a security agreement is not necessary to make the security interest enforceable under Section 9.203（b）（3）;

（2）if the document is presented in a medium other than a written or other tangible medium, the security interest is perfected;and

（3）if the document is presented in a written or other tangible medium and is not a certificated security, chattel paper, a document of title, an instrument, or a letter of credit, the security interest is perfected and has priority over a conflicting security interest in the document so long as the debtor does not have possession of the document.

词汇索引

保兑人	confirmer	第 5.102 条（a）（4）
单据	document	第 5.102 条（a）（6）
兑付	honor	第 5.102 条（a）（8）
记录	record	第 5.102 条（a）（14）
拒付	dishonor	第 5.102 条（a）（5）
开证人	issuer	第 5.102 条（a）（9）
善意	good faith	第 5.102 条（a）（7）
申请人	applicant	第 5.102 条（a）（2）
受益人	beneficiary	第 5.102 条（a）（3）
受益人的继承人	successor of a beneficiary	第 5.102 条（a）（15）
提示	presentation	第 5.102 条（a）（12）
提示人	presenter	第 5.102 条（a）（13）
通知人	adviser	第 5.102 条（a）（1）
信用证	letter of credit	第 5.102 条（a）（10）
指定人	nominated person	第 5.102 条（a）（11）

第6篇　整体转让

ARTICLE 6. BULK TRANSFERS

（已废止）

（REPEALED）

第7篇　所有权凭证

ARTICLE 7. DOCUMENTS OF TITLE

第1章　总　则

PART 1. GENERAL PROVISIONS

第 7.101 条　简称

本篇被引用时可称为《统一商法典——所有权凭证》。

第 7.102 条　定义和定义索引

（a）除上下文另有所指外，在本篇中：

（1）"货物保管人"指通过出具仓单、提单或其他所有权凭证，承认占有货物并约定交付货物的人。

（2）"承运人"指出具提单的人。

（3）"收货人"指提单中注明其名字并承诺向其或其指定人交付货物的人。

（4）"发货人"指提单中注明其名字并将其作为交付货物用于发运的人。

（5）"交货命令"指向承储人、承运人或其他在正常业务中出具仓单或提单的人所发出

§ 7.101. Short Title.

This Article may be cited as Uniform Commercial Code— Documents of Title.

§ 7.102. Definitions and Index of Definitions.

(a) In this Article, unless the context otherwise requires:

(1) "Bailee" means a person that by a warehouse receipt, bill of lading, or other document of title acknowledges possession of goods and contracts to deliver them.

(2) "Carrier" means a person that issues a bill of lading.

(3) "Consignee" means a person named in a bill of lading to which or to whose order the bill promises delivery.

(4) "Consignor" means a person named in a bill of lading as the person from which the goods have been received for shipment.

(5) "Delivery order" means a record that contains an order to deliver goods directed to a warehouse, carrier, or other person that in the

的，指示其交付货物的记录。

ordinary course of business issues warehouse receipts or bills of lading.

（6）［保留］

（6）［Reserved.］

（7）“货物”指为存储合同或运输合同目的被视为可以移动的任何物品。

（7）“Goods” means all things that are treated as movable for the purposes of a contract for storage or transportation.

（8）“开单人”指出具所有权凭证的货物保管人；涉及尚未被接受的交货命令时，也指命令货物占有人交付货物的人。如果任何人的代理人或雇员声称代表前者出具凭证，则只要该代理人或雇员具有出具凭证的真实授权或表见授权，该前者亦属于“开单人”，即使开单人未收到任何货物，或货物的描述不正确，或代理人或雇员以其他方式违反了开单人的指示。

（8）“Issuer” means a bailee that issues a document of title or, in the case of an unaccepted delivery order, the person that orders the possessor of goods to deliver.The term includes a person for which an agent or employee purports to act in issuing a document if the agent or employee has real or apparent authority to issue documents, even if the issuer did not receive any goods, the goods were misdescribed, or in any other respect the agent or employee violated the issuer's instructions.

（9）涉及流通所有权凭证时，“所有权凭证的权利人”指执票人；涉及不可流通所有权凭证时，指根据凭证条款或根据凭证项下之记录中的指示，应向其交付货物的人。

（9）“Person entitled under the document” means the holder, in the case of a negotiable document of title, or the person to which delivery of the goods is to be made by the terms of, or pursuant to instructions in a record under, a nonnegotiable document of title.

（10）［保留］

（10）［Reserved.］

（11）“发运人”指与承运人签订运输合同的人。

（11）“Shipper” means a person that enters into a contract of transportation with a carrier.

（12）“签名”指下列行为，且作出该行为时的意图是通过该行为认证或采纳一项记录：

（12）“Sign” means, with present intent to authenticate or adopt a record:

（A）作出或采纳任何有形符号；或

（A）to execute or adopt a tangible symbol;or

（B）将电子形式的声音、符号或程序附着于该记录，或以符合逻辑的形式连接至该记录。

（B）to attach to or logically associate with the record an electronic sound, symbol, or process.

（13）“承储人”指从事货物收费存储业务的人。

（13）“Warehouse” means a person engaged in the business of storing goods for hire.

（b）其他各篇中适用于本篇的定义及其所在位置：

（b）Definitions in other Articles applying to this Article and the sections in which they appear are:

（1）“买卖合同”　第2.106条

（1）“Contract for sale,” Section 2.106.

（2）“正常业务中的承租方”第2A.103条

（2）“Lessee in ordinary course of business,” Section 2A.103.

（3）“收到”货物　第2.103条

（3）“Receipt” of goods, Section 2.103.

（c）此外，第1篇中的通用定义和解释原则适用于本篇通篇。

（c）In addition, Article 1 contains general definitions and principles of construction and interpretation applicable throughout this Article.

第7.103条　本篇与条约或法律的关系

§ 7.103. Relation of Article to Treaty or Statute.

（a）适用的美国的任何条约或法律，以及本州的任何监管法律，在其适用范围内，效力优于本篇。

（a）This Article is subject to any treaty or statute of the United States or a regulatory statute of this state to the extent the treaty, statute, or regulatory statute is applicable.

（b）如果任何法律对所有权凭证的格式或内容作出规定，或对货物保管人应提供的服务或设施作出规定，或对货物保管人行业作出本篇未特别规定的其他规定，则本篇并不废除或修改该法律。但是，只要任

（b）This Article does not repeal or modify any law prescribing the form or contents of a document of title or the services or facilities to be afforded by a bailee, or otherwise regulating a bailee’s businesses in respects not specifically treated in this Article.However, violation of these laws does not affect the status

何所有权凭证符合所有权凭证的定义，则即使违反前述法律，亦不影响其所有权凭证的地位。

of a document of title that otherwise complies with the definition of a document of title.

（c）本篇修改、限制并取代联邦《国际及国内商业电子签名法》，但并不修改、限制或取代该法的第 7001 条（c）款，也不授权以电子交付方式作出该法第 7003 条（b）款所述的通知。

（c）This Article modifies, limits, and supersedes the federal Electronic Signatures in Global and National Commerce Act, but does not modify, limit, or supersede Section 7001（c） or authorize electronic delivery of any of the notices described in Section 7003（b）.

（d）如果《统一电子交易法》与本篇存在冲突，应以本篇为准。

（d）To the extent there is a conflict between Uniform Electronic Transactions Act and this Article, this Article governs.

第 7.104 条　流通与不可流通所有权凭证

§ 7.104. Negotiable and Nonnegotiable Document of Title.

（a）如果所有权凭证的条款规定，应将货物交付给持票人，或交付给特定人的指定人，该凭证即属于流通所有权凭证。

（a）A document of title is negotiable if by its terms the goods are to be delivered to bearer or to the order of a named person.

（b）上述（a）款以外的其他所有权凭证，均属于不可流通。如果提单规定，货物的收货人为特定人，但同时规定，应仅凭该特定人或另一特定人在签名记录中作出的指示交付货物，该提单亦不因此成为流通所有权凭证。

（b）A document of title other than one described in Subsection（a）is nonnegotiable. A bill of lading that states that the goods are consigned to a named person is not made negotiable by a provision that the goods are to be delivered only against an order in a record signed by the same or another named person.

（c）如果所有权凭证在出具时即载有不可流通的明显标注，则凭证即属于不可流通，无论标注采用何种形式。

（c）A document of title is nonnegotiable if, at the time it is issued, the document has a conspicuous legend, however expressed, that it is nonnegotiable.

第7.105条 以替代媒介再次出具

（a）如果电子所有权凭证的权利人提出要求，则在下列情况下，电子凭证的开单人可以出具实体所有权凭证，用于代替电子凭证：

（1）电子凭证的权利人向开单人交出凭证的控制；并且

（2）实体凭证在出具时注明，该凭证的出具用于代替电子凭证。

（b）在根据（a）款出具实体所有权凭证用于代替电子凭证后：

（1）电子凭证不再具有任何作用或效力；并且

（2）取得实体凭证出具的人，向实体所有权凭证的所有后手权利人担保，在向开单人交出电子凭证的控制时，担保人是电子凭证的权利人。

（c）如果实体所有权凭证的权利人提出要求，则在下列情况下，实体凭证的开单人可以出具电子所有权凭证，用于代替实体凭证：

（1）实体凭证的权利人向开单人交出凭证的控制；并且

§ 7.105. Reissuance in Alternative Medium.

（a）Upon request of a person entitled under an electronic document of title, the issuer of the electronic document may issue a tangible document of title as a substitute for the electronic document if:

（1）the person entitled under the electronic document surrenders control of the document to the issuer;and

（2）the tangible document when issued contains a statement that it is issued in substitution for the electronic document.

（b）Upon issuance of a tangible document of title in substitution for an electronic document of title in accordance with Subsection（a）:

（1）the electronic document ceases to have any effect or validity;and

（2）the person that procured issuance of the tangible document warrants to all subsequent persons entitled under the tangible document that the warrantor was a person entitled under the electronic document when the warrantor surrendered control of the electronic document to the issuer.

（c）Upon request of a person entitled under a tangible document of title, the issuer of the tangible document may issue an electronic document of title as a substitute for the tangible document if:

（1）the person entitled under the tangible document surrenders possession of the document to the issuer;and

（2）电子凭证在出具时注明，该凭证的出具用于代替实体凭证。

（2）the electronic document when issued contains a statement that it is issued in substitution for the tangible document.

（d）在根据（c）款出具电子所有权凭证用于代替实体凭证后：

（d）Upon issuance of the electronic document of title in substitution for a tangible document of title in accordance with Subsection（c）:

（1）实体凭证不再具有任何作用或效力；并且

（1）the tangible document ceases to have any effect or validity;and

（2）取得电子凭证出具的人，向电子所有权凭证的所有后手权利人担保，在向开单人交出实体凭证的控制时，担保人是实体凭证的权利人。

（2）the person that procured issuance of the electronic document warrants to all subsequent persons entitled under the electronic document that the warrantor was a person entitled under the tangible document when the warrantor surrendered possession of the tangible document to the issuer.

第 7.106 条　电子所有权凭证的控制

§ 7.106. Control of Electronic Document of Title.

（a）只要用于证明电子所有权凭证之权利转让的系统能够可靠地证实，电子所有权凭证已出具给或转让给一个人，该人即对该电子凭证拥有控制。

（a）A person has control of an electronic document of title if a system employed for evidencing the transfer of interests in the electronic document reliably establishes that person as the person to which the electronic document was issued or transferred.

（b）如果一个系统中之电子所有权凭证的产生、存储或转让方式符合下列要求，该系统即满足（a）款的规定，且下列人即被视为对电子所有权凭证拥有控制：

（b）A system satisfies Subsection（a）, and a person is deemed to have control of an electronic document of title, if the document is created, stored, and assigned in such a manner that:

（1）凭证只存在一份权威版本，且该版本具有唯一性和

（1）a single authoritative copy of the document exists which is unique, identifiable,

可辨性，且除（4）款、（5）款和（6）款另有规定外，该版本不可更改；

and, except as otherwise provided in Subdivisions（4）,（5）, and（6）, unalterable;

（2）对于声称控制凭证的人，该权威版本确认：

（2）the authoritative copy identifies the person asserting control as:

（A）已将凭证出具给该人；或

（A）the person to which the document was issued;or

（B）如果权威版本注明凭证曾被转让过，该人系取得凭证最新一次转让的人；

（B）if the authoritative copy indicates that the document has been transferred, the person to which the document was most recently transferred;

（3）权威版本被发送至声称拥有控制的人或其指定的保管人，且由该人或该保管人持有；

（3）the authoritative copy is communicated to and maintained by the person asserting control or its designated custodian;

（4）只有在声称拥有控制的人给予同意后，才能制作权威版本的副本或修订本，用于增加或改变权威版本的指定受让人；

（4）copies or amendments that add or change an identified assignee of the authoritative copy can be made only with the consent of the person asserting control;

（5）权威版本的每一个副本，以及该副本的任何副本，都可以容易地看出是副本，而不是权威版本；以及

（5）each copy of the authoritative copy and any copy of a copy is readily identifiable as a copy that is not the authoritative copy;and

（6）权威版本的任何修改，都可以容易地看出是否业经授权。

（6）any amendment of the authoritative copy is readily identifiable as authorized or unauthorized.

第2章　仓单：特殊规定

PART 2. WAREHOUSE RECEIPTS:SPECIAL PROVISIONS

第 7.201 条　可以出具仓单的人；需要保证金的存储

§ 7.201. Person That May Issue a Warehouse Receipt; Storage Under Bond.

（a）任何承储人均可出具

（a）A warehouse receipt may be issued by

仓单。

（b）如果根据法律规定，对于某些货物的存储，包括蒸馏烈性酒和农业商品，必须交纳保证金后才能将货物提出仓库，或必须拥有执照才能出具仓单性质的收据，此时，为该种货物出具的收据，亦被视为仓单，即使出具收据的是货物所有权人而不是承储人。

第 7.202 条　仓单的格式

（a）仓单无须使用特定格式。

（b）如果仓单缺失下列任何一项条款，承储人应对该缺失对任何人造成的损失承担赔偿责任：

（1）存储货物之货仓的位置；

（2）仓单的出具日期；

（3）仓单的唯一识别码；

（4）对于所收到的货物，注明货物应交付给持票人，还是应交付给特定人，还是应交付给特定人或其指定人；

（5）存储费及手续费；但如果货物属于原地存储，且仓单为不可流通仓单，则只要在仓单上注明原地存储之事实即可；

（6）货物的描述，或货物外部包装的描述；

any warehouse.

（b）If goods, including distilled spirits and agricultural commodities, are stored under a statute requiring a bond against withdrawal or a license for the issuance of receipts in the nature of warehouse receipts, a receipt issued for the goods is deemed to be a warehouse receipt even if issued by a person that is the owner of the goods and is not a warehouse.

§ 7.202. Form of Warehouse Receipt.

（a）A warehouse receipt need not be in any particular form.

（b）Unless a warehouse receipt provides for each of the following, the warehouse is liable for damages caused to a person injured by its omission:

（1）the location of the warehouse facility where the goods are stored;

（2）the date of issue of the receipt;

（3）the unique identification code of the receipt;

（4）a statement whether the goods received will be delivered to the bearer, to a named person, or to a named person or its order;

（5）the rate of storage and handling charges, but if goods are stored under a field warehousing arrangement, a statement of that fact is sufficient on a nonnegotiable receipt;

（6）a description of the goods or the packages containing them;

（7）承储人或其代理人的签名；

（7）the signature of the warehouse or its agent;

（8）如果承储人对仓单覆盖的货物拥有所有权，无论是独立所有权，还是按份共有或共同共有的所有权，仓单均应注明此种事实；并且

（8）if the receipt is issued for goods that the warehouse owns, either solely, jointly, or in common with others, the fact of that ownership;and

（9）说明贷款金额，并说明承储人所主张之留置权或担保权益所涉及的债务金额。如果在出具仓单时，承储人或出具仓单的代理人不知道贷款或债务的准确金额，则只需注明贷款已支付或债务已发生的事实和原因即可。

（9）a statement of the amount of advances made and of liabilities incurred for which the warehouse claims a lien or security interest, but if the precise amount of advances made or of liabilities incurred is, at the time of the issue of the receipt, unknown to the warehouse or to its agent that issued the receipt, a statement of the fact that advances have been made or liabilities incurred and the purpose of the advances or liabilities is sufficient.

（c）承储人可在仓单中加入任何条款，只要该条款不与本法抵触，且不削弱第 7.403 条规定的承储人交付货物的义务或第 7.204 条规定的承储人行使谨慎的义务。任何违反此处规定的条款，均属无效。

（c）A warehouse may insert in its receipt any terms that are not contrary to this Act and do not impair its obligation of delivery under Section 7.403 or its duty of care under Section 7.204.Any contrary provisions are ineffective.

第 7.203 条　未收到货物或错误描述货物的责任

§ 7.203. Liability for Nonreceipt or Misdescription.

所有权凭证（提单除外）的当事方或善意支付价值的购买人，只要依赖凭证对货物的描述，即有权在开单人未收到货物或错误描述货物时，就受到的损失从开单人取得损害赔偿，但下列情况除外：

A party to or purchaser for value in good faith of a document of title, other than a bill of lading, that relies upon the description of the goods in the document may recover from the issuer damages caused by the nonreceipt or misdescription of the goods, except to the extent that:

（1）凭证醒目注明，开单人不知道货物是否事实上已全部或部分收到，或是否与描述相符，例如，描述系以商标、标签、种类、数量或状况作出，或仓单（或描述）使用了“内容、状况和质量未知”“据报装有”或具有类似含义的用语；但是，该注明必须系属真实；或

（1）the document conspicuously indicates that the issuer does not know whether all or part of the goods in fact were received or conform to the description, such as a case in which the description is in terms of marks or labels or kind, quantity, or condition, or the receipt or description is qualified by "contents, condition, and quality unknown," "said to contain," or words of similar import, if the indication is true;or

（2）当事方或购买人对于未收到货物或错误描述货物的情况，已通过其他方式得到通知。

（2）the party or purchaser otherwise has notice of the nonreceipt or misdescription.

第 7.204 条 谨慎的义务；通过协议限制承储人的责任

§ 7.204. Duty of Care;Contractual Limitation of Warehouse's Liability.

（a）如果承储人未能以合理谨慎的人在类似情况下应该行使的谨慎照管货物，即应对因此造成的货物遗失或损坏承担赔偿责任。但是，除另有协议外，对于行使该谨慎亦不能避免的损失，承储人不承担赔偿责任。

（a）A warehouse is liable for damages for loss of or injury to the goods caused by its failure to exercise care with regard to the goods that a reasonably careful person would exercise under similar circumstances.However, unless otherwise agreed, the warehouse is not liable for damages that could not have been avoided by the exercise of that care.

（b）仓单或存储协议可以设立条款，对货物遗失或损坏的赔偿金额加以限制，并规定承储人不对超出的金额承担责任。如果该条款对承储人侵占货物供自己使用时的责任加以限制，则该限制无效。货物交管人在签订存储协议时，或在收到仓单后的合理时间内，可

（b）Damages may be limited by a term in the warehouse receipt or storage agreement limiting the amount of liability in case of loss or damage beyond which the warehouse is not liable.Such a limitation is not effective with respect to the warehouse's liability for conversion to its own use.The warehouse's liability, on request of the bailor in a record at the time of signing such storage agreement

以使用记录形式，就存储协议或仓单项下之货物的部分或全部，要求增加承储人的责任。此时，可根据货物价值的增加，提高存储费。

or within a reasonable time after receipt of the warehouse receipt, may be increased on part or all of the goods covered by the storage agreement or the warehouse receipt.In this event, increased rates may be charged based on an increased valuation of the goods.

（c）仓单或存储协议可以设立合理条款，对于因货物存储产生的索赔或诉讼，规定提起索赔或诉讼的方式和时间。

（c）Reasonable provisions as to the time and manner of presenting claims and commencing actions based on the bailment may be included in the warehouse receipt or storage agreement.

第 7.205 条 某些情况下仓单代表的所有权失去效力

如果承储人向正常业务中的买方出售并交付种类物，且承储人从事该类货物买卖的经营，则买方取得货物后，不受制于根据仓单提出的索赔，即使仓单属于流通仓单，且已被正常流通。

§ 7.205. Title Under Warehouse Receipt Defeated in Certain Cases.

A buyer in ordinary course of business of fungible goods sold and delivered by a warehouse that is also in the business of buying and selling such goods takes the goods free of any claim under a warehouse receipt even if the receipt is negotiable and has been duly negotiated.

第 7.206 条 承储人终止存储的权利

（a）承储人可以通知货物的名义持有人及已知对货物主张权益的任何其他人，在所有权凭证规定的存储期限结束时，或如果未规定存储期限，则在作出通知后不少于 30 天的规定时间内，后者应支付所有费用，并从承储人取走货物。如果在通知规定的时间期满时货物未被取走，承储人可根据第 7.210 条将货物出售。

§ 7.206. Termination of Storage at Warehouse's Option.

（a）A warehouse, by giving notice to the person on whose account the goods are held and any other person known to claim an interest in the goods, may require payment of any charges and removal of the goods from the warehouse at the termination of the period of storage fixed by the document of title or, if a period is not fixed, within a stated period not less than 30 days after the warehouse gives notice.If the goods are not removed before the date specified in the notice, the warehouse may sell them pursuant to Section 7.210.

（b）如果承储人善意地相信，在（a）款和第7.210条规定的时间内，货物的价值将损失至或降低至不足承储人留置权的金额，则承储人可在根据（a）款作出的通知中，将取货时间合理缩短。如果届时货物未被取走，承储人可将货物公开出售，但至少应在出售的一星期前登出一次广告或布告。

（b）If a warehouse in good faith believes that goods are about to deteriorate or decline in value to less than the amount of its lien within the time provided in Subsection（a）and Section 7.210, the warehouse may specify in the notice given under Subsection（a）any reasonable shorter time for removal of the goods and, if the goods are not removed, may sell them at public sale held not less than one week after a single advertisement or posting.

（c）如果货物因质量或状况原因，对其他财产、货仓设施或其他人的人身构成危险，且承储人在收货时未得到该质量或状况的通知，承储人可在向所有已知对货物主张权益的人作出合理通知后，不经登出广告或布告，即对货物作出公开或私下出售。承储人如果经合理努力无法将货物售出，即可用任何合法方式处置货物，且不因该处置承担责任。

（c）If, as a result of a quality or condition of the goods of which the warehouse did not have notice at the time of deposit, the goods are a hazard to other property, the warehouse facilities, or other persons, the warehouse may sell the goods at public or private sale without advertisement or posting on reasonable notification to all persons known to claim an interest in the goods.If the warehouse, after a reasonable effort, is unable to sell the goods, it may dispose of them in any lawful manner and does not incur liability by reason of that disposition.

（d）在根据本条出售或以其他方式处置货物之前的任何时间，如果任何根据本篇对货物享有权利的人提出适当请求，承储人即应将货物交付给该人。

（d）A warehouse shall deliver the goods to any person entitled to them under this Article upon due demand made at any time before sale or other disposition under this section.

（e）对于根据本条出售或处置货物后的收益，承储人可以用于支付留置权，但必须保留任何余款，并在任何人要求

（e）A warehouse may satisfy its lien from the proceeds of any sale or disposition under this section but shall hold the balance for delivery on the demand of any person to

取得余款时，将余款交给该人，只要承储人原有义务向该人交付货物。

which the warehouse would have been bound to deliver the goods.

第 7.207 条 货物必须分开存储；种类物

§ 7.207. Goods Must Be Kept Separate; Fungible Goods.

（a）除仓单另有规定外，承储人应将每项仓单所覆盖的货物分开存储，以便在任何时候均可辨别并交付该货物。但是，不同份的种类物可以混合。

（a）Unless the warehouse receipt provides otherwise, a warehouse shall keep separate the goods covered by each receipt so as to permit at all times identification and delivery of those goods.However, different lots of fungible goods may be commingled.

（b）如果不同份的种类物混合在一起，则货物的所有各个权利人将共同拥有该种类物，且承储人对每个所有权人就其份额分别承担责任。如果承储人就一整批种类物超量出具仓单，致使该批种类物无法满足全部仓单，则超量出具之仓单正常流通后的执票人，亦属于货物的权利人。

（b）If different lots of fungible goods are commingled, the goods are owned in common by the persons entitled thereto and the warehouse is severally liable to each owner for that owner's share.If, because of overissue, a mass of fungible goods is insufficient to meet all the receipts the warehouse has issued against it, the persons entitled include all holders to which overissued receipts have been duly negotiated.

第 7.208 条 涂改的仓单

§ 7.208. Altered Warehouse Receipts.

如果实体流通仓单的空白处在未经授权的情况下被填入内容，则支付了价值且未得到无授权通知的善意购买人，可将填入的内容视为业经授权。涉及任何其他未经授权的涂改时，实体仓单或电子仓单可按原始条款对开单人强制履行。

If a blank in a negotiable tangible warehouse receipt has been filled in without authority, a good faith purchaser for value and without notice of the lack of authority may treat the insertion as authorized.Any other unauthorized alteration leaves any tangible or electronic warehouse receipt enforceable against the issuer according to its original tenor.

第 7.209 条 承储人的留置权

§ 7.209. Lien of Warehouse.

（a）承储人就所发生的存

（a）A warehouse has a lien against the

储费或运输费（包括滞期费和码头费）、保险费、人工费、货物目前及未来的费用、保存货物的必要费用，以及依法出售货物的合理费用，对仓单或存储协议所覆盖的货物，或对其所占有之货物的收益，享有对抗货物交管人的留置权。如果该货物的名义持有人还就其所存储之其他货物（无论何时存入）欠付此类费用，且目前的仓单或存储协议规定，承储人就该其他货物的费用亦享有留置权，则无论承储人是否已将该其他货物交付，承储人亦对目前仓单或存储协议所覆盖的货物，或对其所占有之货物的收益，享有留置权。但是，在对抗流通仓单正常流通后取得仓单的人时，承储人的留置权仅限于仓单上注明的费用或费率，或如果仓单上未注明，则限于仓单所覆盖之特定货物在收到后发生的合理存储费用。

bailor on the goods covered by a warehouse receipt or storage agreement or on the proceeds thereof in its possession for charges for storage or transportation, including demurrage and terminal charges, insurance, labor, or other charges, present or future, in relation to the goods, and for expenses necessary for preservation of the goods or reasonably incurred in their sale pursuant to law.If the person on whose account the goods are held is liable for similar charges or expenses in relation to other goods whenever deposited and it is stated in the warehouse receipt or storage agreement that a lien is claimed for charges and expenses in relation to other goods, the warehouse also has a lien against the goods covered by the warehouse receipt or storage agreement or on the proceeds thereof in its possession for those charges and expenses, whether or not the other goods have been delivered by the warehouse. However, as against a person to which a negotiable warehouse receipt is duly negotiated, a warehouse's lien is limited to charges in an amount or at a rate specified in the warehouse receipt or, if no charges are so specified, to a reasonable charge for storage of the specific goods covered by the receipt subsequent to the date of the receipt.

（b）承储人还可就（a）款以外的其他费用，如贷款或利息，以仓单注明的最高费用金额为限，保留第 9 篇项下对抗货物交管人的担保权益。该担

（b）The warehouse may also reserve a security interest under Article 9 against the bailor for the maximum amount specified on the receipt for charges other than those specified in Subsection（a）, such as for money advanced

保权益受第 9 篇的约束。

and interest.A security interest is governed by Article 9.

（c）承储人根据（a）款就费用享有的留置权，以及根据（b）款享有的担保权益，亦可有效对抗将货物委托给货物交管人占有的人，只要该委托的方式，在假设货物交管人将货物质押给支付了价值的善意购买人时，本可构成有效质押。但是，在对抗所有权凭证出具前对货物取得法定权益或完善担保权益的人时，承储人的留置权或担保权益在下列情况下无效：

（c）A warehouse's lien for charges and expenses under Subsection（a）or a security interest under Subsection（b）is also effective against any person that so entrusted the bailor with possession of the goods that a pledge of them by the bailor to a good faith purchaser for value would have been valid.However, the lien or security interest is not effective against a person that before issuance of a document of title had a legal interest or a perfected security interest in the goods and that did not:

（1）该人未将货物或覆盖货物的所有权凭证，交付给或委托给货物交管人或其指定人，使其具有运输、存储或出售货物的实际授权或表见授权，或具有根据第 7.403 条取得货物交付的权力，或具有根据第 2.403 条、第 2A.304 条（a）（2）款、第 2A.305 条（a）（2）款、第 9.320 条或其他法律对货物进行处置的权力；以及

（1）deliver or entrust the goods or any document covering the goods to the bailor or the bailor's nominee with actual or apparent authority to ship, store, or sell;or with power to obtain delivery under Section 7.403;or with power of disposition under Section 2.403, 2A.304（a）（2）, 2A.305（a）（2）, or 9.320 or other statute or rule of law;or

（2）该人未对货物交管人或其指定人取得所有权凭证给予默认。

（2）acquiesce in the procurement by the bailor or its nominee of any document.

（d）如果货物之交存人在存储货物时为货物的合法占有人，且货物为家用货物，则承储人根据（a）款就货物之费用享有的留置权，还可有效对抗

（d）A warehouse's lien on household goods for charges and expenses in relation to the goods under Subsection（a）is also effective against all persons if the depositor was the legal possessor of the goods at the time of deposit.

任何其他人。在本款中，“家用货物”指交存人在家庭中使用的家具、物件或个人物品。

（e）承储人如果自愿交付货物，或不当拒绝交付货物，即丧失对该货物的留置权。

第7.210条　承储人留置权的强制履行

（a）除（b）款另有规定外，承储人为强制履行留置权，可在通知所有已知对货物主张权益的人后，在任何时间和地点，以任何商业上合理的条件，将货物整批或分批进行公开或私下出售。通知必须说明到期应付的金额、拟进行之出售的性质，以及公开出售的时间和地点。即使在承储人选择的出售货物之时间或方式以外，存在能够取得更好售价的时间或方式，该事实本身也不足以说明该项出售未以商业上合理的方式进行。只要承储人在该种货物的任何公认市场上以通常方式出售该货物，或在此种市场上以当时的时价出售该货物，或以符合该种货物经营人所采用的商业上合理的其他方式出售该货物，即属以商业上合理的方式出售该货物。如果出售货物的数量，明显超出偿付债务所必需的数量，则除上句所述的情况外，不属于商业上合理。

In this subsection, “household goods” means furniture, furnishings, or personal effects used by the depositor in a dwelling.

（e）A warehouse loses its lien on any goods that it voluntarily delivers or unjustifiably refuses to deliver.

§ 7.210. Enforcement of Warehouse’s Lien.

（a）Except as otherwise provided in Subsection（b）, a warehouse’s lien may be enforced by public or private sale of the goods, in bulk or in packages, at any time or place and on any terms that are commercially reasonable, after notifying all persons known to claim an interest in the goods.The notification must include a statement of the amount due, the nature of the proposed sale, and the time and place of any public sale. The fact that a better price could have been obtained by a sale at a different time or in a different method from that selected by the warehouse is not of itself sufficient to establish that the sale was not made in a commercially reasonable manner.The warehouse has sold in a commercially reasonable manner if the warehouse sells the goods in the usual manner in any recognized market therefor, sells at the price current in that market at the time of the sale, or has otherwise sold in conformity with commercially reasonable practices among dealers in the type of goods sold.A sale of more goods than apparently necessary to be offered to ensure satisfaction of the obligation is not commercially reasonable, except in cases covered by the preceding sentence.

（b）如果货物不属于商人在其业务过程中提交存储的货物，则只有满足下列条件时，承储人才能强制履行对货物的留置权：

（b）A warehouse's lien on goods, other than goods stored by a merchant in the course of its business, may be enforced only if the following requirements are satisfied:

（1）必须通知所有已知对货物主张权益的人。

（1）All persons known to claim an interest in the goods must be notified.

（2）必须在通知中：逐项列出索赔；说明留置权涉及的货物；要求在收到通知后不少于十天的规定日期付款；醒目注明如果未能在规定时间内付款，将发布出售货物的广告并在规定的时间和地点拍卖货物。

（2）The notification must include an itemized statement of the claim, a description of the goods subject to the lien, a demand for payment within a specified time not less than 10 days after receipt of the notification, and a conspicuous statement that unless the claim is paid within that time the goods will be advertised for sale and sold by auction at a specified time and place.

（3）必须按通知说明的条件出售货物。

（3）The sale must conform to the terms of the notification.

（4）必须在与货物留存地或存储地最接近的适当地点出售货物。

（4）The sale must be held at the nearest suitable place to where the goods are held or stored.

（5）必须在通知规定的时间到期后，在货物出售地公开发行的报纸上每星期一次，连续两个星期登出广告。广告必须描述货物，说明货物之名义持有人的名字，并说明出售货物的时间和地点。出售必须在广告第一次登出的15天后进行。如果出售地无公开发行的报纸，则必须在出售前至少十

（5）After the expiration of the time given in the notification, an advertisement of the sale must be published once a week for two weeks consecutively in a newspaper of general circulation where the sale is to be held.The advertisement must include a description of the goods, the name of the person on whose account the goods are being held, and the time and place of the sale.The sale must take place at least 15 days after the first publication.If

日前，在拟出售之地点的临近区域不少于六处的明显位置贴出布告。

there is no newspaper of general circulation where the sale is to be held, the advertisement must be posted at least 10 days before the sale in not less than six conspicuous places in the neighborhood of the proposed sale.

（c）在根据本条进行出售之前，任何对货物主张权利的人，均可支付足够的金额，用于偿付留置权和根据本条支出的合理费用。此时，除仓单条款和本篇另有规定外，承储人不得出售货物，而必须保留货物。

（c）Before any sale pursuant to this section, any person claiming a right in the goods may pay the amount necessary to satisfy the lien and the reasonable expenses incurred in complying with this section.In that event, the goods may not be sold but must be retained by the warehouse subject to the terms of the receipt and this Article.

（d）在根据本条进行的公开出售中，承储人可以买进货物。

（d）A warehouse may buy at any public sale held pursuant to this section.

（e）即使承储人在强制履行留置权的出售中未能遵守本条规定，善意购买人在取得货物后，亦不受制于任何人的权利，只要承储人的留置权可以有效对抗该人的权利。

（e）A purchaser in good faith of goods sold to enforce a warehouse's lien takes the goods free of any rights of persons against which the lien was valid, despite the warehouse's noncompliance with this section.

（f）对于根据本条出售货物的收益，承储人可以用于支付留置权，但必须保留任何余款，并在任何人要求取得余款时，将余款交给该人，只要承储人原有义务向该人交付货物。

（f）A warehouse may satisfy its lien from the proceeds of any sale pursuant to this section but shall hold the balance, if any, for delivery on demand to any person to which the warehouse would have been bound to deliver the goods.

（g）本条提供的权利，是法律规定的债权人对债务人之所有其他权利的补充。

（g）The rights provided by this section are in addition to all other rights allowed by law to a creditor against a debtor.

（h）如果留置权存在于商

（h）If a lien is on goods stored by a

人在其业务过程中提交存储的货物，则留置权的强制履行，既可根据（a）款进行，亦可根据（b）款进行。

merchant in the course of its business, the lien may be enforced in accordance with Subsection (a) or (b).

（i）承储人如果未能按本条规定出售货物，即应对造成的损失承担责任；如果属于故意，应承担侵占货物的责任。

(i) A warehouse is liable for damages caused by failure to comply with the requirements for sale under this section and, in case of wilful violation, is liable for conversion.

第3章 提单：特殊规定

PART 3. BILLS OF LADING: SPECIAL PROVISIONS

第7.301条 未收到货物或错误描述货物的责任；"据报装有"；"发运人的装货和数量"；不适当处理货物

§ 7.301. Liability for Nonreceipt or Misdescription; "Said to Contain"; "Shipper's Load and Count"; Improper Handling.

（a）以善意支付价值取得不可流通提单的收货人，或流通提单正常流通后的执票人，如果依赖提单对货物的描述或提单所标明的日期，即有权在提单错填日期，或在开单人未收到货物或错误描述货物时，就所受到的损失从开单人取得损害赔偿，除非所有权凭证注明，开单人不知道货物是否事实上已部分或全部收到，或是否与描述相符，例如，描述系以商标、标签、种类、数量或状况作出，或提单（或描述）使用了"包装内之内容或状况不详""据报装有""发运人提供重量、装货及数量"，或类似

(a) A consignee of a nonnegotiable bill of lading which has given value in good faith, or a holder to which a negotiable bill has been duly negotiated, relying upon the description of the goods in the bill or upon the date shown in the bill, may recover from the issuer damages caused by the misdating of the bill or the nonreceipt or misdescription of the goods, except to the extent that the document of title indicates that the issuer does not know whether any part or all of the goods in fact were received or conform to the description, such as in a case in which the description is in terms of marks or labels or kind, quantity, or condition, or the receipt or description is qualified by "contents or condition of contents of packages unknown," "said to contain," "shipper's

的限制用语；但是，该注明必须系属真实。

（b）如果提单的开单人装载货物，则在货物为箱装时，其必须清点箱数；在货物为散装时，其必须核实种类和重量。此时，除包装内的货物存在隐瞒外，“发运人提供重量、装货及数量”或其他表示由发运人提供货物情况的用语，系属无效。

（c）如果发运人自行装载散装货物，但向提单的开单人提供了充分的称重设备，则开单人必须在收到发运人以记录形式提出的称重要求后，在合理时间内核实种类和重量。此时，“发运人提供重量”或其他类似用语，系属无效。

（d）开单人可在提单中加入“发运人提供重量、装货和数量”或其他类似用语，用于表示货物由发运人装载。如果该说明系属真实，开单人对不适当装载造成的损失不承担赔偿责任。但是，省略此种说明，不意味着开单人应对不适当装载造成的损失承担责任。

（e）发运人向开单人保证，其向开单人提供的描述、商标、标签、数字、种类、数量、状况及重量，在发运时系属准确。如果该等情况存在不准确之处，

weight, load and count," or words of similar import, if that indication is true.

（b）If goods are loaded by the issuer of the bill of lading, the issuer shall count the packages of goods if shipped in packages and ascertain the kind and quantity if shipped in bulk and words such as "shipper's weight, load and count," or words of similar import indicating that the description was made by the shipper are ineffective except as to goods concealed by packages.

（c）If bulk goods are loaded by a shipper that makes available to the issuer of the bill of lading adequate facilities for weighing those goods, the issuer shall ascertain the kind and quantity within a reasonable time after receiving the shipper's request in a record to do so.In that case, "shipper's weight" or words of similar import are ineffective.

（d）The issuer, by including in the bill of lading the words "shipper's weight, load and count," or words of similar import, may indicate that the goods were loaded by the shipper, and, if that statement is true, the issuer is not liable for damages caused by the improper loading. However, omission of such words does not imply liability for damages caused by improper loading.

（e）A shipper guarantees to the issuer the accuracy at the time of shipment of the description, marks, labels, number, kind, quantity, condition, and weight, as furnished by the shipper, and the shipper shall indemnify the

发运人应就所造成的损失赔偿开单人。开单人取得此种赔偿的权利，对于开单人根据承运合同向发运人以外任何其他人承担的义务和责任，不具有限制作用。

issuer against damage caused by inaccuracies in those particulars.This right of the issuer to that indemnity does not limit its responsibility or liability under the contract of carriage to any person other than the shipper.

第 7.302 条　联运提单和类似的所有权凭证

§ 7.302. Through Bills of Lading and Similar Documents of Title.

（a）如果开单人出具联运提单或其他所有权凭证，说明部分履约将由开单人的代理人或由其他承运人承担，则在该代理人或该其他承运人违反凭证义务时，开单人仍应对有权根据凭证取得赔偿的人承担责任。但是，如果提单涉及在海外或在与美国大陆本土不相接壤之地域履行的义务，或涉及运输以外的其他义务，则当事方可以通过协议，改变该代理人或该其他承运人违反义务时的责任。

（a）The issuer of a through bill of lading or other document of title embodying an undertaking to be performed in part by a person acting as its agent or by a performing carrier is liable to any person entitled to recover on the document for any breach by the other person or the performing carrier of its obligation under the document.However, to the extent that the bill covers an undertaking to be performed overseas or in territory not contiguous to the continental United States or an undertaking including matters other than transportation, this liability for breach by the other person or the performing carrier may be varied by agreement of the parties.

（b）如果覆盖货物的联运提单或其他所有权凭证，包含由开单人以外的其他人履行部分义务的承诺，则该其他人在收到货物后，应就其自己这部分义务，在占有货物期间，履行开单人的义务。该人根据凭证将货物交付给另一人后，即被解除义务，且不对任何其他人或开单人的违约承担责任。

（b）If goods covered by a through bill of lading or other document of title embodying an undertaking to be performed in part by a person other than the issuer are received by that person, the person is subject, with respect to its own performance while the goods are in its possession, to the obligation of the issuer.The person's obligation is discharged by delivery of the goods to another person pursuant to the document and does not include liability for breach by any other person or by the issuer.

（c）上述（a）款所述的联运提单或其他所有权凭证的开单人，有权从承担运输的承运人或凭证项下违约发生时占有货物的其他人，取得下列损害赔偿：

（c）The issuer of a through bill of lading or other document of title described in Subsection（a）is entitled to recover from the performing carrier, or other person in possession of the goods when the breach of the obligation under the document occurred:

（1）因凭证项下的违约，开单人可能有义务向有权就凭证违约取得赔偿的人支付的赔偿金额。该金额可由任何收据、法院判决或判决副本予以证明；以及

（1）the amount it may be required to pay to any person entitled to recover on the document for the breach, as may be evidenced by any receipt, judgment, or transcript of judgment;and

（2）在有权就凭证违约取得赔偿的人提起的诉讼中，开单人为抗辩而支出的合理费用。

（2）the amount of any expense reasonably incurred by the issuer in defending any action commenced by any person entitled to recover on the document for the breach.

第 7.303 条　改变目的地；改变收货人；改变指示

§ 7.303. Diversion; Reconsignment; Change of Instructions.

（a）除提单另有规定外，承运人在收到下列人的指示后，可以遵从该指示将货物交付给不同于提单注明的人或目的地，或以其他方式处置货物，而无须承担错误交付的责任：

（a）Unless the bill of lading otherwise provides, a carrier may deliver the goods to a person or destination other than that stated in the bill or may otherwise dispose of the goods, without liability for misdelivery, on instructions from:

（1）流通提单的执票人；

（1）the holder of a negotiable bill;

（2）不可流通提单的发货人，即使收货人作出相反指示；

（2）the consignor on a nonnegotiable bill even if the consignee has given contrary instructions;

（3）不可流通提单的收货人，只要发货人未作出相反指示，且货物已到达提单注明的目的地，或收货人占有实体提

（3）the consignee on a nonnegotiable bill in the absence of contrary instructions from the consignor, if the goods have arrived at the billed destination or if the consignee is in

单或控制电子提单；或

possession of the tangible bill or in control of the electronic bill;or

（4）不可流通提单的收货人，只要相对于发货人，该收货人有权处置货物。

（4）the consignee on a nonnegotiable bill, if the consignee is entitled as against the consignor to dispose of the goods.

（b）涉及流通提单时，如果（a）款所述的指示未在提单上注明，则提单正常流通后的受让人，可要求货物保管人按提单原始条款履约。

（b）Unless instructions described in Subsection（a）are included in a negotiable bill of lading, a person to which the bill is duly negotiated may hold the bailee according to the original terms.

第 7.304 条　实体成套提单

§ 7.304. Tangible Bills of Lading in Set.

（a）除国际运输中另有习惯做法外，不得出具一套多份的实体提单。开单人对违反本款造成的损失承担责任。

（a）Except as customary in international transportation, a tangible bill of lading may not be issued in a set of parts.The issuer is liable for damages caused by violation of this subsection.

（b）如果一套多份的实体提单系合法出具，且成套提单中的每一份均有编号，并注明只有在未曾就另一份提单交付货物时，该份提单方为有效，则所有各份构成一项提单。

（b）If a tangible bill of lading is lawfully issued in a set of parts, each of which contains an identification code and is expressed to be valid only if the goods have not been delivered against any other part, the whole of the parts constitutes one bill.

（c）如果一套多份的实体流通提单系合法出具，且各份被流通至不同的人，则首次正常流通的执票人对所有权凭证和货物享有的所有权具有优先权，即使随后的任何执票人已善意地从承运人收到货物，并通过交付其所持的那份提单，解除了承运人的义务。

（c）If a tangible negotiable bill of lading is lawfully issued in a set of parts and different parts are negotiated to different persons, the title of the holder to which the first due negotiation is made prevails as to both the document of title and the goods even if any later holder may have received the goods from the carrier in good faith and discharged the carrier's obligation by surrendering its part.

（d）流通或转让实体成套提单中任何一份的人，对那份

（d）A person that negotiates or transfers a single part of a tangible bill of lading issued in

提单的执票人，承担相当于该份提单为全套提单时的责任。

a set is liable to holders of that part as if it were the whole set.

（e）涉及合法出具的实体成套提单时，货物保管人有义务根据本篇第4章的规定，在收到首先提示的那份提单时即交付货物。货物保管人如此交付货物后，即被解除对全套提单的义务。

（e）The bailee is obliged to deliver in accordance with Part 4 against the first presented part of a tangible bill of lading lawfully issued in a set.Delivery in this manner discharges the bailee's obligation on the whole bill.

第7.305条　目的地出具提单

§ 7.305. Destination Bills.

（a）承运人可以根据发货人的要求，不在发运地向发货人出具提单，而在目的地出具提单，或在要求中指定的任何其他地点出具提单。

（a）Instead of issuing a bill of lading to the consignor at the place of shipment, a carrier, at the request of the consignor, may procure the bill to be issued at destination or at any other place designated in the request.

（b）当货物处在运输途中时，如果任何人对于控制货物享有优于承运人的权利，且该人提出要求，并交出覆盖货物的流通在外的提单或其他收据的占有或控制，则除第7.105条另有规定外，开单人可在该人要求中指定的任何地点，出具替代提单。

（b）Upon request of any person entitled as against a carrier to control the goods while in transit and on surrender of possession or control of any outstanding bill of lading or other receipt covering the goods, the issuer, subject to Section 7.105, may procure a substitute bill to be issued at any place designated in the request.

第7.306条　涂改的提单

§ 7.306. Altered Bills of Lading.

如果未经授权，提单被涂改或在空白处被填入任何内容，提单应按原始条款强制履行。

An unauthorized alteration or filling in of a blank in a bill of lading leaves the bill enforceable according to its original tenor.

第7.307条　承运人的留置权

§ 7.307. Lien of Carrier.

（a）承运人就收到货物后的存储或运输费用（包括滞期

（a）A carrier has a lien on the goods covered by a bill of lading or on the proceeds

费和码头费）、运输过程中保存货物的必要费用，以及依法出售货物的合理费用，对提单覆盖的货物，或对其占有之货物的收益，享有留置权。但是，在对抗通过支付价值取得流通提单的购买人时，承运人的留置权仅限于提单上或相关费率表上注明的费用；如果未注明，则限于合理费用。

thereof in its possession for charges after the date of the carrier's receipt of the goods for storage or transportation, including demurrage and terminal charges, and for expenses necessary for preservation of the goods incident to their transportation or reasonably incurred in their sale pursuant to law.However, against a purchaser for value of a negotiable bill of lading, a carrier's lien is limited to charges stated in the bill or the applicable tariffs or, if no charges are stated, a reasonable charge.

（b）如果法律要求承运人收取并承运货物，则承运人根据（a）款就货物费用享有的留置权，可以有效对抗发货人或货物的任何权利人，除非承运人曾得到通知，即发货人缺乏将货物抵偿上述费用的授权。根据（a）款取得的任何其他留置权，可以有效对抗发货人，以及允许货物交管人控制或占有货物的任何人，除非承运人曾得到通知，即货物交管人缺乏该授权。

（b）A lien for charges and expenses under Subsection（a）on goods that the carrier was required by law to receive for transportation is effective against the consignor or any person entitled to the goods unless the carrier had notice that the consignor lacked authority to subject the goods to those charges and expenses.Any other lien under Subsection（a）is effective against the consignor and any person that permitted the bailor to have control or possession of the goods unless the carrier had notice that the bailor lacked authority.

（c）如果承运人自愿交付货物，或不正当地拒绝交付货物，即丧失对该货物的留置权。

（c）A carrier loses its lien on any goods that it voluntarily delivers or unjustifiably refuses to deliver.

第 7.308 条　承运人留置权的强制履行

§ 7.308. Enforcement of Carrier's Lien.

（a）承运人为强制履行留置权，可在通知所有已知对货物主张权益的人后，在任何时间和地点，以任何商业上合理

（a）A carrier's lien on goods may be enforced by public or private sale of the goods, in bulk or in packages, at any time or place and on any terms that are commercially reasonable, after

的条件，将货物整批或分批进行公开或私下出售。通知必须说明到期应付的金额、拟进行之出售的性质，以及公开出售的时间和地点。即使在承运人选择的出售货物之时间或方式以外，存在能够取得更好售价的时间或方式，该事实本身也不足以说明该项出售未以商业上合理的方式进行。只要承运人在该种货物的任何公认市场上以通常方式出售该货物，或在此种市场上以当时的时价出售该货物，或以符合该种货物经营人采用的商业上合理的其他方式出售该货物，即属以商业上合理的方式出售该货物。如果出售货物的数量，明显超出偿付债务所必需的数量，则除上句所述的情况外，不属商业上合理。

notifying all persons known to claim an interest in the goods.The notification must include a statement of the amount due, the nature of the proposed sale, and the time and place of any public sale.The fact that a better price could have been obtained by a sale at a different time or in a different method from that selected by the carrier is not of itself sufficient to establish that the sale was not made in a commercially reasonable manner.The carrier has sold goods in a commercially reasonable manner if the carrier sells the goods in the usual manner in any recognized market therefor, sells at the price current in that market at the time of the sale, or has otherwise sold in conformity with commercially reasonable practices among dealers in the type of goods sold.A sale of more goods than apparently necessary to be offered to ensure satisfaction of the obligation is not commercially reasonable, except in cases covered by the preceding sentence.

（b）在根据本条进行出售之前，任何对货物主张权利的人，均可支付足够的金额，用于偿付留置权和根据本条支出的合理费用。此时，除提单条款和本篇另有规定外，承运人不得出售货物，而必须保留货物。

（b）Before any sale pursuant to this section, any person claiming a right in the goods may pay the amount necessary to satisfy the lien and the reasonable expenses incurred in complying with this section.In that event, the goods may not be sold but must be retained by the carrier, subject to the terms of the bill of lading and this Article.

（c）在根据本条进行的公开出售中，承运人可以买进货物。

（c）A carrier may buy at any public sale pursuant to this section.

（d）即使承运人在强制履

（d）A purchaser in good faith of goods

行留置权的出售中未能遵守本条规定，善意购买人在取得货物后，亦不受制于任何人的权利，只要承运人的留置权可以有效对抗该人的权利。

sold to enforce a carrier's lien takes the goods free of any rights of persons against which the lien was valid, despite the carrier's noncompliance with this section.

（e）对于根据本条出售货物的收益，承运人可以用于支付留置权，但必须保留任何余款，并在任何人要求取得余款时，将余款交给该人，只要承运人原有义务向该人交付货物。

（e）A carrier may satisfy its lien from the proceeds of any sale pursuant to this section but shall hold the balance, if any, for delivery on demand to any person to which the carrier would have been bound to deliver the goods.

（f）本条提供的权利，是法律规定的债权人对债务人之所有其他权利的补充。

（f）The rights provided by this section are in addition to all other rights allowed by law to a creditor against a debtor.

（g）承运人可以选择根据（a）款或根据第7.210条（b）款强制履行留置权。

（g）A carrier's lien may be enforced pursuant to either Subsection（a）or the procedure set forth in Section 7.210（b）.

（h）承运人如果未能按本条规定出售货物，应对造成的损失承担责任；如果属于故意，应承担侵占货物的责任。

（h）A carrier is liable for damages caused by failure to comply with the requirements for sale under this section and, in case of wilful violation, is liable for conversion.

第7.309条　谨慎的义务；通过协议限制承运人的责任

§ 7.309. Duty of Care; Contractual Limitation of Carrier's Liability.

（a）承运人无论出具的是流通提单还是不可流通提单，均必须以合理谨慎的人在类似情况下应该行使的谨慎照管货物。如果任何法律规定，公共承运人应对非疏忽性损失承担责任，该法律不受本款影响。

（a）A carrier that issues a bill of lading, whether negotiable or nonnegotiable, shall exercise the degree of care in relation to the goods which a reasonably careful person would exercise under similar circumstances. This subsection does not affect any statute, regulation, or rule of law that imposes liability upon a common carrier for damages not caused by its negligence.

（b）承运人可在提单或运输协议中规定，只要承运人基于价值收费，且发货人被告知和被给予机会申报较高价值，则承运人对损失的赔偿，即不超过提单或运输协议中注明的价值。但是，涉及承运人侵占货物供自己使用时，对承运人责任进行限制的上述条款，即属无效。

(b) Damages may be limited by a term in the bill of lading or in a transportation agreement that the carrier's liability may not exceed a value stated in the bill or transportation agreement if the carrier's rates are dependent upon value and the consignor is afforded an opportunity to declare a higher value and is advised of the opportunity. However, such a limitation is not effective with respect to the carrier's liability for conversion to its own use.

（c）提单或运输协议可以设立合理条款，规定就运输提起索赔或诉讼的时间和方式。

(c) Reasonable provisions as to the time and manner of presenting claims and commencing actions based on the shipment may be included in a bill of lading or a transportation agreement.

第4章 仓单和提单：一般义务

PART 4. WAREHOUSE RECEIPTS AND BILLS OF LADING: GENERAL OBLIGATIONS

第 7.401 条 仓单或提单的非正常出具；开单人的非正常行为

§ 7.401. Irregularities in Issue of Receipt or Bill or Conduct of Issuer.

即使存在下列情况，本篇就所有权凭证对开单人规定的义务，仍然适用于该凭证：

The obligations imposed by this Article on an issuer apply to a document of title even if:

（1）凭证的出具、格式或内容不符合本篇或其他法律的规定；

(1) the document does not comply with the requirements of this Article or of any other statute, rule, or regulation regarding its issue, form, or content;

（2）开单人违反了约束其商业活动的法律；

(2) the issuer violated laws regulating the conduct of its business;

（3）在凭证出具时，货物保管人系凭证所覆盖之货物的所有权人；或

（3）the goods covered by the document were owned by the bailee when the document was issued;or

（4）出具凭证的人不是承储人，但凭证却注明为仓单。

（4）the person issuing the document is not a warehouse but the document purports to be a warehouse receipt.

第 7.402 条　所有权凭证的副本；超量出具

§ 7.402. Duplicate Document of Title; Overissue.

如果开单人出具的覆盖货物的所有权凭证尚流通在外，则该凭证的任何副本，或显示覆盖同一货物且由同一开单人出具的其他所有权凭证，不赋予对货物的任何权利，但涉及下列情况时另有规定的除外：一套多份实体提单；种类物超量出具的凭证；凭证遗失、被盗或损毁后出具的替代凭证；根据第 7.105 条出具的替代凭证。如果开单人超量出具凭证，或未能在副本上醒目注明为副本，则应对造成的损失承担责任。

A duplicate or any other document of title purporting to cover goods already represented by an outstanding document of the same issuer does not confer any right in the goods, except as provided in the case of tangible bills of lading in a set of parts, overissue of documents for fungible goods, substitutes for lost, stolen, or destroyed documents, or substitute documents issued pursuant to Section 7.105.The issuer is liable for damages caused by its overissue or failure to identify a duplicate document by a conspicuous notation.

第 7.403 条　承储人或承运人交付货物的义务；免责

§ 7.403. Obligation of Warehouse or Carrier to Deliver;Excuse.

（a）只要所有权凭证的权利人遵守了（b）款和（c）款，货物保管人即应向其交付货物，除非货物保管人能够证明：

（a）A bailee shall deliver the goods to a person entitled under a document of title if the person complies with Subsections（b）and（c）, unless and to the extent that the bailee establishes any of the following:

（1）已将货物交付给另一人，且在对抗上述权利人时，该另一人有权收到货物；

（1）delivery of the goods to a person whose receipt was rightful as against the claimant;

（2）货物发生损坏、延迟、

（2）damage to or delay, loss, or destruction

遗失或灭失，且货物保管人不承担责任；

of the goods for which the bailee is not liable;

（3）已将货物出售或作其他处置，用于依法强制履行留置权，或依法终止承储人的存储；

（3）previous sale or other disposition of the goods in lawful enforcement of a lien or on a warehouse's lawful termination of storage;

（4）卖方已根据第2.705条的规定，或出租方已根据第2A.526条的规定，行使了阻止交付货物的权利；

（4）the exercise by a seller of its right to stop delivery pursuant to Section 2.705 or by a lessor of its right to stop delivery pursuant to Section 2A.526;

（5）已根据第7.303条，改变了货物的目的地或收货人，或对货物作了其他处置；

（5）a diversion, reconsignment, or other disposition pursuant to Section 7.303;

（6）货物保管人已被解除责任或已履行义务，或享有其他可对抗上述权利人的相应抗辩；或

（6）release, satisfaction, or any other fact affording a personal defense against the claimant; or

（7）货物保管人享有任何其他合法的免责理由。

（7）any other lawful excuse.

（b）对所有权凭证所覆盖之货物主张权利的人，必须偿付货物保管人的留置权，只要货物保管人提出此种要求，或法律规定货物保管人必须收取费用后才能交付货物。

（b）A person claiming goods covered by a document of title shall satisfy the bailee's lien if the bailee so requests or the bailee is prohibited by law from delivering the goods until the charges are paid.

（c）如果任何人对货物主张权利，则除涉及第7.503条（a）款所述的情况外，即所有权凭证并不赋予该人对货物的任何权利，否则：

（c）Unless a person claiming the goods is one against which the document of title does not confer a right under Section 7.503（a）:

（1）根据凭证主张货物权利的人，应交出覆盖货物并流通在外之流通所有权凭证的占

（1）the person claiming under a document shall surrender possession or control of any outstanding negotiable document covering the

有或控制，用于注销凭证，或注明已交付的那部分货物；并且

（2）货物保管人应注销凭证，或在凭证上醒目注明已交付的那部分货物；否则，其应对凭证正常流通后取得凭证的人承担责任。

goods for cancellation or indication of partial deliveries;and

（2）the bailee shall cancel the document or conspicuously indicate in the document the partial delivery or be liable to any person to which the document is duly negotiated.

第 7.404 条 根据所有权凭证善意交付货物后不承担责任

如果货物保管人以善意并根据所有权凭证条款或本篇规定收取货物，并已交付货物或以其他方式处置货物，货物保管人即不就该货物承担责任，即使存在下列情况：

（1）向货物保管人交付货物的人，不具有取得所有权凭证或处置货物的授权；或

（2）从货物保管人接受货物交付的人，不具有接受货物的授权。

§ 7.404. No Liability for Good Faith Delivery Pursuant to Document of Title.

A bailee that in good faith has received goods and delivered or otherwise disposed of the goods according to the terms of a document of title or pursuant to this Article is not liable for the goods even if:

（1）the person from which the bailee received the goods did not have authority to procure the document or to dispose of the goods;or

（2）the person to which the bailee delivered the goods did not have authority to receive the goods.

第5章 仓单和提单：流通和转让

PART 5. WAREHOUSE RECEIPTS AND BILLS OF LADING:NEGOTIATION AND TRANSFER

第 7.501 条 流通的方式；正常流通的条件

（a）下列原则适用于实体流通所有权凭证：

（1）如果凭证的原始条款

§ 7.501. Form of Negotiation and Require–ments of Due Negotiation.

（a）The following rules apply to a negotiable tangible document of title:

（1）If the document’s original terms run

是向特定人的指定人交付货物，则在该特定人作出背书并交付后，凭证即完成流通。如果该特定人作出空白背书，或背书给持票人，任何人均可仅凭交付使凭证流通。

to the order of a named person, the document is negotiated by the named person's indorsement and delivery. After the named person's indorsement in blank or to bearer, any person may negotiate the document by delivery alone.

（2）如果凭证的原始条款是向持票人交付货物，则凭证可仅凭交付而流通。

（2）If the document's original terms run to bearer, it is negotiated by delivery alone.

（3）如果凭证的原始条款是向特定人的指定人交付货物，则把凭证交付给该特定人，具有相当于该凭证被流通的效果。

（3）If the document's original terms run to the order of a named person and it is delivered to the named person, the effect is the same as if the document had been negotiated.

（4）将凭证背书给特定人后，需要该特定人作出背书并交付，凭证才能再度流通。

（4）Negotiation of the document after it has been indorsed to a named person requires indorsement by the named person as well as delivery.

（5）如果按照本款规定的方式，将凭证流通给任何以善意支付价值购买凭证的执票人，且该人购买时未得到凭证上存在任何人对凭证持有抗辩或权利主张的通知，该凭证的流通即为正常流通，除非能够证明，该流通不属于正常商业活动或融资活动，或涉及为清偿或支付金钱债务而接受凭证。

（5）A document is duly negotiated if it is negotiated in the manner stated in this subsection to a holder that purchases it in good faith, without notice of any defense against or claim to it on the part of any person, and for value, unless it is established that the negotiation is not in the regular course of business or financing or involves receiving the document in settlement or payment of a monetary obligation.

（b）下列原则适用于电子流通所有权凭证：

（b）The following rules apply to a negotiable electronic document of title:

（1）如果凭证的原始条款是向特定人的指定人交付货物，或是向持票人交付货物，则凭证只要被交付给另一人，即完

（1）If the document's original terms run to the order of a named person or to bearer, the document is negotiated by delivery of the document to another person. Indorsement by the

成流通。凭证的流通，无须该特定人作出背书。

named person is not required to negotiate the document.

（2）如果凭证的原始条款是向特定人的指定人交付货物，且该特定人对凭证拥有控制，则该控制的效果，相当于凭证已被流通。

（2）If the document's original terms run to the order of a named person and the named person has control of the document, the effect is the same as if the document had been negotiated.

（3）如果按照本款规定的方式，将凭证流通给任何以善意支付价值购买凭证的执票人，且该人购买时未得到凭证上存在任何人对凭证持有抗辩或权利主张的通知，该凭证的流通即为正常流通，除非能够证明，该流通不属于正常商业活动或融资活动，或涉及为清偿或支付金钱债务而接受凭证。

（3）A document is duly negotiated if it is negotiated in the manner stated in this subsection to a holder that purchases it in good faith, without notice of any defense against or claim to it on the part of any person, and for value, unless it is established that the negotiation is not in the regular course of business or financing or involves taking delivery of the document in settlement or payment of a monetary obligation.

（c）对不可流通所有权凭证作出背书，不能使凭证转变为流通凭证，也不能给受让人增加权利。

（c）Indorsement of a nonnegotiable document of title neither makes it negotiable nor adds to the transferee's rights.

（d）在流通提单上注明货物到达时的联系人，并不限制提单的流通性，也不构成对提单购买人的通知，即该联系人对货物拥有权益。

（d）The naming in a negotiable bill of lading of a person to be notified of the arrival of the goods does not limit the negotiability of the bill or constitute notice to a purchaser of the bill of any interest of that person in the goods.

第 7.502 条　正常流通赋予的权利

§ 7.502. Rights Acquired by Due Negotiation.

（a）除第 7.205 条和第 7.503 条另有规定外，通过正常流通取得流通所有权凭证的执票人，取得下列权利：

（a）Subject to Sections 7.205 and 7.503, a holder to which a negotiable document of title has been duly negotiated acquires thereby:

（1）对凭证的所有权；

（1）title to the document;

（2）对货物的所有权；

（3）代理法或禁止自相矛盾法所提供的全部权利，包括在涉及凭证出具后交付给货物保管人的货物时，对该货物的权利；以及

（4）要求开单人根据所有权凭证条款，履行持有或交付货物之直接责任的权利，且该权利不受开单人任何抗辩或权利主张的对抗，除非抗辩或权利主张系根据所有权凭证条款或本篇规定提出。涉及交货命令时，货物保管人只有在接受命令后才承担责任；执票人所取得的权利，是开单人和任何背书人有义务致使货物保管人接受该命令。

（b）除第7.503条另有规定外，即使所有权凭证所代表的货物被阻止交付，或即使货物保管人已交出货物，通过正常流通取得的所有权和其他权利，仍然保持有效；并且，即使存在下列情况，该所有权和其他权利亦不受削弱：

（1）该正常流通或任何先前的正常流通构成违反义务；

（2）任何人由于不实陈述、欺诈、事故、误解、胁迫、遗失、被盗或侵占，失去实体流通凭证的占有，或失去电子流通凭证的控制；或

（2）title to the goods;

（3）all rights accruing under the law of agency or estoppel, including rights to goods delivered to the bailee after the document was issued;and

（4）the direct obligation of the issuer to hold or deliver the goods according to the terms of the document free of any defense or claim by the issuer except those arising under the terms of the document or under this Article.In the case of a delivery order, the bailee's obligation accrues only upon the bailee's acceptance of the delivery order and the obligation acquired by the holder is that the issuer and any indorser will procure the acceptance of the bailee.

（b）Subject to Section 7.503, title and rights acquired by due negotiation are not defeated by any stoppage of the goods represented by the document of title or by surrender of the goods by the bailee and are not impaired even if:

（1）the due negotiation or any prior due negotiation constituted a breach of duty;

（2）any person has been deprived of possession of a negotiable tangible document or control of a negotiable electronic document by misrepresentation, fraud, accident, mistake, duress, loss, theft, or conversion;or

（3）货物或凭证在此之前已被出售给或转让给第三人。

（3）a previous sale or other transfer of the goods or document has been made to a third person.

第 7.503 条 某些情况下货物的所有权凭证失去效力

§ 7.503. Document of Title to Goods Defeated in Certain Cases.

（a）如果任何人在所有权凭证出具之前，对货物拥有合法权益或完善担保权益，则在对抗该人时，不能基于所有权凭证主张对货物的任何权利，只要：

（a）A document of title confers no right in goods against a person that before issuance of the document had a legal interest or a perfected security interest in the goods and that did not:

（1）该人未将货物或覆盖货物的凭证，交付给或委托给货物交管人或其指定人，使其具有发运、存储或出售货物的实际授权或表见授权，或具有根据第 7.403 条收取货物交付的权力，或具有根据第 2.403 条、第 2A.304 条（a）（2）款、第 2A.305 条（a）（2）款、第 9.320 条以及其他法律处置货物的权力；以及

（1）deliver or entrust the goods or any document covering the goods to the bailor or the bailor's nominee with actual or apparent authority to ship, store, or sell; with power to obtain delivery under Section 7.403;or with power of disposition under Section 2.403, 2A.304（a）（2）, 2A.305（a）（2）, or 9.320 or other statute or rule of law;or

（2）该人未对货物交管人或其指定人取得所有权凭证给予默认。

（2）acquiesce in the procurement by the bailor or its nominee of any document.

（b）如果交货命令尚未获得接受，则基于该命令对货物的所有权，受制于通过正常流通取得覆盖货物之流通仓单或流通提单的人的权利。基于该命令的所有权，如同开单人或其受让人的权利一样，有可能如第 7.504 条所述失去效力。

（b）Title to goods based upon an unaccepted delivery order is subject to the rights of any person to which a negotiable warehouse receipt or bill of lading covering the goods has been duly negotiated.That title may be defeated under Section 7.504 to the same extent as the rights of the issuer or a transferee from the issuer.

（c）如果提单被出具给货物递送人，则基于该提单取得的对货物的所有权，受制于任何人通过正常流通取得货物递送人自己出具之提单后拥有的权利。但是，承运人如果基于自己之提单，根据本篇第4章的规定交付了货物，即被解除交货的义务。

（c）Title to goods based upon a bill of lading issued to a freight forwarder is subject to the rights of any person to which a bill issued by the freight forwarder is duly negotiated. However, delivery by the carrier in accordance with Part 4 pursuant to its own bill of lading discharges the carrier's obligation to deliver.

第7.504条 非正常流通赋予的权利；改变货物目的地的效力；阻止交付货物

§ 7.504. Rights Acquired in Absence of Due Negotiation; Effect of Diversion; Stoppage of Delivery.

（a）所有权凭证（无论流通凭证或不可流通凭证）的受让人，如果只取得凭证的交付，但未取得凭证的正常流通，则只取得转让人拥有的或有实际授权转让的所有权和权利。

（a）A transferee of a document of title, whether negotiable or nonnegotiable, to which the document has been delivered but not duly negotiated, acquires the title and rights that its transferor had or had actual authority to convey.

（b）涉及不可流通所有权凭证时，在货物保管人收到转让通知之前（不包括之后），凭证受让人的权利在对抗下列人时，系属无效：

（b）In the case of a nonnegotiable document of title, until but not after the bailee receives notice of the transfer, the rights of the transferee may be defeated:

（1）转让人之任何债权人，只要该债权人有权根据第2.402条或第2A.308条视转让为无效；

（1）by those creditors of the transferor that could treat the transfer as void under Section 2.402 or 2A.308;

（2）转让人之正常业务中的买方，只要货物保管人已将货物交付给该买方，或已收到有关该买方之权利的通知；

（2）by a buyer from the transferor in ordinary course of business if the bailee has delivered the goods to the buyer or received notification of the buyer's rights;

（3）转让人之正常业务中的承租方，只要货物保管人已

（3）by a lessee from the transferor in ordinary course of business if the bailee has

将货物交付给该承租方，或已收到有关该承租方之权利的通知；或

delivered the goods to the lessee or received notification of the lessee's rights;or

（4）货物保管人，只要货物保管人与转让人的交易系以善意进行。

（4）as against the bailee, by good faith dealings of the bailee with the transferor.

（c）涉及不可流通提单时，如果发货人改变货物目的地，或改变其他运输条款，致使货物保管人未向收货人交付货物，且货物已被交付给正常业务中的买方或承租方，收货人即丧失对货物的所有权；无论如何，收货人均丧失对抗货物保管人的权利。

（c）A diversion or other change of shipping instructions by the consignor in a nonnegotiable bill of lading which causes the bailee not to deliver the goods to the consignee defeats the consignee's title to the goods if the goods have been delivered to a buyer in ordinary course of business or a lessee in ordinary course of business and in any event defeats the consignee's rights against the bailee.

（d）卖方可以根据第 2.705 条，或出租方可以根据第 2A.526 条，阻止不可流通所有权凭证项下的交货，但应遵守该条款有关适当通知的规定。货物保管人对于遵从卖方或出租方指示而受到的损失或产生的费用，有权要求卖方或出租方给予补偿。

（d）Delivery of the goods pursuant to a nonnegotiable document of title may be stopped by a seller under Section 2.705 or a lessor under Section 2A.526, subject to the requirements of due notification in those sections.A bailee honoring the seller's or lessor's instructions is entitled to be indemnified by the seller or lessor against any resulting loss or expense.

第 7.505 条　背书人不是其他当事方的保证人

§ 7.505. Indorser Not Guarantor for Other Parties.

涉及货物保管人出具的实体所有权凭证时，背书人不因在凭证上作出背书而对货物保管人或前手背书人的违约承担责任。

The indorsement of a tangible document of title issued by a bailee does not make the indorser liable for any default by the bailee or previous indorsers.

第 7.506 条　缺少背书的交付；要求补充背书的权利

涉及实体流通所有权凭证时，受让人有权要求转让人实际履行补充必要背书的义务。只有完成对背书的补充，转让才从该时起构成流通。

§ 7.506. Delivery Without Indorsement; Right to Compel Indorsement.

The transferee of a negotiable tangible document of title has a specifically enforceable right to have its transferor supply any necessary indorsement, but the transfer becomes a negotiation only as of the time the indorsement is supplied.

第 7.507 条　流通或交付所有权凭证时的担保

为取得价值而流通或交付所有权凭证的人（第 7.508 条所述的纯粹中间人除外），除另有协议外，仅向其直接购买人作出以下担保，作为出售或出租货物时所作之担保的补充：

（1）凭证系属真实；

（2）转让人不了解有损凭证效力或价值的事实；以及

（3）对于凭证的所有权，以及凭证所覆盖之货物的所有权，该流通或交付系属正当和充分有效。

§ 7.507. Warranties on Negotiation or Delivery of Document of Title.

If a person negotiates or delivers a document of title for value, otherwise than as a mere intermediary under Section 7.508, unless otherwise agreed, the transferor warrants to its immediate purchaser only in addition to any warranty made in selling or leasing the goods that:

（1）the document is genuine;

（2）the transferor does not have knowledge of any fact that would impair the document's validity or worth;and

（3）the negotiation or delivery is rightful and fully effective with respect to the title to the document and the goods it represents.

第 7.508 条　收款银行对所有权凭证的担保

如果已知收款银行或其他中间人系接受委托代表他人持有所有权凭证，或系接受委托通过交付该凭证，就汇票或其他权利主张进行收款，则该银行或中间人在交付所有权凭证

§ 7.508. Warranties of Collecting Bank as to Documents of Title.

A collecting bank or other intermediary known to be entrusted with documents of title on behalf of another or with collection of a draft or other claim against delivery of documents warrants by the delivery of the documents only its own good faith and authority even if

时，只担保其自身的善意和授权，即使该银行或中间人已购买了用于收款的权利主张或汇票，或已为其提供贷款。

the collecting bank or other intermediary has purchased or made advances against the claim or draft to be collected.

第 7.509 条　足以符合商业合同

所有权凭证是否足以履行买卖合同或租赁合同的义务，或是否足以满足信用证的条件，应根据第 2 篇、第 2A 篇或第 5 篇确定。

§ 7.509. Adequate Compliance With Commercial Contract.

Whether a document of title is adequate to fulfill the obligations of a contract for sale, a contract for lease, or the conditions of a letter of credit is determined by Article 2, 2A, or 5.

第6章　仓单和提单：其他规定

PART 6. WAREHOUSE RECEIPTS AND BILLS OF LADING: MISCELLANEOUS PROVISIONS

第 7.601 条　所有权凭证的遗失、被盗或损毁

（a）如果所有权凭证遗失、被盗或损毁，法院可以判决交付货物或出具替代凭证。货物保管人不因遵守法院判决对任何人承担责任。涉及流通所有权凭证时，只有在权利主张人交付保证金之后，法院才可判决交付货物或出具替代凭证，除非法院认定，因凭证之占有或控制未被交出而可能受到损失的人，已就该损失获得充分保护。涉及不可流通所有权凭证时，法院可以决定是否需要保证金。在根据本款提起的诉讼中，法院还有权判决支付货

§ 7.601. Lost, Stolen, or Destroyed Documents of Title.

（a）If a document of title is lost, stolen, or destroyed, a court may order delivery of the goods or issuance of a substitute document and the bailee may without liability to any person comply with the order.If the document was negotiable, a court may not order delivery of the goods or issuance of a substitute document without the claimant's posting security unless it finds that any person that may suffer loss as a result of nonsurrender of possession or control of the document is adequately protected against the loss.If the document was nonnegotiable, the court may require security.The court may also order payment of the bailee's reasonable costs and attorney's fees in any action under this

物保管人的合理费用和律师费。

（b）如果货物保管人在未得到法院判决的情况下，将货物交付给声称遗失流通所有权凭证的人，货物保管人应对因此受到损失的人承担责任。如果交货非以善意作出，货物保管人应承担侵占货物的责任。如果善意交付货物，且权利主张人向货物保管人交付了至少两倍于货物当时价值的保证金，用于补偿因该交付受到损失并在货物交付后一年内发出索赔通知的人，则该交付即不属于侵占货物。

subsection.

(b) A bailee that without court order delivers goods to a person claiming under a missing negotiable document of title is liable to any person injured thereby.If the delivery is not in good faith, the bailee is liable for conversion. Delivery in good faith is not conversion if the claimant posts security with the bailee in an amount at least double the value of the goods at the time of posting to indemnify any person injured by the delivery that files a notice of claim within one year after the delivery.

第 7.602 条　扣押流通所有权凭证覆盖的货物

除非所有权凭证最初基于货物的交付而出具，而交付货物的人本身不具有处置货物的权力，否则，只要覆盖货物的流通所有权凭证尚流通在外，即不能通过司法程序，使留置权附着于货物保管人占有的货物，除非首先向货物保管人交还凭证的占有或控制，或首先由法院禁止凭证流通。在向货物保管人或法院交还凭证的占有或控制之前，不得通过司法程序强迫货物保管人交付货物。购买人如果通过支付价值购买凭证，且购买时未得到上述司法程序或禁令的通知，即不受

§ 7.602. Attachment of Goods Covered by Negotiable Document of Title.

Unless a document of title was originally issued upon delivery of the goods by a person that did not have power to dispose of them, a lien does not attach by virtue of any judicial process to goods in the possession of a bailee for which a negotiable document of title is outstanding unless possession or control of the document is first surrendered to the bailee or the document's negotiation is enjoined. The bailee may not be compelled to deliver the goods pursuant to process until possession or control of the document is surrendered to the bailee or to the court.A purchaser of the document for value without notice of the process or injunction takes free of the lien imposed by judicial process.

制于该司法程序设立的留置权。

第 7.603 条　冲突的权利主张；相向诉讼

如果不止一人对货物主张所有权或占有权，货物保管人在有合理时间确定此种对抗主张的有效性或作出相向诉讼之前，没有义务交付货物。货物保管人要作出相向诉讼，可以就拒绝交付货物的诉讼提出抗辩，也可以主动提起诉讼。

§ 7.603. Conflicting Claims; Interpleader.

If more than one person claims title to or possession of the goods, the bailee is excused from delivery until the bailee has a reasonable time to ascertain the validity of the adverse claims or to commence an action for interpleader. The bailee may assert an interpleader either in defending an action for nondelivery of the goods or by original action.

词汇索引

超量出具	overissue	第 7.402 条
承储人	warehouse	第 7.102 条（a）（13）
承运人	carrier	第 7.102 条（a）（2）
发货人	consignor	第 7.102 条（a）（4）
发运人	shipper	第 7.102 条（a）（11）
货物	goods	第 7.102 条（a）（7）
货物保管人	bailee	第 7.102 条（a）（1）
交货命令	delivery order	第 7.102 条（a）（5）
开单人	issuer	第 7.102 条（a）（8）
签名	sign	第 7.102 条（a）（12）
收货人	consignee	第 7.102 条（a）（3）
所有权凭证的权利人	person entitled under the document	第 7.102 条（a）（9）
正常流通	due negotiation	第 7.501 条

第8篇　投资证券

ARTICLE 8. INVESTMENT SECURITIES

第1章　简称和一般事项

PART 1. SHORT TITLE AND GENERAL MATTERS

第 8.101 条　简称

本篇被引用时可称为《统一商法典——投资证券》。

第 8.102 条　定义

（a）在本篇中：

（1）“对立主张”指主张人声称对金融资产拥有财产权益，并声称另一人对该金融资产的持有、转让或支配，构成对主张人权利的侵犯。

（2）涉及票式证券时，“持票式”指证券的一种格式，即证券根据其条款，而不是基于背书，应向证券证书的持票人付款。

（3）“经纪人”指联邦证券法所定义的经纪人或经营人，但不排除以该身份从事业务的银行。

（4）“票式证券”指由证书代表的证券。

§ 8.101. Short Title.

This Article may be cited as Uniform Commercial Code—Investment Securities.

§ 8.102. Definitions.

（a）In this Article:

（1）“Adverse claim” means a claim that a claimant has a property interest in a financial asset and that it is a violation of the rights of the claimant for another person to hold, transfer, or deal with the financial asset.

（2）“Bearer form,” as applied to a certificated security, means a form in which the security is payable to the bearer of the security certificate according to its terms but not by reason of an indorsement.

（3）“Broker” means a person defined as a broker or dealer under the federal securities laws, but without excluding a bank acting in that capacity.

（4）“Certificated security” means a security that is represented by a certificate.

（5）“清算公司”指：

（A）根据联邦证券法注册为“清算机构”的人；

（B）任何联邦储备银行；或

（C）就金融资产提供清算或结算业务的任何其他人，只要其根据联邦证券法本应注册为清算机构，但符合免予注册的条件；并且，其作为清算公司的活动，包括发布规则，受联邦政府或州政府的管辖。

（6）“传送”指：

（A）发送已签署的书面材料；或

（B）发送信息，只要发送方式符合发送人和接收人之间的协议。

（7）“权利持有人”指在证券中间人的记录中，被注明持有可对抗该证券中间人之证券权利的人。如果任何人根据第8.501条（b）（2）款或（3）款取得证券权利，则该人即为权利持有人。

（8）涉及对金融资产拥有证券权利的权利持有人时，“权利命令”指该权利持有人向证券中间人传送的通知，指示该中间人转让或赎兑该金融资产。

（9）除第8.103条另有规

（5）“Clearing corporation” means:

（A）a person that is registered as a “clearing agency” under the federal securities laws;

（B）a federal reserve bank;or

（C）any other person that provides clearance or settlement services with respect to financial assets that would require it to register as a clearing agency under the federal securities laws but for an exclusion or exemption from the registration requirement, if its activities as a clearing corporation, including promulgation of rules, are subject to regulation by a federal or state governmental authority.

（6）“Communicate” means to:

（A）send a signed writing;or

（B）transmit information by any mechanism agreed on by the persons transmitting and receiving the information.

（7）“Entitlement holder” means a person identified in the records of a securities intermediary as the person having a security entitlement against the securities intermediary. If a person acquires a security entitlement by virtue of Section 8.501（b）（2）or（3）, that person is the entitlement holder.

（8）“Entitlement order” means a notification communicated to a securities intermediary directing transfer or redemption of a financial asset to which the entitlement holder has a security entitlement.

（9）“Financial asset,” except as otherwise

定外，“金融资产”指：

（A）证券；

（B）任何人的债务，或对任何人或任何人之财产或企业持有的份额、参股或其他权益，只要该债务或权益实际在或其类型可以在金融市场上进行交易或买卖，或只要其在发行或交易区域属于投资媒介；或

（C）证券中间人在证券账户中为另一人持有的任何财产，只要该证券中间人与该另一人明确约定，该财产应被视为本篇项下的金融资产。

（D）根据上下文，“金融资产”可以指一项权益本身，也可以指证明任何人对该权益之主张权的工具，包括票式证券、无票证券、证券证书、或证券权利。

（10）[保留]

（11）“背书”指在登记式证券证书上或在独立文件上作出的仅有名字的签名，或伴有其他文字的签名，用于转让或赎兑该证券，或提供转让或赎兑该证券的权力。

（12）“指示”指发送给无票证券之发行人的通知，命令其就证券转让作出登记，或命令其赎兑证券。

provided in Section 8.103, means:

（A） a security;

（B） an obligation of a person or a share, participation, or other interest in a person or in property or an enterprise of a person that is, or is of a type, dealt in or traded on financial markets or that is recognized in any area in which it is issued or dealt in as a medium for investment;or

（C） any property that is held by a securities intermediary for another person in a securities account if the securities intermediary has expressly agreed with the other person that the property is to be treated as a financial asset under this Article.

（D） As context requires, the term means either the interest itself or the means by which a person's claim to it is evidenced, including a certificated or uncertificated security, a security certificate, or a security entitlement.

（10） [Reserved]

（11） “Indorsement” means a signature that alone or accompanied by other words is made on a security certificate in registered form or on a separate document for the purpose of assigning, transferring, or redeeming the security or granting a power to assign, transfer, or redeem it.

（12） “Instruction” means a notification communicated to the issuer of an uncertificated security that directs that the transfer of the security be registered or that the security be redeemed.

（13）涉及票式证券时，“登记式”指下列证券格式：

（A）证券证书上注明了证券的权利人；并且

（B）可以将证券的转让登记在发行人设立或代表发行人设立的证券转让账册上，或证券证书规定可以进行此种登记。

（13）“Registered form,” as applied to a certificated security, means a form in which:

（A）the security certificate specifies a person entitled to the security;and

（B）a transfer of the security may be registered on books maintained for that purpose by or on behalf of the issuer, or the security certificate so states.

（14）“证券中间人”指：

（A）清算公司；或

（B）在正常业务中为他人掌管证券账户并以该身份作为的人，包括银行或经纪人。

（14）“Securities intermediary” means:

（A）a clearing corporation;or

（B）a person, including a bank or broker, that in the ordinary course of its business maintains securities accounts for others and is acting in that capacity.

（15）除第 8.103 条另有规定外，“证券”指发行人的债务，或对发行人或发行人之财产或企业持有的份额、参股或其他权益；并且：

（A）由持票式或登记式的证券证书所代表，或其转让可以登记在发行人设立或代表发行人设立的证券转让账册上；

（B）属于一个类别或一个系列之一，或根据其条款可被分割成一个类别或一个系列的份额、参股、权益或债务；并且

（C）还：

（i）实际在或其类型可以

（15）“Security,” except as otherwise provided in Section 8.103, means an obligation of an issuer or a share, participation, or other interest in an issuer or in property or an enterprise of an issuer:

（A）that is represented by a security certificate in bearer or registered form, or the transfer of which may be registered on books maintained for that purpose by or on behalf of the issuer;

（B）that is one of a class or series or by its terms is divisible into a class or series of shares, participations, interests, or obligations;and

（C）that:

（i）is, or is of a type, dealt in or traded on

在证券交易所或证券市场进行交易或买卖；或

securities exchanges or securities markets; or

（ii）属于投资媒介，且其条款明确规定系本篇管辖的证券。

（ii）is a medium for investment and by its terms expressly provides that it is a security governed by this Article.

（16）“证券证书”指代表证券的证书。

（16）“Security certificate” means a certificate representing a security.

（17）“证券权利”指本篇第 5 章所述的权利持有人对金融资产享有的权利和财产权益。

（17）“Security entitlement” means the rights and property interest of an entitlement holder with respect to a financial asset specified in Part 5.

（18）“无票证券”指非由证书代表的证券。

（18）“Uncertificated security” means a security that is not represented by a certificate.

（b）适用于本篇的其他定义及其所在位置：

（b）Other definitions applying to this Article and the sections in which they appear are:

“适格人”　第 8.107 条

“控制”　第 8.106 条

“交付”　第 8.301 条

“投资公司证券”　第 8.103 条

“发行人”　第 8.201 条

“超量发行”　第 8.210 条

“受保护购买人”　第 8.303 条

“证券账户”　第 8.501 条

Appropriate person Section 8.107

Control Section 8.106

Delivery Section 8.301

Investment company security Section 8.103

Issuer Section 8.201

Overissue Section 8.210

Protected purchaser Section 8.303

Securities account Section 8.501

（c）此外，第 1 篇中的通用定义和解释原则适用于本篇通篇。

（c）In addition, Article 1 contains general definitions and principles of construction and interpretation applicable throughout this Article.

（d）为本篇目的而对任何人、任何业务或任何交易之性质所作的规定，不能决定该人、该业务或该交易在其他法律或

（d）The characterization of a person, business, or transaction for purposes of this Article does not determine the characterization of the person, business, or transaction for

规则下的性质。

第 8.103 条 某些债务和权益属于证券还是金融资产的认定原则

（a）公司、商业信托、股份公司或类似实体所发行的份额或类似的股本权益属于证券。

（b）投资公司证券属于证券。“投资公司证券”指根据联邦投资公司法注册为投资公司的任何实体所发行的份额或类似的股本权益；或指按前述方式注册的按份投资信托中的权益；或指按前述方式注册的面额证券公司发行的面额证券。“投资公司证券”不包括保险公司出具的保险单、定期人寿保险单或年金合同。

（c）合伙或有限责任公司中的权益不属于证券，除非该权益在证券交易所或证券市场上进行交易或买卖，或该权益的条款明确规定其为受本篇管辖的证券，或该权益为投资公司证券。但是，如果合伙或有限责任公司中的权益存在于证券账户中，该权益即属于金融资产。

（d）构成证券证书的书面文件，即使同时满足第 3 篇的规定，亦由本篇管辖，而不由第 3 篇管辖。但是，如果第 3

purposes of any other law, regulation, or rule.

§ 8.103. Rules for Determining Whether Certain Obligations and Interests Are Securities or Financial Assets.

（a）A share or similar equity interest issued by a corporation, business trust, joint stock company, or similar entity is a security.

（b）An investment company security is a security. “Investment company security” means a share or similar equity interest issued by an entity that is registered as an investment company under the federal investment company laws, an interest in a unit investment trust that is so registered, or a face-amount certificate issued by a face-amount certificate company that is so registered. “Investment company security” does not include an insurance policy or endowment policy or annuity contract issued by an insurance company.

（c）An interest in a partnership or limited liability company is not a security unless it is dealt in or traded on securities exchanges or in securities markets, its terms expressly provide that it is a security governed by this Article, or it is an investment company security.However, an interest in a partnership or limited liability company is a financial asset if it is held in a securities account.

（d）A writing that is a security certificate is governed by this Article and not by Article 3, even though it also meets the requirements of that Article.However, a negotiable instrument

篇项下的流通票据存在于证券账户中，即属于金融资产。

governed by Article 3 is a financial asset if it is held in a securities account.

（e）清算公司向其会员发行的选购权或类似债务，不属于证券，但属于金融资产。

（e）An option or similar obligation issued by a clearing corporation to its participants is not a security, but is a financial asset.

（f）第 9.102 条（a）（15）款所定义的商品合同，不属于证券或金融资产。

（f）A commodity contract, as defined in Section 9.102（a）（15）, is not a security or a financial asset.

（g）第 1.201 条（b）（16）款所定义的所有权凭证，不属于金融资产，除非第 8.102 条（a）（9）（C）款适用于该凭证。

（g）A document of title, as defined in Section 1.201（b）（16）, is not a financial asset unless Section 8.102（a）（9）（C）applies.

第 8.104 条　证券、金融资产或其中权益的取得

§ 8.104. Acquisition of Security or Financial Asset or Interest Therein.

（a）在下列情况下，一个人取得本篇项下的证券或其中的权益：

（a）A person acquires a security or an interest therein under this Article if:

（1）该人系根据第 8.301 条取得证券交付的购买人；或

（1）the person is a purchaser to whom a security is delivered pursuant to Section 8.301;or

（2）该人根据第 8.501 条取得对证券的证券权利。

（2）the person acquires a security entitlement to the security pursuant to Section 8.501.

（b）任何人取得对金融资产的证券权利后，即取得本篇项下的金融资产（证券除外）或其中的权益。

（b）A person acquires a financial asset, other than a security, or an interest therein, under this Article, if the person acquires a security entitlement to the financial asset.

（c）任何人取得对证券或对其他金融资产的证券权利后，即享有本篇第 5 章规定的权利；但是，该人仅在第 8.503 条规定的范围内，成为证券中间人持有之证券、证券权利或其他

（c）A person who acquires a security entitlement to a security or other financial asset has the rights specified in Part 5, but is a purchaser of any security, security entitlement, or other financial asset held by the securities intermediary only to the extent provided in

金融资产的购买人。

（d）如果任何人被其他法律、规则或协议要求，向另一人转让、交付、提示、交出或交换证券或金融资产，或以其他方式使该另一人占有该证券或金融资产，则除情况显示存在其他要求外，只要前者使该另一人根据（a）款或（b）款取得该证券或金融资产中的权益，前者即满足了上述法律、规则或协议的要求。

Section 8.503.

（d）Unless the context shows that a different meaning is intended, a person who is required by other law, regulation, rule, or agreement to transfer, deliver, present, surrender, exchange, or otherwise put in the possession of another person a security or financial asset satisfies that requirement by causing the other person to acquire an interest in the security or financial asset pursuant to Subsection（a）or（b）.

第 8.105 条 对立主张的通知

§ 8.105. Notice of Adverse Claim.

（a）在下列情况下，一个人被视为得到对立主张的通知：

（1）该人知道该对立主张；

（2）该人所了解的事实足以表明，极有可能存在对立主张，但该人故意回避可以证明存在对立主张的信息；或

（3）根据法律，该人有义务调查是否存在对立主张，且所要求的调查能够证明对立主张的存在。

（a）A person has notice of an adverse claim if:

（1）the person knows of the adverse claim;

（2）the person is aware of facts sufficient to indicate that there is a significant probability that the adverse claim exists and deliberately avoids information that would establish the existence of the adverse claim;or

（3）the person has a duty, imposed by statute or regulation, to investigate whether an adverse claim exists, and the investigation so required would establish the existence of the adverse claim.

（b）知道代表人转让或已经转让金融资产或其中的权益，不意味着有义务询问交易的正当性，也不构成对立主张的通知。但是，如果一个人知道，

（b）Having knowledge that a financial asset or interest therein is or has been transferred by a representative imposes no duty of inquiry into the rightfulness of a transaction and is not notice of an adverse claim.However,

代表人在任何交易中转让了金融资产或其中的权益，且该交易或其收益的使用，系为代表人的个人利益，或以其他方式构成了违反义务，该人即被视为得到对立主张的通知。

a person who knows that a representative has transferred a financial asset or interest therein in a transaction that is, or whose proceeds are being used, for the individual benefit of the representative or otherwise in breach of duty has notice of an adverse claim.

（c）任何行为或事件，如果赋予一项权利，可以要求证券证书所代表的主债务即时履行，或如果设定一个日期，规定应在该日或之后提示或交还证书，用于赎兑或交换，此时，该行为或事件本身并不构成对立主张的通知，除非涉及以下转让：

（c）An act or event that creates a right to immediate performance of the principal obligation represented by a security certificate or sets a date on or after which the certificate is to be presented or surrendered for redemption or exchange does not itself constitute notice of an adverse claim except in the case of a transfer more than:

（1）涉及为赎兑或交换所设定的提示或交还日期时，超过该日期一年以上的转让；或

（1）one year after a date set for presentment or surrender for redemption or exchange;or

（2）涉及为取得付款所设定的提示或交还证书的日期时，超过该日期六个月以上的转让，但前提是在该日期存在可供支付的款项。

（2）six months after a date set for payment of money against presentation or surrender of the certificate, if money was available for payment on that date.

（d）在证券证书存在下列情况下，票式证券的购买人被视为得到对立主张的通知：

（d）A purchaser of a certificated security has notice of an adverse claim if the security certificate:

（1）无论证书是持票式还是登记式，该证书之背书已注明"用于收款"或"用于交还"，或注明用于转让以外的其他目的；或

（1）whether in bearer or registered form, has been indorsed "for collection" or "for surrender" or for some other purpose not involving transfer;or

（2）证书为持票式，且明确注明系转让人以外之其他人

（2）is in bearer form and has on it an unambiguous statement that it is the property of

的财产；但是，如果证书上只有一个名字，该事实并不构成上述注明。

a person other than the transferor, but the mere writing of a name on the certificate is not such a statement.

（e）如果根据第9篇登记融资声明，该登记不构成金融资产存在对立主张的通知。

（e）Filing of a financing statement under Article 9 is not notice of an adverse claim to a financial asset.

第8.106条　控制

§ 8.106. Control.

（a）将持票式的票式证券交付给购买人后，购买人即取得对证券的控制。

（a）A purchaser has control of a certificated security in bearer form if the certificated security is delivered to the purchaser.

（b）将登记式的票式证券交付给购买人后，在下列情况下，购买人取得对证券的控制：

（b）A purchaser has control of a certificated security in registered form if the certificated security is delivered to the purchaser and:

（1）证书被有效背书给购买人，或被作出有效空白背书；或

（1）the certificate is indorsed to the purchaser or in blank by an effective indorsement;or

（2）通过原始发行登记或发行人的转让登记，证书被登记在购买人名字之下。

（2）the certificate is registered in the name of the purchaser, on original issue or registration of transfer by the issuer.

（c）在下列情况下，购买人被视为取得对无票证券的控制：

（c）A purchaser has control of an uncertificated security if:

（1）无票证券被交付给购买人；或

（1）the uncertificated security is delivered to the purchaser;or

（2）发行人同意遵从购买人发起的指示，而无须再经注册所有权人的同意。

（2）the issuer has agreed that it will comply with instructions originated by the purchaser without further consent by the registered owner.

（d）在下列情况下，购买人被视为取得对证券权利的控制：

（d）A purchaser has control of a security entitlement if:

（1）购买人成为权利持有人；

（1）the purchaser becomes the entitlement holder;

（2）证券中间人同意遵从购买人发起的权利命令，而无须再经权利持有人的同意；或

（2）the securities intermediary has agreed that it will comply with entitlement orders originated by the purchaser without further consent by the entitlement holder;or

（3）另一人代表购买人控制证券权利；或在取得对证券权利的控制后，承认代表购买人持有控制。

（3）another person has control of the security entitlement on behalf of the purchaser or, having previously acquired control of the security entitlement, acknowledges that it has control on behalf of the purchaser.

（e）如果权利持有人将证券权利中的权益赋予自己的证券中间人，证券中间人即被视为取得控制。

（e）If an interest in a security entitlement is granted by the entitlement holder to the entitlement holder's own securities intermediary, the securities intermediary has control.

（f）购买人只要满足（c）款或（d）款的要求，即取得控制，即使（c）款中的注册所有权人或（d）款中的权利持有人保留了权利，有权对无票证券或证券权利作出替换，或有权向发行人或证券中间人发起指示或权利命令，或有权以其他方式处置无票证券或证券权利。

（f）A purchaser who has satisfied the requirements of Subsection（c）or（d）has control, even if the registered owner in the case of Subsection（c）or the entitlement holder in the case of Subsection（d）retains the right to make substitutions for the uncertificated security or security entitlement, to originate instructions or entitlement orders to the issuer or securities intermediary, or otherwise to deal with the uncertificated security or security entitlement.

（g）发行人或证券中间人在未得到注册所有权人或权利持有人同意的情况下，不得签订（c）（2）款或（d）（2）款所述的协议；但即使注册所有权人或权利持有人发出签订该

（g）An issuer or a securities intermediary may not enter into an agreement of the kind described in Subsection（c）（2）or（d）（2）without the consent of the registered owner or entitlement holder, but an issuer or a securities intermediary is not required to enter into such

协议的指示，发行人或证券中间人亦非必须签订该协议。发行人或证券中间人签订该协议后，无须向其他当事方确认该协议的存在，除非注册所有权人或权利持有人要求作出确认。

an agreement even though the registered owner or entitlement holder so directs.An issuer or securities intermediary that has entered into such an agreement is not required to confirm the existence of the agreement to another party unless requested to do so by the registered owner or entitlement holder.

第 8.107 条　背书、指示或权利命令的生效条件

§ 8.107. Whether Indorsement, Instruction, or Entitlement Order Is Effective.

（a）“适格人”指下列人：

（1）涉及一项背书时，指证券证书注明的或有效记名背书注明的将对证券享有权利的人；

（2）涉及一项指示时，指无票证券的注册所有权人；

（3）涉及一项权利命令时，指权利持有人；

（4）当（1）款、（2）款或（3）款规定的人已去世时，指其他法律规定的该人的继承人，或指代表该人处置遗产的私人代表人；或

（5）当（1）款、（2）款或（3）款规定的人不具有行为能力时，指该人的监护人、保护人，或根据其他法律有权力转让该人之证券或金融资产的人。

（b）背书、指示或权利命令在下列情况下系属有效：

（1）由适格人作出；

（a）“Appropriate person” means:

（1）with respect to an indorsement, the person specified by a security certificate or by an effective special indorsement to be entitled to the security;

（2）with respect to an instruction, the registered owner of an uncertificated security;

（3）with respect to an entitlement order, the entitlement holder;

（4）if the person designated in Subdivision（1）,（2）, or（3）is deceased, the designated person's successor taking under other law or the designated person's personal representative acting for the estate of the decedent;or

（5）if the person designated in Subdivision（1）,（2）, or（3）lacks capacity, the designated person's guardian, conservator, or other similar representative who has power under other law to transfer the security or financial asset.

（b）An indorsement, instruction, or entitlement order is effective if:

（1）it is made by the appropriate person;

（2）由适格人的代表人作出，只要根据代理法，该代表人有权力代表适格人转让证券或金融资产；或在涉及指示或权利命令时，只要根据第 8.106 条（c）（2）款或（d）（2）款，作出该指示或命令的人拥有控制；或

（2）it is made by a person who has power under the law of agency to transfer the security or financial asset on behalf of the appropriate person, including, in the case of an instruction or entitlement order, a person who has control under Section 8.106（c）（2）or（d）（2）; or

（3）得到适格人的批准，或适格人无权主张其无效。

（3）the appropriate person has ratified it or is otherwise precluded from asserting its ineffectiveness.

（c）即使存在下列情况，代表人作出的背书、指示或权利命令亦属有效：

（c）An indorsement, instruction, or entitlement order made by a representative is effective even if:

（1）代表人未遵从本应遵从的指示，或未遵守管辖代表人关系的州法，包括要求代表人对该交易事先取得法院批准的法律；或

（1）the representative has failed to comply with a controlling instrument or with the law of the state having jurisdiction of the representative relationship, including any law requiring the representative to obtain court approval of the transaction;or

（2）代表人作出背书、指示或权利命令的行为，或使用该交易之收益的行为，在其他方面违反了代表人的义务。

（2）the representative's action in making the indorsement, instruction, or entitlement order or using the proceeds of the transaction is otherwise a breach of duty.

（d）当任何人被说明具有代表人身份时，如果证券被登记在该代表人名字之下，或被记名背书给该代表人，或如果证券账户被掌管在该代表人名字之下，则即使该人在作出背书、指示或权利命令时，已不再具有所说明的身份，其所作的背书、指示或权利命令亦属

（d）If a security is registered in the name of or specially indorsed to a person described as a representative, or if a securities account is maintained in the name of a person described as a representative, an indorsement, instruction, or entitlement order made by the person is effective even though the person is no longer serving in the described capacity.

有效。

（e）背书、指示或权利命令的有效性，应以其作出的日期为准。背书、指示或权利命令，不因情况随后发生变化而失去效力。

（e）Effectiveness of an indorsement, instruction, or entitlement order is determined as of the date the indorsement, instruction, or entitlement order is made, and an indorsement, instruction, or entitlement order does not become ineffective by reason of any later change of circumstances.

第 8.108 条　直接持有时的担保

§ 8.108. Warranties in Direct Holding.

（a）任何人如果向支付了价值的购买人转让票式证券，即向购买人作出下列担保；或如果通过背书作出转让，背书人即向任何后手购买人作出下列担保：

（a）A person who transfers a certificated security to a purchaser for value warrants to the purchaser, and an indorser, if the transfer is by indorsement, warrants to any subsequent purchaser, that:

（1）证书系属真实，且不存在重大涂改；

（1）the certificate is genuine and has not been materially altered;

（2）转让人或背书人不知道可能有损证券有效性的事实；

（2）the transferor or indorser does not know of any fact that might impair the validity of the security;

（3）证券不存在对立主张；

（3）there is no adverse claim to the security;

（4）转让不违反任何转让限制；

（4）the transfer does not violate any restriction on transfer;

（5）当通过背书作出转让时，背书系由适格人作出，或如果背书系由代理人作出，该代理人具有代表适格人的实际授权；并且

（5）if the transfer is by indorsement, the indorsement is made by an appropriate person, or if the indorsement is by an agent, the agent has actual authority to act on behalf of the appropriate person;and

（6）转让在所有其他方面均属有效和正当。

（6）the transfer is otherwise effective and rightful.

（b）如果无票证券被转让

（b）A person who originates an instruction

给支付了价值的购买人，且任何人发起指示，要求对该转让作出登记，则该发起人即向该购买人担保：

for registration of transfer of an uncertificated security to a purchaser for value warrants to the purchaser that:

（1）指示系由适格人作出，或如果指示系由代理人作出，该代理人具有代表适格人的实际授权；

（1）the instruction is made by an appropriate person, or if the instruction is by an agent, the agent has actual authority to act on behalf of the appropriate person;

（2）证券系属有效；

（2）the security is valid;

（3）证券不存在对立主张；并且

（3）there is no adverse claim to the security; and

（4）在指示被提示给发行人时：

（4）at the time the instruction is presented to the issuer:

（A）购买人有权登记该转让；

（A）the purchaser will be entitled to the registration of transfer;

（B）发行人将对该转让作出登记，且除指示中已说明的权利主张外，购买人的登记不受制于任何留置权、担保权益、限制或索赔；

（B）the transfer will be registered by the issuer free from all liens, security interests, restrictions, and claims other than those specified in the instruction;

（C）转让不违反任何转让限制；并且

（C）the transfer will not violate any restriction on transfer;and

（D）所指示的转让在所有其他方面均属有效和正当。

（D）the requested transfer will otherwise be effective and rightful.

（c）任何人如果向支付了价值的购买人转让无票证券，但未就该转让发起指示，即担保：

（c）A person who transfers an uncertificated security to a purchaser for value and does not originate an instruction in connection with the transfer warrants that:

（1）无票证券系属有效；

（1）the uncertificated security is valid;

（2）证券不存在对立主张；

（2）there is no adverse claim to the security;

（3）转让不违反任何转让限制；并且

（3）the transfer does not violate any restriction on transfer;and

（4）转让在所有其他方面均属有效和正当。

（d）在证券证书上作出背书的人向发行人担保：

（1）证券不存在对立主张；并且

（2）背书系属有效。

（e）任何人如果发起指示，要求对无票证券的转让作出登记，即向发行人担保：

（1）指示系属有效；并且

（2）该指示被提示给发行人时，购买人将是有权登记该转让的人。

（f）任何人如果为登记转让或为取得付款或交换而提示票式证券，即向发行人担保，其有权取得登记、付款或交换；但是，支付了价值且未得到对立主张通知的购买人，在取得转让登记后，仅担保其不知道在必要背书中存在无授权签名。

（g）如果任何人作为另一人的代理人向购买人交付票式证券，且收到证书交付的人知道被代理人的真实身份，且代理人交付的证书系从被代理人收到，或从被代理人指定的另一人收到，此时，交付证券证书的人仅担保，其拥有代表被代理人作为的授权，且不知道该票式证券存在对立主张。

（4）the transfer is otherwise effective and rightful.

（d）A person who indorses a security certificate warrants to the issuer that:

（1）there is no adverse claim to the security;and

（2）the indorsement is effective.

（e）A person who originates an instruction for registration of transfer of an uncertificated security warrants to the issuer that:

（1）the instruction is effective;and

（2）at the time the instruction is presented to the issuer the purchaser will be entitled to the registration of transfer.

（f）A person who presents a certificated security for registration of transfer or for payment or exchange warrants to the issuer that the person is entitled to the registration, payment, or exchange, but a purchaser for value and without notice of adverse claims to whom transfer is registered warrants only that the person has no knowledge of any unauthorized signature in a necessary indorsement.

（g）If a person acts as agent of another in delivering a certificated security to a purchaser, the identity of the principal was known to the person to whom the certificate was delivered, and the certificate delivered by the agent was received by the agent from the principal or received by the agent from another person at the direction of the principal, the person delivering the security certificate warrants only that the delivering person has authority to act for the principal and does not know of any adverse claim to the certificated security.

（h）受担保方如果在收到证券证书后再次作出交付，或如果在付款之后根据债务人的命令，将证券证书交付给另一人，即仅承担（g）款项下代理人所作的担保。

（h）A secured party who redelivers a security certificate received, or after payment and on order of the debtor delivers the security certificate to another person, makes only the warranties of an agent under Subsection（g）.

（i）除（g）款另有规定外，代表客户作为的经纪人，向发行人和购买人承担（a）款至（f）款的担保。经纪人如果向客户交付证券证书，或将客户登记为无票证券的所有权人，即向客户承担（a）款或（b）款项下的担保，并享有本条项下购买人的权利和待遇。对于以代理人身份作为的经纪人，其所作的担保，是客户所作相关担保之补充担保；其所享的担保，是客户所享相关担保之补充担保。

（i）Except as otherwise provided in Subsection（g）, a broker acting for a customer makes to the issuer and a purchaser the warranties provided in Subsections（a）-（f）. A broker that delivers a security certificate to its customer, or causes its customer to be registered as the owner of an uncertificated security, makes to the customer the warranties provided in Subsection（a）or（b）, and has the rights and privileges of a purchaser under this section.The warranties of and in favor of the broker acting as an agent are in addition to applicable warranties given by and in favor of the customer.

第8.109条 间接持有时的担保

§ 8.109. Warranties in Indirect Holding.

（a）任何人如果向证券中间人发起权利命令，即向该证券中间人担保：

（a）A person who originates an entitlement order to a securities intermediary warrants to the securities intermediary that:

（1）权利命令系由适格人作出；或如果权利命令系由代理人作出，则该代理人具有代表适格人作为的实际授权；并且

（1）the entitlement order is made by an appropriate person, or if the entitlement order is by an agent, the agent has actual authority to act on behalf of the appropriate person;and

（2）证券权利不存在对立

（2）there is no adverse claim to the

主张。

（b）任何人如果向证券中间人交付证券证书，用于贷记证券账户，或如果就无票证券发起指示，要求将无票证券贷记至证券账户，即向证券中间人承担第 8.108 条（a）款或（b）款规定的担保。

（c）证券中间人如果向权利持有人交付证券证书，或将权利持有人登记为无票证券的所有权人，即向权利持有人承担第 8.108 条（a）款或（b）款规定的担保。

第 8.110 条　适用范围；法律选择

（a）下列事项由（d）款所述的发行人所在州的法律管辖：

（1）证券的合法性；

（2）发行人就转让作出登记的权利和义务；

（3）发行人就转让所作登记的有效性；

（4）当任何人对证券提出对立主张时，发行人是否对该人承担任何义务；以及

（5）在任何人取得票式证券或无票证券的转让登记后，或取得无票证券的控制后，是否可向该人提出对立主张。

security entitlement.

(b) A person who delivers a security certificate to a securities intermediary for credit to a securities account or originates an instruction with respect to an uncertificated security directing that the uncertificated security be credited to a securities account makes to the securities intermediary the warranties specified in Section 8.108(a) or (b).

(c) If a securities intermediary delivers a security certificate to its entitlement holder or causes its entitlement holder to be registered as the owner of an uncertificated security, the securities intermediary makes to the entitlement holder the warranties specified in Section 8.108 (a) or (b).

§ 8.110. Applicability; Choice of Law.

(a) The local law of the issuer's jurisdiction, as specified in Subsection (d), governs:

(1) the validity of a security;

(2) the rights and duties of the issuer with respect to registration of transfer;

(3) the effectiveness of registration of transfer by the issuer;

(4) whether the issuer owes any duties to an adverse claimant to a security;and

(5) whether an adverse claim can be asserted against a person to whom transfer of a certificated or uncertificated security is registered or a person who obtains control of an uncertificated security.

（b）下列事项由（e）款所述的证券中间人所在州的法律管辖：

（1）有关从证券中间人取得证券权利的问题；

（2）证券中间人和权利持有人基于证券权利产生的权利和义务；

（3）当任何人对证券权利提出对立主张时，证券中间人是否对该人承担任何义务；以及

（4）在任何人从证券中间人取得证券权利后，或从权利持有人购买证券权利或其权益后，是否可向该人提出对立主张。

（b）The local law of the securities intermediary's jurisdiction, as specified in Subsection（e）, governs:

（1）acquisition of a security entitlement from the securities intermediary;

（2）the rights and duties of the securities intermediary and entitlement holder arising out of a security entitlement;

（3）whether the securities intermediary owes any duties to an adverse claimant to a security entitlement;and

（4）whether an adverse claim can be asserted against a person who acquires a security entitlement from the securities intermediary or a person who purchases a security entitlement or interest therein from an entitlement holder.

（c）是否可向取得证券证书交付的人提出对立主张，应由交付证书时证书所在州的法律管辖。

（c）The local law of the jurisdiction in which a security certificate is located at the time of delivery governs whether an adverse claim can be asserted against a person to whom the security certificate is delivered.

（d）"发行人所在州"指证券发行人注册成立的州，或如果该州法律允许，指发行人指定的另一州。根据本州法律注册成立的发行人，可以指定另一州的法律，作为管辖（a）（2）款至（5）款事项的法律。

（d）"Issuer's jurisdiction" means the jurisdiction under which the issuer of the security is organized or, if permitted by the law of that jurisdiction, the law of another jurisdiction specified by the issuer.An issuer organized under the law of this state may specify the law of another jurisdiction as the law governing the matters specified in Subsections（a）（2）-（5）.

（e）为本条目的，证券中间人所在州应根据下列原则

（e）The following rules determinc a securities intermediary's jurisdiction for

确定：

（1）如果证券中间人和权利持有人有关证券账户的协议明确规定，为本章、本篇或本法目的，应以某州为证券中间人所在州，则该州即为其所在州。

purposes of this section:

（1）If an agreement between the securities intermediary and its entitlement holder governing the securities account expressly provides that a particular jurisdiction is the securities intermediary's jurisdiction for purposes of this Part, this Article, or this Act, that jurisdiction is the securities intermediary's jurisdiction.

（2）如果（1）款不适用，且证券中间人和权利持有人有关证券账户的协议明确规定，该协议受某州的法律管辖，则该州即为证券中间人所在州。

（2）If Subdivision（1）does not apply and an agreement between the securities intermediary and its entitlement holder governing the securities account expressly provides that the agreement is governed by the law of a particular jurisdiction, that jurisdiction is the securities intermediary's jurisdiction.

（3）如果（1）款和（2）款均不适用，且证券中间人和权利持有人有关证券账户的协议明确规定，证券账户被掌管在位于某州的办公室，则该州即为证券中间人所在州。

（3）If neither Subdivision（1）nor Subdivision（2）applies and an agreement between the securities intermediary and its entitlement holder governing the securities account expressly provides that the securities account is maintained at an office in a particular jurisdiction, that jurisdiction is the securities intermediary's jurisdiction.

（4）如果前述任何一款均不适用，则账户报告单中所注明的为权利持有人账户提供服务之营业厅的所在州，即为证券中间人所在州。

（4）If none of the preceding subdivisions applies, the securities intermediary's jurisdiction is the jurisdiction in which the office identified in an account statement as the office serving the entitlement holder's account is located.

（5）如果前述任何一款均不适用，则证券中间人首席执行官之办公室的所在州，即为

（5）If none of the preceding subdivisions applies, the securities intermediary's jurisdiction is the jurisdiction in which the chief

证券中间人所在州。

executive office of the securities intermediary is located.

（f）证券中间人所在州不由下列决定：

（f）A securities intermediary's jurisdiction is not determined by:

（1）代表金融资产之证书的实际所在州；

（1）the physical location of certificates representing financial assets;

（2）涉及权利持有人对金融资产的证券权利时，金融资产发行人的注册成立州；或

（2）the jurisdiction in which is organized the issuer of the financial asset with respect to which an entitlement holder has a security entitlement;or

（3）账户之数据处理设备或其他记账工作设备的所在州。

（3）the location of facilities for data processing or other recordkeeping concerning the account.

第 8.111 条　清算公司规则

§ 8.111. Clearing Corporation Rules.

清算公司为约束与其成员之间的权利和义务而制定的规则，即使与本篇冲突，且影响到未同意该规则的另一当事方，亦属有效。

A rule adopted by a clearing corporation governing rights and obligations among the clearing corporation and its participants in the clearing corporation is effective even if the rule conflicts with this Article and affects another party who does not consent to the rule.

第 8.112 条　债权人查封书

§ 8.112. Creditor's Legal Process.

（a）如果债权人要查封债务人对票式证券的权益，除（d）款另有规定外，只能通过查封官实际获取该证券证书作出查封。但是涉及已将证书交还给发行人的票式证券时，债权人可以通过向发行人送达查封书，查封该票式证券。

（a）The interest of a debtor in a certificated security may be reached by a creditor only by actual seizure of the security certificate by the officer making the attachment or levy, except as otherwise provided in Subsection（d）.However, a certificated security for which the certificate has been surrendered to the issuer may be reached by a creditor by legal process on the issuer.

（b）如果债权人要查封债务人对无票证券的权益，除（d）款另有规定外，只能通过在发

（b）The interest of a debtor in an uncertificated security may be reached by a creditor only by legal process on the issuer at

行人首席执行官美国办公室所在地，向发行人送达查封书。

its chief executive office in the United States, except as otherwise provided in Subsection（d）.

（c）如果债权人要查封债务人对证券权利的权益，除（d）款另有规定外，只能通过对掌管债务人证券账户的证券中间人送达查封书。

（c）The interest of a debtor in a security entitlement may be reached by a creditor only by legal process on the securities intermediary with whom the debtor's securities account is maintained, except as otherwise provided in Subsection（d）.

（d）如果受担保方占有票式证券的证书，或如果无票证券系登记在受担保方的名字之下，或如果证券权利系掌管在受担保方的名字之下，则债权人要查封债务人对该证券的权益或该证券权利中的权益，可以通过对受担保方送达查封书。

（d）The interest of a debtor in a certificated security for which the certificate is in the possession of a secured party, or in an uncertificated security registered in the name of a secured party, or in a security entitlement maintained in the name of a secured party may be reached by a creditor by legal process on the secured party.

（e）如果债务人系票式证券、无票证券或证券权利的所有权人，债权人有权获得有适当管辖权之法院的协助，通过禁止令或其他方法，获取该票式证券、无票证券或证券权利，或实现法律或衡平原则所允许的但通过其他司法程序难以实现的财产追索。

（e）A creditor whose debtor is the owner of a certificated security, uncertificated security, or security entitlement is entitled to aid from a court of competent jurisdiction, by injunction or otherwise, in reaching the certificated security, uncertificated security, or security entitlement or in satisfying theclaim by means allowed at law or in equity in regard to property that cannot readily be reached by other legal process.

第 8.113 条　反欺诈法不适用

§ 8.113. Statute of Frauds Inapplicable.

出售或购买证券的合同，或该合同的修改，无论是否存在被强制履行一方签名的书面文件或业经认证的记录，均可强制履行，即使该合同或该修

A contract or modification of a contract for the sale or purchase of a security is enforceable whether or not there is a writing signed or record authenticated by a party against whom enforcement is sought, even if the contract or

改无法在订立后一年内履行。

modification is not capable of performance within one year of its making.

第 8.114 条 票式证券的证据规则

如果就票式证券对发行人提起诉讼，应适用下列原则：

（1）除在诉答程序中被特别否定外，证券证书上或必要背书上的每个签名，均可作为证据被采纳。

（2）如果对任何签名的有效性存在争议，主张该签名有效的当事方，应承担签名有效性的举证责任，但该签名应被假定系属真实或业经授权。

（3）如果证券证书上的签名得到采纳或证明，则证书持有人只要出示证书，即有权据其索赔，除非被告能够证明，存在涉及证券合法性的抗辩或瑕疵。

（4）如果能够证明存在抗辩或瑕疵，则原告应承担举证责任，证明该抗辩或瑕疵不能对抗该原告或原告所代表的人。

§ 8.114. Evidentiary Rules Concerning Certificated Securities.

The following rules apply in an action on a certificated security against the issuer:

（1）Unless specifically denied in the pleadings, each signature on a security certificate or in a necessary indorsement is admitted.

（2）If the effectiveness of a signature is put in issue, the burden of establishing effectiveness is on the party claiming under the signature, but the signature is presumed to be genuine or authorized.

（3）If signatures on a security certificate are admitted or established, production of the certificate entitles a holder to recover on it unless the defendant establishes a defense or a defect going to the validity of the security.

（4）If it is shown that a defense or defect exists, the plaintiff has the burden of establishing that the plaintiff, or some person under whom the plaintiff claims, is a person against whom the defense or defect cannot be asserted.

第 8.115 条 证券中间人和其他人不向对立主张人承担责任

如果任何人对金融资产提出对立主张，根据有效的权利命令转让了金融资产的证券中间人，或根据客户或被代理人的指示处理了金融资产的经纪

§ 8.115. Securities Intermediary and Others Not Liable to Adverse Claimant.

A securities intermediary that has transferred a financial asset pursuant to an effective entitlement order, or a broker or other agent or bailee that has dealt with a financial asset at the direction of its customer

人、其他代理人或保管人，不对该主张人承担责任，除非该证券中间人、经纪人、其他代理人或保管人：

（1）在作出上述行动之前，已收到有适当管辖权之法院的查封令、禁止令，或禁止其采取上述行动的其他查封书，且有合理机会据以作为；

（2）与违法者合谋侵犯该主张人的权利；或

（3）涉及被盗的证券证书时，在收到对立主张的通知后作出上述行动。

or principal, is not liable to a person having an adverse claim to the financial asset, unless the securities intermediary, or broker or other agent or bailee:

（1）took the action after it had been served with an injunction, restraining order, or other legal process enjoining it from doing so issued by a court of competent jurisdiction and had a reasonable opportunity to act on the injunction, restraining order, or other legal process;

（2）acted in collusion with the wrongdoer in violating the rights of the adverse claimant;or

（3）in the case of a security certificate that has been stolen, acted with notice of the adverse claim.

第 8.116 条　证券中间人作为支付了价值的购买人

证券中间人如果收到金融资产，且为权利持有人的利益，设立了对该金融资产的证券权利，即属于支付了价值的购买人。证券中间人如果从另一证券中间人取得对金融资产的证券权利，且为权利持有人的利益，设立了对该金融资产的证券权利，即属于通过支付价值取得该证券权利。

§ 8.116. Securities Intermediary as Purchaser for Value.

A securities intermediary that receives a financial asset and establishes a security entitlement to the financial asset in favor of an entitlement holder is a purchaser for value of the financial asset.A securities intermediary that acquires a security entitlement to a financial asset from another securities intermediary acquires the security entitlement for value if the securities intermediary acquiring the security entitlement establishes a security entitlement to the financial asset in favor of an entitlement holder.

第2章　发行和发行人

PART 2. ISSUE AND ISSUER

第 8.201 条　发行人

（a）涉及证券项下的义务或对证券的抗辩时，“发行人”包括下列人：

（1）该人（鉴证受托人、登记人、转让代理人或其他类似的人除外）在证券证书上注明其名字，或授权注明其名字，用于证明在该人财产中或在某个企业中的份额、参股或其他权益，或用于证明该人有义务履行由该证书所代表的某种义务；

（2）该人在其财产中或在某个企业中创设份额、参股或其他权益，或承担某种义务，只要该创设或承担构成无票证券；

（3）该人直接或间接在其权利或财产中创设份额化权益，只要该权益由证券证书所代表；或

（4）该人为本条所描述的另一发行人承担了责任，或取代了另一发行人。

（b）涉及证券项下的义务或对证券的抗辩时，保证人在所作保证之限度内，被视为发行人，无论其责任是否注明在证券证书上。

（c）涉及转让登记时，“发行人”指证券转让账册的持有

§ 8.201. Issuer.

（a）With respect to an obligation on or a defense to a security, “issuer” includes a person that:

（1）places or authorizes the placing of its name on a security certificate, other than as authenticating trustee, registrar, transfer agent, or the like, to evidence a share, participation, or other interest in its property or in an enterprise or to evidence its duty to perform an obligation represented by the certificate;

（2）creates a share, participation, or other interest in its property or in an enterprise, or undertakes an obligation, that is an uncertificated security;

（3）directly or indirectly creates a fractional interest in its rights or property, if the fractional interest is represented by a security certificate;or

（4）becomes responsible for, or in place of, another person described as an issuer in this section.

（b）With respect to an obligation on or defense to a security, a guarantor is an issuer to the extent of its guaranty, whether or not its obligation is noted on a security certificate.

（c）With respect to a registration of a transfer, “issuer” means a person on whose

系代表该人作出。

behalf transfer books are maintained.

第 8.202 条 发行人的责任和抗辩；瑕疵或抗辩的通知

§ 8.202. Issuer's Responsibility and Defenses; Notice of Defect or Defense.

（a）票式证券的条款包括：证书上注明的条款，以及证书中引用并构成证券组成部分的其他票据、债券或单据，或宪法、法律、规则、条例、命令或类似规范，只要此种引用性条款不与证书上注明的条款相冲突。上述条款甚至可以对抗支付了价值且未得到通知的购买人。但是，如果证券的合法性存在瑕疵，则对于支付了价值的购买人，本款所述的引用，本身并不构成有关该瑕疵的通知，即使证书上已明确注明，任何人只要接受证书，即表示承认收到该通知。无票证券的条款包括：任何票据、债券或单据上注明的条款，以及作为证券发行依据的宪法、法律、规则、条例、命令或类似规范中包含的条款。

（a）Even against a purchaser for value and without notice, the terms of a certificated security include terms stated on the certificate and terms made part of the security by reference on the certificate to another instrument, indenture, or document or to a constitution, statute, ordinance, rule, regulation, order, or the like to the extent the terms referred to do not conflict with terms stated on the certificate. A reference under this subsection does not of itself charge a purchaser for value with notice of a defect going to the validity of the security, even if the certificate expressly states that a person accepting it admits notice.The terms of an uncertificated security include those stated in any instrument, indenture, or document or in a constitution, statute, ordinance, rule, regulation, order, or the like pursuant to which the security is issued.

（b）如果发行人主张证券无效，应适用下列原则：

（b）The following rules apply if an issuer asserts that a security is not valid:

（1）证券即使在发行时存在有关其合法性的瑕疵，只要非由政府或政府机构发行，即在支付了价值且未得到该瑕疵通知之购买人持有期间，具有法律效力，除非该瑕疵构成对宪法的违反。即使违反宪法，

（1）A security other than one issued by a government or governmental subdivision, agency, or instrumentality, even though issued with a defect going to its validity, is valid in the hands of a purchaser for value and without notice of the particular defect unless the defect involves a violation of a constitutional

证券在支付了价值且未得到该瑕疵通知之购买人持有期间，仍具有法律效力，但不包括原始发行中的购买人。

（2）只有在下列情况下，上述（1）款才适用于政府或政府机构发行人：

（A）有关该发行的法律要求已基本得到遵守；或

（B）发行人就发行的全部证券或特定证券，已收到很大部分的对价，且所说明的发行理由，系发行人有权力借款或发行证券的理由。

（c）除第8.205条另有规定外，票式证券如果不具真实性，即构成完全抗辩，甚至可以对抗支付了价值且未得到通知的购买人。

（d）证券发行人的所有其他抗辩，包括票式证券的未交付或附条件交付，均不能对抗支付了价值且在取得票式证券时未得到该抗辩通知的购买人。

（e）如果证券合同规定，或有关证券发行或分销的计划或安排规定，该合同、计划或安排“以实际发行为准”或“以实际分销为准”，则任何当事方在证券性质发生重大变化时取消证券合同的权利，不受本条

provision.In that case, the security is valid in the hands of a purchaser for value and without notice of the defect, other than a purchaser who takes by original issue.

（2）Subdivision（1）applies to an issuer that is a government or governmental subdivision, agency, or instrumentality only if:

（A）there has been substantial compliance with the legal requirements governing the issue;or

（B）the issuer has received a substantial consideration for the issue as a whole or for the particular security and a stated purpose of the issue is one for which the issuer has power to borrow money or issue the security.

（c）Except as otherwise provided in Section 8.205, lack of genuineness of a certificated security is a complete defense, even against a purchaser for value and without notice.

（d）All other defenses of the issuer of a security, including nondelivery and conditional delivery of a certificated security, are ineffective against a purchaser for value who has taken the certificated security without notice of the particular defense.

（e）This section does not affect the right of a party to cancel a contract for a security “when, as and if issued” or “when distributed” in the event of a material change in the character of the security that is the subject of the contract or in the plan or arrangement pursuant to which the security is to be issued or

的影响。

（f）如果证券中间人持有证券，而权利持有人对该证券拥有证券权利，则发行人在权利持有人直接持有证券时无权主张的抗辩，亦无权对该证券中间人主张。

第 8.203 条　过期即构成瑕疵或抗辩的通知

除涉及被撤销的回购外，如果一项行为或事件，创设一项权利，即有权要求票式证券所代表的主债务即时履行，或规定一个日期，即在该日期或其后，必须提示或交还证券，用于赎兑或交换，此时，在该行为或事件发生后，购买人即被视为就该证券发行中的瑕疵或就发行人的抗辩得到通知，只要：

（1）该行为或事件要求，在收到证券证书的提示或交还时，支付款项、交付票式证券，或登记无票证券转让（其中任何一项或多项）；并且，在规定的付款日或交换日，存在可用的款项或证券；并且，购买人从该日期起一年之后才取得证券；或

（2）该行为或事件不在（1）款范围以内，且购买人从规定的交还日、提示日或履约日起两年之后才取得证券。

distributed.

（f）If a security is held by a securities intermediary against whom an entitlement holder has a security entitlement with respect to the security, the issuer may not assert any defense that the issuer could not assert if the entitlement holder held the security directly.

§ 8.203. Staleness as Notice of Defect or Defense.

After an act or event, other than a call that has been revoked, creating a right to immediate performance of the principal obligation represented by a certificated security or setting a date on or after which the security is to be presented or surrendered for redemption or exchange, a purchaser is charged with notice of any defect in its issue or defense of the issuer if the act or event:

（1）requires the payment of money, the delivery of a certificated security, the registration of transfer of an uncertificated security, or any of them on presentation or surrender of the security certificate, the money or security is available on the date set for payment or exchange, and the purchaser takes the security more than one year after that date;or

（2）is not covered by Subdivision（1）and the purchaser takes the security more than two years after the date set for surrender or presentation or the date on which performance became due.

第 8.204 条　发行人限制转让的效力

发行人对证券转让的限制，即使在其他方面系属合法，亦不能对抗不知道该限制的人，除非：

（1）证券为票式证券，且该限制被醒目注明在证券证书上；或

（2）证券为无票证券，且注册所有权人已得到该限制的通知。

§ 8.204. Effect of Issuer's Restriction on Transfer.

A restriction on transfer of a security imposed by the issuer, even if otherwise lawful, is ineffective against a person without knowledge of the restriction unless:

（1）the security is certificated and the restriction is noted conspicuously on the security certificate;or

（2）the security is uncertificated and the registered owner has been notified of the restriction.

第 8.205 条　证券证书上无授权签名的效力

发行之前或发行过程中在证券证书上作出的无授权签名不具效力，但对于支付了价值的票式证券购买人，该签名具有效力，只要该购买人未得到该签名缺乏授权的通知，且签名系由下列人作出：

（1）鉴证受托人、登记人、转让代理人，其他受发行人委托签署该证券证书或类似之证券证书的人，或受发行人委托就签署该证券证书或类似之证券证书做直接准备的人；或

（2）发行人的雇员，或（1）款中任何人的雇员，只要其受委托负责处理该证券证书。

§ 8.205. Effect of Unauthorized Signature on Security Certificate.

An unauthorized signature placed on a security certificate before or in the course of issue is ineffective, but the signature is effective in favor of a purchaser for value of the certificated security if the purchaser is without notice of the lack of authority and the signing has been done by:

（1）an authenticating trustee, registrar, transfer agent, or other person entrusted by the issuer with the signing of the security certificate or of similar security certificates or with the immediate preparation for signing of any of them;or

（2）an employee of the issuer, or of any of the persons listed in Subdivision（1）, entrusted with responsible handling of the security certificate.

第 8.206 条 证券证书的添补完整或涂改

（a）证券证书如果载有发行或转让所必需的签名，但在任何其他方面不完整，则：

（1）任何人均可在授权范围内将空白处添补完整；并且

（2）即使证券证书空白处填入的内容不正确，支付了价值且未得到此种错误之通知的购买人，仍可按添补完整后的证券证书强制履行。

（b）完整的证券证书被不适当涂改后（包括欺诈性涂改），仍可强制履行，但只能按原始条款强制履行。

§ 8.206. Completion or Alteration of Security Certificate.

（a）If a security certificate contains the signatures necessary to its issue or transfer but is incomplete in any other respect:

（1）any person may complete it by filling in the blanks as authorized;and

（2）even if the blanks are incorrectly filled in, the security certificate as completed is enforceable by a purchaser who took it for value and without notice of the incorrectness.

（b）A complete security certificate that has been improperly altered, even if fraudulently, remains enforceable, but only according to its original terms.

第 8.207 条 发行人对注册所有权人的权利和义务

（a）发行人或债券受托人，在收到登记式的票式证券之转让登记的适当提示之前，或在收到无票证券之转让登记指示的适当提示之前，可将证券的注册所有权人视为唯一有权进行投票、获得通知，以及通过其他方式行使所有权人之全部权利和权力的人。

（b）证券的注册所有权人对回购、补缴额外股金或类似事项的责任，不受本篇影响。

§ 8.207. Rights and Duties of Issuer With Respect to Registered Owners.

（a）Before due presentment for registration of transfer of a certificated security in registered form or of an instruction requesting registration of transfer of an uncertificated security, the issuer or indenture trustee may treat the registered owner as the person exclusively entitled to vote, receive notifications, and otherwise exercise all the rights and powers of an owner.

（b）This Article does not affect the liability of the registered owner of a security for a call, assessment, or the like.

第 8.208 条 鉴证受托人、登记人和转让代理人之签名的效力

（a）任何人如果以鉴证受

§ 8.208. Effect of Signature of Authenticating Trustee, Registrar, or Transfer Agent.

（a）A person signing a security certificate

托人、登记人、转让代理人或类似之其他人的身份，在证券证书上签名，即向支付了价值且未得到任何特定瑕疵通知的票式证券购买人担保：

（1）证书系属真实；

（2）该签名人具有参与该证券发行的能力，且未超出从发行人获得的授权范围；以及

（3）该签名人有合理理由相信，该票式证券的发行格式和数量，与发行人取得的授权相符。

（b）除另有协议外，上述（a）款项下的签名人，不在其他方面对证券的合法性承担责任。

第 8.209 条 发行人的留置权

发行人对票式证券的留置权，必须醒目注明在证券证书上，才能有效对抗购买人。

第 8.210 条 超量发行

（a）在本条中，"超量发行"指证券的发行数量超出发行人之机构权力所允许发行的数量；但是，如果在出现超量发行后，采取适当行动纠正了超量，则该发行不属于超量发行。

（b）除（c）款和（d）款另有规定外，如果本篇的任何

as authenticating trustee, registrar, transfer agent, or the like warrants to a purchaser for value of the certificated security, if the purchaser is without notice of a particular defect, that:

（1）the certificate is genuine;

（2）the person's own participation in the issue of the security is within the person's capacity and within the scope of the authority received by the person from the issuer;and

（3）the person has reasonable grounds to believe that the certificated security is in the form and within the amount the issuer is authorized to issue.

（b）Unless otherwise agreed, a person signing under Subsection（a）does not assume responsibility for the validity of the security in other respects.

§ 8.209. Issuer's Lien.

A lien in favor of an issuer on a certificated security is valid against a purchaser only if the right of the issuer to the lien is noted conspicuously on the security certificate.

§ 8.210. Overissue.

（a）In this section, "overissue" means the issue of securities in excess of the amount the issuer has corporate power to issue, but an overissue does not occur if appropriate action has cured the overissue.

（b）Except as otherwise provided in Subsections（c）and（d）, the provisions of

条款，对证券赋予效力，或强制要求证券之发行或再发行，但该等生效、发行或再发行将引起超量发行，则对于超量发行部分，该条款不适用。

this Article that validate a security or compel its issue or reissue do not apply to the extent that validation, issue, or reissue would result in overissue.

（c）如果任何人有权取得证券的发行或生效，且存在合理机会可以购买相同的证券，且该购买不构成超量发行，则该人可以强制发行人购买该证券，并交付该证券（如果是票式证券）或登记其转让（如果是无票证券），但该人应交出其持有的证券证书。

（c）If an identical security not constituting an overissue is reasonably available for purchase, a person entitled to issue or validation may compel the issuer to purchase the security and deliver it if certificated or register its transfer if uncertificated, against surrender of any security certificate the person holds.

（d）如果不存在购买证券的合理机会，有权取得发行或生效的人，可就该人或最后支付价值之购买人为证券支付的金额，从发行人处取得赔偿，再加上从该人提出主张之日起的利息。

（d）If a security is not reasonably available for purchase, a person entitled to issue or validation may recover from the issuer the price the person or the last purchaser for value paid for it with interest from the date of the person's demand.

第3章　票式证券和无票证券的转让

PART 3. TRANSFER OF CERTIFICATED AND UNCERTIFICATED SECURITIES

第8.301条　交付

（a）票式证券在下列时间被视为交付给购买人：

（1）购买人取得证券证书的占有；

（2）另一人（证券中间人除外）代表购买人取得证券证

§ 8.301. Delivery.

（a）Delivery of a certificated security to a purchaser occurs when:

（1）the purchaser acquires possession of the security certificate;

（2）another person, other than a securities intermediary, either acquires possession of the

书的占有；或在其取得证书的占有后，承认代表购买人持有证书；或

security certificate on behalf of the purchaser or, having previously acquired possession of the certificate, acknowledges that it holds for the purchaser;or

（3）证券中间人代表购买人取得证券证书的占有，但是，证书必须为登记式，且（i）登记在购买人名下，（ii）规定向购买人的指定人付款，或（iii）通过有效背书，记名背书给购买人，且未曾背书给证券中间人，也未曾有过空白背书。

（3）a securities intermediary acting on behalf of the purchaser acquires possession of the security certificate, only if the certificate is in registered form and is（i）registered in the name of the purchaser,（ii）payable to the order of the purchaser, or（iii）specially indorsed to the purchaser by an effective indorsement and has not been indorsed to the securities intermediary or in blank.

（b）无票证券在下列时间被视为交付给购买人：

（b）Delivery of an uncertificated security to a purchaser occurs when:

（1）发行人在原始发行或转让登记中，将购买人登记为注册所有权人；或

（1）the issuer registers the purchaser as the registered owner, on original issue or registration of transfer;or

（2）另一人（证券中间人除外）代表购买人成为无票证券的注册所有权人，或在成为注册所有权人后，承认代表购买人持有权益。

（2）another person, other than a securities intermediary, either becomes the registered owner of the uncertificated security on behalf of the purchaser or, having previously become the registered owner, acknowledges that it holds for the purchaser.

第 8.302 条 购买人的权利

§ 8.302. Rights of Purchaser.

（a）除（b）款和（c）款另有规定外，票式证券或无票证券的购买人，取得其转让人所拥有的或有权力转让的对证券的全部权利。

（a）Except as otherwise provided in Subsections（b）and（c）, a purchaser of a certificated or uncertificated security acquires all rights in the security that the transferor had or had power to transfer.

（b）有限权益的购买人，只在所购买之权益的范围内取得权利。

（b）A purchaser of a limited interest acquires rights only to the extent of the interest purchased.

（c）如果票式证券的购买人作为前手持有人，曾得到对立主张的通知，该购买人即不能通过从受保护购买人处取得证券来改善自己的地位。

（c）A purchaser of a certificated security who as a previous holder had notice of an adverse claim does not improve its position by taking from a protected purchaser.

第 8.303 条　受保护购买人

§ 8.303. Protected Purchaser.

（a）票式证券、无票证券或该证券之权益的购买人，在满足下列条件时，即属于“受保护购买人”：

（1）支付了价值；

（2）未得到证券存在对立主张的通知；并且

（3）取得了对票式证券或无票证券的控制。

（b）受保护购买人除取得购买人的权利外，其对证券的权利，不受制于任何对立主张。

（a）“Protected purchaser” means a purchaser of a certificated or uncertificated security, or of an interest therein, who:

（1）gives value;

（2）does not have notice of any adverse claim to the security;and

（3）obtains control of the certificated or uncertificated security.

（b）In addition to acquiring the rights of a purchaser, a protected purchaser also acquires its interest in the security free of any adverse claim.

第 8.304 条　背书

§ 8.304. Indorsement.

（a）背书可以是空白背书，也可以是记名背书。空白背书包括背书给持票人的背书。记名背书注明接受证券转让的人，或注明有权力转让证券的人。持有人可将空白背书转化为记名背书。

（b）如果证券证书代表多个单位，且发行人的意图是每个单位可以单独转让，则当背书显示转让证券证书的部分单位时，该背书在其转让范围内系属有效。

（a）An indorsement may be in blank or special.An indorsement in blank includes an indorsement to bearer.A special indorsement specifies to whom a security is to be transferred or who has power to transfer it.A holder may convert a blank indorsement to a special indorsement.

（b）An indorsement purporting to be only of part of a security certificate representing units intended by the issuer to be separately transferable is effective to the extent of the indorsement.

（c）无论是记名背书还是空白背书，只有记载背书的证书被交付后才构成转让；如果背书记载在另外的文件上，则只有证书和该文件都被交付后才构成转让。

（c）An indorsement, whether special or in blank, does not constitute a transfer until delivery of the certificate on which it appears or, if the indorsement is on a separate document, until delivery of both the document and the certificate.

（d）如果登记式的证券证书在缺少必要背书的情况下被交付给购买人，则只有在补齐背书后，购买人才能成为受保护购买人。但是，在对抗转让人时，转让在交付时即属完成，且购买人有权要求转让人实际补齐任何必要背书。

（d）If a security certificate in registered form has been delivered to a purchaser without a necessary indorsement, the purchaser may become a protected purchaser only when the indorsement is supplied.However, against a transferor, a transfer is complete on delivery and the purchaser has a specifically enforceable right to have any necessary indorsement supplied.

（e）对证券证书作出持票式背书，可能构成证书存在对立主张的通知，但在其他方面，不影响持有人取得登记的权利。

（e）An indorsement of a security certificate in bearer form may give notice of an adverse claim to the certificate, but it does not otherwise affect a right to registration that the holder possesses.

（f）除另有协议外，作出背书的人只承担第 8.108 条规定的义务，而没有义务保证发行人会兑付证券。

（f）Unless otherwise agreed, a person making an indorsement assumes only the obligations provided in Section 8.108 and not an obligation that the security will be honored by the issuer.

第 8.305 条　指示

§ 8.305. Instruction.

（a）如果指示由适格人发起，但在其他任何方面不完整，则任何人均可在授权范围内将其添补完整。发行人可以基于添补完整的指示作为，即使添补时发生错误。

（a）If an instruction has been originated by an appropriate person but is incomplete in any other respect, any person may complete it as authorized and the issuer may rely on it as completed, even though it has been completed incorrectly.

（b）除另有协议外，发起

（b）Unless otherwise agreed, a person

指示的人只承担第8.108条规定的义务，而没有义务保证发行人会兑付证券。

initiating an instruction assumes only the obligations imposed by Section 8.108 and not an obligation that the security will be honored by the issuer.

第8.306条　对签名、背书或指示作出保证的效力

§ 8.306. Effect of Guaranteeing Signature, Indorsement, or Instruction.

（a）对证券证书之背书人的签名作出保证的人，担保在该签名的当时：

（1）签名系属真实；

（2）签名人系作出背书的适格人，或如果签名人系代理人，其具有代表适格人作为的实际授权；并且

（3）签名人具有作出签名的法定能力。

（a）A person who guarantees a signature of anindorser of a security certificate warrants that at the time of signing:

（1）the signature was genuine;

（2）the signer was an appropriate person to indorse or, if the signature is by an agent, the agent had actual authority to act on behalf of the appropriate person;and

（3）the signer had legal capacity to sign.

（b）对指示之发起人的签名作出保证的人，担保在该签名的当时：

（1）签名系属真实；

（2）签名人系发起指示的适格人，或如果签名人系代理人，其具有代表适格人作为的实际授权；但是，指示中注明为注册所有权人的人，必须事实上确系注册所有权人，而签名的该保证人对此事实不作出保证；并且

（3）签名人具有作出签名的法定能力。

（b）A person who guarantees a signature of the originator of an instruction warrants that at the time of signing:

（1）the signature was genuine;

（2）the signer was an appropriate person to originate the instruction or, if the signature is by an agent, the agent had actual authority to act on behalf of the appropriate person, if the person specified in the instruction as the registered owner was, in fact, the registered owner, as to which fact the signature guarantor does not make a warranty;and

（3）the signer had legal capacity to sign.

（c）对指示之发起人的签名作出特别保证的人，除作出与（b）款所述之签名保证人相

（c）A person who specially guarantees the signature of an originator of an instruction makes the warranties of a signature guarantor

同的担保外，还同时担保，在该指示被提示给发行人时：

（1）指示中被注明为无票证券注册所有权人的人，将会成为注册所有权人；并且

（2）指示中所要求的无票证券的转让登记，将会得到发行人的登记，且除指示中另有注明外，该转让不受制于任何留置权、担保权益、限制或索赔。

（d）上述（a）款和（b）款项下的保证人，或（c）款项下的特别保证人，不在其他方面担保转让的正当性。

（e）对证券证书之背书作出保证的人，除作出与（a）款所述之签名保证人相同的担保外，还同时担保转让在所有各个方面的正当性。

（f）涉及无票证券的转让时，对转让指示作出保证的人，除作出与（c）款所述之签名特别保证人相同的担保外，还同时担保转让在所有各个方面的正当性。

（g）发行人不得规定，对签名的特别保证、对背书的保证或对指示的保证，系登记转让的条件。

（h）依赖上述保证取得或交易证券的人，是本条项下之

under Subsection（b）and also warrants that at the time the instruction is presented to the issuer:

（1）the person specified in the instruction as the registered owner of the uncertificated security will be the registered owner;and

（2）the transfer of the uncertificated security requested in the instruction will be registered by the issuer free from all liens, security interests, restrictions, and claims other than those specified in the instruction.

（d）A guarantor under Subsections（a）and（b）or a special guarantor under Subsection（c）does not otherwise warrant the rightfulness of the transfer.

（e）A person who guarantees an indorsement of a security certificate makes the warranties of a signature guarantor under Subsection（a）and also warrants the rightfulness of the transfer in all respects.

（f）A person who guarantees an instruction requesting the transfer of an uncertificated security makes the warranties of a special signature guarantor under Subsection（c）and also warrants the rightfulness of the transfer in all respects.

（g）An issuer may not require a special guaranty of signature, a guaranty of indorsement, or a guaranty of instruction as a condition to registration of transfer.

（h）The warranties under this section are made to a person taking or dealing with

担保的受益人。保证人如果违反保证，应就该受益人受到的损失承担赔偿责任。如果任何人为背书人或指示发起人之签名、背书或指示作出保证，则背书人或指示人应在该保证人因违反保证而受到损失时，向该保证人作出赔偿。

the security in reliance on the guaranty, and the guarantor is liable to the person for loss resulting from their breach.An indorser or originator of an instruction whose signature, indorsement, or instruction has been guaranteed is liable to a guarantor for any loss suffered by the guarantor as a result of breach of the warranties of the guarantor.

第 8.307 条　购买人取得转让登记要件的权利

§ 8.307. Purchaser's Right to Requisites for Registration of Transfer.

除另有协议外，证券转让人在收到适当要求后，应向购买人提供转让授权的证明，或提供登记该证券转让所必须的任何其他要件。但是，如果该转让未支付价值，则转让人无须遵从该要求，除非购买人支付必要的费用。如果转让人未能在合理时间内遵从该要求，购买人可以拒绝或取消该转让。

Unless otherwise agreed, the transferor of a security on due demand shall supply the purchaser with proof of authority to transfer or with any other requisite necessary to obtain registration of the transfer of the security, but if the transfer is not for value, a transferor need not comply unless the purchaser pays the necessary expenses.If the transferor fails within a reasonable time to comply with the demand, the purchaser may reject or rescind the transfer.

第4章　登　记

PART 4. REGISTRATION

第 8.401 条　发行人登记转让的义务

§ 8.401. Duty of Issuer to Register Transfer.

（a）如果就登记式的票式证券向发行人作出提示，要求发行人对该证券的转让作出登记，或如果就一项指示向发行人作出提示，要求发行人对无票证券的转让作出登记，则发行人应按要求对转让作出登记，

（a）If a certificated security in registered form is presented to an issuer with a request to register transfer or an instruction is presented to an issuer with a request to register transfer of an uncertificated security, the issuer shall register the transfer as requested if:

只要：

（1）根据证券的条款，要求登记转让的人，有权将证券登记在自己名下；

（1）under the terms of the security the person seeking registration of transfer is eligible to have the security registered in its name;

（2）作出背书或指示的人，系适格人或系拥有实际授权代表适格人作为的代理人；

（2）the indorsement or instruction is made by the appropriate person or by an agent who has actual authority to act on behalf of the appropriate person;

（3）背书或指示的真实和授权已得到合理确认（第 8.402 条）；

（3）reasonable assurance is given that the indorsement or instruction is genuine and authorized（Section 8.402）；

（4）适用的税收法律已得到遵守；

（4）any applicable law relating to the collection of taxes has been complied with;

（5）转让不违反发行人根据第 8.204 条设定的任何转让限制；

（5）the transfer does not violate any restriction on transfer imposed by the issuer in accordance with Section 8.204;

（6）任何请求发行人不得登记转让的要求，尚未按第 8.403 条所述发生效力；或发行人已遵守了第 8.403 条（b）款，但并未收到第 8.403 条（d）款所述的查封书或保证金；并且

（6）a demand that the issuer not register transfer has not become effective under Section 8.403, or the issuer has complied with Section 8.403（b）but no legal process or indemnity bond is obtained as provided in Section 8.403（d）；and

（7）转让在事实上系属正当，或受让人系属受保护购买人。

（7）the transfer is in fact rightful or is to a protected purchaser.

（b）如果发行人有义务登记证券转让，但不合理地延迟登记，或未能登记，或拒绝登记，即应对提示票式证券或登记指示的人或其被代理人因此受到的损失承担责任。

（b）If an issuer is under a duty to register a transfer of a security, the issuer is liable to a person presenting a certificated security or an instruction for registration or to the person's principal for loss resulting from unreasonable delay in registration or failure or refusal to register the transfer.

第 8.402 条 对背书或指示的有效性作出确认

（a）发行人为确认每个必要背书或每项指示均属真实和业经授权，可以要求获得下列确认：

（1）在所有情况下均可要求，就作出背书之人或发起指示之人的签名获得保证；涉及一项指示时，可以要求就指示发起人的真实身份获得合理确认；

（2）当作出背书的人或发起指示的人系代理人时，可以要求就其签名的实际授权获得适当确认；

（3）当作出背书的人或发起指示的人系诚信受托人，且根据第 8.107 条(a)(4)款或(5)款作为时，可以要求就该受托人的任命或任职获得适当证明；

（4）当诚信受托人不止一人时，可以要求就所有应签名的人均已签名之事实获得合理确认；以及

（5）当作出背书的人或发起指示的人不在本款之其他条款所述范围内时，可以根据该案的情况，要求获得尽可能接近本款规定的适当确认。

（b）发行人可以要求获得本条范围以外的其他合理确认。

§ 8.402. Assurance That Indorsement or Instruction Is Effective.

（a）An issuer may require the following assurance that each necessary indorsement or each instruction is genuine and authorized:

（1）in all cases, a guaranty of the signature of the person making an indorsement or originating an instruction, including, in the case of an instruction, reasonable assurance of identity;

（2）if the indorsement is made or the instruction is originated by an agent, appropriate assurance of actual authority to sign;

（3）if the indorsement is made or the instruction is originated by a fiduciary pursuant to Section 8.107（a）（4）or（5）, appropriate evidence of appointment or incumbency;

（4）if there is more than one fiduciary, reasonable assurance that all who are required to sign have done so;and

（5）if the indorsement is made or the instruction is originated by a person not covered by another provision of this subsection, assurance appropriate to the case corresponding as nearly as may be to the provisions of this subsection.

（b）An issuer may elect to require reasonable assurance beyond that specified in this section.

（c）在本条中：

（1）“任命或任职的适当证明”：

（A）在涉及由法院任命或批准的诚信受托人时，指法院或法院官员签发或命令签发或监督签发的证书，且该证书系在转让提示前60日内签发；或

（B）在任何其他情况下，指任命书的副本，或发行人合理认可的相关负责人签发的或代表该人签发的证明书；或如果缺少此种任命书或证明书，指发行人合理认可的其他适当证明。

（2）签名的“保证”，指发行人合理认可的相关负责人签署的保证，或代表该人签署的保证。发行人可就负责人的范围制定标准，但该标准不得明显不合理。

第8.403条　请求发行人不得登记转让

（a）任何人如果系作出背书或发起指示的适格人，即可向发行人发起请求，要求发行人不得就证券转让作出登记。通知应指明注册所有权人，说明证券所属的发行项目，并提供请求人的联系地址。只有在发行人收到请求的时间和方式使发行人有合理机会据以作为

（c）In this section:

（1）“Appropriate evidence of appointment or incumbency” means:

（A）in the case of a fiduciary appointed or qualified by a court, a certificate issued by or under the direction or supervision of the court or an officer thereof and dated within 60 days before the date of presentation for transfer;or

（B）in any other case, a copy of a document showing the appointment or a certificate issued by or on behalf of a person reasonably believed by an issuer to be responsible or, in the absence of that document or certificate, other evidence the issuer reasonably considers appropriate.

（2）“Guaranty of the signature” means a guaranty signed by or on behalf of a person reasonably believed by the issuer to be responsible.An issuer may adopt standards with respect to responsibility if they are not manifestly unreasonable.

§ 8.403. Demand That Issuer Not Register Transfer.

（a）A person who is an appropriate person to make an indorsement or originate an instruction may demand that the issuer not register transfer of a security by communicating to the issuer a notification that identifies the registered owner and the issue of which the security is a part and provides an address for communications directed to the person making the demand.The demand is effective only if it is

时，请求方为有效。

received by the issuer at a time and in a manner affording the issuer reasonable opportunity to act on it.

（b）在请求发行人不得登记转让的请求产生效力后，如果任何人就登记式的票式证券向发行人作出提示，要求对该证券的转让作出登记，或如果就一项指示向发行人作出提示，要求对无票证券的转让作出登记，发行人即应迅即通知下列两者：（i）请求发行人不得登记转让的人，并在通知时使用该人提供的地址；以及（ii）提示证券或发起指示并要求进行转让登记的人；此时，通知中应说明：

（b）If a certificated security in registered form is presented to an issuer with a request to register transfer or an instruction is presented to an issuer with a request to register transfer of an uncertificated security after a demand that the issuer not register transfer has become effective, the issuer shall promptly communicate to（i）the person who initiated the demand at the address provided in the demand and（ii）the person who presented the security for registration of transfer or initiated the instruction requesting registration of transfer a notification stating that:

（1）已收到票式证券的提示，要求进行转让登记，或已收到指示，要求进行无票证券的转让登记；

（1）the certificated security has been presented for registration of transfer or the instruction for registration of transfer of the uncertificated security has been received;

（2）在此之前，已收到不得登记转让的请求；以及

（2）a demand that the issuer not register transfer had previously been received;and

（3）发行人将在自己通知中注明的期限内，暂停转让登记，以便让提出不得登记之请求的人有机会取得查封书或支付保证金。

（3）the issuer will withhold registration of transfer for a period of time stated in the notification in order to provide the person who initiated the demand an opportunity to obtain legal process or an indemnity bond.

（c）上述（b）（3）款所述的时间期限，不得超过通知日期后三十天，但只要不是明显不合理，发行人可以规定短于上述的期限。

（c）The period described in Subsection（b）（3）may not exceed 30 days after the date of communication of the notification.A shorter period may be specified by the issuer if it is not manifestly unreasonable.

（d）如果提出不得登记之请求的人未能在发行人之通知规定的时间内满足下列条件，则发行人在根据有效的背书或指示作出转让登记后，不对请求人受到的损失承担责任：

（d）An issuer is not liable to a person who initiated a demand that the issuer not register transfer for any loss the person suffers as a result of registration of a transfer pursuant to an effective indorsement or instruction if the person who initiated the demand does not, within the time stated in the issuer's communication, either:

（1）从有适当管辖权的法院取得适当的禁令或其他查封书，禁止发行人登记转让；或

（1）obtain an appropriate injunction, restraining order, or other process from a court of competent jurisdiction enjoining the issuer from registering the transfer;or

（2）向发行人交付充分的赔偿保证金，即根据发行人的判断，足以保护发行人及任何转让代理人、登记人或发行人之其他代理人的保证金，使其不因拒绝登记转让而受到损失。

（2）file with the issuer an indemnity bond, sufficient in the issuer's judgment to protect the issuer and any transfer agent, registrar, or other agent of the issuer involved from any loss it or they may suffer by refusing to register the transfer.

（e）如果发行人根据无效的背书或指示登记转让，本条不免除其应承担的责任。

（e）This section does not relieve an issuer from liability for registering transfer pursuant to an indorsement or instruction that was not effective.

第 8.404 条　错误登记

§ 8.404. Wrongful Registration.

（a）除第 8.406 条另有规定外，发行人如果将证券转让登记给无权获得登记的人，即应承担错误登记转让的责任，只要该转让登记：

（a）Except as otherwise provided in Section 8.406, an issuer is liable for wrongful registration of transfer if the issuer has registered a transfer of a security to a person not entitled to it, and the transfer was registered:

（1）系根据无效的背书或指示作出；

（1）pursuant to an ineffective indorsement or instruction;

（2）系在有关不得登记转让的请求已根据第 8.403 条（a）

（2）after a demand that the issuer not register transfer became effective under Section

款发生效力之后作出，且发行人未遵守第8.403条（b）款的规定；

8.403（a）and the issuer did not comply with Section 8.403（b）;

（3）系在发行人已收到有适当管辖权之法院的适当禁令或其他查封书之后作出，而该禁令或其他查封书禁止发行人登记转让，且发行人有合理机会据以作为；或

（3）after the issuer had been served with an appropriate injunction, restraining order, or other process from a court of competent jurisdiction enjoining it from registering the transfer, and the issuer had a reasonable opportunity to act on the injunction, restraining order, or other legal process;or

（4）系由发行人与违法方合谋作出。

（4）by an issuer acting in collusion with the wrongdoer.

（b）根据（a）款对错误登记转让承担责任的发行人，在收到要求后，应向有权取得证券的人，提供相同的票式证券或无票证券，以及由于错误登记致使该人未能收到的任何付款或分红。如果因此造成超量发行，发行人向该人提供相同证券的责任，应根据第8.210条确定。

（b）An issuer that is liable for wrongful registration of transfer under Subsection（a）on demand shall provide the person entitled to the security with a like certificated or uncertificated security and any payments or distributions that the person did not receive as a result of the wrongful registration.If an overissue would result, the issuer's liability to provide the person with a like security is governed by Section 8.210.

（c）除（a）款或有关税收的法律另有规定外，发行人如果根据有效的背书或指示作出登记，即不对所有权人或其他人因证券转让登记受到的损失承担责任。

（c）Except as otherwise provided in Subsection（a）or in a law relating to the collection of taxes, an issuer is not liable to an owner or other person suffering loss as a result of the registration of a transfer of a security if registration was made pursuant to an effective indorsement or instruction.

第8.405条　证券证书遗失、损毁或错拿后的替换

§ 8.405. Replacement of Lost, Destroyed, or Wrongfully Taken Security Certificate.

（a）如果票式证券的所有

（a）If an owner of a certificated security,

权人声称证书遗失、损毁或错拿，则无论证券是登记式还是持票式，发行人均必须发行新的证书，只要该所有权人：

（1）提出补发新证书的要求，且发行人尚未得到受保护购买人已取得该原始证书的通知；

（2）向发行人提供充分的赔偿保证金；并且

（3）满足发行人提出的任何其他合理要求。

（b）在新的证券证书发行之后，如果受保护购买人提示原始证书，要求登记转让，发行人必须作出登记，除非该登记会构成超量发行。如果构成超量发行，发行人的责任应根据第 8.210 条确定。发行人除对赔偿保证金享有权利外，还可从取得新证书的人收回新证书；或在涉及之后从该人取得新证书的人时，从该后人收回新证书，但受保护购买人除外。

whether in registered or bearer form, claims that the certificate has been lost, destroyed, or wrongfully taken, the issuer shall issue a new certificate if the owner:

（1）so requests before the issuer has notice that the certificate has been acquired by a protected purchaser;

（2）files with the issuer a sufficient indemnity bond;and

（3）satisfies other reasonable requirements imposed by the issuer.

（b）If, after the issue of a new security certificate, a protected purchaser of the original certificate presents it for registration of transfer, the issuer shall register the transfer unless an overissue would result.In that case, the issuer's liability is governed by Section 8.210. In addition to any rights on the indemnity bond, an issuer may recover the new certificate from a person to whom it was issued or any person taking under that person, except a protected purchaser.

第 8.406 条 证券证书遗失、损毁或错拿后通知发行人的义务

如果证券证书遗失、损毁或错拿，但所有权人未能在得到该情况的通知后，在合理时间内通知发行人，且发行人在收到通知前登记了证券转让，则对于发行人根据第 8.404 条作出的转让登记，或根据第

§ 8.406. Obligation to Notify Issuer of Lost, Destroyed, or Wrongfully Taken Security Certificate.

If a security certificate has been lost, destroyed, or wrongfully taken, and the owner fails to notify the issuer of that fact within a reasonable time after the owner has notice of it and the issuer registers a transfer of the security before receiving notification, the owner may not assert against the issuer a claim

8.405条发行的新的证券证书，所有权人无权对发行人提出索赔。

for registering the transfer under Section 8.404 or a claim to a new security certificate under Section 8.405.

第8.407条 鉴证受托人、转让代理人和登记人

§ 8.407. Authenticating Trustee, Transfer Agent, and Registrar.

任何人如果系发行人的鉴证受托人、转让代理人、登记人或其他代理人，并代表发行人登记证券转让、发行新的证券证书或无票证券，或注销被收回的证券证书，即对票式证券或无票证券的持有人或所有权人，承担与发行人履行该等职责时同样的义务。

A person acting as authenticating trustee, transfer agent, registrar, or other agent for an issuer in the registration of a transfer of its securities, in the issue of new security certificates or uncertificated securities, or in the cancellation of surrendered security certificates has the same obligation to the holder or owner of a certificated or uncertificated security with regard to the particular functions performed as the issuer has in regard to those functions.

第5章 证券权利

PART 5. SECURITY ENTITLEMENTS

第8.501条 证券账户；从证券中间人取得证券权利

§ 8.501. Securities Account; Acquisition of Security Entitlement From Securities Intermediary.

（a）“证券账户”指根据协议用于贷记金融资产的账户，且掌管账户的人根据协议向账户受益人承诺，后者有权行使金融资产项下的权利。

（a）“Securities account” means an account to which a financial asset is or may be credited in accordance with an agreement under which the person maintaining the account undertakes to treat the person for whom the account is maintained as entitled to exercise the rights that comprise the financial asset.

（b）除（d）款和（e）款另有规定外，一个人在下列情况下被视为取得证券权利：

（1）证券中间人在账目中

（b）Except as otherwise provided in Subsections（d）and（e）, a person acquires a security entitlement if a securities intermediary:

（1）indicates by book entry that a

注明，金融资产被贷记至该人的证券账户；

financial asset has been credited to the person's securities account;

（2）证券中间人从该人收到金融资产，或为该人取得金融资产，且无论何种情况，在接受该资产后贷记至该人的证券账户；或

（2）receives a financial asset from the person or acquires a financial asset for the person and, in either case, accepts it for credit to the person's securities account;or

（3）根据其他法律或规则，证券中间人承担将金融资产贷记至该人证券账户的义务。

（3）becomes obligated under other law, regulation, or rule to credit a financial asset to the person's securities account.

（c）只要（b）款的任何一项条件得到满足，该人即享有证券权利，即使证券中间人本身不持有该金融资产。

（c）If a condition of Subsection（b）has been met, a person has a security entitlement even though the securities intermediary does not itself hold the financial asset.

（d）如果证券中间人为另一人持有金融资产，且该金融资产登记在后者名下，或应向后者的指定人付款，或被记名背书给后者，并且，该金融资产未曾背书给证券中间人，也未有过空白背书，则后者即被视为直接持有该金融资产，而不被视为对该金融资产持有证券权利。

（d）If a securities intermediary holds a financial asset for another person, and the financial asset is registered in the name of, payable to the order of, or specially indorsed to the other person and has not been indorsed to the securities intermediary or in blank, the other person is treated as holding the financial asset directly rather than as having a security entitlement with respect to the financial asset.

（e）证券的发行，本身不能证明证券权利。

（e）Issuance of a security is not establishment of a security entitlement.

第 8.502 条　对权利持有人提出对立主张

§ 8.502. Assertion of Adverse Claim Against Entitlement Holder.

就金融资产提起的对立主张诉讼，无论是基于侵占、取回权、推定信托、衡平留置权或其他理论，均不能对抗根据第 8.501 条通过支付价值取得

An action based on an adverse claim to a financial asset, whether framed in conversion, replevin, constructive trust, equitable lien, or other theory, may not be asserted against a person who acquires a security entitlement

证券权利且未得到对立主张通知的人。

under Section 8.501 for value and without notice of the adverse claim.

第 8.503 条　权利持有人对证券中间人持有的金融资产享有财产权益

§ 8.503. Property Interest of Entitlement Holder in Financial Asset Held by Securities Intermediary.

（a）为使证券中间人能够就一项特定金融资产项下的全部证券权利作出清偿，证券中间人对该金融资产所持有的全部权益，均应被视为代表权利持有人持有，而不属于证券中间人的财产。因此，除第 8.511 条另有规定外，该权益不得用于清偿证券中间人的债权人。

（a）To the extent necessary for a securities intermediary to satisfy all security entitlements with respect to a particular financial asset, all interests in that financial asset held by the securities intermediary are held by the securities intermediary for the entitlement holders, are not property of the securities intermediary, and are not subject to claims of creditors of the securities intermediary, except as otherwise provided in Section 8.511.

（b）对于证券中间人持有的特定金融资产，权利持有人根据（a）款对该特定金融资产享有的财产权益，是该金融资产中全部权益按比例计算的财产权益，无论权利持有人何时取得证券权利，也无论证券中间人何时对金融资产取得权益。

（b）An entitlement holder's property interest with respect to a particular financial asset under Subsection（a）is a pro rata property interest in all interests in that financial asset held by the securities intermediary, without regard to the time the entitlement holder acquired the security entitlement or the time the securities intermediary acquired the interest in that financial asset.

（c）权利持有人根据（a）款对特定金融资产享有的财产权益，仅可通过行使权利持有人在第 8.505 条至第 8.508 条项下的权利，对证券中间人强制履行。

（c）An entitlement holder's property interest with respect to a particular financial asset under Subsection（a）may be enforced against the securities intermediary only by exercise of the entitlement holder's rights under Sections 8.505-8.508.

（d）权利持有人根据（a）款对特定金融资产享有的财产权益，只有在下列情况下，才

（d）An entitlement holder's property interest with respect to a particular financial asset under Subsection（a）may be enforced

可对金融资产或其权益的购买人强制履行：

against a purchaser of the financial asset or interest therein only if:

（1）证券中间人已提起或已被提起破产申请；

（1）insolvency proceedings have been initiated by or against the securities intermediary;

（2）证券中间人对金融资产的权益，已不能充分满足全部权利持有人对金融资产的证券权利；

（2）the securities intermediary does not have sufficient interests in the financial asset to satisfy the security entitlements of all of its entitlement holders to that financial asset;

（3）证券中间人将金融资产或其权益转让给该购买人的行为，违反了证券中间人在第8.504条项下的义务；并且

（3）the securities intermediary violated its obligations under Section 8.504 by transferring the financial asset or interest therein to the purchaser;and

（4）该购买人不受（f）款的保护。

（4）the purchaser is not protected under Subsection（f）.

（e）受托人或其他清算人可以代表对特定金融资产享有证券权利的全部权利持有人，向该购买人追索该金融资产或其权益。如果该受托人或其他清算人放弃行使该权利，则任何权利持有人均可在其证券权利未得到充分满足的情况下，就其在金融资产中的权益向该购买人索赔。

（e）The trustee or other liquidator, acting on behalf of all entitlement holders having security entitlements with respect to a particular financial asset, may recover the financial asset, or interest therein, from the purchaser.If the trustee or other liquidator elects not to pursue that right, an entitlement holder whose security entitlement remains unsatisfied has the right to recover its interest in the financial asset from the purchaser.

（f）权利持有人根据（a）款项下对金融资产之财产权益所提起的诉讼，无论是基于侵占、取回权、推定信托、衡平留置权还是其他理论，在任何购买人支付了价值，取得了控制，且未与证券中间人合谋违反证券中间人在第8.504条项

（f）An action based on the entitlement holder's property interest with respect to a particular financial asset under Subsection（a）, whether framed in conversion, replevin, constructive trust, equitable lien, or other theory, may not be asserted against any purchaser of a financial asset or interest therein who gives value, obtains control, and does not

下之义务的情况下，即不能对抗金融资产或其权益的该购买人。

act in collusion with the securities intermediary in violating the securities intermediary's obligations under Section 8.504.

第 8.504 条 证券中间人掌管金融资产的义务

§ 8.504. Duty of Securities Intermediary to Maintain Financial Asset.

（a）证券中间人为其权利持有人设立证券权利后，应根据全部证券权利的总和，迅即取得相应数量的金融资产并掌管该资产。证券中间人可以直接掌管该金融资产，也可以通过一个或多个其他证券中间人掌管。

（a）A securities intermediary shall promptly obtain and thereafter maintain a financial asset in a quantity corresponding to the aggregate of all security entitlements it has established in favor of its entitlement holders with respect to that financial asset.The securities intermediary may maintain those financial assets directly or through one or more other securities intermediaries.

（b）对于证券中间人根据（a）款有义务掌管的金融资产，证券中间人不得向他人赋予该资产中的任何证券权利，除非得到其权利持有人的另行同意。

（b）Except to the extent otherwise agreed on by its entitlement holder, a securities intermediary may not grant any security interests in a financial asset it is obligated to maintain pursuant to Subsection（a）.

（c）证券中间人在下列情况下被视为满足（a）款的要求：

（c）A securities intermediary satisfies the duty in Subsection（a）if:

（1）证券中间人根据与权利持有人达成的协议履行了义务；或

（1）the securities intermediary acts with respect to the duty as agreed on by the entitlement holder and the securities intermediary;or

（2）在没有协议的情况下，证券中间人根据合理的商业标准，对于金融资产的取得和掌管，行使了适当谨慎。

（2）in the absence of agreement, the securities intermediary exercises due care in accordance with reasonable commercial standards to obtain and maintain the financial asset.

（d）如果清算公司本身系认购权或类似义务的义务人，且清算公司的权利持有人对该

（d）This section does not apply to a clearing corporation that is itself the obligor of an option or similar obligation to which its

义务持有证券权利，则本条不适用于该清算公司。

entitlement holders have security entitlements.

第 8.505 条 证券中间人对于付款和分红的义务

§ 8.505. Duty of Securities Intermediary With Respect to Payments and Distributions.

（a）证券中间人应采取相应行动，获取金融资产发行人作出的付款或分红。在下列情况下，证券中间人被视为履行了该义务：

（a）A securities intermediary shall take action to obtain a payment or distribution made by the issuer of a financial asset.A securities intermediary satisfies the duty if:

（1）证券中间人根据与权利持有人达成的协议履行了义务；或

（1）the securities intermediary acts with respect to the duty as agreed on by the entitlement holder and the securities intermediary;or

（2）在没有协议的情况下，证券中间人根据合理的商业标准，对于付款或分红的获取，行使了适当谨慎。

（2）in the absence of agreement, the securities intermediary exercises due care in accordance with reasonable commercial standards to attempt to obtain the payment or distribution.

（b）证券中间人在收到金融资产发行人作出的付款或分红后，即就该付款或分红向权利持有人承担义务。

（b）A securities intermediary is obligated to its entitlement holder for a payment or distribution made by the issuer of a financial asset if the payment or distribution is received by the securities intermediary.

第 8.506 条 证券中间人根据权利持有人之指示行使权利的义务

§ 8.506. Duty of Securities Intermediary to Exercise Rights as Directed by Entitlement Holder.

证券中间人在收到权利持有人的指示后，应根据该指示行使对金融资产的权利。在下列情况下，证券中间人被视为履行了该义务：

A securities intermediary shall exercise rights with respect to a financial asset if directed to do so by an entitlement holder.A securities intermediary satisfies the duty if:

（1）证券中间人根据与权利持有人达成的协议履行了义

（1）the securities intermediary acts with respect to the duty as agreed on by

务；或

the entitlement holder and the securities intermediary;or

（2）在没有协议的情况下，证券中间人将权利持有人置于可以直接行使该权利的地位，或根据合理的商业标准，对于遵从权利持有人的指示，行使了适当谨慎。

（2）in the absence of agreement, the securities intermediary either places the entitlement holder in a position to exercise the rights directly or exercises due care in accordance with reasonable commercial standards to follow the direction of the entitlement holder.

第 8.507 条　证券中间人遵从权利命令的义务

§ 8.507. Duty of Securities Intermediary to Comply With Entitlement Order.

（a）证券中间人应遵从适格人发起的权利命令，只要证券中间人已有合理机会确认该权利命令系属真实且业经授权，且证券中间人有合理机会据以作为。在下列情况下，证券中间人被视为履行了该义务：

（a）A securities intermediary shall comply with an entitlement order if the entitlement order is originated by the appropriate person, the securities intermediary has had reasonable opportunity to assure itself that the entitlement order is genuine and authorized, and the securities intermediary has had reasonable opportunity to comply with the entitlement order.A securities intermediary satisfies the duty if:

（1）证券中间人根据与权利持有人达成的协议履行了义务；或

（1）the securities intermediary acts with respect to the duty as agreed on by the entitlement holder and the securities intermediary;or

（2）在没有协议的情况下，证券中间人根据合理的商业标准，对于遵从权利命令，行使了适当谨慎。

（2）in the absence of agreement, the securities intermediary exercises due care in accordance with reasonable commercial standards to comply with the entitlement order.

（b）证券中间人如果根据无效的权利命令转让金融资产，即应为金融资产的权利人重新设立证券权利。如果错误转让致使该人未收到付款或分红，

（b）If a securities intermediary transfers a financial asset pursuant to an ineffective entitlement order, the securities intermediary shall reestablish a security entitlement in favor of the person entitled to it and pay or credit

证券中间人应向该人付款或提供贷记。证券中间人如果不重新设立证券权利，即应向权利持有人就其受到的损失作出赔偿。

any payments or distributions that the person did not receive as a result of the wrongful transfer.If the securities intermediary does not reestablish a security entitlement, the securities intermediary is liable to the entitlement holder for damages.

第 8.508 条 证券中间人有义务变更权利持有人地位至其他形式的证券持有

证券中间人应根据权利持有人的指示，将该持有人的证券权利，变更为该权利持有人有权使用并且可行的其他持有方式，或将金融资产转让至权利持有人在其他证券中间人的证券账户。在下列情况下，证券中间人被视为履行了该义务：

（1）证券中间人根据与权利持有人达成的协议履行了义务；或

（2）在没有协议的情况下，证券中间人根据合理的商业标准，对于遵从权利持有人的指示，行使了适当谨慎。

§ 8.508. Duty of Securities Intermediary to Change Entitlement Holder's Position to Other Form of Security Holding.

A securities intermediary shall act at the direction of an entitlement holder to change a security entitlement into another available form of holding for which the entitlement holder is eligible or to cause the financial asset to be transferred to a securities account of the entitlement holder with another securities intermediary.A securities intermediary satisfies the duty if:

（1）the securities intermediary acts as agreed on by the entitlement holder and the securities intermediary;or

（2）in the absence of agreement, the securities intermediary exercises due care in accordance with reasonable commercial standards to follow the direction of the entitlement holder.

第 8.509 条 其他法律或规则对证券中间人义务的规定；证券中间人履行义务的方式；权利持有人行使权利的方式

（a）涉及证券中间人在第 8.504 条至第 8.508 条项下的义务时，如果其实质内容在其他

§ 8.509. Specification of Duties of Securities Intermediary by Other Statute or Regulation;Manner of Performance of Duties of Securities Intermediary and Exercise of Rights of Entitlement Holder.

（a）If the substance of a duty imposed on a securities intermediary by Sections 8.504-8.508 is the subject of another statute,

法律或规则中亦有规定，则只要遵守了该法律或规则，证券中间人即被视为履行了该义务。

regulation, or rule, compliance with that statute, regulation, or rule satisfies the duty.

（b）如果该其他法律或规则，或证券中间人与权利持有人之间的协议，未对证券中间人履行义务或权利持有人行使权利的具体标准作出规定，则证券中间人应按商业上合理的方式履行义务，而权利持有人应按商业上合理的方式行使权利。

（b）To the extent that specific standards for the performance of the duties of a securities intermediary or the exercise of the rights of an entitlement holder are not specified by another statute, regulation, or rule or by agreement between the securities intermediary and the entitlement holder, the securities intermediary shall perform its duties and the entitlement holder shall exercise its rights in a commercially reasonable manner.

（c）证券中间人在履行第8.504条至第8.508条规定的义务时，该义务受制于证券中间人的下列权利：

（c）The obligation of a securities intermediary to perform the duties imposed by Sections 8.504-8.508 is subject to:

（1）基于与权利持有人达成之担保协议或基于其他原因，证券中间人就担保权益享有的权利；以及

（1）rights of the securities intermediary arising out of a security interest under a security agreement with the entitlement holder or otherwise;and

（2）根据其他法律或规则，或根据协议，在权利持有人未能向证券中间人履行义务时，证券中间人暂停履行自己义务的权利。

（2）rights of the securities intermediary under another law, regulation, rule, or agreement to withhold performance of its duties as a result of unfulfilled obligations of the entitlement holder to the securities intermediary.

（d）第8.504条至第8.508条并不要求证券中间人采取被其他法律或规则禁止的行为。

（d）Sections 8.504-8.508 do not require a securities intermediary to take any action that is prohibited by another statute, regulation, or rule.

第8.510条　从权利持有人处取得证券权利之购买人的权利

§ 8.510. Rights of Purchaser of Security Entitlement From Entitlement Holder.

（a）如果不涉及第9篇优

（a）In a case not covered by the priority

先权规则范围内或（c）款范围内的情况，则就金融资产或证券权利提起的对立主张诉讼，无论是基于侵占、取回权、推定信托、衡平留置权还是其他理论，在购买人支付了价值，未得到对立主张的通知，并取得了控制的情况下，均不能对抗从权利持有人取得证券权利或其中权益的购买人。

rules in Article 9 or the rules stated in Subsection（c）, an action based on an adverse claim to a financial asset or security entitlement, whether framed in conversion, replevin, constructive trust, equitable lien, or other theory, may not be asserted against a person who purchases a security entitlement, or an interest therein, from an entitlement holder if the purchaser gives value, does not have notice of the adverse claim, and obtains control.

（b）如果原本无权根据第8.502条对权利持有人提出对立主张，则对于从该权利持有人购买证券权利或其中权益的人，亦无权对其提出对立主张。

（b）If an adverse claim could not have been asserted against an entitlement holder under Section 8.502, the adverse claim cannot be asserted against a person who purchases from the entitlement holder a security entitlement or an interest therein.

（c）如果不涉及第9篇优先权规则范围内的情况，证券权利或其中权益的购买人，只要支付了价值并取得控制，在对抗购买了证券权利或其中权益但未取得控制的购买人时，前者享有优先权。除（d）款另有规定外，在已取得控制的各个购买人之间，优先权的先后顺序，应根据下列时间的先后顺序确定：

（c）In a case not covered by the priority rules in Article 9, a purchaser for value of a security entitlement, or an interest therein, who obtains control has priority over a purchaser of a security entitlement, or an interest therein, who does not obtain control.Except as otherwise provided in Subsection（d）, purchasers who have control rank according to priority in time of:

（1）如果购买人根据第8.106条（d）（1）款取得控制，应根据购买人成为证券权利所在之证券账户受益人的时间确定；

（1）the purchaser's becoming the person for whom the securities account, in which the security entitlement is carried, is maintained, if the purchaser obtained control under Section 8.106（d）（1）;

（2）如果购买人根据第8.106

（2）the securities intermediary's

条（d）（2）款取得控制，应根据证券中间人作出同意的时间确定，即同意就证券权利已经所在或即将所在之证券账户，遵从购买人的权利命令；或

agreement to comply with the purchaser's entitlement orders with respect to security entitlements carried or to be carried in the securities account in which the security entitlement is carried, if the purchaser obtained control under Section 8.106（d）（2）;or

（3）如果购买人根据第8.106条（d）（3）款从另一人取得控制，应根据该另一人假设为受担保方时，本款为其规定之优先权的顺序确定。

（3）if the purchaser obtained control through another person under Section 8.106（d）（3）, the time on which priority would be based under this subsection if the other person were the secured party.

（d）如果证券中间人系购买人，则其权利优于取得了控制的冲突购买人，除非该证券中间人另有约定。

（d）A securities intermediary as purchaser has priority over a conflicting purchaser who has control unless otherwise agreed on by the securities intermediary.

第8.511条 担保权益持有人与权利持有人之间的优先顺序

§ 8.511. Priority Among Security Interests and Entitlement Holders.

（a）除（b）款和（c）款另有规定外，如果证券中间人对特定金融资产的权益，不足以充分满足证券中间人对下列两类人的全部债务，即权利持有人对金融资产持有的证券权利，以及证券中间人之债权人对金融资产持有的担保权益，此时，权利持有人（债权人除外）的权利，优于债权人的权利。

（a）Except as otherwise provided in Subsections（b）and（c）, if a securities intermediary does not have sufficient interests in a particular financial asset to satisfy both its obligations to entitlement holders who have security entitlements to that financial asset and its obligation to a creditor of the securities intermediary who has a security interest in that financial asset, the claims of entitlement holders, other than the creditor, have priority over the claim of the creditor.

（b）涉及证券中间人持有的金融资产时，如果证券中间人的债权人就该金融资产持有担保权益，而证券权利人就该金融资产持有证券权利，此时，

（b）A claim of a creditor of a securities intermediary who has a security interest in a financial asset held by a securities intermediary has priority over claims of the securities intermediary's entitlement holders who have

只要债权人对金融资产拥有控制，债权人的权利即享有优先权。

（c）如果清算公司的金融资产，不足以充分满足其对下列两类人的全部债务，即权利持有人对金融资产持有的证券权利，以及清算公司之债权人对金融资产持有的担保权益，此时，债权人的权利优于权利持有人的权利。

security entitlements with respect to that financial asset if the creditor has control over the financial asset.

（c）If a clearing corporation does not have sufficient financial assets to satisfy both its obligations to entitlement holders who have security entitlements with respect to a financial asset and its obligation to a creditor of the clearing corporation who has a security interest in that financial asset, the claim of the creditor has priority over the claims of entitlement holders.

词汇索引

续表

证券账户	securities account	第 8.501 条（a）
证券证书	security certificate	第 8.102 条（a）（16）
证券中间人	securities intermediary	第 8.102 条（a）（14）
指示	instruction	第 8.102 条（a）（12）

第9篇　担保交易

ARTICLE 9. SECURED TRANSACTIONS

第1章　简称、定义和一般概念

PART 1. SHORT TITLE, DEFINITIONS, AND GENERAL CONCEPTS

第 9.101 条　简称

本篇被引用时可称为《统一商法典——担保交易》。

第 9.102 条　定义和定义索引

（a）在本篇中：

（1）“添附物”指以物理方式与其他货物结合的货物，且在结合后，原有货物并不丧失其本身特征。

（2）“应收款”指基于下列原因而取得的就金钱债务收款的权利，无论该权利是否已通过履约赚取：（i）出售、出租、许可、转让或以其他方式处置财产，无论已经作出或将要作出；（ii）提供服务，无论已经提供或将要提供；（iii）出具保险单，无论已经出具或将要出具；（iv）承担次级义务，无论

§ 9.101. Short Title.

This Article may be cited as Uniform Commercial Code— Secured Transactions.

§ 9.102. Definitions and Index of Definitions.

（a）In this Article:

（1）“Accession” means goods that are physically united with other goods in such a manner that the identity of the original goods is not lost.

（2）“Account,” except as used in “account for,” means a right to payment of a monetary obligation, whether or not earned by performance,（i）for property that has been or is to be sold, leased, licensed, assigned, or otherwise disposed of,（ii）for services rendered or to be rendered,（iii）for a policy of insurance issued or to be issued,（iv）for a secondary obligation incurred or to be incurred,（v）for energy provided or to be provided,（vi）for the

已经承担或将要承担；(v) 提供能源，无论已经提供或将要提供；(vi) 根据包租合同或其他合同，提供船舶的使用或租用；(vii) 信用卡或借记卡的使用，或其中信息的使用，或与该卡结合使用之信息的使用，或 (viii) 抽彩或其他靠概率取胜之游戏的中奖，只要该抽彩或游戏系由州政府组织或发起，或由州政府许可或授权经营该抽彩或游戏之人组织或发起。“应收款”包括医疗保险应收款。“应收款”不包括：(i) 由动产契据或票据证明的收款权利；(ii) 商业侵权索赔；(iii) 存款账户；(iv) 投资财产；(v) 信用证权利或信用证；或 (vi) 因出借或出售金钱或资金而取得的收款权利，但基于下列活动产生的收款权利除外：信用卡或借记卡的使用，或其中信息的使用，或与该卡结合使用之信息的使用。

use or hire of a vessel under a charter or other contract, (vii) arising out of the use of a credit or charge card or information contained on or for use with the card, or (viii) as winnings in a lottery or other game of chance operated or sponsored by a state, governmental unit of a state, or person licensed or authorized to operate the game by a state or governmental unit of a state.The term includes health-care-insurance receivables.The term does not include (i) rights to payment evidenced by chattel paper or an instrument, (ii) commercial tort claims, (iii) deposit accounts, (iv) investment property, (v) letter-of-credit rights or letters of credit, or (vi) rights to payment for money or funds advanced or sold, other than rights arising out of the use of a credit or charge card or information contained on or for use with the card.

(3)“应收款债务人”指就应收款、动产契据或一般无形财产承担义务的人，但不包括有义务支付流通票据的人，即使该票据构成动产契据的一部分。

(3) “Account debtor” means a person obligated on an account, chattel paper, or general intangible.The term does not include persons obligated to pay a negotiable instrument, even if the instrument constitutes part of chattel paper.

(4)“账目”指下列记录：

(4) “Accounting,” except as used in “accounting for,” means a record:

(A) 业经受担保方认证；

(A) authenticated by a secured party;

(B) 标明至某日为止的未

(B) indicating the aggregate unpaid

偿担保债务总额，只要该日不早于或不晚于记录日35天以上；以及

secured obligations as of a date not more than 35 days earlier or 35 days later than the date of the record;and

（C）以合理细节说明债务的构成内容。

（C）identifying the components of the obligations in reasonable detail.

（5）“农业留置权”指农产品中的下列权益：

（5）“Agricultural lien” means an interest in farm products:

（A）该权益系为担保基于下列原因产生的付款或履约义务：

（A）that secures payment or performance of an obligation for:

（i）债务人为自己的农业生产获得了货物或服务；或

（i）goods or services furnished in connection with a debtor's farming operation;or

（ii）债务人为自己的农业生产租用了不动产并应支付租金；

（ii）rent on real property leased by a debtor in connection with its farming operation;

（B）该权益系为下列人的利益依法自动产生：

（B）that is created by statute in favor of a person that:

（i）在正常业务活动中，为债务人的农业生产，向债务人提供货物或服务的人；或

（i）in the ordinary course of its business furnished goods or services to a debtor in connection with a debtor's farming operation;or

（ii）将不动产出租给债务人，用于债务人之农业生产的人；并且

（ii）leased real property to a debtor in connection with the debtor's farming operation;and

（C）该权益的有效性不取决于上述人是否占有相关动产。

（C）whose effectiveness does not depend on the person's possession of the personal property.

（6）“开采状担保物”指：

（6）“As-extracted collateral” means:

（A）受下列担保权益约束的石油、天然气或其他矿物：

（A）oil, gas, or other minerals that are subject to a security interest that:

（i）设立担保权益之债务人在开采前即对矿物持有权益；并且

（i）is created by a debtor having an interest in the minerals before extraction;and

（ii）担保权益在矿物开采

（ii）attaches to the minerals as extracted;or

后立即发生附着；或

（B）在井口或矿口销售石油、天然气或其他矿物所产生的应收款，且债务人在开采前即对矿物持有权益。

（B）accounts arising out of the sale at the wellhead or minehead of oil, gas, or other minerals in which the debtor had an interest before extraction.

（7）“认证”指：

（7）“Authenticate” means:

（A）签名；或

（A）to sign;or

（B）作出一项符号或以其他方式采纳一项符号，或对一项记录的整体或任何部分进行加密处理或作出类似处理，且认证人当时具有证明自己身份并采纳或接受一项记录的意图。

（B）to execute or otherwise adopt a symbol, or encrypt or similarly process a record in whole or in part, with the present intent of the authenticating person to identify the person and adopt or accept a record.

（8）“银行”指从事银行业务的组织，包括储蓄银行、储贷协会、信贷合作社和信托公司。

（8）“Bank” means an organization that is engaged in the business of banking.The term includes savings banks, savings and loan associations, credit unions, and trust companies.

（9）“现金收益”指以金钱、支票、存款账户或类似形式存在的收益。

（9）“Cash proceeds” means proceeds that are money, checks, deposit accounts, or the like.

（10）“产权证书”指下列产权证书：根据法律规定，相关担保权益必须记录在该证书上，并以此作为担保权益就担保物取得优于留置权债权人之权利的前提条件，或作为担保权益取得该优先权后必须完成的手续。

（10）“Certificate of title” means a certificate of title with respect to which a statute provides for the security interest in question to be indicated on the certificate as a condition or result of the security interest's obtaining priority over the rights of a lien creditor with respect to the collateral.

（11）“动产契据”指同时证明金钱债务和下列任何一项内容的记录：特定货物中的担保权益；特定货物中以及该货物所使用之软件中的担保权益；

（11）“Chattel paper” means a record or records that evidence both a monetary obligation and a security interest in specific goods, a security interest in specific goods and software used in the goods, a security interest

特定货物中的担保权益以及该货物所使用之软件的许可；特定货物的租赁；特定货物的租赁以及该货物所使用之软件的许可。在本款中，“金钱债务”指以货物作为担保的金钱债务，或因货物租赁承担的金钱债务，也包括货物所使用之软件引起的金钱债务。“金钱债务”不包括（i）使用或租用船舶之包租合同或其他合同，或（ii）证明收款权利的记录，如果该权利产生于信用卡或借记卡的使用，或其中信息的使用，或与该卡结合使用之信息的使用。如果多项记录共同证明一项交易，且记录中包括一项或一系列票据，则该多项记录共同构成动产契据。

in specific goods and license of software used in the goods, a lease of specific goods, or a lease of specific goods and license of software used in the goods.In this subdivision, “monetary obligation” means a monetary obligation secured by the goods or owed under a lease of the goods and includes a monetary obligation with respect to software used in the goods. The term does not include（i）charters or other contracts involving the use or hire of a vessel or（ii）records that evidence a right to payment arising out of the use of a credit or charge card or information contained on or for use with the card.If a transaction is evidenced by records that include an instrument or series of instruments, the group of records taken together constitutes chattel paper.

（12）“担保物”指设有担保权益或农业留置权的财产。“担保物”包括：

（A）担保权益所附着的收益；

（B）已出售的应收款、动产契据、无形支付或本票；以及

（C）处于寄售状态的货物。

（12）“Collateral” means the property subject to a security interest or agricultural lien. The term includes:

（A）proceeds to which a security interest attaches;

（B）accounts, chattel paper, payment intangibles, and promissory notes that have been sold;and

（C）goods that are the subject of a consignment.

（13）“商业侵权索赔”指下列侵权索赔：

（A）索赔人是组织；或

（B）索赔人是个人，但该

（13）“Commercial tort claim” means a claim arising in tort with respect to which:

（A）the claimant is an organization;or

（B）the claimant is an individual and the

索赔：

（i）发生在索赔人业务或专业活动中；并且

（ii）不涉及因人身伤害或死亡引起的损害赔偿。

claim:

(i) arose in the course of the claimant's business or profession;and

(ii) does not include damages arising out of personal injury to or the death of an individual.

（14）"商品账户"指由商品中间人掌管，用于为商品客户记录商品合同的账户。

(14) "Commodity account" means an account maintained by a commodity intermediary in which a commodity contract is carried for a commodity customer.

（15）"商品合同"指商品期货合同、商品期货合同的期权、商品期权或其他合同，只要该合同或期权：

(15) "Commodity contract" means a commodity futures contract, an option on a commodity futures contract, a commodity option, or another contract if the contract or option is:

（A）在商品交易所买卖或受其规则约束，且根据联邦商品法，该交易所系该类合同的合约市场；或

（B）在外国商品交易所或交易市场买卖，且记录在商品中间人为商品客户设立的账册中。

(A) traded on or subject to the rules of a board of trade that has been designated as a contract market for such a contract pursuant to federal commodities laws;or

(B) traded on a foreign commodity board of trade, exchange, or market and is carried on the books of a commodity intermediary for a commodity customer.

（16）"商品客户"指商品中间人在自己账册中为其记录商品合同的人。

(16) "Commodity customer" means a person for which a commodity intermediary carries a commodity contract on its books.

（17）"商品中间人"指：

(17) "Commodity intermediary" means a person that:

（A）根据联邦商品法注册的收取期货佣金的商人；或

（B）在其正常业务中，为交易所提供清算或结算服务的人，且联邦商品法规定该交易

(A) is registered as a futures commission merchant under federal commodities law;or

(B) in the ordinary course of its business provides clearance or settlement services for a board of trade that has been designated

所系合约市场。

as a contract market pursuant to federal commodities law.

（18）“传送”指：

（A）发送书面或其他有形记录；

（B）按发送人和接收人同意的任何方式传送记录；或

（C）涉及融资声明登记处接收或发出的记录时，按登记处规则指定的任何方式传送记录。

（19）“寄售受托人”指接受寄售货物之交付的商人。

（20）“寄售”指任何人将货物交付给商人用于出售的交易（无论交易采用何种形式），且在该交易中：

（A）该商人：

（i）从事该类货物交易，且商号名字不同于货物交付人的名字；

（ii）不是拍卖人；并且

（iii）其债权人通常不知道其在很大程度上从事销售他人货物；

（B）每次交付的货物在交付时总值达到或超过 1000 美元；

（C）货物在即将交付之前不属于消费品；并且

（D）该交易不属于为担保一项债务而设立担保权益。

（21）“寄售委托人”指向

（18）“Communicate” means:

（A）to send a written or other tangible record;

（B）to transmit a record by any means agreed upon by the persons sending and receiving the record;or

（C）in the case of transmission of a record to or by a filing office, to transmit a record by any means prescribed by filing-office rule.

（19）“Consignee” means a merchant to which goods are delivered in a consignment.

（20）“Consignment” means a transaction, regardless of its form, in which a person delivers goods to a merchant for the purpose of sale and:

（A）the merchant:

（i）deals in goods of that kind under a name other than the name of the person making delivery;

（ii）is not an auctioneer;and

（iii）is not generally known by its creditors to be substantially engaged in selling the goods of others;

（B）with respect to each delivery, the aggregate value of the goods is $1,000 or more at the time of delivery;

（C）the goods are not consumer goods immediately before delivery;and

（D）the transaction does not create a security interest that secures an obligation.

（21）“Consignor” means a person that

寄售受托人交付用于寄售之货物的人。

delivers goods to a consignee in a consignment.

（22）“消费者债务人”指消费者交易中的债务人。

（22）“Consumer debtor” means a debtor in a consumer transaction.

（23）“消费品”指主要用于个人、家庭或家用的货物，或为此种使用而购买的货物。

（23）“Consumer goods” means goods that are used or bought for use primarily for personal, family, or household purposes.

（24）“消费品交易”指下列消费者交易：

（24）“Consumer-goods transaction” means a consumer transaction in which:

（A）个人主要为个人、家庭或家用目的承担债务；并且

（A）an individual incurs an obligation primarily for personal, family, or household purposes;and

（B）以消费品中的担保权益担保该债务。

（B）a security interest in consumer goods secures the obligation.

（25）“消费者义务人”指义务人是个人，且在主要为个人、家庭或家用目的进行的交易中，承担交易项下的债务。

（25）“Consumer obligor” means an obligor who is an individual and who incurred the obligation as part of a transaction entered into primarily for personal, family, or household purposes.

（26）“消费者交易”指下列交易：

（26）“Consumer transaction” means a transaction in which

（i）个人主要为个人、家庭或家用目的承担债务；

（i）an individual incurs an obligation primarily for personal, family, or household purposes,

（ii）债务由担保权益担保；以及

（ii）a security interest secures the obligation, and

（iii）主要出于个人、家庭或家用目的，持有或获取担保物。“消费者交易”包括消费品交易。

（iii）the collateral is held or acquired primarily for personal, family, or household purposes.The term includes consumer-goods transactions.

（27）“延展声明”指融资声明的下列修订文件：

（27）“Continuation statement” means an amendment of a financing statement that:

（A）使用档案号指明所涉

（A）identifies, by its file number, the initial

及的原始融资声明；并且

（B）说明是该融资声明的延展声明，或说明申报目的是延长融资声明的有效期。

financing statement to which it relates;and

（B）indicates that it is a continuation statement for, or that it is filed to continue the effectiveness of, the identified financing statement.

（28）“债务人”指：

（A）对担保物拥有权益（担保权益或其他留置权除外）的人，无论该人是否为义务人；

（B）应收款、动产契据、无形支付或本票的卖方；或

（C）寄售受托人。

（28）“Debtor” means:

（A）a person having an interest, other than a security interest or other lien, in the collateral, whether or not the person is an obligor;

（B）a seller of accounts, chattel paper, payment intangibles, or promissory notes;or

（C）a consignee.

（29）“存款账户”指由银行掌管的活期账户、定期账户、储蓄账户、存折账户或类似账户。“存款账户”也包括不可流通存款凭证，但不包括以票据证明的投资财产或账户。

（29）“Deposit account” means a demand, time, savings, passbook, or similar account maintained with a bank.The term includes a nonnegotiable certificate of deposit.The term does not include investment property or accounts evidenced by an instrument.

（30）“凭证”指所有权凭证或第 7.201 条（b）款所述的收据。

（30）“Document” means a document of title or a receipt of the type described in Section 7.201（b）.

（31）“电子动产契据”指证明该契据的记录系由储存在电子介质中的信息组成。

（31）“Electronic chattel paper” means chattel paper evidenced by a record or records consisting of information stored in an electronic medium.

（32）“不动产他项权”指除所有权外的不动产权利，包括不动产抵押权和其他不动产留置权。

（32）“Encumbrance” means a right, other than an ownership interest, in real property.The term includes mortgages and other liens on real property.

（33）“设备”指除库存、农产品和消费品外的货物。

（33）“Equipment” means goods other than inventory, farm products, or consumer goods.

（34）“农产品”指债务人在农业生产中经营的下列货物（生长中的树木除外）：

（34）“Farm products” means goods, other than standing timber, with respect to which the debtor is engaged in a farming operation and which are:

（A）已经种植、正在种植或将要种植的作物，包括：

（A）crops grown, growing, or to be grown, including:

（i）树木、藤木或灌木产出的作物；以及

（i）crops produced on trees, vines, and bushes;and

（ii）水产作业产出的水产品；

（ii）aquatic goods produced in aquacultural operations;

（B）已出生或待出生的家畜，包括水产作业产出的水产品；

（B）livestock, born or unborn, including aquatic goods produced in aquacultural operations;

（C）农业生产中使用的或产出的原料；或

（C）supplies used or produced in a farming operation;or

（D）未经加工的作物或家畜产品。

（D）products of crops or livestock in their unmanufactured states.

（35）“农业生产”指养育、种植、繁殖、催肥或放牧，以及其他的农业、家畜或水产经营。

（35）“Farming operation” means raising, cultivating, propagating, fattening, grazing, or any other farming, livestock, or aquacultural operation.

（36）“档案号”指根据第9.519条（a）款分配给原始融资声明的号码。

（36）“File number” means the number assigned to an initial financing statement pursuant to Section 9.519（a）.

（37）“登记处”指第9.501条规定的用于登记融资声明的办公处所。

（37）“Filing office” means an office designated in Section 9.501 as the place to file a financing statement.

（38）“登记处规则”指根据第9.526条制定的规则。

（38）“Filing-office rule” means a rule adopted pursuant to Section 9.526.

（39）“融资声明”指由原始融资声明及登记在案的涉及该声明之其他记录组成的记录总和。

（39）“Financing statement” means a record or records composed of an initial financing statement and any filed record relating to the initial financing statement.

（40）“不动产附着物登记”指所登记的融资声明覆盖已经成为或将要成为不动产附着物的货物，并满足第 9.502 条（a）款和（b）款的规定。“不动产附着物登记”也指所登记的融资声明覆盖公用事业传输企业的货物，且该货物已经成为或将要成为不动产附着物。

（40）“Fixture filing” means the filing of a financing statement covering goods that are or are to become fixtures and satisfying Sections 9.502（a）and（b）.The term includes the filing of a financing statement covering goods of a transmitting utility that are or are to become fixtures.

（41）“不动产附着物”指与特定不动产发生紧密联系的货物，且该联系致使货物中的权益在不动产所在地受不动产法的约束。

（41）“Fixtures” means goods that have become so related to particular real property that an interest in them arises under the real property law of the state in which the real property is situated.

（42）“一般无形财产”指包括诉权在内的除下列财产外的任何动产：应收款、动产契据、商业侵权索赔、存款账户、凭证、货物、票据、投资财产、信用证权利、信用证或金钱，或尚未开采的石油、天然气或其他矿物。“一般无形财产”包括无形支付和软件。

（42）“General intangible” means any personal property, including things in action, other than accounts, chattel paper, commercial tort claims, deposit accounts, documents, goods, instruments, investment property, letter-of-credit rights, letters of credit, money, and oil, gas, or other minerals before extraction. The term includes payment intangibles and software.

（43）[保留]

（43）[Reserved]

（44）“货物”指在担保权益发生附着时可以移动的所有物品。“货物”包括：

（44）“Goods” means all things that are movable when a security interest attaches.The term includes

（i）不动产附着物；

（i）fixtures,

（ii）生长中的树木，只要根据不动产转让合同或买卖合同，树木将被砍伐和移走；

（ii）standing timber that is to be cut and removed under a conveyance or contract for sale,

（iii）动物待出生的幼仔；

（iii）the unborn young of animals,

（iv）已经种植、正在种植

（iv）crops grown, growing, or to be grown,

或将要种植的作物，即使其生长于树木、藤木或灌木上；以及

even if the crops are produced on trees, vines, or bushes, and

（v）工厂预制房屋。

（v）manufactured homes.

“货物”也包括植入货物的计算机软件，以及软件交易中提供的支持性信息，只要：

The term also includes a computer program embedded in goods and any supporting information provided in connection with a transaction relating to the program if

（i）根据软件与货物的结合方式，习惯上认为软件构成货物的组成部分；或

（i）the program is associated with the goods in such a manner that it customarily is considered part of the goods, or

（ii）取得货物所有权的人，同时取得与货物有关之软件的使用权。

（ii）by becoming the owner of the goods, a person acquires a right to use the program in connection with the goods.

如果包含计算机软件的货物，仅系软件安装的介质，则该计算机软件不属于“货物”。“货物”也不包括应收款、动产契据、商业侵权索赔、存款账户、凭证、一般无形财产、票据、投资财产、信用证权利、信用证或金钱，或尚未开采的石油、天然气或其他矿物。

The term does not include a computer program embedded in goods that consist solely of the medium in which the program is embedded.The term also does not include accounts, chattel paper, commercial tort claims, deposit accounts, documents, general intangibles, instruments, investment property, letter-of-credit rights, letters of credit, money, or oil, gas, or other minerals before extraction.

（45）“政府机构”指美国联邦政府、州政府或外国政府的任何部门、机构、县、区、市或其他组织。“政府机构”也包括具有独立公司身份的组织，只要该组织根据美国联邦法律，有权发行豁免所得税的债券。

（45）“Governmental unit” means a subdivision, agency, department, county, parish, municipality, or other unit of the government of the United States, a state, or a foreign country. The term includes an organization having a separate corporate existence if the organization is eligible to issue debt on which interest is exempt from income taxation under the laws of the United States.

（46）“医疗保险应收款”

（46）“Health care insurance receivable”

指相关保险单项下的权益或索赔权，即基于已经提供或即将提供的医疗产品或服务，就金钱债务获得付款的权利。

means an interest in or claim under a policy of insurance that is a right to payment of a monetary obligation for health care goods or services provided or to be provided.

（47）“票据”指流通票据，或下列其他书面文件：证明有权就金钱债务获得付款的文件，且文件本身不属于担保协议或租约，且文件的类型系在正常业务过程中，可在完成必要背书或转让手续后，通过交付进行转让。“票据”不包括：

（47）“Instrument” means a negotiable instrument or any other writing that evidences a right to the payment of a monetary obligation, is not itself a security agreement or lease, and is of a type that in ordinary course of business is transferred by delivery with any necessary indorsement or assignment.The term does not include

（i）投资财产；

（i）investment property,

（ii）信用证；

（ii）letters of credit,

（iii）证明有权获得付款的书面文件，且该权利产生于信用卡或借记卡的使用，或其中信息的使用，或与该卡结合使用之信息的使用；或

（iii）writings that evidence a right to payment arising out of the use of a credit or charge card or information contained on or for use with the card, or

（iv）不可流通存款凭证。

（iv）nonnegotiable certificates of deposit.

（48）“库存”指除农产品外的下列货物：

（48）“Inventory” means goods, other than farm products, that:

（A）任何人作为出租方出租的货物；

（A）are leased by a person as lessor;

（B）任何人持有的用于出售或出租的货物，或用于服务合同项下向他人供应的货物；

（B）are held by a person for sale or lease or to be furnished under a contract of service;

（C）任何人根据服务合同向他人供应的货物；或

（C）are furnished by a person under a contract of service;or

（D）属于原料或半成品的货物，或属于业务中使用或消耗的材料。

（D）consist of raw materials, work in process, or materials used or consumed in a business.

（49）“投资财产”指证券（包

（49）“Investment property” means a

括票式证券和无票证券）、证券权利、证券账户、商品合同或商品账户。

security, whether certificated or uncertificated, security entitlement, securities account, commodity contract, or commodity account.

（50）涉及注册成立的组织时，“注册成立州”指该组织系根据该州的法律注册成立。

（50）“Jurisdiction of organization,” with respect to a registered organization, means the jurisdiction under whose law the organization is organized.

（51）“信用证权利”指信用证项下获得付款或履约的权利，无论受益人是否已要求行使该权利，也无论受益人当时是否有权提出该要求。受益人就信用证项下之付款或履约提出要求的权利，本身不属于“信用证权利”。

（51）“Letter-of-credit right” means a right to payment or performance under a letter of credit, whether or not the beneficiary has demanded or is at the time entitled to demand payment or performance.The term does not include the right of a beneficiary to demand payment or performance under a letter of credit.

（52）“留置权债权人”指：

（A）通过扣押、查封或类似程序，对财产取得留置权的债权人；

（B）为债权人利益所作之转让中的受让人（从转让时起）；

（C）破产案件中的受托人（从破产申请日起）；或

（D）衡平法中的接收人（从任命时起）。

（52）“Lien creditor” means:

（A）a creditor that has acquired a lien on the property involved by attachment, levy, or the like;

（B）an assignee for benefit of creditors from the time of assignment;

（C）a trustee in bankruptcy from the date of the filing of the petition;or

（D）a receiver in equity from the time of appointment.

（53）“工厂预制房屋”指可以整体或分成不同部位运输的结构，其在运输时主体的宽度为 8 英尺或以上，长度为 40 英尺或以上，或其在场地安装后，主体的面积为 320 平方英尺或以上，且该结构建于永久性底架之上，但可以有也可以

（53）“Manufactured home” means a structure, transportable in one or more sections, that, in the traveling mode, is eight body feet or more in width or 40 body feet or more in length, or, when erected on site, is 320 or more square feet, and that is built on a permanent chassis and designed to be used as a dwelling with or without a permanent foundation when

没有永久性地基；其设计目的是连接到必要公用设施上作为住宅使用，并内含上下水、取暖、空调和电气系统。“工厂预制房屋”也包括符合本款除尺寸外全部要求的其他任何结构，只要制造商按美国住房及城市发展部部长的规定，自愿进行注册登记，并满足美国法典第42章规定的标准。

connected to the required utilities, and includes the plumbing, heating, air-conditioning, and electrical systems contained therein.The term includes any structure that meets all of the requirements of this subdivision except the size requirements and with respect to which the manufacturer voluntarily files a certification required by the United States secretary of housing and urban development and complies with the standards established under Title 42 of the United States Code.

（54）“工厂预制房屋交易”指：

（54）“Manufactured-home transaction” means a secured transaction:

（A）在工厂预制房屋（作为库存的工厂预制房屋除外）上设立价款担保权益的担保交易；或

（A）that creates a purchase-money security interest in a manufactured home, other than a manufactured home held as inventory;or

（B）将工厂预制房屋（作为库存的工厂预制房屋除外）作为主要担保物的担保交易。

（B）in which a manufactured home, other than a manufactured home held as inventory, is the primary collateral.

（55）“不动产抵押权”指作为付款或履约义务的担保，在不动产（包括不动产附着物）上通过约定而设立的权益。

（55）“Mortgage” means a consensual interest in real property, including fixtures, that secures payment or performance of an obligation.

（56）“新债务人”指涉及另一人之前签订的担保协议时，根据第9.203条（d）款成为受该担保协议约束之债务人的人。

（56）“New debtor” means a person that becomes bound as debtor under Section 9.203（d）by a security agreement previously entered into by another person.

（57）“新价值”指：

（i）金钱；

（ii）财产、服务或新信贷的金钱价值；或

（57）“New value” means

（i）money,

（ii）money’s worth in property, services, or new credit, or

（iii）获得财产权益转让之受让人对该财产权益的放弃。“新价值”不包括用于代替另一项债务的债务。

（iii）release by a transferee of an interest in property previously transferred to the transferee. The term does not include an obligation substituted for another obligation.

（58）“非现金收益”指除现金收益外的收益。

（58）“Noncash proceeds” means proceeds other than cash proceeds.

（59）“不可流通存款凭证”指银行签署的下列书面文件：

（59）“Nonnegotiable certificate of deposit” means a writing signed by a bank that:

（A）文件表面注明系存款凭证（如第3.104条所定义）或入账收据；

（A）states on its face that it is a certificate of deposit, as defined in Section 3.104, or receipt for a book entry;

（B）文件确认银行收到一定数额的金钱，且附有明示协议或默示协议，即银行有义务归还该数额的金钱；以及

（B）contains an acknowledgement that a sum of money has been received by the bank, with an express or implied agreement that the bank will repay the sum of money;and

（C）文件不属于流通票据。

（C）is not a negotiable instrument.

（60）涉及由担保物中担保权益或农业留置权所担保的债务时，“义务人”指：

（60）“Obligor” means a person that, with respect to an obligation secured by a security interest in or an agricultural lien on the collateral,

（i）承担付款或履约义务的人；

（i）owes payment or other performance of the obligation,

（ii）为担保该付款或履约义务，提供除担保物外其他财产的人；或

（ii）has provided property other than the collateral to secure payment or other performance of the obligation, or

（iii）就付款或履约义务，以其他方式承担全部或部分责任的人。“义务人”不包括信用证的开证人或指定人。

（iii）is otherwise accountable in whole or in part for payment or other performance of the obligation.The term does not include issuers or nominated persons under a letter of credit.

（61）除在第9.310条（c）款中另有含义外，“原始债务人”指作为债务人签订担保协议的人，但新债务人随后根据

（61）“Original debtor,” except as used in Section 9.310（c）, means a person that, as debtor, entered into a security agreement to which a new debtor has become bound under

第 9.203 条（d）款受该担保协议的约束。

Section 9.203（d）.

（62）“无形支付”是一般无形财产的一种，即其中应收款债务人的主要义务为金钱债务。

（62）“Payment intangible” means a general intangible under which the account debtor’s principal obligation is a monetary obligation.

（63）个人的“关联人”指：

（63）“Person related to,” with respect to an individual, means:

（A）该个人的配偶；

（A）the spouse of the individual;

（B）该个人或其配偶的兄弟姐妹；

（B）a brother, brother-in-law, sister, or sister-in-law of the individual;

（C）该个人或其配偶的直系长辈或直系后代；或

（C）an ancestor or lineal descendant of the individual or the individual’s spouse;or

（D）该个人或其配偶的任何其他具有血缘或婚姻关系的亲戚，只要他们与该个人居于同一家庭。

（D）any other relative, by blood or marriage, of the individual or the individual’s spouse who shares the same home with the individual.

（64）组织的“关联人”指：

（64）“Person related to,” with respect to an organization, means:

（A）控制该组织的人，受该组织控制的人，或与该组织共同受他人控制的人，无论直接或间接控制；

（A）a person directly or indirectly controlling, controlled by, or under common control with the organization;

（B）该组织的行政官或董事，或就该组织行使类似职权的人；

（B）an officer or director of, or a person performing similar functions with respect to, the organization;

（C）上述（A）款中任何人的行政官或董事，或行使类似职权的人；

（C）an officer or director of, or a person performing similar functions with respect to, a person described in Paragraph（A）;

（D）上述（A）、（B）或（C）款中任何个人的配偶；或

（D）the spouse of an individual described in Paragraph（A）,（B）, or（C）;or

（E）上述（A）、（B）、（C）或（D）款中任何个人具有血

（E）an individual who is related by blood or marriage to an individual described in Paragraph

缘或婚姻关系的亲戚，只要他们与该个人居于同一家庭。

（65）除在第9.609条（b）款中另有含义外，“收益”指下列财产：

（A）担保物被出售、出租、许可、交换或以其他方式处置后的全部所得；

（B）担保物收获或分得的全部所得；

（C）担保物带来的权利；

（D）担保物发生灭失、不符合合同、使用受到干扰、缺陷、权利受到侵犯或损坏后引起的索赔权，但不超过担保物的价值；或

（E）担保物发生灭失、不符合合同、缺陷、权利受到侵犯或损坏后有权得到的保险赔偿，但不超过担保物的价值，并不超过债务人或受担保方有权获得的付款。

（66）“本票”指下列票据：该票据证明支付金钱债务的承诺，而不证明付款命令，也不包含银行的确认，即已收到用于存款的一定数额的金钱或资金。

（67）“建议”指由受担保方认证的记录，其中包含相关条款，即受担保方愿意根据第9.620条、第9.621条和第9.622条收取担保物，用于全部或部

（A），（B），（C），or（D）and shares the same home with the individual.

（65）“Proceeds,” except as used in Section 9.609（b），means the following property:

（A）whatever is acquired upon the sale, lease, license, exchange, or other disposition of collateral;

（B）whatever is collected on, or distributed on account of, collateral;

（C）rights arising out of collateral;

（D）to the extent of the value of collateral, claims arising out of the loss, nonconformity, or interference with the use of, defects or infringement of rights in, or damage to the collateral;or

（E）to the extent of the value of collateral and to the extent payable to the debtor or the secured party, insurance payable by reason of the loss or nonconformity of, defects or infringement of rights in, or damage to the collateral.

（66）“Promissory note”means an instrument that evidences a promise to pay a monetary obligation, does not evidence an order to pay, and does not contain an acknowledgement by a bank that the bank has received for deposit a sum of money or funds.

（67）“Proposal”means a record authenticated by a secured party that includes the terms on which the secured party is willing to accept collateral in full or partial satisfaction of the obligation it secures pursuant to Sections 9.620,

分清偿担保物所担保的债务。

（68）“公共融资项目”指具有下列特征的担保交易：

（A）项目包括债券发行；

（B）所发行的全部或部分债券，标明具有20年以上的初始期限；并且

（C）州政府或州政府机构系其中的债务人、义务人、受担保方、应收款债务人或就担保物承担义务的其他人、担保债务的转让人或受让人，或担保权益的转让人或受让人。

（69）涉及受担保方提供的贷款或其他价值时，“根据承诺”指根据受担保方承担的义务，无论随后发生之违约事件或其他超出受担保方控制之事件，是否解除了或有可能解除受担保方的义务。

（70）“记录”指记载在实体介质上的信息，或存储在电子介质或其他介质上并可读取的信息。

（71）“注册成立的组织”指完全根据任何一州法律或美国联邦法律注册成立的组织，且该州或美国必须设有显示该组织已经注册成立的公开记录。

9.621, and 9.622.

（68）“Public-finance transaction” means a secured transaction in connection with which:

（A）debt securities are issued;

（B）all or a portion of the securities issued have an initial stated maturity of at least 20 years;and

（C）the debtor, obligor, secured party, account debtor or other person obligated on collateral, assignor or assigneeof a secured obligation, or assignor or assignee of a security interest is a state or a governmental unit of a state.

（69）“Pursuant to commitment,” with respect to an advance made or other value given by a secured party, means pursuant to the secured party’s obligation, whether or not a subsequent event of default or other event not within the secured party’s control has relieved or may relieve the secured party from its obligation.

（70）“Record,” except as used in “for record,” “of record,” “record or legal title,” and “record owner,” means information that is inscribed on a tangible medium or that is stored in an electronic or other medium and is retrievable in perceivable form.

（71）“Registered organization” means an organization organized solely under the law of a single state or the United States and as to which the state or the United States must maintain a public record showing the organization to have been organized.

（72）“次义务人”指下列义务人：

（A）该义务人的义务具有次级性质；或

（B）就担保物所担保的债务，该义务人拥有对债务人或另一义务人的索赔权，或对其中任何一人之财产的索赔权。

（73）“受担保方”指：

（A）担保协议所设立或提供之担保权益的受益人，无论所担保的债务是否已清偿；

（B）持有农业留置权的人；

（C）寄售委托人；

（D）向其出售应收款、动产契据、无形支付或本票的人；

（E）受益于所设立或提供之担保权益或农业留置权的受托人、债券受托人、代理人、担保物代理人或其他代表人；或

（F）根据第2.401条、第2.505条、第2.711条（c）款、第2A.508条（e）款、第4.210条或第5.118条所产生之担保权益的持有人。

（74）“担保协议”指设立或提供担保权益的协议。

（75）涉及记录或通知时，“发送”指：

（72）“Secondary obligor” means an obligor to the extent that:

（A）the obligor’s obligation is secondary;or

（B）the obligor has a right of recourse with respect to an obligation secured by collateral against the debtor, another obligor, or property of either.

（73）“Secured party” means:

（A）a person in whose favor a security interest is created or provided for under a security agreement, whether or not any obligation to be secured is outstanding;

（B）a person that holds an agricultural lien;

（C）a consignor;

（D）a person to which accounts, chattel paper, payment intangibles, or promissory notes have been sold;

（E）a trustee, indenture trustee, agent, collateral agent, or other representative in whose favor a security interest or agricultural lien is created or provided for;or

（F）a person that holds a security interest arising under Section 2.401, 2.505, 2.711（c）, 2A.508（e）, 4.210, or 5.118.

（74）“Security agreement” means an agreement that creates or provides for a security interest.

（75）“Send,” in connection with a record or notification, means:

（A）在落实了邮费或传送费并标明了当时情况下为合理的地址后，投入邮箱、交付传送或以任何其他惯常通信手段发出；或

（B）使记录或通知在按（A）款规定适当发送时本应收到的时间之内收到。

（A）to deposit in the mail, deliver for transmission, or transmit by any other usual means of communication, with postage or cost of transmission provided for, addressed to any address reasonable under the circumstances;or

（B）to cause the record or notification to be received within the time that it would have been received if properly sent under Paragraph（A）.

（76）“软件”指计算机程序，也包括在与该程序相关之交易中所提供的支持性信息。符合“货物”定义的计算机程序，不属于“软件”。

（76）“Software” means a computer program and any supporting information provided in connection with a transaction relating to the program.The term does not include a computer program that is included in the definition of“goods.”

（77）“州”指美国的任何州、哥伦比亚特区、波多黎各、美属维尔京群岛以及受美国管辖的地域或岛屿。

（77）“State” means a state of the United States, the District of Columbia, Puerto Rico, the United States Virgin Islands, or any territory or insular possession subject to the jurisdiction of the United States.

（78）“支持性债务”指对应收款、动产契据、凭证、一般无形财产、票据或投资财产之付款或履约具有支持作用的信用证权利或次级义务。

（78）“Supporting obligation” means a letter-of-credit right or secondary obligation that supports the payment or performance of an account, chattel paper, a document, a general intangible, an instrument, or investment property.

（79）“实体动产契据”指证明动产契据的记录由记载于实体介质上的信息组成。

（79）“Tangible chattel paper” means chattel paper evidenced by a record or records consisting of information that is inscribed on a tangible medium.

（80）“终止声明”指融资声明的下列修订文件：

（A）文件通过注明原始融

（80）“Termination statement” means an amendment of a financing statement that:

（A）identifies, by its file number,

资声明的档案号，指明其所涉及的原始融资声明；并且

（B）文件说明其系终止声明，或说明被指明的融资声明不再有效。

（81）“公用事业传输企业”指主要从事下列业务的人：

（A）经营铁路、地下铁、地面轨道车辆或有轨电车；

（B）以电子、电磁或光输方式进行通信传输；

（C）通过管道或污水管传送货物；或

（D）传输（或生产并传输）电力、蒸气、天然气或水。

（b）其他各篇中适用于本篇的定义：

“申请人” 第5.102条

“受益人” 第5.102条

“经纪人” 第8.102条

“票式证券” 第8.102条

“支票” 第3.104条

“清算公司” 第8.102条

“买卖合同” 第2.106条

“控制”（涉及所有权凭证时）第7.106条

“客户” 第4.104条

“权利持有人” 第8.102条

“金融资产” 第8.102条

“正当执票人” 第3.302条

“开证人”（涉及信用证或信用证权利时） 第5.102条

“发行人”（涉及证券时）

the initial financing statement to which it relates;and

（B）indicates either that it is a termination statement or that the identified financing statement is no longer effective.

（81）“Transmitting utility” means a person primarily engaged in the business of:

（A）operating a railroad, subway, street railway, or trolley bus;

（B）transmitting communications electrically, electromagnetically, or by light;

（C）transmitting goods by pipeline or sewer;or

（D）transmitting or producing and transmitting electricity, steam, gas, or water.

（b）The following definitions in other Articles apply to this Article:

“Applicant” Section 5.102.

“Beneficiary” Section 5.102.

“Broker” Section 8.102.

“Certificated security” Section 8.102.

“Check” Section 3.104.

“Clearing corporation” Section 8.102.

“Contract for sale” Section 2.106.

“Control”（with respect to a document of title）Section 7.106.

“Customer” Section 4.104.

“Entitlement holder” Section 8.102.

“Financial asset” Section 8.102.

“Holder in due course” Section 3.302.

“Issuer”（with respect to a letter of credit or letter-of-credit right）Section 5.102.

“Issuer”（with respect to a security）Section

第 8.201 条

“租赁” 第 2A.103 条

“租赁协议” 第 2A.103 条

“租赁合同” 第 2A.103 条

“租赁权益” 第 2A.103 条

“承租方” 第 2A.103 条

“正常业务中的承租方” 第 2A.103 条

“出租方” 第 2A.103 条

“出租方残余权益” 第 2A.103 条

“信用证” 第 5.102 条

“商人” 第 2.104 条

“流通票据” 第 3.104 条

“指定人” 第 5.102 条

“本票” 第 3.104 条

“信用证收益” 第 5.114 条

“证明” 第 3.103 条

“买卖” 第 2.106 条

“证券账户” 第 8.501 条

“证券中间人” 第 8.102 条

“证券” 第 8.102 条

“证券证书” 第 8.102 条

“证券权利” 第 8.102 条

“无票证券” 第 8.102 条

（c）第 1 篇中的通用定义和解释原则适用于本篇通篇。

第 9.103 条 价款担保权益；付款的使用；举证责任

（a）在本条中：

8.201.

“Lease” Section 2A.103.

“Lease agreement” Section 2A.103.

“Lease contract” Section 2A.103.

“Leasehold interest” Section 2A.103.

“Lessee” Section 2A.103.

“Lessee in ordinary course of business” Section 2A.103.

“Lessor” Section 2A.103.

“Lessor’s residual interest” Section 2A.103.

“Letter of credit” Section 5.102.

“Merchant” Section 2.104.

“Negotiable instrument” Section 3.104.

“Nominated person” Section 5.102.

“Note” Section 3.104.

“Proceeds of a letter of credit” Section 5.114.

“Prove” Section 3.103.

“Sale” Section 2.106.

“Securities account” Section 8.501.

“Securities intermediary” Section 8.102.

“Security” Section 8.102.

“Security certificate” Section 8.102.

“Security entitlement” Section 8.102.

“Uncertificated security” Section 8.102.

（c）Article 1 contains general definitions and principles of construction and interpretation applicable throughout this Article.

§ 9.103. Purchase-Money Security Interest; Application of Payments; Burden of Establishing.

（a）In this section:

（1）“价款担保物”指用于担保价款债务的货物或软件，且该担保物系该价款债务产生的原因。

（1）“Purchase-money collateral” means goods or software that secures a purchase-money obligation incurred with respect to that collateral.

（2）“价款债务”指义务人为下列目的而承担的债务：用于支付担保物的部分或全部价款；或用于支付向债务人提供的价值，以使债务人能够获得担保物的权利或使用，但该价值必须实际用于该目的。

（2）“Purchase-money obligation” means an obligation of an obligor incurred as all or part of the price of the collateral or for value given to enable the debtor to acquire rights in or the use of the collateral if the value is in fact so used.

（b）在下列情况下，货物中的担保权益属于价款担保权益：

（b）A security interest in goods is a purchase-money security interest:

（1）担保权益涉及的货物属于价款担保物；

（1）to the extent that the goods are purchase-money collateral with respect to that security interest;

（2）当担保权益存在于现在或曾经是价款担保物的库存中时，担保权益系用于担保其他库存引起的价款债务，且受担保方目前或曾经就该其他库存持有价款担保权益；以及

（2）if the security interest is in inventory that is or was purchase-money collateral, also to the extent that the security interest secures a purchase-money obligation incurred with respect to other inventory in which the secured party holds or held a purchase-money security interest;and

（3）担保权益系用于担保由软件引起的价款债务，且受担保方目前或曾经就该软件持有价款担保权益。

（3）also to the extent that the security interest secures a purchase-money obligation incurred with respect to software in which the secured party holds or held a purchase-money security interest.

（c）在下列情况下，软件中的担保权益属于价款担保权益，只要担保权益同时用于担保由货物引起的价款债务，且

（c）A security interest in software is a purchase-money security interest to the extent that the security interest also secures a purchase-money obligation incurred with respect to

受担保方目前或曾经就该货物持有价款担保权益：

goods in which the secured party holds or held a purchasc-money security interest if:

（1）债务人通过一项交易取得软件的权益，且该交易与债务人取得货物权益之交易属于同一交易；并且

（1）the debtor acquired its interest in the software in an integrated transaction in which it acquired an interest in the goods;and

（2）债务人取得软件权益的主要目的，是使用货物中的软件。

（2）the debtor acquired its interest in the software for the principal purpose of using the software in the goods.

（d）寄售委托人对寄售货物的担保权益，属于库存中的价款担保权益。

（d）The security interest of a consignor in goods that are the subject of a consignment is a purchase-money security interest in inventory.

（e）在消费品交易以外的交易中，如果担保权益在何种程度上构成价款担保权益取决于付款是否用于支付一项特定债务，则该付款必须按下列方法使用：

（e）In a transaction other than a consumer-goods transaction, if the extent to which a security interest is a purchase-money security interest depends on the application of a payment to a particular obligation, the payment must be applied:

（1）按当事方约定的合理使用方法使用；

（1）in accordance with any reasonable method of application to which the parties agree;

（2）如果当事方未约定合理方法，按义务人在付款时或付款前表达的意图使用；或

（2）in the absence of the parties’ agreement to a reasonable method, in accordance with any intention of the obligor manifested at or before the time of payment;or

（3）如果当事方未约定合理方法，且义务人也未及时表达意图，则按下列顺序使用：

（3）in the absence of an agreement to a reasonable method and a timely manifestation of the obligor’s intention, in the following order:

（A）用于无担保债务；以及

（A）to obligations that are not secured;and

（B）如果存在一项以上的担保债务，则用于价款担保权

（B）if more than one obligation is secured, to obligations secured by purchase-

益所担保的债务，从其中最先发生的债务开始使用。

money security interests in the order in which those obligations were incurred.

（f）在消费品交易以外的交易中，即使存在下列情况，价款担保权益亦不失去其价款担保权益的地位：

（f）In a transaction other than a consumer-goods transaction, a purchase-money security interest does not lose its status as such, even if:

（1）价款担保物同时担保价款债务以外的债务；

（1）the purchase-money collateral also secures an obligation that is not a purchase-money obligation;

（2）价款担保物以外的担保物同时担保价款债务；或

（2）collateral that is not purchase-money collateral also secures the purchase-money obligation;or

（3）价款债务已发生续期、再融资、合并或改组。

（3）the purchase-money obligation has been renewed, refinanced, consolidated, or restructured.

（g）在消费品交易以外的交易中，主张价款担保权益的受担保方应承担举证责任，证明担保权益在何种程度上构成价款担保权益。

（g）In a transaction other than a consumer-goods transaction, a secured party claiming a purchase-money security interest has the burden of establishing the extent to which the security interest is a purchase-money security interest.

（h）将（e）款、（f）款和（g）款限定为仅适用于非消费品交易，目的在于使法院可以自行决定适用于消费品交易的适当规则。但是，法院不应根据上述限制，来推断消费品交易中适当规则的性质。法院可以继续使用任何已确立的方法。

（h）The limitation of the rules in Subsections（e），（f），and（g）to transactions other than consumer-goods transactions is intended to leave to the court the determination of the proper rules in consumer-goods transactions.The court may not infer from that limitation the nature of the proper rule in consumer-goods transactions and may continue to apply established approaches

第9.104条　对存款账户的控制

§ 9.104. Control of Deposit Account.

（a）在下列情况下，受担

（a）A secured party has control of a deposit

保方对存款账户拥有控制：

（1）受担保方是银行，且掌管该存款账户；

（2）在业经认证的记录中，债务人、受担保方和银行同意，银行将根据受担保方的指示处置存款账户中的资金，而无须另行征得债务人的同意；或

（3）受担保方就该存款账户成为银行的客户。

（b）受担保方如果满足（a）款的要求，即对存款账户拥有控制，即使债务人保留了权利，亦有权通过作出指示处置账户中的资金。

account if:

（1）the secured party is the bank with which the deposit account is maintained;

（2）the debtor, secured party, and bank have agreed in an authenticated record that the bank will comply with instructions originated by the secured party directing disposition of the funds in the deposit account without further consent by the debtor;or

（3）the secured party becomes the bank's customer with respect to the deposit account.

（b）A secured party that has satisfied Subsection（a）has control, even if the debtor retains the right to direct the disposition of funds from the deposit account.

第9.105条　对电子动产契据的控制

如果构成动产契据的记录按照下列方式产生、存储和转让，受担保方即对电子动产契据拥有控制：

（1）该记录只存在一份权威版本，且该版本具有唯一性和可辨性，且除下述(4)款、(5)款和（6）款另有规定外，该版本不可更改；

（2）该版本指明受担保方是该记录的受让人；

（3）该版本被传送给受担保方或其指定的保管人，并由受担保方或该保管人保管；

§ 9.105. Control of Electronic Chattel Paper.

A secured party has control of electronic chattel paper if the record or records comprising the chattel paper are created, stored, and assigned in such a manner that:

（1）a single authoritative copy of the record or records exists that is unique, identifiable and, except as otherwise provided in Subdivisions（4）,（5）, and（6）, unalterable;

（2）the authoritative copy identifies the secured party as the assignee of the record or records;

（3）the authoritative copy is communicated to and maintained by the secured party or its designated custodian;

（4）如果要对权威版本指明的受让人作出添加或改变，只有在受担保方参与的情况下，才有可能就该版本制作副本或进行修订；

（4）copies or revisions that add or change an identified assignee of the authoritative copy can be made only with the participation of the secured party;

（5）权威版本的每一个副本，以及该副本的任何副本，都可以容易地看出是副本，而不是权威版本；并且

（5）each copy of the authoritative copy and any copy of a copy is readily identifiable as a copy that is not the authoritative copy;and

（6）权威版本的任何修改，都可以被容易地看出是否业经授权。

（6）any revision of the authoritative copy is readily identifiable as an authorized or unauthorized revision.

第9.106条　对投资财产的控制

§ 9.106. Control of Investment Property.

（a）应根据第8.106条确定一个人是否对票式证券、无票证券或证券权利拥有控制。

（a）A person has control of a certificated security, uncertificated security, or security entitlement as provided in Section 8.106.

（b）在下列情况下，受担保方对商品合同拥有控制：

（b）A secured party has control of a commodity contract if:

（1）受担保方是掌管该商品合同的商品中间人；或

（1）the secured party is the commodity intermediary with which the commodity contract is carried;or

（2）商品客户、受担保方和商品中间人同意，商品中间人将根据受担保方的指示使用商品合同分得的任何价值，而无须另行取得商品客户的同意。

（2）the commodity customer, secured party, and commodity intermediary have agreed that the commodity intermediary will apply any value distributed on account of the commodity contract as directed by the secured party without further consent by the commodity customer.

（c）如果受担保方对证券账户或商品账户项下的全部证券权利或全部商品合同拥有控制，即等于对该证券账户或商

（c）A secured party having control of all security entitlements or commodity contracts carried in a securities account or commodity account has control over the securities account

品账户拥有控制。

or commodity account.

第 9.107 条　对信用证权利的控制

§ 9.107. Control of Letter-of-Credit Right.

如果开证人或任何指定人根据第 5.114 条（c）款，或根据适用法或惯例，已对信用证收益的转让给予同意，则只要受担保方有权要求该开证人或指定人付款或履约，受担保方即对信用证权利拥有控制。

A secured party has control of a letter-of-credit right to the extent of any right to payment or performance by the issuer or any nominated person if the issuer or nominated person has consented to an assignment of proceeds of the letter of credit under Section 5.114（c）or otherwise applicable law or practice.

第 9.108 条　描述的充分性

§ 9.108. Sufficiency of Description.

（a）除（c）款、（d）款和（e）款另有规定外，对动产或不动产的描述，只要能够合理指明被描述的财产，即为充分，无论描述是否具体。

（a）Except as otherwise provided in Subsections（c）,（d）, and（e）, a description of personal or real property is sufficient, whether or not it is specific, if it reasonably identifies what is described.

（b）除（d）款另有规定外，使用下列描述方式指明担保物，属于合理指明：

（b）Except as otherwise provided in Subsection（d）, a description of collateral reasonably identifies the collateral if it identifies the collateral by:

（1）具体列出担保物；

（1）specific listing;

（2）列出担保物种类；

（2）category;

（3）除（e）款另有规定外，按本法定义的类别描述担保物；

（3）except as otherwise provided in Subsection（e）, a type of collateral defined in this Act;

（4）说明担保物的数量；

（4）quantity;

（5）说明计算或分配的公式或程序；或

（5）computational or allocational formula or procedure;or

（6）除（c）款另有规定外，使用任何其他方式，只要能客观辨别担保物。

（6）except as otherwise provided in Subsection（c）, any other method, if the identity of the collateral is objectively determinable.

（c）对担保物的描述，如果使用“债务人的全部财产”“债

（c）A description of collateral as “all the debtor's assets” or “all the debtor's personal

务人的全部动产”或具有类似含义的文字，不属于合理指明担保物。

property” or using words of similar import does not reasonably identify the collateral.

（d）除（e）款另有规定外，对证券权利、证券账户或商品账户的下列描述，属于充分：

（d）Except as otherwise provided in Subsection（e）, a description of a security entitlement, securities account, or commodity account is sufficient if it describes:

（1）使用证券权利、证券账户或商品账户此类用词描述担保物，或将担保物称为投资财产；或

（1）the collateral by those terms or as investment property;or

（2）对作为其基础的金融资产或商品合同作出描述。

（2）the underlying financial asset or commodity contract.

（e）涉及下列担保物时，如果仅以本法定义的担保物类别进行描述，不属于充分：

（e）A description only by type of collateral defined in this Act is an insufficient description of:

（1）担保物系商业侵权索赔；或

（1）a commercial tort claim;or

（2）涉及消费者交易时，担保物系消费品、证券权利、证券账户或商品账户。

（2）in a consumer transaction, consumer goods, a security entitlement, a securities account, or a commodity account.

第9.109条　范围

§ 9.109. Scope.

（a）除（c）款、（d）款和（e）款另有规定外，本篇适用于：

（a）Except as otherwise provided in Subsections（c）,（d）, and（e）, this Article applies to:

（1）以合同方式在动产或不动产附着物上设立担保权益的交易，无论交易采用何种形式；

（1）a transaction, regardless of its form, that creates a security interest in personal property or fixtures by contract;

（2）农业留置权；

（2）an agricultural lien;

（3）应收款、动产契据、无形支付或本票的买卖；

（3）a sale of accounts, chattel paper, payment intangibles, or promissory notes;

（4）寄售；

（4）a consignment;

（5）如第 9.110 条所述，根据第 2.401 条、第 2.505 条、第 2.711 条（c）款或第 2A.508 条（e）款产生的担保权益；以及

（5）a security interest arising under Section 2.401, 2.505, 2.711（c）, or 2A.508（e）, as provided in Section 9.110;and

（6）根据第 4.210 条或第 5.118 条产生的担保权益。

（6）a security interest arising under Section 4.210 or 5.118.

（b）即使担保债务本身系由不受本篇管辖之交易或权益所担保，本篇对该担保债务中担保权益的适用亦不受影响。

（b）The application of this Article to a security interest in a secured obligation is not affected by the fact that the obligation is itself secured by a transaction or interest to which this Article does not apply.

（c）涉及下列情况时，本篇不适用：

（c）This Article does not apply to the extent that:

（1）美国的任何法律或条约具有优于本篇的效力；

（1）a statute, regulation, or treaty of the United States preempts this Article;

（2）涉及本州或本州政府机构设立的担保权益时，本州其他法律明确规定，该法适用于该担保权益的设立、完善、优先顺序或强制履行；

（2）another statute of this state expressly governs the creation, perfection, priority, or enforcement of a security interest created by this state or a governmental unit of this state;

（3）涉及外州或外国或其政府机构设立的担保权益时，该外州或外国法律（普遍适用于担保权益的一般法除外）明确规定，该法适用于该担保权益的设立、完善、优先顺序或强制履行；或

（3）a statute of another state, a foreign country, or a governmental unit of another state or a foreign country, other than a statute generally applicable to security interests, expressly governs creation, perfection, priority, or enforcement of a security interest created by the state, country, or governmental unit;or

（4）如果信用证项下之指定人或身为受让人之受益人的权利，根据第 5.114 条享有独立性和优先性，则在该规定的范围内，本篇不适用。

（4）the rights of a transferee beneficiary or nominated person under a letter of credit are independent and superior under Section 5.114.

（d）本篇不适用于下列：

（d）This Article does not apply to:

（1）地主留置权（农业留置权除外）；

（1）a landlord's lien, other than an agricultural lien;

（2）因提供服务或材料而依法自动取得的留置权（农业留置权除外）；但是，该服务或材料之留置权的优先顺序由第9.333条规定；

（2）a lien, other than an agricultural lien, given by statute or other rule of law for services or materials, but Section 9.333 applies with respect to priority of the lien;

（3）雇员工资或其他报酬之索赔权的转让；

（3）an assignment of a claim for wages, salary, or other compensation of an employee;

（4）如果应收款、动产契据、无形支付或本票的买卖，属于运营业务之出售交易的组成部分，且产生于该运营业务，则本篇不适用于该应收款、动产契据、无形支付或本票的买卖；

（4）a sale of accounts, chattel paper, payment intangibles, or promissory notes as part of a sale of the business out of which they arose;

（5）仅用于收款目的而对应收款、动产契据、无形支付或本票作出的转让；

（5）an assignment of accounts, chattel paper, payment intangibles, or promissory notes that is for the purpose of collection only;

（6）合同项下收款权利的转让，只要受让人亦承担合同项下的履约义务；

（6）an assignment of a right to payment under a contract to an assignee that is also obligated to perform under the contract;

（7）单独一项无形支付、本票或应收款的转让，只要该转让系用于向受让人部分或充分清偿前存债务；

（7）an assignment of a single account, payment intangible, or promissory note to an assignee in full or partial satisfaction of a preexisting indebtedness;

（8）保险单项下之权益或索赔权的转让，但是，当医疗服务提供者系转让人或受让人时，医疗保险应收款的转让以及收款权的随后转让除外；此外，第9.315条和第9.322条适用于保险单项下之权益或索赔

（8）a transfer of an interest in or an assignment of a claim under a policy of insurance, other than an assignment by or to a health care provider of a health-care-insurance receivable and any subsequent assignment of the right to payment, but Sections 9.315 and 9.322 apply with respect to proceeds and

权之转让的收益，以及收益的优先顺序；

priorities in proceeds;

（9）由法院判决书所代表之权利的转让；但是，如果以收款权作为担保物，则有关该收款权的判决除外；

（9）an assignment of a right represented by a judgment, other than a judgment taken on a right to payment that was collateral;

（10）扣减权或抵销权，但是：

（10）a right of recoupment or set-off, but:

（A）涉及对存款账户行使的扣减权或抵销权时，该权利的有效性受第 9.340 条的约束；并且

（A）Section 9.340 applies with respect to the effectiveness of rights of recoupment or set-off against deposit accounts;and

（B）应收款债务人的抗辩或索赔受第 9.404 条的约束；

（B）Section 9.404 applies with respect to defenses or claims of an account debtor;

（11）不动产（包括不动产项下之租赁或租金）中之权益或留置权的设立或转让；购买不动产权益之地契合同中，出售人和买受人的权益；或不动产权益之购买选择权合同中，选择权提供人和选择权接受人的权益；但是，下列条款的相关规定应予适用：

（11）the creation or transfer of an interest in or lien on real property, including a lease or rents thereunder, the interest of a vendor or vendee in a contract for deed to purchase an interest in real property, or the interest of an optionor or optionee in an option to purchase an interest in real property, except to the extent that provision is made for:

（A）第 9.203 条和第 9.308 条对不动产留置权的规定；

（A）liens on real property in Sections 9.203 and 9.308;

（B）第 9.334 条对不动产附着物的规定；

（B）fixtures in Section 9.334;

（C）第 9.501 条、第 9.502 条、第 9.512 条、第 9.516 条和第 9.519 条对不动产附着物登记的规定；以及

（C）fixture filings in Sections 9.501, 9.502, 9.512, 9.516, and 9.519;and

（D）第 9.604 条对同时覆盖动产和不动产之担保协议的

（D）security agreements covering personal and real property in Section 9.604;

规定；

（12）因侵权产生之索赔权（商业侵权索赔除外）的转让；但是，此种索赔权的收益以及收益的优先顺序，受第9.315条和第9.322条的约束；或

（12）an assignment of a claim arising in tort, other than a commercial tort claim, but Sections 9.315 and 9.322 apply with respect to proceeds and priorities in proceeds;or

（13）消费者交易中存款账户（不可流通存款凭证除外）的转让；但是，此种账户的收益以及收益的优先顺序，受第9.315条和第9.322条的约束。

（13）an assignment of a deposit account, other than a nonnegotiable certificate of deposit, in a consumer transaction, but Sections 9.315 and 9.322 apply with respect to proceeds and priorities in proceeds.

（e）将本篇适用于应收款、动产契据、无形支付或本票的买卖，目的不在于重新定义该买卖的性质，使其成为就债务设立担保的交易，而只是为相关通知提供一个登记系统，用于保护该类财产的购买人。在任何意义上，如果不存在欺诈或故意不实陈述，则只要当事方将此种财产买卖的性质确定为买卖，该交易即确定地属于买卖，而不属于担保交易；并且，所有权（无论法定或衡平所有权）即转移至作为财产购买人的当事方，无论受担保方是否对债务人持有追索权，无论债务人是否有权获得财产的剩余部分，也无论当事方协议的其他条款如何规定。

（e）The application of this Article to the sale of accounts, chattel paper, payment intangibles, or promissory notes is not to recharacterize that sale as a transaction to secure indebtedness but to protect purchasers of those assets by providing a notice filing system.For all purposes, in the absence of fraud or intentional misrepresentation, the parties' characterization of a transaction as a sale of such assets shall be conclusive that the transaction is a sale and is not a secured transaction and that title, legal and equitable, has passed to the party characterized as the purchaser of those assets regardless of whether the secured party has any recourse against the debtor, whether the debtor is entitled to any surplus, or any other term of the parties' agreement.

第9.110条 根据第2篇或第2A篇产生的担保权益

§ 9.110. Security Interests Arising Under Article 2 or 2A.

根据第2.401条、第2.505

A security interest arising under Section

条、第 2.711 条（c）款或第 2A.508 条（e）款产生的担保权益，受本篇的约束。但是，在债务人占有货物之前：

（1）即使不满足第 9.203 条（b）（3）款的条件，该担保权益仍可强制履行；

（2）该担保权益无须登记亦可获得完善；

（3）债务人违约后，受担保方的权利受第 2 篇或第 2A 篇的约束；以及

（4）该担保权益优于债务人设立的其他冲突担保权益。

2.401, 2.505, 2.711（c）, or 2A.508（e）is subject to this Article.However, until the debtor obtains possession of the goods:

（1）the security interest is enforceable, even if Section 9.203（b）（3）has not been satisfied;

（2）filing is not required to perfect the security interest;

（3）the rights of the secured party after default by the debtor are governed by Article 2 or 2A;and

（4）the security interest has priority over a conflicting security interest created by the debtor.

第2章　担保协议的效力；担保权益的附着；担保协议当事方的权利

PART 2. EFFECTIVENESS OF SECURITY AGREEMENT; ATTACHMENT OF SECURITY INTEREST;RIGHTS OF PARTIES TO SECURITY AGREEMENT

第 9.201 条　担保协议之效力的一般原则

（a）除本法另有规定外，在当事方之间，以及在对抗担保物购买人或在对抗债权人时，担保协议的效力根据其条款确定。

（b）受本篇约束的交易，亦同时受为消费者制定不同规则之其他适用法的约束。

（c）如果本篇的规定与（b）款所述的法律存在冲突，后者

§ 9.201. General Effectiveness of Security Agreement.

（a）Except as otherwise provided by this Act, a security agreement is effective according to its terms between the parties, against purchasers of the collateral, and against creditors.

（b）A transaction subject to this Article is subject to any applicable rule of law that establishes a different rule for consumers.

（c）In case of conflict between this Article and a rule of law, statute, or regulation

具有优先效力。未能遵守（b）款所述的法律，只产生该法规定的后果。

described in Subsection（b）, the rule of law, statute, or regulation controls.Failure to comply with a statute or regulation described in Subsection（b）has only the effect the statute or regulation specifies.

（d）本篇：

（1）不使违反（b）款所述之法律的任何费率、费用、协议或做法产生效力；并且

（2）不使该法适用于其本来不适用的交易。

（d）This Article does not:

（1）validate any rate, charge, agreement, or practice that violates a rule of law, statute, or regulation described in Subsection（b）;or

（2）extend the application of the rule of law, statute, or regulation to a transaction not otherwise subject to it.

第 9.202 条　担保物所有权无关紧要

除涉及寄售或涉及应收款、动产契据、无形支付或本票的买卖时另有规定外，无论担保物的所有权由受担保方持有还是由债务人持有，本篇有关权利和义务的条款均同样适用。

§ 9.202. Title to Collateral Immaterial.

Except as otherwise provided with respect to consignments or sales of accounts, chattel paper, payment intangibles, or promissory notes, the provisions of this Article with regard to rights and obligations apply whether title to collateral is in the secured party or the debtor.

第 9.203 条　担保权益的附着和强制履行；收益；支持性债务；形式要求

（a）担保权益就担保物对债务人产生强制履行力的时间，即为担保权益附着于担保物的时间，除非通过协议明确推迟附着的时间。

（b）除（c）款至（j）款另有规定外，只有在下列情况下，才可就担保物对债务人和第三方强制履行担保权益：

（1）已支付价值；

§ 9.203. Attachment and Enforceability of Security Interest; Proceeds; Supporting Obligations; Formal Requisites.

（a）A security interest attaches to collateral when it becomes enforceable against the debtor with respect to the collateral, unless an agreement expressly postpones the time of attachment.

（b）Except as otherwise provided in Subsections（c）-（j）, a security interest is enforceable against the debtor and third parties with respect to the collateral only if:

（1）value has been given;

（2）债务人对担保物拥有权利，或有权力向受担保方转让担保物的权利；并且

（2）the debtor has rights in the collateral or the power to transfer rights in the collateral to a secured party;and

（3）下列条件之一得到满足：

（3）one of the following conditions is met:

（A）债务人已对包含担保物描述的担保协议作出认证；当担保权益覆盖待砍伐树木时，担保协议还同时包含对相关土地的描述；

（A）the debtor has authenticated a security agreement that provides a description of the collateral and, if the security interest covers timber to be cut, a description of the land concerned;

（B）担保物不属于票式证券，且根据债务人的担保协议，受担保方根据第 9.313 条占有担保物；

（B）the collateral is not a certificated security and is in the possession of the secured party under Section 9.313 pursuant to the debtor's security agreement;

（C）担保物属于登记式的票式证券，且根据债务人的担保协议，已按第 8.301 条的规定将证券证书交付给受担保方；或

（C）the collateral is a certificated security in registered form and the security certificate has been delivered to the secured party under Section 8.301 pursuant to the debtor's security agreement;or

（D）担保物属于存款账户、电子动产契据、投资财产、信用证权利或电子凭证，且根据债务人的担保协议，受担保方根据第 7.106 条、第 9.104 条、第 9.105 条、第 9.106 条或第 9.107 条，取得对担保物的控制。

（D）the collateral is deposit accounts, electronic chattel paper, investment property, letter-of-credit rights, or electronic documents, and the secured party has control under Section 7.106, 9.104, 9.105, 9.106, or 9.107 pursuant to the debtor's security agreement.

（c）上述（b）款受制于下列各款：有关收款银行之担保权益的第 4.210 条；有关信用证开证人或指定人之担保权益的第 5.118 条；有关根据第 2 篇或第 2A 篇产生之担保权益的第 9.110 条；以及有关投资财产中

（c）Subsection（b）is subject to Section 4.210 on the security interest of a collecting bank, Section 5.118 on the security interest of a letter-of-credit issuer or nominated person, Section 9.110 on a security interest arising under Article 2 or 2A, and Section 9.206 on security interests in investment property.

之担保权益的第 9.206 条。

（d）如果基于本篇以外的其他法律或基于合同而出现下列情况，一人即成为受另一人签订之担保协议约束的债务人：

（d）A person becomes bound as debtor by a security agreement entered into by another person if, by operation of law other than this Article or by contract:

（1）担保协议产生了在前者财产上设立担保权益的效力；或

（1）the security agreement becomes effective to create a security interest in the person's property;or

（2）前者对后者的债务（包括担保协议所担保的债务）承担总体义务，并取得或继承后者的全部或几乎全部财产。

（2）the person becomes generally obligated for the obligations of the other person, including the obligation secured under the security agreement, and acquires or succeeds to all or substantially all of the assets of the other person.

（e）如果新债务人成为受另一人签订之担保协议约束的债务人，则：

（e）If a new debtor becomes bound as debtor by a security agreement entered into by another person:

（1）只要担保协议对新债务人的现有财产和后得财产作出描述，该协议即满足（b）（3）款的要求；并且

（1）the agreement satisfies Subsection（b）（3）with respect to existing or after-acquired property of the new debtor to the extent the property is described in the agreement;and

（2）无须另行签订协议，该财产中的担保权益即具有强制履行力。

（2）another agreement is not necessary to make a security interest in the property enforceable.

（f）担保物中的担保权益发生附着后，受担保方即取得第 9.315 条所述的对收益的权利；同时，该附着亦构成担保物的支持性债务中担保权益的附着。

（f）The attachment of a security interest in collateral gives the secured party the rights to proceeds provided by Section 9.315 and is also attachment of a security interest in a supporting obligation for the collateral.

（g）动产或不动产中的担保权益或其他留置权，如果用

（g）The attachment of a security interest in a right to payment or performance secured

于担保获得付款或履约的权利，则在该权利中的担保权益发生附着后，即同时使该动产或不动产中的担保权益、不动产抵押权，或其他留置权中的担保权益发生附着。

by a security interest or other lien on personal or real property is also attachment of a security interest in the security interest, mortgage, or other lien.

（h）证券账户中的担保权益发生附着后，即同时构成该证券账户内证券权利中之担保权益的附着。

（h）The attachment of a security interest in a securities account is also attachment of a security interest in the security entitlements carried in the securities account.

（i）商品账户中的担保权益发生附着后，即同时构成商品账户内商品合同中之担保权益的附着。

（i）The attachment of a security interest in a commodity account is also attachment of a security interest in the commodity contracts carried in the commodity account.

（j）涉及矿物（包括石油和天然气）时，如果受担保方根据本篇，在矿物开采出来后立即对矿物享有担保权益，且根据适用法，该担保权益构成对开采前矿物的留置权，则该财产中的担保权益即构成开采前和开采后连续无间断的单一留置权。本款是对本款生效日期之前存在之本州法律的描述，并适用于矿物（包括石油和天然气），无论矿物于何时开采。

（j）If a secured party holds a security interest that applies under this Article to minerals, including oil and gas, upon their extraction and the security interest also qualifies under applicable law as a lien on those minerals before their extraction, the security interest before and after production is a single continuous and uninterrupted lien on the property.This subsection is a statement of the law of this state as it existed before the effective date of this subsection and applies with respect to minerals, including oil and gas, regardless of when the minerals were extracted.

第 9.204 条　后得财产；未来贷款

§ 9.204. After–Acquired Property; Future Advances.

（a）除（b）款另有规定外，担保协议可在今后取得的财产中设立担保权益，或对设立此种担保权益作出规定。

（a）Except as provided in Subsection（b）, a security agreement may create or provide for a security interest in after-acquired collateral.

（b）有关后得财产的条款，不能使担保权益附着于：

（b）A security interest does not attach under a term constituting an after-acquired property clause to:

（1）消费品（作为附加担保而提供的添附物除外），除非在受担保方支付价值后10日内，债务人取得对消费品的权利；或

（1）consumer goods, other than an accession when given as additional security, unless the debtor acquires rights in them within 10 days after the secured party gives value;or

（2）商业侵权索赔。

（2）a commercial tort claim.

（c）担保协议可以规定担保物系担保未来贷款或其他价值，或规定应收款、动产契据、无形支付或本票的出售系用于未来贷款或其他价值，无论贷款或其他价值是否系根据承诺提供。

（c）A security agreement may provide that collateral secures, or that accounts, chattel paper, payment intangibles, or promissory notes are sold in connection with, future advances or other value, whether or not the advances or value are given pursuant to commitment.

第9.205条 允许使用或处置担保物

§ 9.205. Use or Disposition of Collateral Permissible.

（a）仅有下列情况存在，不使担保权益失去效力，亦不构成欺诈：

（a）A security interest is not invalid or fraudulent against creditors solely because:

（1）债务人有权利或有实际可能：

（1）the debtor has the right or ability to:

（A）使用、混合或处置全部或部分担保物，包括被退回或被收回的货物；

（A）use, commingle, or dispose of all or part of the collateral, including returned or repossessed goods;

（B）就担保物作出收款、和解、强制履行或其他行为；

（B）collect, compromise, enforce, or otherwise deal with collateral;

（C）接受担保物的退回，或收回担保物；或

（C）accept the return of collateral or make repossessions; or

（D）使用、混合或处置收益；或

（D）use, commingle, or dispose of proceeds; or

（2）受担保方未能要求债

（2）the secured party fails to require

务人就收益作出说明或更新担保物。

the debtor to account for proceeds or replace collateral.

（b）如果担保权益的附着、完善或强制履行取决于受担保方对担保物的占有，则本条并不降低对占有的要求。

（b）This section does not relax the requirements of possession if attachment, perfection, or enforcement of a security interest depends upon possession of the collateral by the secured party.

第 9.206 条　购买或交付金融资产时产生的担保权益

§ 9.206. Security Interest Arising in Purchase or Delivery of Financial Asset.

（a）在下列情况下，以证券中间人为受益人的担保权益附着于下列人所持有的证券权利：

（a）A security interest in favor of a securities intermediary attaches to a person's security entitlement if:

（1）该人通过该证券中间人购买金融资产，且在该交易中，该人有义务在购买时向该证券中间人支付购价；并且

（1）the person buys a financial asset through the securities intermediary in a transaction in which the person is obligated to pay the purchase price to the securities intermediary at the time of the purchase;and

（2）在买方向证券中间人作出付款前，证券中间人将金融资产贷记于买方的证券账户。

（2）the securities intermediary credits the financial asset to the buyer's securities account before the buyer pays the securities intermediary.

（b）上述（a）款所述的担保权益，系用于担保该人支付金融资产购价的义务。

（b）The security interest described in Subsection（a）secures the person's obligation to pay for the financial asset.

（c）如果任何人交付票式证券，或交付由书面文件代表的其他金融资产，则在下列情况下，以该人为受益人的担保权益附着于该证券或金融资产：

（c）A security interest in favor of a person that delivers a certificated security or other financial asset represented by a writing attaches to the security or other financial asset if:

（1）该证券或金融资产：

（1）the security or other financial asset:

（A）系在正常业务过程中，在完成任何必要背书或转让程

（A）in the ordinary course of business is transferred by delivery with any necessary

序后，通过交付而转让；并且

（B）系根据从事此类证券或金融资产之业务的人之间的协议而交付；并且

（2）该协议要求在交付时付款。

（d）上述（c）款所述的担保权益，系用于担保为该交付作出付款的义务。

indorsement or assignment;and

（B）is delivered under an agreement between persons in the business of dealing with such securities or financial assets;and

（2）the agreement calls for delivery against payment.

（d）The security interest described in Subsection（c）secures the obligation to make payment for the delivery.

第 9.207 条　受担保方占有或控制担保物时的权利和义务

§ 9.207. Rights And Duties of Secured Party Having Possession or Control of Collateral.

（a）除（d）款另有规定外，受担保方在照管和保存其占有的担保物时，有义务行使合理谨慎。涉及动产契据或票据时，除另有协议外，合理谨慎还包括采取必要步骤，以保留对抗前手当事方的权利。

（a）Except as otherwise provided in Subsection（d）, a secured party shall use reasonable care in the custody and preservation of collateral in the secured party's possession. In the case of chattel paper or an instrument, reasonable care includes taking necessary steps to preserve rights against prior parties unless otherwise agreed.

（b）除（d）款另有规定外，在受担保方占有担保物时：

（b）Except as otherwise provided in Subsection（d）, if a secured party has possession of collateral:

（1）为照管、保存、使用或营运担保物而发生的合理费用，包括保险费、税费和其他费用，由债务人承担，并以担保物担保；

（1）reasonable expenses, including the cost of insurance and payment of taxes or other charges, incurred in the custody, preservation, use, or operation of the collateral are chargeable to the debtor and are secured by the collateral;

（2）意外灭失或损坏的风险，在有效保险覆盖范围以外的，由债务人承担；

（2）the risk of accidental loss or damage is on the debtor to the extent of any deficiency in any effective insurance coverage;

（3）受担保方应使担保物保持在可分辨状态，但种类物

（3）the secured party shall keep the collateral identifiable, but fungible collateral

可以混合；并且

（4）受担保方可以使用或营运担保物，只要：

（A）目的在于保存担保物或其价值；

（B）有适当管辖权的法院发出许可令；或

（C）符合债务人同意的方式和限度，但涉及消费品时除外。

（c）除（d）款另有规定外，根据第7.106条、第9.104条、第9.105条、第9.106条或第9.107条占有或控制担保物的受担保方：

（1）可将担保物取得的收益（金钱或资金除外）作为附加担保；

（2）应将担保物获得的金钱或资金用于减少所担保的债务，除非已将其汇付给债务人；并且

（3）可在担保物上设立担保权益。

（d）如果受担保方是应收款、动产契据、无形支付或本票的买方，或是寄售委托人，则：

（1）上述（a）款不适用，除非受担保方根据协议享有下列权利：

（A）在就担保物未获收款时作出倒账；或

may be commingled;and

（4）the secured party may use or operate the collateral:

（A）for the purpose of preserving the collateral or its value;

（B）as permitted by an order of a court having competent jurisdiction;or

（C）except in the case of consumer goods, in the manner and to the extent agreed by the debtor.

（c）Except as otherwise provided in Subsection（d）, a secured party having possession of collateral or control of collateral under Section 7.106, 9.104, 9.105, 9.106, or 9.107:

（1）may hold as additional security any proceeds, except money or funds, received from the collateral;

（2）shall apply money or funds received from the collateral to reduce the secured obligation, unless remitted to the debtor;and

（3）may create a security interest in the collateral.

（d）If the secured party is a buyer of accounts, chattel paper, payment intangibles, or promissory notes or a consignor:

（1）Subsection（a）does not apply unless the secured party is entitled under an agreement:

（A）to charge back uncollected collateral;or

（B）基于应收款债务人或担保物其他次义务人未能付款或发生其他违约，对该债务人或义务人行使充分的或有限的追索；并且

（2）上述（b）款和（c）款不适用。

第9.208条 受担保方控制担保物时的进一步义务

（a）如果不存在尚未清偿的担保债务，且受担保方未就提供贷款、承担债务或以其他方式支付价值作出承诺，则应适用本条。

（b）如果债务人提出业经认证的要求，则在收到要求后10天内：

（1）根据第9.104条（a）（2）款控制存款账户的受担保方，应向掌管存款账户的银行发送业经认证的说明，从此解除该银行服从受担保方指示的义务；

（2）根据第9.104条（a）（3）款控制存款账户的受担保方：

（A）应将存款账户中的存款余额支付给债务人；或

（B）应将存款余额转存到债务人名字之下的存款账户；

（3）根据第9.105条控制电子动产契据的受担保方（买

（B）otherwise to full or limited recourse against the debtor or a secondary obligor based on the nonpayment or other default of an account debtor or other obligor on the collateral;and

（2）Subsections（b）and（c）do not apply.

§ 9.208. Additional Duties of Secured Party Having Control of Collateral.

（a）This section applies to cases in which there is no outstanding secured obligation and the secured party is not committed to make advances, incur obligations, or otherwise give value.

（b）Within 10 days after receiving an authenticated demand by the debtor:

（1）a secured party having control of a deposit account under Section 9.104（a）（2）shall send to the bank with which the deposit account is maintained an authenticated statement that releases the bank from any further obligation to comply with instructions originated by the secured party;

（2）a secured party having control of a deposit account under Section 9.104（a）（3）shall:

（A）pay the debtor the balance on deposit in the deposit account;or

（B）transfer the balance on deposit into a deposit account in the debtor's name;

（3）a secured party, other than a buyer, having control of electronic chattel paper under

方除外）：

（A）应将电子动产契据的权威版本传送给债务人或其指定的保管人；

（B）当债务人指定的保管人同时是代表受担保方掌管电子动产契据权威版本的指定保管人时，应向该保管人发送业经认证的记录，从此解除该保管人服从受担保方指示的义务，同时指示该保管人从此服从债务人的指示；并且

（C）应采取适当行动，以使债务人或其指定的保管人在添加或改变权威版本注明的受让人时，可就权威版本制作副本，或对权威版本进行修订，而无须取得受担保方的同意；

（4）根据第 8.106 条（d）（2）款或第 9.106 条（b）款控制投资财产的受担保方，应向掌管证券权利或商品合同的证券中间人或商品中间人发送业经认证的记录，从此解除该证券中间人或商品中间人服从受担保方之权利命令或指示的义务；

（5）根据第 9.107 条控制信用证权利的受担保方，应向每一个尚有义务向受担保方付

Section 9.105 shall:

（A）communicate the authoritative copy of the electronic chattel paper to the debtor or its designated custodian;

（B）if the debtor designates a custodian that is the designated custodian with which the authoritative copy of the electronic chattel paper is maintained for the secured party, communicate to the custodian an authenticated record releasing the designated custodian from any further obligation to comply with instructions originated by the secured party and instructing the custodian to comply with instructions originated by the debtor;and

（C）take appropriate action to enable the debtor or its designated custodian to make copies of or revisions to the authoritative copy that add or change an identified assignee of the authoritative copy without the consent of the secured party;

（4）a secured party having control of investment property under Section 8.106（d）（2）or 9.106（b）shall send to the securities intermediary or commodity intermediary with which the security entitlement or commodity contract is maintained an authenticated record that releases the securities intermediary or commodity intermediary from any further obligation to comply with entitlement orders or directions originated by the secured party;

（5）a secured party having control of a letter-of-credit right under Section 9.107 shall send to each person having an unfulfilled

款或交付信用证收益的人发送业经认证的记录，从此解除该人向受担保方付款或交付信用证收益的义务；以及

obligation to pay or deliver proceeds of the letter of credit to the secured party an authenticated release from any further obligation to pay or deliver proceeds of the letter of credit to the secured party;and

（6）控制电子凭证的受担保方：

（6）a secured party having control of an electronic document shall:

（A）应将电子凭证的控制交给债务人或其指定的保管人；

（A）give control of the electronic document to the debtor or its designated custodian;

（B）当债务人指定的保管人同时是代表受担保方掌管电子凭证权威版本的指定保管人时，应向该保管人发送业经认证的记录，从此解除该保管人服从受担保方指示的义务，同时指示该保管人从此服从债务人的指示；并且

（B）if the debtor designates a custodian that is the designated custodian with which the authoritative copy of the electronic document is maintained for the secured party, communicate to the custodian an authenticated record releasing the designated custodian from any further obligation to comply with instructions originated by the secured party and instructing the custodian to comply with instructions originated by the debtor;and

（C）应采取适当行动，以使债务人或其指定的保管人在添加或改变权威版本注明的受让人时，可就权威版本制作副本，或对权威版本进行修订，而无须征得受担保方的同意。

（C）take appropriate action to enable the debtor or its designated custodian to make copies of or revisions to the authoritative copy which add or change an identified assignee of the authoritative copy without the consent of the secured party.

第9.209条　应收款债务人收到转让通知后受担保方的义务

§ 9.209. Duties of Secured Party if Account Debtor Has Been Notified of Assignment.

（a）除（c）款另有规定外，在下列情况下，应适用本条：

（a）Except as otherwise provided in Subsection（c）, this section applies if:

（1）不存在尚未清偿的担保债务；并且

（1）there is no outstanding secured obligation;and

（2）受担保方未就提供贷款、承担债务或以其他方式支付价值作出承诺。

（2）the secured party is not committed to makc advances, incur obligations, or otherwise give value.

（b）如果按第9.406条（a）款所述，应收款债务人已得到受担保方作为受让人取得转让的通知，则受担保方在收到债务人业经认证的要求后，应在10天内向应收款债务人发送业经认证的记录，从此解除应收款债务人对受担保方的义务。

（b）Within 10 days after receiving an authenticated demand by the debtor, a secured party shall send to an account debtor that has received notification of an assignment to the secured party as assignee under Section 9.406（a）an authenticated record that releases the account debtor from any further obligation to the secured party.

（c）如果转让属于应收款、动产契据或无形支付的买卖，则本条不适用于该转让。

（c）This section does not apply to an assignment constituting the sale of an account, chattel paper, or payment intangible.

第9.210条　对账请求；担保物清单请求；债务清单请求

§ 9.210. Request for Accounting; Request Regarding List of Collateral or Statement of Account.

（a）在本条中：

（a）In this section:

（1）“请求”指（2）款、（3）款或（4）款所述种类的记录。

（1）“Request” means a record of a type described in Subdivision（2），（3），or（4）.

（2）“对账请求”指债务人作出的业经认证的下列记录：在合理指明请求所涉及的交易或关系后，请求接收人就担保物所担保的尚未清偿的债务予以列明。

（2）“Request for an accounting” means a record authenticated by a debtor requesting that the recipient provide an accounting of the unpaid obligations secured by collateral and reasonably identifying the transaction or relationship that is the subject of the request.

（3）“担保物清单请求”指债务人作出的业经认证的下列记录：在合理指明请求所涉及的交易或关系后，提供债务人认为正确的用于债务担保的担保物清单，并请求接收人对清单作出批准或纠正。

（3）“Request regarding a list of collateral” means a record authenticated by a debtor requesting that the recipient approve or correct a list of what the debtor believes to be the collateral securing an obligation and reasonably identifying the transaction or relationship that is the subject of the request.

（4）“债务清单请求”指债务人作出的业经认证的下列记录：在合理指明请求所涉及的交易或关系后，提供债务人认为正确的至特定日期为止由担保物所担保的未偿债务总额，并请求接收人对清单作出批准或纠正。

（4）“Request regarding a statement of account” means a record authenticated by a debtor requesting that the recipient approve or correct a statement indicating what the debtor believes to be the aggregate amount of unpaid obligations secured by collateral as of a specified date and reasonably identifying the transaction or relationship that is the subject of the request.

（b）除（c）款、（d）款、（e）款和（f）款另有规定外，受担保方（应收款、动产契据、无形支付或本票的买方和寄售委托人除外）在收到请求后14天内，应以下列方式满足该请求：

（b）Subject to Subsections（c），（d），（e），and（f），a secured party, other than a buyer of accounts, chattel paper, payment intangibles, or promissory notes or a consignor, shall comply with a request within 14 days after receipt:

（1）涉及对账请求时，应向债务人发送业经认证的账目；以及

（1）in the case of a request for an accounting, by authenticating and sending to the debtor an accounting;and

（2）涉及担保物清单请求或债务清单请求时，应向债务人发送业经认证的批准或纠正。

（2）in the case of a request regarding a list of collateral or a request regarding a statement of account, by authenticating and sending to the debtor an approval or correction.

（c）受担保方如果对债务人拥有之特定种类担保物的全部，均主张担保权益，则为满足担保物清单请求，可在收到请求后的十四天内向债务人发送业经认证的声明，说明受担保方的该主张。

（c）A secured party that claims a security interest in all of a particular type of collateral owned by the debtor may comply with a request regarding a list of collateral by sending to the debtor an authenticated record including a statement to that effect within 14 days after receipt.

（d）一个人如果收到担保物清单请求，但在收到请求时对担保物不主张权益，而是曾

（d）A person that receives a request regarding a list of collateral, claims no interest in the collateral when it receives the request,

经对担保物主张过权益，则应在收到请求后十四天内，通过向债务人发送业经认证的下列记录满足该请求：

（1）声明不对担保物主张权益；并且

（2）提供接收人之担保物权益的受让人或继承人的名字和邮寄地址，只要接收人知道该名字和地址。

（e）一个人如果收到对账请求或债务清单请求，但在收到请求时对该债务不主张权益，而是曾经对该债务主张过权益，则应在收到请求后十四天内，通过向债务人发送业经认证的下列记录满足该请求：

（1）声明不对该债务主张权益；并且

（2）提供接收人对该债务之权益的受让人或继承人的名字和邮寄地址，只要接收人知道该名字和地址。

（f）对于本条所述的请求，债务人有权每六个月内获得一次免费答复。对于额外的答复，受担保方可以每次收取不超过 25 美元的费用。

and claimed an interest in the collateral at an earlier time shall comply with the request within 14 days after receipt by sending to the debtor an authenticated record:

（1）disclaiming any interest in the collateral;and

（2）if known to the recipient, providing the name and mailing address of any assignee of or successor to the recipient's interest in the collateral.

（e）A person that receives a request for an accounting or a request regarding a statement of account, claims no interest in the obligations when it receives the request, and claimed an interest in the obligations at an earlier time shall comply with the request within 14 days after receipt by sending to the debtor an authenticated record:

（1）disclaiming any interest in the obligations;and

（2）if known to the recipient, providing the name and mailing address of any assignee of or successor to the recipient's interest in the obligations.

（f）A debtor is entitled without charge to one response to a request under this section during any six-month period.The secured party may require payment of a charge not exceeding $25 for each additional response.

第3章　完善和优先顺序

PART 3. PERFECTION AND PRIORITY

第 9.301 条　约束担保权益之完善和优先顺序的法律

除第 9.303 条至第 9.306 条另有规定外，有关担保物中担保权益之完善方式、完善或不完善的效力，以及优先顺序的适用法，应按下列原则确定：

（1）除本条另有规定外，当债务人位于某州时，担保物中担保权益之完善方式、完善或不完善的效力，以及优先顺序，受该州法律的约束。

（2）当担保物位于某州时，担保物中占有性担保权益之完善方式、完善或不完善的效力，以及优先顺序，受该州法律的约束。

（3）除（4）款另有规定外，当实体流通凭证、货物、票据、金钱或实体动产契据位于某州时，下列事项受该州法律的约束：

（A）通过不动产附着物登记，完善货物中的担保权益；

（B）完善待砍伐树木中的担保权益；以及

（C）涉及担保物中非占有性担保权益时，完善或不完善

§ 9.301. Law Governing Perfection and Priority of Security Interests.

Except as otherwise provided in Sections 9.303 through 9.306, the following rules determine the law governing perfection, the effect of perfection or nonperfection, and the priority of a security interest in collateral:

（1）Except as otherwise provided in this section, while a debtor is located in a jurisdiction, the local law of that jurisdiction governs perfection, the effect of perfection or nonperfection, and the priority of a security interest in collateral.

（2）While collateral is located in a jurisdiction, the local law of that jurisdiction governs perfection, the effect of perfection or nonperfection, and the priority of a possessory security interest in that collateral.

（3）Except as otherwise provided in Subdivision（4）, while tangible negotiable documents, goods, instruments, money, or tangible chattel paper is located in a jurisdiction, the local law of that jurisdiction governs:

（A）perfection of a security interest in the goods by filing a fixture filing;

（B）perfection of a security interest in timber to be cut;and

（C）the effect of perfection or nonperfection and the priority of a nonpossessory security

的效力，以及优先顺序。

（4）当井源或矿源位于某州时，开采状担保物中担保权益之完善方式、完善或不完善的效力，以及优先顺序，受该州法律的约束。

第 9.302 条　约束农业留置权之完善和优先顺序的法律

当农产品位于某州时，农产品中农业留置权之完善方式、完善或不完善的效力，以及优先顺序，受该州法律的约束。

第 9.303 条　约束产权证书覆盖之货物中担保权益之完善和优先顺序的法律

（a）本条适用于由产权证书覆盖的货物，即使颁发证书的州与货物或与债务人没有其他联系。

（b）如果向相关机构递交了有效的产权证书申请和所需费用，则从递交之时起，货物即被视为具有产权证书。如果产权证书根据证书颁发州的法律失去效力，或如果另一州就该货物随后颁发产权证书，则从两者中先发生的时间起，货物即被视为不再具有原产权证书。

（c）如果货物具有产权证书，从货物获得产权证书时起至货物不再具有该证书时止，

interest in the collateral.

（4）The local law of the jurisdiction in which the wellhead or minehead is located governs perfection, the effect of perfection or nonperfection, and the priority of a security interest in as-extracted collateral.

§ 9.302. Law Governing Perfection and Priority of Agricultural Liens.

While farm products are located in a jurisdiction, the local law of that jurisdiction governs perfection, the effect of perfection or nonperfection, and the priority of an agricultural lien on the farm products.

§ 9.303. Law Governing Perfection and Priority of Security Interests in Goods Covered by a Certificate of Title.

（a）This section applies to goods covered by a certificate of title, even if there is no other relationship between the jurisdiction under whose certificate of title the goods are covered and the goods or the debtor.

（b）Goods become covered by a certificate of title when a valid application for the certificate of title and the applicable fee are delivered to the appropriate authority.Goods cease to be covered by a certificate of title at the earlier of the time the certificate of title ceases to be effective under the law of the issuing jurisdiction or the time the goods become covered subsequently by a certificate of title issued by another jurisdiction.

（c）The local law of the jurisdiction under whose certificate of title the goods are covered governs perfection, the effect of perfection or

对于由产权证书覆盖的货物，其中担保权益之完善方式、完善或不完善的效力，以及优先顺序，受产权证书颁发州法律的约束。

nonperfection, and the priority of a security interest in goods covered by a certificate of title from the time the goods become covered by the certificate of title until the goods cease to be covered by the certificate of title.

第 9.304 条 约束存款账户中担保权益之完善和优先顺序的法律

§ 9.304. Law Governing Perfection and Priority of Security Interests in Deposit Accounts.

（a）对于银行掌管的存款账户，存款账户中担保权益之完善方式、完善或不完善的效力，以及优先顺序，受银行所在州法律的约束。

（a）The local law of a bank's jurisdiction governs perfection, the effect of perfection or nonperfection, and the priority of a security interest in a deposit account maintained with that bank.

（b）为本章目的，应按下列原则确定银行所在州：

（b）The following rules determine a bank's jurisdiction for purposes of this Part:

（1）如果银行和债务人之间有关存款账户的协议明确规定，为本章、本篇或本法目的，某州为银行所在州，则该州即为银行所在州。

（1）If an agreement between the bank and its customer governing the deposit account expressly provides that a particular jurisdiction is the bank's jurisdiction for purposes of this Part, this Article, or this Act, that jurisdiction is the bank's jurisdiction.

（2）如果（1）款不适用，但银行和债务人之间有关存款账户的协议明确规定，协议受某州法律的约束，则该州即为银行所在州。

（2）If Subdivision（1）does not apply and an agreement between the bank and its customer governing the deposit account expressly provides that the agreement is governed by the law of a particular jurisdiction, that jurisdiction is the bank's jurisdiction.

（3）如果（1）款和（2）款均不适用，但银行和债务人之间有关存款账户的协议明确规定，该账户由银行在某州的营业处掌管，则该州即为银行所在州。

（3）If neither Subdivision（1）nor Subdivision（2）applies and an agreement between the bank and its customer governing the deposit account expressly provides that the deposit account is maintained at an office in a particular jurisdiction, that jurisdiction is the bank's jurisdiction.

（4）如果上述任何一款均不适用，但账户报告单上注明了为该客户之账户提供服务的营业处，则该营业处所在州即为银行所在州。

（4）If none of the preceding subdivisions applies, the bank's jurisdiction is the jurisdiction in which the office identified in an account statement as the office serving the customer's account is located.

（5）如果上述任何一款均不适用，则银行首席行政官办公室的所在州即为银行所在州。

（5）If none of the preceding subdivisions applies, the bank's jurisdiction is the jurisdiction in which the chief executive office of the bank is located.

第 9.305 条　约束投资财产中担保权益之完善和优先顺序的法律

§ 9.305. Law Governing Perfection and Priority of Security Interests in Investment Property.

（a）除（c）款另有规定外，应适用下列原则：

（a）Except as otherwise provided in Subsection（c）, the following rules apply:

（1）当证券证书位于某州时，其所代表的票式证券中担保权益之完善方式、完善或不完善的效力，以及优先顺序，受证券证书所在州法律的约束。

（1）While a security certificate is located in a jurisdiction, the local law of that jurisdiction governs perfection, the effect of perfection or nonperfection, and the priority of a security interest in the certificated security represented thereby.

（2）无票证券中担保权益之完善方式、完善或不完善的效力，以及优先顺序，受第 8.110 条（d）款所述的发行人所在州法律的约束。

（2）The local law of the issuer's jurisdiction as specified in Section 8.110（d）governs perfection, the effect of perfection or nonperfection, and the priority of a security interest in an uncertificated security.

（3）证券权利或证券账户中担保权益之完善方式、完善或不完善的效力，以及优先顺序，受第 8.110 条（e）款所述的证券中间人所在州法律的约束。

（3）The local law of the securities intermediary's jurisdiction as specified in Section 8.110（e）governs perfection, the effect of perfection or nonperfection, and the priority of a security interest in a security entitlement or securities account.

（4）商品合同或商品账户

（4）The local law of the commodity

中担保权益之完善方式、完善或不完善的效力，以及优先顺序，受商品中间人所在州法律的约束。

intermediary's jurisdiction governs perfection, the effect of perfection or nonperfection, and the priority of a security interest in a commodity contract or commodity account.

（b）为本章目的，应按下列原则确定商品中间人所在州：

（b）The following rules determine a commodity intermediary's jurisdiction for purposes of this Part:

（1）如果商品中间人和商品客户之间有关商品账户的协议明确规定，为本章、本篇或本法目的，某州为商品中间人所在州，则该州即为商品中间人所在州。

（1）If an agreement between the commodity intermediary and commodity customer governing the commodity account expressly provides that a particular jurisdiction is the commodity intermediary's jurisdiction for purposes of this Part, this Article, or this Act, that jurisdiction is the commodity intermediary's jurisdiction.

（2）如果（1）款不适用，但商品中间人和商品客户之间有关商品账户的协议明确规定，协议受某州法律的约束，则该州即为商品中间人所在州。

（2）If Subdivision（1）does not apply and an agreement between the commodity intermediary and commodity customer governing the commodity account expressly provides that the agreement is governed by the law of a particular jurisdiction, that jurisdiction is the commodity intermediary's jurisdiction.

（3）如果（1）款和（2）款均不适用，但商品中间人和商品客户之间有关商品账户的协议明确规定，账户由商品中间人在某州的营业处掌管，则该州即为商品中间人所在州。

（3）If neither Subdivision（1）nor Subdivision（2）applies and an agreement between the commodity intermediary and commodity customer governing the commodity account expressly provides that the commodity account is maintained at an office in a particular jurisdiction, that jurisdiction is the commodity intermediary's jurisdiction.

（4）如果上述任何一款均不适用，但账户报告单上注明了为该客户之账户提供服务的

（4）If none of the preceding subdivisions applies, the commodity intermediary's jurisdiction is the jurisdiction in which the

营业处，则该营业处所在州即为商品中间人所在州。

office identified in an account statement as the office serving the commodity customer's account is located.

（5）如果上述任何一款均不适用，则商品中间人首席行政官办公室的所在州即为商品中间人所在州。

（5）If none of the preceding subdivisions applies, the commodity intermediary's jurisdiction is the jurisdiction in which the chief executive office of the commodity intermediary is located.

（c）下列事项受债务人所在地的州法约束：

（1）通过登记完善投资财产中的担保权益；

（2）涉及经纪人或证券中间人在投资财产中设立的担保权益时，担保权益的自动完善；以及

（3）涉及商品中间人在商品合同或商品账户中设立的担保权益时，担保权益的自动完善。

（c）The local law of the jurisdiction in which the debtor is located governs:

（1）perfection of a security interest in investment property by filing;

（2）automatic perfection of a security interest in investment property created by a broker or securities intermediary;and

（3）automatic perfection of a security interest in a commodity contract or commodity account created by a commodity intermediary.

第 9.306 条　约束信用证权利中担保权益之完善和优先顺序的法律

§ 9.306. Law Governing Perfection and Priority of Security Interests in Letter-of-Credit Rights.

（a）除（c）款另有规定外，当开证人或指定人所在州为某州时，信用证权利中担保权益之完善方式、完善或不完善的效力，以及优先顺序，受开证人或指定人所在州法律的约束。

（a）Subject to Subsection（c）, the local law of the issuer's jurisdiction or a nominated person's jurisdiction governs perfection, the effect of perfection or nonperfection, and the priority of a security interest in a letter-of-credit right if the issuer's jurisdiction or nominated person's jurisdiction is a state.

（b）为本章目的，涉及第 5.116 条所述的信用证权利时，如果开证人或指定人的义务受

（b）For purposes of this Part, an issuer's jurisdiction or nominated person's jurisdiction is the jurisdiction whose law governs the

某州法律的约束，该州即为开证人或指定人所在州。

liability of the issuer or nominated person with respect to the letter-of-credit right as provided in Section 5.116.

（c）如果担保权益只能根据第 9.308 条（d）款获得完善，则本条不适用。

（c）This section does not apply to a security interest that is perfected only under Section 9.308（d）.

第 9.307 条 债务人所在地

§ 9.307. Location of Debtor.

（a）在本条中，“营业地”指债务人从事业务的地点。

（a）In this section, “place of business” means a place where a debtor conducts its affairs.

（b）除本条另有规定外，应根据下列原则确定债务人所在地：

（b）Except as otherwise provided in this section, the following rules determine a debtor’s location:

（1）如果债务人是个人，则其主要居所即为所在地。

（1）A debtor who is an individual is located at the individual’s principal residence.

（2）如果债务人是组织，且只有一个营业地，则其营业地即为所在地。

（2）A debtor that is an organization and has only one place of business is located at its place of business.

（3）如果债务人是组织，且有一个以上营业地，则其首席行政官办公室的所在地即为所在地。

（3）A debtor that is an organization and has more than one place of business is located at its chief executive office.

（c）只有满足下列条件时，上述（b）款才适用：债务人的居所、营业地或首席行政官办公室所在地（以适用者为准）之所在州，其法律必须原则上要求，非占有性担保权益的有关情况，需要通过登记或记录使公众得知，并且，该登记或记录，是使该担保权益就担保物取得优于留置权债权人之优先权的条件，或是取得该优先

（c）Subsection（b）applies only if a debtor’s residence, place of business, or chief executive office, as applicable, is located in a jurisdiction whose law generally requires information concerning the existence of a nonpossessory security interest to be made generally available in a filing, recording, or registration system as a condition or result of the security interest’s obtaining priority over the rights of a lien creditor with respect to the collateral.If Subsection（b）does not apply, the

权后必须完成的手续。如果（b）款不适用，则债务人的所在地为哥伦比亚特区。

debtor is located in the District of Columbia.

（d）一个人即使不再存在，或不再拥有居所或营业地，其仍被视为继续位于（b）款或（c）款规定的所在地。

（d）A person that ceases to exist, have a residence, or have a place of business continues to be located in the jurisdiction specified by Subsections（b）and（c）.

（e）如果一个组织根据某州的法律注册成立，则该州即为所在地。

（e）A registered organization that is organized under the law of a state is located in that state.

（f）除（i）款另有规定外，涉及根据美国联邦法律注册成立的组织，以及非根据美国联邦法律或任何州法律注册成立的银行分行或代理处时，应根据下列原则确定所在地：

（f）Except as otherwise provided in Subsection（i）, a registered organization that is organized under the law of the United States and a branch or agency of a bank that is not organized under the law of the United States or a state are located:

（1）如果美国联邦法律规定了其所在州，则该州即为所在地；

（1）in the state that the law of the United States designates, if the law designates a state of location;

（2）如果美国联邦法律允许此种注册成立的组织、分行或代理处规定其所在州，则此种注册成立的组织、分行或代理处所规定的州，即为其所在地；或

（2）in the state that the registered organization, branch, or agency designates, if the law of the United States authorizes the registered organization, branch, or agency to designate its state of location;or

（3）如果（1）款和（2）款均不适用，则哥伦比亚特区即为所在地。

（3）in the District of Columbia, if neither Subdivision（1）nor Subdivision（2）applies.

（g）注册成立之组织的所在地，在下列情况下仍为（e）款或（f）款规定的州：

（g）A registered organization continues to be located in the jurisdiction specified by Subsection（e）or（f）notwithstanding:

（1）该组织在其注册成立地发生暂停、撤销、取缔或过

（1）the suspension, revocation, forfeiture, or lapse of the registered organization's status

期；或

（2）该组织发生解散、清盘或注销。

（h）美国的所在地为哥伦比亚特区。

（i）如果非根据美国联邦法律或任何州法律注册成立之银行的所有分行或代理处，都只在同一个州取得执照，则该银行任何一个分行或代理处的所在地，均为其取得执照的州。

（j）在最新修订的《1958年联邦航空法》中，外国航空公司的所在地，为代表该航空公司收取诉讼通知之代理人的指定办公地。

（k）本条只适用于本章目的。

第 9.308 条 担保权益或农业留置权获得完善的时间；完善的持续性

（a）除本条及第 9.309 条另有规定外，在担保权益已发生附着，且第 9.310 条至第 9.316 条对获得完善所规定的全部适用条件均已满足后，担保权益即获得完善。如果该等适用条件在附着发生前即已满足，则担保权益在发生附着时获得完善。

（b）在农业留置权已生效，且第 9.310 条对获得完善所规

as such in its jurisdiction of organization;or

（2）the dissolution, winding up, or cancellation of the existence of the registered organization.

（h）The United States is located in the District of Columbia.

（i）A branch or agency of a bank that is not organized under the law of the United States or a state is located in the state in which the branch or agency is licensed, if all branches and agencies of the bank are licensed in only one state.

（j）A foreign air carrier under the Federal Aviation Act of 1958, as amended, is located at the designated office of the agent upon which service of process may be made on behalf of the carrier.

（k）This section applies only for purposes of this Part.

§ 9.308. When Security Interest or Agricultural Lien Is Perfected;Continuity of Perfection.

（a）Except as otherwise provided in this section and Section 9.309, a security interest is perfected if it has attached and all of the applicable requirements for perfection in Sections 9.310 through 9.316 have been satisfied.A security interest is perfected when it attaches if the applicable requirements are satisfied before the security interest attaches.

（b）An agricultural lien is perfected if it has become effective and all of the applicable

定的全部适用条件均已满足后，农业留置权即获得完善。如果该等适用条件在农业留置权生效前即已满足，则农业留置权在生效时即获得完善。

requirements for perfection in Section 9.310 have been satisfied.An agricultural lien is perfected when it becomes effective if the applicable requirements are satisfied before the agricultural lien becomes effective.

（c）如果担保权益或农业留置权先通过本篇规定的任何一种方法获得完善，其后又通过本篇规定的另一种方法获得完善，则只要在两次完善之间不存在不完善的期间，该担保权益或农业留置权即被视为始终保持完善。

（c）A security interest or agricultural lien is perfected continuously if it is originally perfected by one method under this Article and is later perfected by another method under this Article, without an intermediate period when it was unperfected.

（d）担保物中的担保权益获得完善后，即同时使该担保物之支持性债务中的担保权益获得完善。

（d）Perfection of a security interest in collateral also perfects a security interest in a supporting obligation for the collateral.

（e）获得付款或履约之权利中的担保权益获得完善后，即同时使担保该权利之动产或不动产中的担保权益、不动产抵押权，或其他留置权中的担保权益获得完善。

（e）Perfection of a security interest in a right to payment or performance also perfects a security interest in a security interest, mortgage, or other lien on personal or real property securing the right.

（f）证券账户中的担保权益获得完善后，即同时使证券账户项下之证券权利中的担保权益获得完善。

（f）Perfection of a security interest in a securities account also perfects a security interest in the security entitlements carried in the securities account.

（g）商品账户中的担保权益获得完善后，即同时使商品账户项下之商品合同中的担保权益获得完善。

（g）Perfection of a security interest in a commodity account also perfects a security interest in the commodity contracts carried in the commodity account.

第 9.309 条 发生附着时即获得完善的担保权益

下列担保权益在发生附着时即获得完善：

（1）消费品中的价款担保权益；但是，如果消费品受第 9.311 条（a）款所述法律或条约的约束，则在第 9.311 条（b）款对该消费品另有规定时除外；

（2）应收款或无形支付的转让，只要该转让无论单独计算，还是与同一受让人获得的其他转让合并计算，均不构成转让人未结应收款或无形支付之重要部分的转让；

（3）无形支付的买卖；

（4）本票的买卖；

（5）涉及向医疗用品或医疗服务提供者转让医疗保险应收款时，因该转让引起的担保权益；

（6）根据第 2.401 条、第 2.505 条、第 2.711 条（c）款或第 2A.508 条（e）款产生的担保权益，但仅适用于债务人尚未取得担保物占有的情况；

（7）收款银行根据第 4.210 条取得的担保权益；

（8）开证人或指定人根据第 5.118 条取得的担保权益；

（9）根据第 9.206 条（c）款因交付金融资产取得的担保权益；

§ 9.309. Security Interest Perfected Upon Attachment.

The following security interests are perfected when they attach:

（1）a purchase money security interest in consumer goods, except as otherwise provided in Section 9.311（b）with respect to consumer goods that are subject to a statute or treaty described in Section 9.311（a）;

（2）an assignment of accounts or payment intangibles that does not by itself or in conjunction with other assignments to the same assignee transfer a significant part of the assignor's outstanding accounts or payment intangibles;

（3）a sale of a payment intangible;

（4）a sale of a promissory note;

（5）a security interest created by the assignment of a health-care-insurance receivable to the provider of the health care goods or services;

（6）a security interest arising under Section 2.401, 2.505, 2.711（c）, or 2A.508（e）, until the debtor obtains possession of the collateral;

（7）a security interest of a collecting bank arising under Section 4.210;

（8）a security interest of an issuer or nominated person arising under Section 5.118;

（9）a security interest arising in the delivery of a financial asset under Section 9.206（c）;

（10）经纪人或证券中间人在投资财产中设立的担保权益；

（10）a security interest in investment property created by a broker or securities intermediary;

（11）商品中间人在商品合同或商品账户中设立的担保权益；

（11）a security interest in a commodity contract or a commodity account created by a commodity intermediary;

（12）为转让人全体债权人利益所作的转让，以及受让人随后作出的转让；

（12）an assignment for the benefit of all the creditors of the transferor and subsequent transfers by the assignee thereunder;

（13）因转让去世者遗产之收益权产生的担保权益；以及

（13）a security interest created by an assignment of a beneficial interest in a decedent's estate;and

（14）涉及个人在博彩或赌博游戏中赢取的应收款时，个人对该应收款的买卖。

（14）a sale by an individual of an account that is a right to payment of winnings in a lottery or other game of chance.

第 9.310 条　必须通过登记获得完善的担保权益或农业留置权；登记条款不适用的担保权益和农业留置权

§ 9.310. When Filing Required to Perfect Security Interest or Agricultural Lien; Security Interests and Agricultural Liens to Which Filing Provisions Do Not Apply.

（a）除（b）款和第 9.312 条（b）款另有规定外，所有的担保权益和农业留置权，均必须通过登记融资声明获得完善。

（a）Except as otherwise provided in Subsection（b）and Section 9.312（b）, a financing statement must be filed to perfect all security interests and agricultural liens.

（b）下列担保权益的完善，无须登记融资声明：

（b）The filing of a financing statement is not necessary to perfect a security interest:

（1）根据第 9.308 条（d）款、（e）款、（f）款或（g）款获得完善的担保权益；

（1）that is perfected under Section 9.308（d）,（e）,（f）, or（g）;

（2）根据第 9.309 条在发生附着时即获得完善的担保权益；

（2）that is perfected under Section 9.309 when it attaches;

（3）受第 9.311 条（a）款所述法律或条约约束之财产中

（3）in property subject to a statute, regulation, or treaty described in Section 9.311

的担保权益；

（4）涉及货物保管人占有的货物时，货物中根据第9.312条（d）（1）款或（2）款获得完善的担保权益；

（5）涉及票式证券、凭证、货物或票据中的担保权益时，根据第9.312条（e）款、（f）款或（g）款，不经登记、控制或占有而获得完善的担保权益；

（6）第9.313条所述的受担保方所占有之担保物中的担保权益；

（7）涉及票式证券中的担保权益时，根据第9.313条通过向受担保方交付证券证书而获得完善的担保权益；

（8）涉及存款账户、电子动产契据、电子凭证、投资财产或信用证权利中的担保权益时，根据第9.314条通过取得控制而获得完善的担保权益；

（9）收益中根据第9.315条获得完善的担保权益；

（10）根据第9.316条获得完善的担保权益；或

（11）第9.343条所述的石油或天然气生产中或其收益中的担保权益。

（c）受担保方在转让完善担保权益或农业留置权时，无须作出本篇规定的登记，即可使担保权益在对抗原始债务人

(a);

(4) in goods in possession of a bailee that is perfected under Section 9.312(d)(1) or (2);

(5) in certificated securities, documents, goods, or instruments which is perfected without filing, control or possession under Section 9.312 (e), (f), or (g);

(6) in collateral in the secured party's possession under Section 9.313;

(7) in a certificated security that is perfected by delivery of the security certificate to the secured party under Section 9.313;

(8) in deposit accounts, electronic chattel paper, electronic documents, investment property, or letter-of-credit rights that is perfected by control under Section 9.314;

(9) in proceeds that is perfected under Section 9.315;

(10) that is perfected under Section 9.316;or

(11) in oil or gas production or their proceeds under Section 9.343.

(c) If a secured party assigns a perfected security interest or agricultural lien, a filing under this Article is not required to continue the perfected status of the security interest against

的债权人和受让人时，保持完善。

creditors of and transferees from the original debtor.

第 9.311 条 受某些法律或条约约束之财产中担保权益的完善

§ 9.311. Perfection of Security Interests in Property Subject to Certain Statutes, Regulations, and Treaties.

（a）除（d）款另有规定外，为完善下列财产中的担保权益，无须登记融资声明，且登记亦不具有任何效力：

（a）Except as otherwise provided in Subsection（d）, the filing of a financing statement is not necessary or effective to perfect a security interest in property subject to:

（1）受美国联邦法律或条约约束的财产，只要在涉及该财产中之担保权益在何种条件下优于留置权债权人之权利的问题时，该法律或条约的效力优于第 9.310 条（a）款；

（1）a statute, regulation, or treaty of the United States whose requirements for a security interest's obtaining priority over the rights of a lien creditor with respect to the property preempt Section 9.310（a）;

（2）受本州下列法律约束的财产：《交通法》中有关机动车产权证书的规定，《公园及野生动物法》中有关船舶和外装马达产权证书的规定，《行业法》中有关工厂预制房屋产权证书的规定，或有关公用事业企业之担保票据的法律规定；或

（2）the following statutes of this state:Transportation Code,relating to the certificates of title for motor vehicles;Parks and Wildlife Code,relating to the certificates of title for vessels and outboard motors;Occupations Code, relating to the documents of title for manufactured homes;or the law relating to utility security instruments;or

（3）受另一州产权证书法约束的财产，只要该法规定，将担保权益注明在产权证书上，是该担保权益就该财产取得优于留置权债权人之权利的前提条件，或是取得该优先权后必须完成的手续。

（3）a certificate of title statute of another jurisdiction that provides for a security interest to be indicated on the certificate as a condition or result of the security interest's obtaining priority over the rights of a lien creditor with respect to the property.

（b）如果要取得优于留置权债权人之权利的权利，遵守

（b）Compliance with the requirements of a statute, regulation, or treaty described

（a）款所述的法律或条约，即相当于登记了本篇项下的融资声明。除（d）款以及有关由产权证书所覆盖之货物的第 9.313 条和第 9.316 条（d）款和（e）款另有规定外，受（a）款所述之法律或条约约束之财产中的担保权益，只能通过遵守该法律或条约的规定获得完善；并且，即使担保物的使用发生变化或占有发生转移，通过此种方式获得完善的担保权益，仍继续保持完善。

in Subsection（a）for obtaining priority over the rights of a lien creditor is equivalent to the filing of a financing statement under this Article.Except as otherwise provided in Subsection（d）and Sections 9.313 and 9.316（d）and（e）for goods covered by a certificate of title, a security interest in property subject to a statute, regulation, or treaty described in Subsection（a）may be perfected only by compliance with those requirements, and a security interest so perfected remains perfected notwithstanding a change in the use or transfer of possession of the collateral.

（c）除（d）款以及第 9.316 条（d）款和（e）款另有规定外，通过遵守（a）款所述法律或条约获得完善的担保权益，其完善的期间和续期由该法律或条约规定，但担保权益的其他方面受本篇约束。

（c）Except as otherwise provided in Subsection（d）and Sections 9.316（d）and（e）, duration and renewal of perfection of a security interest perfected by compliance with the requirements prescribed by a statute, regulation, or treaty described in Subsection（a）are governed by the statute, regulation, or treaty.In other respects, the security interest is subject to this Article.

（d）如果受（a）（2）款所述法律约束的担保物，被任何从事该类货物出售业务的人，为出售或出租目的作为库存持有，或作为库存以出租方的身份出租，则在担保物作为库存的期间，本条不适用于该人在该担保物中设立的担保权益。

（d）During any period in which collateral subject to a statute specified in Subsection（a）（2）is inventory held for sale or lease by a person or leased by that person as lessor and that person is in the business of selling goods of that kind, this section does not apply to a security interest in that collateral created by that person.

第 9.312 条 动产契据、存款账户、凭证、凭证覆盖的货物、票据、投资财产、信用证权利以及金钱中担保权益的完善；通过许可性登记获得完善；无须登记或转移占有的临时完善

（a）动产契据、流通凭证、票据或投资财产中的担保权益，可以通过登记获得完善。

（b）除第 9.315 条（c）款和（d）款对收益另有规定外：

（1）存款账户中的担保权益，只能通过取得第 9.314 条所述的控制获得完善；

（2）并且，除第 9.308 条（d）款另有规定外，信用证权利中的担保权益，只能通过取得第 9.314 条所述的控制获得完善；以及

（3）金钱中的担保权益，只能通过受担保方取得第 9.313 条所述的占有获得完善。

（c）如果货物保管人已出具覆盖货物的流通凭证，则在其占有货物期间：

（1）可以通过完善凭证中的担保权益，使货物中的担保权益获得完善；并且

（2）凭证中的完善担保权益，优于该期间内货物中以其他方式获得完善的担保权益。

§ 9.312. Perfection of Security Interests in Chattel Paper, Deposit Accounts, Documents, and Goods Covered by Documents, Instruments, Investment Property, Letter-of-Credit Rights, and Money;Perfection by Permissive Filing; Temporary Perfection Without Filing or Transfer of Possession.

（a）A security interest in chattel paper, negotiable documents, instruments, or investment property may be perfected by filing.

（b）Except as otherwise provided in Sections 9.315（c）and（d）for proceeds:

（1）a security interest in a deposit account may be perfected only by control under Section 9.314;

（2）and except as otherwise provided in Section 9.308（d）, a security interest in a letter-of-credit right may be perfected only by control under Section 9.314;and

（3）a security interest in money may be perfected only by the secured party's taking possession under Section 9.313.

（c）While goods are in the possession of a bailee that has issued a negotiable document covering the goods:

（1）a security interest in the goods may be perfected by perfecting a security interest in the document;and

（2）a security interest perfected in the document has priority over any security interest that becomes perfected in the goods by another method during that time.

（d）如果货物保管人已出具覆盖货物的不可流通凭证，则在其占有货物期间，可以通过下列方式完善货物中的担保权益：

（1）以受担保方的名字出具凭证；

（2）使货物保管人收到受担保方权益的通知；或

（3）就货物作出登记。

（e）票式证券、流通凭证或票据中的担保权益发生附着后，可以无须登记，也无须占有或控制担保物，而在20天内保持完善，只要担保权益产生于业经认证之担保协议项下提供的新价值。

（f）流通凭证中的完善担保权益，或货物保管人（已就货物出具流通凭证的除外）所占有之货物中的完善担保权益，在受担保方为下列目的将货物或覆盖货物的凭证提供给债务人后，可以无须登记而在20天内保持完善：

（1）为最终出售或交换；或

（2）为装货、卸货、存储、运输、转运、制造或加工，或为出售或交换而做的其他准备活动。

（g）票式证券或票据中的完善担保权益，在受担保方为下列目的将证券证书或票据交

（d）While goods are in the possession of a bailee that has issued a nonnegotiable document covering the goods, a security interest in the goods may be perfected by:

（1）issuance of a document in the name of the secured party;

（2）the bailee's receipt of notification of the secured party's interest;or

（3）filing as to the goods.

（e）A security interest in certificated securities, negotiable documents, or instruments is perfected without filing or the taking of possession or control for a period of 20 days from the time it attaches to the extent that it arises for new value given under an authenticated security agreement.

（f）A perfected security interest in a negotiable document or goods in possession of a bailee, other than one that has issued a negotiable document for the goods, remains perfected for 20 days without filing if the secured party makes available to the debtor the goods or documents representing the goods for the purpose of:

（1）ultimate sale or exchange;or

（2）loading, unloading, storing, shipping, transshipping, manufacturing, processing, or otherwise dealing with them in a manner preliminary to their sale or exchange.

（g）A perfected security interest in a certificated security or instrument remains perfected for 20 days without filing if the

付给债务人后，可以无须登记而在二十天内保持完善：

（1）为最终出售或交换；或

（2）为提示、收款、强制履行、续延或转让登记。

（h）在（e）款、（f）款和（g）款规定的 20 天期限之后，只有遵守本篇规定，担保权益才能获得完善。

第 9.313 条　受担保方取得占有或交付后无须登记而获得完善的担保权益

（a）除（b）款另有规定外，受担保方可以通过占有担保物，使实体流通凭证、货物、票据、金钱或实体动产契据中的担保权益获得完善。受担保方可以根据第 8.301 条，通过取得票式证券的交付，使其中的担保权益获得完善。

（b）涉及由本州产权证书覆盖的货物时，只有在第 9.316 条（d）款所述的情况下，受担保方才可以通过占有货物，使其中的担保权益获得完善。

（c）如果担保物不是票式证券，也不是凭证覆盖的货物，且占有担保物的人，不是债务人或受担保方，也不是债务人在正常业务中出租担保物后的承租方，则受担保方在下列情

secured party delivers the security certificate or instrument to the debtor for the purpose of:

（1）ultimate sale or exchange;or

（2）presentation, collection, enforcement, renewal, or registration of transfer.

（h）After the 20-day period specified in Subsection（e）,（f）, or（g）expires, perfection depends upon compliance with this Article.

§ 9.313. When Possession by or Delivery to Secured Party Perfects Security Interest Without Filing.

（a）Except as otherwise provided in Subsection（b）, a secured party may perfect a security interest in tangible negotiable documents, goods, instruments, money, or tangible chattel paper by taking possession of the collateral.A secured party may perfect a security interest in certificated securities by taking delivery of the certificated securities under Section 8.301.

（b）With respect to goods covered by a certificate of title issued by this state, a secured party may perfect a security interest in the goods by taking possession of the goods only in the circumstances described in Section 9.316（d）.

（c）With respect to collateral other than certificated securities and goods covered by a document, a secured party takes possession of collateral in the possession of a person other than the debtor, the secured party, or a lessee of the collateral from the debtor in the ordinary

况下被视为占有担保物：

（1）占有担保物的人，在业经认证的记录中声明，其为受担保方的利益占有担保物；或

（2）占有担保物的人在取得占有之前，在业经认证的记录中声明，其将为受担保方的利益占有担保物。

（d）如果只有通过受担保方占有担保物，担保权益才能获得完善，则在受担保方取得占有之前，担保权益不能获得完善；并且，只有受担保方保持占有，担保权益才能保持完善。

（e）如果根据第8.301条交付登记式的票式证券，则证券中的担保权益，通过交付获得完善，且在债务人取得证券证书的占有之前，该交付使担保权益保持完善。

（f）占有担保物的人，无须声明其为受担保方的利益占有担保物。

（g）如果任何人声明，其为受担保方的利益占有担保物：

（1）即使该声明侵犯了债务人的权利，该声明在（c）款或第8.301条（a）款意义上仍然有效；并且

（2）除该人另有约定或除本篇以外的其他法律另有规定

course of the debtor's business when:

(1) the person in possession authenticates a record acknowledging that it holds possession of the collateral for the secured party's benefit;or

(2) the person takes possession of the collateral after having authenticated a record acknowledging that it will hold possession of collateral for the secured party's benefit.

(d) If perfection of a security interest depends upon possession of the collateral by a secured party, perfection occurs no earlier than the time the secured party takes possession and continues only while the secured party retains possession.

(e) A security interest in a certificated security in registered form is perfected by delivery when delivery of the certificated security occurs under Section 8.301 and remains perfected by delivery until the debtor obtains possession of the security certificate.

(f) A person in possession of collateral is not required to acknowledge that it holds possession for a secured party's benefit.

(g) If a person acknowledges that it holds possession for the secured party's benefit:

(1) the acknowledgment is effective under Subsection (c) or Section 8.301 (a), even if the acknowledgment violates the rights of a debtor;and

(2) unless the person otherwise agrees or law other than this Article otherwise provides,

外，该人不对受担保方承担任何义务，也无须向另一人确认该声明。

（h）占有担保物的受担保方即使向任何人交付担保物，只要该人不是债务人，也不是债务人在正常业务中出租担保物后的承租方，受担保方即不属于放弃担保物的占有，只要其在交付担保物之前或同时，向该人作出下列指示：

（1）为受担保方的利益占有担保物；或

（2）应将担保物交还给受担保方。

（i）即使（h）款所述的交付侵犯了债务人的权利，受担保方亦不属于放弃担保物的占有。收到（h）款所述之担保物交付的人，除另有约定或除本篇以外的其他法律另有规定外，不对受担保方承担任何义务，也无须向另一人确认该交付。

the person does not owe any duty to the secured party and is not required to confirm the acknowledgment to another person.

（h）A secured party having possession of collateral does not relinquish possession by delivering the collateral to a person other than the debtor or a lessee of the collateral from the debtor in the ordinary course of the debtor's business if the person was instructed before the delivery or is instructed contemporaneously with the delivery:

（1）to hold possession of the collateral for the secured party's benefit;or

（2）to redeliver the collateral to the secured party.

（i）A secured party does not relinquish possession, even if a delivery under Subsection（h）violates the rights of a debtor.A person to which collateral is delivered under Subsection（h）does not owe any duty to the secured party and is not required to confirm the delivery to another person unless the person otherwise agrees or law other than this Article otherwise provides.

第 9.314 条　通过取得控制获得完善

（a）投资财产、存款账户、信用证权利、电子动产契据或电子凭证中的担保权益，可以根据第 7.106 条、第 9.104 条、第 9.105 条、第 9.106 条或第 9.107 条，通过对担保物取得控制获得完善。

§ 9.314. Perfection by Control.

（a）A security interest in investment property, deposit accounts, letter-of-credit rights, electronic chattel paper, or electronic documents may be perfected by control of the collateral under Section 7.106, 9.104, 9.105, 9.106, or 9.107.

（b）涉及存款账户、电子动产契据、信用证权利或电子凭证中的担保权益时，在受担保方取得控制后，担保权益即根据第7.106条、第9.104条、第9.105条或第9.107条，通过取得控制获得完善；并且，只有受担保方保持控制，担保权益才能通过保持控制而保持完善。

（b）A security interest in deposit accounts, electronic chattel paper, letter-of-credit rights, or electronic documents is perfected by control under Section 7.106, 9.104, 9.105, or 9.107 when the secured party obtains control and remains perfected by control only while the secured party retains control.

（c）受担保方对投资财产取得控制后，其中的担保权益即根据第9.106条，通过取得控制获得完善，且在下列情况发生前，通过保持控制而保持完善：

（c）A security interest in investment property is perfected by control under Section 9.106 from the time the secured party obtains control and remains perfected by control until:

（1）受担保方失去控制；并且

（1）the secured party does not have control;and

（2）发生以下情况之一：

（2）one of the following occurs:

（A）当担保物是票式证券时，债务人占有证券证书；

（A）if the collateral is a certificated security, the debtor has or acquires possession of the security certificate;

（B）当担保物是无票证券时，发行人将债务人登记为注册所有权人；或

（B）if the collateral is an uncertificated security, the issuer has registered or registers the debtor as the registered owner;or

（C）当担保物是证券权利时，债务人成为权利持有人。

（C）if the collateral is a security entitlement, the debtor is or becomes the entitlement holder.

第9.315条　担保物被处置后受担保方的权利和对收益的权利

§ 9.315. Secured Party's Rights on Disposition of Collateral and in Proceeds.

（a）除本篇和第2.403条（b）款另有规定外：

（a）Except as otherwise provided in this Article and Section 2.403（b）:

（1）担保物被出售、出租、许可、交换或作其他处置后，其中的担保权益或农业留置权继续存在，除非受担保方给予授权，使担保物在处置后不受制于该担保权益或农业留置权；并且

（1）a security interest or agricultural lien continues in collateral notwithstanding sale, lease, license, exchange, or other disposition thereof unless the secured party authorized the disposition free of the security interest or agricultural lien;and

（2）担保权益附着于担保物的任何可分辨收益。

（2）a security interest attaches to any identifiable proceeds of collateral.

（b）即使收益已与其他财产混合：

（b）Proceeds that are commingled with other property are identifiable proceeds:

（1）当收益是货物时，收益在第 9.336 条所述的限度内属于可分辨收益；以及

（1）if the proceeds are goods, to the extent provided by Section 9.336;and

（2）当收益不是货物时，在受担保方有任何识别方法（包括使用公平原则）对收益进行分辨的限度内，收益属于可分辨收益，只要本篇以外的法律允许使用该方法分辨被混合的该类财产。

（2）if the proceeds are not goods, to the extent that the secured party identifies the proceeds by a method of tracing, including application of equitable principles, that is permitted under law other than this Article with respect to commingled property of the type involved.

（c）只要原始担保物中的担保权益原为完善，收益中的担保权益即为完善。

（c）A security interest in proceeds is a perfected security interest if the interest in the original collateral was perfected.

（d）收益中的完善担保权益，在附着于收益后的第 21 天失去完善性，除非：

（d）A perfected security interest in proceeds becomes unperfected on the 21st day after the security interest attaches to receipt of the proceeds unless:

（1）下列条件得到满足：

（1）the following conditions are satisfied:

（A）已登记的融资声明覆盖原始担保物；

（A）a filed financing statement covers the original collateral;

（B）允许通过在融资声明登记处作出登记，使收益所属

（B）the proceeds are collateral in which a security interest may be perfected by filing in

种类之担保物中的担保权益获得完善；并且

（C）没有使用现金收益取得该收益；

（2）收益为可分辨现金收益；或

（3）收益中的担保权益在附着于收益时或在其后20天内，根据（c）款以外的规定获得完善。

（e）如果已登记的融资声明覆盖原始担保物，则收益中根据（d）（1）款保持完善的担保权益，在下列两种情况中迟者发生时失去完善性：

（1）已登记的融资声明根据第9.515条到期失效，或根据第9.513条终止；或

（2）担保权益附着于收益后已满21天。

第9.316条 适用法改变后担保权益保持完善

（a）根据第9.301条（1）款或第9.305条（c）款规定之州法获得完善的担保权益，在下列情况中最早者发生后失去完善性：

（1）根据该州法律，完善本应失去效力的时间；

（2）债务人所在地换至另一州后已满四个月；或

the office in which the financing statement has been filed;and

（C）the proceeds are not acquired with cash proceeds;

（2）the proceeds are identifiable cash proceeds;or

（3）the security interest in the proceeds is perfected other than under Subsection（c）when the security interest attaches to the proceeds or within 20 days thereafter.

（e）If a filed financing statement covers the original collateral, a security interest in proceeds that remains perfected under Subsection（d）（1）becomes unperfected at the later of:

（1）when the effectiveness of the filed financing statement lapses under Section 9.515 or is terminated under Section 9.513;or

（2）the 21st day after the security interest attaches to the proceeds.

§ 9.316. Continued Perfection of Security Interest Following Change in Governing Law.

（a）A security interest perfected pursuant to the law of the jurisdiction designated in Section 9.301（1）or 9.305（c）remains perfected until the earliest of:

（1）the time perfection would have ceased under the law of that jurisdiction;

（2）the expiration of four months after a change of the debtor's location to another jurisdiction;or

（3）担保物转让后已满一年，且受让人因该转让成为债务人，且其所在地为另一州。

（3）the expiration of one year after a transfer of collateral to a person that thereby becomes a debtor and is located in another jurisdiction.

（b）如果（a）款所述的担保权益，在所述情况中最早者发生前，根据该另一州法律获得完善，则该担保权益随后将保持完善。如果该担保权益在该最早者发生时，尚未根据另一州法律获得完善，则该担保权益即失去完善性，且在对抗支付了价值的担保物购买人时，被视为从未获得过完善。

（b）If a security interest described in Subsection（a）becomes perfected under the law of the other jurisdiction before the earliest time or event described in that subsection, it remains perfected thereafter.If the security interest does not become perfected under the law of the other jurisdiction before the earliest time or event, it becomes unperfected and is deemed never to have been perfected as against a purchaser of the collateral for value.

（c）只要担保物不是产权证书覆盖的货物，也不是由货物构成的开采状担保物，担保物中占有性担保权益在下列情况下即一直保持完善：

（c）A possessory security interest in collateral, other than goods covered by a certificate of title and as-extracted collateral consisting of goods, remains continuously perfected if:

（1）担保物位于某州，且其中的担保权益根据该州法律获得完善；

（1）the collateral is located in one jurisdiction and subject to a security interest perfected under the law of that jurisdiction;

（2）担保物随后被带入另一州；并且

（2）thereafter the collateral is brought into another jurisdiction;and

（3）担保物进入该另一州后，担保权益根据该另一州的法律获得完善。

（3）upon entry into the other jurisdiction, the security interest is perfected under the law of the other jurisdiction.

（d）除（e）款另有规定外，涉及产权证书覆盖的货物时，如果货物中的担保权益，在货物获得本州的产权证书之前，已通过任何方式根据另一州法律获得完善，则该担保权

（d）Except as otherwise provided in Subsection（e）, a security interest in goods covered by a certificate of title that is perfected by any method under the law of another jurisdiction when the goods become covered by a certificate of title from this state remains

益将保持完善，直至在货物假设未获得本州产权证书的情况下，该担保权益根据该另一州法律本应失去完善性的时间。

perfected until the security interest would have become unperfected under the law of the other jurisdiction had the goods not become so covered.

（e）如果第9.311条（b）款或第9.313条对完善性的相关要求未能在下列情况中较早者发生前获得满足，则在对抗支付了价值的货物购买人时，上述（d）款所述的担保权益即失去完善性，且被视为从未获得过完善：

（e）A security interest described in Subsection（d）becomes unperfected as against a purchaser of the goods for value and is deemed never to have been perfected as against a purchaser of the goods for value if the applicable requirements for perfection under Section 9.311（b）or 9.313 are not satisfied before the earlier of:

（1）根据该另一州法律，在货物假设未获得本州产权证书时，该担保权益本应失去完善性的时间；或

（1）the time the security interest would have become unperfected under the law of the other jurisdiction had the goods not become covered by a certificate of title from this State;or

（2）货物获得本州产权证书后已满四个月。

（2）the expiration of four months after the goods had become so covered.

（f）涉及存款账户、信用证权利或投资财产时，如果其中的担保权益根据银行、开证人、指定人、证券中间人或商品中间人（以适用者为准）所在州的法律获得完善，则该担保权益在下列情况中较早者发生后失去完善性：

（f）A security interest in deposit accounts, letter-of-credit rights, or investment property that is perfected under the law of the bank's jurisdiction, the issuer's jurisdiction, a nominated person'sjurisdiction, the securities intermediary's jurisdiction, or the commodity intermediary's jurisdiction, as applicable, remains perfected until the earlier of:

（1）根据该州法律，该担保权益本应失去完善性的时间；或

（1）the time the security interest would have become unperfected under the law of that jurisdiction;or

（2）担保物所在州变换至另一州后已满四个月。

（2）the expiration of four months after a change of the applicable jurisdiction to another jurisdiction.

（g）如果（f）款所述的担保权益根据该另一州的法律获得完善，且早于该款所述时间中较早者，则该担保权益随后将保持完善。如果该担保权益在该较早者发生时，尚未根据该另一州的法律获得完善，则该担保权益即失去完善性，且在对抗支付了价值的担保物购买人时，被视为从未获得过完善。

（g）If a security interest described in Subsection（f）becomes perfected under the law of the other jurisdiction before the earlier of the time or the end of the period described in that subsection, it remains perfected thereafter.If the security interest does not become perfected under the law of the other jurisdiction before the earlier of that time or the end of that period, it becomes unperfected and is deemed never to have been perfected as against a purchaser of the collateral for value.

第 9.317 条 优于或不受制于担保权益或农业留置权的权益

§ 9.317. Interests That Take Priority Over or Take Free of Security Interest or Agricultural Lien.

（a）担保权益或农业留置权，次于下列人的权利：

（a）A security interest or agricultural lien is subordinate to the rights of:

（1）根据第 9.322 条享有优先权的人；以及

（1）a person entitled to priority under Section 9.322;and

（2）除（e）款另有规定外，在下列情况中较早者发生前成为留置权债权人的人：

（2）except as otherwise provided in Subsection（e）, a person that becomes a lien creditor before the earlier of the time:

（A）担保权益或农业留置权获得完善；或

（A）the security interest or agricultural lien is perfected;or

（B）已满足第 9.203 条（b）（3）款所述条件的任何一项，且已登记覆盖担保物的融资声明。

（B）one of the conditions specified in Section 9.203（b）（3）is met and a financing statement covering the collateral is filed.

（b）除（e）款另有规定外，实体动产契据、实体凭证、货物、票据或证券证书的买方（受担保方除外），只要在支付价值和接受担保物交付时，不知道担保权益或农业留置权的存在，

（b）Except as otherwise provided in Subsection（e）, a buyer, other than a secured party, of tangible chattel paper, tangible documents, goods, instruments, or a security certificate takes free of a security interest or agricultural lien if the buyer gives value

且担保权益或农业留置权当时尚未获得完善，即不受制于担保物中的担保权益或农业留置权。

and receives delivery of the collateral without knowledge of the security interest or agricultural lien and before it is perfected.

（c）除（e）款另有规定外，货物的承租方，只要在支付价值和接受担保物交付时，不知道担保权益或农业留置权的存在，且担保权益或农业留置权当时尚未获得完善，即不受制于担保物中的担保权益或农业留置权。

（c）Except as otherwise provided in Subsection（e）, a lessee of goods takes free of a security interest or agricultural lien if the lessee gives value and receives delivery of the collateral without knowledge of the security interest or agricultural lien and before it is perfected.

（d）一般无形财产的被许可方，或应收款、电子动产契据、电子凭证、一般无形财产或投资财产（票式证券除外）的买方（受担保方除外），只要在支付价值时，不知道担保权益的存在，且担保权益当时尚未获得完善，即不受制于担保物中的担保权益。

（d）A licensee of a general intangible or a buyer, other than a secured party, of accounts, electronic chattel paper, electronic documents, general intangibles, or investment property other than a certificated security takes free of a security interest if the licensee or buyer gives value without knowledge of the security interest and before it is perfected.

（e)除第9.320条和第9.321条另有规定外，如果在债务人收到担保物交付之前或其后20天内，任何人就价款担保权益登记融资声明，则该担保权益优于买方、承租方或留置权债权人的权利，只要该买方、承租方或留置权债权人的权利，产生于担保权益附着之后至登记之前的期间。

（e）Except as otherwise provided in Sections 9.320 and 9.321, if a person files a financing statement with respect to a purchase-money security interest before or within 20 days after the debtor receives delivery of the collateral, the security interest takes priority over the rights of a buyer, lessee, or lien creditor that arise between the time the security interest attaches and the time of filing.

第 9.318 条　收款权利出售后不再保留权益；应收款或动产契据之卖方相对于债权人和购买人的权利和所有权

（a）债务人将应收款、动产契据、无形支付或本票出售后，即不再对所售的担保物保留法定或衡平权益。

（b）债务人将应收款或动产契据出售后，在确定其债权人的权利，以及在确定支付了价值之应收款或动产契据购买人的权利时，在买方之担保权益尚未获得完善的期间，债务人对应收款或动产契据的权利和所有权，被视为相当于债务人所出售的权利和所有权。

第 9.319 条　寄售受托人相对于债权人和购买人的权利和所有权

（a）除（b）款另有规定外，在确定寄售受托人之债权人的权利，以及在确定支付了价值从寄售受托人购买货物之购买人的权利时，在货物由寄售受托人占有的期间，寄售受托人对货物的权利和所有权，被视为相当于寄售委托人拥有或有权力转让的权利和所有权。

（b）在确定寄售受托人之债权人的权利时，如果本章规定寄售委托人持有的完善担保权益优于债权人的权利，则寄

§ 9.318. No Interest Retained in Right to Payment That Is Sold;Rights and Title of Seller of Account or Chattel Paper With Respect to Creditors and Purchasers.

（a）A debtor that has sold an account, chattel paper, payment intangible, or promissory note does not retain a legal or equitable interest in the collateral sold.

（b）For purposes of determining the rights of creditors of, and purchasers for value of an account or chattel paper from, a debtor that has sold an account or chattel paper, while the buyer's security interest is unperfected, the debtor is deemed to have rights and title to the account or chattel paper identical to those the debtor sold.

§ 9.319. Rights and Title of Consignee With Respect to Creditors and Purchasers.

（a）Except as otherwise provided in Subsection（b）, for purposes of determining the rights of creditors of, and purchasers for value of goods from, a consignee, while the goods are in the possession of the consignee, the consignee is deemed to have rights and title to the goods identical to those the consignor had or had power to transfer.

（b）For purposes of determining the rights of a creditor of a consignee, law other than this Article determines the rights and title of a consignee while goods are in the consignee's

售受托人在占有货物期间所拥有的权利和所有权，应根据本篇以外的其他法律确定。

possession if, under this Part, a perfected security interest held by the consignor would have priority over the rights of the creditor.

第 9.320 条 货物的买方

§ 9.320. Buyers of Goods.

（a）除（e）款另有规定外，正常业务中的买方（从农业经营人买进农产品的人除外），不受制于其卖方在担保物中设立的担保权益，即使担保权益已获得完善，且买方知道担保权益的存在。

（a）Except as otherwise provided by Subsection（e）, a buyer in ordinary course of business, other than a person buying farm products from a person engaged in farming operations, takes free of a security interest created by the buyer's seller, even if the security interest is perfected and the buyer knows of its existence.

（b）除（e）款另有规定外，如果一个人主要为个人、家庭或家用目的使用货物，或为该使用而购买货物，则随后从该人购买货物的买方，不受制于货物中的担保权益，即使担保权益已获得完善，只要买方在买进货物时：

（b）Except as otherwise provided in Subsection（e）, a buyer of goods from a person who used or bought the goods for use primarily for personal, family, or household purposes takes free of a security interest, even if perfected, if the buyer buys:

（1）不知道担保权益的存在；

（1）without knowledge of the security interest;

（2）支付了价值；

（2）for value;

（3）主要用于买方个人、家庭或家用目的；并且

（3）primarily for the buyer's personal, family, or household purposes;and

（4）在覆盖货物的融资声明作出登记之前。

（4）before the filing of a financing statement covering the goods.

（c）涉及（b）款所述的货物买方时，如果在卖方所在州作出的登记，对担保权益是否优于买方之权益具有影响，则应根据第 9.316 条（a）款和（b）款，确定卖方所在州之登记的

（c）To the extent that it affects the priority of a security interest over a buyer of goods under Subsection（b）, the period of effectiveness of a filing made in the jurisdiction in which the seller is located is governed by Sections 9.316（a）and（b）.

有效期限。

（d）涉及在井源或矿源处买进或在开采后买进的石油、天然气或其他矿物时，正常业务中的买方不受制于其中的不动产他项权。

（d）A buyer in ordinary course of business buying oil, gas, or other minerals at the wellhead or minehead or after extraction takes free of an interest arising out of an encumbrance.

（e）如果受担保方根据第9.313条占有货物，上述（a）款和（b）款不影响货物中的担保权益。

（e）Subsections（a）and（b）do not affect a security interest in goods in the possession of the secured party under Section 9.313.

第9.321条　正常业务中的一般无形财产之被许可方和货物之承租方

§ 9.321. Licensee of General Intangible and Lessee of Goods In Ordinary Course of Business.

（a）在本条中，“正常业务中的被许可方”指以善意成为一般无形财产被许可方的人，且其不知道该许可侵犯了另一人对该一般无形财产的权利，并以正常方式向经营该类一般无形财产许可业务的人取得许可。如果一项许可符合许可方行业的通常或惯用做法，或符合许可方自己的通常或惯用做法，取得许可的人即属于正常业务中的被许可方。

（a）In this section, “licensee in ordinary course of business” means a person that becomes a licensee of a general intangible in good faith, without knowledge that the license violates the rights of another person in the general intangible, and in the ordinary course from a person in the business of licensing general intangibles of that kind.A person becomes a licensee in the ordinary course if the license to the person comports with the usual or customary practices in the kind of business in which the licensor is engaged or with the licensor’s own usual or customary practices.

（b）涉及非独家许可时，正常业务中的被许可方的权利，不受制于许可方在一般无形财产中设立的担保权益，即使该担保权益已获得完善，且被许可方知道担保权益的存在。

（b）A licensee in ordinary course of business takes its rights under a nonexclusive license free of a security interest in the general intangible created by the licensor, even if the security interest is perfected and the licensee knows of its existence.

（c）正常业务中的承租方

（c）A lessee in ordinary course of

的租赁权益，不受制于出租方在货物中设立的担保权益，即使该担保权益已获得完善，且承租方知道担保权益的存在。

business takes its leasehold interest free of a security interest in the goods created by the lessor, even if the security interest is perfected and the lessee knows of its existence.

第 9.322 条　同一担保物中冲突的各项担保权益或农业留置权之间的优先顺序

§ 9.322. Priorities Among Conflicting Security Interests in and Agricultural Liens on Same Collateral.

（a）除本条另有规定外，同一担保物中冲突的各项担保权益或农业留置权之间的优先顺序，应根据下列原则确定：

（a）Except as otherwise provided in this section, priority among conflicting security interests and agricultural liens in the same collateral is determined according to the following rules:

（1）在冲突的各项完善担保权益或农业留置权之间，优先顺序的先后，取决于作出登记或获得完善之时间的先后。优先权的产生时间，为下列先发生者：首次作出覆盖担保物之登记的时间，或担保权益或农业留置权首次获得完善的时间，只要在该登记或完善之后不存在登记或完善的中断。

（1）Conflicting perfected security interests and agricultural liens rank according to priority in time of filing or perfection. Priority dates from the earlier of the time a filing covering the collateral is first made or the security interest or agricultural lien is first perfected, if there is no period thereafter when there is neither filing nor perfection.

（2）完善的担保权益或农业留置权，优于冲突的不完善担保权益或农业留置权。

（2）A perfected security interest or agricultural lien has priority over a conflicting unperfected security interest or agricultural lien.

（3）如果冲突的各项担保权益或农业留置权均未获得完善，首先附着或生效的担保权益或农业留置权享有优先权。

（3）The first security interest or agricultural lien to attach or become effective has priority if conflicting security interests and agricultural liens are unperfected.

（b）为（a）（1）款目的：

（b）For the purposes of Subsection（a)(1):

（1）担保物中担保权益作出登记或获得完善的时间，也

（1）the time of filing or perfection as to a security interest in collateral is also the time of

是收益中担保权益之登记或完善的时间；并且

（2）如果担保物中担保权益由支持性债务支持，则担保权益作出登记或获得完善的时间，也是支持性债务中担保权益之登记或完善的时间。

（c）除（f）款另有规定外，如果根据第 9.327 条、第 9.328 条、第 9.329 条、第 9.330 条或第 9.331 条，担保物中的任何担保权益优于冲突的担保权益，则享有优先权的担保权益，亦优于下列财产中之冲突的担保权益：

（1）担保物的支持性债务；以及

（2）担保物的收益，只要：

（A）收益中的担保权益已获得完善；

（B）收益系现金收益，或系与担保物同类的财产；并且

（C）涉及收益之收益时，之前的所有收益均系现金收益，或系与担保物同类的财产，或系与担保物有关的应收款。

（d）除（e）款另有规定外，且除（f）款另有规定外，涉及动产契据、存款账户、流通凭证、票据、投资财产或信用证权利时，如果其中的担保权益已获得完善，但不是通过登记

filing or perfection as to a security interest in proceeds;and

（2）the time of filing or perfection as to a security interest in collateral supported by a supporting obligation is also the time of filing or perfection as to a security interest in the supporting obligation.

（c）Except as otherwise provided in Subsection（f）, a security interest in collateral that qualifies for priority over a conflicting security interest under Section 9.327, 9.328, 9.329, 9.330, or 9.331 also has priority over a conflicting security interest in:

（1）any supporting obligation for the collateral;and

（2）proceeds of the collateral if:

（A）the security interest in proceeds is perfected;

（B）the proceeds are cash proceeds or of the same type as the collateral; and

（C）in the case of proceeds that are proceeds of proceeds, all intervening proceeds are cash proceeds, proceeds of the same type as the collateral, or an account relating to the collateral.

（d）Subject to Subsection（e）and except as otherwise provided in Subsection（f）, if a security interest in chattel paper, deposit accounts, negotiable documents, instruments, investment property, or letter-of-credit rights is perfected by a method other than filing,

获得完善，则在担保物收益中冲突的各项完善担保权益之间，优先顺序的先后，取决于作出登记的时间先后。

conflicting perfected security interests in proceeds of the collateral rank according to priority in time of filing.

（e）只有当担保物收益不是现金收益、动产契据、流通凭证、票据、投资财产或信用证权利时，上述（d）款才适用。

（e）Subsection（d）applies only if the proceeds of the collateral are not cash proceeds, chattel paper, negotiable documents, instruments, investment property, or letter-of-credit rights.

（f）上述（a）款至（e）款受制于以下条款：

（f）Subsections（a）-（e）are subject to:

（1）下述（g）款，以及本章的其他条款；

（1）Subsection（g）and the other provisions of this Part;

（2）有关收款银行之担保权益的第 4.210 条；

（2）Section 4.210 with respect to a security interest of a collecting bank;

（3）有关开证人或指定人之担保权益的第 5.118 条；以及

（3）Section 5.118 with respect to a security interest of an issuer or nominated person;and

（4）有关根据第 2 篇或第 2A 篇产生之担保权益的第 9.110 条。

（4）Section 9.110 with respect to a security interest arising under Article 2 or 2A.

（g）担保物中完善的农业留置权，优于同一担保物中冲突的担保权益或农业留置权，只要设立该农业留置权的法律如此规定。

（g）A perfected agricultural lien on collateral has priority over a conflicting security interest in or agricultural lien on the same collateral if the statute creating the agricultural lien so provides.

第 9.323 条　未来贷款

§ 9.323. Future Advances.

（a）除（c）款另有规定外，在确定第 9.322 条（a）（1）款所述的完善担保权益的优先顺序时，作出贷款的时间，即为担保权益获得完善的时间，只要该担保权益系担保下列贷款：

（a）Except as otherwise provided in Subsection（c）, for purposes of determining the priority of a perfected security interest under Section 9.322（a）（1）, perfection of the security interest dates from the time an advance is made to the extent that the security interest secures an advance that:

（1）担保权益处于完善状态时所作的贷款，但该完善：

（1）is made while the security interest is perfected only:

（A）仅根据第9.309条在发生附着时获得完善；或

（A）under Section 9.309 when it attaches;or

（B）仅根据第9.312条（e）款、（f）款或（g）款获得临时完善；并且

（B）temporarily under Section 9.312（e）,（f）, or（g）;and

（2）贷款不是根据承诺作出，即并非基于在担保权益通过第9.309条或第9.312条（e）款、（f）款或（g）款以外之方式获得完善前或处于完善状态时作出的承诺。

（2）is not made pursuant to a commitment entered into before or while the security interest is perfected by a method other than under Section 9.309 or 9.312（e）,（f）, or（g）.

（b）除（c）款另有规定外，如果从任何人成为留置权债权人起45天后作出贷款，则担保该贷款的担保权益，次于该留置权债权人的权利，除非在作出贷款时：

（b）Except as otherwise provided in Subsection（c）, a security interest is subordinate to the rights of a person that becomes a lien creditor to the extent that the security interest secures an advance made more than 45 days after the person becomes a lien creditor unless the advance is made:

（1）贷款人不知道该留置权的存在；或

（1）without knowledge of the lien;or

（2）贷款系根据承诺作出，而作出承诺时不知道该留置权的存在。

（2）pursuant to a commitment entered into without knowledge of the lien.

（c）如果受担保方是应收款、动产契据、无形支付或本票的买方，或是寄售委托人，则（a）款和（b）款不适用于其持有的担保权益。

（c）Subsections（a）and（b）do not apply to a security interest held by a secured party that is a buyer of accounts, chattel paper, payment intangibles, or promissory notes or a consignor.

（d）除（e）款另有规定外，即使货物的买方不属于正常业

（d）Except as otherwise provided in Subsection（e）, a buyer of goods other than a

务中的买方，只要担保权益用于担保在下列较早者发生后作出的贷款，买方即不受制于该担保权益：

（1）受担保方得知买方的购买；或

（2）购买后已满45天。

（e）如果贷款系根据承诺作出，但作出承诺系在得知买方的购买之前，且在该45天期限届满之前，则（d）款不适用。

（f）除（g）款另有规定外，即使货物的承租方不是正常业务中的承租方，只要担保权益用于担保在下列较早者发生后作出的贷款，承租方的租赁权益即不受制于该担保权益：

（1）受担保方得知该租赁；或

（2）租赁合同取得强制履行力后已满45天。

（g）如果贷款系根据承诺作出，但作出承诺系在得知租赁之前，且在该45天期限届满之前，则（f）款不适用。

第9.324条 价款担保权益的优先顺序

（a）除（g）款另有规定外，只要在债务人取得担保物占有时或占有后20天内价款担保权益获得完善，货物（库存或家畜除外）中的完善价款担保权

buyer in ordinary course of business takes free of a security interest to the extent that it secures advances made after the earlier of:

（1）the time the secured party acquires knowledge of the buyer's purchase;or

（2）45 days after the purchase.

（e）Subsection（d）does not apply if the advance is made pursuant to a commitment entered into without knowledge of the buyer's purchase and before the expiration of the 45-day period.

（f）Except as otherwise provided in Subsection（g）, a lessee of goods, other than a lessee in ordinary course of business, takes the leasehold interest free of a security interest to the extent that it secures advances made after the earlier of:

（1）the time the secured party acquires knowledge of the lease;or

（2）45 days after the lease contract becomes enforceable.

（g）Subsection（f）does not apply if the advance is made pursuant to a commitment entered into without knowledge of the lease and before the expiration of the 45-day period.

§ 9.324. Priority of Purchase-Money Security Interests.

（a）Except as otherwise provided in Subsection（g）, a perfected purchase-money security interest in goods other than inventory or livestock has priority over a conflicting security interest in the same goods, and, except

益，优于同一货物中冲突的担保权益；并且，除第 9.327 条另有规定外，货物可分辨收益中的完善担保权益，亦享有优先权。

as otherwise provided in Section 9.327, a perfected security interest in its identifiable proceeds also has priority, if the purchase-money security interest is perfected when thet debtor receives possession of the collateral or within 20 days thereafter.

（b）除（c）款另有规定外，且除（g）款另有规定外，库存中的完善价款担保权益，优于同一库存中冲突的担保权益；当库存之收益是动产契据或票据时，还优于库存之收益中冲突的担保权益，以及该动产契据之收益中冲突的担保权益，只要第 9.330 条如此规定；并且，除第 9.327 条另有规定外，还对库存的可分辨现金收益享有优先权，只要在将库存交付给买方之时或之前收到该收益；但是，所有上述各项，均以下列为条件：

（b）Subject to Subsection（c）and except as otherwise provided in Subsection（g）, a perfected purchase-money security interest in inventory has priority over a conflicting security interest in the same inventory, has priority over a conflicting security interest in chattel paper or an instrument constituting proceeds of the inventory and in proceeds of the chattel paper, if so provided in Section 9.330, and, except as otherwise provided in Section 9.327, also has priority in identifiable cash proceeds of the inventory to the extent the identifiable cash proceeds are received on or before the delivery of the inventory to a buyer, if:

（1）在债务人取得库存的占有时，价款担保权益已经获得完善；

（1）the purchase-money security interest is perfected when the debtor receives possession of the inventory;

（2）价款受担保方向冲突担保权益的持有人发出业经认证的通知，除非被第 9.343 条所免除（石油和天然气生产）；

（2）except where excused by Section 9.343（oil and gas production）, the purchase-money secured party sends an authenticated notification to the holder of the conflicting security interest;

（3）债务人取得库存占有的时间，系在冲突担保权益的持有人收到所需通知后五年之内；并且

（3）the holder of the conflicting security interest receives any required notification within five years before the debtor receives possession of the inventory;and

（4）通知说明，发送通知的人对债务人的库存已经或将要取得价款担保权益，并对库存作出描述。

（4）the notification states that the person sending the notification has or expects to acquire a purchase-money security interest in inventory of the debtor and describes the inventory.

（c）冲突担保权益的持有人，必须在下列时间之前就同类库存登记融资声明，上述（b）（2）款至（4）款才适用：

（c）Subsections（b）（2）-（4）apply only if the holder of the conflicting security interest had filed a financing statement covering the same types of inventory:

（1）当价款担保权益系通过登记获得完善时，在登记日之前；或

（1）if the purchase-money security interest is perfected by filing, before the date of the filing;or

（2）当价款担保权益系根据第9.312条（f）款不经登记或占有而获得临时完善时，在该款规定的20天期限开始之前。

（2）if the purchase-money security interest is temporarily perfected without filing or possession under Section 9.312（f）, before the beginning of the 20-day period under that subsection.

（d）除（e）款另有规定外，且除（g）款另有规定外，如果家畜系农产品，则其中的完善价款担保权益，优于同一家畜中冲突的担保权益；并且，除第9.327条另有规定外，对于家畜的可分辨收益，或未经加工的可分辨产品，其中的完善担保权益，亦享有优先权；但是，所有上述各项，均以下列为条件：

（d）Subject to Subsection（e）and except as otherwise provided in Subsection（g）, a perfected purchase-money security interest in livestock that are farm products has priority over a conflicting security interest in the same livestock, and, except as otherwise provided in Section 9.327, a perfected security interest in their identifiable proceeds and identifiable products in their unmanufactured states also has priority, if:

（1）在债务人取得家畜的占有时，价款担保权益已经获得完善；

（1）the purchase-money security interest is perfected when the debtor receives possession of the livestock;

（2）价款受担保方向冲突担保权益的持有人发出业经认

（2）the purchase-money secured party sends an authenticated notification to the holder

证的通知；

（3）债务人取得家畜占有的时间，系在冲突担保权益的持有人收到所需通知后六个月之内；并且

（4）通知说明，发送通知的人对债务人的家畜已经或将要取得价款担保权益，并对家畜作出描述。

（e）冲突担保权益的持有人，必须在下列时间之前就同类家畜登记融资声明，上述（d）（2）款至（4）款才适用：

（1）当价款担保权益系通过登记获得完善时，在登记日之前；或

（2）当价款担保权益系根据第 9.312 条（f）款不经登记或占有而获得临时完善时，在该款规定的 20 天期限开始之前。

（f）除（g）款另有规定外，软件中的完善价款担保权益，优于同一担保物中冲突的担保权益；并且，除第 9.327 条另有规定外，其可分辨收益中的完善担保权益，亦享有优先权，只要根据本条规定，承载软件之货物中的价款担保权益，对货物或货物的收益亦享有优先权。

of the conflicting security interest;

（3）the holder of the conflicting security interest receives the notification within six months before the debtor receives possession of the livestock;and

（4）the notification states that the person sending the notification has or expects to acquire a purchase-money security interest in livestock of the debtor and describes the livestock.

（e）Subsections（d）（2）-（4）apply only if the holder of the conflicting security interest had filed a financing statement covering the same types of livestock:

（1）if the purchase-money security interest is perfected by filing, before the date of the filing;or

（2）if the purchase-money security interest is temporarily perfected without filing or possession under Section 9.312（f）, before the beginning of the 20-day period under that subsection.

（f）Except as otherwise provided in Subsection（g）, a perfected purchase-money security interest in software has priority over a conflicting security interest in the same collateral, and, except as otherwise provided in Section 9.327, a perfected security interest in its identifiable proceeds also has priority, to the extent that the purchase-money security interest in the goods in which the software was acquired for use has priority in the goods and proceeds of the goods under this section.

（g）如果根据（a）款、（b）款、（d）款或（f）款，一项以上的担保权益就同一担保物享有优先权，则：

（g）If more than one security interest qualifies for priority in the same collateral under Subsection（a），（b），（d），or（f）：

（1）如果一项担保权益所担保的债务，系担保物之价款的全部或部分，而另一项担保权益所担保的债务，系使债务人取得担保物权利或担保物使用而支付的价值，则前一担保权益优于后一担保权益；以及

（1）a security interest securing an obligation incurred as all or part of the price of the collateral has priority over a security interest securing an obligation incurred for value given to enable the debtor to acquire rights in or the use of collateral;and

（2）在所有其他情况下，第9.322条（a）款适用于所有符合条件的担保权益。

（2）in all other cases, Section 9.322（a）applies to the qualifying security interests.

第9.325条 被转让之担保物中担保权益的优先顺序

§ 9.325. Priority of Security Interests in Transferred Collateral.

（a）除（b）款另有规定外，债务人设立的担保权益，在下列情况下，次于另一人在同一担保物中设立的担保权益：

（a）Except as otherwise provided in Subsection（b），a security interest created by a debtor is subordinate to a security interest in the same collateral created by another person if:

（1）债务人取得担保物时，受制于该另一人在担保物中已经设立的担保权益；

（1）the debtor acquired the collateral subject to the security interest created by the other person;

（2）债务人取得担保物时，该另一人设立的担保权益已经获得完善；并且

（2）the security interest created by the other person was perfected when the debtor acquired the collateral;and

（3）该另一人的担保权益随后不存在不完善期间。

（3）there is no period thereafter when the security interest is unperfected.

（b）只有在下列情况下，上述（a）款才会使一项担保权益处于次位：

（b）Subsection（a）subordinates a security interest only if the security interest:

（1）该担保权益原本只能

（1）otherwise would have priority solely

仅根据第 9.322 条（a）款或第 9.324 条享有优先权；或

under Section 9.322（a）or 9.324;or

（2）该担保权益仅基于第 2.711 条（c）款或第 2A.508 条（e）款产生。

（2）arose solely under Section 2.711（c）or 2A.508（e）.

第 9.326 条　新债务人设立之担保权益的优先顺序

§ 9.326. Priority of Security Interests Created by New Debtor.

（a）除（b）款另有规定外，如果新债务人在其拥有权利的担保物中设立担保权益，且该担保权益通过登记融资声明获得完善，且融资声明的有效性完全基于第 9.508 条，此时，如果同一担保物中存在其他担保权益，且该其他担保权益亦已获得完善，但获得完善的方式，不是通过登记有效性完全基于第 9.508 条的融资声明，则前一担保权益，次于后一担保权益。

（a）Subject to Subsection（b）, a security interest created by a new debtor that is perfected by a filed financing statement that is effective solely under Section 9.508 in collateral in which a new debtor has or acquires rights is subordinate to a security interest in the same collateral that is perfected other than by a filed financing statement that is effective solely under Section 9.508.

（b）涉及同一担保物中冲突的各项担保权益时，如果所有的担保权益，均系通过登记有效性完全基于第 9.508 条的融资声明获得完善，则各项担保权益的优先顺序，应根据本章的其他条款确定。但是，如果使新债务人作为债务人受到约束之多项担保协议，并非由同一原始债务人签订，则冲突的担保权益，应按新债务人受到协议约束的时间先后，确定优先顺序的先后。

（b）The other provisions of this Part determine the priority among conflicting security interests in the same collateral perfected by filed financing statements that are effective solely under Section 9.508. However, if the security agreements to which a new debtor became bound as debtor were not entered into by the same original debtor, the conflicting security interests rank according to priority in time of the new debtor's having become bound.

第 9.327 条 存款账户中担保权益的优先顺序

如果同一存款账户中存在冲突的各项担保权益，应按下列原则确定优先顺序：

（1）根据第 9.104 条对存款账户取得控制的受担保方，相对于未取得控制的受担保方，前者的担保权益优于后者的冲突担保权益。

（2）除（3）款和（4）款另有规定外，根据第 9.314 条通过取得控制获得完善的各项担保权益，按取得控制的时间先后，确定优先顺序的先后。

（3）除（4）款另有规定外，掌管存款账户的银行，相对于冲突担保权益的其他受担保方，前者在存款账户中的担保权益享有优先权。

（4）根据第 9.104 条（a）（3）款通过取得控制获得完善的担保权益，优于掌管存款账户之银行的担保权益。

§ 9.327. Priority of Security Interests in Deposit Account.

The following rules govern priority among conflicting security interests in the same deposit account:

（1）A security interest held by a secured party having control of the deposit account under Section 9.104 has priority over a conflicting security interest held by a secured party that does not have control.

（2）Except as otherwise provided in Subdivisions（3）and（4）, security interests perfected by control under Section 9.314 rank according to priority in time of obtaining control.

（3）Except as otherwise provided in Subdivision（4）, a security interest held by the bank with which the deposit account is maintained has priority over a conflicting security interest held by another secured party.

（4）A security interest perfected by control under Section 9.104（a）（3）has priority over a security interest held by the bank with which the deposit account is maintained.

第 9.328 条 投资财产中担保权益的优先顺序

如果同一投资财产中存在冲突的各项担保权益，应按下列原则确定优先顺序：

（1）根据第 9.106 条对投资财产取得控制的受担保方，相对于未取得控制的受担保方，前者的担保权益优于后者的担

§ 9.328. Priority of Security Interests in Investment Property.

The following rules govern priority among conflicting security interests in the same investment property:

（1）A security interest held by a secured party having control of investment property under Section 9.106 has priority over a security interest held by a secured party that does not

保权益。

（2）除（3）款和（4）款另有规定外，如果每个受担保方均根据第9.106条取得控制，则他们的冲突担保权益，应根据下列情况之发生时间的先后，确定优先顺序的先后：

（A）如果担保物是证券，则根据取得控制之时间的先后；

（B）如果担保物是证券账户中的证券权利，并且：

（i）受担保方根据第8.106条（d）（1）款取得控制，则根据受担保方成为证券账户受益人之时间的先后；

（ii）受担保方根据第8.106条（d）（2）款取得控制，则根据证券中间人作出同意之时间的先后，即同意根据受担保方的权利命令，处置证券账户中目前或未来的证券权利；或

（iii）受担保方根据第8.106条（d）（3）款通过另一人取得控制，则该时间为，假设该另一方为受担保方时，其本应享有的优先权时间；或

（C）如果担保物是商品中间人持有的商品合同，则根据满足控制条件之时间的先后，即满足第9.106条（b）（2）款对商品中间人持有或即将持有之商品合同规定的控制条件。

（3）证券中间人对证券权

have control of the investment property.

（2）Except as otherwise provided in Subdivisions（3）and（4）, conflicting security interests held by secured parties each of which has control under Section 9.106 rank according to priority in time of:

（A）if the collateral is a security, obtaining control;

（B）if the collateral is a security entitlement carried in a securities account and:

（i）if the secured party obtained control under Section 8.106（d）（1）, the secured party's becoming the person for which the securities account is maintained;

（ii）if the secured party obtained control under Section 8.106（d）（2）, the securities intermediary's agreement to comply with the secured party's entitlement orders with respect to security entitlements carried or to be carried in the securities account;or

（iii）if the secured party obtained control through another person under Section 8.106（d）（3）, the time on which priority would be based under this subdivision if the other person were the secured party;or

（C）if the collateral is a commodity contract carried with a commodity intermediary, the satisfaction of the requirement for control specified in Section 9.106（b）（2）with respect to commodity contracts carried or to be carried with the commodity intermediary.

（3）A security interest held by a securities

利的担保权益，或对其掌管之证券账户的担保权益，优于其他受担保方的冲突担保权益。

intermediary in a security entitlement or a securities account maintained with the securities intermediary has priority over a conflicting security interest held by another secured party.

（4）商品中间人对商品合同的担保权益，或对其掌管之商品账户的担保权益，优于其他受担保方的冲突担保权益。

（4）A security interest held by a commodity intermediary in a commodity contract or a commodity account maintained with the commodity intermediary has priority over a conflicting security interest held by another secured party.

（5）如果登记式的票式证券中的担保权益，系根据第9.313条（a）款通过取得交付获得完善，而不是根据第9.314条通过取得控制获得完善，则相对于也不是通过取得控制获得完善的冲突担保权益，前者享有优先权。

（5）A security interest in a certificated security in registered form that is perfected by taking delivery under Section 9.313（a）and not by control under Section 9.314 has priority over a conflicting security interest perfected by a method other than control.

（6）经纪人、证券中间人或商品中间人设立的各项冲突担保权益，如果已经获得完善，但没有根据第9.106条取得控制，则一律平等。

（6）Conflicting security interests created by a broker, securities intermediary, or commodity intermediary that are perfected without control under Section 9.106 rank equally.

（7）在所有其他情况下，投资财产中冲突的各项担保权益，应根据第9.322条和第9.323条，确定它们之间的优先顺序。

（7）In all other cases, priority among conflicting security interests in investment property is governed by Sections 9.322 and 9.323.

第9.329条　信用证权利中担保权益的优先顺序

§ 9.329. Priority of Security Interests in Letter-of-Credit Right.

如果同一信用证权利中存在冲突的各项担保权益，应按

The following rules govern priority among conflicting security interests in the same letter-

下列原则确定优先顺序：

（1）根据第9.107条对信用证权利取得控制的受担保方，相对于未取得控制的受担保方，前者的担保权益优于后者的冲突担保权益。

（2）根据第9.314条通过取得控制获得完善的各项担保权益，根据取得控制之时间的先后，确定优先顺序的先后。

of-credit right:

(1) A security interest held by a secured party having control of the letter-of-credit right under Section 9.107 has priority to the extent of its control over a conflicting security interest held by a secured party that does not have control.

(2) Security interests perfected by control under Section 9.314 rank according to priority in time of obtaining control.

第9.330条　动产契据或票据之购买人的优先权

（a）如果动产契据仅被主张为设有担保权益之库存的收益，则在下列情况下，动产契据购买人的权利，优于动产契据中的担保权益：

（1）购买人在正常业务中以善意支付新价值，取得对动产契据的占有，或根据第9.105条取得对动产契据的控制；并且

（2）动产契据并未注明，其已被转让给除购买人外的任何特定受让人。

（b）即使动产契据并非仅被主张为设有担保权益之库存的收益，动产契据购买人的权利，仍然优于动产契据中的担保权益，只要购买人在正常业务中以善意支付新价值，取得对动产契据的占有，或根据第

§ 9.330. Priority of Purchaser of Chattel Paper or Instrument.

(a) A purchaser of chattel paper has priority over a security interest in the chattel paper that is claimed merely as proceeds of inventory subject to a security interest if:

(1) in good faith and in the ordinary course of the purchaser's business, the purchaser gives new value and takes possession of the chattel paper or obtains control of the chattel paper under Section 9.105;and

(2) the chattel paper does not indicate that it has been assigned to an identified assignee other than the purchaser.

(b) A purchaser of chattel paper has priority over a security interest in the chattel paper that is claimed other than merely as proceeds of inventory subject to a security interest if the purchaser gives new value and takes possession of the chattel paper or obtains control of the chattel paper under Section 9.105

9.105条取得对动产契据的控制，且不知道该购买侵犯了受担保方的权利。

in good faith, in the ordinary course of the purchaser's business, and without knowledge that the purchase violates the rights of the secured party.

（c）除第9.327条另有规定外，根据（a）款或（b）款对动产契据享有优先权的购买人，在下列情况下，对动产契据的收益亦享有优先权：

（1）第9.322条规定对收益享有优先权；或

（2）收益系动产契据覆盖的特定货物，或系该特定货物的现金收益，即使购买人在收益中的担保权益尚未获得完善。

（c）Except as otherwise provided in Section 9.327, a purchaser having priority in chattel paper under Subsection（a）or（b）also has priority in proceeds of the chattel paper to the extent that:

（1）Section 9.322 provides for priority in the proceeds;or

（2）the proceeds consist of the specific goods covered by the chattel paper or cash proceeds of the specific goods, even if the purchaser's security interest in the proceeds is unperfected.

（d）除第9.331条（a）款另有规定外，如果票据中的担保权益已经获得完善，但不是通过取得占有获得完善，则只要票据购买人以善意支付价值，取得对票据的占有，且不知道该购买侵犯了受担保方的权利，票据购买人即享有优先权。

（d）Except as otherwise provided in Section 9.331（a），a purchaser of an instrument has priority over a security interest in the instrument perfected by a method other than possession if the purchasergives value and takes possession of the instrument in good faith and without knowledge that the purchase violates the rights of the secured party.

（e）为（a）款和（b）款目的，如果动产契据是库存的收益，则对库存持有价款担保权益的人，即被视为就动产契据支付了新价值。

（e）For purposes of Subsections（a）and（b），the holder of a purchase-money security interest in inventory gives new value for chattel paper constituting proceeds of the inventory.

（f）为（b）款和（d）款目的，如果动产契据或票据注明，其已被转让给除购买人外的特定受担保方，则动产契据或票据

（f）For purposes of Subsections（b）and（d），if chattel paper or an instrument indicates that it has been assigned to an identified secured party other than the purchaser, a

的购买人，即被视为知道该购买侵犯了受担保方的权利。

purchaser of the chattel paper or instrument has knowledge that the purchase violates the rights of the secured party.

第 9.331 条　其他各篇项下票据、凭证和证券之购买人之权利的优先顺序；第 8 篇项下金融资产和证券权利中之权益的优先顺序

§ 9.331. Priority of Rights of Purchasers of Instruments, Documents, and Securities Under Other Articles; Priority of Interests in Financial Assets and Security Entitlements Under Article 8.

（a）本篇不对下列人的权利作出限制：流通票据的正当执票人、通过正常流通取得流通所有权凭证的持有人，或证券的受保护购买人。该等执票人、持有人或购买人的权利，在第 3 篇、第 7 篇和第 8 篇规定的范围内，优于前存的担保权益，即使该前存担保权益已经获得完善。

（a）This Article does not limit the rights of a holder in due course of a negotiable instrument, a holder to which a negotiable document of title has been duly negotiated, or a protected purchaser of a security.These holders or purchasers take priority over an earlier security interest, even if perfected, to the extent provided in Articles 3, 7, and 8.

（b）如果第 8 篇保护任何人不受制于任何权利主张，则本篇不限制该人的权利，也不增加其义务。

（b）This Article does not limit the rights of or impose liability on a person to the extent that the person is protected against the assertion of a claim under Article 8.

（c）根据本篇作出的登记，对于（a）款和（b）款所述的执票人、持有人、购买人或其他人，不构成索赔或抗辩的通知。

（c）Filing under this Article does not constitute notice of a claim or defense to the holders, or purchasers, or persons described in Subsections（a）and（b）.

第 9.332 条　金钱的转移；存款账户中资金的转移

§ 9.332. Transfer of Money; Transfer of Funds From Deposit Account.

（a）金钱的受转移人取得金钱后，不受制于任何担保权益，除非该人与债务人合谋侵犯受担保方的权利。

（a）A transferee of money takes the money free of a security interest unless the transferee acts in collusion with the debtor in violating the rights of the secured party.

（b）存款账户中资金的受转移人，不受制于存款账户中的担保权益，除非该人与债务人合谋侵犯受担保方的权利。

（b）A transferee of funds from a deposit account takes the funds free of a security interest in the deposit account unless the transferee acts in collusion with the debtor in violating the rights of the secured party.

第 9.333 条　某些依法自动产生之留置权的优先顺序

§ 9.333. Priority of Certain Liens Arising by Operation of Law.

（a）在本条中，“占有性留置权”指除担保权益或农业留置权外的下列权益：

（a）In this section, “possessory lien” means an interest, other than a security interest or an agricultural lien:

（1）任何人在其正常业务中就货物提供服务或材料后，以该权益担保另一方之付款或履约的义务；

（1）that secures payment or performance of an obligation for services or materials furnished with respect to goods by a person in the ordinary course of the person's business;

（2）该权益系法律以该人为受益人而自动提供；并且

（2）that is created by statute or rule of law in favor of the person;and

（3）该权益的有效性取决于该人对货物的占有。

（3）whose effectiveness depends on the person's possession of the goods.

（b）货物中的占有性留置权，优于货物中的担保权益，除非设定该留置权的法律明确另有规定。

（b）A possessory lien on goods has priority over a security interest in the goods unless the lien is created by a statute that expressly provides otherwise.

第 9.334 条　不动产附着物和农作物中担保权益的优先顺序

§ 9.334. Priority of Security Interests in Fixtures and Crops.

（a）本篇项下的担保权益，可以设立在属于不动产附着物的货物中，也可以继续存在于随后成为不动产附着物的货物中。担保权益不能根据本篇存在于已用于土地建设工程中的普通建筑材料。

（a）A security interest under this Article may be created in goods that are fixtures or may continue in goods that become fixtures. A security interest does not exist under this Article in ordinary building materials incorporated into an improvement on land.

（b）本篇不妨碍根据不动

（b）This Article does not prevent creation

产法在不动产附着物上设立不动产他项权。

of an encumbrance upon fixtures under real property law.

（c）涉及（d）款至（h）款以外的情况时，不动产附着物中的担保权益，次于相关不动产他项权人或不动产所有权人（债务人除外）的冲突权益。

（c）In cases not governed by Subsections（d）-（h），a security interest in fixtures is subordinate to a conflicting interest of an encumbrancer or owner of the related real property other than the debtor.

（d）除（h）款另有规定外，不动产附着物中的完善担保权益，优于不动产他项权人或不动产所有权人的冲突权益，只要债务人对不动产持有注册权益或占有不动产；并且：

（d）Except as otherwise provided in Subsection（h），a perfected security interest in fixtures has priority over the conflicting interest of an encumbrancer or owner of the real property if the debtor has an interest of record in or is in possession of the real property and:

（1）该担保权益属于价款担保权益；

（1）the security interest is a purchase-money security interest;

（2）不动产他项权人或不动产所有权人的权益，在货物成为不动产附着物之前产生；并且

（2）the interest of the encumbrancer or owner arises before the goods become fixtures;and

（3）该担保权益在货物成为不动产附着物之前，或在其后20天内，通过不动产附着物登记获得完善。

（3）the security interest is perfected by a fixture filing before the goods become fixtures or within 20 days thereafter.

（e）不动产附着物中的完善担保权益，在下列情况下，优于不动产他项权人或不动产所有权人的冲突权益：

（e）A perfected security interest in fixtures has priority over a conflicting interest of an encumbrancer or owner of the real property if:

（1）债务人对不动产持有注册权益或占有不动产，并且，该担保权益：

（1）the debtor has an interest of record in the real property or is in possession of the real property and the security interest:

（A）在不动产他项权人或不动产所有权人的权益获得注

（A）is perfected by a fixture filing before the interest of the encumbrancer or owner is of

册之前，已经通过不动产附着物登记获得完善；并且

record;and

（B）优于不动产他项权人或不动产所有权人的前手所有权人的冲突权益；

（B）has priority over any conflicting interest of a predecessor in title of the encumbrancer or owner;

（2）在货物成为不动产附着物之前，该担保权益通过本篇允许的任何方法获得完善，且不动产附着物属于可方便拆移的下列物品：

（2）before the goods become fixtures, the security interest is perfected by any method permitted by this Article and the fixtures are readily removable:

（A）工厂或办公室的机器；

（A）factory or office machines;

（B）设备，但不主要用于不动产运营，亦不主要为此种目的租赁；或

（B）equipment that is not primarily used or leased for use in the operation of the real property;or

（C）用于替换家用电器的物品，且其属于消费品；

（C）replacements of domestic appliances that are consumer goods;

（3）冲突权益系通过法律或衡平程序取得的不动产留置权，且在该担保权益通过本篇允许的任何方法获得完善后，才取得该留置权；或

（3）the conflicting interest is a lien on the real property obtained by legal or equitable proceedings after the security interest was perfected by any method permitted by this Article;or

（4）该担保权益：

（4）the security interest is:

（A）系在工厂预制房屋交易中，设立在工厂预制房屋中；并且

（A）created in a manufactured home in a manufactured-home transaction;and

（B）根据第9.311条（a）（2）款所述的法律获得完善。

（B）perfected pursuant to a statute described in Section 9.311（a）（2）.

（f）不动产附着物中的担保权益，无论是否获得完善，在下列情况下，均优于不动产他项权人或不动产所有权人的冲突权益：

（f）A security interest in fixtures, whether or not perfected, has priority over the conflicting interest of an encumbrancer or owner of the real property if:

（1）该不动产他项权人或

（1）the encumbrancer or owner has, in an

不动产所有权人在业经认证的记录中，已同意该担保权益，或不再将货物作为不动产附着物主张权益；或

authenticated record, consented to the security interest or disclaimed an interest in the goods as fixtures;or

（2）相对于不动产他项权人或不动产所有权人，债务人有权拆移货物。

（2）the debtor has a right to remove the goods as against the encumbrancer or owner.

（g）即使债务人相对于不动产他项权人或不动产所有权人享有的拆移货物之权利已经终止，担保权益根据（f）（2）款享有的优先权，仍将持续一段合理时间。

（g）The priority of the security interest under Subsection（f）（2）continues for a reasonable time if the debtor's right to remove the goods as against the encumbrancer or owner terminates.

（h）如果不动产抵押权系用于担保土地建设工程中产生的债务，包括购置土地的成本，该不动产抵押权即属于建设抵押权，但该抵押权的注册记录需要如此注明。除（e）款和（f）款另有规定外，不动产附着物中的担保权益，次于建设抵押权，只要在建设完成之前，并在货物成为不动产附着物之前，该抵押记录被登记注册。如果不动产抵押权系用于建设抵押权的再融资，该抵押权与建设抵押权同样享有上述优先权。

（h）A mortgage is a construction mortgage to the extent that it secures an obligation incurred for the construction of an improvement on land, including the acquisition cost of the land, if a recorded record of the mortgage so indicates.Except as otherwise provided in Subsections（e）and（f）, a security interest in fixtures is subordinate to a construction mortgage if a record of the mortgage is recorded before the goods become fixtures before the completion of the construction.A mortgagehas this priority to the same extent as a construction mortgage to the extent that it is given to refinance a construction mortgage.

（i）不动产上生长之农作物中的完善担保权益，优于不动产他项权人或不动产所有权人的冲突权益，只要债务人对不动产持有注册权益或占有不动产。

（i）A perfected security interest in crops growing on real property has priority over a conflicting interest of an encumbrancer or owner of the real property if the debtor has an interest of record in or is in possession of the real property.

第 9.335 条　添附物

（a）担保权益可以设立在添附物中。在担保物随后成为添附物后，担保权益亦可继续存在。

（b）如果在成为添附物时，担保物中的担保权益已经获得完善，担保权益将在担保物中保持完善。

（c）除（d）款另有规定外，添附物中担保权益的优先顺序，应根据本章其他条款确定。

（d）添附物中的担保权益，次于整体货物中的担保权益，只要后者系通过遵守第 9.311 条（b）款所述的产权证书法获得完善。

（e）出现违约后，除本篇第 6 章另有规定外，受担保方可将添附物从其他货物中拆移，只要添附物中的担保权益，优于对整体货物享有权益之每一个人的主张权。

（f）根据（e）款将添附物从其他货物中拆移的受担保方，应迅即就修补整体货物或其他货物之物理损伤所产生的费用，向对整体货物或其他货物持有担保权益、其他留置权或所有权的人（债务人除外）作出补偿。但是，对于整体货物或其他货物因拆移或替换添附物造成的价值降低，受担保方无须

§ 9.335. Accessions.

（a）A security interest may be created in an accession and continues in collateral that becomes an accession.

（b）If a security interest is perfected when the collateral becomes an accession, the security interest remains perfected in the collateral.

（c）Except as otherwise provided in Subsection（d）, the other provisions of this Part determine the priority of a security interest in an accession.

（d）A security interest in an accession is subordinate to a security interest in the whole that is perfected by compliance with the requirements of a certificate-of-title statute under Section 9.311（b）.

（e）After default, subject to Part 6, a secured party may remove an accession from other goods if the security interest in the accession has priority over the claims of every person having an interest in the whole.

（f）A secured party that removes an accession from other goods under Subsection（e）shall promptly reimburse any holder of a security interest or other lien on, or owner of, the whole or the other goods, other than the debtor, for the cost of repair of any physical injury to the whole or the other goods.Thc secured party need not reimburse the holder or owner for any diminution in value of the whole or the other goods caused by the absence of

作出补偿。有权获得补偿的人，在受担保方就履行补偿义务提供充分保证之前，可以拒绝添附物的拆移。

the accession removed or by any necessity for replacing it. A person entitled to reimbursement may refuse permission to remove until the secured party gives adequate assurance for the performance of the obligation to reimburse.

第 9.336 条　融入物

（a）在本条中，“融入物”指以物理方式与其他货物结合的货物，且在结合后的产品或整体中，原有货物失去其本身特征。

（b）担保权益无法存在于融入物本身。但是，在货物成为融入物后，担保权益可以附着于随后形成的产品或整体。

（c）如果担保物成为融入物，担保权益即附着于产品或整体。

（d）如果担保物中的担保权益在担保物成为融入物之前已经获得完善，则根据（c）款附着于产品或整体的担保权益仍保持完善。

（e）除（f）款另有规定外，根据（c）款附着于产品或整体之担保权益的优先顺序，应根据本章其他条款确定。

（f）如果一项以上的担保权益根据（c）款附着于产品或整体，应按下列原则确定优先顺序：

（1）根据（d）款获得完善

§ 9.336. Commingled Goods.

（a）In this section, “commingled goods” means goods that are physically united with other goods in such a manner that their identity is lost in a product or mass.

（b）A security interest does not exist in commingled goods as such.However, a security interest may attach to a product or mass that results when goods become commingled goods.

（c）If collateral becomes commingled goods, a security interest attaches to the product or mass.

（d）If a security interest in collateral is perfected before the collateral becomes commingled goods, the security interest that attaches to the product or mass under Subsection（c）is perfected.

（e）Except as otherwise provided in Subsection（f）, the other provisions of this Part determine the priority of a security interest that attaches to the product or mass under Subsection（c）.

（f）If more than one security interest attaches to the product or mass under Subsection（c）, the following rules determine priority:

（1）A security interest that is perfected

的担保权益，优于在担保物成为融入物时尚未获得完善的担保权益。

under Subsection（d）has priority over a security interest that is unperfected at the time the collateral becomes commingled goods.

（2）如果一项以上的担保权益根据（d）款获得完善，则各项担保权益，应根据担保物在成为融入物时的价值，按比例享有同等优先顺序。

（2）If more than one security interest is perfected under Subsection（d）, the security interests rank equally in proportion to the value of the collateral at the time it became commingled goods.

第 9.337 条 产权证书覆盖之货物中担保权益的优先顺序

§ 9.337. Priority of Security Interests in Goods Covered by Certificate of Title.

如果货物中的担保权益通过另一州法律规定的任何方法获得完善，但本州在该完善期间就货物颁发产权证书，此时，如果产权证书未注明货物设有担保权益，也未注明货物可能设有产权证书未显示的担保权益，则：

If, while a security interest in goods is perfected by any method under the law of another jurisdiction, this state issues a certificate of title that does not show that the goods are subject to the security interest or contain a statement that they may be subject to security interests not shown on the certificate:

（1）货物的买方（从事该种货物销售业务的人除外）不受制于该担保权益，只要买方系在产权证书颁发之后，在不知道该担保权益的情况下，支付价值并取得货物的交付；并且

（1）a buyer of the goods, other than a person in the business of selling goods of that kind, takes free of the security interest if the buyer gives value and receives delivery of the goods after issuance of the certificate and without knowledge of the security interest;and

（2）该担保权益次于货物中的下列冲突担保权益：在产权证书颁发后，且在冲突的受担保方不知道该担保权益的情况下，发生附着并根据第 9.311 条（b）款获得完善的担保权益。

（2）the security interest is subordinate to a conflicting security interest in the goods that attaches, and is perfected under Section 9.311（b）, after issuance of the certificate and without the conflicting secured party's knowledge of the security interest.

第 9.338 条 融资声明登记信息不正确时通过其获得完善之担保权益或农业留置权的优先顺序

如果担保权益或农业留置权通过登记融资声明获得完善，且融资声明包含了第 9.516 条（b）（5）款所述的信息，但在登记时该信息不正确，则：

（1）该担保权益或农业留置权，次于担保物中的完善冲突担保权益，只要冲突担保权益的持有人合理地依赖于不正确的信息支付了价值；并且

（2）担保物的购买人（受担保方除外）不受制于该担保权益或农业留置权，只要购买人合理地依赖于不正确的信息支付了价值，并在涉及实体动产契据、实体凭证、货物、票据或证券证书时，取得了担保物的交付。

第 9.339 条 优先权可以降位

本篇不限制享有优先权的人通过协议降低其优先顺序。

第 9.340 条 扣减权或抵销权对存款账户的效力

（a）除（c）款另有规定外，掌管存款账户的银行，可以针对对存款账户持有担保权益的受担保方，行使扣减权或抵销权。

§ 9.338. Priority of Security Interest or Agricultural Lien Perfected by Filed Financing Statement Providing Certain Incorrect Information.

If a security interest or agricultural lien is perfected by a filed financing statement providing information described in Section 9.516（b）（5）that is incorrect at the time the financing statement is filed:

（1）the security interest or agricultural lien is subordinate to a conflicting perfected security interest in the collateral to the extent that the holder of the conflicting security interest gives value in reasonable reliance upon the incorrect information;and

（2）a purchaser, other than a secured party, of the collateral takes free of the security interest or agricultural lien to the extent that, in reasonable reliance upon the incorrect information, the purchaser gives value and, in the case of tangible chattel paper, tangible documents, goods, instruments, or a security certificate, receives delivery of the collateral.

§ 9.339. Priority Subject to Subordination.

This Article does not preclude subordination by agreement by a person entitled to priority.

§ 9.340. Effectiveness of Right of Recoupment or Set-off Against Deposit Account.

（a）Except as otherwise provided in Subsection（c）, a bank with which a deposit account is maintained may exercise any right of recoupment or set-off against a secured party that holds a security interest in the deposit account.

（b）除（c）款另有规定外，如果受担保方掌管存款账户，则本篇对存款账户中之担保权益的适用，不影响受担保方享有的扣减权或抵销权。

（b）Except as otherwise provided in Subsection（c）, the application of this Article to a security interest in a deposit account does not affect a right of recoupment or set-off of the secured party as to a deposit account maintained with the secured party.

（c）如果受担保方对存款账户持有的担保权益，系根据第9.104条（a）（3）款通过取得控制获得完善，则银行基于对债务人的索赔而对该存款账户行使的抵销权，对于该受担保方系属无效。

（c）The exercise by a bank of a set-off against a deposit account is ineffective against a secured party that holds a security interest in the deposit account that is perfected by control under Section 9.104（a）（3）, if the set-off is based on a claim against the debtor.

第9.341条　银行对存款账户的权利和义务

§ 9.341. Bank's Rights and Duties With Respect to Deposit Account.

除第9.340条（c）款另有规定外，且除银行在业经认证的记录中另有约定外，银行对其掌管之存款账户的权利和义务，不因下列原因终止、暂停或改变：

Except as otherwise provided in Section 9.340（c）, and unless the bank otherwise agrees in an authenticated record, a bank's rights and duties with respect to a deposit account maintained with the bank are not terminated, suspended, or modified by:

（1）针对存款账户而设立、附着或完善担保权益；

（1）the creation, attachment, or perfection of a security interest in the deposit account;

（2）银行知道担保权益的存在；或

（2）the bank's knowledge of the security interest;or

（3）银行收到受担保方的指示。

（3）the bank's receipt of instructions from the secured party.

第9.342条　银行有权拒绝签订或拒绝披露控制协议

§ 9.342. Bank's Right to Refuse to Enter Into or Disclose Existence of Control Agreement.

本篇不要求银行签订第9.104

This Article does not require a bank to

条（a）（2）款所述种类的协议，即使其客户提出要求或作出命令。已经签订此类协议的银行，无须向另一人确认该协议的存在，除非其客户要求银行确认。

enter into an agreement of the kind described in Section 9.104（a）（2）, even if its customer so requests or directs.A bank that has entered into such an agreement is not required to confirm the existence of the agreement to another person unless requested to do so by its customer.

第4章　第三方的权利

PART 4. RIGHTS OF THIRD PARTIES

第 9.401 条　债务人权利的可转让性

（a）除（b）款和第 9.406 条、第 9.407 条、第 9.408 条和第 9.409 条另有规定外，债务人对担保物的权利，是否可以自愿转让或非自愿转让，应根据本篇以外的法律确定。

（b）即使债务人与受担保方之间的协议禁止转让债务人对担保物的权利，或规定转让属于违约，亦不妨碍转让产生效力。

§ 9.401. Alienability of Debtor's Rights.

（a）Except as otherwise provided in Subsection（b）and Sections 9.406, 9.407, 9.408, and 9.409, whether a debtor's rights in collateral may be voluntarily or involuntarily transferred is governed by law other than this Article.

（b）An agreement between the debtor and secured party that prohibits a transfer of the debtor's rights in collateral or makes the transfer a default does not prevent the transfer from taking effect.

第 9.402 条　受担保方不承担债务人的合同责任或侵权责任

在没有其他因素的情况下，担保权益或农业留置权的存在，或债务人取得的处置或使用担保物的授权，不使受担保方对债务人的行为或疏漏承担合同责任或侵权责任。

§ 9.402. Secured Party Not Obligated on Contract of Debtor or in Tort.

The existence of a security interest, agricultural lien, or authority given to a debtor to dispose of or use collateral, without more, does not subject a secured party to liability in contract or tort for the debtor's acts or omissions.

第 9.403 条　不向受让人主张抗辩的协议

（a）在本条中，“价值”具有第 3.303 条(a)款所述的含义。

（b）除本条另有规定外，如果应收款债务人与转让人之间的协议规定，应收款债务人对其可能享有的对抗转让人的索赔或抗辩，不向受让人提出主张，则该协议可由受让人强制履行，只要受让人在取得转让时：

（1）支付了价值；

（2）以善意作为；

（3）未得到被转让财产存在财产权或占有权之主张的通知；并且

（4）涉及有权根据第 3.305 条（a）款强制履行流通票据的人时，未得到可向该人主张之种类的抗辩或扣减权的通知。

（c）对于根据第 3.305 条(b)款可向流通票据正当执票人主张之种类的抗辩，上述（b）款不适用。

（d）在消费者交易中，如果存在可以证明应收款债务人之债务的记录，并且本篇以外的法律要求，该记录本应说明，如果应收款债务人有权向原始债权人主张索赔或抗辩，受让人的权利将受制于该索赔或抗辩；但是，该记录并未包含此

§ 9.403. Agreement Not to Assert Defenses Against Assignee.

（a）In this section, “value” has the meaning provided in Section 3.303（a）.

（b）Except as otherwise provided in this section, an agreement between an account debtor and an assignor not to assert against an assignee any claim or defense that the account debtor may have against the assignor is enforceable by an assignee that takes an assignment:

（1）for value;

（2）in good faith;

（3）without notice of a claim of a property or possessory right to the property assigned;and

（4）without notice of a defense or claim in recoupment of the type that may be asserted against a person entitled to enforce a negotiable instrument under Section 3.305（a）.

（c）Subsection（b）does not apply to defenses of a type that may be asserted against a holder in due course of a negotiable instrument under Section 3.305（b）.

（d）In a consumer transaction, if a record evidences the account debtor’s obligation, law other than this Article requires that the record include a statement to the effect that the rights of an assignee are subject to claims or defenses that the account debtor could assert against the original obligee, and the record does not include such a statement:

种说明；此时：

（1）该记录的效力，与包含此种说明时的效力相同；并且

（1）the record has the same effect as if the record included such a statement;and

（2）应收款债务人有权向受让人主张的索赔和抗辩，与包含此种说明时的范围相同。

（2）the account debtor may assert against an assignee those claims and defenses that would have been available if the record included such a statement.

（e）如果应收款债务人系个人，且主要为个人、家庭或家用目的承担债务，且本篇以外的法律为此制定了不同的规则，则本条受制于该法律。

（e）This section is subject to law other than this Article that establishes a different rule for an account debtor who is an individual and who incurred the obligation primarily for personal, family, or household purposes.

（f）除（d）款另有规定外，如果应收款债务人在协议中规定，不向受让人主张索赔或抗辩，且本篇以外的法律承认该协议的效力，则本条不排除该法律。

（f）Except as otherwise provided in Subsection（d）, this section does not displace law other than this Article that gives effect to an agreement by an account debtor not to assert a claim or defense against an assignee.

第 9.404 条　受让人取得的权利；对抗受让人的索赔和抗辩

§ 9.404. Rights Acquired by Assignee; Claims and Defenses Against Assignee.

（a）除应收款债务人已签署具有强制履行力的放弃索赔或抗辩之协议外，且除（b）款至（e）款另有规定外，受让人的权利受制于下列各项：

（a）Unless an account debtor has made an enforceable agreement not to assert defenses or claims, and subject to Subsections（b）-（e）, the rights of an assignee are subject to:

（1）应收款债务人与转让人之间协议的全部条款，以及从合同之基础交易中产生的任何抗辩或扣减权；以及

（1）all terms of the agreement between the account debtor and assignor and any defense or claim in recoupment arising from the transaction that gave rise to the contract;and

（2）应收款债务人对转让人持有的任何其他抗辩或索赔，只要其产生于应收款债务人收

（2）any other defense or claim of the account debtor against the assignor that accrues before the account debtor receives a notification

到业经转让人或受让人认证之转让通知之前。

of the assignment authenticated by the assignor or the assignee.

（b）除（c）款另有规定外，且除（d）款另有规定外，应收款债务人对抗转让人的索赔，只有在用于减少应收款债务人所欠之债务金额时，才能根据（a）款向受让人提出。

（b）Subject to Subsection（c）and except as otherwise provided in Subsection（d）, the claim of an account debtor against an assignor may be asserted against an assignee under Subsection（a）only to reduce the amount the account debtor owes.

（c）如果债务人系个人，且主要为个人、家庭或家用目的承担债务，且本篇以外的法律为此制定了不同的规则，则本条受制于该法律。

（c）This section is subject to law other than this Article that establishes a different rule for an account debtor who is an individual and who incurred the obligation primarily for personal, family, or household purposes.

（d）在消费者交易中，如果存在可以证明应收款债务人之债务的记录，并且本篇以外的法律要求，该记录本应说明，如果应收款债务人基于对转让人的索赔或抗辩而从受让人取得赔偿，则赔偿金额不得超过该记录中应收款债务人的支付金额；但是，该记录并未包含此种说明；此时，应收款债务人在何种程度上有权基于对转让人的索赔而向受让人提出索赔，应按该记录包含此种说明时的情况确定。

（d）In a consumer transaction, if a record evidences the account debtor's obligation, law other than this Article requires that the record include a statement to the effect that the account debtor's recovery against an assignee with respect to claims and defenses against the assignor may not exceed amounts paid by the account debtor under the record, and the record does not include such a statement, the extent to which a claim of an account debtor against the assignor may be asserted against an assignee is determined as if the record included such a statement.

（e）本条不适用于医疗保险应收款的转让。

（e）This section does not apply to an assignment of a health-care-insurance receivable.

第 9.405 条　被转让之合同的修改

§ 9.405. Modification of Assigned Contract.

（a）修改或替换已被转让的合同，只要以善意作出，即

（a）A modification of or substitution for an assigned contract is effective against

对受让人具有效力。受让人取得被修改或被替换之合同项下的相应权利。转让协议可以规定，该修改或替换属于转让人对合同的违反。本款受制于（b）款至（d）款。

an assignee if made in good faith.The assignee acquires corresponding rights under the modified or substituted contract.The assignment may provide that the modification or substitution is a breach of contract by the assignor.This subsection is subject to Subsections（b）-（d）.

（b）上述（a）款适用于下列情况：

（b）Subsection（a）applies to the extent that:

（1）尚未通过履约完全赚取所转让之合同项下的要求对方作出全部或部分付款的权利；或

（1）the right to payment or a part thereof under an assigned contract has not been fully earned by performance;or

（2）已通过履约完全赚取要求对方作出全部或部分付款的权利，但应收款债务人尚未收到第 9.406 条（a）款所述的转让通知。

（2）the right to payment or a part thereof has been fully earned by performance and the account debtor has not received notification of the assignment under Section 9.406（a）.

（c）如果应收款债务人系个人，且主要为个人、家庭或家用目的承担债务，且本篇以外的法律为此制定了不同的规则，则本条受制于该法律。

（c）This section is subject to law other than this Article that establishes a different rule for an account debtor who is an individual and who incurred the obligation primarily for personal, family, or household purposes.

（d）本条不适用于医疗保险应收款的转让。

（d）This section does not apply to an assignment of a health-care-insurance receivable.

第 9.406 条　应收款债务人的债务解除；转让通知；转让的指明和证明；对应收款、动产契据、无形支付和本票之转让的限制无效

§ 9.406. Discharge of Account Debtor; Notification of Assignment; Identification and Proof of Assignment; Restrictions on Assignment of Accounts, Chattel Paper, Payment Intangibles, and Promissory Notes Ineffective.

（a）除（b）款至（i）款另

（a）Subject to Subsections（b）-（i）,

有规定外，应收款、动产契据或无形支付的应收款债务人，可以通过向转让人付款而获得债务解除，但必须在应收款债务人尚未收到（而不是已经收到）业经转让人或受让人认证的通知，说明已到付款期限或将到付款期限的金额已被转让，因此应向受让人付款。在收到通知之后，应收款债务人可以通过向受让人作出付款而获得债务解除，但不能通过向转让人作出付款而获得债务解除。

an account debtor on an account, chattel paper, or a payment intangible may discharge its obligation by paying the assignor until, but not after, the account debtor receives a notification, authenticated by the assignor or the assignee, that the amount due or to become due has been assigned and that payment is to be made to the assignee.After receipt of the notification, the account debtor may discharge its obligation by paying the assignee and may not discharge the obligation by paying the assignor.

（b）除（h）款另有规定外，为（a）款目的，通知在下列情况下系属无效：

（b）Subject to Subsection（h）, notification is ineffective under Subsection（a）:

（1）通知未合理指明被转让的权利；

（1）if it does not reasonably identify the rights assigned;

（2）应收款债务人和无形支付卖方之间的协议，禁止应收款债务人向卖方以外的人作出付款，且根据本篇以外的法律，该禁止系属有效；或

（2）to the extent that an agreement between an account debtor and a seller of a payment intangible limits the account debtor's duty to pay a person other than the seller and the limitation is effective under law other than this Article;or

（3）通知要求应收款债务人，对于应向受让人支付的任何分期付款中的一期，支付少于全部应付数额的金额，此时，应收款债务人有权视该通知为无效，即使：

（3）at the option of an account debtor, if the notification notifies the account debtor to make less than the full amount of any installment or other periodic payment to the assignee, even if:

（A）仅一部分的应收款、动产契据或无形支付被转让给被指定的受让人；

（A）only a portion of the account, chattel paper, or payment intangible has been assigned to that assignee;

（B）一部分被转让给另一受让人；或

（C）应收款债务人知道，向被指定的受让人的转让系属有限转让。

（c）除（h）款另有规定外，如果应收款债务人提出要求，受让人应及时提供合理证明，证明转让已经发生。如果受让人未满足该要求，应收款债务人可以通过向转让人作出付款而获得债务解除，即使应收款债务人已收到（a）款所述的通知。

（d）除（e）款及第2A.303条和第9.407条另有规定外，且除（h）款另有规定外，涉及应收款债务人和转让人之间的协议时，或涉及本票时，协议或本票的下列条款无效：

（1）该条款规定，涉及应收款、动产契据、无形支付或本票的转让时，或涉及其中担保权益的设立、附着、完善或强制履行时，禁止、限制或要求应收款债务人或本票义务人给予同意；或

（2）该条款规定，该转让或该担保权益的设立、附着、完善或强制履行，可引起应收款、动产契据、无形支付或本票项下的违约、扣减权、索赔、抗辩、终止、终止权或救济。

（B）a portion has been assigned to another assignee;or

（C）the account debtor knows that the assignment to that assignee is limited.

（c）Subject to Subsection（h）, if requested by the account debtor, an assignee shall seasonably furnish reasonable proof that the assignment has been made.Unless the assignee complies, the account debtor may discharge its obligation by paying the assignor, even if the account debtor has received a notification under Subsection（a）.

（d）Except as otherwise provided in Subsection（e）and Sections 2A.303 and 9.407, and subject to Subsection（h）, a term in an agreement between an account debtor and an assignor or in a promissory note is ineffective to the extent that it:

（1）prohibits, restricts, or requires the consent of the account debtor or person obligated on the promissory note to the assignment or transfer of, or the creation, attachment, perfection, or enforcement of a security interest in, the account, chattel paper, payment intangible, or promissory note;or

（2）provides that the assignment or transfer or the creation, attachment, perfection, or enforcement of the security interest may give rise to a default, breach, right of recoupment, claim, defense, termination, right of termination, or remedy under the account, chattel paper, payment intangible, or promissory note.

（e）上述（d）款不适用于无形支付或本票的买卖。

（e）Subsection（d）does not apply to the sale of a payment intangible or promissory note.

（f）除第2A.303条和第9.407条另有规定外，且除（h）款至（i）款另有规定外，如果任何法律规定，涉及应收款或动产契据的转让时，或涉及其中担保权益的设立时，禁止、限制或要求任何政府机构或官员或应收款债务人给予同意，则该法律系属无效，只要：

（f）Except as otherwise provided in Sections 2A.303 and 9.407, and subject to Subsections（h）and（i）, a rule of law, statute, or regulation that prohibits, restricts, or requires the consent of a government, governmental body or official, or account debtor to the assignment or transfer of, or creation of a security interest in, an account or chattel paper is ineffective to the extent that the rule of law, statute, or regulation:

（1）该法律规定，禁止、限制或要求任何政府机构或官员或应收款债务人，对该应收款或动产契据的转让，或对其中担保权益的设立、附着、完善或强制履行，给予同意；或

（1）prohibits, restricts, or requires the consent of the government, governmental body or official, or account debtor to the assignment or transfer of, or the creation, attachment, perfection, or enforcement of a security interest in, the account or chattel paper;or

（2）该法律规定，该转让或该担保权益的设立、附着、完善或强制履行，可引起应收款或动产契据项下的违约、扣减权、索赔、抗辩、终止、终止权或救济。

（2）provides that the assignment or transfer or the creation, attachment, perfection, or enforcement of the security interest may give rise to a default, breach, right of recoupment, claim, defense, termination, right of termination, or remedy under the account or chattel paper.

（g）除（h）款另有规定外，应收款债务人不得放弃或改变其在（b）（3）款项下的选择权。

（g）Subject to Subsection（h）, an account debtor may not waive or vary its option under Subsection（b）（3）.

（h）如果应收款债务人系个人，且主要为个人、家庭或家用目的承担债务，且本篇以

（h）This section is subject to law other than this Article that establishes a different rule for an account debtor who is an individual

外的法律为此制定了不同的规则，则本条受制于该法律。

（i）本条不适用于医疗保险应收款的转让。

and who incurred the obligation primarily for personal, family, or household purposes.

（i）This section does not apply to an assignment of a health-care-insurance receivable.

第 9.407 条 限制租赁权益中或出租方残余权益中担保权益的设立或强制履行

§ 9.407. Restrictions on Creation or Enforcement of Security Interest in Leasehold Interest or in Lessor's Residual Interest.

（a）除（b）款另有规定外，租赁协议中的下列条款无效：

（1）涉及任何一方在租赁合同项下的权益时，或涉及出租方在货物中的残余权益时，该条款规定，禁止、限制或要求租赁的任何一方，对该权益的转让，或对其中担保权益的设立、附着、完善或强制履行，给予同意；或

（2）该条款规定，该转让或该担保权益的设立、附着、完善或强制履行，可引起租赁项下的违约、扣减权、索赔、抗辩、终止、终止权或救济。

（a）Except as otherwise provided in Subsection（b）, a term in a lease agreement is ineffective to the extent that it:

（1）prohibits, restricts, or requires the consent of a party to the lease to the assignment or transfer of, or the creation, attachment, perfection, or enforcement of a security interest in, an interest of a party under the lease contract or in the lessor's residual interest in the goods;or

（2）provides that the assignment or transfer or the creation, attachment, perfection, or enforcement of the security interest may give rise to a default, breach, right of recoupment, claim, defense, termination, right of termination, or remedy under the lease.

（b）除第 2A.303 条（g）款另有规定外，上述（a）（2）款所述的条款，在下列情况下系属有效：

（1）承租方违反该条款的规定，转让承租方对货物的占有权或使用权；或

（2）租赁合同的任何一方

（b）Except as otherwise provided in Section 2A.303（g）, a term described in Subsection（a）（2）is effective to the extent that there is:

（1）a transfer by the lessee of the lessee's right of possession or use of the goods in violation of the term;or

（2）a delegation of a material performance

违反该条款的规定，将其重要履约义务委托他人代为履行。

（c）涉及出租方在租赁合同项下的权益时，或涉及出租方在货物中的残余权益时，该权益中担保权益的设立、附着、完善或强制履行，不构成第 2A.303 条（d）款所述的转让，即该转让不对承租方获得回报履约的前景造成严重损害，或严重改变承租方的义务，或严重增加承租方的负担或风险，除非（并只在其限度内）强制履行已实际导致出租方重要履约义务的委托履行。

第 9.408 条　对本票、医疗保险应收款和某些一般无形财产之转让的限制无效

（a）除（b）款另有规定外，如果本票中的条款，或应收款债务人与任何债务人关于医疗保险应收款或一般无形财产（包括合同、执照、许可或特许）之协议的条款，对于本票、医疗保险应收款或一般无形财产的转让，或对于其中担保权益的设立、附着或完善，禁止、限制或要求本票义务人或应收款债务人给予同意，则在下列情况下，该条款无效：

of either party to the lease contract in violation of the term.

（c）The creation, attachment, perfection, or enforcement of a security interest in the lessor's interest under the lease contract or the lessor's residual interest in the goods is not a transfer that materially impairs the lessee's prospect of obtaining return performance or materially changes the duty of or materially increases the burden or risk imposed on the lessee within the purview of Section 2A.303（d）unless, and then only to the extent that, enforcement actually results in a delegation of material performance of the lessor.

§ 9.408. Restrictions on Assignment of Promissory Notes, Health-Care-Insurance Receivables, and Certain General Intangibles Ineffective.

（a）Except as otherwise provided in Subsection（b）, a term in a promissory note or in an agreement between an account debtor and a debtor that relates to a health-care-insurance receivable or a general intangible, including a contract, permit, license, or franchise, and which term prohibits, restricts, or requires the consent of the person obligated on the promissory note or the account debtor to, the assignment or transfer of, or creation, attachment, or perfection of a security interest in, the promissory note, health-care-insurance receivable, or general intangible, is ineffective to the extent that the term:

（1）该条款妨碍担保权益的设立、附着或完善；或

（2）该条款规定，该转让或该担保权益的设立、附着或完善，可引起本票、医疗保险应收款或一般无形财产项下的违约、扣减权、索赔、抗辩、终止、终止权或救济。

（b）只有当担保权益源于无形支付或本票的买卖时，上述（a）款才适用于无形支付或本票中的担保权益。

（c）如果任何法律规定，涉及本票、医疗保险应收款或一般无形财产（包括应收款债务人与任何债务人之间的合同、执照、许可或特许）的转让时，或涉及其中担保权益的设立时，禁止、限制或要求任何政府机构或官员或本票义务人或应收款债务人给予同意，则该法律系属无效，只要：

（1）该法律妨碍担保权益的设立、附着或完善；或

（2）该法律规定，该转让或该担保权益的设立、附着或完善，可引起本票、医疗保险应收款或一般无形财产项下的违约、扣减权、索赔、抗辩、

（1）would impair the creation, attachment, or perfection of a security interest;or

（2）provides that the assignment or transfer or the creation, attachment, or perfection of the security interest may give rise to a default, breach, right of recoupment, claim, defense, termination, right of termination, or remedy under the promissory note, health-care-insurance receivable, or general intangible.

（b）Subsection（a）applies to a security interest in a payment intangible or promissory note only if the security interest arises out of a sale of the payment intangible or promissory note.

（c）A rule of law, statute, or regulation that prohibits, restricts, or requires the consent of a government, governmental body or official, person obligated on a promissory note, or account debtor to the assignment or transfer of, or creation of a security interest in, a promissory note, health-care-insurance receivable, or general intangible, including a contract, permit, license, or franchise between an account debtor and a debtor, is ineffective to the extent that the rule of law, statute, or regulation:

（1）would impair the creation, attachment, or perfection of a security interest;or

（2）provides that the assignment or transfer or the creation, attachment, or perfection of the security interest may give rise to a default, breach, right of recoupment, claim, defense, termination, right of termination, or

终止、终止权或救济。

remedy under the promissory note, health-care-insurance receivable, or general intangible.

（d）如果本票的条款，或应收款债务人与任何债务人之间协议的条款，涉及医疗保险应收款或一般无形财产，或涉及（c）款所述的法律，且该条款根据本篇以外的法律系属有效，但根据（a）款或（c）款系属无效，此时，该本票、医疗保险应收款或一般无形财产中担保权益的设立、附着或完善：

（d）To the extent that a term in a promissory note or in an agreement between an account debtor and a debtor that relates to a health-care-insurance receivable or general intangible or a rule of law, statute, or regulation described in Subsection（c）would be effective under law other than this Article but is ineffective under Subsection（a）or（c）, the creation, attachment, or perfection of a security interest in the promissory note, health-care-insurance receivable, or general intangible:

（1）不可对本票义务人或应收款债务人强制履行；

（1）is not enforceable against the person obligated on the promissory note or the account debtor;

（2）不对本票义务人或应收款债务人加赋义务或债务；

（2）does not impose a duty or obligation on the person obligated on the promissory note or the account debtor;

（3）不要求本票义务人或应收款债务人承认该担保权益，或向受担保方作出付款或履约，或从受担保方接受付款或履约；

（3）does not require the person obligated on the promissory note or the account debtor to recognize the security interest, pay or render performance to the secured party, or accept payment or performance from the secured party;

（4）不使受担保方有权使用或转让债务人在本票、医疗保险应收款或一般无形财产项下的权利，包括使用或转让债务人在引起本票、医疗保险应收款或一般无形财产之交易中获得的相关信息或材料；

（4）does not entitle the secured party to use or assign the debtor's rights under the promissory note, health-care-insurance receivable, or general intangible, including any related information or materials furnished to the debtor in the transaction giving rise to the promissory note, health-care-insurance receivable, or general intangible;

（5）不使受担保方有权使用、转让、占有或接触本票义务人或应收款债务人的任何商业秘密或保密信息；以及

（5）does not entitle the secured party to use, assign, possess, or have access to any trade secrets or confidential information of the person obligated on the promissory note or the account debtor;and

（6）不使受担保方有权强制履行本票、医疗保险应收款或一般无形财产中的担保权益。

（6）does not entitle the secured party to enforce the security interest in the promissory note, health-care-insurance receivable, or general intangible.

第 9.409 条　对信用证权利之转让的限制无效

§ 9.409. Restrictions on Assignment of Letter-of-Credit Rights Ineffective.

（a）如果信用证的条款，或如果适用于信用证的法律、规则、惯例或做法，对于受益人对信用证权利的转让，或对于其中担保权益的设立，禁止、限制或要求申请人、开证人或指定人给予同意，则在下列情况下，该条款、法律、规则、惯例或做法系属无效：

（a）A term in a letter of credit or a rule of law, statute, regulation, custom, or practice applicable to the letter of credit that prohibits, restricts, or requires the consent of an applicant, issuer, or nominated person to a beneficiary's assignment of or creation of a security interest in a letter-of-credit right is ineffective to the extent that the term or rule of law, statute, regulation, custom, or practice:

（1）其妨碍信用证权利中担保权益的设立、附着或完善；或

（1）would impair the creation, attachment, or perfection of a security interest in the letter-of-credit right;or

（2）其规定该担保权益的设立、附着或完善，可引起信用证权利项下的违约、扣减权、索赔、抗辩、终止、终止权或救济。

（2）provides that the assignment or the creation, attachment, or perfection of the security interest may give rise to a default, breach, right of recoupment, claim, defense, termination, right of termination, or remedy under the letter-of-credit right.

（b）如果信用证的任何条款根据（a）款无效，但根据本篇以外的法律，或根据适用于信用证、信用证项下获得付款

（b）To the extent that a term in a letter of credit is ineffective under Subsection（a）but would be effective under law other than this Article or a custom or practice applicable to the

或其他履约之权利，或信用证收益权之转让的惯例或做法，该条款系属有效，此时，信用证权利中担保权益的设立、附着或完善：

letter of credit, to the transfer of a right to draw or otherwise demand performance under the letter of credit, or to the assignment of a right to proceeds of the letter of credit, the creation, attachment, or perfection of a security interest in the letter-of-credit right:

（1）不可对申请人、开证人、指定人或身为受让人之受益人强制履行；

（1）is not enforceable against the applicant, issuer, nominated person, or transferee beneficiary;

（2）不对申请人、开证人、指定人或身为受让人之受益人加赋义务或债务；以及

（2）imposes no duties or obligations on the applicant, issuer, nominated person, or transferee beneficiary;and

（3）不要求申请人、开证人、指定人或身为受让人之受益人承认该担保权益，或向受担保方作出付款或履约，或从受担保方接受付款或履约。

（3）does not require the applicant, issuer, nominated person, or transferee beneficiary to recognize the security interest, pay or render performance to the secured party, or accept payment or other performance from the secured party.

第5章　登　记

PART 5. FILING

第 9.501 条　登记处

§ 9.501. Filing Office.

（a）除（b）款另有规定外，如果担保权益或农业留置权的完善受本州法律管辖，则用于完善担保权益或农业留置权的融资声明登记处：

（a）Except as otherwise provided in Subsection（b）, if the local law of this state governs perfection of a security interest or agricultural lien, the office in which to file a financing statement to perfect the security interest or agricultural lien is:

（1）应为登记相关不动产抵押记录的办公处，只要：

（1）the office designated for the filing or recording of a record of a mortgage on the related real property, if:

（A）担保物系开采状担保物，或系待砍伐树木；或

（A）the collateral is as-extracted collateral or timber to be cut;or

（B）融资声明系作为不动产附着物登记而进行登记，且作为担保物的货物系不动产附着物，或即将成为不动产附着物；或

（B）the financing statement is filed as a fixture filing and the collateral is goods that are or are to become fixtures;or

（2）在所有其他情况下，应为州务卿办公处；如果作为担保物的货物系不动产附着物，或即将成为不动产附着物，但融资声明不作为不动产附着物登记而进行登记，则登记处亦应为州务卿办公处。

（2）the office of the Secretary of State, in all other cases, including a case in which the collateral is goods that are or are to become fixtures and the financing statement is not filed as a fixture filing.

（b）涉及公用事业传输企业的担保物（包括不动产附着物）时，用于完善其中担保权益的融资声明登记处，应为州务卿办公处。如果融资声明注明，其中任何担保物系不动产附着物，或即将成为不动产附着物，则该融资声明亦同时构成不动产附着物登记。

（b）The office in which to file a financing statement to perfect a security interest in collateral, including fixtures, of a transmitting utility is the office of the Secretary of State. The financing statement also constitutes a fixture filing as to the collateral indicated in the financing statement that is or is to become fixtures.

第 9.502 条　融资声明的内容；不动产抵押记录作为融资声明；登记融资声明的时间

§ 9.502. Contents of Financing Statement;Record of Mortgage as Financing Statement; Time of Filing Financing Statement.

（a）除（b）款另有规定外，融资声明只有达到下列要求，方为充分：

（a）Subject to Subsection（b）, a financing statement is sufficient only if it:

（1）提供了债务人的名字；

（1）provides the name of the debtor;

（2）提供了受担保方或其代表人的名字；并且

（2）provides the name of the secured party or a representative of the secured party;and

（3）注明了融资声明覆盖的担保物。

（3）indicates the collateral covered by the financing statement.

（b）除第9.501条（b）款另有规定外，如果融资声明覆盖开采状担保物或待砍伐树木，或如果融资声明系作为不动产附着物登记而进行登记，且覆盖的货物系不动产附着物，或即将成为不动产附着物，则该融资声明必须同时满足（a）款要求和下列要求，方为充分：

（b）Except as otherwise provided in Section 9.501（b）, to be sufficient, a financing statement that covers as-extracted collateral or timber to be cut, or that is filed as a fixture filing and covers goods that are or are to become fixtures, must satisfy Subsection（a）and also:

（1）注明了覆盖此类担保物；

（1）indicate that it covers this type of collateral;

（2）注明了将在不动产登记处进行登记；

（2）indicate that it is to be filed for record in the real property records;

（3）描述了与担保物有关的不动产，且根据本州法律，假设该描述登记在不动产抵押记录中，其足以构成不动产抵押推定通知；并且

（3）provide a description of the real property to which the collateral is related sufficient to give constructive notice of a mortgage under the law of this state if the description were contained in a record of the mortgage of the real property;and

（4）当债务人对不动产不享有注册权益时，提供了不动产注册所有权人的名字。

（4）if the debtor does not have an interest of record in the real property, provide the name of a record owner.

（c）只有满足下列要求的不动产抵押记录，才可从登记之日起，成为具有不动产附着物登记之效力的融资声明，或成为覆盖开采状担保物或待砍伐树木的融资声明：

（c）A record of a mortgage is effective, from the date of recording, as a financing statement filed as a fixture filing or as a financing statement covering as-extracted collateral or timber to be cut only if:

（1）注明了所覆盖的货物或应收款；

（1）the record indicates the goods or accounts that it covers;

（2）货物系与记录所描述之不动产相关的不动产附着物，或即将成为不动产附着物的货

（2）the goods are or are to become fixtures related to the real property described in the record or the collateral is related to the

物，或担保物系与记录所描述之不动产相关的开采状担保物或待砍伐树木；

real property described in the record and is as-extracted collateral or timber to be cut;

（3）除去未注明即将作出不动产登记外，记录满足了本条对融资声明的所有要求；并且

（3）the record satisfies the requirements for a financing statement in this section other than an indication that it is to be filed in the real property records;and

（4）记录的登记方式系属适当。

（4）the record is duly recorded.

（d）融资声明的登记，可以在签订担保协议之前，也可以在担保权益以其他方式发生附着之前。

（d）A financing statement may be filed before a security agreement is made or a security interest otherwise attaches.

第9.503条　债务人和受担保方的名字

§ 9.503. Name of Debtor and Secured Party.

（a）融资声明只有按下列方式注明债务人的名字，方为充分：

（a）A financing statement sufficiently provides the name of the debtor:

（1）当债务人系注册成立的组织时，融资声明必须提供债务人在注册州公共记录（用于显示债务人已注册成立的公共记录）中注明的名字；

（1）if the debtor is a registered organization, only if the financing statement provides the name of the debtor indicated on the public record of the debtor's jurisdiction of organization that shows the debtor to have been organized;

（2）当债务人系个人的遗产时，融资声明必须提供去世者的名字，并注明债务人为遗产；

（2）if the debtor is a decedent's estate, only if the financing statement provides the name of the decedent and indicates that the debtor is an estate;

（3）当债务人系信托时，或系代表信托持有财产的信托人时，融资声明：

（3）if the debtor is a trust or a trustee acting with respect to property held in trust, only if the financing statement:

（A）必须提供信托成立文件中为信托确定的名字，或如果未确定名字，则提供信托管

（A）provides the name specified for the trust in its organic documents or, if no name is specified, provides the name of the settlor and

理员的名字，同时提供足以把债务人同其他由同一个或多个管理员管理之信托区分开的其他信息；并且

additional information sufficient to distinguish the debtor from other trusts having one or more of the same settlors;and

（B）必须以债务人的名字或以其他方式作出说明，即债务人系信托，或系代表信托持有财产的信托人；以及

（B）indicates, in the debtor's name or otherwise, that the debtor is a trust or is a trustee acting with respect to property held in trust;and

（4）在其他情况下：

（4）in other cases:

（A）如果债务人有名字，融资声明必须提供该债务人个人或组织的名字；以及

（A）if the debtor has a name, only if the financing statement provides the individual or organizational name of the debtor;and

（B）如果债务人没有名字，融资声明必须提供债务人之合伙人、成员、会员或其他组成人员的名字。

（B）if the debtor does not have a name, only if the financing statement provides the names of the partners, members, associates, or other persons comprising the debtor.

（b）根据（a）款提供了债务人名字的融资声明，不因缺少以下而失效：

（b）A financing statement that provides the name of the debtor in accordance with Subsection（a）is not rendered ineffective by the absence of:

（1）债务人的商号或其他名字；或

（1）a trade name or other name of the debtor;or

（2）债务人之合伙人、成员、会员或其他组成人员的名字，除非根据（a）（4）（B）款需要提供。

（2）unless required under Subsection（a）（4）（B）, names of partners, members, associates, or other persons comprising the debtor.

（c）如果融资声明仅提供债务人的商号，不属于对债务人名字的充分说明。

（c）A financing statement that provides only the debtor's trade name does not sufficiently provide the name of the debtor.

（d）未能说明受担保方系他人之代表人，或未能说明受担保方的代表人，不影响融资声明的充分性。

（d）Failure to indicate the representative capacity of a secured party or representative of a secured party does not affect the sufficiency of a financing statement.

（e）一份融资声明可以提供一个以上债务人的名字，以及一个以上受担保方的名字。

（e）A financing statement may provide the namc of more than one debtor and the name of more than one secured party.

第 9.504 条 说明担保物

§ 9.504. Indication of Collateral.

融资声明只要满足以下要求，即被视为充分说明了其所覆盖的担保物：

A financing statement sufficiently indicates the collateral that it covers if the financing statement provides:

（1）融资声明根据第 9.108 条对担保物作出描述；或

（1）a description of the collateral pursuant to Section 9.108;or

（2）融资声明注明，其覆盖全部资产或全部动产。

（2）an indication that the financing statement covers all assets or all personal property.

第 9.505 条 寄售、租赁、其他存储和其他交易：登记及遵守其他法律和条约

§ 9.505. Filing and Compliance With Other Statutes and Treaties for Consignments, Leases, Other Bailments, and Other Transactions.

（a）货物的寄售委托人或出租方，或其他的货物托管人，或许可方，或无形支付或本票的买方，在登记融资声明时，或在根据第 9.311 条（a）款所述之法律或条约作为时，可以使用诸如“寄售委托人”“寄售受托人”“出租方”“承租方”“货物交管人”“货物保管人”“许可方”“被许可方”“所有权人”“注册所有权人”“买方”“卖方”或具有类似含义的称呼，用来代替“受担保方”和“债务人”的称呼。

（a）A consignor, lessor, or other bailor of goods, a licensor, or a buyer of a payment intangible or promissory note may file a financing statement, or may comply with a statute or treaty described in Section 9.311（a）, using the terms “consignor,” “consignee,” “lessor,” “lessee,” “bailor,” “bailee,” “licensor,” “licensee,” “owner,” “registered owner,” “buyer,” or “seller,” or words of similar import, instead of the terms “secured party” and “debtor.”

（b）本章适用于根据（a）款对融资声明作出的登记；在适用的情况下，也适用于对第 9.311 条（b）款的遵守，即通

（b）This Part applies to the filing of a financing statement under Subsection（a）and, as appropriate, to compliance that is equivalent to filing a financing statement under Section

过遵守该款所述的相关法律或条约，取得相当于登记融资声明的效力。但是，该登记或遵守本身，不能确认该担保物是否用于担保一项债务。如果基于其他理由，确认担保物系担保一项债务，则寄售委托人、出租方、货物交管人、许可方、所有权人或买方持有的担保权益，在附着于担保物后，即通过该登记或遵守获得完善。

9.311（b），but the filing or compliance is not of itself a factor in determining whether the collateral secures an obligation.If it is determined for another reason that the collateral secures an obligation, a security interest held by the consignor, lessor, bailor, licensor, owner, or buyer that attaches to the collateral is perfected by the filing or compliance.

第 9.506 条　错误或遗漏的后果

（a）融资声明即使存在次要错误或遗漏，只要实质上满足本章的要求，即属有效，除非该错误或遗漏使融资声明产生严重误导。

（b）除（c）款另有规定外，未能根据第 9.503 条（a）款充分注明债务人名字的融资声明，属于严重误导。

（c）即使融资声明未能根据第 9.503 条（a）款充分注明债务人的名字，但如果基于债务人的正确名字，并使用登记处的标准检索逻辑（如有），可以在登记处通过对记录进行检索找到该融资声明，即不应认为所提供的名字使融资声明产生严重误导。

§ 9.506. Effect of Errors or Omissions.

（a）A financing statement substantially satisfying the requirements of this Part is effective, even if it has minor errors or omissions, unless the errors or omissions make the financing statement seriously misleading.

（b）Except as otherwise provided in Subsection（c），a financing statement that fails sufficiently to provide the name of the debtor in accordance with Section 9.503（a）is seriously misleading.

（c）If a search of the records of the filing office under the debtor’s correct name, using the filing office’s standard search logic, if any, would disclose a financing statement that fails sufficiently to provide the name of the debtor in accordance with Section 9.503（a），the name provided does not make the financing statement seriously misleading.

（d）上述（c）款中的“债务人的正确名字”，为第9.508条（b）款目的，指新债务人的正确名字。

（d）For purposes of Section 9.508（b）, the “debtor’s correct name” in Subsection（c）means the correct name of the new debtor.

第9.507条　某些事件对融资声明有效性的影响

§ 9.507. Effect of Certain Events on Effectiveness of Financing Statement.

（a）在担保物被出售、交换、租赁、许可或以其他方式处置后，只要担保物中的担保权益或农业留置权继续存在，已登记的融资声明即保持有效，即使受担保方知道或同意该处置。

（a）A filed financing statement remains effective with respect to collateral that is sold, exchanged, leased, licensed, or otherwise disposed of and in which a security interest or agricultural lien continues, even if the secured party knows of or consents to the disposition.

（b）除（c）款和第9.508条另有规定外，如果融资声明中提供的信息，在融资声明作出登记后发生变化，形成第9.506条所述的严重误导，融资声明亦不因此失效。

（b）Except as otherwise provided in Subsection（c）and Section 9.508, a financing statement is not rendered ineffective if, after the financing statement is filed, the information provided in the financing statement becomes seriously misleading under Section 9.506.

（c）如果债务人改变名字，且改变程度致使已登记的融资声明根据第9.506条成为严重误导，则：

（c）If a debtor so changes its name that a filed financing statement becomes seriously misleading under Section 9.506:

（1）只要债务人系在改变名字之前或之后四个月内取得担保物，该融资声明即可有效完善担保物中的担保权益；但是

（1）the financing statement is effective to perfect a security interest in collateral acquired by the debtor before, or within four months after, the change;and

（2）如果债务人在改变超过四个月后取得担保物，则融资声明不能有效完善其中的担保权益，除非在改变后四个月内，登记了融资声明修订文件，

（2）the financing statement is not effective to perfect a security interest in collateral acquired by the debtor more than four months after the change, unless an amendment to the financing statement that renders the

使融资声明不再严重误导。

financing statement not seriously misleading is filed within four months after the change.

第 9.508 条　新债务人受到担保协议约束后融资声明的有效性

§ 9.508. Effectiveness of Financing Statement if New Debtor Becomes Bound by Security Agreement.

（a）除本条另有规定外，如果已登记的融资声明注明原始债务人，但新债务人对担保物拥有权利或随后取得权利，则融资声明亦可有效完善担保物中的担保权益，但条件是，假设原始债务人取得对担保物的权利，该融资声明本属有效。

（a）Except as otherwise provided in this section, a filed financing statement naming an original debtor is effective to perfect a security interest in collateral in which a new debtor has or acquires rights to the extent that the financing statement would have been effective had the original debtor acquired rights in the collateral.

（b）如果已登记且根据（a）款具有效力的融资声明，因原始债务人名字与新债务人名字之间的区别，引起第 9.506 条所述的严重误导，则：

（b）If the difference between the name of the original debtor and that of the new debtor causes a filed financing statement that is effective under Subsection（a）to be seriously misleading under Section 9.506:

（1）在新债务人受到第 9.203 条（d）款约束之前及之后四个月内，该融资声明可以有效完善新债务人所取得之担保物中的担保权益；但是

（1）the financing statement is effective to perfect a security interest in collateral acquired by the new debtor before, and within four months after, the new debtor becomes bound under Section 9.203（d）;and

（2）在新债务人受到第 9.203 条（d）款约束超过四个月后，该融资声明即不能有效完善新债务人所取得之担保物中的担保权益，除非在该期限结束之前，登记了注明新债务人名字的原始融资声明。

（2）the financing statement is not effective to perfect a security interest in collateral acquired by the new debtor more than four months after the new debtor becomes bound under Section 9.203（d）unless an initial financing statement providing the name of the new debtor is filed before the expiration of that time.

（c）如果根据第 9.507 条（a）

（c）This section does not apply to

款，已登记的融资声明对担保物继续有效，可以对抗新债务人，则本条不适用于该担保物。

collateral as to which a filed financing statement remains effective against the new debtor under Section 9.507（a）.

第 9.509 条　有权作出登记的人

§ 9.509. Persons Entitled to File a Record.

（a）只有在下列情况下，一个人才有权登记原始融资声明；或才有权登记修订文件，用于增加融资声明覆盖的担保物，或用于给融资声明添加债务人：

（a）A person may file an initial financing statement, amendment that adds collateral covered by a financing statement, or amendment that adds a debtor to a financing statement only if:

（1）债务人在业经认证的记录中，或根据（b）款或（c）款，对该登记给予授权；或

（1）the debtor authorizes the filing in an authenticated record or pursuant to Subsection（b）or（c）;or

（2）登记人在作出登记时持有已经生效的农业留置权，且融资声明仅覆盖其持有农业留置权的担保物。

（2）the person holds an agricultural lien that has become effective at the time of filing and the financing statement covers only collateral in which the person holds an agricultural lien.

（b）债务人或新债务人在对担保协议作出认证后，或在成为受担保协议约束的债务人后，即相当于对覆盖下列担保物的原始融资声明和修订文件给予登记授权：

（b）By authenticating or becoming bound as debtor by a security agreement, a debtor or new debtor authorizes the filing of an initial financing statement, and an amendment, covering:

（1）担保协议所述的担保物；以及

（1）the collateral described in the security agreement;and

（2）根据第 9.315 条（a）（2）款随后成为担保物的财产，无论担保协议是否明确覆盖收益。

（2）property that becomes collateral under Section 9.315（a）（2）, whether or not the security agreement expressly covers proceeds.

（c）如果债务人取得担保物，且根据第 9.315 条（a）（1）款，其中的担保权益或农业留置权继续存在，则债务人被视

（c）By acquiring collateral in which a security interest or agricultural lien continues under Section 9.315（a）（1）, a debtor authorizes the filing of an initial financing

为对登记原始融资声明和修订文件给予授权，覆盖该担保物及根据第9.315条（a）（2）款随后成为担保物的财产。

statement, and an amendment, covering the collateral and property that becomes collateral under Section 9.315（a）（2）.

（d）除增加融资声明覆盖之担保物，或添加融资声明所注明之债务人的修订文件外，只有在下列情况下，一个人才有权登记融资声明修订文件：

（d）A person may file an amendment other than an amendment that adds collateral covered by a financing statement or an amendment that adds a debtor to a financing statement only if:

（1）注册受担保方对该登记给予授权；或

（1）the secured party of record authorizes the filing;or

（2）注册受担保方未能根据第9.513条（a）款或（c）款的要求，登记或发送融资声明的终止声明，而该修订文件是该融资声明的终止声明，且债务人对该登记给予授权，且该终止声明注明，债务人对该登记已给予授权。

（2）the amendment is a termination statement for a financing statement as to which the secured party of record has failed to file or send a termination statement as required by Section 9.513（a）or（c）, the debtor authorizes the filing, and the termination statement indicates that the debtor authorized it to be filed.

（e）如果融资声明存在一个以上的注册受担保方，每个注册受担保方均可对（d）款所述之修订文件的登记给予授权。

（e）If there is more than one secured party of record for a financing statement, each secured party of record may authorize the filing of an amendment under Subsection（d）.

第9.510条　已登记之记录的有效性

§ 9.510. Effectiveness of Filed Record.

（a）只有在登记人根据第9.509条有权作出登记时，已登记的记录方为有效。

（a）A filed record is effective only to the extent that it was filed by a person that may file it under Section 9.509.

（b）任何注册受担保方所授权作出的记录，不影响融资声明对另一注册受担保方的效力。

（b）A record authorized by one secured party of record does not affect the financing statement with respect to another secured party of record.

（c）如果延展声明未能在

（c）A continuation statement that is not

第 9.515 条（d）款规定的六个月期限内登记，则该延展声明即属无效。

filed within the six-month period prescribed by Section 9.515（d）is ineffective.

第 9.511 条　注册受担保方

（a）如果在已登记的原始融资声明中，一个人的名字被注明系受担保方的名字或其代表人的名字，该人即为融资声明的注册受担保方。如果根据第 9.514 条（a）款对原始融资声明作出登记，则其中被注明名字的受让人，即为原始融资声明的注册受担保方。

（b）如果在已登记的融资声明修订文件中，一个人的名字被注明系受担保方的名字或其代表人的名字，修订文件中的该人即为注册受担保方。如果根据第 9.514 条（b）款对修订文件作出登记，则其中被注明名字的受让人，即为注册受担保方。

（c）在被随后登记的融资声明修订文件删除之前，注册受担保方将保持作为注册受担保方。

§ 9.511. Secured Party of Record.

（a）A secured party of record with respect to a financing statement is a person whose name is provided as the name of the secured party or a representative of the secured party in an initial financing statement that has been filed.If an initial financing statement is filed under Section 9.514（a）, the assignee named in the initial financing statement is the secured party of record with respect to the financing statement.

（b）If an amendment of a financing statement that provides the name of a person as a secured party or a representative of a secured party is filed, the person named in the amendment is a secured party of record.If an amendment is filed under Section 9.514（b）, the assignee named in the amendment is a secured party of record.

（c）A person remains a secured party of record until the filing of an amendment of the financing statement that deletes the person.

第 9.512 条　融资声明修订文件

（a）除第 9.509 条另有规定外，一个人可以通过登记修订文件，增加或删除融资声明覆盖的担保物，延展或终止融资

§ 9.512. Amendment of Financing Statement.

（a）Subject to Section 9.509, a person may add or delete collateral covered by, continue or terminate the effectiveness of, or, subject to Subsection（e）, otherwise

声明的有效期，或除（e）款另有规定外，也可以在其他方面修改融资声明包含的信息，只要该修订文件：

amend the information provided in a financing statement by filing an amendment that:

（1）通过引用原始融资声明的档案号，说明修订文件所涉及的融资声明；以及

（1）identifies, by its file number, the initial financing statement to which the amendment relates;and

（2）当修订文件涉及的原始融资声明系在第9.501条（a）（1）款所述的登记处登记时，提供第9.502条（b）款规定的信息。

（2）if the amendment relates to an initial financing statement filed or recorded in a filing office described in Section 9.501（a）（1）, provides the information specified in Section 9.502（b）.

（b）除第9.515条另有规定外，登记修订文件，不延长融资声明的有效期。

（b）Except as otherwise provided in Section 9.515, the filing of an amendment does not extend the period of effectiveness of the financing statement.

（c）如果融资声明修订文件增加担保物，则对于所增加的担保物，修订文件仅从登记之日起生效。

（c）A financing statement that is amended by an amendment that adds collateral is effective as to the added collateral only from the date of the filing of the amendment.

（d）如果融资声明修订文件添加债务人，则对于所添加的债务人，修订文件仅从登记之日起生效。

（d）A financing statement that is amended by an amendment that adds a debtor is effective as to the added debtor only from the date of the filing of the amendment.

（e）修订文件在下列情况下无效：

（e）An amendment is ineffective to the extent it:

（1）试图删除全部债务人，但未能提供即将被融资声明覆盖的任何债务人的名字；或

（1）purports to delete all debtors and fails to provide the name of a debtor to be covered by the financing statement;or

（2）试图删除全部注册受担保方，但未能提供新的注册受担保方的名字。

（2）purports to delete all secured parties of record and fails to provide the name of a new secured party of record.

（f）受担保方可以通过登

（f）A secured party may change the name

记总体修订文件，改变一份以上融资声明中受担保方的名字或邮寄地址，只要该总体修订文件注明受担保方的名字、每一份融资声明的档案号，以及受担保方新的名字或邮寄地址。受担保方还必须按州务卿规定的计算机可读形式，提供登记信息。

or mailing address of the secured party in more than one financing statement by filing a master amendment setting forth the name of the secured party and file number of each financing statement and the new name or mailing address of the secured party.The secured party must also provide filing information in computer-readable form prescribed by the Secretary of State.

第 9.513 条　终止声明

§ 9.513. Termination Statement.

（a）如果融资声明覆盖消费品，且存在下列情况，受担保方即应使融资声明的注册受担保方，就融资声明登记终止声明：

（1）融资声明覆盖的担保物不担保任何债务，且不存在提供贷款、承担债务或以其他方式支付价值的承诺；或

（2）债务人未曾授权登记原始融资声明。

（b）为遵守（a）款，受担保方应使注册受担保方在下列时间内登记终止声明：

（1）如果融资声明覆盖的担保物不担保任何债务，且不存在提供贷款、承担债务或以其他方式支付价值的承诺，则在该情况发生后一个月内；或

（2）在受担保方收到债务人业经认证的要求后 20 天内，如果此期限早于上述期限。

（c）涉及（a）款以外的情

（a）A secured party shall cause the secured party of record for a financing statement to file a termination statement for the financing statement if the financing statement covers consumer goods and:

（1）there is no obligation secured by the collateral covered by the financing statement and no commitment to make an advance, incur an obligation, or otherwise give value;or

（2）the debtor did not authorize the filing of the initial financing statement.

（b）To comply with Subsection（a）, a secured party shall cause the secured party of record to file the termination statement:

（1）within one month after there is no obligation secured by the collateral covered by the financing statement and no commitment to make advances, incur an obligation, or otherwise give value;or

（2）if earlier, within 20 days after the secured party receives an authenticated demand from a debtor.

（c）In cases not governed by Subsection

况时，受担保方在收到债务人业经认证的要求后20天内，应使融资声明的注册受担保方向债务人发送融资声明的终止声明，或在登记处登记终止声明，只要：

(a), within 20 days after a secured party receives an authenticated demand from a debtor, the secured party shall cause the secured party of record for a financing statement to send the debtor a termination statement for the financing statement or file the termination statement in the filing office if:

（1）融资声明覆盖的担保物不担保任何债务，且不存在提供贷款、承担债务或以其他方式支付价值的承诺，除非融资声明覆盖已出售的应收款或动产契据，或覆盖处于寄售的货物；

(1) except in the case of a financing statement covering accounts or chattel paper that has been sold or goods that are the subject of a consignment, there is no obligation secured by the collateral covered by the financing statement and no commitment to make an advance, incur an obligation, or otherwise give value;

（2）融资声明覆盖已出售的应收款或动产契据，但应收款债务人或其他义务人已被解除相关债务；

(2) the financing statement covers accounts or chattel paper that has been sold but as to which the account debtor or other person obligated has discharged its obligation;

（3）融资声明覆盖曾交给债务人用于寄售的货物，但货物不在债务人占有之下；或

(3) the financing statement covers goods that were the subject of a consignment to the debtor but are not in the debtor's possession;or

（4）债务人未曾授权登记原始融资声明。

(4) the debtor did not authorize the filing of the initial financing statement.

（d）除第9.510条另有规定外，在登记处登记终止声明后，其涉及的融资声明即失去效力。除第9.510条另有规定外，为第9.519条（g）款、第9.522条(a)款及第9.523条(c)款目的，如果在登记处就融资声明登记终止声明，且融资声

(d) Except as otherwise provided in Section 9.510, upon the filing of a termination statement with the filing office, the financing statement to which the termination statement relates ceases to be effective.Except as otherwise provided in Section 9.510, for purposes of Sections 9.519 (g), 9.522 (a), and 9.523 (c), the filing with the filing office of a termination

明注明债务人系公用事业传输企业，则该登记亦导致该融资声明的失效。

statement relating to a financing statement that indicates that the debtor is a transmitting utility also causes the effectiveness of the financing statement to lapse.

第 9.514 条　注册受担保方之权力的转让

§ 9.514. Assignment of Powers of Secured Party of Record.

（a）除（c）款另有规定外，如果受担保方已将授权修改融资声明的全部权力转让给受让人，则原始融资声明可以注明此种转让，并提供受让人的名字和邮寄地址，将其作为受担保方的名字和邮寄地址。

（a）Except as otherwise provided in Subsection（c）, an initial financing statement may reflect an assignment of all of the secured party's power to authorize an amendment to the financing statement by providing the name and mailing address of the assignee as the name and address of the secured party.

（b）除（c）款另有规定外，注册受担保方可将授权修改融资声明的全部或部分权力进行注册转让，但应在登记处登记包含下列内容的融资声明修订文件：

（b）Except as otherwise provided in Subsection（c）, a secured party of record may assign of record all or a part of its power to authorize an amendment to a financing statement by filing in the filing office an amendment of the financing statement that:

（1）通过引用原始融资声明的档案号，说明修订文件所涉及的融资声明；

（1）identifies, by its file number, the initial financing statement to which it relates;

（2）提供转让人的名字；以及

（2）provides the name of the assignor;and

（3）提供受让人的名字和邮寄地址。

（3）provides the name and mailing address of the assignee.

（c）如果覆盖不动产附着物之不动产抵押记录，可以有效构成第 9.502 条（c）款所述的具有不动产附着物登记之效力的融资声明，则不动产附着物中担保权益的注册转让，只能根据本篇以外之本州法律规

（c）An assignment of record of a security interest in a fixture covered by a record of a mortgage that is effective as a financing statement filed as a fixture filing under Section 9.502（c）may be made only by an assignment of record of the mortgage in the manner provided by law of this state other than this

定的方式，通过不动产抵押记录的注册转让进行。

Article.

（d）注册受担保方可以通过登记总体转让文件，针对在州务卿处登记的一份以上的融资声明，将受担保方在其项下的全部权利进行注册转让，只要转让文件注明注册受担保方的名字、每一份融资声明的档案号，以及受让人的名字和邮寄地址。受担保方还必须按州务卿规定的计算机可读形式，提供登记信息。

（d）A secured party of record may assign of record all of the secured party's rights under more than one financing statement filed with the Secretary of State by filing a master assignment setting forth the name of the secured party of record and file number of each financing statement and the name and mailing address of the assignee.The secured party must also provide filing information in computer-readable form prescribed by the Secretary of State.

第 9.515 条　融资声明的期限和效力；过期融资声明的效力

§ 9.515. Duration and Effectiveness of Financing Statement; Effect of Lapsed Financing Statement.

（a）除（b）款至（g）款另有规定外，已登记的融资声明，从登记之日起五年内有效。

（a）Except as otherwise provided in Subsections（b）-（g）, a filed financing statement is effective for a period of five years after the date of filing.

（b）除（e）款、（f）款和（g）款另有规定外，为公共融资项目或工厂预制房屋交易登记的原始融资声明，从登记之日起三十年内有效，只要其注明该登记系为公共融资项目或为工厂预制房屋交易。

（b）Except as otherwise provided in Subsections（e）,（f）, and（g）, an initial financing statement filed in connection with a public-finance transaction or manufactured-home transaction is effective for a period of 30 years after the date of filing if it indicates that it is filed in connection with a public-finance transaction or manufactured-home transaction.

（c）已登记的融资声明在有效期到期后失效，除非在到期之前根据（d）款规定登记延展声明。有效期满后，融资声明失去效力，而通过融资声明

（c）The effectiveness of a filed financing statement lapses on the expiration of the period of its effectiveness unless before the lapse a continuation statement is filed pursuant to Subsection（d）.Upon lapse, a financing

获得完善的担保权益或农业留置权即失去完善性，除非担保权益由于其他原因保持完善。如果担保权益或农业留置权因到期而失去完善性，则在对抗支付了价值的担保物购买人时，该担保权益或农业留置权被视为从未获得过完善。

statement ceases to be effective and any security interest or agricultural lien that was perfected by the financing statement becomes unperfected, unless the security interest is perfected otherwise.If the security interest or agricultural lien becomes unperfected upon lapse, it is deemed never to have been perfected as against a purchaser of the collateral for value.

（d）根据适用的情况，延展声明只能在（a）款所述的五年期限或（b）款所述的30年期限到期前的六个月内进行登记。

（d）A continuation statement may be filed only within six months before the expiration of the five-year period specified in Subsection（a）or the 30-year period specified in Subsection（b）, whichever is applicable.

（e）除第9.510条另有规定外，在及时登记延展声明后，原始融资声明的有效期，将从假设未登记延展声明时融资声明本应失效之日起，再延续五年。在该五年期限到期时，融资声明按（c）款规定的同样方式失效，除非在到期前，再根据（d）款登记延展声明。可以按同样方式随后多次登记延展声明，用于延续原始融资声明的有效性。

（e）Except as otherwise provided in Section 9.510, upon timely filing of a continuation statement, the effectiveness of the initial financing statement continues for a period of five years commencing on the day on which the financing statement would have become ineffective in the absence of the filing. Upon the expiration of the five-year period, the financing statement lapses in the same manner as provided in Subsection（c）, unless, before the lapse, another continuation statement is filed pursuant to Subsection（d）.Succeeding continuation statements may be filed in the same manner to continue the effectiveness of the initial financing statement.

（f）如果债务人是公用事业运输企业，且登记的融资声明也如此注明，则在登记终止声明之前，融资声明一直有效。

（f）If a debtor is a transmitting utility and a filed financing statement so indicates, the financing statement is effective until a termination statement is filed.

（g）如果不动产抵押记录可以有效作为具有不动产附着物登记之效力的融资声明，或作为有效覆盖第9.502条（c）款所述的开采状担保物或待砍伐树木的融资声明，则在不动产抵押获得解除或获得注册清偿之前，或在不动产抵押记录由于其他原因对不动产失去效力之前，该记录可继续有效地作为具有不动产附着物登记之效力的融资声明，或作为有效覆盖开采状担保物或待砍伐树木的融资声明。

（g）A record of a mortgage that is effective as a financing statement filed as a fixture filing or as a financing statement covering as-extracted collateral or timber to be cut under Section 9.502（c）remains effective as a financing statement filed as a fixture filing or as a financing statement covering as-extracted collateral or timber to be cut until the mortgage is released or satisfied of record or its effectiveness otherwise terminates as to the real property.

第9.516条 构成登记的条件；登记的有效性

§ 9.516. What Constitutes Filing; Effectiveness of Filing.

（a）除（b）款另有规定外，只要将一项记录传送给登记处并提示支付登记费，或只要登记处接受一项记录，即构成登记。

（a）Except as otherwise provided in Subsection（b）, communication of a record to a filing office and tender of the filing fee or acceptance of the record by the filing office constitutes filing.

（b）如果登记处由于下列原因拒绝接受一项记录，则登记未完成：

（b）Filing does not occur with respect to a record that a filing office refuses to accept because:

（1）该记录未以登记处规定的传送方式或媒介传送；

（1）the record is not communicated by a method or medium of communication authorized by the filing office;

（2）未提示支付等于或大于规定金额的登记费；

（2）an amount equal to or greater than the applicable filing fee is not tendered;

（3）登记处由于下列原因无法将该记录编目：

（3）the filing office is unable to index the record because:

（A）涉及原始融资声明时，该记录未提供债务人的名字；

（A）in the case of an initial financing statement, the record does not provide a name for the debtor;

（B）涉及修订文件或纠错声明时，该记录：

（B）in the case of an amendment or correction statement, the record:

（i）未按第9.512条或第9.518条的要求（以适用者为准）指明原始融资声明；或

（i）does not identify the initial financing statement as required by Section 9.512 or 9.518, as applicable;or

（ii）所指明的原始融资声明根据第9.515条已超过有效期；

（ii）identifies an initial financing statement whose effectiveness has lapsed under Section 9.515;

（C）当原始融资声明注明债务人为个人并提供了债务人名字时，或当修订文件注明债务人为个人并提供了债务人名字但其涉及的融资声明未曾提供该名字时，该记录未提供债务人的姓氏；或

（C）in the case of an initial financing statement that provides the name of a debtor identified as an individual or an amendment that provides a name of a debtor identified as an individual that was not previously provided in the financing statement to which the record relates, the record does not identify the debtor's last name;or

（D）涉及在第9.501条（a）（1）款所述登记处登记的记录时，该记录未就涉及的不动产作出充分描述；

（D）in the case of a record filed or recorded in the filing office described in Section 9.501（a）（1）, the record does not provide a sufficient description of the real property to which it relates;

（4）涉及原始融资声明时，或涉及添加注册受担保方的修订文件时，该记录未提供注册受担保方的名字和邮寄地址；

（4）in the case of an initial financing statement or an amendment that adds a secured party of record, the record does not provide a name and mailing address for the secured party of record;

（5）涉及原始融资声明时，或涉及提供债务人名字但相关融资声明未曾提供该名字的修订文件时，该记录：

（5）in the case of an initial financing statement or an amendment that provides a name of a debtor that was not previously provided in the financing statement to which the amendment relates, the record does not:

（A）未能提供债务人的邮

（A）provide a mailing address for the

寄地址；

（B）未能说明债务人系个人还是组织；或

（C）在融资声明注明债务人系组织时：

（i）未能提供债务人组织的类型；

（ii）未能提供债务人的注册成立地；或

（iii）未能提供债务人的组织代码，或未能注明债务人没有代码；

（6）涉及第9.514条（a）款所述在原始融资声明中注明的转让时，或涉及根据第9.514条（b）款登记的修订文件时，该记录未提供受让人的名字和邮寄地址；

（7）涉及延展声明时，该记录未在第9.515条（d）款规定的六个月期限内登记；或

（8）该记录未以行业标准格式作出，包括根据州务卿制定之规则采纳的全国标准格式，或国际商业管理者协会批准的格式。

（c）为（b）款目的：

（1）如果登记处无法读取或识别记录中的信息，该记录即被视为未提供信息；以及

（2）如果记录未按第9.512条、第9.514条或第9.518条的规定，标明其为修订文件，或

debtor;

（B）indicate whether the debtor is an individual or an organization;or

（C）if the financing statement indicates that the debtor is an organization, provide:

（i）a type of organization for the debtor;

（ii）a jurisdiction of organization for the debtor;or

（iii）an organizational identification number for the debtor or indicate that the debtor has none;

（6）in the case of an assignment reflected in an initial financing statement under Section 9.514（a）or an amendment filed under Section 9.514（b）, the record does not provide a name and mailing address for the assignee;

（7）in the case of a continuation statement, the record is not filed within the six-month period prescribed by Section 9.515（d）;or

（8）the record is not on an industry standard form, including a national standard form or a form approved by the International Association of Commercial Administrators, adopted by rule by the secretary of state.

（c）For purposes of Subsection（b）:

（1）a record does not provide information if the filing office is unable to read or decipher the information;and

（2）a record that does not indicate that it is an amendment or identify an initial financing statement to which it relates, as required by

指明其涉及的原始融资声明，该记录即被视为原始融资声明。

Section 9.512, 9.514, or 9.518, is an initial financing statement.

（d）如果传送给登记处的记录提示支付登记费，但登记处因（b）款以外的原因拒绝接受该记录，则该记录仍构成有效登记的记录，但不能对抗担保物购买人，只要其合理依赖了档案中不存在该记录的情况支付了价值。

（d）A record that is communicated to the filing office with tender of the filing fee, but that the filing office refuses to accept for a reason other than one set forth in Subsection（b）, is effective as a filed record except as against a purchaser of the collateral that gives value in reasonable reliance upon the absence of the record from the files.

第 9.517 条　错误编目的影响

§ 9.517. Effect of Indexing Errors.

登记处未能对一项记录作出正确编目，不影响已登记之记录的有效性。

The failure of the filing office to index a record correctly does not affect the effectiveness of the filed record.

第 9.518 条　指出不准确记录或错误登记

§ 9.518. Claim Concerning Inaccurate or Wrongfully Filed Record.

（a）如果任何人认为，在登记处编目于其名字之下的任何记录不准确，或属于错误登记的记录，则该人可以在登记处登记纠错声明。

（a）A person may file in the filing office a correction statement with respect to a record indexed there under the person's name if the person believes that the record is inaccurate or was wrongfully filed.

（b）纠错声明必须：

（b）A correction statement must:

（1）通过引用该记录所涉及的原始融资声明的档案号，指明纠错声明所涉及的记录；

（1）identify the record to which it relates by the file number assigned to the initial financing statement to which the record relates;

（2）说明其系纠错声明；并且

（2）indicate that it is a correction statement;and

（3）提供该人认为记录不准确的理由，并说明其认为应如何纠正记录的不准确之处；或提供其认为登记属于错误登记的理由。

（3）provide the basis for the person's belief that the record is inaccurate and indicate the manner in which the person believes the record should be amended to cure any inaccuracy or provide the basis for the person's belief that the record was wrongfully filed.

（c）登记纠错声明，不影响原始融资声明或其他已登记之记录的有效性。

（c）The filing of a correction statement does not affect the effectiveness of an initial financing statement or other filed record.

第 9.518（增）条 欺诈性登记

§ 9.518（Supplementary）. Fraudulent Filing.

（a）任何人不得故意或默认允许融资声明被提交登记，或致使融资声明被提交登记，只要该人知道，该融资声明：

（1）系属伪造；

（2）包含重大不实陈述；或

（3）缺乏根据。

（a）A person may not intentionally or knowingly present for filing or cause to be presented for filing a financing statement that the person knows:

（1）is forged;

（2）contains a material false statement;or

（3）is groundless.

（b）违反（a）款的人，应向融资声明所覆盖之财产的所有权人就下列各项作出赔偿：

（1）5000 美元或所有权人的实际损失，以高者为准；

（2）法院费用；以及

（3）合理的律师费。

（b）A person who violates Subsection（a）is liable to the owner of property covered by the financing statement for:

（1）the greater of $5,000 or the owner's actual damages;

（2）court costs;and

（3）reasonable attorney's fees.

（c）违反（a）款的人，还可能因触犯《刑法典》被刑事起诉。

（c）A person who violates Subsection（a）also may be prosecuted under Penal Code.

（d）涉及（a）款所述的欺诈性融资声明时，其所覆盖之财产的所有权人，还可以在有管辖权的法院起诉，寻求实际履行，包括但不限于删除欺诈性融资声明。登记欺诈性融资声明的人，应向胜诉的原告赔偿合理的律师费和法院费用。如果登记欺诈性融资声明的人

（d）An owner of property covered by a fraudulent financing statement described in Subsection（a）also may file suit in a court of suitable jurisdiction requesting specific relief, including, but not limited to, release of the fraudulent financing statement. A successful plaintiff is entitled to reasonable attorney's fees and costs of court assessed against the person who filed the fraudulent financing

无法找到，或如果其为虚构的人，财产的所有权人可以针对已知或未知的被告，在起诉法院所在地公开发行的报纸上公示送达起诉书。

statement.If the person who filed the fraudulent financing statement cannot be located or is a fictitious person, the owner of the property may serve the known or unknown defendant through publication in a newspaper of general circulation in the county in which the suit is brought.

第 9.519 条　记录的编号、保存和编目；提供记录信息

§ 9.519. Numbering, Maintaining, and Indexing Records; Communicating Information Provided in Records.

（a）对于在登记处登记的每一份记录，登记处均应：

（1）为已登记的记录发放具有唯一性的序号；

（2）为已登记的记录制作记录，其中包含为已登记之记录所发放的序号，以及登记的日期和时间；

（3）对已登记的记录进行保存并供公众查阅；以及

（4）根据（c）款、（d）款和（e）款，为已登记的记录编目。

（b）除（i）款另有规定外，2002 年 1 月 1 日之后发放的登记序号，必须包含一个满足下列要求的数字：

（1）该数字根据数学方法，取自或联至该登记序号中的其他数字；并且

（2）该数字可以协助登记处确认，发送出去的登记序号中，是否存在单个数字或位置

（a）For each record filed in a filing office, the filing office shall:

（1）assign a unique number to the filed record;

（2）create a record that bears the number assigned to the filed record and the date and time of filing;

（3）maintain the filed record for public inspection;and

（4）index the filed record in accordance with Subsections（c），（d），and（e）.

（b）Except as provided in Subsection（i），a file number assigned after January 1, 2002, must include a digit that:

（1）is mathematically derived from or related to the other digits of the file number;and

（2）aids the filing office in determining whether a number communicated as the file number includes a single-digit or transpositional

排列的错误。

（c）除（d）款和（e）款另有规定外，登记处应该：

（1）按照债务人的名字，对原始融资声明编目，并且，对与该原始融资声明有关的所有已登记的记录编目，且编目方法必须能够把原始融资声明与涉及该融资声明的所有已登记的记录联系起来；并且

（2）如果记录提供了相关融资声明中以前不曾提供的债务人名字，则应按照以前不曾提供的该债务人的名字，同时为该记录另行编目。

（d）如果融资声明作为不动产附着物登记而进行登记，或覆盖开采状担保物或待砍伐树木，则必须对融资声明进行注册登记，且登记处应按下列方式编目：

（1）根据所描述的不动产，应将债务人和每一个注册所有权人均假设为不动产抵押中的抵押人，并据此将融资声明登记在融资声明所注明之债务人的名下和每个注册所有权人的名下；以及

（2）如果本州法律规定，应将不动产抵押的目录登记在抵押权人的名字之下，则应将受担保方假设为不动产抵押中

error.

（c）Except as otherwise provided in Subsections（d）and（e）, the filing office shall:

（1）index an initial financing statement according to the name of the debtor and index all filed records relating to the initial financing statement in a manner that associates with one another an initial financing statement and all filed records relating to the initial financing statement;and

（2）index a record that provides a name of a debtor that was not previously provided in the financing statement to which the record relates also according to the name that was not previously provided.

（d）If a financing statement is filed as a fixture filing or covers as-extracted collateral or timber to be cut, it must be filed for record and the filing office shall index it:

（1）under the names of the debtor and of each owner of record shown on the financing statement as if they were the mortgagors under a mortgage of the real property described;and

（2）to the extent that the law of this state provides for indexing of records of mortgages under the name of the mortgagee, under the name of the secured party as if the secured

的抵押权人，并据此将融资声明登记在受担保方的名下，或如果编目是根据不动产描述排序，则应假设融资声明是所述不动产的抵押记录，并相应将其登记在受担保方的名字之下。

party were the mortgagee thereunder, or, if indexing is by description, as if the financing statement were a record of a mortgage of the real property described.

（e）如果融资声明作为不动产附着物登记而进行登记，或覆盖开采状担保物或待砍伐树木，则对于根据第9.514条（a）款登记的转让，或根据第9.514条(b)款登记的修订文件，登记处应按下列方式编目：

（e）If a financing statement is filed as a fixture filing or covers as-extracted collateral or timber to be cut, the filing office shall index an assignment filed under Section 9.514（a）or an amendment filed under Section 9.514（b）:

（1）转让或修订文件应登记在转让人的名字之下，如同其为不动产转让人；以及

（1）under the name of the assignor as grantor;and

（2）如果本州法律规定，不动产抵押的转让记录应登记在不动产受让人的名字之下，则该记录即应登记在受让人的名字之下。

（2）to the extent that the law of this state provides for indexing a record of the assignment of a mortgage under the name of the assignee, under the name of the assignee.

（f）登记处应保持下列功能：

（f）The filing office shall maintain a capability:

（1）能够根据债务人的名字调取记录，以及根据原始融资声明的档案号调取与其相关的记录；并且

（1）to retrieve a record by the name of the debtor and by the file number assigned to the initial financing statement to which the record relates;and

（2）能够把原始融资声明与每一个相关的已登记的记录联系起来，并进行调取。

（2）to associate and retrieve with one another an initial financing statement and each filed record relating to the initial financing statement.

（g）只有在融资声明根据

（g）The filing office may not remove a

第 9.515 条就全部的注册受担保方均失去效力满一年后，登记处才能将融资声明中的债务人名字从目录中删除。

debtor's name from the index until one year after the effectiveness of a financing statement naming the debtor lapses under Section 9.515 with respect to all secured parties of record.

（h）除（i）款另有规定外，登记处应按登记处规则中的时间和方式，履行（a）款至（e）款的行为，但不得超过登记处收到相关记录后两个营业日。

（h）Except as provided in Subsection（i）, the filing office shall perform the acts required by Subsections（a）-（e）at the time and in the manner prescribed by filing-office rule, but not later than two business days after the filing office receives the record in question.

（i）上述（b）款和（h）款不适用于第 9.501 条（a）（1）款所述的登记处。

（i）Subsections（b）and（h）do not apply to a filing office described in Section 9.501（a）（1）.

第 9.520 条　接受和拒绝接受记录

§ 9.520. Acceptance and Refusal to Accept Record.

（a）如果存在第 9.516 条（b）款所列的原因，登记处应拒绝接受一项记录的登记，且只能因该款所列的原因拒绝接受一项记录的登记。

（a）A filing office shall refuse to accept a record for filing for a reason set forth in Section 9.516（b）and may refuse to accept a record for filing only for a reason set forth in Section 9.516（b）.

（b）登记处如果拒绝接受一项记录的登记，应向提交记录的人，就拒绝的事实和原因作出说明，并同时说明，假设登记处接受了该记录，该记录本应享有的登记日期和时间。该说明应按登记处规则中的时间和方式予以发送，但在涉及第 9.501 条（a）（2）款所述的登记处时，在任何情况下，都不得超过登记处收到记录后两个工作日。

（b）If a filing office refuses to accept a record for filing, it shall communicate to the person that presented the record the fact of and reason for the refusal and the date and time the record would have been filed had the filing office accepted it.The communication must be made at the time and in the manner prescribed by filing-office rule, but in the case of a filing office described in Section 9.501（a）（2）, in no event more than two business days after the filing office receives the record.

（c）已登记的融资声明，

（c）A filed financing statement satisfying

只要满足第9.502条(a)款和(b)款的要求，即为有效，即使登记处根据（a）款本来应该拒绝接受登记。但是，如果已登记的融资声明包含第9.516条（b）（5）款所述的信息，而信息在登记融资声明时不正确，则应适用第9.338条。

Sections 9.502（a）and（b）is effective, even if thc filing office is required to refuse to accept it for filing under Subsection（a）.However, Section 9.338 applies to a filed financing statement providing information described in Section 9.516（b）（5）that is incorrect at the time the financing statement is filed.

（d）如果向登记处发送的记录涉及一个以上债务人的信息，则本章独立适用于每一个债务人。

（d）If a record communicated to a filing office provides information that relates to more than one debtor, this Part applies as to each debtor separately.

第9.521条　书面融资声明和修订文件的统一格式

§ 9.521. Uniform Form of Written Financing Statement and Amendment.

（a）除第9.516条（b）款另有规定外，接受书面记录的登记处，不得拒绝接受按行业标准格式作出的书面原始融资声明，包括根据州务卿所制定之规则采纳的全国标准格式及国际商业管理者协会批准的格式。

（a）Except as provided by Section 9.516（b）, a filing office that accepts written records may not refuse to accept a written initial financing statement on an industry standard form, including a national standard form or a form approved by the International Association of Commercial Administrators, adopted by rule by the secretary of state.

（b）除第9.516条（b）款另有规定外，接受书面记录的登记处，不得拒绝接受按行业标准格式作出的书面记录，包括根据州务卿所制定之规则采纳的全国标准格式及国际商业管理者协会批准的格式。

（b）Except as provided by Section 9.516（b）, a filing office that accepts written records may not refuse to accept a written record on an industry standard form, including a national standard form or a form approved by the International Association of Commercial Administrators, adopted by rule by the secretary of state.

第9.522条　记录的保存和销毁

§ 9.522. Maintenance and Destruction of Records.

（a）在已登记的融资声明

（a）The filing office shall maintain a

根据第 9.515 条对全部的注册受担保方均已到期后，登记处应将载有其中信息的记录至少再保存一年。必须能够使用债务人的名字和原始融资声明的档案号对该记录进行调取。

record of the information provided in a filed financing statement for at least one year after the effectiveness of the financing statement has lapsed under Section 9.515 with respect to all secured parties of record.The record must be retrievable by using the name of the debtor and by using the file number assigned to the initial financing statement to which the record relates.

（b）除有关公共记录处理的法律另有规定外，登记处可以即时销毁证明融资声明的任何书面记录。但是，登记处如果销毁书面记录，即应对融资声明保存另一份符合（a）款要求的记录。

（b）Except to the extent that a statute governing disposition of public records provides otherwise, the filing office immediately may destroy any written record evidencing a financing statement.However, if the filing office destroys a written record, it shall maintain another record of the financing statement that complies with Subsection（a）.

第 9.523 条　登记处提供的信息；记录之买卖或许可

§ 9.523. Information From Filing Office; Sale or License of Records.

（a）如果提交书面记录登记的人索取登记回执，则登记处应向该人发送该记录的图像，显示根据第 9.519 条（a）（1）款发放给该记录的序号，以及该记录的登记日期和时间。但是，如果该人向登记处提供该记录的副本，则作为替代方法，登记处可以：

（a）If a person that files a written record requests an acknowledgment of the filing, the filing office shall send to the person an image of the record showing the number assigned to the record pursuant to Section 9.519（a）（1）and the date and time of the filing of the record. However, if the person furnishes a copy of the record to the filing office, the filing office may instead:

（1）在该副本上注明根据第 9.519 条（a）（1）款发放给该记录的序号，以及该记录的登记日期和时间；并且

（1）note upon the copy the number assigned to the record pursuant to Section 9.519（a）（1）and the date and time of the filing of the record;and

（2）将该副本发送给该人。

（2）send the copy to the person.

（b）如果一个人登记的记

（b）If a person files a record other

录不是书面记录，登记处应向该人发送具有下列内容的确认：

than a written record, the filing office shall communicate to the person an acknowledgment that provides:

（1）记录中包含的信息；

（1）the information in the record;

（2）根据第9.519条（a）（1）款发放给该记录的序号；以及

（2）the number assigned to the record pursuant to Section 9.519（a）（1）;and

（3）记录的登记日期和时间。

（3）the date and time of the filing of the record.

（c）任何人只要提出获得下列信息的要求，登记处即应以记录形式，将信息发送给或以其他形式提供给该人：

（c）The filing office shall communicate or otherwise make available in a record the following information to any person that requests it:

（1）截至登记处所注明的日期和时间（但该日期不得早于登记处收到该要求前三个工作日），档案中是否存在：

（1）whether there is on file on a date and time specified by the filing office, but not a date earlier than three business days before the filing office receives the request, any financing statement that:

（A）指向任何特定债务人的融资声明，或如果该人提供了地址，指向位于该特定地址之特定债务人的融资声明；

（A）designates a particular debtor or, if the request so states, designates a particular debtor at the address specified in the request;

（B）根据第9.515条尚未就全部的注册受担保方过期的融资声明；以及

（B）has not lapsed under Section 9.515 with respect to all secured parties of record;and

（C）根据第9.515条已经过期，但登记处根据第9.522条（a）款存有记录的融资声明（如果该人要求予以说明）；

（C）if the request so states, has lapsed under Section 9.515 and a record of which is maintained by the filing office under Section 9.522（a）;

（2）每一份此种融资声明的登记日期和时间；以及

（2）the date and time of filing of each financing statement;and

（3）每一份此种融资声明中包含的信息。

（3）the information provided in each financing statement.

（d）在履行（c）款项下的

（d）In complying with its duty under

义务时，登记处可以使用任何媒介提供信息。但在被要求时，登记处应通过出具书面证明发送信息。

Subsection（c），the filing office may communicate information in any medium. However, if requested, the filing office shall communicate information by issuing its written certificate.

（e）登记处应按登记处规则中的时间和方式，履行（a）款至（d）款要求的行为，但不得晚于登记处收到要求后两个工作日。

（e）The filing office shall perform the acts required by Subsections（a）-（d）at the time and in the manner prescribed by filing-office rule, but not later than two business days after the filing office receives the request.

（f）州务卿应至少每周一次，通过可使用的任何媒介，在非独家和整体打包的基础上，以出售或许可形式，向公众提供根据本章在州务卿处登记的所有记录的副本。

（f）At least weekly, the Secretary of State shall offer to sell or license to the public on a nonexclusive basis, in bulk, copies of all records filed with the Secretary under this Part, in every medium from time to time available to the Secretary.

第 9.524 条　登记处的延迟

§ 9.524. Delay by Filing Office.

在下列情况下，登记处对超出本章时间期限的延迟不承担责任：

Delay by the filing office beyond a time limit prescribed by this Part is excused if:

（1）延迟源于通信或计算机设施故障、战争、紧急情况、设备失效或其他超出登记处控制的情况；并且

（1）the delay is caused by interruption of communication or computer facilities, war, emergency conditions, failure of equipment, or other circumstances beyond control of the filing office;and

（2）根据当时情况，登记处已作出合理努力。

（2）the filing office exercises reasonable diligence under the circumstances.

第 9.525 条　费用

§ 9.525. Fees.

（a）除（e）款和（f）款另有规定外，为本章项下之记录［但（b）款所述类别的原始融资声明除外］登记和编目的费用为：

（a）Except as otherwise provided in Subsections（e）and（f），the fee for filing and indexing a record under this Part, other than an initial financing statement of the kind described in Subsection（b），is:

（1）如果记录用书面传送，且为一页至两页纸，费用为 15 美元；

（1）$15 if the record is communicated in writing and consists of one or two pages;

（2）如果记录用书面传送，且超出两页纸，费用为 30 美元；以及

（2）$30 if the record is communicated in writing and consists of more than two pages;and

（3）如果记录用登记处规则允许的其他媒介作出，费用为 5 美元。

（3）$5 if the record is communicated by another medium authorized by filing-office rule.

（b）除（e）款另有规定外，为下列类别的原始融资声明登记和编目的费用为：

（b）Except as otherwise provided in Subsection（e）, the fee for filing and indexing an initial financing statement of the following kinds is:

（1）如果融资声明注明，登记系为公共融资项目，费用为六十美元；以及

（1）$60 if the financing statement indicates that it is filed in connection with a public-finance transaction;and

（2）如果融资声明注明，登记系为工厂预制房屋交易，费用为 60 美元。

（2）$60 if the financing statement indicates that it is filed in connection with a manufactured-home transaction.

（c）编目时需要输入的名字数量，不影响（a）款和（b）款中的费用金额。

（c）The number of names required to be indexed does not affect the amount of the fee in Subsections（a）and（b）.

（d）涉及向登记处提出的询问时，包括档案中是否存在指向任何特定债务人的融资声明，答复此种询问的费用为：

（d）The fee for responding to a request for information from the filing office, including for communicating whether there is on file any financing statement naming a particular debtor, is:

（1）如果询问以书面发送，费用为 15 美元；以及

（1）$15 if the request is communicated in writing;and

（2）如果询问以登记处规则允许的另一种媒介发送，费用为登记处设定的金额。

（2）an amount established by the filing office if the request is communicated by another medium authorized by filing-office rule.

（e）如果一项不动产抵押记录，可以有效作为具有不动产附着物登记之效力的融资声明，或有效作为覆盖第9.502条（c）款所述的开采状担保物或待砍伐树木的融资声明，则本条不要求就该不动产抵押记录收取融资声明的费用，但是，该不动产抵押记录本来应收取的登记费和解押费仍然适用。

（e）This section does not require a fee with respect to a record of a mortgage that is effective as a financing statement filed as a fixture filing or as a financing statement covering as-extractedcollateral or timber to be cut under Section 9.502（c）.However, the recording and satisfaction fees that otherwise would be applicable to the record of the mortgage apply.

（f）涉及第9.512条（f）款项下的总体修订文件，或第9.514条（d）款项下的总体转让文件时，登记、编目及提供登记数据的登记费为500美元。如果总体声明覆盖的融资声明超过50个，则每增加一个，加收50美分。

（f）The filing fee for filing, indexing, and furnishing filing data about a statement of master amendment under Section 9.512（f）or master assignment under Section 9.514（d）is $500 plus 50 cents for each financing statement covered by the master statement in excess of 50.

第9.526条 登记处规则

§ 9.526. Filing–Office Rules.

（a）州务卿应制定并公布实施本篇的规则。登记处规则必须与本篇相符。

（a）The Secretary of State shall adopt and publish rules to implement this Article.The filing-office rules must be consistent with this Article.

（b）为使登记处的规则与做法，与基本采纳了本章之其他州登记处的规则与做法相协调，并为使登记处使用的技术，与基本采纳了本章的其他州登记处的技术相兼容，州务卿在制定、修改和废除登记处规则时，在符合本篇目的、政策和条款的情况下，应该：

（b）To keep the filing-office rules and practices of the filing office in harmony with the rules and practices of filing offices in other jurisdictions that enact substantially this Part, and to keep the technology used by the filing office compatible with the technology used by filing offices in other jurisdictions that enact substantially this Part, the Secretary of State, so far as is consistent with the purposes, policies, and provisions of this Article, in adopting, amending, and repealing filing-office rules, shall:

（1）咨询基本采纳了本章之其他州登记处；

（1）consult with filing offices in other jurisdictions that enact substantially this Part;

（2）参考公司管理者国际协会或其继任组织制定的《示范管理规则》最新版本；以及

（2）consult the most recent version of the Model Administrative Rules promulgated by the International Association of Corporation Administrators or any successor organization;and

（3）参考基本采纳了本章之其他州登记处使用的规则、做法和技术。

（3）take into consideration the rules and practices of, and the technology used by, filing offices in other jurisdictions that enact substantially this Part.

第 9.527 条　报告的义务

§ 9.527. Duty to Report.

在每个单数年份的一月一日之前，州务卿应向立法机构报告登记处的运行情况。报告必须就下列情况作出说明：

The Secretary of State shall report before January 1 of each odd-numbered year to the Legislature on the operation of the filing office. The report must contain a statement of the extent to which:

（1）登记处规则与基本采纳了本章之其他州登记处规则之间的差异程度及差异原因；以及

（1）the filing-office rules are not in harmony with the rules of filing offices in other jurisdictions that enact substantially this Part and the reasons for these variations;and

（2）登记处规则与公司管理者国际协会或其继任组织制定的《示范管理规则》最新版本之间的差异程度及差异原因。

（2）the filing-office rules are not in harmony with the most recent version of the Model Administrative Rules promulgated by the International Association of Corporation Administrators, or any successor organization, and the reasons for these variations.

第6章　违　约

PART 6. DEFAULT

第 9.601 条　发生违约后的权利；司法强制履行；寄售委托人；应收款、动产契据、无形支付或本票的买方

§ 9.601. Rights After Default; Judicial Enforcement; Consignor or Buyer of Accounts, Chattel Paper, Payment Intangibles, or Promissory Notes.

（a）发生违约后，受担保方享有本章提供的权利，且除第 9.602 条另有规定外，还享有当事方协议提供的权利。受担保方：

（a）After default, a secured party has the rights provided in this Part and, except as otherwise provided in Section 9.602, those provided by agreement of the parties.A secured party:

（1）可以就索赔寻求法院判决，可以变现担保物，也可以通过任何其他可用的司法程序强制履行其索赔、担保权益或农业留置权；并且

（1）may reduce a claim to judgment, foreclose, or otherwise enforce the claim, security interest, or agricultural lien by any available judicial procedure;and

（2）如果担保物系凭证，则既可以就凭证采取行动，也可以就凭证覆盖的货物采取行动。

（2）if the collateral is documents, may proceed either as to the documents or as to the goods they cover.

（b）受担保方如果占有担保物或根据第 7.106 条、第 9.104 条、第 9.105 条、第 9.106 条或第 9.107 条控制担保物，即享有第 9.207 条规定的权利和义务。

（b）A secured party in possession of collateral or control of collateral under Section 7.106, 9.104, 9.105, 9.106, or 9.107 has the rights and duties provided in Section 9.207.

（c）上述（a）款和（b）款中的权利可以叠加，并可以同时行使。

（c）The rights under Subsections（a）and（b）are cumulative and may be exercised simultaneously.

（d）除（g）款和第 9.605 条另有规定外，发生违约后，债务人和义务人享有本章及当事方协议提供的权利。

（d）Except as otherwise provided in Subsection（g）and Section 9.605, after default, a debtor and an obligor have the rights provided in this Part and by agreement of the parties.

（e）如果受担保方已就其

（e）If a secured party has reduced its

索赔取得法院判决，则在执行判决中通过查封担保物所取得的留置权，将溯及至下列最早的日期：

（1）担保物中担保权益或农业留置权获得完善的日期；

（2）覆盖担保物之融资声明的登记日期；或

（3）设定农业留置权之法律规定的任何日期。

（f）司法执行中的出售，属于本条规定的通过司法程序进行担保权益或农业留置权的变现。受担保方可以在该出售中购买，且其后在持有担保物时，不受制于本篇的任何其他要求。

（g）除第 9.607 条（c）款另有规定外，如果受担保方系寄售委托人，或系应收款、动产契据、无形支付或本票的买方，本章不向该受担保方施加义务。

第 9.602 条　权利和义务的放弃和变更

除第 9.624 条另有规定外，对于下列各条中的原则，只要涉及向债务人或义务人提供权利，或向受担保方施加义务，债务人或义务人即不得放弃或变更该等原则：

（1）第 9.207 条（b）（4）（C）

claim to judgment, the lien of any levy that may be made upon the collateral by virtue of an execution based upon the judgment relates back to the earliest of:

（1）the date of the perfection of the security interest or agricultural lien in the collateral;

（2）the date of filing a financing statement covering the collateral;or

（3）any date specified in a statute under which the agricultural lien was created.

（f）A sale pursuant to an execution is a foreclosure of the security interest or agricultural lien by judicial procedure within the meaning of this section.A secured party may purchase at the sale and thereafter hold the collateral free of any other requirements of this Article.

（g）Except as otherwise provided in Section 9.607（c）, this Part imposes no duties upon a secured party that is a consignor or is a buyer of accounts, chattel paper, payment intangibles, or promissory notes.

§ 9.602. Waiver and Variance of Rights and Duties.

Except as otherwise provided in Section 9.624, to the extent that they give rights to a debtor or obligor and impose duties on a secured party, the debtor or obligor may not waive or vary the rules stated in the following listed sections:

（1）Section 9.207（b）（4）（C）, which

款，关于受担保方对担保物的使用和运营；

deals with use and operation of the collateral by the secured party;

（2）第 9.210 条，关于对账请求、担保物清单请求和债务清单请求；

（2）Section 9.210, which deals with requests for an accounting and requests concerning a list of collateral and statement of account;

（3）第 9.607 条（c）款，关于担保物的收款和强制履行；

（3）Section 9.607（c）, which deals with collection and enforcement of collateral;

（4）第 9.608 条（a）款和第 9.615 条（c）款，关于非现金收益的使用和支付，只要该收益系通过收款、强制履行或处置而取得；

（4）Sections 9.608（a）and 9.615（c）to the extent that they deal with application or payment of noncash proceeds of collection, enforcement, or disposition;

（5）第 9.608 条（a）款和第 9.615 条（d）款，关于担保物之剩余部分的结算和支付；

（5）Sections 9.608（a）and 9.615（d）to the extent that they require accounting for or payment of surplus proceeds of collateral;

（6）第 9.609 条，关于非通过司法程序取得担保物占有之受担保方在取得担保物过程中不破坏和平的义务；

（6）Section 9.609 to the extent that it imposes upon a secured party that takes possession of collateral without judicial process the duty to do so without breach of the peace;

（7）第 9.610 条（b）款、第 9.611 条、第 9.613 条和第 9.614 条，关于担保物的处置；

（7）Sections 9.610（b）, 9.611, 9.613, and 9.614, which deal with disposition of collateral;

（8）第 9.615 条（f）款，关于将担保物处置给受担保方、受担保方关联人或次义务人时，不足部分或剩余部分的计算；

（8）Section 9.615（f）, which deals with calculation of a deficiency or surplus when a disposition is made to the secured party, a person related to the secured party, or a secondary obligor;

（9）第 9.616 条，关于对剩余部分或不足部分计算的解释；

（9）Section 9.616, which deals with explanation of the calculation of a surplus or deficiency;

（10）第 9.620 条、第 9.621 条和第 9.622 条，关于收取担

（10）Sections 9.620, 9.621, and 9.622, which deal with acceptance of collateral in

保物用于偿付债务；

（11）第 9.623 条，关于担保物的赎回；

（12）第 9.624 条，关于允许作出的弃权；以及

（13）第 9.625 条和第 9.626 条，关于受担保方未能遵守本篇规定时的责任。

第 9.603 条　规定权利和义务之标准的协议

（a）当事方可以通过协议，就第 9.602 条所述的涉及债务人或义务人之权利或受担保方之义务的原则，制定行使权利和履行义务的标准，但此种标准不得明显不合理。

（b）上述（a）款不适用于第 9.609 条所述的不破坏和平的义务。

第 9.604 条　担保协议覆盖不动产或不动产附着物时的程序

（a）如果担保协议同时覆盖动产和不动产，受担保方可以：

（1）根据本章就动产作为，且不损害其对不动产享有的任何权利；或

（2）根据对不动产享有的权利，同时就动产和不动产作为，此时本章的其他条款不适用。

（b）除（c）款另有规定外，

satisfaction of obligation;

（11）Section 9.623, which deals with redemption of collateral;

（12）Section 9.624, which deals with permissible waivers;and

（13）Sections 9.625 and 9.626, which deal with the secured party's liability for failure to comply with this Article.

§ 9.603. Agreement on Standards Concerning Rights and Duties.

（a）The parties may determine by agreement the standards measuring the fulfillment of the rights of a debtor or obligor and the duties of a secured party under a rule stated in Section 9.602 if the standards are not manifestly unreasonable.

（b）Subsection（a）does not apply to the duty under Section 9.609 to refrain from breaching the peace.

§ 9.604. Procedure if Security Agreement Covers Real Property or Fixtures.

（a）If a security agreement covers both personal and real property, a secured party may proceed:

（1）under this Part as to the personal property without prejudicing any rights with respect to the real property;or

（2）as to both the personal property and the real property in accordance with the rights with respect to the real property, in which case the other provisions of this Part do not apply.

（b）Subject to Subsection（c）, if a

如果担保协议覆盖的货物已经成为或即将成为不动产附着物，则受担保方可以：

（1）根据本章作为；或

（2）根据对不动产享有的权利作为，此时本章的其他条款不适用。

（c）除本章其他条款另有规定外，对不动产附着物持有担保权益的受担保方，如果相对于不动产的全部其他所有权人和不动产他项权人，均享有优先权，则在发生违约后，受担保方可以将担保物从不动产上拆移。

（d）拆移担保物的受担保方，应就拆移所造成之物理损伤的修复费用，迅即对不动产的任何不动产他项权人或所有权人（债务人除外）给予补偿，但受担保方无须就不动产由于缺少或替换被拆移之货物所造成的价值降低，对不动产他项权人或所有权人给予补偿。有权获得补偿的人，在受担保方就履行补偿义务提供充分保证前，可以拒绝该拆移。

security agreement covers goods that are or become fixtures, a secured party may proceed:

（1）under this Part;or

（2）in accordance with the rights with respect to real property, in which case the other provisions of this Part do not apply.

（c）Subject to the other provisions of this Part, if a secured party holding a security interest in fixtures has priority over all owners and encumbrancers of the real property, the secured party, after default, may remove the collateral from the real property.

（d）A secured party that removes collateral shall promptly reimburse any encumbrancer or owner of the real property, other than the debtor, for the cost of repair of any physical injury caused by the removal. The secured party need not reimburse the encumbrancer or owner for any diminution in value of the real property caused by the absence of the goods removed or by any necessity of replacing them.A person entitled to reimbursement may refuse permission to remove until the secured party gives adequate assurance for the performance of the obligation to reimburse.

第9.605条 未知债务人或次义务人

受担保方不因其受担保方的身份，对下列人承担义务：

§ 9.605. Unknown Debtor or Secondary Obligor.

A secured party does not owe a duty based on its status as secured party:

（1）身为债务人或义务人的人，除非受担保方：

（A）知道该人为债务人或义务人；

（B）知道该人的真实身份；并且

（C）知道如何与该人联系；或

（2）登记了针对任何人之融资声明的受担保方或留置权持有人，除非受担保方：

（A）知道被针对的人为债务人；并且

（B）知道该债务人的真实身份。

（1）to a person that is a debtor or obligor, unless the secured party knows:

（A）that the person is a debtor or obligor;

（B）the identity of the person;and

（C）how to communicate with the person;or

（2）to a secured party or lienholder that has filed a financing statement against a person, unless the secured party knows:

（A）that the person is a debtor;and

（B）the identity of the person.

第 9.606 条　农业留置权发生违约的时间

为本章目的，当受担保方根据设立农业留置权之法律有权强制履行该农业留置权时，该时间即为违约的发生时间。

§ 9.606. Time of Default for Agricultural Lien.

For purposes of this Part, a default occurs in connection with an agricultural lien at the time the secured party becomes entitled to enforce the lien in accordance with the statute under which it was created.

第 9.607 条　受担保方的收款和强制履行

（a）如果存在相关约定，或只要发生违约，受担保方即：

（1）可以通知应收款债务人或其他就担保物承担义务的人，向受担保方，或以受担保方为受益人，作出付款或其他形式的履约；

（2）可以收取根据第 9.315

§ 9.607. Collection and Enforcement by Secured Party.

（a）If so agreed, and in any event after default, a secured party:

（1）may notify an account debtor or other person obligated on collateral to make payment or otherwise render performance to or for the benefit of the secured party;

（2）may take any proceeds to which the

条受担保方有权取得的担保物收益；

secured party is entitled under Section 9.315;

（3）可以对应收款债务人或其他就担保物承担义务的人，强制履行其义务，并且，可以就前述人承担的向债务人作出付款或其他形式履约的义务，并针对用于担保前述人之债务的财产，代替行使债务人的权利；

（3）may enforce the obligations of an account debtor or other person obligated on collateral and exercise the rights of the debtor with respect to the obligation of the account debtor or other person obligated on collateral to make payment or otherwise render performance to the debtor, and with respect to any property that secures the obligations of the account debtor or other person obligated on the collateral;

（4）可以将存款账户的余额，用于支付存款账户所担保的债务，只要受担保方对存款账户持有担保权益，且担保权益根据第9.104条（a）（1）款通过取得控制获得完善；并且

（4）if it holds a security interest in a deposit account perfected by control under Section 9.104（a）（1）, may apply the balance of the deposit account to the obligation secured by the deposit account;and

（5）可以指示银行将存款账户的余额支付给受担保方，或以受担保方为受益人作出支付，只要受担保方对存款账户持有担保权益，且担保权益根据第9.104条（a）（2）款或（3）款通过取得控制获得完善。

（5）if it holds a security interest in a deposit account perfected by control under Section 9.104（a）（2）or（3）, may instruct the bank to pay the balance of the deposit account to or for the benefit of the secured party.

（b）必要时，为使受担保方能够根据（a）（3）款代替行使债务人的权利，通过非司法方式强制履行不动产抵押权，受担保方可以在不动产抵押登记处登记下列文件：

（b）If necessary to enable a secured party to exercise under Subsection（a）（3）the right of a debtor to enforce a mortgage nonjudicially, the secured party may record in the office in which a record of the mortgage is recorded:

（1）担保协议的副本，即针对不动产抵押权所担保的债

（1）a copy of the security agreement that creates or provides for a security interest in the

务，在该债务中设立担保权益的协议；以及

obligation secured by the mortgage;and

（2）符合登记要求的受担保方的宣誓证明，其中说明：

（2）the secured party's sworn affidavit in recordable form stating that:

（A）已发生违约；并且

（A）a default has occurred;and

（B）受担保方有权通过非司法方式强制履行不动产抵押权。

（B）the secured party is entitled to enforce the mortgage nonjudicially.

（c）如果存在下列情况，则受担保方应以商业上合理的方式作为：

（c）A secured party shall proceed in a commercially reasonable manner if the secured party:

（1）受担保方决定针对应收款债务人或其他就担保物承担义务的人，强制履行其义务，或就该义务收款；以及

（1）undertakes to collect from or enforce an obligation of an account debtor or other person obligated on collateral;and

（2）受担保方有权针对未获得付款之担保物行使倒账权，或以其他方式对债务人或次义务人行使充分的或有限的追索权。

（2）is entitled to charge back uncollected collateral or otherwise to full or limited recourse against the debtor or a secondary obligor.

（d）受担保方如果根据（c）款获得款项，即有权从中扣除合理的追偿和强制履行费用，包括受担保方支出的合理的律师费和法律费用。

（d）A secured party may deduct from the collections made pursuant to Subsection（c）reasonable expenses of collection and enforcement, including reasonable attorney's fees and legal expenses incurred by the secured party.

（e）应收款债务人、银行或其他就担保物承担义务的人是否对受担保方负有义务，不由本条规定。

（e）This section does not determine whether an account debtor, bank, or other person obligated on collateral owes a duty to a secured party.

第 9.608 条 收款或强制履行之收益的使用；不足部分的责任及剩余部分的权利

§ 9.608. Application of Proceeds of Collection or Enforcement; Liability for Deficiency and Right to Surplus.

（a）如果担保权益或农业

（a）If a security interest or agricultural

留置权用于担保一项债务的支付或履行，应适用下列原则：

lien secures payment or performance of an obligation, the following rules apply:

（1）对于根据第9.607条进行收款或强制履行所获得的现金收益，受担保方应按下列顺序使用或支付：

（1）A secured party shall apply or pay over for application the cash proceeds of collection or enforcement under Section 9.607 in the following order to:

（A）收款和强制履行的合理费用；以及受担保方支出的合理的律师费和法律费用，只要协议允许且法律不禁止；

（A）the reasonable expenses of collection and enforcement and, to the extent provided for by agreement and not prohibited by law, reasonable attorney's fees and legal expenses incurred by the secured party;

（B）债务的偿付，即作为收款和强制履行之依据的担保权益或农业留置权所担保的债务；以及

（B）the satisfaction of obligations secured by the security interest or agricultural lien under which the collection or enforcement is made;and

（C）次级债务的偿付，即作为收款和强制履行之依据的，受制于前述担保权益或农业留置权的任何次级担保权益或其他留置权所担保的债务，只要在收益分配完成之前，受担保方收到业经认证的有关参与收益分配的要求。

（C）the satisfaction of obligations secured by any subordinate security interest in or other lien on the collateral subject to the security interest or agricultural lien under which the collection or enforcement is made if the secured party receives an authenticated demand for proceeds before distribution of the proceeds is completed.

（2）如果受担保方提出要求，次级担保权益或其他留置权的持有人应在合理时间内，就该权益或留置权提供合理证明。如果持有人不予遵从，受担保方即无须遵从该持有人根据（1）（C）款提出的要求。

（2）If requested by a secured party, a holder of a subordinate security interest or other lien shall furnish reasonable proof of the interest or lien within a reasonable time.Unless the holder complies, the secured party need not comply with the holder's demand under Subdivision（1）（C）.

（3）对于根据第9.607条通过收款或强制履行所获得的非现金收益，受担保方无须作

（3）A secured party need not apply or pay over for application noncash proceeds of collection and enforcement under Section

出使用或支付，除非不这样做属于商业上不合理。受担保方如果对非现金收益作出使用或支付，应以商业上合理的方式进行。

（4）受担保方应将剩余部分支付给债务人，而义务人对不足部分应承担责任。

（b）如果基础交易是应收款、动产契据、无形支付或本票的买卖，则债务人无权获得剩余部分，而义务人对不足部分亦不承担责任。

第 9.609 条　发生违约后受担保方取得占有的权利

（a）发生违约后，受担保方：

（1）可以取得担保物的占有；并且

（2）可以在不拆移的情况下使设备失去使用功能，并可以根据第 9.610 条，在债务人的场地处置担保物。

（b）根据（a）款作为时，受担保方可以：

（1）通过司法程序进行；或

（2）不通过司法程序进行，只要能够不破坏和平。

（c）如果存在相关约定，或无论如何只要发生违约，受担保方即可要求债务人把担保物集齐，并在受担保方指定的对双方都合理和方便的地点，

9.607 unless the failure to do so would be commercially unreasonable.A secured party that applies or pays over for application noncash proceeds shall do so in a commercially reasonable manner.

（4）A secured party shall account to and pay a debtor for any surplus, and the obligor is liable for any deficiency.

（b）If the underlying transaction is a sale of accounts, chattel paper, payment intangibles, or promissory notes, the debtor is not entitled to any surplus, and the obligor is not liable for any deficiency.

§ 9.609. Secured Party's Right to Take Possession After Default.

（a）After default, a secured party:

（1）may take possession of the collateral;and

（2）without removal, may render equipment unusable and dispose of collateral on the debtor's premises under Section 9.610.

（b）A secured party may proceed under Subsection（a）:

（1）pursuant to judicial process;or

（2）without judicial process, if it proceeds without breach of the peace.

（c）If so agreed, and in any event after default, a secured party may require the debtor to assemble the collateral and make it available to the secured party at a place to be designated by the secured party that is reasonably

交付给受担保方。

convenient to both parties.

第 9.610 条　发生违约后处置担保物

§ 9.610. Disposition of Collateral After Default.

（a）发生违约后，受担保方可以按担保物当时的状况，或在进行商业上合理的准备或加工后，出售、出租、许可或以其他方式处置部分或全部担保物。

（a）After default, a secured party may sell, lease, license, or otherwise dispose of any or all of the collateral in its present condition or following any commercially reasonable preparation or processing.

（b）处置担保物的各个方面，包括方法、方式、时间、地点及其他条件，都需要商业上合理。只要商业上合理，受担保方在处置担保物时，可以使用公开或私下方式，通过一个或多个合同，整体或分批进行，并在任何时间和地点，以任何合理的条件处置。

（b）Every aspect of a disposition of collateral, including the method, manner, time, place, and other terms, must be commercially reasonable.If commercially reasonable, a secured party may dispose of collateral by public or private proceedings, by one or more contracts, as a unit or in parcels, and at any time and place and on any terms.

（c）受担保方可以按下列方式购买担保物：

（1）通过公开处置购买；或

（2）通过私下处置购买，但是在此种处置中，担保物的种类必须系通常在公认市场上买卖，或通过广泛使用的标准报价买卖。

（c）A secured party may purchase collateral:

（1）at a public disposition;or

（2）at a private disposition only if the collateral is of a kind that is customarily sold on a recognized market or the subject of widely distributed standard price quotations.

（d）买卖、租赁、许可或其他处置方式所使用的合同，应被视为包含所有权、占有权和平安使用的担保条款，以及在自愿处置类似财产时，合同依法自动包含的其他担保条款。

（d）A contract for sale, lease, license, or other disposition includes the warranties relating to title, possession, quiet enjoyment, and the like that by operation of law accompany a voluntary disposition of property of the kind subject to the contract.

（e）受担保方可以对（d）

（e）A secured party may disclaim or

款所述的担保加以排除或修改，只要：

modify warranties under Subsection（d）:

（1）所使用的方式在自愿处置类似财产时，可以有效排除或修改担保；或

（1）in a manner that would be effective to disclaim or modify the warranties in a voluntary disposition of property of the kind subject to the contract of disposition;or

（2）向购买者发送证明处置合同的记录，其中包含对担保的明示排除或修改。

（2）by communicating to the purchaser a record evidencing the contract for disposition and including an express disclaimer or modification of the warranties.

（f）如果记录说明，“在本次处置中，不存在所有权、占有权或平安使用的担保或类似担保”，或使用具有类似含义的文字，该记录即符合（e）款要求，足以排除担保。

（f）A record is sufficient to disclaim warranties under Subsection（e）if it indicates “There is no warranty relating to title, possession, quiet enjoyment, or the like in this disposition” or uses words of similar import.

第 9.611 条　处置担保物前的通知

§ 9.611. Notification Before Disposition of Collateral.

（a）在本条中，“通知日”指下列中较早的日期：

（a）In this section, “notification date” means the earlier of the date on which:

（1）受担保方给债务人和任何次义务人发送业经认证之处置通知的日期；或

（1）a secured party sends to the debtor and any secondary obligor an authenticated notification of disposition;or

（2）债务人和任何次义务人放弃获得通知之权利的日期。

（2）the debtor and any secondary obligor waive the right to notification.

（b）除（d）款另有规定外，受担保方如果根据第 9.610 条处置担保物，即应向（c）款规定的人，发送业经认证的合理的处置通知。

（b）Except as otherwise provided in Subsection（d）, a secured party that disposes of collateral under Section 9.610 shall send to the persons specified in Subsection（c）a reasonable authenticated notification of disposition.

（c）为遵守（b）款规定，受担保方应向下列人发送业经

（c）To comply with Subsection（b）, the secured party shall send an authenticated

认证的处置通知：

notification of disposition to:

（1）债务人；

（1）the debtor;

（2）任何次义务人；以及

（2）any secondary obligor;and

（3）当担保物非属消费品时：

（3）if the collateral is other than consumer goods:

（A）任何其他人，只要在通知日之前，受担保方从其收到了业经认证的对担保物主张权益的通知；

（A）any other person from which the secured party has received, before the notification date, an authenticated notification of a claim of an interest in the collateral;

（B）任何其他受担保方或留置权持有人，只要在通知日前10天以前，其曾对担保物持有担保权益或其他留置权，且该权益通过登记符合下列条件之融资声明获得完善：

（B）any other secured party or lienholder that, 10 days before the notification date, held a security interest in or other lien on the collateral perfected by the filing of a financing statement that:

（i）融资声明指明了该担保物；

（i）identified the collateral;

（ii）截至该日，融资声明根据编目登记在债务人名字之下；并且

（ii）was indexed under the debtor's name as of that date;and

（iii）截至该日，作出登记的登记处，相对于该债务人以及覆盖该担保物的融资声明，是正确的登记处；以及

（iii）was filed in the office in which to file a financing statement against the debtor covering the collateral as of that date;and

（C）任何其他受担保方，只要在通知日前10天以前，其曾对担保物持有担保权益，且该权益通过遵守第9.311条（a）款所述的法律或条约获得完善。

（C）any other secured party that, 10 days before the notification date, held a security interest in the collateral perfected by compliance with a statute, regulation, or treaty described in Section 9.311（a）.

（d）如果担保物易腐或面临价值迅速降低的危险，或属于惯常在公认市场上买卖的种类，则（b）款不适用。

（d）Subsection（b）does not apply if the collateral is perishable or threatens to decline speedily in value or is of a type customarily sold on a recognized market.

（e）受担保方只要做到下列，即满足了（c）（3）（B）款有关通知的要求：

（1）在通知日前不少于 20 天且不多于 30 天之前，受担保方以商业上合理的方式，向（c）（3）（B）款所述的登记处，要求获取目录中登记在债务人名字下的融资声明；并且

（2）在通知日之前，受担保方：

（A）未就所要求的信息收到答复；或

（B）就所要求的信息收到了答复，并向答复中列出的每一个就担保物登记了融资声明的受担保方或其他留置权持有人，发送了业经认证的处置通知。

（e）A secured party complies with the requirement for notification prescribed by Subsection（c）（3）（B）if:

（1）not later than 20 days or earlier than 30 days before the notification date, the secured party requests, in a commercially reasonable manner, information concerning financing statements indexed under the debtor's name in the office indicated in Subsection（c）（3）（B）;and

（2）before the notification date, the secured party:

（A）did not receive a response to the request for information;or

（B）received a response to the request for information and sent an authenticated notification of disposition to each secured party or other lienholder named in that response whose financing statement covered the collateral.

第 9.612 条　处置担保物前之通知的及时性

（a）除（b）款另有规定外，通知是否在合理时间内发出，属于事实问题。

（b）在消费者交易以外的交易中，如果处置通知在违约发生后发送，且在通知中注明的最早处置时间 10 天以前发送，即属于在合理时间内发送。

§ 9.612. Timeliness of Notification Before Disposition of Collateral.

（a）Except as otherwise provided in Subsection（b）, whether a notification is sent within a reasonable time is a question of fact.

（b）In a transaction other than a consumer transaction, a notification of disposition sent after default and 10 days or more before the earliest time of disposition set forth in the notification is sent within a reasonable time before the disposition.

第 9.613 条　处置担保物前之通知的内容和格式：一般规定

除涉及消费品交易外，应适用下列原则：

（1）处置通知只要达到下列要求，内容即为充分：

（A）描述了债务人和受担保方；

（B）描述了计划处置的担保物；

（C）说明了计划处置的方式；

（D）说明了债务人有权就尚未清偿的债务获得账单，并说明了制作账单的费用（如果收费）；并且

（E）说明了公开处置的时间和地点，或如果是其他处置方法，说明了处置的最早时间。

（2）如果通知缺少（1）款规定的任何信息，则通知内容是否仍属充分，属于事实问题。

（3）如果通知实质上提供了（1）款规定的信息，则通知即使存在下列情况，其内容亦属充分：

（A）提供了该款未要求的信息；或

（B）存在不会造成严重误导的次要错误。

（4）通知不需要使用特定用语。

§ 9.613. Contents and Form of Notification Before Disposition of Collateral:General.

Except in a consumer-goods transaction, the following rules apply:

（1）The contents of a notification of disposition are sufficient if the notification:

（A）describes the debtor and the secured party;

（B）describes the collateral that is the subject of the intended disposition;

（C）states the method of intended disposition;

（D）states that the debtor is entitled to an accounting of the unpaid indebtedness and states the charge, if any, for an accounting;and

（E）states the time and place of a public disposition or the time after which any other disposition is to be made.

（2）Whether the contents of a notification that lacks any of the information specified in Subdivision（1）are nevertheless sufficient is a question of fact.

（3）The contents of a notification providing substantially the information specified in Subdivision（1）are sufficient, even if the notification includes:

（A）information not specified by that subdivision;or

（B）minor errors that are not seriously misleading.

（4）A particular phrasing of the notification is not required.

（5）通知的下列格式以及第9.614条（3）款所列的格式，在填写完整后，均被视为提供了充分信息：

担保物处置通知：

致：__________（作为通知接收人之债务人、义务人或其他人的名字）

自：__________（受担保方的名字、地址和电话号码）

债务人名字：____________（只有债务人不是通知接收人时才需要）

（用于公开处置：）

我们将把（描述担保物）公开出售（或，视情况而定，租赁或许可）（给出价最高的合格竞标人），具体如下：

星期和日期：____________

时间：____________________

地点：____________________

（用于私下处置：）

我们将在________（星期及日期）之后的某个时间，把______（描述担保物）私下出售（或，视情况而定，租赁或许可）。

对于我们计划出售（或，视情况而定，租赁或许可）之财产所担保的未偿债务，你有权（在支付____________美元费用后）获取账单。你可以给我们打电话________（电话号码），

（5）The following form of notification and the form appearing in Section 9.614（3）, when completed, each provide sufficient information:

NOTIFICATION OF DISPOSITION OF COLLATERAL

To:__________[Name of debtor, obligor, or other person to which the notification is sent]

From:__________[Name, address, and telephone number of secured party]

Name of Debtor（s）:__________[Include only if debtor（s）are not an addressee]

[For a public disposition:]

We will sell [or lease or license, as applicable] the [describe collateral] [to the highest qualified bidder] in public as follows:

Day and Date:________________________

Time:______________________________

Place:_____________________________

[For a private disposition:]

We will sell [or lease or license, as applicable] the ________[describe collateral] privately sometime after __________[day and date].

You are entitled to an accounting of the unpaid indebtedness secured by the property that we intend to sell [or lease or license, as applicable] [for a charge of $__________]. You may request an accounting by calling us at __________[telephone number].

提出获取账单的要求。

第 9.614 条　处置担保物前之通知的内容和格式：消费品交易

§ 9.614. Contents and Form of Notification Before Disposition of Collateral:Consumer-Goods Transaction.

在消费品交易中，应适用下列原则：

In a consumer-goods transaction, the following rules apply:

（1）处置通知必须包含下列信息：

（1）A notification of disposition must providc the following information:

（A）第 9.613 条（1）款要求的信息；

（A）the information specified in Section 9.613（1）;

（B）向接收通知的人说明其是否对不足部分承担责任；

（B）a description of any liability for a deficiency of the person to which the notification is sent;

（C）提供相关电话号码，即如果希望根据第 9.623 条赎回担保物，可以通过该电话确认应向受担保方支付的金额；以及

（C）a telephone number from which the amount that must be paid to the secured party to redeem the collateral under Section 9.623 is available; and

（D）提供电话号码或邮寄地址，用于提供有关担保物处置和担保债务的进一步信息。

（D）a telephone number or mailing address from which additional information concerning the disposition and the obligation secured is available.

（2）通知不需要使用特定用语。

（2）A particular phrasing of the notification is not required.

（3）下列通知格式在填写完整后，被视为提供了充分信息：

（3）The following form of notification, when completed, provides sufficient information:

__________（受担保方的名字和地址）

__________［Name and address of secured party］

__________（日期）

__________［Date］

我们计划出售财产的通知

NOTICE OF OUR PLAN TO SELL PROPERTY

__________（兼为债务人之

__________［Name and address of any

义务人的名字和地址）

标题：__________（说明交易）

我们持有__________（描述担保物），因为你违反了我们协议中的承诺。

（用于公开处置：）

我们将把__________（描述担保物）公开出售。出售可以包括租赁或许可。

出售信息如下：

日期：____________________

时间：____________________

地点：____________________

如果你愿意，你可以参加出售并带来你的竞标人。

（用于私下处置：）

我们将在__________（日期）之后的某个时间，把________（描述担保物）私下出售。出售可以包括租赁或许可。

从出售获得的钱款，（在支付我们的成本后）将用来减少你所欠的金额________。如果我们获得的钱款少于你的欠债金额，你（视情况而定，将会或将不会）继续就不足部分向我们欠债。如果我们获得的钱款多于你的欠债金额，剩余部分将支付给你，除非我们必须将其支付给其他人。

在我们出售该财产之前的任何时间，你都可以通过向我们支

obligor who is also a debtor]

Subject:________________[Identification of Transaction]

We have your ________________[describe collateral], because you broke promises in our agreement.

[For a public disposition:]

We will sell________________ [describe collateral] at public sale.A sale could include a lease or license.

The sale will be held as follows:

Date:________________________________

Time:________________________________

Place:_______________________________

You may attend the sale and bring bidders if you want.

[For a private disposition:]

We will sell ________ [describe collateral] at private sale sometime after ________ [date]. A sale could include a lease or license.

The money that we get from the sale (after paying our costs) will reduce the amount you owe.If we get less money than you owe, you ________ [will or will not, as applicable] still owe us the difference.If we get more money than you owe, you will get the extra money, unless we must pay it to someone else.

You can get the property back at any time before we sell it by paying us the full amount you

付你的全部欠债金额（而不是只支付过期的金额），包括我们的费用，而将财产取回。要确认你必须支付的准确金额，请给我们打电话__________（电话号码）。

owe（not just the past due payments）, including our expenses.To learn the exact amount you must pay, call us at ________ [telephone number] .

如果你希望我们通过书面形式，向你解释我们如何计算出你欠我们的金额，你可以给我们打电话_________（电话号码）或给我们写信至_________（受担保方的地址），提出书面解释的要求。（如果在近六个月之内，我们曾就你欠我们的金额作出过书面解释，则我们将就此次解释向你收取___________美元的费用）。

If you want us to explain to you in writing how we have figured the amount that you owe us, you may call us at ________ [telephone number] [or write us at ________ [secured party's address] ________] and request a written explanation. [We will charge you $ ________ for the explanation if we sent you another written explanation of the amount you owe us within the last six months.]

如果你对出售需要进一步的信息，请打电话给我们__________（电话号码）或给我们写信至__________（受担保方的地址）。

If you need more information about the sale call us at ____________________ [telephone number] [or write us at [secured party's address] ______________] .

我们同时将这份通知发送给下列人，因为他们对________（描述担保物）享有权益，或在你的协议项下欠有钱款：

__________（所有其他债务人和义务人的名字，如有）

We are sending this notice to the following other people who have an interest in __________ [describe collateral] or who owe money under your agreement:

____________ [Names of all other debtors and obligors, if any]

（4）符合（3）款格式的通知，即使在格式的结尾包含额外的信息，亦属充分。

（4）A notification in the form of Subdivision（3）is sufficient, even if additional information appears at the end of the form.

（5）符合（3）款格式的通知，即使在（1）款不要求的信息中存在错误，只要该错误不对本

（5）A notification in the form of Subdivision（3）is sufficient, even if it includes errors in information not required by Subdivision（1）,

篇提供的权利构成误导，亦属充分。

（6）如果本条项下的通知不符合（3）款的格式，则对于包含（1）款所不要求之信息的后果，应根据本篇以外的法律确定。

第 9.615 条　处置之收益的使用；不足部分的义务及剩余部分的权利

（a）对于根据第 9.610 条作出处置后所获得的现金收益，受担保方应按下列顺序使用或支付：

（1）取回、持有、准备、加工和处置的合理费用；以及受担保方支出的合理的律师费和法律费用，只要协议允许且法律不禁止；

（2）债务的偿付，即作为处置之依据的担保权益或农业留置权所担保的债务；

（3）次级债务的偿付，即担保物中任何次级担保权益或其他留置权所担保的债务，只要：

（A）在收益分配完成之前，受担保方从该次级担保权益或其他留置权的持有人收到业经认证的有关参与收益分配的要求；以及

（B）涉及对担保物享有权益的寄售委托人时，上述次级

unless the error is misleading with respect to rights arising under this Article.

（6）If a notification under this section is not in the form of Subdivision（3）, law other than this Article determines the effect of including information not required by Subdivision（1）.

§ 9.615. Application of Proceeds of Disposition; Liability for Deficiency and Right to Surplus.

（a）A secured party shall apply or pay over for application the cash proceeds of disposition under Section 9.610 in the following order to:

（1）the reasonable expenses of retaking, holding, preparing for disposition, processing, and disposing and, to the extent provided for by agreement and not prohibited by law, reasonable attorney's fees and legal expenses incurred by the secured party;

（2）the satisfaction of obligations secured by the security interest or agricultural lien under which the disposition is made;

（3）the satisfaction of obligations secured by any subordinate security interest in or other subordinate lien on the collateral if:

（A）the secured party receives from the holder of the subordinate security interest or other lien an authenticated demand for proceeds before distribution of the proceeds is completed;and

（B）in a case in which a consignor has an interest in the collateral, the subordinate

担保权益或其他留置权优于寄售委托人的权益；并且

（4）向身为担保物寄售委托人之受担保方的支付，只要受担保方在收益分配完成之前，从该寄售委托人收到业经认证的有关参与收益分配的要求。

（b）如果受担保方提出要求，则次级担保权益或其他留置权的持有人应在合理时间内，就该权益或留置权提供合理证明。如果持有人不予遵从，受担保方即无须遵从该持有人根据（a）（3）款提出的要求。

（c）对于根据第9.610条通过处置所获得的非现金收益，受担保方无须作出使用或支付，除非不这样做属于商业上不合理。受担保方如果对非现金收益作出使用或支付，应以商业上合理的方式进行。

（d）如果作为处置依据的担保权益系用于担保付款或履约，则在作出（a）款要求和（c）款允许的支付和使用后：

（1）受担保方应向债务人结算账目并支付剩余部分，除非（a）（4）款要求受担保方将现金收益支付给寄售委托人，

security interest or other lien is senior to the interest of the consignor;and

（4）a secured party that is a consignor of the collateral if the secured party receives from the consignor an authenticated demand for proceeds before distribution of the proceeds is completed.

（b）If requested by a secured party, a holder of a subordinate security interest or other lien shall furnish reasonable proof of the interest or lien within a reasonable time.Unless the holder does so, the secured party need not comply with the holder's demand under Subsection（a）（3）.

（c）A secured party need not apply or pay over for application noncash proceeds of disposition under Section 9.610 unless the failure to do so would be commercially unreasonable.A secured party that applies or pays over for application noncash proceeds shall do so in a commercially reasonable manner.

（d）If the security interest under which a disposition is made secures payment or performance of an obligation, after making the payments and applications required by Subsection（a）and permitted by Subsection（c）:

（1）unless Subsection（a）（4）requires the secured party to apply or pay over cash proceeds to a consignor, the secured party shall account to and pay a debtor for any surplus;and

或以其为受益人进行使用；并且

（2）义务人对不足部分应承担责任。

（2）the obligor is liable for any deficiency.

（e）如果基础交易是应收款、动产契据、无形支付或本票的买卖，则：

（1）债务人无权获得剩余部分；并且

（2）义务人对不足部分不承担责任。

（e）If the underlying transaction is a sale of accounts, chattel paper, payment intangibles, or promissory notes:

（1）the debtor is not entitled to any surplus;and

（2）the obligor is not liable for any deficiency.

（f）在计算处置后的剩余部分或不足部分时，如果存在下列情况，即应按处置本应产生的收益金额计算，即假设处置符合本章规定，且受让人不是受担保方、受担保方关联人或次义务人时，该处置本应获得的金额：

（1）处置中的受让人是受担保方、受担保方关联人或次义务人；并且

（2）处置的收益金额，与处置符合本章规定，且受让人不是受担保方、受担保方关联人或次义务人时所应获得的金额范围相比，显著偏低。

（f）The surplus or deficiency following a disposition is calculated based on the amount of proceeds that would have been realized in a disposition complying with this Part to a transferee other than the secured party, a person related to the secured party, or a secondary obligor if:

（1）the transferee in the disposition is the secured party, a person related to the secured party, or a secondary obligor;and

（2）the amount of proceeds of the disposition is significantly below the range of proceeds that a complying disposition to a person other than the secured party, a person related to the secured party, or a secondary obligor would have brought.

（g）当处置据以进行的担保权益或农业留置权并不优于其他担保权益或留置权时，只要受担保方在处置中以善意收到现金收益，且不知道接受该

（g）A secured party that receives cash proceeds of a disposition in good faith and without knowledge that the receipt violates the rights of the holder of a security interest or other lien that is not subordinate to the security

现金侵犯了该其他担保权益或留置权之持有人的权利，受担保方即：

interest or agricultural lien under which the disposition is made:

（1）在取得现金收益后，不受制于该其他担保权益或留置权；

（1）takes the cash proceeds free of the security interest or other lien;

（2）没有义务将处置的收益，用于偿付该其他担保权益或留置权所担保的债务；并且

（2）is not obligated to apply the proceeds of the disposition to the satisfaction of obligations secured by the security interest or other lien;and

（3）没有义务就任何剩余部分，向该其他担保权益或留置权的持有人结算账目或作出支付。

（3）is not obligated to account to or pay the holder of the security interest or other lien for any surplus.

第 9.616 条　对剩余部分或不足部分之计算的解释

§ 9.616. Explanation of Calculation of Surplus or Deficiency.

（a）在本条中：

（a）In this section:

（1）“解释”指包含下列内容的书面文件：

（1）“Explanation” means a writing that:

（A）注明了剩余部分或不足部分的金额；

（A）states the amount of the surplus or deficiency;

（B）根据（c）款，就受担保方计算剩余部分或不足部分的方法提供了解释；

（B）provides an explanation in accordance with Subsection（c）of how the secured party calculated the surplus or deficiency;

（C）在适用的情况下，说明了未来之借记、贷记、收费（包括额外的信贷服务费或利息）、返款和费用对剩余部分或不足部分之金额可能产生的影响；以及

（C）states, if applicable, that future debits, credits, charges, including additional credit service charges or interest, rebates, and expenses may affect the amount of the surplus or deficiency;and

（D）提供了电话号码或邮寄地址，用于提供有关交易的进一步信息。

（D）provides a telephone number or mailing address from which additional information concerning the transaction is available.

（2）“请求”指符合下列条件的记录：

（2）“Request” means a record:

（A）业经债务人或消费者义务人的认证；

（A）authenticated by a debtor or consumer obligor;

（B）请求收件人提供解释；以及

（B）requesting that the recipient provide an explanation;and

（C）在担保物根据第9.610条被处置之后发出。

（C）sent after disposition of the collateral under Section 9.610.

（b）在消费品交易中，如果根据第9.615条，债务人有权获得剩余部分，或消费者义务人有义务支付不足部分，则：

（b）In a consumer-goods transaction in which the debtor is entitled to a surplus or a consumer obligor is liable for a deficiency under Section 9.615, the secured party shall:

（1）受担保方应在处置之后，向债务人或消费者义务人（依适用情况）发送解释，并且：

（1）send an explanation to the debtor or consumer obligor, as applicable, after the disposition and:

（A）发送应在受担保方作出下列行为之前或同时进行：向债务人报告账目并支付剩余部分，或在处置后首次向消费者义务人就不足部分提出书面支付要求；并且

（A）before or when the secured party accounts to the debtor and pays any surplus or first makes written demand on the consumer obligor after the disposition for payment of the deficiency;and

（B）发送应在收到请求后十四天内；或

（B）within 14 days after receipt of a request;or

（2）当消费者义务人对不足部分承担责任时，受担保方应在收到请求后十四天内，向消费者义务人发送记录，放弃受担保方对不足部分的权利。

（2）in the case of a consumer obligor who is liable for a deficiency, within 14 days after receipt of a request, send to the consumer obligor a record waiving the secured party's right to a deficiency.

（c）为遵守（a）（1）（B）款的规定，书面文件必须按下列顺序，提供下列信息：

（c）To comply with Subsection（a）（1）（B）, a writing must provide the following information in the following order:

（1）作为处置依据之担保

（1）the aggregate amount of obligations

权益所担保的债务总额；如果该总额已减去了所返还的尚未赚取的利息或信贷服务费，则应说明该事实；并且，计算的截止日应为：

secured by the security interest under which the disposition was made and, if the amount reflects a rebate of unearned interest or credit service charge, an indication of that fact, calculated as of a specified date:

（A）如果受担保方在违约发生后取得担保物的占有，截止日不应超过受担保方取得占有前三十五天；或

（A）if the secured party takes or receives possession of the collateral after default, not more than 35 days before the secured party takes or receives possession;or

（B）如果受担保方在违约发生前取得担保物的占有，或没有取得担保物的占有，截止日不应超过处置前三十五天；

（B）if the secured party takes or receives possession of the collateral before default or does not take possession of the collateral, not more than 35 days before the disposition;

（2）处置的收益金额；

（2）the amount of proceeds of the disposition;

（3）减去收益金额后的债务总额；

（3）the aggregate amount of the obligations after deducting the amount of proceeds;

（4）费用的总额或分类金额，以及费用的类别，包括担保物取回、持有、准备处置、加工和处置的费用，还有受担保方已知的在此次处置中发生的并由担保物所担保的律师费；

（4）the amount, in the aggregate or by type, and types of expenses, including expenses of retaking, holding, preparing for disposition, processing, and disposing of the collateral, and attorney's fees secured by the collateral which are known to the secured party and relate to the current disposition;

（5）贷记的总额或分类金额，以及贷记的类别，包括返还的利息或信贷服务费，即已知的义务人有权获得且尚未包含在（1）款内的金额；以及

（5）the amount, in the aggregate or by type, and types of credits, including rebates of interest or credit service charges, to which the obligor is known to be entitled and which are not reflected in the amount in Subdivision（1）; and

（6）剩余部分或不足部分的金额。

（6）the amount of the surplus or deficiency.

（d）解释不需要使用任何特定用语。解释即使包含次要错误，只要本质上符合（a）款的要求，且该错误不会造成严重误导，即属解释充分。

（d）A particular phrasing of the explanation is not required.An explanation complying substantially with the requirements of Subsection（a）is sufficient, even if it includes minor errors that are not seriously misleading.

（e）债务人或消费者义务人根据本条提出请求时，有权每六个月获得一次免费答复，只要在该期间内，受担保方未根据（b）（1）款向债务人或消费者义务人发送过解释。对于额外的解释，受担保方可以收取每次不超过二十五美元的费用。

（e）A debtor or consumer obligor is entitled without charge to one response to a request under this section during any six-month period in which the secured party did not send to the debtor or consumer obligor an explanation pursuant to Subsection（b）（1）. The secured party may require payment of a charge not exceeding $25 for each additional response.

第 9.617 条　担保物受让人的权利

§ 9.617. Rights of Transferee of Collateral.

（a）违约发生后受担保方对担保物的处置，具有下列效力：

（a）A secured party's disposition of collateral after default:

（1）将债务人对担保物的全部权利转让给支付了价值的受让人；

（1）transfers to a transferee for value all of the debtor's rights in the collateral;

（2）作为处置依据的担保权益被解除；并且

（2）discharges the security interest under which the disposition is made;and

（3）任何次级担保权益或其他留置权被解除。

（3）discharges any subordinate security interest or other subordinate lien.

（b）即使受担保方未能遵守本篇或任何司法程序的要求，以善意作为的受让人取得担保物后，亦不受制于（a）款所述的权利和权益。

（b）A transferee that acts in good faith takes free of the rights and interests described in Subsection（a）, even if the secured party fails to comply with this Article or the requirements of any judicial proceeding.

（c）如果受让人不能免受

（c）If a transferee does not take free of

（a）款所述权利和权益的制约，则该受让人取得担保物后，受制于下列：

（1）债务人对担保物的权利；

（2）作为处置依据的担保权益或农业留置权；以及

（3）任何其他担保权益或留置权。

第9.618条 某些次义务人的权利和义务

（a）次义务人在出现下列情况后，即取得受担保方的权利，并就受担保方的义务，承担履行该义务的责任：

（1）从受担保方取得担保债务的转让；

（2）从受担保方取得担保物的转让，同时，同意取得受担保方的权利，并承担受担保方的义务；或

（3）就担保物代位取得受担保方的权利。

（b）上述（a）款所述的转让或代位：

（1）不属于第9.610条所述的担保物处置；并且

（2）解除受担保方在本篇项下的进一步义务。

第9.619条 注册所有权或法定所有权的转让

（a）在本条中，“转让声明”指业经受担保方认证的包含下

the rights and interests described in Subsection（a）, the transferee takes the collateral subject to:

（1）the debtor’s rights in the collateral;

（2）the security interest or agricultural lien under which the disposition is made;and

（3）any other security interest or other lien.

§ 9.618. Rights and Duties of Certain Secondary Obligors.

（a）A secondary obligor acquires the rights and becomes obligated to perform the duties of the secured party after the secondary obligor:

（1）receives an assignment of a secured obligation from the secured party;

（2）receives a transfer of collateral from the secured party and agrees to accept the rights and assume the duties of the secured party;or

（3）is subrogated to the rights of a secured party with respect to collateral.

（b）An assignment, transfer, or subrogation described in Subsection（a）:

（1）is not a disposition of collateral under Section 9.610;and

（2）relieves the secured party of further duties under this Article.

§ 9.619. Transfer of Record or Legal Title.

（a）In this section, “transfer statement” means a record authenticated by a secured party

列说明的记录：

stating:

（1）债务人已就债务发生违约，且该债务由所描述之担保物担保；

（1）that the debtor has defaulted in connection with an obligation secured by specified collateral;

（2）受担保方已就担保物行使违约后的救济；

（2）that the secured party has exercised its post-default remedies with respect to the collateral;

（3）在行使救济后，受让人已取得债务人对担保物的权利；以及

（3）that, by reason of the exercise, a transferee has acquired the rights of the debtor in the collateral;and

（4）记录中包括了受担保方、债务人和受让人的名字和邮寄地址。

（4）the name and mailing address of the secured party, debtor, and transferee.

（b）转让声明使受让人有权就声明中所描述的担保物，取得债务人对该担保物之全部权利的注册转让，即该担保物从任何官方登记、记录、注册或产权证书系统中的转让。只要向管理系统的官员或办事处提示转让声明，支付应付费用，并交付申请表格，该官员或办事处即应：

（b）A transfer statement entitles the transferee to the transfer of record of all rights of the debtor in the collateral specified in the statement in any official filing, recording, registration, or certificate-of-title system covering the collateral.If a transfer statement is presented with the applicable fee and request form to the official or office responsible for maintaining the system, the official or office shall:

（1）接受转让声明；

（1）accept the transfer statement;

（2）迅速修改其记录并注明该转让；并且

（2）promptly amend its records to reflect the transfer;and

（3）在适用的情况下，以受让人名字颁发适当的新产权证书。

（3）if applicable, issue a new appropriate certificate of title in the name of the transferee.

（c）向受担保方转让担保物的注册所有权或法定所有权，无论系根据（b）款还是以其他方式，其本身不构成本篇所述

（c）A transfer of the record or legal title to collateral to a secured party under Subsection（b）or otherwise is not of itself a disposition of collateral under this Article and does not

的担保物处置，亦不解除受担保方在本篇项下的义务。

of itself relieve the secured party of its duties under this Article.

第 9.620 条　收取担保物作为全部或部分债务的清偿；担保物的强制处置

§ 9.620. Acceptance of Collateral in Full or Partial Satisfaction of Obligation;Compulsory Disposition of Collateral.

（a）除（g）款另有规定外，只有在下列情况下，受担保方才可以收取担保物，作为担保物所担保之全部或部分债务的清偿：

（a）Except as otherwise provided in Subsection（g）, a secured party may accept collateral in full or partial satisfaction of the obligation it secures only if:

（1）债务人根据（c）款同意该收取；

（1）the debtor consents to the acceptance under Subsection（c）;

（2）受担保方在（d）款规定的时间内，对于收取担保物的建议，没有收到业经下列人认证的异议通知：

（2）the secured party does not receive, within the time set forth in Subsection（d）, a notification of objection to the proposal authenticated by:

（A）根据第 9.621 条，受担保方必须向其发送建议的人；或

（A）a person to which the secured party was required to send a proposal under Section 9.621;or

（B）对担保物持有权益的任何其他人（债务人除外），即使该权益次于该建议所涉及的担保权益；

（B）any other person, other than the debtor, holding an interest in the collateral subordinate to the security interest that is the subject of the proposal;

（3）涉及属于消费品的担保物时，债务人在同意该收取时，不占有担保物；并且

（3）if the collateral is consumer goods, the collateral is not in the possession of the debtor when the debtor consents to the acceptance;and

（4）下述（e）款不要求该受担保方处置担保物，或债务人根据第 9.624 条放弃相关要求。

（4）Subsection（e）does not require the secured party to dispose of the collateral or the debtor waives the requirement pursuant to Section 9.624.

（b）除非满足下列条件，否则，对担保物的收取不具效力，即使已尝试收取或已作出

（b）A purported or apparent acceptance of collateral under this section is ineffective unless:

收取：

（1）受担保方在业经认证的记录中同意该收取，或向债务人发送收取建议；并且

（2）上述（a）款的条件获得满足。

（c）为本条目的：

（1）只有债务人以记录的形式，同意该收取的条款，并在违约发生之后认证该记录，债务人才被视为同意以担保物的收取，作为担保物所担保之债务的部分清偿；以及

（2）只有债务人以记录的形式，同意该收取的条款，并在违约发生之后认证该记录，或只有在下列条件满足之后，债务人才被视为同意以担保物的收取，作为担保物所担保之债务的全部清偿：

（A）在违约发生后，受担保方向债务人发送收取建议，且该建议是无条件的，或只规定必须保留或保存不处于受担保方占有下的担保物；

（B）在该建议中，建议收取担保物作为其所担保之债务的全部清偿；以及

（C）在建议发送后二十天内，未收到业经债务人认证的异议通知。

（d）异议通知必须使受担保方在下列时间内收到，才具

（1）the secured party consents to the acceptance in an authenticated record or sends a proposal to the debtor;and

（2）the conditions of Subsection（a）are met.

（c）For purposes of this section:

（1）a debtor consents to an acceptance of collateral in partial satisfaction of the obligation it secures only if the debtor agrees to the terms of the acceptance in a record authenticated after default; and

（2）a debtor consents to an acceptance of collateral in full satisfaction of the obligation it secures only if the debtor agrees to the terms of the acceptance in a record authenticated after default or the secured party:

（A）sends to the debtor after default a proposal that is unconditional or subject only to a condition that collateral not in the possession of the secured party be preserved or maintained;

（B）in the proposal, proposes to accept collateral in full satisfaction of the obligation it secures;and

（C）does not receive a notification of objection authenticated by the debtor within 20 days after the proposal is sent.

（d）To be effective under Subsection（a）（2）, a notification of objection must be

有（a）（2）款所述的效力：

（1）如果对任何人的建议系根据第9.621条发送，则该时间为向该人发送通知后二十天内；以及

（2）在其他情况下：

（A）该时间为第9.621条所述之最后一个通知发送后二十天内；或

（B）如果未发送通知，该时间为债务人根据（c）款同意该收取之前。

（e）已经取得担保物占有的受担保方，应根据第9.610条，在（f）款规定的时间内处置担保物，只要：

（1）涉及消费品的价款担保权益时，60%的现金价格已经支付；或

（2）涉及消费品的非价款担保权益时，所担保之债务之60%的本金金额已经支付。

（f）为遵守（e）款，受担保方应在下列时间内处置担保物：

（1）取得占有之后九十天内；或

（2）任何更长的时间内，只要债务人和所有次义务人在违约之后达成并认证协议，同意该时间。

（g）在消费者交易中，受

received by the secured party:

（1）in the case of a person to which the proposal was sent pursuant to Section 9.621, within 20 days after notification was sent to that person;and

（2）in other cases:

（A）within 20 days after the last notification was sent pursuant to Section 9.621;or

（B）if a notification was not sent, before the debtor consents to the acceptance under Subsection（c）.

（e）A secured party that has taken possession of collateral shall dispose of the collateral pursuant to Section 9.610 within the time specified in Subsection（f）if:

（1）60 percent of the cash price has been paid in the case of a purchase-money security interest in consumer goods;or

（2）60 percent of the principal amount of the obligation secured has been paid in the case of a non-purchase-money security interest in consumer goods.

（f）To comply with Subsection（e）, the secured party shall dispose of the collateral:

（1）within 90 days after taking possession; or

（2）within any longer period to which the debtor and all secondary obligors have agreed in an agreement to that effect entered into and authenticated after default.

（g）In a consumer transaction, a secured

担保方不得以收取担保物作为其所担保之债务的部分清偿。

party may not accept collateral in partial satisfaction of the obligation it secures.

第 9.621 条　建议收取担保物的通知

§ 9.621. Notification of Proposal to Accept Collateral.

（a）希望以收取担保物作为其所担保之债务之全部或部分清偿的受担保方，应将建议发送给：

（a）A secured party that desires to accept collateral in full or partial satisfaction of the obligation it secures shall send its proposal to:

（1）对担保物主张权益的人，只要在债务人同意该收取之前，受担保方已从该人收到业经认证的主张；

（1）any person from which the secured party has received, before the debtor consented to the acceptance, an authenticated notification of a claim of an interest in the collateral;

（2）任何其他受担保方或留置权持有人，只要在债务人同意该收取十天之前，该人对担保物持有通过登记符合下列条件之融资声明而获得完善的担保权益或其他留置权：

（2）any other secured party or lienholder that, 10 days before the debtor consented to the acceptance, held a security interest in or other lien on the collateral perfected by the filing of a financing statement that:

（A）融资声明指向该担保物；

（A）identified the collateral;

（B）截至该日，融资声明在编目中登记在债务人名字之下；以及

（B）was indexed under the debtor's name as of that date;and

（C）截至该日，登记该融资声明的一个或多个登记处，相对于该债务人和覆盖该担保物之融资声明，是正确的登记处；并且

（C）was filed in the office or offices in which to file a financing statement against the debtor covering the collateral as of that date;and

（3）任何其他受担保方，只要在债务人同意该收取十天之前，该人对担保物持有担保权益，且该担保权益通过遵守第 9.311 条（a）款所述的法律

（3）any other secured party that, 10 days before the debtor consented to the acceptance, held a security interest in the collateral perfected by compliance with a statute, regulation, or treaty described in Section 9.311（a）.

或条约获得完善。

（b）受担保方如果希望以收取担保物作为其所担保之债务的部分清偿，则除了（a）款所述的人，还应将建议发送至任何次义务人。

（b）A secured party that desires to accept collateral in partial satisfaction of the obligation it secures shall send its proposal to any secondary obligor in addition to the persons described in Subsection（a）.

第 9.622 条　收取担保物的效力

§ 9.622. Effect of Acceptance of Collateral.

（a）如果受担保方收取担保物，作为其所担保之债务的全部或部分清偿，则：

（a）A secured party's acceptance of collateral in full or partial satisfaction of the obligation it secures:

（1）在债务人同意的限度内，债务获得解除；

（1）discharges the obligation to the extent consented to by the debtor;

（2）债务人对担保物的全部权利，被转让给受担保方；

（2）transfers to the secured party all of a debtor's rights in the collateral;

（3）在债务人同意的限度内，该同意所涉及的担保权益或农业留置权被解除，同时任何次级担保权益或其他次级留置权亦被解除；以及

（3）discharges the security interest or agricultural lien that is the subject of the debtor's consent and any subordinate security interest or other subordinate lien;and

（4）任何其他次级权益均被终止。

（4）terminates any other subordinate interest.

（b）即使受担保方未能遵守本篇，次级权益亦根据（a）款被解除或终止。

（b）A subordinate interest is discharged or terminated under Subsection（a）, even if the secured party fails to comply with this Article.

第 9.623 条　赎回担保物的权利

§ 9.623. Right to Redeem Collateral.

（a）债务人、任何次义务人，或任何其他受担保方或留置权持有人，均可赎回担保物。

（a）A debtor, any secondary obligor, or any other secured party or lienholder may redeem collateral.

（b）希望赎回担保物的人，应作出下列表示：

（b）To redeem collateral, a person shall tender:

（1）清偿担保物所担保的

（1）fulfillment of all obligations secured

全部债务；并且

（2）支付第 9.615 条（a）（1）款所述的合理的费用和律师费。

（c）赎回可在任何时间进行，只要受担保方尚未：

（1）根据第 9.607 条就担保物获得收款；

（2）根据第 9.610 条处置担保物或订立处置合同；或

（3）根据第 9.622 条收取担保物，作为其所担保之债务的全部或部分清偿。

第 9.624 条　弃权

（a）债务人或次义务人可以放弃第 9.611 条项下获得处置通知的权利，但只能通过违约发生之后达成和认证的协议放弃。

（b）债务人可以放弃第 9.620 条（e）款项下要求处置担保物的权利，但只能通过违约发生之后达成和认证的协议放弃。

（c）除消费品交易外，债务人或次义务人可以放弃第 9.623 条项下赎回担保物的权利，但只能通过违约发生之后达成和认证的协议放弃。

第 9.625 条　受担保方未能遵守本篇时的救济

（a）如果能够证明受担保方未根据本篇规定作为，法院可就担保物的收款、强制履行

by the collateral;and

（2）the reasonable expenses and attorneys' fees described in Section 9.615（a）（1）.

（c）A redemption may occur at any time before a secured party:

（1）has collected collateral under Section 9.607;

（2）has disposed of collateral or entered into a contract for its disposition under Section 9.610;or

（3）has accepted collateral in full or partial satisfaction of the obligation it secures under Section 9.622.

§ 9.624. Waiver.

（a）A debtor or secondary obligor may waive the right to notification of disposition of collateral under Section 9.611 only by an agreement to that effect entered into and authenticated after default.

（b）A debtor may waive the right to require disposition of collateral under Section 9.620（e）only by an agreement to that effect entered into and authenticated after default.

（c）Except in a consumer-goods transaction, a debtor or secondary obligor may waive the right to redeem collateral under Section 9.623 only by an agreement to that effect entered into and authenticated after default.

§ 9.625. Remedies for Secured Party's Failure to Comply With Article.

（a）If it is established that a secured party is not proceeding in accordance with this Article, a court may order or restrain collection,

或处置，规定适当的执行条件或禁止条件。

enforcement, or disposition of collateral on appropriate terms and conditions.

（b）除（c）款、（d）款和（f）款另有规定外，任何人如果未能遵守本篇，即应对所造成的损失金额承担赔偿责任。未能遵守本篇所造成的损失，包括债务人无法取得或需要以更高成本取得替代融资的损失。

（b）Subject to Subsections（c），（d），and（f），a person is liable for damages in the amount of any loss caused by a failure to comply with this Article.Loss caused by a failure to comply may include loss resulting from the debtor's inability to obtain, or increased costs of, alternative financing.

（c）除第9.628条另有规定外：

（c）Except as otherwise provided in Section 9.628:

（1）发生违反本篇的情况时，如果任何人当时系债务人或义务人，或当时对担保物持有担保权益或其他留置权，该人即有权就其损失获得（b）款所述的损害赔偿；并且

（1）a person that, at the time of the failure, was a debtor, was an obligor, or held a security interest in or other lien on the collateral may recover damages under Subsection（b）for its loss;and

（2）如果担保物是消费品，只要在受担保方违反本章时，任何人当时系债务人或次义务人，该人即在任何情况下均有权获得不低于信贷服务费金额的赔偿，再加上债务本金金额的10%，或有权获得不低于时间价格差的金额，再加上现金价格的10%。

（2）if the collateral is consumer goods, a person that was a debtor or a secondary obligor at the time a secured party failed to comply with this Part may recover for that failure in any event an amount not less than the credit service charge plus 10 percent of the principal amount of the obligation or the time price differential plus 10 percent of the cash price.

（d）如果债务人所应支付的不足部分根据第9.626条被免除，则其可就损失的担保物之剩余部分获得赔偿。但是，如果债务人或次义务人的不足部分根据第9.626条被免除或降低，即不得在上述赔偿之外，根据（b）款就担保物在收款、

（d）A debtor whose deficiency is eliminated under Section 9.626 may recover damages for the loss of any surplus.However, a debtor or secondary obligor whose deficiency is eliminated or reduced under Section 9.626 may not otherwise recover under Subsection（b）for noncompliance with the provisions of this Part relating to collection, enforcement, disposition,

强制履行、处置或收取中未能遵守本章获得赔偿。

or acceptance.

（e）除了根据（b）款可以获得的任何损害赔偿外，债务人、消费者义务人，或在已登记之记录中被称为债务人的人（以适用者为准），在任何人未能遵守下列条款时，还可以就每次违反获得五百美元的赔偿：

（e）In addition to any damages recoverable under Subsection（b）, the debtor, consumer obligor, or person named as a debtor in a filed record, as applicable, may recover $500 in each case from a person that:

（1）未能遵守第 9.208 条；

（1）fails to comply with Section 9.208;

（2）未能遵守第 9.209 条；

（2）fails to comply with Section 9.209;

（3）登记了根据第 9.509 条（a）款其无权登记的记录；

（3）files a record that the person is not entitled to file under Section 9.509（a）;

（4）未能致使注册受担保方按第 9.513 条（a）款或（c）款的要求，登记或发送终止声明；

（4）fails to cause the secured party of record to file or send a termination statement as required by Section 9.513（a）or（c）;

（5）未能遵守第 9.616 条（b）（1）款，且属于习惯性或经常性违反；或

（5）fails to comply with Section 9.616（b）（1）and whose failure is part of a pattern, or consistent with a practice, of noncompliance;or

（6）未能遵守第 9.616 条（b）（2）款。

（6）fails to comply with Section 9.616（b）（2）.

（f）如果任何人无合理理由而未能遵从第 9.210 条项下的请求，债务人或消费者义务人可以根据（b）款获得损害赔偿，并另外获得每次五百美元的赔偿。对于根据第 9.210 条提出的请求，如果其接收人从未就第 9.210 条所述之请求涉及的担保物或债务主张过权益，则在本款意义上，该人被视为有合理理由不遵从该请求。

（f）A debtor or consumer obligor may recover damages under Subsection（b）and, in addition, $500 in each case from a person that, without reasonable cause, fails to comply with a request under Section 9.210.A recipient of a request under Section 9.210 that never claimed an interest in the collateral or obligations that are the subject of a request under that section has a reasonable excuse for failure to comply with the request within the meaning of this subsection.

（g）如果受担保方未能遵从第 9.210 条所述的担保物清单请求或债务清单请求，则对于合理地因此受到误导的人，受担保方只能就包含在请求中之清单列出的担保权益，提出主张。

(g) If a secured party fails to comply with a request regarding a list of collateral or a statement of account under Section 9.210, the secured party may claim a security interest only as shown in the list or statement included in the request as against a person that is reasonably misled by the failure.

第 9.626 条　不足部分或剩余部分的争议诉讼

§ 9.626. Action in Which Deficiency or Surplus Is in Issue.

（a）除消费者交易外，如果在其他交易引起的诉讼中，不足部分或剩余部分的金额存在争议，应适用下列原则：

(a) In an action arising from a transaction, other than a consumer transaction, in which the amount of a deficiency or surplus is in issue, the following rules apply:

（1）涉及受担保方的收款、强制履行、处置或收取时，除非债务人或次义务人对受担保方是否遵守了本章规定提出质疑，否则受担保方无须证明其遵守了本章的相关规定。

(1) A secured party need not prove compliance with the provisions of this Part relating to collection, enforcement, disposition, or acceptance unless the debtor or a secondary obligor places the secured party's compliance in issue.

（2）如果对受担保方是否遵守了本章存在质疑，则受担保方应就收款、强制履行、处置或收取过程中是否遵守了本章规定，承担举证责任。

(2) If the secured party's compliance is placed in issue, the secured party has the burden of establishing that the collection, enforcement, disposition, or acceptance was conducted in accordance with this Part.

（3）除第 9.628 条另有规定外，如果受担保方不能证明，在取回、强制履行、处置或收取过程中遵守了本章有关规定，则债务人或次义务人对不足部分所承担的责任，将被限于担保债务、费用及律师费之总额超出下列金额中较高者的部分：

(3) Except as otherwise provided in Section 9.628, if a secured party fails to prove that the collection, enforcement, disposition, or acceptance was conducted in accordance with the provisions of this Part relating to collection, enforcement, disposition, or acceptance, the liability of a debtor or a secondary obligor for a deficiency is limited to an amount by which the sum of the secured obligation, expenses, and

attorney's fees exceeds the greater of:

（A）通过收款、强制履行、处置或收取所获得的收益金额；或

（A）the proceeds of the collection, enforcement, disposition, or acceptance; or

（B）假设未遵守规定之受担保方在遵守了本章有关收款、强制履行、处置或收取的规定时，本来可以实现的收益金额。

（B）the amount of proceeds that would have been realized had the noncomplying secured party proceeded in accordance with the provisions of this Part relating to collection, enforcement, disposition, or acceptance.

（4）为（3）（B）款目的，本来可以实现的收益金额，等于担保债务、费用及律师费的总额，除非受担保方能够证明，前一金额低于后一总额。

（4）For purposes of Subdivision（3）（B）, the amount of proceeds that would have been realized is equal to the sum of the secured obligation, expenses, and attorney's fees unless the secured party proves that the amount is less than that sum.

（5）当根据第 9.615 条（f）款计算不足部分或剩余部分时，债务人或义务人有义务证明，处置的收益金额，与处置符合本章规定且受让人不是受担保方、受担保方关联人或次义务人时所应获得的金额范围相比，显著偏低。

（5）If a deficiency or surplus is calculated under Section 9.615（f）, the debtor or obligor has the burden of establishing that the amount of proceeds of the disposition is significantly below the range of prices that a complying disposition to a person other than the secured party, a person related to the secured party, or a secondary obligor would have brought.

（b）规定（a）款仅适用于非消费品交易，目的在于使法院可以自行决定适用于消费品交易的适当规则。但是，法院不应根据上述限制来推断消费品交易中适当规则的性质。法院可以继续使用任何已确立的方法。

（b）The limitation of the rules in Subsection（a）to transactions other than consumer transactions is intended to leave to the court the determination of the proper rules in consumer transactions.Thecourt may not infer from that limitation the nature of the proper rule in consumer transactions and may continue to apply established approaches.

第 9.627 条 确定行为是否属于商业上合理

（a）涉及收款、强制履行、处置或收取时，即使与受担保方所选择的时间或方法相比，存在本来可以获得更高金额的另一时间或另一方法，其本身也不足以妨碍受担保方证明，其作出的收款、强制履行、处置或收取，系属商业上合理。

（b）如果担保物的处置按下列方式进行，即属商业上合理：

（1）在公认市场上以通常方式进行；

（2）在公认市场上以处置时市场上的时价进行；或

（3）以其他方式采用了该类财产之经销商使用的合理商业做法。

（c）如果收款、强制履行、处置或收取获得下列批准，即属商业上合理：

（1）司法程序；

（2）正当成立的债权人委员会；

（3）债权人的代表人；或

（4）代表债权人利益的受让人。

（d）上述（c）款所述的批准并非必需，且没有该批准并

§ 9.627. Determination of Whether Conduct Was Commercially Reasonable.

（a）The fact that a greater amount could have been obtained by a collection, enforcement, disposition, or acceptance at a different time or in a different method from that selected by the secured party is not of itself sufficient to preclude the secured party from establishing that the collection, enforcement, disposition, or acceptance was made in a commercially reasonable manner.

（b）A disposition of collateral is made in a commercially reasonable manner if the disposition is made:

（1）in the usual manner on any recognized market;

（2）at the price current in any recognized market at the time of the disposition;or

（3）otherwise in conformity with reasonable commercial practices among dealers in the type of property that was the subject of the disposition.

（c）A collection, enforcement, disposition, or acceptance is commercially reasonable if it has been approved:

（1）in a judicial proceeding;

（2）by a bona fide creditors’ committee;

（3）by a representative of creditors;or

（4）by an assignee for the benefit of creditors.

（d）Approval under Subsection（c）need not be obtained, and lack of approval does

不意味着收款、强制履行、处置或收取不属商业上合理。

not mean that the collection, enforcement, disposition, or acceptance is not commercially reasonable.

第 9.628 条　受担保方的免责和限制责任；次义务人的责任

§ 9.628. Nonliability and Limitation on Liability of Secured Party; Liability of Secondary Obligor.

（a）除非受担保方知道一个人系债务人或义务人，并知道该人的真实身份，并知道如何与该人联系，否则：

（a）Unless a secured party knows that a person is a debtor or obligor, knows the identity of the person, and knows how to communicate with the person:

（1）对于该人，或对于针对该人登记了融资声明的受担保方或留置权持有人，受担保方不承担违反本篇规定的责任；并且

（1）the secured party is not liable to the person, or to a secured party or lienholder that has filed a financing statement against the person, for failure to comply with this Article;and

（2）受担保方违反本篇规定，不影响该人对不足部分的责任。

（2）the secured party's failure to comply with this Article does not affect the liability of the person for a deficiency.

（b）受担保方不因其受担保方的身份，对下列人承担责任：

（b）A secured party is not liable because of its status as secured party:

（1）身为债务人或义务人的人，除非受担保方：

（1）to a person that is a debtor or obligor, unless the secured party knows:

（A）知道该人系债务人或义务人；

（A）that the person is a debtor or obligor;

（B）知道该人的真实身份；并且

（B）the identity of the person;and

（C）知道如何与该人联系；或

（C）how to communicate with the person;or

（2）登记了针对任何人之融资声明的受担保方或留置权持有人，除非受担保方：

（2）to a secured party or lienholder that has filed a financing statement against a person, unless the secured party knows:

（A）知道被针对的人系债

（A）that the person is a debtor;and

务人；并且

（B）知道该债务人的真实身份。

（c）如果受担保方合理相信，一项交易非属消费品交易或消费者交易，或货物非属消费品，则受担保方不就基于该合理相信的行为或疏漏，向任何人承担责任，且任何人对不足部分的责任也不受影响，只要受担保方的相信是合理地依赖于：

（1）债务人对担保物之使用、取得或持有目的的陈述；或

（2）义务人对担保债务之产生理由的陈述。

（d）受担保方即使未能遵守第9.616条，亦不对任何人承担第9.625条（c）（2）款项下的责任。

（e）受担保方不就任何一项担保债务，承担一次以上的第9.625条（c）（2）款项下的责任。

（B） the identity of the person.

（c） A secured party is not liable to any person, and a person's liability for a deficiency is not affected, because of any act or omission arising out of the secured party's reasonable belief that a transaction is not a consumer-goods transaction or a consumer transaction or that goods are not consumer goods, if the secured party's belief is based on its reasonable reliance on:

（1） a debtor's representation concerning the purpose for which collateral was to be used, acquired, or held;or

（2） an obligor's representation concerning the purpose for which a secured obligation was incurred.

（d） A secured party is not liable to any person under Section 9.625（c）（2） for its failure to comply with Section 9.616.

（e） A secured party is not liable under Section 9.625（c）（2） more than once with respect to any one secured obligation.

词汇索引

续表

工厂预制房屋	manufactured home	第 9.102 条（a）（53）
工厂预制房屋交易	manufactured-home transaction	第 9.102 条（a）（54）
公共融资项目	public-finance transaction	第 9.102 条（a）（68）
公用事业传输企业	transmitting utility	第 9.102 条（a）（81）
货物	goods	第 9.102 条（a）（44）
记录	record	第 9.102 条（a）（70）
寄售	consignment	第 9.102 条（a）（20）
寄售受托人	consignee	第 9.102 条（a）（19）
寄售委托人	consignor	第 9.102 条（a）（21）
价款担保物	purchase-money collateral	第 9.103 条（a）（1）
价款债务	purchase-money obligation	第 9.103 条（a）（2）
价款担保权益	purchase-money security interest	第 9.103 条（c）
开采状担保物	as-extracted collateral	第 9.102 条（a）（6）
库存	inventory	第 9.102 条（a）（48）
留置权债权人	lien creditor	第 9.102 条（a）（52）
农产品	farm products	第 9.102 条（a）（34）
农业留置权	agricultural lien	第 9.102 条（a）（5）
农业生产	farming operation	第 9.102 条（a）（35）
票据	instrument	第 9.102 条（a）（47）
凭证	document	第 9.102 条（a）（30）
认证	authenticate	第 9.102 条（a）（7）
融资声明	financing statement	第 9.102 条（a）（39）
软件	software	第 9.102 条（a）（76）
商品合同	commodity contract	第 9.102 条（a）（15）
商品经纪人	commodity intermediary	第 9.102 条（a）（17）
商品客户	commodity customer	第 9.102 条（a）（16）

续表

商品账户	commodity account	第 9.102 条（a）（14）
商业侵权索赔	commercial tort claim	第 9.102 条（a）（13）
设备	equipment	第 9.102 条（a）（33）
实体动产契据	tangible chattel paper	第 9.102 条（a）（79）
收益	proceeds	第 9.102 条（a）（65）
受担保方	secured party	第 9.102 条（a）（73）
添附物	accession	第 9.102 条（a）（1）
投资财产	investment property	第 9.102 条（a）（49）
完善	perfection	第 9.308 条（a）
无形支付	payment intangible	第 9.102 条（a）（62）
现金收益	cash proceeds	第 9.102 条（a）（9）
消费品	consumer goods	第 9.102 条（a）（23）
消费品交易	consumer-goods transaction	第 9.102 条（a）（24）
消费者交易	consumer transaction	第 9.102 条（a）（26）
消费者义务人	consumer obligor	第 9.102 条（a）（25）
消费者债务人	consumer detor	第 9.102 条（a）（22）
新价值	new value	第 9.102 条（a）（57）
新债务人	new debtor	第 9.102 条（a）（56）
信用证权利	letter-of-credit right	第 9.102 条（a）（51）
修订文件	amendment	第 9.512
延展声明	continuation statement	第 9.102 条（a）（27）
一般无形财产	general intangible	第 9.102 条（a）（42）
医疗保险应收款	health care insurance receivable	第 9.102 条（a）（46）
义务人	obligor	第 9.102 条（a）（60）
银行	bank	第 9.102 条（a）（8）
应收款	account	第 9.102 条（a）（2）

续表

应收款债务人	account debtor	第 9.102 条（a）（3）
关联人	person related to	第 9.102 条（a）（63）
原始债务人	original debtor	第 9.102 条（a）（61）
债务人	debtor	第 9.102 条（a）（28）
账目	accounting	第 9.102 条（a）（4）
政府机构	governmental unit	第 9.102 条（a）（45）
支持性债务	supporting obligation	第 9.102 条（a）（78）
终止声明	termination statement	第 9.102 条（a）（80）
州	state	第 9.102 条（a）（77）
注册成立的组织	registered organization	第 9.102 条（a）（71）
注册成立地	jurisdiction of organization	第 9.102 条（a）（50）

图书在版编目(CIP)数据

美国统一商法典：汉英对照／潘琪译．--2版．--
北京：法律出版社，2020
ISBN 978-7-5197-4806-7

Ⅰ．①美…　Ⅱ．①潘…　Ⅲ．①商法－法典－美国－汉、英　Ⅳ．①D971.239.9

中国版本图书馆CIP数据核字(2020)第153434号

美国统一商法典(中英双语)
MEIGUO TONGYI SHANGFADIAN
(ZHONGYING SHUANGYU)

潘　琪　译

策划编辑　黄琳佳
责任编辑　黄琳佳
装帧设计　鲍龙卉

出版　法律出版社
总发行　中国法律图书有限公司
经销　新华书店
印刷　中煤(北京)印务有限公司
责任校对　王　丰
责任印制　陶　松

编辑统筹　学术·对外出版分社
开本　710毫米×1000毫米　1/16
印张　45.5
字数　737千
版本　2020年10月第2版
印次　2020年10月第1次印刷

法律出版社／北京市丰台区莲花池西里7号(100073)
网址／www.lawpress.com.cn
投稿邮箱／info@lawpress.com.cn
举报维权邮箱／jbwq@lawpress.com.cn
销售热线／400-660-8393
咨询电话／010-63939796

中国法律图书有限公司／北京市丰台区莲花池西里7号(100073)
全国各地中法图分、子公司销售电话：
统一销售客服／400-660-8393/6393
第一法律书店／010-83938432/8433　西安分公司／029-85330678　重庆分公司／023-67453036
上海分公司／021-62071639/1636　深圳分公司／0755-83072995

书号：ISBN 978-7-5197-4806-7　**定价**：488.00元
(如有缺页或倒装，中国法律图书有限公司负责退换)